D0776862

THE PHYSICS OF ELECTRONIC AND ATOMIC COLLISIONS

VII ICPEAC

International Conference on the Physics of Electronic &
Atomic Collisions, 7th, Amsterdam, 1971

The Physics of Electronic
and Atomic Collisions

VII ICPEAC
Amsterdam, The Netherlands   26-30 July, 1971

Invited Papers and Progress Reports

Edited by:

T. R. GOVERS and F. J. DE HEER
FOM Institute, Amsterdam, The Netherlands

NORTH-HOLLAND PUBLISHING COMPANY - AMSTERDAM · LONDON
AMERICAN ELSEVIER PUBLISHING COMPANY, INC. - NEW YORK

© North-Holland Publishing Company – 1972

All rights reserved. No part of this publication may be reproduced, stored in a retrieval system, in any form or by any means, electronic, mechanical, photocopying, recording or otherwise, without the prior permission of the copyright owner.

Library of Congress Catalog Card Number: 78-190292
North-Holland ISBN: 0 7204 02441
American Elsevier ISBN: 0 444 10361 9

Publishers:

North-Holland Publishing Company – Amsterdam
North-Holland Publishing Company, Ltd. – London

Sole distributors for the U.S.A. and Canada:

American Elsevier Publishing Company, Inc.
52 Vanderbilt Avenue, New York, N.Y. 10017

Library
I.U.P.
Indiana, Pa.

539.754 In8p

c.1

Printed in The Netherlands

PREFACE

The present volume contains 29 invited talks and progress reports selected by the program committee of the VII ICPEAC. We are grateful to all contributing authors for making it possible to publish these valuable papers. We are indebted to Dr. T.R. Govers and Dr. F.J. de Heer, the editors, and to Mrs. Louise Roos, the local conference secretary, for the care they took in preparing the papers for the printer. We would also like to thank the North-Holland Publishing Co. for the deligent and efficient way in which they produced not only this book, but also the two volumes containing the abstracts of some 500 contributed papers. Together these books represent the scientific consciousness of the world of atomic- and electronic-collision physics, anno 1971.

As seems to be unavoidable, some irregularities occurred in the compilation of this volume. Professor E.E. Nikitin could not come to Amsterdam and only supplied us with the abstract of his paper included herein; the paper was presented by Professor Yu.N. Demkov at the Conference. The manuscript of Professor Demkov's own talk, which dealt with associative ionization and detachment, did not reach us in time. Professor A. Damburg could not come to the Conference, but he did provide us with the complete manuscript of his paper, and we are glad that it could be included in this book.

Three of our most distinguished colleagues who were alive and active at the time of the Boston conference in 1969 were very much missed in Amsterdam. Among them was the late Professor I. Amdur, the local chairman of the VI ICPEAC. The lasting influence of his personality and of his work was recalled in the opening talk by Professor F.T. Smith. A heavy loss was also caused by the tragic deaths, shortly before the Conference, of Professor R. Wolfgang and Dr. H. Rosenthal; they were still so young and promising.

We hope and are convinced that the next meeting in 1973 with all our friends in Yugoslavia, under the guidance of Dr. B. Cobić, will be as successful as the Amsterdam ICPEAC was. The field of atomic physics still seems to have enough unknown territory to make this possible.

J. Kistemaker, chairman
Local Organizing Committee
VII ICPEAC, Amsterdam 1971

Amsterdam, October 1971

v

ACKNOWLEDGEMENTS

The seventh International Conference of the Physics of Electronic and Atomic Collisions was organized under the auspices of the International Union of Pure and Applied Physics (IUPAP) and the Nederlandse Natuurkundige Vereniging (NNV).

It was sponsored by
- The International Union for Pure and Applied Physics;
- The Dutch Ministry of Education and Sciences;
- The Dutch Ministry of Culture;
- The Amsterdam Municipality;
- UNESCO;
- N.V. Philips' Gloeilampen Fabrieken;
- N.V. Rijn—Schelde Machinefabrieken en Scheepswerven;
- IBM Nederland N.V.;
- N.V. Geveke Fysica;
- N.V. Verenigde Bedrijven Bredero;
- Stichting Fundamenteel Onderzoek der Materie (FOM);
- Stichting Physica
- Royal Dutch Airlines (KLM)

VII ICPEAC

Officers

Chairman
L.M. Branscomb
National Bureau of Standards
Administration Building
Room, A-1138
Washington D.C. 20234, U.S.A.

Secretary
R. Geballe
Department of Physics
University of Washington
Seattle, Washington, 98105,
U.S.A.

Vice Chairman
H. Ehrhardt
Universität Trier-Kaiserslautern
Postfach 1049
675 Kaiserslautern, Germany

Treasurer
F.J. de Heer
FOM-Instituut voor Atoom-
en Molecuulfysica
Kruislaan 407
Amsterdam, the Netherlands

Executive Committee

The above officers (ex officio) and

N.V. Fedorenko
A.F. Ioffe Physico-Technical
Institute
Leningrad K-21, U.S.S.R.

J. Kistemaker
FOM-Instituut voor Atoom- en
Molecuulfysica
Kruislaan 407
Amsterdam, the Netherlands

Program Committee

The executive committee and

M. Barat
Institut d'électronique fondamentale
Faculté des Sciences, Bâtiment 350,
91-Orsay, France

E.E. Nikitin
Institute of Chemical Physics
Vorobyevskoye chaussee 2-B
Moscow, V-334, U.S.S.R.

A.C.H. Smith
Physics Department
University College London
Gower street
London W.C.1, England

VII ICPEAC INVITED TALKS AND PROGRESS REPORTS

REPULSIVE INTERACTIONS OF ATOMS OR IONS
WITH RARE-GAS STRUCTURE

In Memoriam I. Amdur

Felix T. Smith

Stanford Research Institute
333 Ravenswood Avenue
Menlo Park, California 94025, U.S.A.

ABSTRACT:

Current knowledge of repulsive potentials between rare-gas atoms and between them and rare-gas-like ions is surveyed, with emphasis on the comparison of experiment and theory, especially in the region of potential energies between 0.1 and 10 eV. In this region, the repulsion is essentially exponential and arises mainly from the operation of the Pauli exclusion principle on the outer electrons of closed-shell systems. In close encounters, both atoms are distorted and the repulsion energy is approximately the sum of the distortion energies inside each atom. This leads to derivation of a combining law for constructing potentials for mixed systems AB from the symmetric potential for A_2 and B_2. This combining rule is used to develop new connections between ion-atom potentials and the repulsive potentials in the alkali halide gases and solids.

1. Introduction

Those of us who were present at the previous conference of this series in Boston remember Professor Isadore Amdur and are saddened that he is not with us again in Amsterdam. Through the course of these meetings, many of us grew to know Professor Amdur, to respect him for his high standards of science, and to love him for his human sympathy and friendship, his modesty, and his generosity. He would have especially enjoyed being with us in Amsterdam where he spent a recent sabbatical, working with our hosts at the FOM Laboratory.

It is most fitting that we honor him in reviewing his scientific accomplishments in our field and in carrying further the development of new knowledge in a field to which he contributed so much.

As a scientist, Professor Amdur had an unusual consistency of style and of subject matter throughout his career. He chose problems simple in principle, but fundamental and important in nature--first, the recombination of

H atoms, a basic chemical reaction, and then the simplest collisions of atoms, a field in which he began to work more than 30 years ago.

In his first major paper on this topic [1], published in 1940, he announced his intention of devoting particular attention to repulsive interactions in the simplest systems, especially the collisions of He with He. I am sure he did not realize at that time how long that problem would continue to absorb much of his attention before it would be definitively disposed of in his 1967 work with Professor Jordan [2].

Professor Amdur worked in a number of related fields, including colli-sional interactions involving molecules and studies of transport properties and their connection with collision properties, but this paper must be limited to a selected portion of his work and the related work of others. I shall devote this review to the present status of our knowledge and understanding of the repul-sive interactions of rare-gas atoms and of ions with rare-gas structure. After a survey of the experimental and theoretical position with regard to the best studied of these systems, I will turn to a topic with which Professor Amdur was especially concerned, namely, the proper formulation of combining rules for predicting the repulsive potential of some species AB from a knowledge of the potential of the related species AA and BB. Finally I will turn briefly to another topic with which Amdur himself was long concerned and to which he was making a contribution at the end of his life, namely, the relationship between the potentials of neutral species and the repulsive part of the inter-action in the related alkali halide molecules and crystals.

2. Atom-atom potentials

Most of our knowledge of the repulsive interactions of neutral species has been obtained through experiments designed somewhat as shown in the sketch in fig. 1 [3]. Ions produced in the ion source are accelerated to a few hundred or a few thousand eV and pass through an aperture where many of them are neutralized either in grazing collisions with the wall or by collisions with the background gas. Beyond the aperture, the remaining ions are deflect-ed away by an electrostatic field, and a fast neutral beam proceeds onward into a region where it interacts with a target gas. Finally, those atoms that have not been removed from the beam are accepted through the final aper-ture and measured at the detector.

Conceptually, this is a chemist's experiment, modeled on the measurement of optical absorption as a function of distance. In a sense, atoms deflected from the beam so as to miss the detector can be considered as absorbed. In

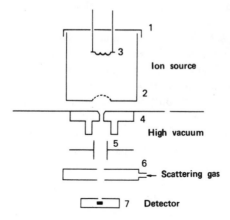

Fig. 1. Principal features of the Amdur beam experiment. Anode 1, cathode 2, filament 3, accelerating electrode 4, deflecting condenser 5, scattering chamber 6, detector 7.

fact, however, as fig. 2 illustrates, the analysis of the scattering experiment must be much more sophisticated. The effective angular aperture of the detector depends on the location at which the scattering event occurs in both the longitudinal and radial directions. Consequently, the analysis of the experiments requires a careful evaluation of geometric factors, including the distribution of fast particles in the incident beam. In the analysis of these experimental

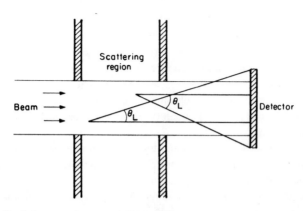

Fig. 2. Details of the scattering region. The angle of acceptance θ_L depends on the location of the scattering event.

factors, the group at MIT has gradually developed more and more sophisticated methods.

This type of measurement is best suited to exploring the repulsive region of interatomic potentials in the energy range lying between a few tenths of an eV and 10 or 20 eV. The actual experiments are conducted with beams of particles with kinetic energies between a few hundred and a few thousand eV; this energy range is suitable both for production of neutral beams by charge transfer and for their detection on a target either by thermal effects or by kinetic ejection of electrons. The actual region of the potential explored is lower than the kinetic energy of the particles by a factor of the order of 100, because only small-angle scattering is really being investigated. Roughly, the potential is probed at energies measured by the product of the scattering angle (in radians) and the kinetic energy. In Amdur's experiments, the region explored is one in which simple repulsive effects predominate (especially for closed-shell atoms, where the attractive dispersion forces are small) and it lies below the region where inelastic effects become important. When the potential energy exceeds about 10 or 20 eV, the collisions become strong enough to promote electrons into excited states, and inelastic effects can no longer be neglected. The experiments of Amdur therefore explore a region where the physical effects are comparatively simple, and the results should be susceptible to interpretation in a simple and uniform way.

It has long been customary to analyze the experimental data using as trial form for the potential an inverse power of r, the internuclear distance: $V = Br^{-s}$. The exponent s and the coefficient B are found by a fitting procedure. An exponential potential, $V = Ae^{-br}$, is known to give a much better representation, but leads to a more complicated functional form for the deflection function and consequently for the tedious analysis of geometric effects. However, computer programs have been developed at MIT for carrying out the analysis in the exponential form. Nevertheless, any given experiment can only probe a small region in r, and therefore the logarithmic slope b cannot be very well defined by a single set of measurements. The best results, as in the case of He_2, are obtained by combining the results of a number of experiments using different pieces of apparatus designed to probe different regions of the potentials.

For many years, the repetition and improvement of these experiments were prompted by a long-standing but gradually decreasing discrepancy between theory and experiment in the crucial case of the He_2 potential, a discrepancy that also prompted continuing work on the theoretical side.

The present state of these investigations is shown in fig. 3, in which we see the three most reliable measurements from MIT (in Amdur's estimation) [2],

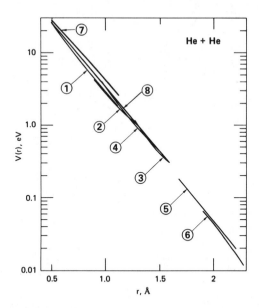

Fig. 3. Potential: He + He.
Experimental curves: 1 [2], 2 [4], 3 [5], 4 [6] from scattering; 5 [7], 6 [8] from transport and virial data. Theoretical curves: 7 [9], and 8 [10].

[4], [5], together with measurements by a substantially similar technique by Kamnev and Leonas [6] in Moscow as well as results obtained from transport properties and virial coefficients [7], [8]. Also plotted are the important theoretical results of Phillipson [9] and the even more reliable recent results of Matsumoto, Bender and Davidson [10]. The final result is an essentially perfect agreement between the data of the latest and best calculations and those of the most careful experiments. After many years of effort in both experiment and theory, this celebrated discrepancy has been entirely re-solved, and a long-standing problem may be considered closed. That this satis-factory solution has at length been attained must be attributed largely to the persistence with which Professor Amdur kept returning to this problem until it was truly and finally solved.

At this Conference, the field of interest in He_2 collisions has clearly shifted to interactions at larger distances and to thermal or even cryogenic energies, and into the outer attractive region of the potential.

Figures 4 and 5 show similar data for the systems Ar_2 and HeAr. It may be noted from these figures that the best theoretical results, using careful and

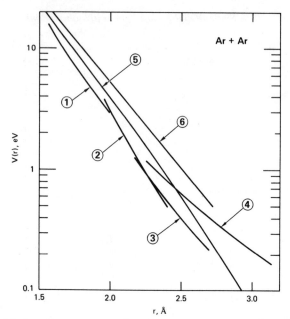

Fig. 4. Potential: Ar + Ar.
Experimental: 1 [11], 2 [12], 3 [13], 4 [6] from scattering; 5 [14] from shock compression.
Theoretical: 6 [15].

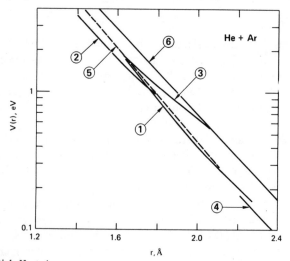

Fig. 5. Potential: He + Ar.
Experimental: 1 [16], 2 [12], 3 [6] from scattering; 4 [17] from diffusion.
Combining Rule (geometric mean): 5 [3f].
Theoretical: 6 [18].

extensive molecular orbital calculations, uniformly exceed the experimental results by a considerable amount. It may be suspected that this discrepancy results in part from the difficulty of including enough configurations for calculations in systems involving atoms as big as argon. If so, it is to be hoped that the next few years will see a considerable reduction in the gap. In addition, these figures show a good deal more discrepancy between the various experiments than in the He_2 system, which has been much more thoroughly studied than any of the others.

In fig. 5, we show in addition to the experimental and theoretical results an estimate (shown by the dashed curve) made by Amdur by combining the results of the He_2 and the Ar_2 potentials to predict the HeAr potential [3f]. For this prediction, Amdur used his best fit to the experimental data for the two symmetric potentials and assumed that the potentials could be combined, at least approximately, by a geometric mean rule to estimate the asymmetric potential:

$$V_{12}(r) \approx [V_{11}(r) V_{22}(r)]^{1/2}. \tag{1}$$

For an exponential potential,

$$V_{ii} = A_{ii} \exp(-b_{ii}r), \tag{2}$$

the result is

$$V_{12}(r) \approx A_{12} \exp(-b_{12}r), \tag{3}$$

$$b_{12} \approx \tfrac{1}{2}(b_1 + b_2), \tag{4}$$

$$A_{12} \approx (A_{11}A_{22})^{1/2}. \tag{5}$$

Empirically the result shown in fig. 5 is quite gratifying. However, as Amdur often pointed out, a good theoretical justification for this plausible procedure has always been lacking.

In fig. 6, we show in one plot a large number of experimental results for the three systems, He_2 HeAr, and Ar_2 (included are additional experimental results of varying reliability beyond those shown in figs. 3 to 5). This figure shows strikingly the common tendency of these systems to show a simple exponential repulsive potential in the domain of potential energies from about 0.1 to 10 eV, i.e., over at least two decades. In addition, the three

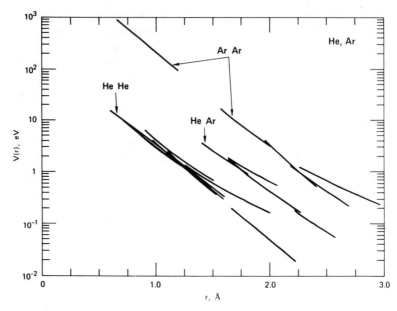

Fig. 6. Experimental potential data: He + He, He + Ar, and Ar + Ar. Data as in figs. 3-5, with additions: He + He [19]; Ar + Ar [20].

curves are substantially parallel, i.e. the exponential fall-off is substantially the same in the three potentials. Finally, the three curves are evenly spaced, with the HeAr case lying equidistant from the other two. This spacing can be considered as arising either from a simple vertical displacement from one curve to the next, reflecting the concept of the geometric mean rule, or from a horizontal displacement from curve to curve, representing an increase in size as one goes from He to Ar in one or both of the collision partners. As long as the curves are substantially simple exponentials with the same exponential constant, there is no way of choosing between these points of view. However, the geometric-mean concept appears to require comparing the potentials at equal internuclear distances, which does not seem really appropriate when dealing with atoms which we usually consider to be of different sizes. On the other hand, the concept of shifting the curves in the radial direction implies comparing collision radii at equal interaction energies instead of comparing interaction energies at equal radii.

The exponential behavior of these repulsive potentials has been known for a long time, and similar behavior occurs in the repulsive portion of the inter-actions in the alkali halide molecules and crystals; this type of interaction is fundamental for the Born-Mayer theory of the alkali halide crystals. Since the 1920s, this exponential repulsion has been explained as due to the Pauli exclusion principle operating when the electrons in the outer orbitals of two neighboring atoms begin to overlap. The overlap in question occurs in the exponential tails of the electron densities in the two atoms, and the exponential increase in the repulsion energies at smaller distances is assumed to be directly related to the exponential increase in the amount of overlap. The concept is illustrated in fig. 7, where the solid curves schematically represent the electron density associated with the orbitals in the outer shells. The increase in size of the heavier atoms is then associated with the existence of nodes in the wave functions and the filling of inner shells. This overlap model suggests the basis for the quantitative estimation of repulsion energies by perturbation theory and related methods.

The theoretical calculations of these repulsive potentials are of two principal types: detailed molecular structure calculations, and approximations based on the Thomas-Fermi-Dirac (TFD) statistical model. Thorough molecular orbital calculations are available for rare-gas colliding systems up to and including Ar, but the best agreement between theory and experiment is obtained only in the first row of the Periodic Table, including the Ne-Ne collision.

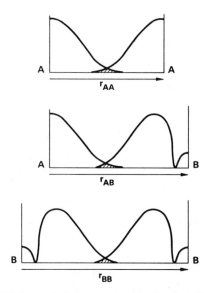

Fig. 7. The overlap model. Outer shell electron densities for dissimilar atoms (schematic).

Various forms of the statistical theory are available for use in the case of heavier systems. Abrahamson has carried out extensive calculations using a TFD theory for all the rare gas combinations [21], but the expressions he used have been criticized [22], [23] and the potential energies appear to be too high by 30% or more for many of the heavier systems. The same procedure was applied by Menendez [24] and others to the collision of alkali ions with rare gases, and these results are presumably afflicted by the same errors. An improved calculation by Gaydaenko and Nikulin [25] is available for all neutral atoms up to and including Xe. For the ion-atom case there exist careful calculations by Sida [26] for the two systems K^+ + Ar and Ca^{++} + Ne. A new and interesting application of the TFD concepts, including terms introduced by Brueckner [27] and others, is being carried out by Kim and Gordon [28], and the results look extremely promising in such systems as Ar_2, where good agreement with the experiments is obtained.

It is clear from a plot such as that in fig. 6 that the difference in radii between two different atoms of the rare gases is a well-defined quantity sub-

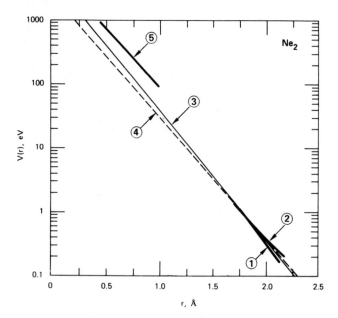

Fig. 8. Potential: Ne + Ne.
Experimental: 1 [29], 2 [6], 5 [30].
Theory: 3 [15], 4 [25].

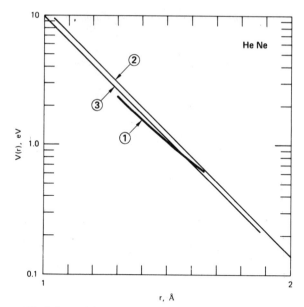

Fig.9. Potential: He + Ne.
Experimental: 1 [6].
Theory: 2 [18], 3 [25], geometric-mean combining rule.

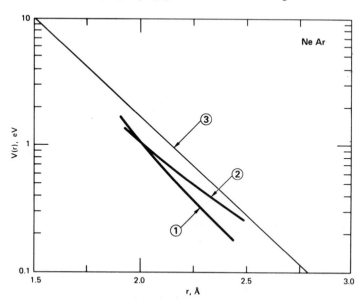

Fig. 10. Potential: Ne + Ar.
Experimental: 1 [31], 2 [6].
Theory: 3 [18].

Table 1

Collison radii (r) and radial differences (both in Å) for various rare-gas systems, evaluated at a standard potential energy of 1 eV. The last column represents the average of all available data.

Y	r(YHe)	r(YAr)	$\frac{1}{2}r(Y_2)$	r(YHe)$-r(He_2)$	r(YAr)$-r$(HeAr)	$\frac{1}{2}r(Y_2)-\frac{1}{2}r(He_2)$	r(Y)$-r$(He) average
He	1.30	1.78	0.65	0	0	0	0
Ne	1.53	2.03	0.89	0.23	0.25	0.24	0.24
Ar	1.78	2.29	1.145	0.48	0.51	0.495	0.50
Kr	2.00	2.67	1.28	0.70	0.89	0.63	0.70
Xe	2.00	2.63	1.42	0.70	0.85	0.77	0.75

Table 2

Comparison of the average radial differences of table 1 with those predicted by Pauling [32]. The collision radii given by Pauling [32] are also listed. Distances are in Å.

Y	Collisional average (1 eV)	Crystal (Pauling)	
	$r(Y) - r(He)$	$r_{cr}(Y) - r_{cr}(He)$	$r_{cr}(Y)$
He	0	0	0.93
Ne	0.24	0.19	1.12
Ar	0.50	0.60	1.54
Kr	0.70	0.75	1.69
Xe	0.75	0.96	1.90

stantially independent of energy over a wide range. On the other hand, the atomic radii themselves are energy dependent, and perhaps should be defined at a standard potential energy. Radii defined at 1 eV will clearly be quite different from radii defined at thermal energies.

The same concepts apply to the other rare gases. A reasonable amount of information, both theoretical and experimental, is available for the systems

Table 3

Exponential constant (b), range ($\rho = b^{-1}$) and size (X) for a number of rare-gas-like systems. The interaction potential was represented by $V(r) = A\exp(-br)$. The size X, defined by $X = \ln(A/\rho F_0)$ was computed by using standard force, $F_0 = 1$ eV/Å. "T" and "E" refer to theoretical and experimental data, respectively; "g" and "s" indicate gaseous and solid state systems.

	$Be^{++}He$	Li^+He	He_2	H^-He	Li^+H^- (g)	
$b(Å^{-1})$	5.7	5.1	4.10	2.04	2.79	
$\rho = b^{-1}$, (Å)	0.175	0.196	0.244	0.491	0.358	
X (Å)	1.430	1.560	1.630	1.769	1.961	

	$Ca^{++}Ne$		Ne_2		Na^+F^- (g)	Na^+F^- (s)
b ($Å^{-1}$)	5.0		4.57		3.60	3.03
ρ (Å)	0.200		0.219		0.278	0.330
X (Å)	2.165		2.138		2.369	2.20

	$K^+Ar(T)$	$Ar_2(E)$	Cl^-Ar	K^+Cl^- (g)	K^+Cl^- (s)
b ($Å^{-1}$)	3.6	3.90	2.59	3.01	2.97
ρ (Å)	0.277	0.256	0.386	0.332	0.337
X (Å)	2.615	2.612	2.750	3.035	2.91

Ne_2, HeNe, and NeAr, illustrated in figs. 8, 9, and 10. Smaller amounts of information of lesser reliability, but still of some value, are available for the other rare gases as well. Tables 1 and 2 present a selection of data on the collision radii and the radial differences between various species evaluated at the standard potential energy of 1 eV. These can be compared with estimates made by Pauling [32], derived from interpolation between neighbouring alkali and halide ions in crystals and referring to a lower effective repulsive energy. Nevertheless, the radial differences are reasonably comparable.

Table 3 shows information on the best-determined exponential constants for rare-gas systems; it is clear that these are not truly identical from system to system and that the constant in question is larger for Ne than for either He or Ar. Naively, one would expect this quantity to vary smoothly with the ionization potential, and such evidence as there is seems to indicate that such a relationship holds for all of the rare gases with eight electrons in the outer shell. Possibly the fact that He appears to be softer than Ne, despite its higher ionization potential, is related to the number of electrons available to create the repulsive field.

3. Ion-atom potentials

Turning now to closed shell ions colliding with rare gases, fig. 11 shows data for K^+ + Ar, a system that was investigated by Amdur and others at the FOM Laboratory [33], [34]. It has also been studied by the MIT group in the last year or two, and their paper on the subject was presented at this Conference [35] as was another by Inouye and Kita [36]. Except for the first set of measurements, which appear to be low in absolute value, these results are in substantial agreement with one another and also with the theory of Sida [26], which was based on a Thomas-Fermi-Dirac procedure. Figure 12 shows another system that has been thoroughly investigated, Li^+ + He. Here, however, the experimental techniques differ. Zehr and Berry [37] used a retarding potential to discriminate against ions scattered through angles greater than a certain minimum deflection, thereby obtaining an estimate of the potential. The SRI group [38] used differential scattering to determine the potential. These results are in substantial agreement with the theoretical potentials that have been determined by three groups [39], [40], [41], and the deviations between experimental and theoretical results at small r are explained by the opening of inelastic channels in the experimental measurements. The potential for Li^+ + He is therefore as well established as that for He_2, and the theoretical estimates should be used.

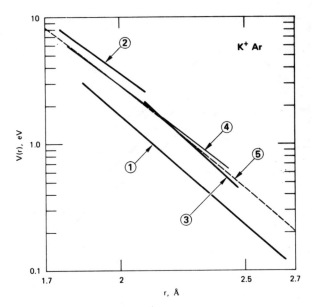

Fig. 11. Potential: K^+ + Ar.
Experimental: 1 [33, 34], 2 and 3 [35], 4 [36].
Theory: 5 [26].

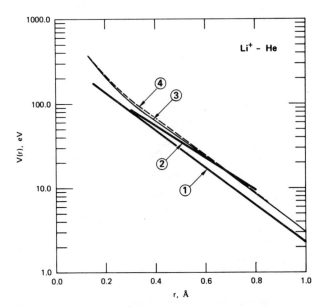

Fig. 12. Potential: Li^+He.
Experimental: 1 [37], 2 [38].
Theory: 3 [39], 4 [40, 41].

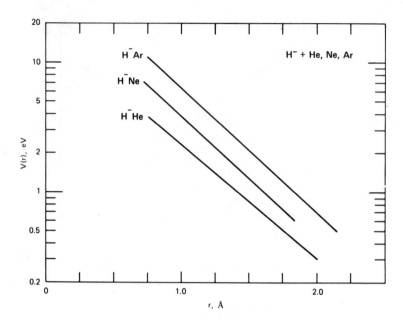

Fig. 13. Potentials: $H^- +$ He, Ne, Ar [42].

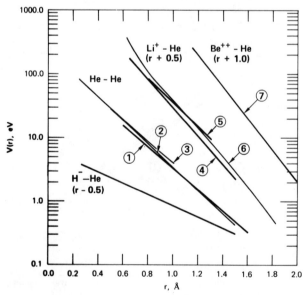

Fig. 14. Potentials: $He^- + H^-$ He, Li^+, Be^{++}.
Curves: He + He: 1 most probable experimental value, 2 [10], 3 [9];
He + Li^+: 4 [37], 5 [38], 6 [39];
He + Be^{++}: 7 [43];
H^- + He: [42].

In fig. 13 we show the experimentally determined potentials for H^- as scattered by He, Ne, and Ar, and in fig. 14 we show all the systems isoelectronic with He_2, including the recent results of Giffin and Berry [43] on Be^{++} + He. Figure 14 illustrates particularly clearly a systematic change in the slopes of the semi-log plots, showing a slight steepening toward heavier positive ions and a large fall-off in slope in going from He to H^-. This illustrates an effect that might be expected on physical grounds, namely, that the hardness or softness of the interaction depends mostly on the softer of the two partners. The same is shown in the values tabulated in table 3. This result, which is physically plausible, tends to make questionable the geometric-mean combining rule, since a geometric mean for the potentials leads to an arithmetic mean for the exponential constant. With an arithmetic mean, the harder of the two collision partners would tend to control the slope instead of the softer. Physical intuition and the results of table 3 suggest that a better combining rule would be based on a mean between the reciprocals of the exponential constants instead of those constants themselves.

4. The combining rule

4.1. *The distortion model*

To discuss the combining rule in a more quantitative way, I wish to call your attention to the existence of another model that is superficially different from the picture of overlap between the colliding atoms. This is the distortion model, which is to be considered complementary to the overlap model, and not in contradiction to it. Presumably, similar results could be obtained by using either point of view, but each one is illuminating in its own way. The distortion model is based on the fact that we are dealing with closed-shell atoms, electrons of which cannot in fact overlap into the region occupied by electrons of the other atom because of the Pauli exclusion principle, unless they are promoted into a very much higher excited state. Consequently, we can picture the situation as one in which each atom is distorted by the presence of its neighbor in such a way that the electron clouds in the two atoms avoid overlapping each other. The electron clouds of the two atoms can then be considered as terminating at a common surface lying somewhere between the two atomic centers. While this surface need not be planar (except in encounters between identical atoms), it is reasonable in most cases to assume that it is approximately so. The situation is then as pictured in fig. 15. Each atom is distorted in much the same way as a fast tennis ball when it collides with the racket. The interaction energy is then made up principally of the distortion energies internal to the colliding atoms.

DISTORTION AND DIPOLE MOMENTS

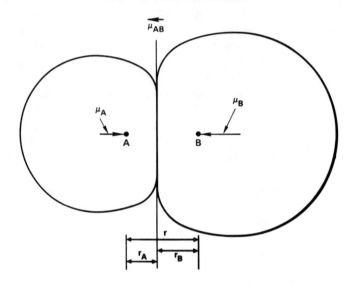

Fig. 15. Atomic distortion in rare-gas collisions. Effective distortion radii r_A, r_B and dipole moments (schematic).

One of the consequences of this atomic distortion is the continuum infrared absorption seen in mixtures of neutral gases, including rare-gas mixtures. The distortion picture was applied especially clearly by Matcha and Nesbet [18] to this problem. The atomic distortion in each atom creates a temporary dipole moment; in the case of collisions of unlike atoms, this results in the existence of a transient dipole for the diatomic pair. Matcha and Nesbet have exploited this model in the particular case of the three rare-gas pairs, HeNe, HeAr, and NeAr, for which they have done careful molecular-orbital calculations of the repulsive potential and the resulting dipole moments. They point out that the resultant dipole moment should be the difference between the internal dipole moments induced by the distortion in each of the two colliding atoms. What has not been noticed previously is that this model leads to a simple derivation of a combining rule for deducing the repulsive potentials between unlike atoms from those for the two like pairs.

In the case of identical atoms, it is clear that the dividing surface between the two atoms in the collision must lie halfway between the nuclei. For an unlike pair, as shown in fig. 15, this surface may be assumed to remain planar, but to be placed at some unknown distance r_A part-way along the distance r

between the nuclei of A and B. The potential is the sum of two terms, the distortion energies of atoms A and B, depending on r_A and $r_B = r - r_A$, each of which is known if the potentials V_{AA} and V_{BB} are known. The sole uncertainty is the location of the dividing surface, r_A. Clearly this surface will place itself in such a position that the total potential V_{AB} is minimized:

$$V_{AB}(r) = \tfrac{1}{2} V_{AA}(2r_A) + \tfrac{1}{2} V_{BB}(2r_B),\tag{6}$$

$$r_A + r_B = r,\tag{7}$$

$$\partial V_{AB}(r, r_A)/\partial r_A = 0,\tag{8}$$

$$(dV_{AA}(r)/dr)_{r=2r_A} = (dV_{BB}(r)/dr)_{r=2r_B}.\tag{9}$$

The condition for determining r_A is then that the restoring forces arising from the distortion in the two atoms are equal and opposite.

This condition allows us to obtain a combining law for any functional form of the distortion energies in the two symmetric systems. We can now apply it in particular to the simple case where these potentials are exponential. In this case, it is convenient to write the exponentials in the following form, where we use a range ρ, the reciprocal of the exponential constant b used previously:

$$V_{11} = A_{11} \exp(-r/\rho_{11}),\tag{10}$$

$$V_{22} = A_{22} \exp(-r/\rho_{22}).\tag{11}$$

It is an accident resulting from the exponential nature of the force law that the two terms in the combined potential for the asymmetric case coalesce into a single exponential term with a range that is just the arithmetic mean of the ranges for the two symmetric systems:

$$V_{12} = A_{12} \exp(-r/\rho_{12}),\tag{12}$$

$$\rho_{12} = \tfrac{1}{2}(\rho_{11} + \rho_{22}).\tag{13}$$

The pre-exponential constants combine in a slightly more complicated way:

$$(A_{12}/\rho_{12})^{2\rho_{12}} = (A_{11}/\rho_{11})^{\rho_{11}} (A_{22}/\rho_{22})^{\rho_{22}}.\tag{14}$$

Explicitly, we have:

$$r_A \left(\frac{1}{\rho_{11}} + \frac{1}{\rho_{22}} \right) = \frac{r}{\rho_{22}} + \frac{1}{2} \ell n \left(\frac{A_{11} \rho_{22}}{\rho_{11} A_{22}} \right) . \tag{15}$$

These results are exact for the exponential potential, and they can be used over local regions for other potentials that can be approximated by exponentials.

The limitations of these results should be emphasized. The principal one arises from the assumption that the interaction is mainly caused by the internal distortion of each of the two colliding atoms and that long-range forces between the two atoms or between their component parts are unimportant. As we will see, this condition is increasingly violated in harder collisions, particularly when the collision energy exceeds 10 eV. Secondly, this result depends on the approximation that the distortion surface is planar; this condition gradually loses its validity as the two colliding atoms become very different in size and in the tightness with which their outer electrons are bound. Thirdly, this model holds only for situations involving closed shells and should not be applied where valence forces may occur. Fourthly, however, we may point out that the model may have some approximate usefulness where the colliding partners are not spherically symmetric atoms but small molecules, which often can, at least approximately, be treated by replacing them by equivalent spheres.

Now let us consider some of the consequences of the combining rule arising from the distortion model. Firstly, we note that it is the ranges ρ that are averaged and not their reciprocals. This corresponds with the intuitive physical argument that the forces are dominated by the softer and not the harder of the two partners. Secondly, we see from the combining rule for the pre-exponential factors that the equation reduces to the geometric mean if the ranges ρ are approximately equal, a condition that in fact does often apply. This shows in a gratifying way that the geometric mean rule can indeed be justified under some circumstances and that the new distortion rule is an improvement with a larger range of validity.

4.2. Applications

There are various ways in which a combining rule can be used. Not only can potentials for asymmetric systems be deduced from those for symmetric ones, but one may go in other directions to obtain symmetric potentials from asymmetric ones. The principal cases are the following:

(a)   (AA, BB) → (AB)

(b)   (AA, AB) → (BB)

(c)   (AB, BC, CA) → (AA, BB, CC) .

Of these, the third possibility, the deduction of three symmetric potentials from three asymmetric ones, is the most stringent test of the capabilities of a combining rule. Fortunately in the three systems, HeNe, HeAr, and NeAr, we have in the calculations of Matcha and Nesbet [18] just the material for such a test. In fig. 16, we show the results of applying the combining rule to Matcha and Nesbet's data to deduce potentials for the systems He_2, Ne_2, and Ar_2. When the distortion combining rule is used, we obtain from Matcha and Nesbet a potential for He_2 that is completely indistinguishable from the best theoretical potential, that of Matsumoto et al. [10]; similarly the results for Ne_2 and Ar_2 are very close to the best calculations, those of Gilbert and Wahl [15]. In contrast, we can apply the same procedure to extract poten-

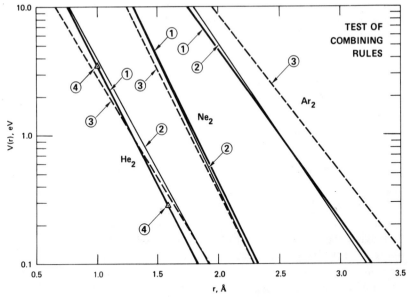

Fig. 16. Test of combining rules.
Potentials for He_2, Ne_2, Ar_2 deduced from data of [18] for HeNe, HeAr, NeAr: 1, curves deduced by the distortion rule; 3, curves deduced by the geometric mean. Direct calculation: 2, curves of [15]; 4, points from [10]. The distortion combining rule gives the following values for A(eV) and ρ(Å): He_2: 252.92 and 0.2336; Ne_2: 3493.0 and 0.2222; Ar_2: 2081.8 and 0.3282.

tials by the geometric mean combining rule, and the results are shown on the dashed curves on the same figure. The results convincingly show the superiority of the distortion combining law, and they also show the excellence of the Matcha and Nesbet calculations. (However, as seen earlier, their calculations resemble Gilbert and Wahl's in overestimating the potentials involving Ar.)

As I have mentioned, the distortion model was originally applied in the treatment of dipole moments. The dipole moments of each of the colliding molecules increase as the distortion increases, and these opposing dipoles exert a repulsive force on each other. There results a contribution to the potential that should strictly be added to the contribution arising from the internal distortion of the two atoms:

$$V(r) = V_{dis}(r) + V_\mu(r) . \tag{16}$$

This dipole-dipole repulsion term is of the form

$$V_\mu(r) = \frac{2\mu_A(r_A)\mu_B(r_B)}{r^3} \tag{17}$$

The individual dipole moments are probably close to exponential functions:

$$\mu_A(r_A) \approx M_A \exp(-\lambda_A r_A) . \tag{18}$$

Using (15), we find then

$$V_\mu(r) = Wr^{-3}\exp(-\bar{\lambda}r), \tag{19}$$

where

$$\bar{\lambda} = (\rho_{11}\lambda_A + \rho_{22}\lambda_B)/\rho_{11} + \rho_{22}), \tag{19a}$$

$$W = 2M_A M_B(A_{11}\rho_{22}/\rho_{11}A_{22})^y, \tag{19b}$$

and

$$y = \tfrac{1}{2}(\lambda_A - \lambda_B)\rho_{11}\rho_{22}/(\rho_{11} + \rho_{22}) . \tag{19c}$$

To evaluate the importance of this term, information is needed on the dipole moments of the individual atoms as a function of the distance to the distorting plane at r_A or r_B. Such information is not directly available, but a rough estimate based on Matcha and Nesbet's calculation [18] of the resultant diatomic dipole moments suggests that the dipole-dipole energy may become important when the total interaction potential is of the order 10 eV or more and that it will be comparatively unimportant for most of the range considered here. Nevertheless this dipole-dipole term is of great interest since it shows the origin of the deviation from the exponential behavior and the beginning of an influence of the coulomb interactions that become greater and greater as the two nuclei approach each other and penetrate the shielding electron clouds. Initially, this effect is dominated by a term of the form r^{-3}, but as the penetration increases one may expect it to be converted to an ion-dipole term behaving as r^{-2}, and ultimately to a shielded coulomb term going as r^{-1}:

$$V(r) \approx A e^{-br} (r \text{ large})$$

$$\rightarrow W r^{-3} \exp(-\bar{\lambda} r)$$

$$\rightarrow N r^{-2} \exp(-\gamma r)$$

$$\rightarrow \frac{Z_1 Z_2 e^2}{r} \exp(-cr) \ (r \rightarrow 0). \tag{20}$$

In this way we see an illuminating physical origin for the transition, which is in fact seen both in the numerical results of TFD calculations and of more sophisticated models and in the experimental results, where the effects of the various electronic shells may be also seen.

If a dipole-dipole or other long-range term is important in the repulsive potential, it is of course possible to include it explicitly in the expression for the total energy that is to be minimized in locating the distortion plane at r_A. Such a procedure makes it possible to extend the combining rule to regions of higher potentials and shorter internuclear distances. The cost will be slightly a greater complexity in the expressions and possibly a greater use of simple numerical methods.

Let us now return to the region of lower energies where the dipole-dipole term can be safely neglected. Re-examining the combining rule for the pre-exponential constants, we are led to define a new quantity of the dimensions of length, which we may term the atomic size, X, by taking logarithms on both sides of eq. (14). To do this, it is convenient to introduce a standard force F_0 to make the coefficients inside the logarithm appropriately dimensionless:

$$X = \rho \ln(A/\rho F_0). \tag{21}$$

The atomic size is then dependent on the standard force, which measures the magnitude of the distortion of each of the colliding atoms. Thus we see that it is better to compare atomic sizes at a standard restoring force, instead of at a common value of the repulsive potential energy. It is convenient to take as standard force $F_0 = 1$ eV/Å. Using the definition (21), the combining rule for the pre-exponential constant A becomes simply an arithmetic-mean combining rule for the size parameter X:

$$X_{12} = \tfrac{1}{2} (X_{11} + X_{22}) .\tag{22}$$

Furthermore, an exponential potential can be written in terms of the two parameters with dimensions of length X and ρ and the unit force F_0:

$$V = \rho F_0 \exp [(X - r)/\rho] .\tag{23}$$

This form for the potential is in fact identical with the Born-Mayer repulsive term if the range parameters ρ are essentially identical, as they appear to be in the alkali halide crystals (but in the crystal theory, the nearest-neighbor spacing d_0 appears instead of X; however, both quantities reflect the effect of the ionic size).

In tables 3 and 4 we present a number of values of the range parameter ρ and size parameter X for various colliding systems, extracted either from experimental or theoretical information. Furthermore, we can use the combining rules in their simplest forms to obtain parameters for the distortion potentials of other colliding pairs that have not been directly measured or are not accessible to easy measurement. Using data on the three systems for which collisions with H^- have been studied, we can obtain the estimates of these parameters for the hypothetical collisions of H^- with H^-. The numbers are reasonably comparable, and we take their average as a best value. Similarly, we can obtain parameters of the distortion potential for $Li^+ + Li^+$. Finally, using the combining rule again, we can estimate the distortion potential for the molecule Li^+H^-. In using the combining rule in this case, we are dealing with a highly unfavorable example, since the notion of a planar boundary is very inappropriate to the tightly bound Li^+ embedded in the loose H^-.

In a similar way, we show estimates obtained for the system K^+Cl^-. For the collisions of Cl^- with the rare gases, we can use the data from the FOM Laboratory [34]. For K^+ collisons we have in addition the new work from MIT [35] and from Japan [36], reported at this meeting, and the theoretical estimate of Sida [26] for K^+ Ar. In this case there are two difficulties: (1) there is a discrepancy between the theoretical and experimental potentials for Ar_2, so that the range ρ is still rather uncertain; (2) there is a lack of confirming data from more than one laboratory on Cl^- collisions with the rare gases and a need for more refined geometrical analysis of the FOM measurements, before the absolute magnitude of the potential curves (i.e., the size parameter X) can be considered well established.

The results are then compared in table 4 with known information about

Library
I.U.P.
Indiana, Pa.

539.754 In8p
c.1

Table 4
Range (ρ) and size (X): connection between neutrals, ions and alkali halides. (Values in
Å, see also caption of table 3.)

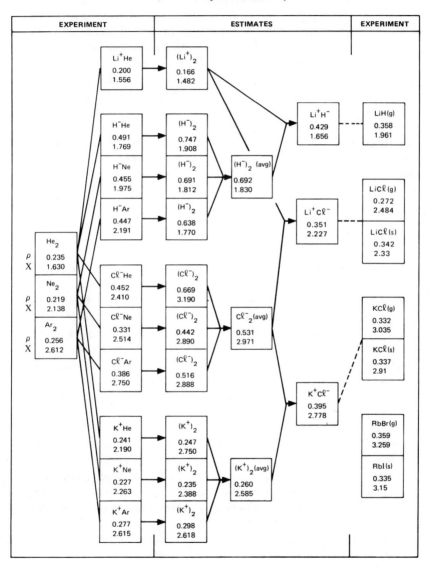

the alkali halides and hydrides, which we will shortly discuss in more detail. These results, based in many cases on data of uncertain accuracy, are at any rate suggestive of the connection that can be made between gas-phase collision data and the repulsive parameters of the alkali halides. In the near future, I hope that this connection will become better established, leading either to better agreement or to systematic disagreements that may reveal meaningful physical effects. For this purpose, we need more collision studies on ion-atom systems by various techniques including differential scattering and the retarding-potential method. Since a combination of theoretical and experimental approaches will lead to the most rapid and assured progress, particular attention should be devoted to the lighter species, i.e., various combination including F^-, Ne, and Na^+ as well as H^-, He, and Li^+. However, the heavier species and various mixed combinations should not be neglected, especially since new developments in the statistical (TFD) theoretical approach promise to make these accessible to reliable prediction.

5. Alkali halides

Having shown how the combining rules can be used to make a connection with the parameters of the repulsive potential for the alkali halides, let us look at the existing experimental information on those ionic but rare-gas-like systems. The connection between the rare gases and the alkali halides was in fact an old interest of Professor Amdur, and the problem of applying information from the neutral rare gases to predict the repulsive interaction in the alkali halides was the subject of an interesting piece of work that was partially completed at the time of his death. I will return to this contribution of Amdur after briefly describing the current situation with regard to these important substances.

Historically, the alkali halides were first studied in solids, and a long series of important papers beginning with several by Max Born have been devoted to the development of a theory of their structure [44]. The repulsive interaction of the closed shells plays an important part in this development. The experimental data include compressibilities and other thermodynamic properties, measurements of the equilibrium ionic spacings, and heats of vaporization. In addition, ultrasonic measurements are now providing further information of impressive accuracy on some of the important parameters of the crystals [45]. From these pieces of information, one can obtain estimates of the effective potential and several of its derivatives at the equilibrium spacing, and by subtraction of the ionic term and of a Van der Waals term, a good estimate of the repulsion potential can be obtained. This repulsion potential has usually been assumed to have the Born-Mayer form, as justified in eq. (23).

The alkali halide molecules have been extensively studied in recent years, and highly refined spectroscopic information is available on them. From their heats of formation we know the equilibrium value of their potential, and from spectroscopic data we know very precisely their equilibrium internuclear distances, dipole moments, and no less than the first four derivatives of the potential at the equilibrium spacing. This spacing is a good deal smaller than the spacing in the related crystal, so that much information is available that can be used to construct potential curves.

Customarily, it is assumed that the potential for the alkali halide molecules is of the form originally given by Rittner [46] :

$$U_{12}(r) = \frac{e^2}{r} - \frac{(\alpha_1 + \alpha_2)e^2}{2r^4}$$

$$- \frac{2\alpha_1\alpha_2 e^2}{r^7} - \frac{C_6}{r^6} + V_{rep}(r),$$

where α_1 and α_2 are the atomic polarizabilities and C_6 the Van der Waals constant. Using experimental data and this potential form, one can obtain estimates of the repulsive part of the potential at the equilibrium spacing, its slope, and higher derivatives [47]. In fig. 17 we present the existing information on these repulsive potentials for alkali halides [48]. Fig. 17 shows that the slopes about the two (gas and solid) equilibrium distances consistently fail to give a proper fit. This suggests a systematic error in the Rittner potential or in the estimates used for the polarizabilities in it. Since that potential omits consideration of the ion-dipole and dipole-dipole terms produced by the distortion of the electron clouds, we believe that the discrepancy can be explained and remedied. In the meanwhile, the best information now available has been used to compute the estimated range and size parameters for these species shown in table 5.

In table 6, the information on the diatomic size parameters of the alkali halides from table 5 is used to deduce differences in sizes of the various alkali and halide ions; the gaseous diatomic and the crystal results are reasonably in concordance with each other. In table 7 the crystal and gaseous data are used to estimate values of the ionic sizes themselves, using only one piece of collisional information, the ratio between the sizes of K^+ and Cl^- from data in table 4. At present, the data used are of uncertain reliability, and the self-consistency of the general pattern appears reasonably encouraging, at least

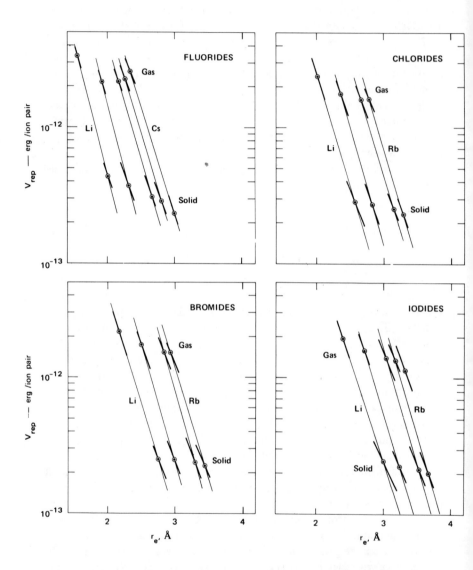

Fig. 17. Repulsive potentials for alkali halides. The short, heavy lines indicate potential energies derived from experimental data. The light lines are drawn between the gas and solid equilibrium points [48].

Table 5
Range (ρ) and size (X) in alkali halides (in Å); see also caption of table 3.

		F⁻		Cℓ⁻		Br⁻		I⁻	
		ρ	X	ρ	X	ρ	X	ρ	X
Li⁺	g	0.2640	2.110	0.2722	2.484	0.2742	2.609	0.2802	2.803
	s	0.299	1.98	0.342	2.33	0.353	2.46	0.430	2.56
Na⁺	g	0.2783	2.369	0.2954	2.750	0.3129	2.892	0.3131	3.071
	s	0.330	2.20	0.317	2.62	0.340	2.72	0.386	2.85
K⁺	g	0.3096	2.632	0.3324	3.035	0.3453	3.172	0.3489	3.370
	s	0.334	2.48	0.337	2.91	0.335	3.03	0.355	3.17
Rb⁺	g	0.3257	2.750	0.3532	3.163	0.3587	3.295	0.3623	3.479
	s	0.328	2.62	0.318	3.04	0.335	3.15	0.337	3.34
Cs⁺	g	0.3453	2.878	0.3517	3.282	0.3105	3.374	0.3187	3.572
	s	0.282	2.81						

enough to warrant further measurements and calculations to make better estimates of these various parameters. It is interesting that the ratio of sizes of K^+ to Cl^- obtained by using collision data, 0.87, is closer to the value of 0.95 obtained by Fumi and Tosi [49] than to the traditional value of 0.73.

These preliminary results, encouraging as they are, suggest some directions for future research in gas-phase ion-atom collisions as well as on the alkali halides themselves to develop and exploit these connections further. A number of questions are left open. Firstly, can a repulsive potential be defined unambiguously in principle and separated in a unique way from the various longer-range terms, including ion-distortion dipole and induced dipole terms and dipole-dipole terms? Secondly, to what extent can the repulsive term be treated as a simple exponential and how important is its possible slow deviation from the exponential form? (Such a deviation would lead to slightly different values of ρ and X when the potential is evaluated at different values of R, and this might cause small systematic variations between the gaseous and crystal values). Thirdly, to what extent is the distortion potential, ap-

Table 6
Size differences in alkali and alkali ions (in Å) obtained from the data of table 5.

			ΔX(H–F)		ΔX(F–Cl)		ΔX(Cl–Br)		ΔX(Br–I)		ΔX(alk⁺) avg.	final avg.
	(g)	LiH	0.149	LiF	0.374	LiCl	0.225	LiBr	0.194	LiI		
	(s)				0.35		0.13		0.10			
ΔX(Li–Na)	(g)				0.259		0.266		0.283		0.268	0.269	0.267
	(s)				0.22		0.29		0.26		0.29	0.265	
	(g)			NaF	0.381	NaCl	0.142	NaBr	0.179	NaI		
	(s)				0.42		0.10		0.13			
ΔX(Na–K)	(g)				0.263		0.285		0.280		0.299	0.282	0.291
	(s)				0.28		0.29		0.31		0.32	0.30	
	(g)			KF	0.403	KCl	0.137	KBr	0.198	KI		
	(s)				0.43		0.12		0.14			
ΔX(K–Rb)	(g)				0.118		0.128		0.123		0.109	0.120	0.130
	(s)				0.14		0.13		0.12		0.17	0.14	
	(g)			RbF	0.413	RbCl	0.132	RbBr	0.184	RbI		
	(s)				0.42		0.11		0.19			
ΔX(Rb–Cs)	(g)				0.128		0.119		0.079		0.093	0.105	0.122
	(s)				0.19							0.19	
	(g)			CsF	0.404	CsCl	0.092	CsBr	0.198	CsI		
ΔX(hal⁻) avg.	(g)		0.149		0.395		0.144		0.191			
	(s)				0.405		0.105		0.14			
Final average			0.149		0.400		0.125		0.165			

Table 7

Ionic and atomic sizes (in Å). X: estimated from alkali halides, based on $X_s(KCl) = 2.91$, $X(K^+)/X(Cl^-) = 1.293/1.484$, and size differences from table 6; X_0: estimated from collision data, table 3; lower bounds in parentheses are based on data from table 1, assuming that ρ increases regularly from Ne to Xe.

	X	X_0		X	X_0		X_0
Li$^+$	0.797	0.741	H$^-$	1.006	0.915	He	0.815
Na$^+$	1.064		F$^-$	1.155		Ne	1.069
K$^+$	1.355	1.293	Cl$^-$	1.555	1.484	Ar	1.306
Rb$^+$	1.485		Br$^-$	1.680		Kr	(> 1.52)
Cs$^+$	1.707		I$^-$	1.845		Xe	(> 1.57)

propriate to the solid different from the distortion potential for the gaseous alkali halides as a consequence of the greater symmetry of the distortion in the crystal lattice? (Presumably this difference will be small, since nearest-neighbor distances in crystals are rather large and the total overlap or distortion energy is small; nevertheless, this difference should be evaluated quantitatively.)

In 1968, on empirical and intuitive grounds, Gilbert [50] proposed the same definitions and the same additivity rules for the range ρ and size X that are here

Table 8

Properties of KCl: comparison of estimates by Amdur [50] with experimental data.

	Estimate		Experiment	
	Gas	Solid	Gas	Solid
r_e (Å)	2.61	3.05	2.67	3.11
D (eV), E_0 (eV)	5.13	7.22	5.00	7.38
$\nu \times 10^{12}$ (cm^{-1}) $\beta_0 \times 10^{12}$ (cm^2/dyne)	9.53	5.66	8.43	5.20

r_e: Equilibrium distance (gaseous molecule), lattice spacing (solid).

D: Dissociation energy; E_0: heat of sublimation.

ν: Fundamental vibration frequency.

β_0: Compressibility.

(Solid properties at 0 K.)

deduced from the distortion model, and justified them on the basis of the regularities existing in the data on the alkali halide molecules and crystals. He also obtained the form (23) for the Born-Mayer potential. His work, of which I was not aware until the present paper was in proof, provides further support for the distortion model. In addition to using the experimental data from the alkali halide molecules and crystal, Gilbert calculated the exponential repulsion for Li_2^{++}, obtaining the values $\rho = 0.139$ Å and $X = 1.341$ Å (at $F_0 = 1$ eV/Å; all results for X have been converted from Gilbert's value of $F_0 = 0.72$ eV/Å). In comparing these with the estimates in table 4, 0.166 and 1.482 Å, one should note that Gilbert expected his results to be slightly ($\lesssim 5\%$) smaller than the true values because of expansion and correlation errors. Using this calculation and the known information about the alkali halides, he could obtain ρ and X for all the individual ions. In particular, his results give for K_2^{++} the values 0.212 and 2.418 Å, to be compared with 0.260 and 2.585 Å (table 4), and for Cl_2^{--} the values 0.475 and 3.643 Å, to be compared with 0.531 and 2.971 Å. His resulting size ratio of K^+ to Cl^- of 0.66 is probably too small. The size differences ΔX between the successive alkali ions from Li^+ to Cs^+ obtained by Gilbert are 0.256, 0.282, 0.124, and 0.143 Å, close to the values in the last column of table 6; his differences ΔX between successive halide ions from F^- to I^- are 0.510, 0.157, and 0.239, significantly ($\geq 25\%$) larger than the values in the last row of table 6.

We have just been discussing in brief the information about parameters of the repulsive potential obtainable from data on the alkali halides. In the last years of his life, Professor Amdur was actively engaged in this field, following the opposite course of predicting the properties of the alkali halide gases and crystals by transferring to these species the information already known about the repulsive potential from measurements on the related rare gases. While his full work has not yet been revised for publication, Amdur published some of his initial results in a survey article published in 1967 [51]. In table 8, we reproduce some of these results and compare them with the observed values. The closeness of agreement is an impressive confirmation of the close connection that exists between the repulsive forces in these ionic materials and those in the superficially exceedingly different and inert rare gases.

In his last work, Professor Amdur was leading the way to an improved understanding and unification of our knowledge of the rare gases and of the alkali halides. It was no doubt partially for this reason that he studied, and stimulated others to study, the intermediate collisions between the closed-shell ions and the rare gases. These lines of work are being continued. Some of the results were presented in papers at this Conference. In the next few years much more will be done to exploit the legacy left us by Isadore Amdur and to carry further the search for an understanding of many of the processes to which he devoted so much enthusiasm and thought.

Acknowledgments

It is a pleasure to acknowledge the invaluable help of Drs. R. E. Olson and D. D. Cubicciotti in the preparation of this paper. I also wish to thank Professor J. E. Jordan for his help in connection with Professor Amdur's work on the alkali halides.

References

[1] I. Amdur and H. Pearlman, J. Chem. Phys. 8 (1940) 7.
[2] J.E. Jordan and I. Amdur, J. Chem. Phys. 46 (1967) 165.
[3] For reviews of the method and its results, see
   (a) E.A. Mason and and J.T. Vanderslice, in: *Atomic and Molecular Processes*, ed. D.R. Bates (Academic Press, New York, 1962), p. 663.
   (b) I. Amdur and J.E. Jordan, in: *Molecular Beams*, (Advan. Chem. Phys., ed. J. Ross, Vol. 10 (Interscience Publishers, New York, 1966), p. 29.
   (c) R.B. Bernstein and J.T. Muckerman, in: *Interatomic Forces*, Advan. Chem. Phys., ed. J.O. Hirschfelder, Vol. 12 (Interscience Publishers, New York, 1967), p. 389.
   (d) I. Amdur, in: *Methods of Experimental Physics*, eds. B. Bederson and W.L. Fite, Vol. 7A, (Academic Press, New York, 1968), p. 341.
   (e) V.B. Leonas and E.V. Samuilov, Teplofiz. Vysokikh Temp. 4 (1966) 710; English Transl.: High Temp. 4 (1966) 664.
   (f) J.E. Jordan, E.A. Mason and I. Amdur, *Molecular Beams in Chemistry*. To appear in: *Physical Methods of Chemistry*, eds. A. Weissberger and B.W. Rossiter (John Wiley and Sons, Inc. Interscience Publishers, New York).
[4] I. Amdur, J.E. Jordan and S.O. Colgate, J. Chem. Phys. 34 (1961) 1525.
[5] I. Amdur and A.L. Harkness, J. Chem. Phys. 22 (1954) 664.
[6] A.B. Kamnev and V.B. Leonas, Dokl. Akad. Nauk. SSR 162, (1965) 798; English Transl.: Soviet Phys.-Dokl. 10 (1965) 529.
[7] N.C. Blais and J.B. Mann, J. Chem. Phys. 32, (1960) 1459.
[8] E.A. Mason and W.E. Rice, J. Chem. Phys. 22, (1954) 522.
[9] P.E. Philipson, Phys. Rev. 125, (1962) 1981.
[10] G.H. Matsumoto, C.F. Bender, and E.R. Davidson, J. Chem. Phys. 46 (1967) 402.
[11] I. Amdur, J.E. Jordan and R.R. Bertrand in: *Atomic Collision Processes*, ed. M.R.C. McDowell (North-Holland Publ. Co., Amsterdam, 1964) p. 934.
[12] S.O. Colgate, J.E. Jordan, I. Amdur and E.A. Mason, J. Chem. Phys. 51 (1969) 968.
[13] I. Amdur and E.A. Mason, J. Chem. Phys. 22 (1954) 670.
[14] R.N. Keeler, M. van Thiel and B.J. Alder, Physica 31 (1965) 1437.

[15] T.L. Gilbert and A.C. Wahl, J. Chem. Phys. 47 (1967) 3425.

[16] I. Amdur, E.A. Mason and A.L. Harkness, J. Chem. Phys. 22 (1954) 1071.

[17] R.E. Walker and A.A. Westenberg, J. Chem. Phys. 31 (1959) 519.

[18] R.L. Matcha and R.K. Nesbet, Phys. Rev. 160 (1967) 72.

[19] W.J. Savola, F.J. Eriksen and E. Pollack, Bull. Amer. Phys. Soc. 16 (1971) 208.

[20] H.W. Berry, Phys. Rev. 75 (1949) 913.

[21] A.A. Abrahamson, Phys. Rev. 130 (1963) 693; 133 (1964) A990; 178 (1969) 76.

[22] K. Günther, Ann. Phys (Leipzig) 14 (1964) 296.

[23] P.T. Wedepohl, J. Phys. B1 (1968) 307.

[24] M.G. Menendez, M.J. Redmon and J.F. Aebischer, Phys. Rev. 180 (1969) 69.

[25] V.I. Gaydaenko and V.K. Nikulin, Chem. Phys. Letters 7 (1970) 360.

[26] D.W. Sida, Phil. Mag. 2 (1957) 761.

[27] See, for instance, K.A. Brueckner, in: *Atomic Physics,* eds. B. Bederson, V.W. Cohen and F.M.J. Pichanick (Plenum Press, New York, 1969) p. 111.

[28] R.E. Gordon, private communication.

[29] I. Amdur and E.A. Mason, J. Chem. Phys. 23 (1955) 415.

[30] H.W. Berry, Phys. Rev. 99 (1955) 553.

[31] I. Amdur and E.A. Mason, J. Chem. Phys. 25 (1956) 632.

[32] L. Pauling, *The Nature of the Chemical Bond* (Cornell University Press, Ithaca, New York, 1939, 1940, 1960).

[33] I. Amdur, H. Inouye, A.J.H. Boerboom, A.N. van de Steege, J. Los and J. Kistemaker, Physica 41 (1969) 566.

[34] A.J.H. Boerboom, H. van Dop and J. Los, Physica 46 (1970) 458.

[35] I. Amdur, J.E. Jordan, L.W-M. Fung, R.L. Hance, E. Hulpke and S.E. Johnson, *VII ICPEAC, Abstracts of Papers,* eds. L.M. Branscomb et al., Vol. 2 (North-Holland Publishing Co., Amsterdam, 1971), p. 955.

[36] H. Inouye and S. Kita, *ICPEAC, Abstracts of Papers,* Eds. L.M. Branscomb et al.,Vol. 2 (North-Holland Publishing Co., Amsterdam, 1971), p. 948.

[37] F.J. Zehr and H.W. Berry, Phys. Rev. 159 (1967) 13.

[38] W. Aberth and D.C. Lorents, Phys. Rev. 182 (1969) 162; R.E. Olson, F.T. Smith and C.R. Mueller, Phys. Rev. A1 (1970) 27.

[39] G.W. Catlow, M.R.C. McDowell, J.J. Kaufman, L.M. Sachs and E.S. Chang, J. Phys. B 3 (1970) 833.

[40] C.R. Fischer, J. Chem. Phys. 48 (1968) 215.

[41] B.F. Junker and J.C. Browne, *VII ICPEAC, Abstracts of Papers,* ed. I. Amdur, (MIT Press, Cambridge, Mass., 1969), p. 220.

[42] T.L. Bailey, C.J. May and E.E. Muschlitz, Jr., J. Chem. Phys. 26 (1957) 1446; E.A. Mason and J.T. Vanderslice, J. Chem. Phys. 28 (1958) 253.

[43] W.C. Giffen and H.W. Berry, Phys. Rev. A3 (1971) 635.

[44] Reviews by
    (a)   M.P. Tosi, in: *Solid State Physics,* eds. F. Seitz and D. Turnbull, Vol. 16 (Academic Press, New York, 1964), p. 1.
    (b)   T.C. Waddington, Advan. Inorg. Chem. and Radiochem. 1 (1959) 157.

[45] R.W. Roberts and C.S. Smith, J. Phys. Chem. Solids 31 (1970) 619; 31 (1970) 2397.

[46] E.S. Rittner, J. Chem. Phys. 19 (1951) 1030.

[47] Dr. D.D. Cubicciotti has kindly assembled and analyzed the current spectroscopic and thermochemical data on the alkali-halide molecules.

[48] Data on solids from [44(a)], on molecules from [47]; figures provided by
Dr. D.D. Cubicciotti.
[49] F.G. Fumi and M.P. Tosi, J. Phys. Chem. Solids 25 (1964) 31; see especially·
table 10.
[50] T.L. Gilbert, J. Chem. Phys. 49 (1968) 2640.
[51] I. Admur, Entropie 18 (1967) 73.

Physics of Electronic and Atomic Collisions, VII ICPEAC, 1971 — North-Holland (1972)

NON-ADIABATIC THEORY IN ATOM-ATOM COLLISIONS

E.E. NIKITIN*

Institute of Chemical Physics, Moscow, USSR

Non-adiabatic transitions in collisions of atoms A and B are defined as transitions between adiabatic electronic terms of the quasimolecule AB induced by the relative motion of nuclei A and B.

1. The atomic-collision theory formulated in the adiabatic electronic basis-set of functions has two major advantages over alternative formulations:

a) regions of the strong coupling are more or less localised, their actual extension being dependent on the velocity;

b) there are broad regions where the system AB evolves adiabatically; this is of importance for the semi-classical description of a collision when different classical trajectories are associated with different adiabatic potentials.

It follows from a) and b) that the scattering matrix S can be constructed as a product of adiabatic evolution matrices, A_k, and transition matrices, T_k, which connect neighbouring A-matrices.

However, there are some disadvantages of the adiabatic representation such as:

c) the coupling between states does not vanish at large interatomic separations, though being weak for low energy;

d) the coupling between states occurs via a differential operator (kinetic energy of nuclei); this implies that weak coupling cannot be treated by the usual perturbation technique.

These shortcomings are of no importance for low-energy collisions if the proper perturbation approach is used.

2. As the transition matrix T depends only on the local behaviour of electronic terms, it is possible to suggest different general models which consitute "pieces" to approximate the real situation:

a) *the linear model* originally formulated in the semi-classical approximations by Landau and Zener; this model has been recently extended to the

---

* The paper was presented by Prof. Yu.N. Demkov; the abstract only was submitted.

quantal region and developed to provide the correct phase of the oscillating transition probality;

b) *hypergeometric models* which presumably give the most general analytical solution of two-state semi-classical equations;

c) *the matching model* which uses the sudden approximation to calculate the T-matrix.

3. The non-adiabatic theory discussed is illustrated by certain collision processes which can be interpreted in terms of the above models:

a) oscillatory behaviour of the differential cross-section near a threshold of atomic excitation (large excitation energy);

b) velocity dependence of the total cross-section for a non-resonant process (small excitation energy);

c) relation among cross-sections for relaxations of atomic multipole moments in a degenerate electronic state with the angular momentum j (zero excitation energy).

Physics of Electronic and Atomic Collisions, VII ICPEAC, 1971 – North-Holland (1972)

STRUCTURE OF TOTAL CROSS-SECTIONS FOR DIABATIC PROCESSES IN SLOW ATOMIC COLLISIONS

S.V.BOBASHEV

A.F.Ioffe Physico-Technical Institute,
USSR Academy of Sciences, Leningrad, USSR

Experimental and theoretical investigations are discussed which deal with the interference of energetically neighbouring quasi-molecular terms giving rise to oscillatory structure of total cross-sections for diabatic processes in slow ion-atom collisions.

1. Introduction

The present paper discusses the phenomenon of interference of quasi-molecular states excited coherently in slow atomic collisions. This phenomenon results in an oscillatory structure of the total cross-sections for inelastic processes with a large resonance defect, due to the diabatic interaction at large internuclear distances which occurs during the separation of the collision partners.

In recent experimental observations to be discussed below, it has been found that in collisions of heavy atomic particles in the hecto- and kiloelectronvolt energy range, the excitation functions of spectral lines have a complicated oscillatory structure. We shall deal with such excitation processes which are accompanied by a considerable energy transfer, so that the interaction of the elastic and inelastic scattering channels can exhibit and oscillatory behaviour in differential scattering cross-sections only.

A qualitative hypothesis, which explained the structure of the total cross-sections for inelastic scattering channels, has been advanced by Rosenthal [1] and later independently by Bobashev [2]. According to this hypothesis, when two atomic particles approach each other, the quasi-molecular ground state term crosses in succession two energetically neighbouring vacant quasi-molecular terms which are populated coherently. When the particles separate, a diabatic interaction arises between these terms, either as a result of terms crossing [1] or because of their close approach [2]. Important here is the assumption that this second interaction, leading to interference, occurs at large internuclear separations. As a result, the probability of separation along of each of the two inelastic scattering channels turns out to be a harmonically oscillating functions of the inverse relative velocity of the atomic particles. The oscillation frequency depends only very weakly on the impact parameter. This is connected with the fact that the impact parameters essential for the inelastic processes under consideration, are significantly smaller than the internuclear distances at which the interaction of terms arises during the separation of the particles. Therefore integration over the impact parameter does not result in the disappearance of oscillations in total cross-sections.

In this paper we will not touch upon the well-known oscillations of differential cross-sections for inelastic processes as function of energy [3]. These oscillations, predicted by Landau and Stückelberg [4], are due to the two alternative possibilities of passage of the pseudo-crossing point during the collision process.

Also, we will not discuss the recently discovered oscillatory structure of total cross-sections for resonant and quasi-resonant charge exchange [5]. This structure is due to the interference of the elastic and inelastic scattering channels. Such interference is not obscured by the integration over impact parameters provided that the relevant phase difference passes through a stationary region. This is the case when there is a maximum in the difference between the interfering energy terms, or when the scattering occurs from a central potential "core" [5,6].

2. Observations of oscillations of optical excitation functions: qualitative hypothesis

Since 1965 the emission of spectral lines in slow ion-atom collisions has been actively studied in a number of laboratories [7−17]. The intensity of lines in the visible part of the spectrum has been studied as a function of ion laboratory energy, $E \leqslant 10$ keV, for collisions between He^+, Ne^+, Ar^+, K^+ and Cs^+ and the noble gases He, Ne, Ar, Kr and Xe. Not dwelling upon the technique of these experimental studies, we shall refer here to two important results noted by several authors. It has been found that in many instances the intensities of the lines under study rise sharply from the experimental thresholds, and that they reach high values at relative kinetic energies of some tens of eV. The experimental thresholds, i.e. the values of the relative kinetic energy at which the sensitivity of the recording devices permits the quanta with a specific wavelength to be detected, have turned out to be somewhat higher than the excitation thresholds for the given spectral line as determined by the laws of energy and momentum conservation. In this case the collision process is described by a simple scheme. As the nuclei of the interacting partners approach each other, the electronic term of the ground state (when both partners are not excited) crosses in succession the electronic terms corresponding to excited states. If only two states are considered, the probability of their non-adiabatic interaction is described by the Landau–Zener theory [4,18].

It has been found, too, that the excitation functions of almost all spectral lines in the visible spectral region exhibit a more or less complicated structure, which, in a number of cases, takes the shape of well-pronounced oscillations. As an example, figs. 1a, b show two experimental curves, measured by Dworetsky et al. [8] and by Tolk et al. [13], which clearly display both peculiarities.

The papers of Matveyev et al. [19,20] describe the excitation of resonance lines of alkali ions and noble-gas atoms in collisions of Na+, K+, Rb+ and Cs+ with He, Ne and Ar at energies ≤ 10 keV. Other studies deal with excitation functions of vacuum-UV lines, emitted by noble-gas atoms in collisions of He+ with He [22] and of He+ with He, Ne, Ar, Kr and Xe [21].

These measurements [2,19–22] have shown that, in general, the excitation functions for resonance lines exhibit similar features as those for visible lines,

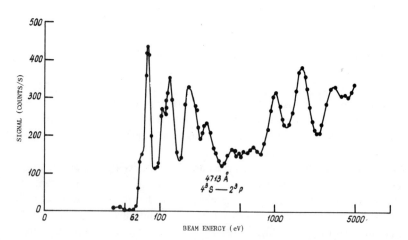

Fig. 1a. Excitation function for the λ 4713 Å line of HeI ($4^3S \rightarrow 2^3P$) for He+ incident on He. (From [8].)

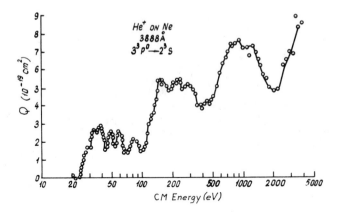

Fig. 1b. Excitation function for the λ 3888 Å line of HeI ($3^3P^0 \to 2^3S$) for He$^+$ incident on Ne. (From [13a].)

although it should be emphasized that in the case of resonance lines these peculiarities in the behaviour of excitation cross-sections are particularly pronounced.

Now we shall discuss in more detail the results of studies [2] dealing with regular oscillations of the total cross-section for excitation of neon resonance lines arising in collisions of fast Na$^+$ ions with neon:

$$\text{Na}^+ + \text{Ne} \to \text{Na}^+ + \text{Ne}^+ \underset{\searrow \; \lambda\,743.7\,\text{Å}}{\overset{\nearrow \; \lambda\,735.9\,\text{Å}}{}} \qquad (1)$$

Fig. 2 shows the experimental excitation functions for these Ne lines plotted versus the inverse velocity v^{-1} of the Na$^+$ ions. It is seen from fig. 2 that the 8 maxima of the excitation cross-section curve for the λ 735.9 Å NeI line are equidistant on a v^{-1} scale with an accuracy of 5% or better. The mean distance between the maxima is equal to $\Delta(v^{-1}) = (2.7\pm0.13) \times 10^{-8}$ s/cm.

Let us now consider the qualitative hypothesis proposed by Rosenthal [1] and later by Bobashev [2] to interprete the oscillations of total cross-sections for excitation of resonance spectral lines. Let us assume that with Na$^+$ and Ne approaching each other, the ground-state energy of the quasi-molecule (NaNe)$^+$ follows the curve 0 (see fig. 3a) and crosses the two vacant states 1 and 2 of the quasi-molecule at the points R_1 and R_2, where these states are populated according to the Landau–Zener scheme. Then, as the particles

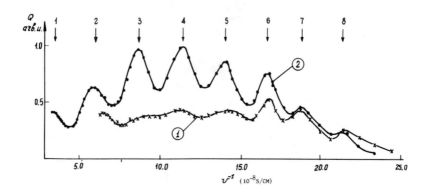

Fig. 2. Cross-sections for emission of resonances lines of neon [2] (curve $1 - \lambda$ 735.9 Å; curve $2 - \lambda$ 743.7 Å), plotted as a function of inverse relative velocity (v^{-1}) for Na^+ incident on Ne. The emitting states are $2p^5(^2P^0_{1/2})3s$ and $2p^5(^2P^0_{3/2})3s$, respectively (cf. fig. 3b).

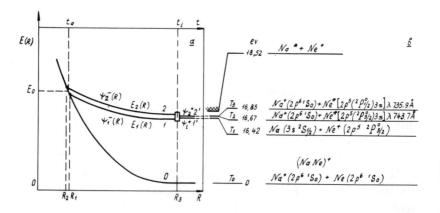

Fig. 3a. Schematic representation of the model involving two regions of interaction, used in the discussion of diabatic Na^+-Ne collisions. 3b. Energetic location of low-lying terms of the $(NaNe)^+$ quasi-molecule at $R \rightarrow \infty$.

separate, an additional non-adiabatic interaction between states 1 and 2 occurs at a large internuclear distance, R_3, far from the points R_1 and R_2 $(R_3 \gg R_1, R_2)$. This interaction gives rise to two states (see fig. 3) which emit resonance lines of NeI (term $2'$) and to the charge exchange of Na^+ with neon atoms into the ground state of the Na atom (term $1'$):

$$Na^+ + Ne \rightarrow Na + Ne^+ . \tag{2}$$

Let us assume that the process of population takes place at a point $R = R_0 (R_0 = R_1 = R_2)$ and at a time $t = t_0$. For the purposes of this paper let us not distinguish between the two excited states of neon, assuming that they correspond to only one state at infinity ($2'$ in fig. 3a)*.

The wave function of the system for a region $t_0 - t_1$ at $t \rightarrow t_1$ at the left (see fig. 3a) takes the form:

$$\psi = b_1 \psi_1^-(R) \cdot \exp\left[-\frac{i}{\hbar} \int_{t_0}^{t_1} E_1(R) dt\right] + b_2 \psi_2^-(R) \cdot \exp\left[-\frac{i}{\hbar} \int_{t_0}^{t_1} E_2(R) dt\right] \tag{3}$$

where b_1 and b_2 are time-dependent amplitudes of states 1 and 2 formed after double passage through the regions R_1 and R_2. Assume that in the region $R = R_3$ $(t = t_1)$ (denoted by a rectangle in fig. 3a) a "strong" diabatic interaction takes place. Then in the region $t > t_1$ at $t \rightarrow t_1$ at the right, the wave function of the system will take the form

$$\psi = \left\{\frac{b_1}{\sqrt{2}} \cdot \exp\left[-\frac{i}{\hbar} \int_{t_0}^{t_1} E_1(R) dt\right] + \frac{b_2}{\sqrt{2}} \cdot \exp\left[-\frac{i}{\hbar} \int_{t_0}^{t_1} E_2(R) dt\right]\right\} \psi_1^+ +$$

$$+ \left\{\frac{b_1}{\sqrt{2}} \cdot \exp\left[-\frac{i}{\hbar} \int_{t_0}^{t_1} E_1(R) dt\right] - \frac{b_2}{\sqrt{2}} \cdot \exp\left[-\frac{i}{\hbar} \int_{t_0}^{t_1} E_2(R) dt\right]\right\} \psi_2^+ . \tag{4}$$

Here $\psi_{1,2}^+ = (\psi_1^- \pm \psi_2^-)/\sqrt{2}$ are the wave functions of atomic states (fig. 3b). The probability, W, for the system to remain in either the ψ_1^+ or the ψ_2^+ state is thus equal to

* This is a rough assumption, since actually not only the two excited states of neon corresponding to allowed transitions should be taken into account, but also the two metastable states, whose population characteristics in the collision process under consideration are completely unknown.

$$W_{1,2} = \tfrac{1}{2}(|b_1|^2 + |b_2|^2) \pm 2\mathrm{Re}\frac{b_1 \cdot b_2^*}{2} \cdot \exp\left[-\frac{i}{\hbar}\int_{t_0}^{t_1}[E_2(R) - E_1(R)]\,dt\right]. \quad (5)$$

Now we shall be only interested in the oscillatory part of the total cross-section, so let us consider only the second term in expression (5). Substitute $s\exp(i\phi)$ for the product $b_1 \cdot b_2^*$ and introduce the radial velocity v_R instead of the time t:

$$v_R = \frac{dR}{dt} = \left[\frac{2}{\mu}\left(E - E_0 - \frac{\rho^2 E}{R^2}\right)\right]^{1/2}.$$

Here μ is the reduced mass of the colliding particles, $E_0 = E(R_0)$ the pseudo-crossing ordinate (fig. 3a), ρ the impact parameter, and E the energy of relative motion of the particles at infinity. In order to obtain the oscillatory part of the total cross-section $\Delta Q(E)$, we integrate the second term in expression (5) over all impact parameters from $\rho = 0$ to $\rho_m = R_0(1 - E_0/E)^{1/2}$, assuming $E_2(R) - E_1(R) = \Delta E$:

$$\Delta Q(E) = 2\pi \int_0^{\rho m} s\rho d\rho \cos\left(\int_{R_0}^{R_3}\frac{\Delta E}{\hbar v_R}\,dR + \phi\right). \quad (6)$$

Below are discussed the results of a theoretical study [23], where the conditions are derived for which integration over the impact parameter in (6) does not suppress the appearance of oscillations in total cross sections. To analyse the situation *qualitatively* let us assume a moment that the argument of the cosine in expression (6) does not depend on ρ and that the radial velocity, v_R, is equal to the velocity at infinity, $v = (2E/\mu)^{1/2}$. Let us also take ϕ to be small and independent of the impact parameter, then:

$$\Delta Q(E) = \pi s R_0^2 \cos\frac{\Delta E \cdot \Delta R}{\hbar \cdot v}, \quad (7)$$

where $\Delta R = R_3 - R_0$. It is seen that on satisfying all these assumptions the total cross-sections for the two inelastic processes $2'$ and $1'$ (fig. 3a) will oscillate with a frequency determined by the quantity $\Delta E \cdot \Delta R/\hbar$ and the extrema on the cross-section curves will be equidistant on a v^{-1} scale.

It has been pointed out by Bobashev [2] on the basis of these qualitative considerations that the second inelastic channel interfering with the excitation

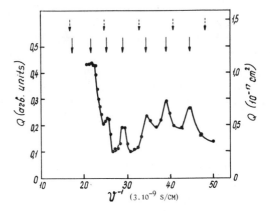

Fig. 4. The absolute value of the cross-section for the charge exchange $Na^+ + Ne \rightarrow Na +$ $+ Ne^+$ [24] as a function of inverse velocity of the ions v^{-1}. Arrows show the position of maxima, dotted arrows show the position of maxima of the excitation cross-section (1) of fig. 2a.

channel $(2')$ is the charge exchange of Na^+ ions with Ne atoms $(1')$, since at infinity the charge exchange term is energetically close to the excitation terms (fig. 3b). It seemed [2] that the charge exchange cross-section $(1')$ should oscillate in the opposite phase with process $(2')$. The charge exchange was recently measured by Latipov and Shaporenko [24]; the absolute value of the cross-section is plotted in fig. 4 as a function of v^{-1}. It does oscillate, but the oscillation period is about half as large as that for process $(2')$. The mean distance between the maxima is $\Delta(v^{-1}) = 1.3 \times 10^{-8}$ s/cm [24]. The authors of paper [24] have suggested that this change in oscillation period is explicable if three rather than two terms interacting at large nuclear separations are considered: one term corresponding to charge exchange (T_1) and the two others corresponding to excitation of resonance lines (T_2, T_3). Indeed, it is seen from fig. 3b that energy differences between these terms at large internuclear separations are nearly equal:

$$T_3 - T_2 = 0.18 \text{ eV} , \qquad T_2 - T_1 = 0.23 \text{ eV} .$$

A necessary condition underlying the hypothesis described here is the presence of crossing or strong convergence of quasi-molecular terms at large internuclear separations. A calculation for the structure of terms of the $(He^+ He)$ system performed by Rosenthal [1] confirms the existence of pseudo-crossings at sufficiently large R ($R_x \approx 15$ a.u. for the 3^1S and 3^3S levels of the He atom).

Let us proceed to theoretical studies made by Ankudinov et al. [23], where the above hypothesis has been treated *quantitatively*. The problem of oscillations of total cross-sections for inelastic processes in atomic collisions has been considered and conditions have been derived for which the oscillation of the excitation probability of a given inelastic process is retained in the cross-section after integrating over the impact parameter.

3. The interference of quasi-molecular states and the structure of total cross-sections

Following the study by Ankudinov et al. [23], let us consider the problem of collision of two atomic particles X and Y which may lead to the formation of either X′ and Y′ or X″ or Y″ particles. Thus, two inelastic processes interact:

$$X + Y \rightarrow X' + Y', \qquad X + Y \rightarrow X'' + Y''. \tag{8}$$

It is convenient to present the scheme of terms of a quasi-molecule produced in collision in a form as shown in fig. 5, where the left part corresponds to the approach of the particles and the right part to their separation. Index 0

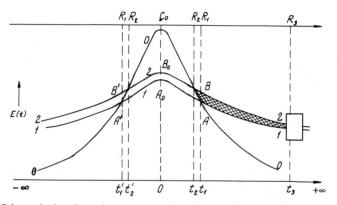

Fig. 5. Schematic time-dependent representation of a model as that of fig. 3a. (From [23].)

designates the ground term X + Y while indexes 1 and 2 are for the excited states, X' + Y' and X'' + Y'', respectively. As the particles approach each other, the energy of the quasi-molecule changes along the curve 0. In the points of pseudo-crossing R_1 and R_2 ($t=t'_1, t'_2, t_2, t_1$) the two excited states 1 and 2 are populated, $t = 0$ corresponding to the turning point. In the R_3 ($t=t_3$) region after separation of the particles, these states interact non-adiabatically, The terms are considered to interact only in the vicinity of the points R_1, R_2 and R_3; in the remaining regions of internuclear separation the wave function of the system changes adiabatically and takes the form:

$$\psi = b_0(t)\psi_0(R) + b_1(t)\psi_1(R) + b_2(t)\psi_2(R) , \tag{9}$$

where $\psi_0(R)$, $\psi_1(R)$ and $\psi_2(R)$ are the wave functions of the states 0, 1, 2 of the quasi-molecule at an internuclear separation R. The coefficients $b_0(t)$, $b_1(t)$ and $b_2(t)$ depend on time only through the phase factors

$$\exp\left(-\frac{i}{\hbar}\int^t E_i(R)\,dt\right) ,$$

where $E_i(R)$ is the energy of the corresponding states. The problem is solved in two stages. First the amplitudes $b_1(t)$ and $b_2(t)$ are determined immediately after the states 1 and 2 are populated at the point R_1; then their interference due to interaction of terms at large internuclear separation R_3 is to be considered. Colliding particles are taken to move uniformly and rectilinearly, i.e. the kinetic energy of the relative motion is greater than the potential energy of their interaction.

Each pseudo-crossing has been considered in terms of a "two-level" model according to the Landau–Zener scheme: it is assumed that the pseudo-crossing points are sufficiently isolated from each other and situated sufficiently far from the turning point.

Following Zener [18], a relationship can be found between the amplitudes of states 1 and 2 on the left of a pseudo-crossing point $t = t_k$ (b_1^- and b_2^-) and those on the right of this point (b_1^+ and b_2^+):

$$b_1^+ = g_k b_1^- + s_k^* b_2^- , \qquad b_2^+ = -s_k b_1^- + g_k b_2^- . \tag{10}$$

In these formulae:

$$g_k = \exp(-\pi\gamma_k) , \tag{11}$$

$$s_k = \frac{\sqrt{2\pi\gamma_k}}{\Gamma(1+i\gamma_k)} \exp\left\{-\tfrac{1}{2}\pi\gamma_k +i\gamma_k \ln\gamma_k +i\pi/4\right\}, \tag{12}$$

where γ_k is the Landau–Zener parameter:

$$\gamma_k = V_k^2/\hbar v_R |\Delta F_k|, \tag{13}$$

V_k is the matrix element of interaction connecting two crossing terms, ΔF_k is the force difference corresponding to these terms at the crossing point, v_R is the radial relative velocity at this point.

In order to obtain expressions for the amplitudes of states 1, 2 immediately after population at the point R_1, it is necessary to apply expressions (10) successively to all crossings occurring from $t = -\infty$ to $t = t_1$ inclusive, taking into account the initial conditions $|b_0(-\infty)| = 1, b_1(-\infty) = b_2(-\infty) = 0$.

Of course, in addition, account must be taken of an adiabatic change of phase in between crossings. Omitting the expressions for the amplitudes $b_1(t_1)$ and $b_2(t_1)$ [23], we shall write straight away the formulae for the excitation probabilities of states 1 and 2 after passing twice the region of pseudo-crossings in a three-term model (fig. 5):

$$|b_1(t_1)|^2 = 2p_1(1-p_1)\{1-p_2+p_2^2-(1-p_2)\cos(\chi_1-\chi_2) +$$

$$+ p_2(1-p_2)\cos\chi_2 -p_2 \cos\chi_1\}, \tag{14}$$

$$|b_2(t_1)|^2 = 2p_1 p_2(1-p_2)(1-\cos\chi_2). \tag{15}$$

Here the following designations are introduced:

$$p_k - g_k^2 = \exp(-2\pi\gamma_k)$$

which is the probability of remaining in a given state at the kth crossing;

$$\chi_k = 2\phi_k + \frac{1}{\hbar} \int_{t_{k'}}^{t_k} (E_k-E_0)\,\mathrm{d}t, \tag{16}$$

where ϕ_k is the phase of the s_k factor:

$$\phi_k = \gamma_k \ln\gamma_k + \pi/4 - \arg\Gamma(1+i\gamma_k). \tag{17}$$

Consider the region $t = t_3 (R=R_3)$ where, according to the hypothesis formulated above, an additional non-adiabatic interaction occurs as the particles separate. Near R_3 and on the left of it, the amplitudes $b_1^-(t_3)$ and $b_2^-(t_3)$ differ from $b_1(t_1)$ and $b_2(t_1)$ only by corresponding phase factors. On the right of R_3 the amplitudes of these states acquire other values: $b_1^+(t_3)$ and $b_2^+(t_3)$, each of which is a linear combination of $b_1^-(t_3)$ and $b_2^-(t_3)$.

We shall consider two variants of the interaction involving the mixing of states after separation of the particles. If one assumes, in accordance with Rosenthal [1], that the terms 1 and 2 cross at $R = R_3$ (see fig. 6a), then the relation between $b_1^+(t_3)$, $b_2^+(t_3)$ and $b_1^-(t_3)$, $b_2^-(t_3)$ is given by formulae (10–13).

In the second case, when a non-adiabatic interaction is caused by a sharp convergence of terms in the region $R = R_3$ (fig. 6b), the results of Demkov's paper may be used [25]. We assume the diagonal Hamiltonian matrix elements H_{11} and H_{22} to be constant in the R_3 region, and the non-diagonal elements decreasing following the law $\exp(-\lambda R)$. As the convergence occurs at large internuclear separations R, we can put $R = vt$. It is convenient to choose R_3 (and so t_3) in such a manner that at this point

$$H_{12} = H_{21} = \tfrac{1}{2} k (H_{22} - H_{11}) \exp \{ -\lambda (R-R_3) \} . \tag{18}$$

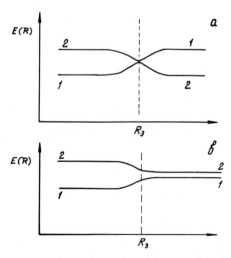

Fig. 6. Detail of the long-range interaction region of figs. 3a and 5: a) pseudo-crossing of terms; b) sharp convergence of terms. (From [23].)

Here $k = \pm 1$, depending on the sign of the non-diagonal matrix element. In the region of $R \approx R_3$ the terms draw close together (fig. 6b) and the adiabatic wave functions adjust to the transition from the molecular wave functions (ψ_1^-, ψ_2^-) to the functions of isolated atoms (ψ_1^+, ψ_2^+) (see fig. 3a).

In the region of term convergence, the solution of Schrodinger's equation [23] with an appropriate selection of phases yields a relationship between the coefficients $b_1^+(t_3)$, $b_2^+(t_3)$ and $b_1^-(t_3)$, $b_2^-(t_3)$ which is expressed by formulae (10) where, however, g_3 and s_3 take the following values:

$$g_3 = (1 + e^{-\pi \delta})^{-1/2} , \qquad s_3 = (1 + e^{\pi \delta})^{-1/2} e^{2i\delta} , \qquad (19)$$

and

$$\delta = (H_{22} - H_{11})/2\hbar\lambda\upsilon . \qquad (20)$$

From (19) it is clear that as $\lambda \to 0$ (a very smooth convergence of terms), $s_3 \to 0$, $g_3 \to 1$, and there is no transition. At large λ (strong convergence of terms) the states are completely mixed and $g_3 = s_3 = 1/\sqrt{2}$.

The population probabilities for states 1 and 2 after collision are determined by the values of $b_1^+(t_3)$ and $b_2^+(t_3)$:

$$|b_1^+(t_3)|^2 = W_1 + \Delta W , \qquad |b_2^+(t_3)|^2 = W_2 - \Delta W . \qquad (21)$$

We are interested only in the interference term of these expressions, ΔW, dependent on the shape of the energy terms 1 and 2 in the $R_3 - R_1$ region:

$$\Delta W = 2p_1 \left[p_2 p_3 (1-p_1)(1-p_2)(1-p_3) \right]^{1/2} \{ \cos(\chi+\chi_1-\chi_2) -$$

$$- \cos(\chi+\chi_1) + (1-p_2)\cos(\chi+\chi_2) - p_2 \cos(\chi-\chi_2) - (1-2p_2)\cos\chi \} , \qquad (22)$$

where $p_3 = g_3^2$. The phases χ_1 and χ_2 are determined by eq. (16), while the phase χ is given by:

$$\chi = \frac{1}{\hbar} \int_{t_1}^{t_3} (E_2 - E_1) dt + \frac{1}{\hbar} \int_{t_2}^{t_1} (E_2 - E_0) dt + \phi_1 - \phi_2 + \phi_3 . \qquad (23)$$

Here ϕ_3 is the phase of the s_3 factor, which is equal to $+2\delta$ if the energy terms 1 and 2 approach each other at R_3, and which is given by formula (17) if they cross.

Total cross-sections for inelastic processes are obtained by integration of expressions (21) over the impact parameter. As the phases χ_1 and χ_2 depend strongly on the impact parameter, the terms comprising $\cos(\chi+\chi_1)$, $\cos(\chi+\chi_2)$ and $\cos(\chi-\chi_2)$ in expression (22) do not contribute to the total cross-sections. Also we shall not take into account the term $\cos(\chi+\chi_1-\chi_2)^*$. And so, only the term with $\cos\chi$ is left in expression (22).

To obtain explicit expressions for the total cross-sections, let us consider the case when γ_1 and γ_2 are small. This may be the case, for instance, when term 0 rises much more steeply in the region of R_1 and R_2 than terms 1 and 2 do. Then the oscillatory part of the total cross-section will be:

$$\Delta Q = 8\pi^2 \, [p_3(1-p_3)]^{1/2} \int_0^{\rho\max} \sqrt{\gamma_1\gamma_2} \, \cos\chi(\rho)\rho \, d\rho \; . \tag{24}$$

Now we shall discuss the behaviour of the phase χ (23) in detail. At small γ_1 and γ_2 we have $\phi_1 = \phi_2 = \pi/4$. The second integral in (23) is much smaller than the first one, since $E_2(R) - E_0(R)$ in the interval t_2, t_1 does not exceed $E_2(R) - E_1(R)$ and the interval $t_1 - t_2$ itself is smaller than $t_3 - t_1$. To transform the first integral, replace t by the internuclear distance $R = \sqrt{\rho^2 + v^2 t^2}$. Then:

$$\chi(\rho) = \frac{1}{\hbar v} \int_{R_1}^{R_3} [E_2(R) - E_1(R)] \left[1 - \frac{\rho^2}{R^2} \right]^{-1/2} dR + \phi_3 \; . \tag{25}$$

If $\cos\chi(\rho)$ undergoes a considerable number of oscillations as ρ changes from 0 to R_2, ΔQ will be small and the oscillatory structure will not reveal itself in the total cross-sections. For the oscillations not to be suppressed by integration over ρ, it is essential that the phase $\chi(\rho)$ be only weakly dependent on ρ; ϕ_3 does not depend on ρ, neither in the case of the term convergence when $\phi_3 = 2\delta$, nor in the case of crossing (17). Let us write $\chi(\rho)$ in the form:

$$\chi(\rho) = [u_0 + u(\rho)]/v + \phi_3 \; , \tag{26}$$

where

---

* The difference $\chi_1 - \chi_2$ may be small if the energy terms 1 and 2 are close to each other in the region of $R < R_2$; then the term $\cos(\chi+\chi_1-\chi_2)$ should be taken into account and added to the last term in expression (22).

$$u_0 = \frac{1}{\hbar} \int\limits_{R_1}^{R_3} \Delta E(R)\, dR \; , \tag{27}$$

$$u(\rho) = \frac{1}{\hbar} \int\limits_{R_1}^{R_3} \Delta E(R) \left[\left(1 - \frac{\rho^2}{R^2}\right)^{-1/2} - 1 \right] dR \; . \tag{28}$$

Assuming that $R_3 \gg R_1$ and taking into account that $\rho < R_1$ we obtain the following estimates for u_0 and $u(\rho)$:

$$u_0 \approx R_3 \Delta E/\hbar \; , \qquad u(\rho) \approx R_1 \Delta E'/\hbar \; . \tag{29}$$

Here ΔE and $\Delta E'$ are some mean values of the term difference $E_2(R) - E_1(R)$, with only the separation region about R_1 being essential for $\Delta E'$. If $R_3 \gg R_1$, a velocity range can be found where

$$R_1 \Delta E'/\hbar < v < R_3 \Delta E/\hbar \; . \tag{30}$$

Within this range of velocities the quantity $u(\rho)/v$ under the cos sign can be neglected (cf. (24) and (26)) and $\cos \chi$ can then be extracted from under the integral in formula (24). Condition (30) is very important for determining the energy region in which we can hope to observe oscillations of total cross-sections. After integrating over ρ in formula (24), we finally obtain:

$$\Delta Q = [Q_{1L} Q_{2L} p_3 (1-p_3)]^{1/2} \cos \chi(0) \; , \tag{31}$$

where

$$Q_{kL} = 8\pi^2 V_k^2 R_k^2 \left(v^2 - \frac{2E_k}{\mu}\right)^{1/2} \Big/ \hbar |\Delta F_k| v^2 \tag{32}$$

is the Landau [26] cross-section, μ is the reduced mass of the colliding particles and where v_k^2, E_k and ΔF_k are evaluated at the crossing point $R = R_k$.

Total cross-sections of inelastic processes in the same approximation are determined by the formulae:

$$Q_1 = Q_{1L} p_3 + Q_{2L} (1-p_3) + \Delta Q \; , \tag{33}$$

$$Q_2 = Q_{1L} (1-p_3) + Q_{2L} p_3 - \Delta Q \; . \tag{34}$$

It will be recalled that in formulae $(31,33,34)$ $p_3 = \exp(-2\pi\gamma_3)$ if during separation of the particles the interaction of terms is due to their crossing $(\gamma_3 = V_3^2/\hbar v|\Delta F_3|)$. If the interaction is connected with term convergence, then $p_3 = (1 + \exp -\pi\delta)^{-1}$, where δ is determined from formulae (20).

Thus, as is seen from the final formulae $(31,33,34)$, within the range of velocities determined by inequality (30), the interference of two states during separation of the particles results in oscillation of the total cross-sections of the inelastic processes involved, with the cross-sections for both channels oscillating in opposite phase.

The oscillatory part of the total cross-sections is due only to the last member in expression (22). It stems from the intereference of amplitudes connected to passage along $0A'B'B_0B2$ and $0A'B'B_0BA1$ respectively (fig. 5), so that up to the point B the interfering paths coincide. The oscillation phase is therefore independent of the shape of terms in the region $R < R_2$. Thus, if in the region $R < R_2$ there are some term interactions not taken into account in the model discussed, this will not alter the oscillation phase, though its amplitude may change.

Let us now consider the velocity dependence of the oscillation phase. In the case of converging terms the oscillation phase is:

$$\chi(0) = \frac{1}{\hbar v} \int_{R_1}^{R_3} \Delta E(R)\,dR + \frac{H_{22} - H_{11}}{\hbar\lambda v}. \tag{35}$$

It is seen that in this case the total cross-sections are harmonic functions of v^{-1}.

In the case of term crossing, the quantity ϕ_3 which enters into the determination of $\chi(0)$ depends in a complicated manner on the velocity. Fig. 7 shows ϕ_3 as a function of γ_3. It is seen from the figure, that the oscillations can be harmonic in v^{-1} in two extreme cases: if $\gamma_3 \ll 1$ then $\phi_3 = \pi/4$ and

$$\chi(0) = \frac{1}{\hbar v} \int_{R_1}^{R_3} \Delta E(R)\,dR + \pi/4 ; \tag{36}$$

if, on the other hand, $\gamma_3 > 1$ then $\phi_3 = \gamma_3$ and

$$\chi(0) = \frac{1}{\hbar v} \int_{R_1}^{R_3} \Delta E(R)\,dR + \frac{V_3^2}{\hbar v|\Delta F_3|}. \tag{37}$$

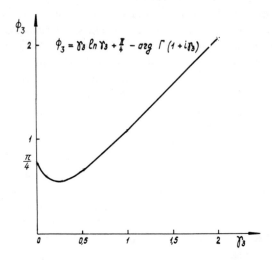

Fig. 7. Relation between the phase ϕ_3 and the corresponding Landau–Zener parameter (cf. eqs. (13) and (17)).

It should be noted that if γ_3 and δ are large compared to unity, then p_3 will be small, indicating that the interaction of terms at large internuclear distance is negligible. Consequently, if the experimental depth of modulation is not small (the maximum depth of modulation is 50%), it can be stated that the last members in expressions (35) and (37) are not large and that the period of oscillations is practically equal to $2\pi/u_0$ where $u_0 \approx R_3 \Delta E/\hbar$. The period is determined by the area between terms 1 and 2 in the interval from R_1 to R_3 (the shaded area in fig. 5).

The formulae for total cross-sections (31), (33), (34) are obtained on the assumption that the quantities γ_1 and γ_2 describing the population of terms 1 and 2 are small. In the case of arbitrary γ_1 and γ_2 the expressions for total cross-sections are rather cumbersome. Note an interesting qualitative feature which may arise in this case. The coefficient of $\cos \chi$ in expression (22) includes a factor $(1-2p_2)$ which becomes zero when $p_2 = 1/2$. In the vicinity of the corresponding energy a disturbance of the oscillation pattern and a change of the phase by π is therefore possible. In our opinion this circumstance is responsible for the complicated shape of the excitation function in fig. 1a, which represents data obtained by Dworetsky et al. [8] for emission of the λ 4713 Å line in He$^+$ + He collisions. At a He$^+$ energy $E \approx 500$ eV, a drastic change in the oscillation phase can be observed.

4. Analysis of experimental data

On the basis of the theory discussed above we shall now analyse some recent experimental data relevant to the measurement of structure in total cross-sections for inelastic processes. Fig. 8a represents the curve for the total cross-section Q for excitation of the $[2p^5(^2P^0_{1/2})3s]$ state of NeI (curve 1 in fig. 2) and fig. 8b the quantity $\Delta Q/Q_a$ where Q_a is the smooth part of the cross-section and ΔQ its oscillatory part. The full curve is a graph of the function $0.25 \cos(u_0/v+\pi/4)$ at $u_0 = 2.3 \times 10^{-8}$ cm/s.

The experimental curve exhibits a number of features which follow directly from the above calculation. In particular, if numerous oscillations are detected, one can expect the maxima to be equidistant on a v^{-1} scale, at any rate, at greater velocities. In the case of term *crossing* at large internuclear separation, the modulation depth can possibly decrease in the region of great velocities (if $\gamma_3 \to 0$, then $p_3 \to 1$). If the terms *approach* each other, the modulation depth at large velocities should be independent of velocity (if $\delta \to 0$, then $p_3 \to 1/2$). In the low-velocity range oscillations in total cross-section may become irregular and less pronounced, owing to the averaging over the impact parameter (violation of inequality (30)) as well as to the decrease in interaction efficiency ($p_3 \to 0$ when $\gamma_3 \to \infty$, $p_3 \to 1$ when $\delta \to \infty$ and in both cases the mixing of states disappears). Since the modulation depth in fig. 8a is rather large (25%) and depends only weakly on velocity, we may conclude that the population probabilities of the interacting levels in the region of R_1 and R_2 do not differ strongly from each other and that the interaction at large separations is effective enough.

The initial phase, ϕ_3, also is determined by the nature of the interaction. In the case of term crossing $\phi_3 \to \pi/4$ as $v \to \infty$ (see fig. 7). This suggests, that in the case of excitation of NeI resonance lines (fig. 8a) a crossing of terms takes place at large separation R, as the initial phase, according to fig. 8b, is $\pi/4$. If the terms approach each other at large R, then $\phi_3 \to 0$ as $v \to \infty$ (35). In [13] excitation functions are given for a number of spectral lines in the process $He^+ + Ne$. In fig. 9 the intensity of the HeI line λ 4713 Å ($4^3S \to 2^3P$) is plotted against $1/(E-U)^{1/2}$, where E is the center of mass energy and U is the energy defect of the reaction [13]. An interesting feature of this curve is the fact that the oscillation period varies with velocity, which is, seemingly, connected with the behaviour of the phase ϕ_3 (fig. 7).

Below are presented two experimental measurements where one can distinctly observe that the total cross-sections for two energetically close inelastic channels oscillate in opposite phase. The graph in fig. 10 is taken from the work of Rosenthal and Foley [1]. It relates to the structure of the excitation

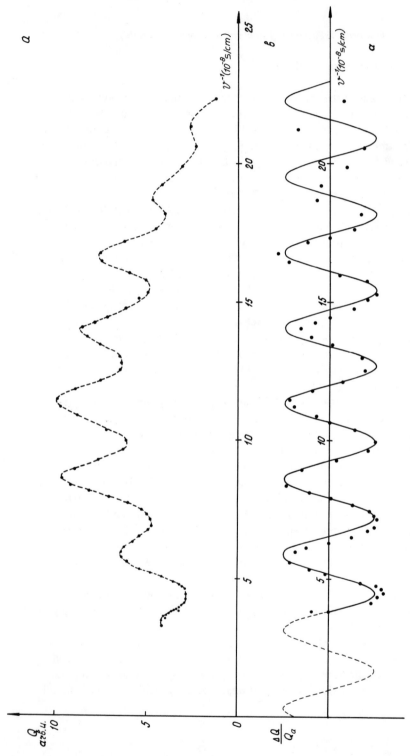

Fig. 8a, b. The oscillatory part ΔQ of the intensity of the λ 736 Å line of NeI in relation to the smooth component Q_a; points: the experiment; full line: the function $0.25 \cos{(2.3 \times 10^8/\upsilon + \pi/4)}$ [4]; dashed line in a: the high velocity part of the curve, where experimental points are lacking. (From [23].)

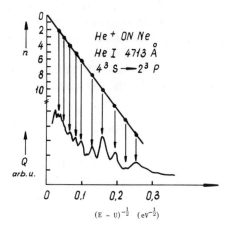

Fig. 9. Relative emission cross-section for the λ 4713 Å line of HeI (4^3S$\rightarrow 2^3$P) for He$^+$ incident on Ne as a function of $1/(E-U)^{1/2}$. E is the center of mass energy and U the energy defect of the reaction. The straight line is a linear least-squares fit of the phase integer n versus the location of the cross-section maxima on the abscissa. (From [13b].)

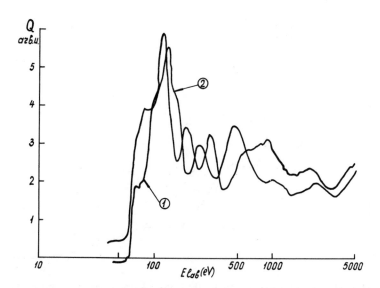

Fig. 10. Excitation functions of HeI lines for He$^+$ incident on He [8]. Curve 1: λ 7281 Å (3^1S$\rightarrow 2^1$P); curve 2: λ 7065 Å (3^3S$\rightarrow 2^3$P^0). (From [1].)

function of visible He lines in the processes $He^+ + He$ [8] . In the middle of the energy range the excitation cross-sections for the 3^1S ar.d 3^3S states oscillate in opposite phase and the maxima are almost equidistant on a v^{-1} scale [1] .

In the work of Bobashev and Kritskii [27] experimental data are represented on the excitation function of the HeI resonance line λ 584.3 Å in the process

$$Na^+ + He \rightarrow Na^+ + He^* - 21.22 \ eV \ . \tag{38}$$

In fig. 11 the cross-section for excitation of this HeI line is compared with the excitation function of the Na yellow doublet $Na(3p^2P_{1/2,3/2})$ in the process:

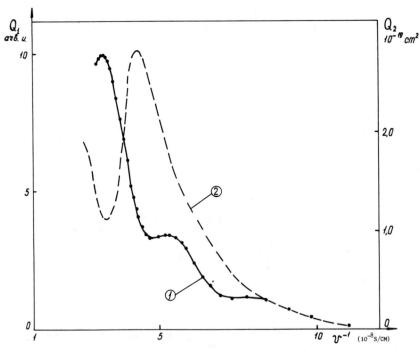

Fig. 11. (1) Emission cross-section Q_1 for the λ 584.3 Å line of HeI in the process $Na^+ + He \rightarrow Na^+ + He^{\bar{*}}$ [27] . (2) Cross-section Q_2 for emission of the yellow Na doublet in the reaction $Na^+ + He \rightarrow Na^* + He^+$ [28] , plotted to a v^{-1} scale. (From [27] .)

$$Na^+ + He \rightarrow Na^* + He^+ - 21.55 \text{ eV} \tag{39}$$

taken from ref. [28]. It should be noted, too, that the three maxima of the excitation function for the λ 584.3 Å line are approximately equidistant on the v^{-1} scale.

Consider another experimental indication of the existence of diabatic interaction at large internuclear separations. It can be concluded from fig. 3a that the cross-section for a transition from state $1'$ to state $2'$ (and vice versa) must be a large one, as it is determined by the —large— magnitude of $R_3(\sigma_{2'\leftrightarrow1'}\sim\pi R_3^2)$. In fig. 12 absolute cross-sections are plotted for excitation of ArI resonance lines in the process

$$K^+ + Ar \rightarrow K^+ + Ar^* \begin{cases} \lambda \text{ 1066 Å} \\ \lambda \text{ 1048 Å} \end{cases} \tag{40}$$

These measurements have recently been carried out by the author using the apparatus described in [2,19]. Absolute values of the cross-sections have been estimated on the basis of data on the angular analysis of inelastically scattered ions K^+ in reaction (40) [29]. The absolute values obtained in this way are reliable within a factor of two. By analogy with processes (1) and (2) it can be

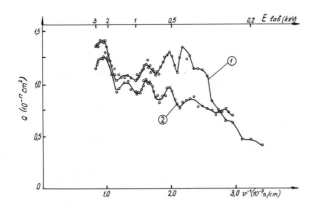

Fig. 12. The emission cross-section for resonance lines of ArI in the collision process $K^+ + Ar$ as a function of the inverse velocity (v^{-1}) of the K^+ ions. 1: λ 1048.2 Å; 2: λ 1066.7 Å.

supposed that the oscillations of the cross-sections in fig. 12 are due to inter-ference of the excitation channel and the charge exchange channel:

$$K^+ + Ar \rightarrow K + Ar^+ . \tag{41}$$

Consequently, we can expect that the effective cross-section for the charge exchange of fast Ar^+ ions on K atoms,

$$K + Ar^+ \rightarrow K^+ + Ar^* , \tag{42}$$

is sufficiently large, i.e. significantly larger than the cross-section for reaction (40). Fig. 13 shows the dependence of the cross-section for reaction (42) on the energy of the Ar^+ ions obtained in [30]. The authors of this paper sup-posed that due to a small resonance defect in reaction (42) Ar^+ ions capture an electron mainly in the excited 4s and 4p states of the Ar atom. The cross-section for charge exchange (8×10^{-15} cm^2 at $E = 1.5$ keV) is much larger than the excitation cross-section (40) which amounts to about 3×10^{-17} cm^2 (within a factor of two) at the same ion energy.

The magnitude of the oscillation period taken from experiment permits the distance R_3 to be related to the mean difference of energies, ΔE, between interacting levels. Indeed, $\Delta E \cdot \Delta R/\hbar \approx u_0$ and assuming $R_3 \gg R_1$ it is possi-ble, knowing the distance between the oscillation maxima $\Delta(v^{-1})$, to deter-mine the values of $\Delta E \cdot \Delta R$, where $\Delta R = R_3 - R_1$:

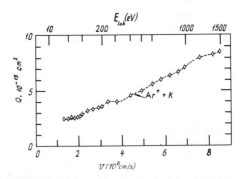

Fig. 13. Absolute charge exchange cross-section for Ar^+ incident on K, plotted against the velocity of the Ar^+ ions [30].

$$\Delta R \cdot \Delta E = \frac{2\pi\hbar}{\Delta(v^{-1})} . \tag{43}$$

For the system $(K \ Ar)^+$ we can estimate R_3 as 14 a.u. and $\Delta E \approx 1.7$ eV. Table 1 gives values of the quantity $\Delta E \cdot \Delta R$ for those processes where the oscillation period was measured. It is seen from table 1, that the quantity $\Delta E \cdot \Delta R$ changes only weakly in passing from one process to another.

Table 1
Experimental $\Delta E \cdot \Delta R$ values for diabatic processes showing oscillations in their total cross-sections.

Processes	Ref.	$\Delta E \cdot \Delta R$ (eV·cm)
$Na^+ + Ne$, NeI λ 735.9 Å	[2]	1.5×10^{-7}
$Na^+ + Ne \rightarrow Na + Ne^+$	[24]	3.07×10^{-7}
$He^+ + Ne$, NeI λ 7032 Å	[13]	1.24×10^{-7}
NeII λ 3482 Å		0.88×10^{-7}
HeI λ 3889 Å		0.9×10^{-7}
HeI λ 4713 Å		2.0×10^{-7}
$Na^+ + He$, HeI λ 584 Å	[27]	1.6×10^{-7}
$K^+ + Ar$, ArI λ 1048 Å		1.2×10^{-7}

Conclusion

The occurrence of oscillations in the excitation probability for a given state of a system of two atomic particles is due to the existence of alternative channels leading to that state (this is also true for Landau–Stückelberg oscillations). Each pair of channels corresponds to an oscillation mode whose phase is determined by an area ($\int^t \Delta E \cdot dt$), defined by these channels in the diagram illustrating the time dependence of the system's energy. If this area depends weakly on the impact parameter, the oscillations will also appear in the total cross-section, the oscillation frequency on a v^{-1} scale being proportional to the area enclosed by the two potential energy curves in the diagram of the dependence of the system's energy on internuclear separation. One can conceive of a case, shown in fig. 14, when three terms interact at large internuclear separations. This situation differs from that shown in fig. 3a only in that the coherent population of states 1 and 2 occurs through an intermediate

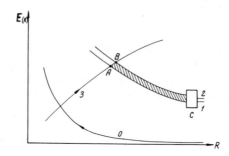

Fig. 14. Schematic representation of the interaction of three terms at large internuclear separations. (From [23].)

term 3. Oscillations of the population probability for states 1 and 2 are associated in this case with the existence of a closed "loop" ABC.

If the behaviour of quasi-molecular terms at large separations involves the formation of such a "loop", the probability oscillations will also appear in the total cross-sections for inelastic channels 1 and 2, since the magnitude of the loop area is practically independent of the impact parameter.

If several inelastic channels interact at large internuclear separations, there will possibly occur several "loops" and, correspondingly, several oscillation modes in the cross-sections for these channels.

In this paper only total cross-sections of inelastic processes have been dealt with. Of course, the interaction of terms should manifest itself in differential cross-sections [3]. The oscillations due to this interaction, as compared to the Landau–Stückelberg oscillations, have a significantly larger period and show up only in the energy dependence of differential cross-sections.

The experimental data and theoretical studies mentioned above indicate convincingly that the phenomenon of interference of two quasi-molecular states coherently excited in atomic collisions determines to a great extent the structure of total cross-sections for inelastic scattering channels in atomic collisions. It is hoped that a further progress in investigations of this phenomenon will lead to a better understanding of the mechanism of diabatic interaction in atomic collisions. In particular, it will be possible to develop methods for calculating the shape of the quasi-molecular terms in the region of large internuclear separations where there occurs a rearrangement of the quasi-molecular wave functions to the wave functions for the states of the final products of an atomic collision. From the experimental point of view the analysis of the magnitude and structure of the cross-section for a given inelastic interaction enables us to predict the atomic processes having large cross-sections and, consequently, will play an important part in the understanding of various phenomena in nature.

Acknowledgements

I am deeply indebted to Professor Dukelskii, Professor V.I.Perel', Dr. V. Ankudinov, and Dr. N.Tolk for valuable discussions during the preparation of this report.

References

[1] H.Rosenthal, *VI ICPEAC, Abstracts of Papers*, ed. I.Amdur (MIT Press, Cambridge, Mass., 1969) p. 302;
H.Rosenthal and H.M.Foley, Phys. Rev. Letters *23* (1969) 1480.
[2] S.V.Bobashev, ZhETF Pis. Red. *11* (1970) 389; [English Transl.: Soviet Phys.-JETP Letters *11* (1970) 260].
[3] D.Coffey, Jr., D.C.Lorents and F.T.Smith, Phys. Rev. *187* (1969) 201.
[4] L.D.Landau, Physik. Z. Sowjetunion *2* (1932) 46;
E.C.G.Stückelberg, Helv. Phys. Acta *5* (1932) 369.
[5] F.J.Smith, Phys. Letters *20* (1966) 271;
F.J.Smith, *VI ICPEAC, Abstracts of Papers*, ed. I.Amdur (MIT Press, Cambridge, Mass., 1969) p. 1069.
[6] J.Perel, R.H.Vernon and H.L.Daley, Phys. Rev. *138* (1965) A937;
J.Perel and H.L.Daley, *VI ICPEAC, Abstracts of Papers*, ed. I.Amdur (MIT Press, Cambridge, Mass., 1969) p. 1055;
Z.Z.Latypov, N.V.Fedorenko, I.P.Flaks and A.A.Shaporenko, ZhETF Pis. Red. *11* (1970) 189; [English Transl.: Soviet Phys. -JETP Letters *11* (1970) 116];
W.L.McMillan, Phys. Rev. A *4* (1971) 69.
[7] M.Lipeles, R.Novick and N.Tolk, Phys. Rev. Letters *15* (1965) 815.
[8] S.Dworetsky, R.Novick, W.W.Smith and N.Tolk, Phys. Rev. Letters *18* (1967) 939.
[9] S.H.Dworetsky and R.Novick, Phys. Rev. Letters *23* (1969) 1484.
[10] M.Lipeles, R.D.Swift, M.S.Longmire and M.P.Weinered, Phys. Rev. Letters *24* (1970) 799.
[11] D.Jaecks, F.J. de Heer and A.Salop, Physica *36* (1967) 606.
[12] F.J.de Heer, D.Jaecks, A.Salop, L.Wolterbeek Muller and B.F.J.Luyken, *V ICPEAC, Abstracts of Papers*, eds. I.P.Flaks and E.S.Solovyov (Publishing House "Nauka", Leningrad, 1967) p. 283.
[13] (a) N.Tolk and C.W.White, *VI ICPEAC, Abstracts of Papers*, ed. I.Amdur (MIT Press, Cambridge, Mass., 1969) p. 309;
(b) N.H.Tolk, C.W.White, S.H.Dworetsky and L.A.Farrow, Phys. Rev. Letters *25* (1970) 1251.

[14] H.Anderson, K.Jensen, J.Koch, K.Pedersen and E.Veje, *VI ICPEAC, Abstracts of Papers,* ed. I.Amdur (MIT Press, Cambridge, Mass., 1969) p. 223.

[15] S.S.Pop, I.Yu.Krivsky, I.P.Zapesochny and M.V.Baletskaya, Zh. Eksp. Teor. Fiz. *59* (1970) 696; [English Transl.: Soviet Phys. -JETP *32* (1971) 380].

[16] S.S.Pop, I.Yu.Krivsky, I.P.Zapesochny and M.V.Baletskaya, Zh. Eksp. Teor. Fiz. *58* (1970) 810; [English Transl.: Soviet Phys. -JETP *31* (1970) 434].

[17] I.P.Zapesochny, A.N.Zavilopulo and O.B.Shpenik, Opt. Spektrosk. *28* (1970) 856; [English Transl.: Opt. Spectrosc. *28* (1970) 465].

[18] C.Zener, Proc. Roy. Soc., Ser. A *137* (1934) 696.

[19] V.B.Matveyev, S.V.Bobashev and V.M.Dukelskii, Zh. Eksp. Teor. Fiz. *55* (1968) 781; [English Transl.: Soviet Phys. -JETP *28* (1969) 404].

[20] V.B.Matveyev, S.V.Bobashev and V.M.Dukelski, Zh. Eksp. Teor. Fiz. *57* (1969) 1534; [English Transl.: Soviet Phys. -JETP *30* (1970) 829].

[21] F.J.de Heer, B.F.J.Luyken, D.Jaecks and L.Wolterbeek Muller, Physica *41* (1969) 588.

[22] S.H.Dworetsky, R.Novick and N.Tolk, *VI ICPEAC, Abstracts of Papers,* ed. I.Amdur (MIT Press, Cambridge, Mass., 1969) p. 294.

[23] V.A.Ankudinov, S.V.Bobashev and V.I.Perel, Zh. Eksp. Teor. Fiz. *60* (1971) 906; [English Transl.: Soviet Phys. -JETP *33* (1971) 490].

[24] Z.Z.Latypov and A.A.Shaporenko, ZhETF Pis. Red. *12* (1970) 177; [English Transl. Soviet Phys. -JETP Letters *12* (1970) 123].

[25] Yu.N.Demkov, Zh. Eksp. Teor. Fiz. *45* (1963) 196; [English Transl.: Soviet Phys. -JETP *18* (1964) 138].

[26] L.D.Landau and E.M.Lifshitz, *Quantum Mechanics; Non-Relativistic Theory,* 2nd ed. (Pergamon Press, Oxford, 1965).

[27] S.V.Bobashev and V.A.Kritskii, ZhETF Pis. Red. *12* (1970) 280; [English Transl.: Soviet Phys. -JETP Letters *12* (1970) 189].

[28] W.Maurer and K.Mehnert, Z. Phys. *106* (1937) 453.

[29] V.V.Afrosimov, Yu.S.Gordeev, V.M.Lavrov and S.G.Shchemelinin, ZhETF Pis. Red. *12* (1971) 455; [English Transl.: Soviet Phys. -JETP Letters *12* (1970) 317].

[30] J.R.Peterson and D.C.Lorents, Phys. Rev. *182* (1969) 152.

Physics of Electronic and Atomic Collisions, VII ICPEAC, 1971 – North-Holland (1972)

COLLISIONAL TRANSFER BETWEEN
FINE-STRUCTURE LEVELS

L.KRAUSE

Department of Physics, University of Windsor,
Windsor, Ontario, Canada

A survey is presented of recent experiments dealing with the transfer of excitation between fine-structure levels, induced in collisions between excited alkali atoms and unexcited alkali atoms, noble gas atoms or molecules. In addition to traditional studies of atoms excited to their resonance states, investigations of interactions involving more highly excited atoms are also reported. These indicate that cross-sections for adiabatic atom-atom collisions of similar type (alkali-alkali or alkali-noble gas) vary inversely with the energy gap between the appropriate fine-structure states and obey Franck's rule, no matter whether atoms in resonance states or in more highly excited states take part in the interaction. Cross-sections for collisions with molecules are significantly larger than for collisions with noble gas atoms and exhibit different variations with temperature. Further progress has been made in studies of mixing between Zeeman sublevels and the results appear to invalidate the selection rule $m_J \nleftrightarrow -m_J$. New examples are reported of coherence transfer in atomic collisions.

1. Introduction

The study of interactions between excited atoms and ground state atoms or molecules, is attracting the interest of a growing group of physicists and chemists, as may be seen by the number of contributions on this subject at this and other similar conferences. Excitation transfer and quenching of resonance radiation were studied during the first 30 years of this century and, after a period of dormancy, interest in these collisional phenomena was revived in the 1950's by the work of R.Seiwert in Berlin and of the author's group in Windsor. Experimental and theoretical investigations of low-energy collisions involving excited atoms are now being pursued in several research institutes with a wide geographical distribution. The studies of such interactions provide an important check on our understanding of atomic structure and of quantum mechanical calculations. The results are also found very useful by scientists and engineers working in a variety of fields both pure and applied. It has been suggested, for instance [1,2], that collisional mixing between fine-structure states in O, C^+ and Si^+, may constitute a possible cooling mechanism in interstellar space. Collisional effects are even more important in processes that take place in the earth's atmosphere, especially collisions involving metastable ^1D oxygen atoms and $^1\Delta_g$ oxygen molecules. The considerable effort which is being put into laser research and development, draws heavily on the information furnished by basic research on low-energy atomic and molecular collisions, information which is also crucial to the understanding of chemical reactions in the gas phase. Many phenomena are studied under conditions such that the distribution functions of local thermodynamic equilibrium are not applicable. This results in a demand for atomic cross-sections, rate constants and lifetimes, needed for the detailed computation of occupation numbers.

For fairly obvious reasons, the resonance states of mercury and of the alkali atoms were frequently chosen to study the processes of excitation transfer. These states are spectroscopically accessible, emit spectral lines with large oscillator strengths and are well enough separated from other states so that experiments need not be complicated by cascade effects. The fine-structure splittings in the alkali atoms are sufficiently large so that (with the exception of lithium) the resonance doublets can be easily separated and yet the energy defects between them can be spanned collisionally by drawing energy from the kinetic energy continuum. The collisional transfer of excitation between fine-structure states of the same atom or of different atoms, manifests itself by the emission of sensitized fluorescence. The early work dealing with sensitized fluorescence has been discussed by Mitchell and Zemansky [3] and by Pringsheim [4]. Reviews of more recent experiments on collisions between excited and unexcited atoms have been provided by Seiwert [5] and by Kraulinya [6], whose two monographs (in Russian) give particular emphasis on the experimental work carried out in the Soviet Union. Gilmore, Bauer and McGowan [7] covered collisions with both atoms and molecules in their review of atomic and molecular excitation mechanisms, while comprehensive accounts of experiments dealing with interactions between excited atoms and molecules may be found in Callear's two articles [8,9].

This report is intended to provide a survey of the results obtained from recent experimental studies of sensitized fluorescence in systems containing alkali atoms. Where appropriate, mention will also be made of collisional depolarization and coherence transfer phenomena, which have been the object of some recent interest.

2. Atomic fluorescence

When a pure sample of metal vapor at low density is irradiated with the appropriate resonance radiation, the atoms become excited to their resonance states and, in decaying, emit resonance fluorescence which is of the same frequency as the exciting radiation. If resonance fluorescence is excited in a vapor at a somewhat higher density (sodium or potassium above 5×10^{-7} Torr), the fluorescent light does not reach the observer directly but becomes re-absorbed and re-emitted by the ground-state atoms in the fluorescence vessel. This re-absorption gives rise to a phenomenon known as imprisonment or trapping of resonance radiation, which manifests itself by an increase in the observed mean lifetime of the resonance state. In all experiments dealing with resonance fluorescence, the problem of radiation trapping must be resolved, as otherwise the experimental results will be subject to serious error. One way of avoiding the issue is to work at very low vapor densities at which radiation is not imprisoned, provided that one can tolerate the very low resulting fluorescent intensities. At pressures above 10^{-5} Torr, inelastic collisions between the excited and ground-state atoms begin to influence the properties of the fluorescent light. During such a collision, excitation may be transferred, producing an excited atom of the same or different species (if other atomic species have been added to the system), so that the resulting fluorescence includes frequency components additional to that present in the exciting light. These additional components are commonly known as sensitized fluorescence. Their presence may be due to collisions in which the ground-state atoms receive part of the transferred energy, become excited and decay optically, or to collisions with atoms or molecules which, serving merely as carriers of kinetic energy, remain in their electronic ground-states and cause the primarily excited atom to be transferred to another excited state. Both cases are illustrated in fig. 1, which shows the energy levels involved in the sensitized fluorescence of potassium and rubidium, induced in collisions between excited potassium and ground-state rubidium atoms [10,11]. When only the $4^2P_{1/2}$ or the $4^2P_{3/2}$ state in potassium is excited by irradiation with monochromatic light, the excited potassium atom, when colliding with a ground-state rubidium atom, may either be transferred to the other fine-structure state with the excess of energy being supplied from or released to the kinetic energy of relative motion, or the excitation may be transferred to the rubidium atom, leaving it in the $5^2P_{1/2}$ or $5^2P_{3/2}$ state. The three processes take place simultaneously, though with different probabilities, and give rise to sensitized fluorescence which consists of three spectral components.

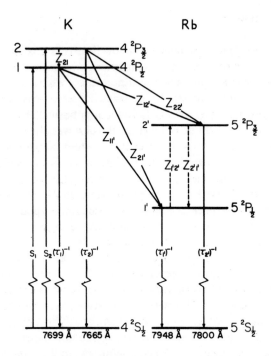

Fig. 1. Energy levels involved in the sensitized fluorescence of potassium and rubidium induced in collisions between excited potassium and ground-state rubidium atoms. The s coefficients refer to excitation by the absorption of photons, τ^{-1} to radiative decay, and Z to radiationless transfer of energy by inelastic collisions. (From [27].)

3. Apparatus

The basic experimental method of investigating sensitized fluorescence in atomic vapors has not altered much since the early experiments of Wood [12] and Lochte-Holtegreven [13], even though considerable improvement in the various techniques has been made because of technological advances. A fluorescence vessel containing the metallic vapor, pure or mixed with another vapor or gas, is mounted in an oven whose temperature can be measured and controlled accurately, and the gaseous mixture is irradiated with the appropriate resonance radiation emitted by a spectral lamp. The resulting fluorescence is monitored at right angles to the direction of irradiation by a suitable light detector. A representative arrangement of such apparatus is shown in fig. 2.

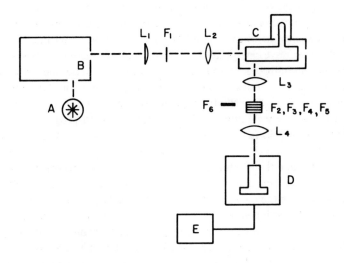

Fig. 2. Schematic diagram of apparatus used for studies of sensitized fluorescence. A, spectral lamp; B, monochromator; C, fluorescence cell in over; D, photomultiplier in cryostat; E, preamplifier and scaler; L_{1-4}, condensing lenses; F_{1-5}, interference filters; F_6, neutral density filter. (From [28].)

It is of crucial importance to the success of the experiments that the resonance lines used to excite the fluorescence, should be of high and constant intensity and of small width, and should not be self-reversed. When the gaseous mixture in the fluorescence vessel is kept at pressures of at most a few Torr, as is frequently done in fluorescence experiments, the resonance absorption lines are extremely narrow. For maximal efficiency of excitation, the profiles of the lines in the exciting light should match the absorption profiles as closely as possible, otherwise much of the light emitted by the spectral lamp will be wasted. Even more serious consequences result from self-reversal of the exciting lines, as changes in the pressure of the fluorescing mixture will cause the absorption profile to be shifted along the steep trough in the exciting line, with a consequent rapid variation in the fluorescent intensity. There seems little doubt that electrodeless discharges and hollow cathode discharges are preferable as light sources for fluorescence experiments. An electrodeless discharge in a bulb containing a small amount of the appropriate metal with 1–2 Torr of a noble gas (to carry the discharge) can be excited directly with an r.f. oscillator. It produces intense and unreversed resonance lines, whose profiles can be controlled by varying the temperature of the small reservoir at the bottom of the bulb and thus the vapor pressure of the metal [14]. Such a discharge can also be excited by microwaves, either by directing these onto the discharge bulb from a horn or by mounting the bulb in a tunable microwave cavity [15,16]. The advent of tunable dye-lasers has opened a new era in light sources for the excitation of atomic fluorescence. An increasing number of descriptions of these may be found in the literature [17] and populations of alkali atoms excited to their ^2P resonance states, approaching the theoretical limit of 50%, have been reported [18].

The fluorescent cells in use today tend to be variations on Wood's original design. A typical cell includes two windows at right angles to one another, which make possible the excitation and observation of fluorescence such that the paths of the exciting and fluorescent light in the vapor are extremely small, thus reducing the re-absorption and trapping of resonance radiation. The cell is usually equipped with a side-arm which contains the liquid metal and the temperature of which is lower than that of the main cell. Although completely sealed fluorescence cells have been used in many experiments, there is a significant risk that the metal sample in a sealed tube may become contaminated by gaseous impurities adsorbed on the walls of the cell. Experience has shown that a fluorescence cell connected to a pumping system by a narrow-bore (2 mm) tube does not suffer from such disadvantages.

The most common detector of the fluorescent light is the photomultiplier tube which must be selected for proper spectral sensitivity of the photocathode and adequate response time. Because fluorescent light is frequently very faint, considerations of signal-to-noise ratio are paramount and, when dealing with signals in the red region of the spectrum, it is necessary to refrigerate the photomultiplier. Its output signal can be measured with a good electrometer amplifier which should have low noise, fast response and a zero-suppresion feature. If there is a large background component, such as black body radiation from an oven, it is necessary to employ lock-in techniques. If the actual fluorescent light is extremely faint, photon counting methods are preferable, provided that the photomultiplier tube has suitable dark-noise characteristics and that a discriminator is included in the counting circuit.

4. Excitation transfer between fine-structure states in alkali atoms

Until recently, most studies of collisional excitation transfer in alkali atoms have dealt with the $^2P_{1/2}$ and $^2P_{3/2}$ resonance sub-states. The experimental procedure usually involves the excitation of one ^2P fine-structure state by the appropriate component of the resonance doublet and the mea-

surement of the relative intensities of both components present in the fluorescent light. The appearance of the second component, known as sensitized
fluorescence, is due to inelastic collisions between the excited and unexcited
atoms present in the mixture.

The excitation transfer may be considered as proceeding according to the
following equation:

$$M(n^2P_{1/2}) + X + \Delta E \leftrightarrow M(n^2P_{3/2}) + X , \tag{1}$$

where M represents the excited alkali atom and X is an alkali or other atom in
its ground state. ΔE is the energy defect between the resonance substates,
which is drawn from or converted into kinetic energy of relative motion of
the collision partners and which equals 18 cm^{-1} for sodium, 57 cm^{-1} for
potassium, 238 cm^{-1} for rubidium and 554 cm^{-1} for cesium.

4.1. *Collisions between alkali atoms of the same species*

Extensive experimental studies of mixing between ^{2}P resonance substates
in alkali atoms, induced in collisions between excited and unexcited atoms of
the same species, have been carried out in recent years by the author's group
in Windsor. The experiments were performed at very low alkali-vapor pressures
so that trapping of resonance radiation could be avoided. The cross-sections
for ^{2}P mixing in sodium [19], potassium [20], rubidium [21] and cesium
[22] have been reported in the literature, as have been theoretical cross-
sections calculated by Dashevskaya et al. [23], which are about one order of
magnitude smaller than the experimental values.

Quite recently the group of Berlande at Saclay has been investigating collisional excitation transfer between higher fine-structure states in cesium, induced in collisions between excited and unexcited cesium atoms. Taking advantage of the nearly exact coincidence between the energies of the
$8^2P_{1/2} - 6^2S_{1/2}$ transition in cesium and the $3^3P_1 - 2^3S_1$ transition in
helium, they used a helium spectral lamp to excite the Cs $8^2P_{1/2}$ state and, by
measuring the relative intensities of fluorescent components emitted from
closely lying levels, determined the cross-sections for the processes
$8^2P_{3/2} \leftarrow 8^2P_{1/2}$ and $4^2F_{5/2,7/2} \leftarrow 8^2S_{1/2}$ [24] as well as $7^2D_{3/2} \leftarrow 8^2P_{1/2}$
and $7^2D_{5/2} \leftarrow 8^2P_{1/2}$ [25]. They were also able to estimate cross-sections for
the transitions $8^2P_{1/2} \rightarrow 8^2S_{1/2}, 8^2P_{1/2} \rightarrow 4^2F, 8^2P_{3/2} \rightarrow 8^2S_{1/2}$ and
$8^2P_{3/2} \rightarrow 4^2F$ [25].

The group at Windsor found the cross-sections for mixing between the
resonance fine-structure states in potassium, rubidium and cesium to vary inversely as ΔE (the fine-structure splitting) and thus to obey Franck's rule [26]

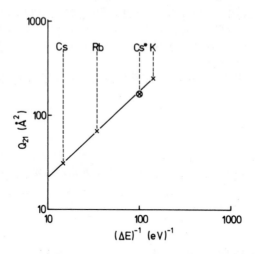

Fig. 3. The relationship between the cross sections $Q_{21}(^2P_{3/2}\rightarrow{}^2P_{1/2})$ and the fine-structure splitting ΔE for collisions between alkali atoms of like species. The point Cs^* refers to the transition $8^2P_{3/2} \rightarrow 8^2P_{1/2}$, all others indicate transitions between resonance sublevels.

(in sodium ΔE is so small that it no longer limits the cross section). The cross section for $8^2P_{3/2} - 8^2P_{1/2}$ mixing in cesium does also obey the same empirical relation as may be seen in fig. 3. Thus there is good correlation between the results of the Saclay and Windsor groups.

4.2. Collisions between dissimilar alkali atoms

When an excited alkali atom collides with a ground-state alkali atom of a different species, electronic excitation energy may be transferred in one of two ways represented by the following typical equations:

$$K(4^2P_{3/2}) + Rb(5^2S_{1/2}) \leftrightarrow K(4^2P_{1/2}) + Rb(5^2S_{1/2}) + \Delta E , \qquad (2)$$

$$K(4^2P_{3/2}) + Rb(5^2S_{1/2}) \leftrightarrow K(4^2S_{1/2}) + Rb(5^2P_{3/2}) + \Delta E' , \qquad (3)$$

where ΔE is the fine-structure splitting in potassium and $\Delta E'$ is the energy interval between the $K(4^2P_{3/2})$ and $Rb(5^2P_{3/2})$ states. Here the interaction is somewhat different from that occurring in collisions between identical partners, and the cross-sections are smaller. Eq. (2) represents mixing between the ^2P resonance states of an atom, induced in a collision with an atom of a

Table 1
Cross-sections for K → Rb excitation transfer ($Å^2$)

Collisional Process	$\Delta E'$ (cm^{-1})	Experimental cross-sections		Theoretical
		Hrycyshyn [28]	Stacey [30]	Dashevskaya [31]
$K(4^2P_{1/2}) \rightarrow Rb(5^2P_{3/2})$	168	40	5.3	10
$K(4^2P_{3/2}) \rightarrow Rb(5^2P_{3/2})$	225	27	5.5	
$K(4^2P_{1/2}) \rightarrow Rb(5^2P_{1/2})$	409	2.7	2.3	4
$K(4^2P_{3/2}) \rightarrow Rb(5^2P_{1/2})$	466	1.9	2.5	

different species, while eq. (3) describes excitation transfer from one species to the other. During the past two or three years, the former process has been studied experimentally in K-Rb mixtures by Hrycyshyn and Krause [27] and the latter processes have been investigated by Hrycyshyn and Krause [28], Ornstein and Zare [29] and Stacey and Zare [30]. The theoretical aspects of excitation transfer between two dissimilar alkali atoms were considered by Nikitin and co-workers [31]. The cross-sections for K→Rb excitation transfer, reported by the various authors, are summarized in table 1. It may be seen that there is considerable divergence between the theoretical and experimental results and, also, that there is no complete agreement between the various experimental cross-sections. It is not surprising that the experimental values agree only within an order of magnitude with the calculated cross-sections, bearing in mind the difficulties associated with such calculations, and even this degree of agreement should be regarded as gratifying. Of the four experimental K-Rb cross-sections determined both by Hrycyshyn and Krause [28] and by Stacey and Zare [30], two are in good agreement and the other two are not. There are no obvious reasons to account for the discrepancies but it should be noted that the four cross-sections quoted by Hrycyshyn and Krause decrease with increasing energy differences $\Delta E'$ as do also similar cross-sections for Rb-Cs collisions [32], while no such dependence on $\Delta E'$ is borne out in the results of Stacey and Zare.

4.3. Collisions between alkali and noble gas atoms

In the process of mixing between fine-structure states in alkali atoms, induced in collisions with ground-state noble gas atoms, the noble gas acts as a carrier of kinetic energy which is interconverted with the electronic excitation energy of the alkali atoms.

Studies of sensitized fluorescence in alkali atoms, induced in collisions

with noble gas atoms, have been carried out for over 40 years. They have
mostly dealt with the $^2P_{3/2} - {}^2P_{1/2}$ excitation transfer between resonance
fine-structure states, for which both experimental and theoretical collision
cross-sections have been reported [33–36], with agreement at least within an
order of magnitude and sometimes much better [37]. Gallagher [38] found
that the ^2P mixing cross-sections for rubidium and cesium vary with temperature according to a power law $Q \propto T^n$, where $2 \leqslant n \leqslant 4.5$.

At present, collisional excitation transfer between fine-structure states of
more highly excited alkali atoms is being investigated experimentally and
theoretically. The cross-sections for the process $8^2P_{3/2} \leftarrow 8^2P_{1/2}$ in cesium,
induced in collisions with noble gases, were determined by Pimbert et al. [39].
Cross sections for the transfers $7^2D_{3/2} \leftarrow 8^2P_{1/2}$ and $7^2D_{5/2} \leftarrow 8^2P_{1/2}$ were
reported at this conference [25], as were the results of a theoretical investiga-
tion of excitation transfer in collisions of highly excited alkali atoms [40].
The $6^2P_{3/2} - 6^2P_{1/2}$ excitation transfer in rubidium is now being investigated
in Windsor [41]. Table 2 shows a comparison of some alkali-neon cross-sections. There is little doubt that the cross-sections exhibit a roughly inverse dependence on ΔE, the fine-structure splitting, no matter whether the excitation
transfer takes place between the fine-structure components in the first excited state (potassium), the second (rubidium) or the third (cesium). In this
respect the cross-sections are consistent with those for the adiabatic ^2P mixing collisions between alkali atoms of the same species, which were found to
obey Franck's rule (see fig. 3). It has also been found that these cross-sections
do not show the rapid variation with temperature found by Gallagher [38] for
the alkali resonance fine-structure states [39].

Table 2

Cross-sections for fine-structure mixing in some excited alkali atoms, induced in collisions
with neon atoms.

Collision partners	Excitation transfer process	ΔE (cm^{-1})	T (K)	Cross-sections (Å)	Reference
K- -Ne	$K(4^2P_{3/2} \leftarrow 4^2P_{1/2})$	57	368	14.3	[20]
K- -Ne	$K(4^2P_{3/2} \rightarrow 4^2P_{1/2})$	57	368	9.5	[20]
Rb- -Ne	$Rb(6^2P_{3/2} \leftarrow 6^2P_{1/2})$	77.4	445	8.6	[41]
Rb- -Ne	$Rb(6^2P_{3/2} \rightarrow 6^2P_{1/2})$	77.4	445	5.8	[41]
Cs- -Ne	$Cs(8^2P_{3/2} \leftarrow 8^2P_{1/2})$	82.6	420	4.4	[39]
Cs- -Ne	$Cs(8^2P_{3/2} \leftarrow 8^2P_{1/2})$	88.6	620	6.3	[39]

4.4. Collisions between alkali atoms and molecules

Until recently, except for Lochte–Holtgreven's [13] early experiments, all studies of interactions between excited metal atoms and ground-state molecules dealt with the quenching process (in the case of mercury also with the transfer to the 6^3P_0 metastable state). Yet, when investigating the quenching of alkali resonance radiation, it should be borne in mind that significant transfer of excitation does take place between the ^2P fine-structure states, often with a cross-section larger than the quenching cross-section.

During the past few years, several experimental studies have been reported, dealing with excitation transfer between the resonance fine-structure states of alkali atoms, induced in collisions with molecules. The ^2P mixing process in sodium has been investigated by Stupavsky and Krause [42], in potassium by McGillis and Krause [43], in rubidium by Bellisio, Davidovits and Kindlmann [44] and by Hrycyshyn and Krause [45] and in cesium by McGillis and Krause [46]. The experiments were carried out using methods of sensitized fluorescence and apparatus similar to that depicted in fig. 2. In order to extract the mixing cross-sections from the fluorescent intensity measurements, it is necessary to solve rate equations which include quenching terms as well as mixing terms, because in the vapor-gas mixture, quenching and mixing processes occur simultaneously, though with different probabilities [47]. A perusal of the cross-sections which may be found in the various references cited above, leads to the immediate conclusion that in the cases of adiabatic collisions, involving rubidium and cesium, the ^2P mixing cross-sections for collisions with molecules are very much larger than for collisions with noble gas atoms. A theoretical model for the collisional process, which involves the formation of an intermediate ionic complex [48], successfully explained these large differences in the cases of the $Cs-N_2$ and $Rb-N_2$ interactions, and permitted the calculation of cross-sections which agreed with experimental results.

The general mechanism of excitation transfer in collisions with molecules and particularly the role of the molecular vibrational and rotational levels in the interaction, are not fully understood. It is difficult to explain the large sizes of the cross-sections on the basis of a resonant energy transfer to the vibrational states, which would require significantly more energy than is released in the atomic transition [49]. On the other hand, correlations between the sizes of the cross-sections and possible resonances with the molecular rotational transitions are rather uncertain [46]. Some additional light may have been thrown upon this problem by a recent series of experiments, in which ^2P mixing in cesium [50,51] and rubidium [52], induced in collisions

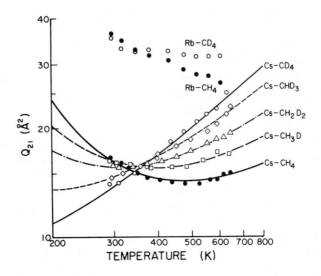

Fig. 4. The variations with temperature of the total cross-sections for $^2P_{3/2} \rightarrow {}^2P_{1/2}$ mixing in cesium and rubidium, induced in collisions with deuterated methane molecules. The points are experimental and the curves represent fits of eq. (4).

with various molecules, has been investigated in relation to temperature. Some of the experimental results are shown in fig. 4. The temperature dependence of the cross-sections differs markedly from that observed with noble gas atoms as collision partners [38]. An isotope effect is also apparent, which has been observed as well in the cross-sections for collisions between cesium and isotopic hydrogens and ethanes [51]. A semi-empirical analysis of the process, carried out on the basis of an extension of Light, Ross and Shuler's [53] model of reactive hard spheres, leads to the following relation between the cross-section and the temperature:

$$Q_{21}(T) = CT(I/I_0)(2 - \beta x_0 + \beta^2 x_0^2) \tag{4}$$

where Q_{21} is the cross-section for $^2P_{1/2} \leftarrow {}^2P_{3/2}$ excitation transfer, T is the absolute temperature, C is a constant, I is the moment of inertia of the particular deuterated methane molecule, I_0 is the moment of inertia of CH_4 and βx_0 represents the threshold energy for the interaction, divided by kT [50]. Fig. 4 shows approximate fits of eq. (4) to the experimental results, the analysis of which indicated the presence of a slightly attractive potential at the critical distance of approach. This conclusion is consistent with the results obtained by Baylis [54] who calculated interatomic potentials for alkali-noble gas atomic pairs and predicted the existence of shallow potential wells at large interatomic distances. The predicted depths of these wells for cesium are in the range $10-1000$ cm^{-1}, in which also lie the values E^* obtained by Walentynowicz, Phaneuf and Krause [50].

Studies of excitation transfer induced in collisions with molecules were not limited to fine-structure states of alkali atoms. Excitation transfer from the $6^2D_{3/2}$ to the $6^2D_{5/2}$ state in thallium was investigated in a Hanle experiment by Rityn, Chaika and Cherenkovskii [55], who obtained cross-sections of 12 Å^2 for collisions with nitrogen and 16 Å^2 with hydrogen. Slightly earlier, Doemeny, van Itallie and Martin [56] observed fluorescence from crossed molecular beams and measured relative cross-sections for the energy transfer $Hg(6^3P_2\rightarrow6^3P_1)$ induced in collisions with various molecules. Their values are: CO: 1.00 (normalized); N$_2$: 0.71; H$_2$: 0.42; D$_2$: 0.10; CH$_4$: 0.62; CD$_4$: 0.21. The results were interpreted qualitatively on the basis of energy transfer to the molecular vibrational states.

5. Transfer of excitation from mercury to other metallic atoms

Mercury may be easily excited to the 6^3P_1 state by 2537 Å radiation or by electron impact, and the excitation energy may be removed partly or totally in collisions with unexcited atoms or molecules. It is generally recognized that collisions with noble gas atoms do not result in excitation transfer to the 6^3P_0 metastable state nor in quenching to the 6^1S_0 ground state [57–59]. On the other hand, the occurrence of collisional excitation transfer from the $Hg(6^3P_1)$ state to closely lying levels of other atoms has been known for many years, and the effect has been studied extensively with various atoms as collision partners. The first experiments dealing with mercury-thallium collisions were performed by Cario and Franck [60], and mercury-sodium collisions were investigated by Beutler and Josephy [61]. Recently, extensive experimental work on this subject has been carried out by the group of Frish in Leningrad and of Kraulinya in Riga [62]. In her experiments, Kraulinya optically excited the Hg 6^3P_1 state and followed the excitation transfer to the various levels in the collision partner by measuring the intensities of the collisionally sensitized lines. In this way she determined a large number of collision cross-sections for excitation transfer from mercury to sodium [63], thallium [64], cadmium [65], zinc [65] and indium [66]. The experiments were carried out at quite high mercury-vapor pressures and some unexpectedly large cross-sections were reported. For instance, a cross-section of 1 Å^2

was found for the transfer $Hg\ 6^3P_1 \rightarrow Cd\ 5^1S_0$, over an energy gap of
$8756\ cm^{-1}$ [67]. It was suggested that this and other large cross-sections in
systems involving mercury, might be due to the formation of molecular complexes: $Hg\ 6^3P_0 + Hg\ 6^1S_0 \rightarrow Hg_2(^3O_u^-)$, whose vibrational levels are in near
resonance with the appropriate levels in cadmium, zinc or indium [65,66].
Although no molecules were present in these systems to populate the $Hg\ 6^3P_0$
metastable state, it is possible that at the relatively high mercury vapor densities some $Hg\ 6^3P_1$ atoms could have been transferred to the 6^3P_0 state in
binary collisions with ground-state mercury atoms [68].

The problem of excitation transfer from the 6^3P_1 state in mercury to
various levels in sodium is being re-investigated by Czajkowski at Windsor, but
at mercury-vapor pressures about three orders of magnitude lower than those
employed by Kraulinya.

6. Collisional depolarization effects in alkali atoms

During recent years several investigations have been reported on transitions
between m_J sublevels of resonance states in alkali atoms and the subject continues to attract the attention of both experimentalists and theoreticians [69].
m_J mixing within the $^2P_{1/2}$ resonance fine-structure state, induced in collisions
with noble gas atoms, has been investigated in potassium using a modified
Zeeman scanning method [70], and in rubidium and cesium by means of
Hanle experiments [71]. More recently, m_J mixing in the $^2P_{3/2}$ state of potassium has also been studied at kilogauss fields, permitting the determination of
disorientation and disalignment cross-sections [72]. The experimental work
was parallelled by the theoretical studies of Baylis [69] and of Okunevich and
Perel [73]. The large cross-sections for m_J mixing in the $^2P_{1/2}$ state of potassium indicated the apparent breakdown of the time-reversal selection rule, according to which the collisional mixing between the $m_J = +1/2$ and $m_J = -1/2$
states should be forbidden. It was suggested that this breakdown was due to
the proximity of the $^2P_{3/2}$ state in potassium and that the rule should hold
rigorously in rubidium and cesium [74]. New results for cesium have just
been obtained by Guiry and Krause in Windsor [75], who carried out Zeeman
scanning experiments at magnetic fields in the vicinity of 9 kG, populating
selectively the $(m_J=-1/2, m_I=-7/2)$ substate of the $^2P_{1/2}$ fine-structure state,
and observing the decay of circular polarization induced in collisions with
noble gas atoms. The cross-sections for m_J mixing are shown in table 3 and
are compared with values obtained by Gallagher [71] in Hanle experiments.
These new results provide conclusive evidence against the existence of the

Table 3
Cross-sections for $m_J = +1/2 \leftrightarrow m_J = -1/2$ transitions in the $^2P_{1/2}$ resonance state of cesium, induced in collisions with noble gas atoms.

Collision partners	Collision cross-sections (Å^2)	
	Guiry [75]	Gallagher [71]
Cs- -He	6	2.1
Cs- -Ne	2	0.8
Cs- -Ar	5	1.7
Cs- -Kr	19	
Cs- -Xe	36	

selection rule, evidence which is also supported by the recent theoretical work of Okunevich and Perel [73].

Mention should also be made of recent experimental work on the collisional depolarization of the $^2P_{3/2}$ resonance states in sodium and potassium. The effect of depolarizing collisions is being observed in Hanle experiments at low magnetic fields. Tudorache [76] reported a cross-section of 180 Å^2 for argon-induced depolarization in sodium, which agrees within an order of magnitude with Gallagher's estimated value [71]. Niewitecka [77] has just measured a similar cross-section of 22 Å for potassium-helium collisions and is continuing her study with other noble gas atoms and simple molecules.

7. Transfer of coherence in atomic collisions

The transfer of coherence in atomic collisions has been observed some years ago by Gough [78], who studied collisional excitation transfer between mercury and cadmium atoms and who noted the partial transfer of polarization and thus of spatial coherence from mercury to cadmium. Similar effects have been reported by Kraulinya et al. [79], who investigated excitation transfer from mercury to thallium.

Collisional coherence transfer from the $^2P_{1/2}$ to the $^2P_{3/2}$ resonance states in sodium and potassium is also being investigated in a series of Hanle experiments. The $m_J = +1/2$ Zeeman sublevel of the $^2P_{1/2}$ state is populated by excitation with circularly polarized light and the excited (and polarized) alkali atoms, in colliding with noble gas atoms present in the fluorescence vessel, are transferred to the various Zeeman sublevels of the $^2P_{3/2}$ state. Their polarization is however, partly conserved in the collision, resulting in the appearance

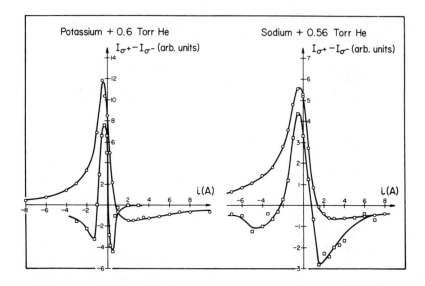

Fig. 5. Transfer of coherence from $^2P_{1/2}$ to $^2P_{3/2}$ in sodium and potassium. In both cases the broader curves represent the ordinary Hanle effect in the $^2P_{3/2}$ state, and the narrower curves represent the Hanle effect in the sensitized fluorescence. (1 A=9.7 G.)

of a Hanle signal in the sensitized fluorescence. Such transfer of coherence has been demonstrated in the cases of sodium [80] and potassium [77], with helium acting as the buffer gas. Fig. 5 shows sensitized Hanle curves for sodium and potassium. Both are significantly narrower than the corresponding ordinary Hanle curves and both show inversion of the signal or their wings, which is probably due to the de-coupling of the nuclear spin by the magnetic field [80,81]. The cross-sections for polarization transfer from the $3^2P_{1/2}$ state to the $3^2P_{3/2}$ state in sodium, incuded in collisions with noble gas atoms, which have been determined by Elbel and Schneider [81], amount to roughly 25 percent of the corresponding cross sections for excitation transfer [34] (about 22 $Å^2$ as compared to 90 $Å^2$).

References

[1] A.Dalgarno, Rev. Mod. Phys. *39* (1967) 850.
[2] A.Dalgarno, Rev. Mod. Phys. *39* (1967) 858.
[3] A.C.G.Mitchell and M.W.Zemansky, *Resonance Radiation and Excited Atoms* (Cambridge University Press, London, 1961).

[4] P.Pringsheim, *Fluorescence and Phosphorescence* (Interscience, New York, 1949).
[5] R.Seiwert, Erg. Ex. Naturwiss. *47* (1968) 143.
[6] E.K.Kraulinya, *Sensitized Fluorescence in Mixtures of Metal Vapors, Vols. I and II* (Latvian State University, Riga, 1968, 1969).
[7] F.R.Gilmore, E.Bauer and J.W.McGowan, J. Quant. Spectrosc. Radiat. Transfer *9* (1969) 157.
[8] A.B.Callear, Appl. Opt. , Supplement on Chemical Lasers (1965).
[9] A.B.Callear and J.D.Lambert, in: *Comprehensive Chemical Kinetics*, eds. C.H. Bamford and C.F.H.Tipper, *Vol. 3* (Elsevier, Amsterdam, 1969) p. 182.
[10] E.S.Hrycyshyn and L.Krause, Can. J. Phys. *47* (1969) 215.
[11] E.S.Hrycyshyn and L.Krause, Can. J. Phys. *47* (1969) 223.
[12] R.W.Wood and L.Dunoyer, Phil. Mag. *27* (1914) 1018.
[13] W.Lochte-Holtgreven, Z. Phys. *47* (1928) 362.
[14] W.Berdowski, T.Shiner and L.Krause, Appl. Opt. *6* (1967) 1683.
[15] F.C.Fehsenfeld, K.M.Evenson and H.P.Broida, Rev. Sci. Instrum. *36* (1965) 294.
[16] R.M.Dagnall and T.S.West, Appl. Opt. *7* (1968) 1287.
[17] A.J.Gibson, J. Phys. E *2* (1969) 802.
[18] H.Walter and J.L.Hall, Appl. Phys. Letters *17* (1970) 239.
[19] J.Pitre and L.Krause, Can. J. Phys. *46* (1968) 125.
[20] G.D.Chapman and L.Krause, Can. J. Phys. *44* (1966) 753.
[21] A.G.A.Rae and L.Krause, Can. J. Phys. *43* (1965) 1574.
[22] M.Czajkowski and L.Krause, Can. J. Phys. *43* (1965) 1259.
[23] E.I.Dashevskaya, E.E.Nikitin, A.I.Voronin and A.A.Zembekov, Can. J. Phys. *48* (1970) 981.
[24] M.Pimbert, J.-L.Rocchiccioli and J.Cuvellier, C.R.Acad. Sci., Ser. B *270* (1970) 684.
[25] M.Pimbert, J.Cuvellier, J.Pascale and F.Gounand, *VII ICPEAC, Abstracts of Papers*, eds. L.M.Branscomb et al., Vol. 1 (North-Holland Publ. Co., Amsterdam, 1971) p. 667.
[26] J.Franck, Naturwissenschaften *14* (1929) 211.
[27] E.S.Hrycyshyn and L.Krause, Can. J. Phys. *47* (1969) 223.
[28] E.S.Hrycyshyn and L.Krause, Can. J. Phys. *47* (1969) 215.
[29] M.H.Ornstein and R.N.Zare, Phys. Rev. *181–1* (1969) 214.
[30] V.Stacey and R.N.Zare, Phys. Rev. A*1* (1970) 1125.
[31] E.I.Dashevskaya, A.I.Voronin and E.E.Nikitin, Can. J. Phys. *47* (1969) 1237.
[32] M.Czajkowski, D.A.McGillis and L.Krause, Can. J. Phys. *44* (1966) 741.
[33] L.Krause, Appl. Opt. *5* (1966) 1375.
[34] J.Pitre and L.Krause, Can. J. Phys. *45* (1967) 2671.
[35] E.I.Dashevskaya and E.E.Nikitin, Opt. Spektrosk. *22* (1967) 886; [English Transl.: Opt. Spectrosc. *22* (1967) 473].
[36] E.I.Dashevskaya, E.E.Nikitin and A.I.Reznikov, J. Chem. Phys. *53* (1970) 1175.
[37] R.H.G.Reid and A.Dalgarno, Chem. Phys. Letters *6* (1970) 85.
[38] A.Gallagher, Phys. Rev. *172–1* (1968) 88.
[39] M.Pimbert, J.Rocchiccioli, J.Cuvellier and J.Pascale, C.R. Acad. Sci., Ser. B *271* (1970) 415.
[40] A.A.Zembekov, E.E.Nikitin and A.I.Reznikov, *VII ICPEAC, Abstracts of Papers*, eds. L.M.Branscomb et al., Vol. 2 (North-Holland Publ. Co., Amsterdam, 1971) p. 680.

[41] E.S.Hrycyshyn, I.Siara and L.Krause, Can. J. Phys. (to be published).
[42] M.Stupavsky and L.Krause, Can. J. Phys. 46 (1968) 2127; Ibid. 47 (1969) 1249.
[43] D.A.McGillis and L.Krause, Can. J. Phys. 46 (1968) 25.
[44] J.A.Bellisio, P.Davidovits and P.J.Kindlmann, J. Chem. Phys. 48 (1968) 2376.
[45] E.S.Hrycyshyn and L.Krause, Can. J. Phys. 48 (1970) 2761.
[46] D.A.McGillis and L.Krause, Can. J. Phys. 46 (1968) 1051.
[47] D.A.McGillis and L.Krause, Phys. Rev. 153–1 (1967) 44.
[48] E.A.Andreev and A.I.Voronin, Chem. Phys. Letters 3 (1969) 488.
[49] D.A.McGillis and L.Krause, Can. J. Phys. 47 (1969) 473.
[50] E.Walentynowicz, R.A.Phaneuf, W.E.Baylis and L.Krause, Can. J. Phys. (to be published).
[51] E.Walentynowicz, R.A.Phaneuf and L.Krause, Can. J. Phys. (to be published).
[52] R.A.Phaneuf and L.Krause, Can. J. Phys. (to be published).
[53] J.C.Light, J.Ross and K.E.Shuler, in: Kinetic Processes in Gases and Plasmas, ed. A.R.Hochstim (Academic Press, New York, 1969) p. 281.
[54] W.E.Baylis, J. Chem. Phys. 51 (1969) 2665.
[55] E.Rityn, M.Chaika and V.Cherenkovskii, Opt. Spektrosk. 28 (1970) 636 [English Transl.: Opt. Spectrosc. 28 (1970) 344].
[56] L.J.Doemeny, F.J.van Itallie and R.M.Martin, Chem. Phys. Letters 4 (1969) 302.
[57] J.P.Barrat, D.Casalta, J.L.Cojan and J.Hamel, J. Phys. (Paris) 27 (1966) 608.
[58] A.I.Voronin and V.A.Kvlividze, Theor. Chim. Acta 8 (1967) 334.
[59] J.Pitre, J.S.Deech and L.Krause, VII ICPEAC, Abstracts of Papers, eds. L.M.Branscomb et al., Vol. 2 (North-Holland Publ. Co., Amsterdam, 1971) p. 671.
[60] G.Cario and J.Franck, Z. Phys. 17 (1923) 202.
[61] B.Beutler and H.Josephy, Z. Phys. 53 (1929) 747.
[62] E.Kraulinya, A.Lezdin and M.Jansons, VII ICPEAC, Abstracts of Papers, eds. L.M. Branscomb et al. (North-Holland Publ. Co., Amsterdam, 1971) Vol. 1, p. 615.
[63] E.K.Kraulinya, Opt. Spektrosk. 17 (1964) 464; [English Transl.: Opt. Spectrosc. 17 (1964) 250].
[64] E.K.Kraulinya and A.E.Lezdin, Opt. Spektrosk. 20 (1966) 539; [English Transl.: Opt. Spectrosc. 20 (1966) 304].
[65] E.K.Kraulinya and M.G.Arman, Opt. Spektrosk. 26 (1969) 511; [English Transl.: Opt. Spectrosc. 26 (1969) 285].
[66] E.K.Kraulinya and M.L.Jansons, Opt. Spektrosk. 29 (1970) 445; [English Transl.: Opt. Spectrosc. 29 (1970) 239].
[67] E.N.Morozov and M.L.Sosinskii, Opt. Spektrosk. 26 (1969) 506; [English Transl.: Opt. Spectrosc. 26 (1969) 282].
[68] B.V.Waddell and G.S.Hurst, J. Chem. Phys. 53 (1970) 3892.
[69] W.E.Baylis, VII ICPEAC, Abstracts of Papers, eds. L.M.Branscomb et al., Vol. 2 (North-Holland Publ. Co., Amsterdam, 1971) p. 677.
[70] W.Berdowski and L.Krause, Phys. Rev. 165 (1968) 158.
[71] A.Gallagher, Phys. Rev. 157 (1967) 68.
[72] W.Berdowski, T.Shiner and L.Krause, Phys. Rev. A 4 (1971) 984.
[73] A.I.Okunevich and V.I.Perel, Zh. Eksp. Teor. Fiz. 58 (1970) 666; [English Transl.: Soviet Phys.-JETP 31 (1970) 356].
[74] F.A.Franz, Proceedings of the Intern. Conf. on Opt. Pumping, Warsaw, 1968.
[75] J.Guiry and L.Krause, Phys. Rev. (to be published).

[76] S.T.Tudorache, Rev. Roum. Phys. *15* (1970) 269.
[77] B.Niewitecka, Ph. D. Thesis (University of Windsor) 1972.
[78] W.Gough, Proc. Phys. Soc. *90* (1967) 287.
[79] E.K.Kraulinya, O.S.Sametis and A.P.Bryukhovetskii, Opt. Spektrosk. *29* (1970) 423; [English Transl.: Opt. Spectrosc. *29* (1970) 227].
[80] M.Elbel, B.Niewitecka and L.Krause, Can. J. Phys. *48* (1970) 2996.
[81] M.Elbel and W.Schneider, Z. Phys. *241* (1971) 244.

Physics of Electronic and Atomic Collisions, VII ICPEAC, 1971 — North-Holland (1972)

COINCIDENCE STUDIES OF ELEMENTARY PROCESSES IN COLLISIONS OF HYDROGEN PARTICLES WITH ATOMS AND MOLECULES

V.V. AFROSIMOV

A.F. Ioffe Physico-Technical Institute,
USSR Academy of Sciences, Leningrad, USSR

This paper gives a review of some experimental investigations of elementary atomic collision processes, in which a simultaneous analysis is made of the final charge states of both collision partners. A description is given of the delayed-coincidence method employed in these studies. The possibilities of this technique are illustrated by measurements of the cross-section for a number of elementary processes occurring in collisions of fast hydrogen particles (protons, negative hydrogen ions, and hydrogen atoms) with rare-gas atoms and diatomic molecules in the energy range of 5-50 keV.

1. Introduction

The interaction of the simplest atomic particles, i.e. positive and negative hydrogen ions (H^+ and H^-) and hydrogen atoms (H^0) with atoms and molecules seems to be the case which has so far been studied most thoroughly in the field of atomic collisions. The interest shown in the interaction of hydrogen particles with other atomic particles is understandable: the data on the elementary processes involved are of importance to hydrogen-plasma physics and astrophysics, and the theoretical analysis of the results, whose possibilities are, unfortunately, still limited, turns out to be the simplest in this case. The present paper deals with experimental studies of elementary processes of change in charge states in atomic collisions involving fast hydrogen particles. The scheme of such processes (subsequently referred to as "elementary processes", for the sake of briefness) can be written in the following traditional form:

$$\vec{H}^{k+} + B^0 \rightarrow \vec{H}^{m+} + B^{n+} + (m+n-k)e , \tag{1}$$

where $\vec{H}$ is the fast hydrogen particle, k and m are its initial and final charge states, respectively, which can take only 3 values: $+1$, 0 and -1; $\tilde{B}^0$ is the target atom which is transformed into an n-charged ion by the collision. Abbreviated notations of the process ($komn$) and of its cross-section (σ_{on}^{km}) which we commonly use, refer to initial (k and o) and final (m and n) charge states of the interacting particles.

Up to now, the methods used in investigations of the elementary processes discussed in this paper, have been based upon the analysis and detection of either the fast collision products ($\vec{H}^{m+}$) or the slow ions (B^{n+}) and electrons produced in the gas target. The application of just these methods has furnished almost all information available at present on elementary processes in atomic collisions. As this information accumulates, however, its limitations become more evident. The analysis of one of the particles participating in the collision does not yield, in most cases, a direct information on the cross-section for the processes (σ_{on}^{km}). If the total charge of positive ions or electrons formed in the gas is measured (it is usually done by means of the condenser technique), then the cross-section for the formation of positive ions (σ_+) and electrons (σ_-) measured in this case turns out to be a summation over all the states of the products:

$$\sigma_+ = \sum_m \sum_n n\, \sigma_{on}^{km} \; ; \qquad \sigma_- = \sum_m \sum_n (m+n-k)\, \sigma_{on}^{km} \; .$$

If, again, the charge of either the fast or the slow ion is analyzed, the measured cross-section for the formation of the particle analyzed in a particular charge state turns out to be a summation over all the charge states of the second, non-observed, particle. Thus, the cross-sections for the formation of m-charged fast ions and n-charged slow ions may be written in the form

$$\sigma^{km} = \sum_n \sigma_{on}^{km} \; ; \qquad \sigma_{on} = \sum_m \sigma_{on}^{km} \; .$$

Of course, situations are not excluded, where some elementary process is the only possible one or where it occurs with a predominant probability. In this case the detection of one of the particles suffices to find out whether the process takes place and to measure its cross-section. Such cases, however, are rare.

The problem of detailed studies of elementary processes and of the mechanism of inelastic atomic collisions strongly calls for working out a "complete" experiment in which the state of the system could be determined both before and after collision.

A natural first step towards such a "complete" experiment is proceeding to the study of individual elementary collisions with simultaneous analysis of the final charge state of both interacting atomic particles. Both partners in the same collision act can be identified by means of the coincidence technique well-known in nuclear physics.

The investigations of elementary processes in atomic collisions with registration of both collision products were carried out first at the A.F. Ioffe Physico-Technical Institute, USSR, in 1963 [1] and then at the University of Connecticut, USA in 1965 [2]. These first experiments using the coincidence technique in collision physics were devoted to the investigation of scattering and inelastic energy losses in violent atomic collisions. The investigations into elementary processes of change of charge states and measurements of cross-sections for these processes by means of the coincidence method [3-5] have been carried out in A.F. Ioffe Institute since 1967.

2. Experimental arrangement used in the investigation of elementary processes

Obviously, an experimental arrangement designed to investigate the elementary processes $Komn$, is to make possible effective collection, simulaneous analysis of charge states and registration in the counting mode of scattered beam particles as well as of slow ions produced in the gas. The scheme of a device for measuring cross-sections of the elementary processes by the coincidence method [3] is shown in fig. 1. The monoenergetic ion beam, separated by a magnetic monochromator M and collimated by a series of slits, enters through the slit S_6 into the collision chamber filled with gas. The fast particles pass through the exit slit S_7 into the magnetic analyser A_3, where they are analyzed according to their charge state. The charged particles are registered by the detector D_1, and the neutral particles by the detector D_2. The slow ions produced in the gas are extracted by the electric field of the condenser K, focused by the electrostatic lens and then directed into the lateral magnetic analyser A_2. In the analyser, the ions are further accelerated and analysed according to the charge states and then registered by the detector D_3. The electric pulses which appear during the registration of individual particles at the detector output are fed into the delayed-coincidence circuit. The delay of pulses introduced in the fast-particle registration is necessary because of the difference in the time-of-flight of the fast particles and of the slow ions, travelling from the place where the collision occurred to the detector.

Between the monochromator of the primary beam and the chamber C_3, two other collision chambers, C_1 and C_2, are mounted. They can be filled with gas and can produce mono-energetic fast atom beams by charge ex-

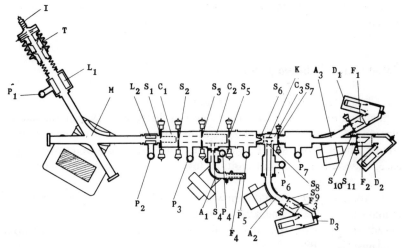

Fig. 1. Scheme of the experimental arrangement used in the investigation of elementary charge changing processes by the coincidence method [3]. I: ion source; T: accelerating tube; M: magnetic mass-monochromator; L_1 and L_2: ion-beam focussing lenses; C_1 and C_2: collision chambers for charge exchange of ions and for measurement of the total cross-section of ionization and charge exchange; C_3: collision chamber for measurement of cross-sections for elementary processes by the coincidence method; K: condenser extracting slow ions; A_2: slow-ion analyser; A_3: fast-ion analyser; D_1, D_2, D_3: individual particle detectors; F_1-F_4: particle collectors; S_1-S_7: slits that can be controlled without breaking the vacuum; P_1-P_7: diffusion pumps.

change. They can also be used to measure the total cross-sections for the formation of slow positive ions, σ_+, and free electrons, σ_-, by the potential method in the way described in ref. [6]. The magnetic analyser A_1, connected to one of the chambers, allows the measurement of the total cross-sections for the formation of slow ions with a particular charge state, σ_{on}, by the method proposed in ref. [7]. The change-over from the measurement of the total cross-sections $(\sigma_+, \sigma_-, \sigma_{on})$ by ion- and electron-current registration to the measurement of the cross-sections of elementary processes, σ_{on}^{km}, by the coincidence method with individual particle registration, requires control of the primary beam intensities within a broad range. For this purpose, two systems of quadrupole lenses L_1 and L_2 are placed in the primary beam path, in front of the collision chambers.

The dimensions and position of the slits in the apparatus are controlled without breaking the vacuum. Owing to the differential pumping, the pressure differences existing between the collision chambers (pressure $P \approx 10^{-4}$

Torr) and the other parts of the apparatus ($P < 10^{-6}$ Torr) are localized at the slits.

3. Collision of hydrogen particles with atoms

3.1. Classification of elementary processes

Elementary processes involving changes in charge states, which can take place in collisions of H^+, H^o and H^- with atoms, are classified in several main groups. The classification of the processes is based on the qualitative differences between the electron transitions involved. The basic types of elementary processes are:

a. Processes of *pure capture*, in which electrons of one particle transit to bound states in the second particle. In thise case no free electrons are produced: $m + n - k = 0$ (see eq. (1)). The simplest capture process is the charge exchange: $\vec{H^+} + B^o \rightarrow \vec{H^o} + B^+$.

b. Processes of *pure ionization*, which result only in the transition of target atom electrons into the continuum. The analogous processes with the removal of electrons from the incident particle are called *pure stripping*. In processes of ionization and stripping, free electrons are produced, $m + n - k > 0$ and $m \geqslant k$. The simplest processes of ionization and stripping are: $\vec{H^+} + B^o \rightarrow \vec{H^+} + B^+ + e$ and $\vec{H^o} + B^o \rightarrow \vec{H^+} + B^o + e$, respectively.

c. Processes of *capture with ionization*, in which a fraction of the electrons, removed from one of the particles, transits to the continuum, while the remainder is captured by the other particle. In this case too, free electrons are produced, $m + n - k > 0$, while $m < k$. The simplest process of capture with ionization is $\vec{H^+} + B^o \rightarrow \vec{H^o} + B^{2+} + e$.

The first two types of processes are well-known. The assumption about the existence of processes of the third type was made in our papers as early as 1956 [6,7]. However, there was no direct evidence about the existence of these processes, because they cannot be singled out by ordinary methods of analysis of one of the collision products.

3.2. Elementary processes in collisions of H^+, H^o and H^- with atoms of noble gases

Investigations carried out so-far by the coincidence technique have shown that, during ion-atom collisions, all the types of elementary processes listed above occur: pure capture, pure ionization, and capture with ionization. The simplest elementary processes resulting in changes of charge states take place in collisions of protons with helium atoms: $\vec{H^+} + He$ (see table 1). A simulta-

Table 1

Processes with changes in charge states in collisions $\vec{H}^+ - He$

Number of the process	Scheme of the process	Abbreviated designation of the process	Designation of the cross-section	Type of the process
1	$\vec{H}^+ + He \rightarrow \vec{H}^+ + He^+ + e$	1011	σ_{01}^{11}	Ionization
2	$\rightarrow \vec{H}^+ + He^{2+} + 2e$	1012	σ_{02}^{11}	Double ionization
3	$\rightarrow \vec{H}^0 + He^+$	1001	σ_{01}^{10}	Capture (charge exchange)
4	$\rightarrow \vec{H}^0 + He^{2+} + e$	1002	σ_{02}^{10}	Capture with ionization
5	$\rightarrow \vec{H}^- + He^{2+}$	10–12	σ_{02}^{1-1}	Double capture

neous analysis of the final charge states of both particles made it possible to measure separately the cross-sections of all five elementary processes which are possible in this case [8] (fig. 2). The two processes: pure ionization with the removal of one electron: 1011 (process 1 in table 1), and pure capture of one electron by the proton (charge exchange): 1001 (process 3), produce singly charged ions: He^+. The other three processes, pure ionization with the

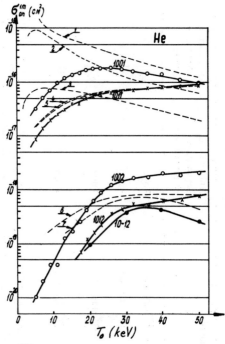

Fig. 2. Cross-sections σ_{0n}^{1m} for elementary processes with changes in charge states, 10 mn, in collisions of protons with helium atoms [8]. The final charge states of the fast particles are indicated as follows: $m = +1$: $-\times-\times-$; $m = 0$: $-\circ-\circ-$; $m = -1$: $---$
Abbreviated notations for the processes are given on the corresponding curves. Schemes of the processes are given in table 1. Curves 1 and 2: quantum-mechanical calculations of the charge exchange cross-section taking into account different final states [11], and one final state (1s) [10] respectively; curves 3 and 5: classical calculations of the cross-sections of charge exchange and ionization with the removal of one electron [14,15]; curve 4: quantum-mechanical calculations of ionization with the removal of one electron [12,13]; curve 6: classical cross-section calculations for ionization with removal of two electrons [14]; curve 7: experimental cross-sections for two-electron capture by protons in helium, σ^{1-1} [9]. (From [8].)

removal of two electrons: 1012 (process 2), pure capture of two electrons by protons (double charge exchange): 10–12 (process 5), and capture of one electron with simultaneous ionization: 1002 (process 4), produce doubly charged ions, He^{2+}. Within practically the whole range of incident proton energies investigated in [8], T_0 = 5-50 keV, the process of pure capture, 1001, plays an essential part in the formation of singly charged ions, He^+. However, the role of pure ionization, 1011, increases with increasing T_0 and, at $T_0 \approx$ 50 keV, the pure ionization and pure capture cross-sections become equal. Among the processes producing doubly charged ions, He^{2+}, the process of capture with ionization, 1002, has the highest cross-section. The latter is three times higher than the cross-section for pure ionization with the removal of two electrons, 1012, which is the second largest. The process of pure capture of two electrons by protons, 10–12, resulting in the formation of the fast negative hydrogen ions, has the smallest cross-section.

It is interesting to note that, by analysing just one collision product, it is possible, even in this simplest case of H^+ incident on He, to measure the cross-section of only one of the processes mentioned, i.e. the process 10–12. This can be done by the registration of fast negative hydrogen ions because, during the formation of these ions, the target-particle must be in the charge state He^{2+}. The cross-section σ^{1-1} for the production of fast negative hydrogen ions in helium, obtained by Fogel et al. [9], is represented by curve 7 in fig. 2. Figure 2 also shows the results of theoretical calculations of elementary processes resulting in changes of charge states. The quantum-mechanical cross-section calculations for charge exchange taking into account one (1s) and several final states, performed by Bransden et al. [10] and by Mapleton [11] respectively, as well as the calculations for ionization by Mapleton [12] and Peach [13] have been performed in the Born-approximation. The classical calculations by Gryzinsky [14–15] have been performed on the basis of the model of binary Coulomb collisions of protons with atomic electrons. In these calculations the atomic electrons are not considered to be at rest, as was assumed in Thompson's ionization theory, but they are allowed to exhibit a distribution in velocities.

Analysis of experimental results has shown that the conclusions about the relative role of different elementary processes in the formation of slow ions for the case $\vec{H}^+$ − He also hold for the interaction of protons with more complex atoms. The existence of processes of capture with ionization explains the well-known fact that cross-sections for the formation of multicharged ions (σ_{on}, $n > 1$) in collisions of protons with atoms have the highest values at incident proton velocities, $v \approx e^2/\hbar$. This circumstance makes it also explicable to a great extent why the maximum cross-section values for the formation of slow multi-charged ions by protons, σ_{on}, considerably exceed those for the formation of ions with the same charge in electron collisions. Actually, in electron impact, ion formation is possible only as a result of the pure ionization processes. As an illustration, data are given in fig. 3 for cross-sections of elementary processes resulting in the formation of triply-charged argon ions, Ar^{3+}, in $\vec{H}^+-$ Ar collisions. Figure 3 shows that the highest cross-sections belong to the process associated with the capture of an electron by the proton (capture with ionization, 1003). The process of pure ionization, 1013, begins to play an important role only at incident proton energies of several tens of keV.

The difference between the mechanism of interaction of protons with atoms and that involved in electron-atom collisions is not only evident in processes of capture with ionization, but also in processes of pure ionization by protons which can also be investigated by the coincidence technique. Contrary to processes of capture with ionization, processes of pure ionization by protons do not have a cross-section maximum in the region of the incident proton velocities $v \approx e^2/\hbar$. However, the relative yield of multi-charged ions in pure ionization of atoms by protons can have the maximum at the velocities $v \approx e^2/\hbar$. Figure 4 shows data on the relative probabilities q_n (in per cent) of pure ionization by protons with the removal of one, two or three electrons ($n = 1, 2, 3$) from He, Ne, Ar, Kr and Xe. The relative probabilities q_n are connected with the cross-sections of the elementary processes of pure

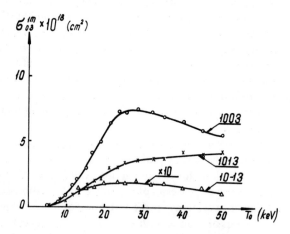

Fig. 3. Cross-sections for elementary processes of the type 10 m3, leading to the formation of slow triply-charged ions Ar^{3+} in $\vec{H}^+$-Ar collisions. (From [4].)

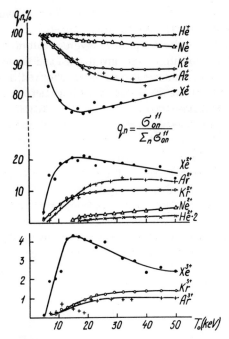

Fig. 4. Relative probabilities for the removal of one, two an three electrons in the pure ionization of rare-gas atoms by protons. The ions produced are indicated on the corresponding curves. (From [8].)

ionization by the relation

$$q_n = \sigma_{on}^{11} \Big/ \sum_n \sigma_{on}^{11} .$$

For the light atoms He and Ne, the relative probability of pure ionization with the removal of two electrons constantly increases with increasing energy of the incident protons. In heavy gases this probability shows a maximum which is especially clear in the case of xenon. The same also holds for the probability of ionization with the removal of three electrons. The results given in fig. 4 show that the relative probability of pure ionization with the removal of several electrons in heavy gases turns out to be the highest at proton velocities close to the velocities of the outer atomic electrons.

Interesting characteristics of the mechanism of proton-atom interactions can be observed by studying the charge composition, i.e. the relative probabilities P_m of the final charge states $m = 1, 0$ or -1 of the hydrogen particles, for the different charge states n of the atomic target.

In our work [16], collisions of protons, hydrogen atoms and negative hydrogen ions with xenon atoms were investigated and the formation of xenon ions with charges from $n = 1$ to $n = 4$ was observed. The investigated elementary processes involve a wide range of energy defects: 1.5 eV are liberated in the charge exchange 1001 for the pair $\vec{H}^+ - \vec{Xe}$ ($\vec{H}^+ + Xe \rightarrow$ $H^0 + Xe^+$), 124 eV are absorbed in the ionization with stripping (0014) for the pair $\vec{H}^0 - Xe$ ($\vec{H}^0 + Xe \rightarrow \vec{H}^+ + Xe^{4+} + 5e$). The distribution in charges of fast hydrogen particles is expected to depend on the charge state of the xenon ions. Figure 5 gives data on P_m ($m = +1, 0$ and -1) for different charges ($n = 1$ to 4) of xenon ions produced in single collisions.

It can be seen from fig. 5 that the charge composition of the fast hydrogen particles depends only slightly on the charge state of the slow xenon ions. It is an interesting fact that, although the beam fractions P_+, P_0 and P_- presented in fig. 5 concern single collisions, their values are close to those of the

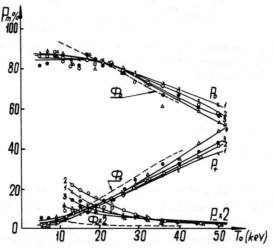

Fig. 5. Relative probabilities P_m for formation of fast hydrogen particles with final charge $m = +1, 0$ and -1, in single collisions between $\vec{H}^0$ and Xe leading to the formation of xenon ions of various charges. The charge of the xenon ions, $n = 1, 2, 3$ and 4, is indicated by numbers on the corresponding curves. ϕ_+, ϕ_0 and ϕ_- are the equilibrium fractions of, respectively, protons, hydrogen atoms and negative hydrogen ions in multiple collisions of fast hydrogen particles with Xe atoms, on passage through a thick target of xenon gas. (From [16].)

so-called equilibrium fractions $\phi_m(\phi_+, \phi_0$ and $\phi_-)$ which result from multiple collisions during the passage of hydrogen particles through a thick xenon target.

It could be expected too, that the charge composition of fast particles after collision depends on the initial state of these particles. Figure 6 shows the probabilities P_+, P_0 and P_- corresponding to collisions of different fast particles, $\vec{H}^+$, $\vec{H}^0$ and $\vec{H}^-$, with xenon atoms, resulting in the formation of Xe^{2+}. It can be seen that the charge composition of the hydrogen particles after collision depends little on their initial charge.

The observed characteristics suggest that it is possible to distinguish two stages in the inelastic collision of a hydrogen particle with a many-electron atom. In the first stage, as the nuclei approach each other, the fast hydrogen particle crosses the electronic shell of the atom, bringing about its excitation, while the particle itself "forgets" its initial charge state. In the second stage, during scattering, the fast particle passes through the outer shells interacting with weakly bound electrons. The distribution of the final charge states of the fast particles which is thus established, closely resembles the equilibrium

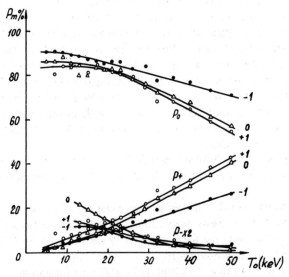

Fig. 6. Relative probabilities P_m for formation of fast hydrogen particles with final charge states $m = +1, 0$ and -1 in single collisions $\vec{H}^+ - Xe$, $\vec{H}^0 - Xe$ and $\vec{H}^- - Xe$, leading to the formation of doubly charged xenon ions ($n=2$). The initial charge of the fast hydrogen particle, $k = +1, 0$ and -1, is indicated by a number on the corresponding curve. (From [16].)

distribution; it depends on the velocity of the incident particles, but only weakly on their initial state and on the total inelastic energy transferred to the target-atom. The excited states of the atoms can decay by the removal of a different number of electrons with the formation of a slow ion having a corresponding charge state.

4. Collisions of hydrogen particles with molecules

The use of the coincidence technique in the investigation of collisions in which molecules take part, appears to offer even more advantages over standard methods of analysis of only one of the collision partners. This is due to the fact that the pattern of elementary processes involving molecules is much more complex than that for atomic targets, because besides the capture and removal of electrons, the dissociation of the target-molecule is also possible. As a consequence, the possibilities of studying elementary processes by usual methods prove to be very limited, while the coincidence technique permits practically all elementary processes to be separated in this case too. For the investigation of the collisions in which molecules take part, a more complicated technique is needed. As a result of dissociation, three atomic particles appear after collision rather than two, thus complicating the application of the coincidence technique. In addition to this, the dissociation products can possess considerable kinetic energies. The magnitudes of these energies depend on the electronic state of the molecule target before dissociation. This makes the experiment difficult, but at the same time provides a source of important information, for if the initial kinetic energies of the dissociation products are measured, one can determine the electronic state of the molecular system resulting from the collision.

It is appropriate to illustrate the whole picture of elementary processes involving molecules by considering the simplest case, i.e. the collision $\vec{H}^+ - H_2$.

The scheme of possible changes in charge state of the incident particles, as was mentioned above, is extremely simple. As the result of the collision the proton can either retain its charge state, or by electron capture turn into a fast atom, $\vec{H}^0$, or a negative ion, $\vec{H}^-$.

The scheme of possible transitions resulting in the formation of ions from the hydrogen molecule, is somewhat more complex and it is convenient to consider it using the well-known diagram of the potential-energy curves for this system [17]. Figure 7 shows curves which represent the ground-state of the H_2 molecule ($^1\Sigma_g^+$), the ground-state of the molecular ion H_2^+ ($1s\sigma_g$), the

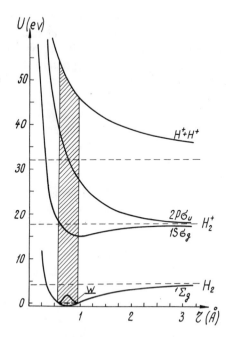

Fig. 7. Dependence of the interaction potential on internuclear distance r for the hydrogen molecule (H_2), the hydrogen molecular ion (H_2^+) and two protons ($H^+ + H^+$) [17]. The energies of H_2, H_2^+, H^+ and H^+ at $r = \infty$ are indicated by horizontal dashed lines.

repulsive state of the H_2^+ ion ($2p\sigma_u$) and the Coulomb interaction of two protons ($H^+ + H^+$).*

Figure 7 illustrates the transitions resulting in the formation of the H_2^+ and H^+ ions form the molecular target, thus making possible an estimate of the kinetic energies which these ions obtain as the result of such transitions. In satisfying the Franck-Condon principle, electronic transitions occur in the region of internuclear distances corresponding to the ground vibrational state of the H_2 molecule. This region is indicated in fig. 7 by a hatched band. The

_____

* Between the curves $2p\sigma_u$ and ($H^+ + H^+$) there are also a number of repulsive curves corresponding to different excited electronic states of the H_2^+ ion. However, for a qualitative analysis of the scheme of transitions associated with change in charge states, it is sufficient to consider only the four curves given in fig. 7. In fact, transitions to each curve corresponding to electronic excitation of the H_2^+ ion, and transitions to the curve $2p\sigma_u$, lead to the dissociation of the H_2^+ ion into a hydrogen atom and a proton ($H_2^+ \rightarrow H + H^+$); the difference lies only in the state of the hydrogen atom.

transition $1s\sigma_g \leftarrow {}^1\Sigma_g^+$ mostly leads to the formation of the H_2^+ molecular ion in different vibrational states and practically without kinetic energy transfer. However, in a transition to that part of the curve $1s\sigma_g$, which lies above the dissociation limit for the H_2^+ ion, corresponding to the smallest internuclear distances in the hatched region in fig. 7, the dissociation of the H_2^+ ion should occur with the formation of a hydrogen atom and a proton with very low kinetic energies. The second transition, $2p\sigma_u \leftarrow {}^1\Sigma_g^+$, is related to the formation of a hydrogen atom and a proton with mean kinetic energies of ≈ 7 eV (at the maximum of the energy distribution). And, finally, the transition $(H^+ + H^+) \leftarrow {}^1\Sigma_g^+$ results in the formation of two protons with the mean kinetic energy of ≈ 9 eV.

The possible processes involving changes in charge states in $\vec{H}^+ - H_2$ collisions are summarized in table 2. In addition to the reaction schemes (column 2), this table gives the state of the molecular target which is excited by the collision (column 3), the mean kinetic energies of the fragment ions (column 4), and the symbols for the cross-sections for the various processes (column 5). In these symbols, the upper indices indicate the initial (1) and the final (1, 0 or −1) charge states of the incident particles, respectively, while the lower indices indicate the initial charge states of the target molecule (0) and the corresponding fragments produced as a result of the collision (H_2^+, H and H^+). It can be seen from table 2 that in processes $1 - 3$ the fast protons retain their charge state (the ionization-process group), in processes $4 - 6$ they transform into fast atoms (the group of processes connected with one-electron capture by the proton), and in process 7 they change into fast negative ions (the process with two-electron capture by the proton). The result of processes 1 and 4 is the formation of a slow molecular ion, H_2^+, while the other processes produce one proton or even two protons at once in the target gas.

It is interesting to note that, to-date, of all the processes listed in table 2 only the cross-section for the process with double capture (process 7) was measured directly. Since the hydrogen molecule has only two electrons, this process, analogous to reaction 5 in table 1, is the only one resulting in the formation of fast negative ions $\vec{H}^-$, and its cross-section coincides with the total cross-section for double capture, σ^{1-1}, obtained by the measurement of the total yield of fast $\vec{H}^-$ ions. All other cross-sections presently known, i.e. the total cross-section for the capture of one electron by the fast proton, σ^{10}, and the total cross-sections for the formation of H_2^+ ions, $\sigma_{H_2^+}$, and of protons, σ_{H^+}, in the target gas, represent the sum of cross-sections for various of the elementary processes listed in table 2.* (See footnote on page 99.)

The cross-sections of all the processes given in Table 2 have been determined as described in our paper [18] : all atomic particles produced in each individual collision of a proton with a hydrogen molecule were detected by means of the delayed-coincidence technique. Elementary processes which resulted in the formation of various charged particles, fast $\vec{H}^+$, $\vec{H}^0$ or $\vec{H}^-$ and slow H_2^+ or H^+, were separated by the analysis of these particles in magnetic analysers. To separate processes in which one or two protons at a time are produced from the target molecule, (i.e. to separate processes 2a, 2b from process 3 and processes 5a, 5b from process 6) we used the difference in pulse amplitudes appearing at the output of the slow-ion detector when one proton and a pair of protons were registered. In addition, we carried out [18] separation of processes resulting in the same changes of charge states but involving different electronic states in the excitation of the target molecule (processes 2a and 2b, as well as 5a and 5b). For such differentiation, apart from the coincidence technique, the analysis of kinetic energies of protons produced by dissociation was used. In order to separate protons of different kinetic energies we varied the extraction field in the collision chamber as well as the time delay introduced in the channel registering the fast particles. A similar technique was applied in our investigations of elementary processes in the interaction between hydrogen particles H^+, H^0, H^- with more complex molecules (e.g. N_2, CO).

As an illustration of the results, figure 8 shows the cross-sections for the processes leading to the formation of $\vec{H}_2^+$ molecular ions in collisions of fast protons and hydrogen atoms with hydrogen molecules. Two cross-sections, $\sigma_{0H_2^+}^{10}$ and $\sigma_{0H_2^+}^{11}$ refer to the case of $\vec{H}^+ - H_2$, while the other three, $\sigma_{0H_2^+}^{00}$, $\sigma_{0H_2^+}^{01}$ and $\sigma_{0H_2^+}^{0-}$ refer to the case of $\vec{H}^0 - H_2$.

In the case of fast protons the basic process for H_2^+ formation is pure capture, $\sigma_{0H_2^+}^{10}$. However, the role of pure ionization, $\sigma_{0H_2^+}^{11}$, increases with increasing energy of the incident protons and at energies of the order of 45 keV the cross-sections of pure capture and ionization are equal. In the case of fast atoms, the basic process for H_2^+ formation is pure ionization of the molecule. In the low-energy region the process with the second largest cross-section is the capture of an electron by the atom, while in the high energy region it is

---

* Besides those shown in the table one more elementary process is also possible, i.e. the reaction $\vec{H}^+ + H_2 \rightarrow \vec{H}^+ + H^+ + H^-$; its cross-section can be determined directly by the registration of one of the particles - the slow negative ion H^-, owing to the fact that the dissociation $H_2 \rightarrow H^+ + H^-$ is the only source of slow H^- ions during the $\vec{H}^+ + H_2$ collision. However, as the experimental estimates of the total cross-section for the formation of slow H^- ions, σ_{H^-}, reported in ref. [18] have shown, the value of σ_{H^-} is one order of magnitude smaller than the cross-section of any other process mentioned in table 2.

Table 2

Processes with changes in charge states in collisions $\vec{H}^+ + H_2$

Number of the process	Scheme of the process	Final state of the molecular system	Mean energy of the slow ion (eV)	Designation of the cross-section	Type of process
1	$\vec{H}^+ + H_2 \to \vec{H}^+ + H_2 + e$	$1s\sigma_g$	≈ 0	$\sigma^{11}_{0H_2^+}$	Pure ionization
2a	$\vec{H}^+ + H_2 \to \vec{H}^+ + H + H^+ + e$	$1s\sigma_g$	≈ 0	$\sigma^{11}_{0(H,H^+)}$	Ionization with dissociation
2b		$2p\sigma_u$ and the excited states	≈ 7		
3	$\vec{H}^+ + H_2 \to \vec{H}^+ + 2H^+ + 2e$	$H^+ + H^+$	≈ 9	$\sigma^{11}_{0(H^+,H^+)}$	Double ionization
4	$\vec{H}^+ + H_2 \to \vec{H}^0 + H_2^+$	$1s\sigma_g$	≈ 0	$\sigma^{10}_{0H_2^+}$	Pure capture (charge exchange)
5a	$\vec{H}^+ + H_2 \to \vec{H}^0 + H + H^+$	$1s\sigma_g$	≈ 0	$\sigma^{10}_{0(H^+,H)}$	Capture with dissociation
5b		$2p\sigma_u$ and the excited states	≈ 7		
6	$\vec{H}^+ + H_2 \to \vec{H}^0 + 2H^+ + e$	$H^+ + H^+$	≈ 9	$\sigma^{10}_{0(H^+,H^+)}$	Capture with ionization
7	$\vec{H}^+ + H_2 \to \vec{H}^- + 2H^+$	$H^+ + H^+$	≈ 9	$\sigma^{1-1}_{0(H^+,H^+)}$	Double capture

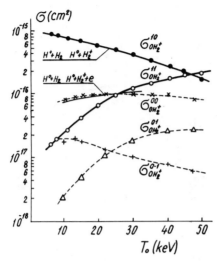

Fig. 8. Cross-section for elementary processes producing molecular ions H_2^+ in collisions of protons [18] and hydrogen atoms with hydrogen molecules. Full lines: data for the pair $\vec{H}^+ + H_2$, dashed lines: data for the pair $\vec{H}^0 - H_2$.

the ionization of the molecule with simultaneous stripping of the fast atom. It is interesting to notice that, at velocities lower than that of an electron in the Bohr 1s orbit, the cross-section for pure ionization is larger for atoms than for protons.

The cross-sections resulting in the formation of protons from hydrogen molecules are given in fig. 9. The largest cross-section in the entire energy range is that for capture with dissociation from repulsive states (process 5b). The next largest one is that for capture with ionization (process 6). At proton energies exceeding 30 keV, this process gives the largest contribution to the total production of slow protons, due to the fact that it results in simultaneous production of two protons while its cross-section is only 1.5 times smaller than that for process 5b.

Collisions of hydrogen particles with many-electron diatomic molecules are accompanied by elementary processes which in number by far exceed those in the case of hydrogen molecules, due to the possibility of the formation of multiply charged atomic-and molecular ions. The application of the coincidence technique, however, together with the analysis of the collision products by means of magnetic and electric fields and by time-of-flight measurements, permits the elementary processes to be successfully separated in these cases too. As an example, fig. 10 shows the data on the cross-sections

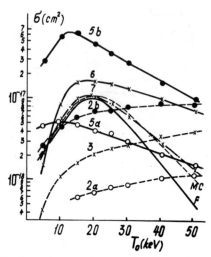

Fig. 9. Cross-sections for elementary processes resulting in the formation of protons from the H_2 molecule in collisions of protons with hydrogen molecules [18].————: processes associated with the capture of one electron by the incident proton; —·—·—: process associated with the capture of two electrons by the incident proton (double capture); —————: processes associated with ionization. The electronic states of the molecular target after collision are: $\bigcirc$: $1s\sigma_g$; $\bullet$: $2p\sigma_u$ and excited electronic states of H_2^+; $\times$: $H^+ + H^+$. Data for the cross-section of double capture: F - from ref. [9]; MC - from ref. [19]. The numbers on the curves correspond to the ordinal numbers of the processes given in table 2. (From [18].)

for pure ionization processes in collisions between $\overrightarrow{H}^+$ and CO in which the target molecule or its fragments take various charge states and the incident proton retains its initial charge. Characteristic for the dissociative ionization of the CO molecule is a predominant formation of positive carbon ions.

The detailed study of elementary processes by the coincidence technique also opens up other possibilities. For instance, the availability of the cross-section data for all elementary processes makes it possible to evaluate the relative probabilities of collision-induced transitions of a molecular system into different electronic states. Figure 11 shows data for the relative probabilities for transitions yielding $1s\sigma_g$ or $2p\sigma_u$ H_2^+ ions, or two slow protons in collisions of protons with hydrogen molecules. It is an interesting fact that the relative probabilities for transitions into higher electronic states are maximum at energies of the order of 20 keV, which corresponds to velocities close to that of an electron in the Bohr 1s orbit. This result is characteristic of an inelastic interaction of atomic particles in the medium velocity region and is

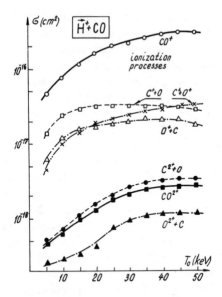

Fig. 10. Cross-sections for the elementary processes of pure ionization in collisions between $\vec{H}^+$ and CO. The final charge states of the target molecule are indicated on the corresponding curves.

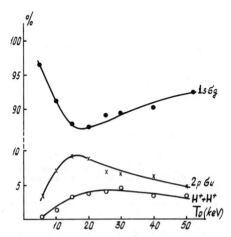

Fig. 11. Relative probabilities for transitions of $H_2(^1\Sigma_g^+)$ to different electronic states during collisions of protons with hydrogen molecules. The final states are indicated on the corresponding curves. (From [18].)

in agreement with the conclusions reached from the analysis of processes in collisions of hydrogen particles with atoms (see fig. 4).

The study of the probabilities for various electronic transitions makes it possible to elucidate whether the electronic transitions in the collision of atomic particles with the molecular gas targets take place in accordance with the Franck-Condon principle. It can be seen from fig. 7 that part from the transitions from the ground state of the H_2 molecule to the lower $1s\sigma_g$ state of the H_2^+ ion can lead to dissociation. According to the calculations [20, 21] for the Franck-Condon transitions and to the experimental data for electron collisions with H_2 molecules [22–24] where the Franck-Condon principle must be complied with, the dissociation probability in the transition into the $1s\sigma_g$ state is about 1%. Figure 12 presents our experimental data on relative probabilities of dissociation in transitions $1s\sigma_g \leftarrow {}^1\Sigma_g^+$ for collisions of $\vec{H}^+$ and $\vec{H}^0$ with H_2 molecules in different processes: stripping, ionization and capture. It is seen that when the energy of the incident particles, T_0, is high, the dissociation probability for all processes is independent of T_0 and equals $\approx$ 1%, which corresponds to transitions satisfying the Franck-Condon principle. At $T_0 < 20$ keV the dissociation probability in processes of ionization and stripping increases, which points to a violation of the Franck-Condon principle in these transitions. This can be explained by the fact that ionization and stripping occur at smaller impact parameters than capture processes. At small impact parameters, an essential role is played by the effect of direct transfer

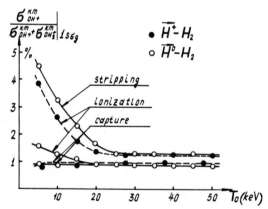

Fig. 12. Probability ratio for the formation of protons and H_2^+ ions in the processes of stripping, ionization and capture were the H_2 molecule is transferred from the ground state $({}^1\Sigma_g^+)$ to the $(1s\sigma_g)$ state of H_2^+. $\circ$: data for the pair $\vec{H}^0-H_2$; $\bullet$: data for the pair $\vec{H}^+-H_2$.

of the kinetic energy from the incident proton to the nuclei of the molecule, which indeed leads to an increase in the dissociation probability. The calculations of cross-sections for the kinetic-energy transfer from protons to H_2 molecules, and the contribution of this transfer to dissociation, are in good agreement with the observed violation of the Franck-Condon principle.

In conclusion, it has to be pointed out that even the results available at present, demonstrate clearly enough the many possibilities of the coincidence technique in the investigation of elementary collision processes. In spite of some complicacies in its application, this method possesses a number of purely methodical advantages. For example, the results of these measurements are only slightly sensitive to the purity of the gas and to the existence of parasitic effects on surfaces. These effects, associated with the interaction of one of the particles with the impurities or surfaces, are, as a rule, automatically excluded because of the selection of the second collision partner according to impulse (or energy) and time-of-flight. Investigations by means of the coincidence technique allow an increase in the variety of information available on atomic collisions, even for the relatively simple and previously well-known cases. A considerable amount of the information collected could not be obtained at all if traditional methods of analysis of one of the particles were used.

The value of the investigation of elementary collision events consists in the possibility to determine a whole set of parameters of the detected process. Owing to this, it is possible to choose experimental conditions which very closely approximate those considered in the theoretical treatment of atomic collisions. Thus, in addition to the possibility of obtaining qualitatively new information, important from the practical point of view, the investigation of elementary collision events offers suitable conditions for achieving progress in the realization of a detailed model for inelastic atomic collisions.

References

[1] V.V. Afrosimov, Yu.S. Gordeev, M.N. Panov and N.V. Fedorenko, *C.R. VI Conf. Internat. Phénom. Ioniz. Gaz* (Proc. VI ICIPG), Eds. P. Hubert and E. Crémieu-Alcan, Vol. I, (Centre de Documentations Universitaires, Paris, 1964) p. 111; V.V. Afrosimov, Yu.S. Gordeev, M.N. Panov and N.V. Fedorenko, Zh. Tekh. Fiz., *34* (1964) 1613; *34* (1964) 1624; *34* (1964) 1637; [English Transl.: Soviet Phys.-Tech. Phys. *9* (1965) 1248; *9* (1965) 1256; *9* (1965) 1265].

[2] E. Everhardt and Q.C. Kessel, Phys. Rev. Letters *14* (1965) 247; Q.C. Kessel, A. Russek and E. Everhart, Phys. Rev. Letters *14* (1965) 484; Q.C. Kessel and E. Everhart, Phys. Rev. *146* (1966) 16.

[3] V.V. Afrosimov, Yu.A. Mamaev, M.N. Panov, V. Uroshevich and N.V. Fedorenko, Zh. Tekh. Fiz. *37* (1967) 550; [English Transl.: Soviet Phys.-Tech. Phys. *12* (1967) 394].

[4] V.V. Afrosimov, Yu.A. Mamaev, M.N. Panov and V. Uroshevich, Zh. Tekh. Fiz. *37* (1967) 717; [English Transl.: Soviet Phys.-Tech. Phys. *12* (1967) 5121.

[5] V.V. Afrosimov, Yu.A. Mamaev, M.N. Panov and N.V. Fedorenko, *V ICPEAC, Abstracts of Papers*, Eds. I.P. Flaks and E.S. Solovyov, (Publishing House "Nauka", Leningrad, 1967) p. 210.

[6] N.V. Fedorenko, V.V. Afrosimov and D.M. Kaminker, Zh. Tekh. Fiz., *26* (1956) 1929; [English Transl.: Soviet Phys-Techn. Phys. *11* (1956) 1861].

[7] N.V. Fedorenko and V.V. Afrosimov, Zh. Tekh. Fiz. *26* (1956) 1941; [English Transl.: Soviet Phys.-Tech. Phys. *1*, (1956) 1872].

[8] V.V. Afrosimov, Yu.A. Mamaev, M.N. Panov and N.V. Fedorenko, Zh. Tekh. Fiz. *39* (1969) 159; [English Transl.: Soviet Phys.-Tech. Phys. *14* (1969) 109].

[9] Ya.M. Fogel, R.V. Mitin, F.V. Kozlov and N.D. Romashko, Zh. Eksp. Fiz. *35* (1958) 565; [English Transl.: Soviet Phys.-JETP *8* (1958) 390].

[10] B.H. Bransden, A. Dalgarno and N.M. King, Proc. Phys. Soc. *A67* (1954) 1075.

[11] R.A. Mapleton, Phys. Rev. *122* (1961) 528.

[12] R.A. Mapleton, Phys. Rev. *109* (1958) 1166.

[13] G. Peach, Proc. Phys. Soc. *85* (1965) 709.

[14] M. Gryzinsky, Report N. 488/XVIII, Institute of Nuclear Research, Warsaw (June 1963).

[15] M. Gryzinsky, Phys. Rev. *138 A* (1965) 336.

[16] V.V. Afrosimov, Yu.A. Mamaev, M.N. Panov and N.V. Fedorenko, Zh. Eksp. Teor. Fiz. *55* (1968) 97; [English Transl.: Soviet Phys.-JETP *28* (1969) 521.

[17] D.R. Bates, K. Ledsham and A.L. Stewart, Phil. Trans. A *246* (1963) 215.

[18] V.V. Afrosimov, G.A. Leiko, Yu.A. Mamaev and M.N. Panov, Zh. Eksp. Teor. Fiz., *56* (1969) 1204; [English Transl.: Soviet Phys.-JETP *29* (1969) 648].

[19] G.W. McClure, Phys. Rev. *132* (1963) 1636.

[20] S. Rothenberg and E.R. Davidson, J. Mol. Spectrosc. *22* (1967) 1.

[21] D. Villarejo, J. Chem. Phys. *49* (1968) 2523.

[22] W. Bleakney, E.U. Condon and L.G. Smith, J. Phys. Chem. *41* (1937) 197.

[23] N. Bauer and J.Y. Beach, J. Chem. Phys. *15* (1947) 150.

[24] O.A. Shaeffer and J..M. Hastings, J. Chem. Phys. *18* (1950) 1048.

Physics of Electronic and Atomic Collisions, VII ICPEAC, 1971 — North-Holland (1972)

INTRODUCTION TO INNER-SHELL
EXCITATION AND DE-EXCITATION PROCESSES*

M.E. RUDD

*Behlen Laboratory of Physics, University of Nebraska, Lincoln
Nebraska, 68508
U.S.A.*

Various simple and complex atomic states involving inner-shell vacancies are discussed and shown on an energy level diagram. Comparison is made between the excitation produced by photon, electron, proton, and heavy ion bombardment. Several mechanisms of inner-shell excitation are examined; especially the electron promotion mechanism of Fano and Lichten, and the methods by which it has been used to determine the energy dependence of excitation by heavy ions. The basic de-excitation mechanisms, X-ray emission and Auger electron emission, and combinations of these are considered. The need to define the fluorescence yield separately for each state, rather than just for each shell, is pointed out.

1. Introduction

Inner-shell vacancy states in heavy atoms have been studied for many years by the X-rays emitted or absorbed. The lower energy states of lighter atoms have come under study more recently as X-ray techniques have improved and magnetic and electrostatic instruments have been developed to analyze Auger electrons.

This paper discusses, in an introductory way, the types of vacancy states that can be excited, the way these states are excited by collisions with different projectiles, and the various modes of decay of such states. Emphasis is placed on recent advances particularly in the experimental work.

* Research sponsored by the National Science Foundation.

2. States of atoms with inner-shell vacancies

Vacancy states of heavy atoms are often displayed on a diagram such as that in fig. 1 in which the energies of individual electrons are plotted rather than the energies of the atom. The level at the bottom represents the situation where the atom has lost one K-electron. Electrons from other shells can "fall" into the vacancy and give up the excess energy in the form of an X-ray. Transitions between states on such a diagram are called "diagram lines". Other transitions which do not fit this scheme are called non-diagram or satellite lines. When one considers the atom as a whole this diagram is inverted. This is because an atom is in a very highly excited state when it has a K vacancy and thus on an energy level diagram for the atom it ought to be near the top rather than at the bottom as in this diagram.

When dealing with excitation of more than one electron, or when discussing states which are not simple vacancy states, this type of diagram is not adequate. I have suggested [1] a somewhat different type of energy level diagram such as that shown in fig. 2 for argon in which different charge states of an atom are

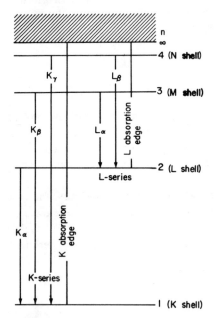

Fig. 1. Energy levels of electrons in various shells of an atom with several possible X-ray transitions shown.

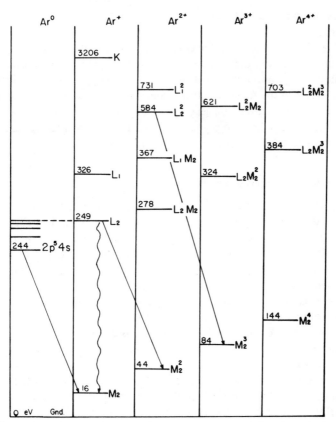

Fig. 2. Energy level diagram of argon with various vacancy and excited states. Auger transitions shown by slanting lines. X-ray transitions shown by wavy lines.

grouped in different columns. All energies are measured relative to the ground state of the atom. An atom can decay from a vacancy state, such as the L_2 state (L_3 is omitted for clarity) either by photon emission to the ground state of Ar^+ as shown by the wavy line, or by Auger emission to the ground state of Ar^{2+} as shown by the slanting line. The energy of the emitted electron or photon is equal to the difference between the energies of the initial and final states. Also shown is one of many possible Rydberg series, this one being formed by exciting the 2p electron to the n = 4,5 . . . shell rather than removing it entirely. The series limit, of course, is the L_2 vacancy state. Simple removal of inner-shell electrons gives rise to diagram lines in X-ray and Auger spectroscopy while satellite lines arise from any of the more complex states indicated.

Larkins [2] has calculated the energies of several states with double vacancies in inner shells and they are also shown in fig. 2. Experimental evidence for such states was given by Ogurtsov and co-workers [3] who found structure at 500 eV in the Auger spectrum from Ar^+-Ar collisions. Such double vacancies may, in addition, be accompanied by outer-shell excitations or vacancies. One cannot hope to plot all possible states but diagrams of this type can be made to show any chosen class of states in detail.

3. Excitation by various projectiles

The first Born approximation predicts in general that the excitation produced by different charged particles should depend only on their charge and velocity provided that the velocity is large compared to that of the electrons of interest in the target atom. Furthermore, if the velocity is high enough not only should electrons and protons produce the same excitation, but it should also be the same as that produced by photons.

Let us examine some experiments where the same type of spectrum has been measured using two different types of excitation to see to what extent these predictions hold true and what differences do appear.

Figure 3 shows measurements by Krause, et al. [4] of the K-L^2 diagram lines and the KL-L^3 satellite lines of neon excited by 1.5 keV photons and by 3.2 keV electrons. The difference in the relative values of the satellite intensities in the two cases is only 3%. Not only are the total satellite intensities practically the same, but the details of the two spectra are essentially identical. The same similarity between electron and photon excitation is evident in the X-ray spectra of silicon measured by Graeffe, et al. [5]

Next compare in fig. 4 the $L_{2,3}$ Auger spectra from argon and the 4 keV electron impact data of Mehlhorn and Stahlherm [6] with the 275 keV proton impact data of Volz and Rudd [7]. The spectra are very similar, but these are diagram lines only and no satellites are shown. When the satellite spectra are examined we find that the satellite-to-diagram intensity ratio is about twice as great for protons than for electrons. We can make a similar comparison for neon using the 300 keV proton data of Edwards and Rudd [8] and the electron data of Körber and Mehlhorn [9] and Krause, et al. [4] from 3–10 keV. Here the satellite-to-total intensity ratio is 0.46 for proton excitation and only 0.21 for electron impact. This seems to indicate that at least for the few cases for which such measurements are available, protons are relatively much more effective in producing satellite states than electrons.

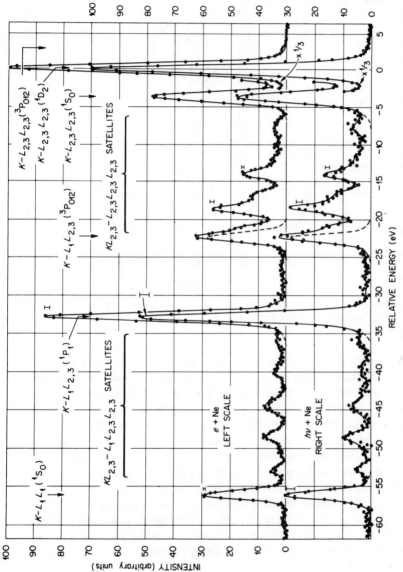

Fig. 3. Spectra of K Auger electrons from neon excited by 3.2 keV electrons and by photons of 1.5 keV. Note the strong similarity. From Krause et al. [4].

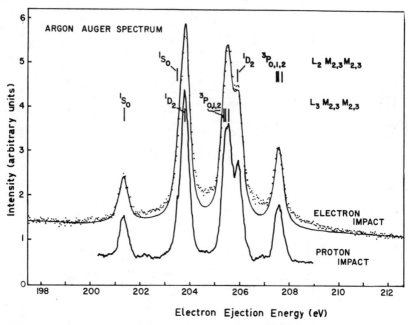

Electron Ejection Energy (eV)

Fig. 4. Spectra of $L_{2,3}$ Auger electrons from argon excited by 4 keV electrons and 275 keV protons. Electron data from Mehlhorn and Stahlherm [6] and proton data from Volz and Rudd [7].

When we come to a comparison of inner-shell excitations caused by protons and by heavier, more complex ions, we find great differences. Consider fig. 5 showing the electron spectra from H^+-Ar and Ar^+-Ar collisions. In the proton case, a relatively few sharp, well defined peaks appear, most of which can be identified as Auger transitions from either simple inner-shell vacancies or from states due to one inner-shell plus one outer-shell vacancy. In sharp contrast, the spectrum from Ar^+ impacts shows no lines from simple vacancy states and, in fact, no sharp lines at all. It appears to consist of a great many lines too close to be resolved. A partial resolution was made by Rudd, et al. [10] which also showed another feature of such symmetric collisions. Electrons from the moving projectile are shifted in energy from those ejected from the stationary target in a way which depends on the angle and energies involved [10]. This Doppler shift complicates an already complicated spectrum even further.

The change in the electron spectrum with Ar^+ energy is shown in fig. 6, which represents unpublished work done at Nebraska. Note that as the energy

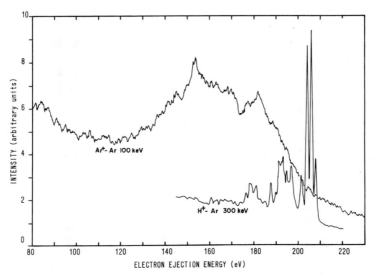

Fig. 5. Spectra of electrons from argon bombarded by protons and by Ar$^+$ ions. Proton data from Volz and Rudd [7], Ar$^+$ data by author.

increases, some features of the spectrum remain fixed (eg. the "peak" at about 180 eV) but the general outline of the spectrum shifts to lower energies as the projectile energy is increased.

Larkins [2] has suggested that this shift of the electron spectrum with ion beam energy can be explained by supposing that more energetic projectiles produce more vacancies in the valence shell in addition to the inner-shell vacancy. His calculations indicate that this will cause a shift of the energy of the corresponding Auger lines downward (and X-ray lines upward) as the impact energy goes up. Then under poor resolution large groups of lines constituting a broad peak would appear to shift with changing projectile energy. Thomson, et al. [11] have done an experiment which provides clear evidence that this effect does indeed take place. They have energy spectra of electrons detected in coincidence with scattered argon ions of various charge states which emitted them after Ar$^+$-Ar collisions. Their spectra show a definite downward shift of the peak as the charge state increases.

Burch, Richard and Blake [12] have measured K X-ray spectra from iron under bombardment by 5 MeV protons and by 30 MeV oxygen ions. The two spectra bear some resemblance to the argon spectra of fig. 5 in that proton impact produces a few sharp lines while impact by a heavier ion yields a broad, poorly resolved peak probably consisting of many satellite lines with

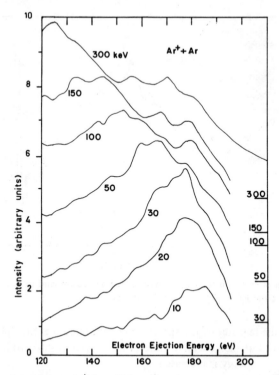

Fig. 6. Electron spectra from Ar$^+$-Ar collisions at various energies measured at 160° from the beam. Zero baseline for 10 and 20 keV data is the axis; other baselines as marked. Data by author.

little if any of the diagram lines remaining. They identify lines from the oxygen bombardment as being from iron ions which have one, two and possibly three vacancies in the $L_{2,3}$ shell in addition to the K vacancy. This lends support to the suggestion of Larkins.

This cannot be the whole story, however, since it is found that the shift of the spectra not only depends on impact energy, but also on the angle of observation of the electron as predicted by assuming a Doppler shift. We may safely conclude that both effects are present and neither can be ignored.

Part of the difference between the two spectra of fig. 5 is due to the factor of 11 in the velocities of the two projectiles. But a more important factor is that different mechanisms are important for the excitation in the two cases. These will be discussed in the next section.

A considerable amount of information about excitation of inner shells in heavy ion collisions has resulted from the measurements of inelastic energy loss made by the groups at Leningrad [13], Connecticut [14], Aarhus [15] and Albuquerque [16]. In this work measurements are made of the distance of closest approach r_o, the inelastic energy loss Q, and in some cases the charge states and energies of one or both of the scattered and recoil particles. For example, Fastrup, and co-workers [15] have made such studies for seven different projectiles with atomic numbers ranging from 13 to 25 with argon as a target. In all cases they find an energy loss spectrum exhibiting three distinct peaks over a narrow range of distances of closest approach. These energy losses, labelled Q_I, Q_{II}, and Q_{III}, are interpreted as follows. Q_I is due to M-shell excitation of both colliding systems. Q_{II} is the Q_I excitation plus the production of one $L_{2,3}$ vacancy in the lower Z partner. Q_{III} is the Q_I excitation plus two vacancies in the lower Z partner. The probability of creation of an $L_{2,3}$ vacancy decreases from near unity for small r_o rapidly to near zero above a critical r_o.

4. Mechanisms of inner-shell excitation

4.1. *Direct Coulomb ejection*

For simple charged projectiles such as electrons and protons the major contribution to the ejection of electrons from atoms is through the direct Coulomb interaction between the projectile and one electron of the target. This is probably also the primary mechanism for inner-shell electron ejection for this type of collision.

Calculations have been made using the binary encounter model which describe this mechaism quite well. Recent versions of this model by Gerjuoy [17] and by Vriens [18] are of quite wide applicability. Garcia [19] has made calculations on this model especially for K-vacancy production by proton impact taking account of the deflection of the projectile and uses a simple way of scaling the cross-sections for various targets. His results compare well with X-ray data on various targets as seen in fig. 7.

In recently published work [20], my colleagues and I have shown that reasonably good agreement between experimental and theoretical differential cross-sections can be obtained by calculating the binary encounter partial cross-sections separately for each shell and adding them.

Quantum methods are also used to calculate the inner-shell excitation and subsequent Auger or X-ray yields. The theory of X-ray production by heavy, charged particles has been discussed by Merzbacher and Lewis [21] and also in a semi-classical approximation by Hansteen and Mosebekk [22]. At Ne-

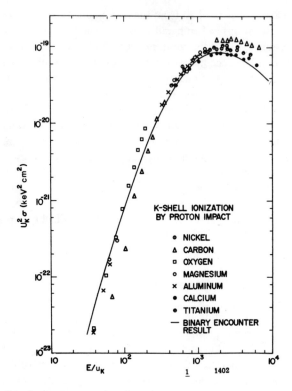

Fig. 7. K-shell ionization cross-sections by proton impact. Solid curve, binary encounter theory; indicated points, various scaled experimental result. From Garcia [19].

braska we have used the Born approximation with hydrogen ground state wave functions [23] to calculate the angular distribution of electrons ejected from various targets. Again, partial cross-sections for the various shells can be added to yield reasonable results [20]. Figure 8 shows that inner shells contribute substantially to the cross-section for certain parameters, notably at high ejection energies and large angles. The agreement is not good although it would be much worse without taking account of the inner shell.

4.2. Electron promotion

When heavy ions carrying many electrons impinge on target atoms, a new excitation mechanism comes into play that is not present when electrons or photons are used as projectiles, and is not usually important for protons. This

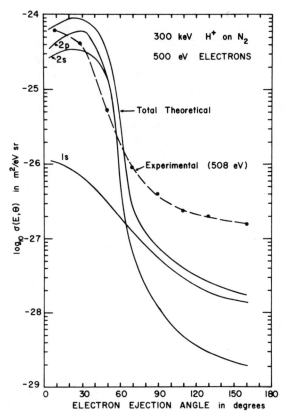

Fig. 8. Angular distribution of 500 eV electrons from nitrogen. Experimental values compared with Born approximation calculations for three subshells. From Rudd et al. [20].

results in the very different energy spectrum of electrons from H^+-Ar and Ar^+-Ar collisions which we already saw in fig. 5.

The mechanism referred to is that of electron promotion first proposed by Fano and Lichten [24] and developed by Lichten [25]. According to this model, close collisions of ions and atoms result in formation of temporary molecules with the atomic electrons going into various molecular orbitals. If the nuclei come close enough together for two molecular orbitals to cross, then upon separation of the nuclei the electron may find itself in a higher energy state of the atom. This can happen both for outer- and inner-shell electrons. In the latter case, the atom can end up with an inner-shell vacancy.

However, there are so many combinations of vacancies and inner- and outer-shell excitations that the spectrum becomes very complex.

This mechanism is most effective in exciting electrons when a shell of the projectile has about the same binding energy as a given shell of the target. For example, the K shell of oxygen has roughly the same binding energy as the L shell of argon so a collision between these atoms would have a high probability of promotion of an electron from one or both of those shells. The reason for this, of course, is that the potential curves of the molecular orbitals do not cross if the energies are too different and then the probability of a transition is very small. This is beautifully shown in the data of three different experimenters who measured the X-ray cross section or yield of a given target as a function of the atomic number of the bombarding projectile. Figure 9 shows the results of Saris [26] who used argon as a target. A periodic rise and fall of the cross-section is evident with maxima for those atoms which have shells of nearly the same binding energy as the $L_{2,3}$ shell of the target. Kavanagh and co-workers at Livermore [27] have demonstrated clearly the same behavior with copper as a target. Similar results on copper have also

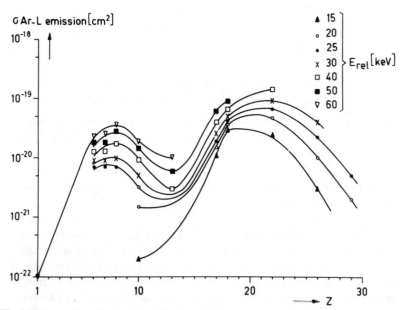

Fig. 9. Cross-sections for Ar L-shell X-ray emission vs. atomic number of the projectile. From Saris [26].

been obtained by Cairns, Holloway and Nelson [28] but in addition to the expected maxima they find unexplained maxima for the rare gas projectiles.

We turn next to the question of the dependance of the inner-shell vacancy production cross-section on the energy E of the projectile ion. There have been two attempts at applying the Fano-Lichten theory to this problem.

Fortner and co-workers [29] assume that the electron excitation occurs at the level-crossing distance and that the probability of excitation obeys the Landau-Zener theory. Their resulting expression is

$$\sigma(E) = 4\pi\alpha r_x^2 \left[Q_3(y/V) - Q_3(2y/V)\right],$$

where $Q_n(x) = \int_1^\infty \exp(-xt)\, t^{-n}dt$ and V is the relative velocity at infinite distance of separation. The parameter α is the probability of formation of the given configuration and y is a parameter which serves as a scale factor for the velocity. In deriving this expression they make two further assumptions, however. One is to neglect the potential energy at the distance of closest approach compared to the ion energy. The other is that only one level-crossing is considered.

Kessel [30, 31] has suggested a very simple model in which it is assumed that the trajectory is calculated from classical mechanics and that the probability of a transition is zero if the distance of closest approach r_0 is larger than some critical distance r_c, and is a constant P_c, independent of velocity, when $r_0 < r_c$. These simple considerations lead to the cross-section equation

$$\sigma(E) = P_c \pi r_c^2 \left[1 - V(r_c)/E\right].$$

If one uses a screened Coulomb potential for V it is easy to make calculations from this equation. The resulting expression has no adjustable constants except P_c and experimental data are available to give this for a number of collision partners.

The results for the L-excitation of argon by Ar^+ are shown in fig. 10 for this equation and for Fortner's model along with X-ray data of Saris and Onderdelinden [33] and Auger electron data of Cacak et al. [31].

The most striking distinction between the two theoretical treatments is that the Kessel equation predicts a threshold while the Fortner model does not. Actually the latter has thrown out the threshold by the assumption that $V(r) \ll E$, an assumption which could probably be omitted without too much additional complexity. It is obvious from the experimental data that there is indeed a threshold followed by a sharp rise and this is matched reasonably well by the Kessel equation. Cairns and co-workers [28] have also found that the characteristic X-rays generated in collisions of heavy ions with copper

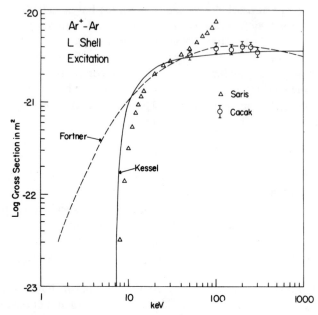

Fig. 10. Cross-sections for production of L-shell vacancies in argon vs. energy of Ar+ projectile. Solid line, Kessel model [30, 31]. Dashed line, Fortner model [29]. Cacak data from Auger electron spectra [31]. Saris data from X-ray spectra [33].

show a definite threshold. On the other hand, Der et al. [32] have K X-ray data which tends to agree with the Fortner model.

There is also a disagreement between the models and also between the experiments at high energies. The data of Saris increase while the Fortner model cross-sections decrease. The Kessel model yields a constant value and this tends to be verified both by the data of Cacak and of Cairns. Additional experimental work at higher energies would be useful.

4.3. Electron shake-off

When an electron is ejected, particularly an inner-shell electron, the rest of the electrons suddenly find themselves in a different potential; that is, they see a different effective nuclear charge. The initial state then is spread out over all the possible states of the new Z and the final state is a linear combination of all such states. Some of these states are continuum states in which case we have electron shake-off, while others are excited states and then we have excitation by shake-up. Shake-off is one of the important mechanisms for double ionization, especially for light elements, and therefore is one way satellite states are produced.

The sudden approximation predicts a shake-off probability which is independent of the specific cause of the change in effective charge provided the change is rapid enough. This leads to the conclusion that the satellite ratio should be the same regardless of the type of projectile causing the initial excitation if it is fast enough. As we have seen, there is considerable evidence that this is true for photon and electron excitation but does not appear to hold for proton excitation. However, this may simply indicate that other mechanisms of double ionization are important for that case or that the proton velocities were not great enough.

Theoretical and experimental studies of beta emission and of photoelectron emission have yielded a fairly complete understanding of the shake-off mechanism. Especially noteworthy is the work of the Oak Ridge group [34].

4.4. Other mechanisms of inner-shell excitation

Charge transfer is effective not only in removing outer-shell electrons from a target atom, but inner-shell electrons as well. Vinogradov and Shevel'ko [35] have shown, in fact, that in calculating both total and partial cross-sections for charge transfer to protons, the contribution of the inner shells in many cases is actually larger than that from the outer shells especially at high energies.

It should be noted that while in charge transfer the projectile is usually considered to carry along the captured electron in a bound state, it has recently been shown that the electron may also be transferred to a continuum state of the projectile. Theoretical work on this effect has been done by Salin [36] and by Macek [37]. Experimental verification has been made by Harrison and Lucas [38] and by Crooks and Rudd [39].

Other mechanisms of inner-shell vacancy production such as internal conversion and capture will not be discussed here.

5. Mechanisms of de-excitation

Since 1925, when Auger first interpreted the electron ejection process which bears his name, it has been understood that there are two basic ways by which an atom or ion with a vacancy in an inner shell can decay, namely X-ray emission and Auger electron emission. The branching ratio between these competing processes is measured by the fluorescence yield ω which is defined as the ratio of the number of decays by photon emission to the total number of decays from a given state. Thus ω_K, ω_L, ω_M, represent the fluorescence yield of the atom from K,L,M, etc. vacancy states.

A full understanding of the process of de-excitation would involve knowing what the transition rate is from each given initial vacancy state to each possible final state by each mechanism. Experimentally, we approach the problem by measuring line intensities in X-ray and Auger spectra and also lifetimes. This assumes that the resolution is great enough that individual transitions can be observed and that the energies are known well enough that identifications can be made. In X-ray work high resolution analysis is done with a crystal spectrometer or a grazing incidence grating. Auger electrons are energy analyzed by electrostatic or magnetic analyzers of various configurations. Unfortunately, much work is done at low resolution so that the measured quantities are simply averages weighted in some unknown way over many states.

In addition to the two basic processes of de-excitation more complex mechanisms are possible. Carlson and Krause have presented evidence [40] for a double Auger process from charge state measurements in rare gases. An example is the K-L^3 process which in neon occurs 7.5% of the time. Cooper and LaVilla [41] recently reported direct evidence of a "semi-Auger" process in which the $L_{2,3}$ hole in Ar, Cl, or K is filled by one $M_{2,3}$ electron while another electron is excited to conserve angular momentum.

Other combination processes are the radiative Auger transition in which an electron and photon are simultaneously emitted, and the cascade process. In a cascade an Auger transition, for example, from an L vacancy state may leave two M-shell vacancies. Each of these in turn could lead to two N-shell vacancies, and so forth. If the atom has enough shells, the final result could be a loss of all or most of the outer electrons. As pointed out by Krause [42], the effect of such a cascade would be devastating to a molecule since molecular bonding depends on the outer-shell electrons.

The fluorescence yield has been measured over the years by a number of different methods of varying accuracy and also has been calculated from the theoretical transition rates for production of radiation and Auger electrons. Early work in this area is summarized by Burhop [43]. A more recent review of the subject has been given by Fink,Jopson,Mark and Swift [44]. Recent theoretical contributions have been made by Callan [45],Rubenstein [46], McGuire [47],Kostroun and co-workers [48] and by Walters and Bhalla [49]. The last named recently presented nonrelativistic calculations of K Auger and K X-ray transition rates and fluorescence yields using the Hartree-Fock-Slater approach with various exchange approximations. Their results are given in fig. 11.

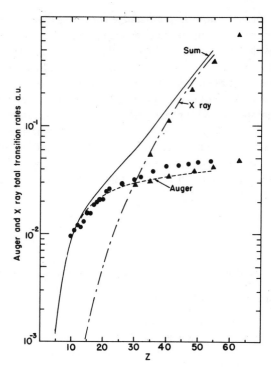

Fig. 11. Nonrelativistic total K-shell X-ray and Auger transition rates vs. atomic number. From Walters [49].

K fluorescence yields are often approximated by the simple formula $\omega_K = (1+A/Z^4)^{-1}$ with $A \approx 10^{-6}$. This expression was derived by Wentzel [50] by assuming the Auger yield was constant with respect to Z while X-ray transitions vary as Z^4. Figure 11 from Walters and Bhalla shows clearly that these are approximations only and that there is a considerably different behavior at low values of Z.

The fluorescence yield has been taken to be a definite quantity for each sub-shell of each atomic species. This implies that the de-excitation process is independent of the mode by which the excitation took place. Most of the lifetimes are long enough to make this a plausible assumption. However, care needs to be exercised. In fig. 10 the X-ray data of Saris and the Auger electron data of Cacak vary in quite different ways with ion energy where they overlap. If those data were used to calculate the fluorescence yield, it would have varied by a factor of 2 or more for different energies of excitation. What this evidently means, if both sets of data are correct, is that as the energy is varied different sets of complex states are being excited in different proportions. Since neither experiment had the resolution to distinguish separate states, the cross-sections are for the sum of all states yielding X-rays or Auger electrons in the range of energies accepted by the detectors.

It appears that the fluorescence yield not only has to be defined separately for each atomic species and for each shell, but also for each state associated with a given vacancy. As we saw earlier, an inner-shell electron can be either excited or removed and can be accompanied by the excitation and/or removal of electrons from other shells and there is no reason to expect that all states associated with a given inner-shell vacancy should have the same ratio of X-ray-to-Auger yield.

References

[1] M.E. Rudd, in: *Proceedings of the Second Oak Ridge Conference on the Use of Small Accelerators for Teaching and Research,* Ed. Jerome L. Duggan, (Oak Ridge Associated Universities, 1970 p. 305.
[2] F.P. Larkins, J. Phys. B*4* (1971) 1.
[3] G.N. Ogurtsov, I.P. Flaks and S.V. Avakyan, Zh. Tekh. Fiz. *40* (1970) 2124; [English Transl.: Soviet Phys.-Tech. Phys. *15* (1971) 1656].
[4] M.O. Krause, F.A. Stevie, L.J. Lewis, T.A. Carlson and W.E. Moddeman, Phys. Letters *31A* (1970) 81.
[5] G. Graeffe, J. Siivola, J. Utriainen, M. Linkoaho and T. Åberg, Phys. Letters *29A* (1969) 464.
[6] W. Mehlhorn and D. Stahlherm, Z. Phys. *217* (1968) 294.
[7] D.J. Volz and M.E. Rudd, Phys. Rev. A *2* (1970) 1395.
[8] A.K. Edwards and M.E. Rudd, Phys. Rev. *170* (1968) 140.
[9] H. Körber and W. Mehlhorn, Z. Phys. *191* (1966) 217.
[10] M.E. Rudd, T. Jorgensen, Jr. and D.J. Volz, Phys. Rev. *151* (1966) 28.
[11] G.M. Thomson, P.C. Laudieri and E. Everhart, Phys. Rev. A *I* (1970) 1439.
[12] D. Burch, Patrick Richard and R.L. Blake, Phys. Rev. Letters *22* (1971) 1355.
[13] V.V. Afrosimov, Yu.S. Gordeev, M.N. Panov and N.V. Fedorenko, Zh. Tekh. Fiz. *34* (1964) 1624; [English Transl.: Soviet Phys.-Techn. Phys. *9* (1965) 1256].
[14] Q.C. Kessel and E. Everhart, Phys. Rev. *146* (1966) 16.
[15] B. Fastrup, G. Hermann and K.J. Smith, Phys. Rev. A 3 (1971) 1591.
[16] F.W. Bingham, Phys. Rev. *182* (1969) 180.
[17] E. Gerjuoy, Phys. Rev. *148* (1966) 54.
[18] L. Vriens, Proc. Phys. Soc. (London) *90* (1967) 935.
[19] J.D. Garcia, Phys. Rev. A *1* (1970) 1402.
[20] M.E. Rudd, D. Gregoire and J.B. Crooks, Phys. Rev. A *3* (1971) 1635.
[21] E. Merzbacher and H.W. Lewis, in: Handbuch der Physik, Ed. S. Flügge, Vol. 34 (Springer-Verlag, Berlin, 1958) p. 166.
[22] J.M. Hansteen and O.P. Mosebekk, Z. Physik *234* (1970) 281.

[23] C.E. Kuyatt and T. Jorgensen, Jr., Phys. Rev. *130* (1963) 1444.

[24] U. Fano and W. Lichten, Phys. Rev. Letters *14* (1965) 627.

[25] William Lichten, Phys. Rev. *164* (1967) 131.

[26] F.W. Saris, Physica *52* (1971) 290.

[27] T.M. Kavanagh, M.E. Cunningham, R.C. Der, R.J. Fortner, J.M. Khan, E.J. Zaharis and J.D. Garcia, Phys. Rev. Letters *25* (1970) 1473.

[28] J.A. Cairns, D.F. Holloway and R.S. Nelson, in: *Atomic Collision Phenomena in Solids*, Ed. D.W. Palmer, M.W. Thompson and P.D. Townsend (North-Holland Co., 1970) p. 541.

[29] R.J. Fortner, B.P. Curry, R.C. Der, T.M. Kavanagh and J.M. Khan, Phys. Rev. *185* (1969) 164.

[30] Q.C. Kessel, Bull. Amer. Phys. Soc. *14* (1966) 946.

[31] R.K. Cacak, Q.C. Kessel and M.E. Rudd, Phys. Rev. A. *2* (1970) 1327.

[32] R.C. Der, R.J. Fortner, T.M. Kavanagh and J.M. Khan, Phys. Rev. Letters *24* (1970) 1272.

[33] F.W. Saris and D. Onderdelinden, Physica *49* (1970) 441.

[34] Eg. see T.A. Carlson, W.E. Moddeman and M.O. Krause, Phys. Rev. A *1* (1970) 1406, and references contained therein.

[35] A.V. Vinogradov and V.P. Shevel'ko, Zh. Eksp. Teor. Fiz. *59* (1970) 593; [English Transl.: Soviet Phys.-JETP *32* (1971) 323].

[36] A. Salin, J. Phys. B, Ser. 2, 2 (1969) 631.

[37] J. Macek, Phys. Rev. A *1* (1970) 235.

[38] K.G. Harrison and M.W. Lucas, Phys. Letters *33A* (1970) 142.

[39] G.B. Crooks and M.E. Rudd, Phys. Rev. Letters *25* (1970) 1599.

[40] Thomas A. Carlson and Manfred O. Krause, Phys. Rev. Letters *14* (1965) 390; and *17* (1966) 1079.

[41] J.W. Cooper and R.E. LaVilla, Phys. Rev. Letters *25*, (1970) 1745.

[42] M.O. Krause, *Rearrangement of Inner-Shell Ionized Atoms*, paper presented at the C.N.R.S. Colloquium *Les Processus Electroniques Simples et Multiples du Domaine X et X-UV*, Paris, 1970, to be published in J. Phys. (Paris).

[43] E.H.S. Burhop, *The Auger Effect and other Radiationless Transitions* (Cambridge University Press, London, 1952 Ch. 4.

[44] R.W. Fink, R.C. Jopson, H. Mark and C.D. Swift, Rev. Mod. Phys. *38* (1966) 513.

[45] E.J. Callan, Phys. Rev. *124* (1961) 793.

[46] R.A. Rubenstein, Ph.D. thesis, University of Illinois 1965, unpublished.

[47] E.J. McGuire, Phys. Rev. *185* (1969) 1; Phys. Rev. A *2* (1970) 273.

[48] V.O. Kostroun, M.H. Chen and B. Craseman, Phys. Rev. A *3* (1971) 533.

[49] D.L. Walters and C.P. Bhalla, Phys. Rev. A *3* (1971) 1919.

[50] G. Wentzel, Z. Phys. *43* (1927) 524.

Physics of Electronic and Atomic Collisions, VII ICPEAC, 1971 – North-Holland (1972)

INNER-SHELL EXCITATIONS IN ION-ATOM COLLISIONS

QUENTIN C. KESSEL*

Institute of Physics, University of Aarhus
DK-8000 Aarhus C, Denmark

Experimental and theoretical investigations undertaken during the past decade have clearly established that inner shells of atoms may become excited when heavy ions strike heavy atoms at keV energies. These excitations have been shown to correspond to the production of electron vacancies in the excited shells. For symmetric collisions, the excitations seem best described by a model proposed by Fano and Lichten which makes use of the theory of molecular orbitals. Recent investigations by Fastrup and co-workers indicate the possible extension of this model to asymmetric collisions and provide data that might be used to determine the correct interaction mechanism for K-shell excitations.

1. Introduction

This progress report will be limited to the consideration of those inner-shell excitations which are produced when heavy ions collide with heavy atoms. The excitations in question have been observed to occur when the inner electron shells surrounding two heavy nuclei are made to interpenetrate during an atomic collision. Although it was not initially obvious, it is now generally acknowledged that these excitations represent the removal of one or more electrons from the inner shells of these atoms. When these vacancies are filled, the excitation energy of the system is removed through the emission of photons and electrons. Usually some of these photons and electrons have energies characteristic of the atomic shells in which the initial vacancies were produced and are thus characteristic X-rays and Auger electrons.

The experiments for investigating these excitations fall into two categories: First, it is possible to measure the inelastic energy loss Q, of single collisions in which inner-shell vacancies are produced. The inelastic energy

* Permanent address: Department of Physics, The University of Connecticut, Storrs, Connecticut, 06268, U.S.A.

losses, or Q values, provide quantitative information about the excitation
energy required for the production of inner-shell vacancies. The second cate-
gory includes those experiments which measure the energies and intensities of
the characteristic X-rays and Auger electrons that are emitted when these
vacancies are filled. As other papers in this volume emphasize this latter group
experiments, I will devote most of my report to the inelastic energy loss experiments.

2. Early experiments

Let me start by turning the clock back about ten years [1]. By 1961, the
laboratories of Professor Fedorenko at the A.F. Ioffe Physical-Technical Institute and of Professor Everhart at the University of Connecticut had shown
that unexpectedly high ionization states resulted when heavy ions encountered heavy atoms in violent collisions. I say "unexpectedly" because prior to
these experiments, many investigators thought in terms of single electron
capture- and loss cross-sections. The removal of 5 and 6 electrons in a single
collision, as was demonstrated by these laboratories, was simply not expected.

Morgan and Everhart [2] took the next logical step when they measured
the inelastic energy losses of those collisions which resulted in these anoma-
lously high charge states. For certain Ar^+ - Ar collisions, the energy losses
showed that three different types of collisions were occurring, each having its
own characteristic inelastic energy loss. The collisions with the lowest energy
loss, less than 100 eV, were easily accounted for because this loss corre-
sponded to the approximate sum of the ionization energies of the electrons
removed by the collision. The other losses, however, were about 200 eV and
400 eV higher than this, and their origin was not obvious. Subsequently, the
groups in Leningrad and Connecticut developed coincidence apparatus to
explore these losses further [3–5]. Figure 1 summarizes the Ar^+- Ar energy
loss data from Connecticut together with more recent data obtained with
higher energy ions beams [6]. It is possible to associate a distance of closest
approach r_o, with each combination of incident ion energy E_o, and scattering
angle θ [7]. This figure shows the average $\bar{Q}$ values plotted versus r_o for a
wide range of incident ion energies. Each contour shows data for one ion
energy, and the larger distances of closest approach for a given contour correspond to the more gentle, small-angle collisions. There are several regions of
interest here: For large values of r_o, $\bar{Q}$ is less than 100 eV, and these excitations concern only the outer shells of the two atoms. The discrete increases,

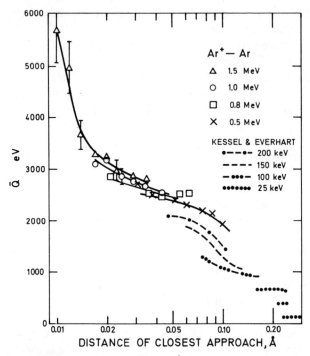

Fig. 1. The average inelastic energy loss $\bar{Q}$ for Ar^+- Ar collisions is plotted versus the distance of closest approach with the incident energy as a parameter. The data of Kessel and Everhart [5] are indicated (Kessel et al. [6]).

first observed by Morgan and Everhart, are evident at r_o equal to 0.24 Å. As the classical radius for the L-shell of argon is about 0.18 Å, these excitations occur only after the L-shells surrounding the two nuclei have begun to inter-penetrate. After a region of relative inactivity, further interpenetration results in another large increase in $\bar{Q}$, this time at r_o equal to about 0.10 Å. A third region of interest occurs between 0.01 Å and 0.02 Å. Here, where the K-shells begin to interpenetrate, $\bar{Q}$ rises dramatically once again.

The explanation for these steps in the inelastic energy-loss spectrum was not obvious. Coincidence experiments were able to show that the discrete steps at 0.24 Å were due to L-shell excitations [8], but the exact nature of these excitations was still unknown. It seemed unlikely that any L-shell electrons could be knocked out by the slow moving argon nuclei. It remained for Professors Fano and Lichten [9, 10] to suggest that inner-shell electrons might be removed through a molecular mechanism.

3. The molecular orbital model

In what has become known at the "Fano-Lichten Model," the general concepts of the Born-Oppenheimer approximation have been extended to keV collisions between heavy ions. In this model, the colliding atoms are treated as a diatomic molecule whose interatomic separation varies during the collision. The molecular quantum numbers, having little importance for the widely separated atoms, become dominating factors as the collision brings the nuclei close together. Figure 2 is a correlation diagram showing the behavior of the diabatic (H_2^+-like), one-electron molecular orbitals for a symmetric system. Of particular interest is the $4f\sigma$ orbital. When the two nuclei ap-

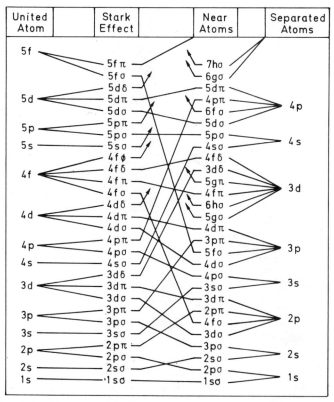

Fig. 2. Correlation diagram for the diabatic, one-electron molecular orbitals of a symmetric molecule (Lichten [10]).

proach, electrons in this orbital experience a large increase in their principle
quantum number. This demonstrates the "promotion mechanism" noted by
Hund in 1927 [11]. Fano and Lichten pointed out that if these promoted
electrons fail to return to their original atomic orbitals when the nuclei separate, then inner-shell vacancies will have been produced. Figure 3 shows the
corresponding diabatic, one-electron curves drawn by Fano and Lichten for
the Ar-Ar system [9, 10]. They suggested that the excitations occuring at
0.24 Å (0.48 a.u.) might be due to the promotion of one or two 4fσ electrons. Electrons with an energy appropriate to be ascribed to such a mechanism were observed shortly thereafter [12]. The other excitations in the inelastic energy loss spectrum are also fairly well explained within this framework.

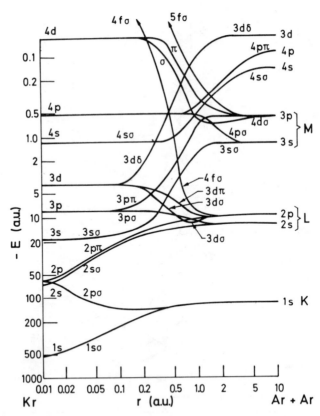

Fig. 3. Semi-quantitative energy levels for the diabatic, one-electron molecular orbitals of
the Ar-Ar system (Lichten [10]).

These experimental and theoretical investigations may be considered an important milestone in our understanding of inner-shell excitations. The demonstration that these excitations do correspond to the production of inner-shell vacancies, opened a new field of research. It allowed the techniques developed for single collision experiments to be applied to those problems which had previously been in the almost exclusive domain of the X-ray physicists. Furthermore, the differential techniques used for single collisions provide information not normally available from X-ray measurements. The latter are usually "total" in nature and cannot associate a specific impact parameter with a particular excitation.

Needless to say, the Fano-Lichten curves represent not a finished model but, rather, a starting point for future investigations. If the model does hold, it represents a surprising extension in our understanding of the quantum mechanics of molecules. If the Born-Oppenheimer separation is indeed valid for these interactions, there remain a number of important theroretical investigations to be done. For example, just why is the Born-Oppenheimer separation apparently successful here? The answer to this is not obvious. Also, if these qualitative one-electron orbitals explain the data this well, would more exact calculations be useful? It should be noted here that Thulstrup and Johansen of Aarhus have presented the results of such a calculation for the Ne^{+}- Ne system at this meeting. What about asymmetric collisions? Fastrup and co-workers have collected a large volume of very interesting data for asymmetric collisions [14, 15]. Although I believe that no theoretical papers on this subject were submitted to this conference, several investigators are considering this problem [16].

Let us now turn to the more recent experiments. Considerable progress has been made in determining the conditions under which vacancies are produced. This information can be used not only to determine the positions of important level crossings, but also to determine corresponding transition probabilities.

4. Recent progress

4.1. *L-shell excitations*

It has been shown that the first two L vacancies produced in Ar^{+}- Ar collisions are produced independently, and it is therefore possible to define and calculate a single electron promotion probability α, from the data for these excitations [17]. Figure 4 shows α plotted versus r_0 for Ar^{+}- Ar collisions. The behavior of this excitation function is just what the Fano-Lichten model

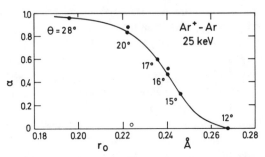

Fig. 4. The one-electron promotion probability α, plotted versus the distance of closest approach r_0, for Ar^+- Ar collisions (Everhart and Kessel [17]).

predicts. There is a sharp threshold centered at about 0.24 Å. Unless the collision brings the nuclei close enough together for a level crossing to occur, there is no excitation. For this excitation in Ar^+- Ar collisions, we see that α rapidly approaches unity. This is in keeping with the concept of the highly promoted $4f\sigma$ orbital crossing many other orbitals. Statistically, that situation would give a high transition probability because the likelihood of a $4f\sigma$ electron returning to its atomic orbital would be small.

The geometric nature of the cross section for producing this excitation is also evident from the figure. The cross section would have a sharp threshold because if the collision energy were not sufficient to bring the nuclei to within 0.24 Å of each other in a head-on collision, no excitation would occur. At high energies, where the impact parameter and r_0 become approximately equal, the cross section for electron emission would be approximately two (there are two electrons being promoted) times πr_0^2 or about 3×10^{-17} cm^2.

The possible extension of these concepts to asymmetric collisions is made evident by an excellent series of experiments performed by Fastrup and co-workers [14]. They choose several elements adjacent to argon in the periodic table and observed similar excitations when they used these ions as projectiles incident upon argon targets. Their values for α are shown in fig. 5. Not only do these curves establish the existence of these excitations for asymmetric collisions, but Fastrup and co-workers observed another curious phenomenon. They found that the vacancies were produced preferentially in the L shell of the lighter element. For the Al^+- Ar collisions, both vacancies were produced in the aluminum ion while for Mn^+- Ar collisions, both vacancies were produced in the argon atom. For Cl^+- Ar collisions, vacancies were produced in the L shells of each participant; but again, they were produced preferentially in the ligher partner.

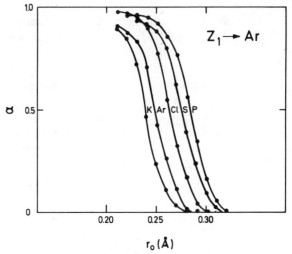

Fig. 5. The one-electron promotion probability α, plotted versus the distance of closest approach r_0, for several ions incident on Ar (Fastrup et al. [14]).

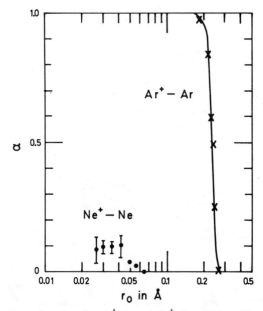

Fig. 6. A comparison of α values for Ar^+- Ar and Ne^+- Ne collisions (Kessel et al. [18]).

4.2. K-shell excitations

Excitation of K shells in heavy ion-atom collisions were first observed in the Connecticut laboratory in 1966 [18], and it was apparent that a fundamental difference exists between K-shell and L-shell excitations. Figure 6 compares the α versus r_o curves for Ar^+- Ar and Ne^+- Ne collisions. The Ne excitation is not so sharply defined with respect to r_o, and it has a maximum value that is considerably less than unity.

Lichten was able to explain these differences within the framework of molecular orbital theory, and fig. 7 shows his curves for the Ne - Ne system [10]. He argued that the only possible K-shell interaction would involve a rotational coupling of the 2pσ and 2pπ molecular orbitals. It should be noted

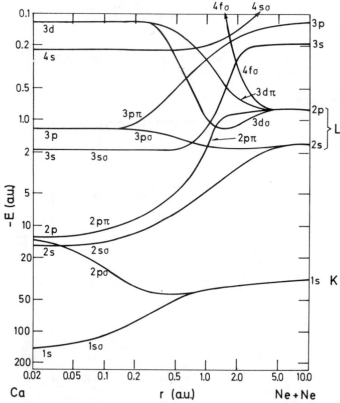

Fig. 7. Semi-quantitative energy levels for the diabatic, one-electron molecular orbitals of the Ne-Ne system (Lichten [10]).

that these orbitals do not actually cross each other. Since in the formation of the Ne^+- Ne molecule only a fraction of the molecules will have a $2p\pi$ vacancy, the probability of promoting a K-shell electron in such a collision would be much less than unity. He also made the asertion, subsequently verified [19], that a promotion would be twice as likely to occur if doubly ionized projectiles were used. In this case there would exist twice as many $2p\pi$ vacancies into which a K-shell electron might be promoted.

This remarkable success of Lichten's gives one hope that we might be able to gain more information about these interactions from K-shell excitations than is possible from L-shell excitations. The L-shell promotion appears to involve many crossings and it is difficult to extract specific level-crossing information from the data. However, for K-shell promotion, it appears that we have only to concern ourselves with transitions between a small number of orbitals. Furthermore, it should be possible to extract more information from the experimental promotion probabilities since they will not immediately saturate at unity as they did for the argon L-shell excitations.

With these facts in mind, Fastrup and co-workers [15] have been investigating K-shell excitations in Z_1- Ne collisions. I have enjoyed the very great privilege of being one of Fastrup's co-workers in this latter series of experiments. Figure 8 (from this work) shows the probability for producing a K-shell vacancy P_{II}, in Ne^+- Ne collisions plotted versus the product $E_0\theta$. To

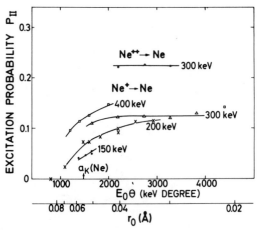

Fig. 8. The excitation probability, P_{II}, for producing an inner-shell vacancy in Ne^+- Ne collision, plotted versus $E_0\theta$, the product of the incident ion energy and the scattering angle of the collision (Fastrup et al. [15]).

a first approximation, this product is a single valued function of r_0. In this figure, larger values of $E_0\theta$ correspond to the more violent collisions having a smaller value of r_0. As in the previous work, and in keeping with the molecular orbital model, a threshold is observed; however, for the first time, a velocity dependence for the excitation is also evident. This is information of a more advanced nature than we have considered previously. If this excitation is due to a rotational coupling of the 2pσ and 2pπ orbitals, it may be possible to determine the behavior of the rotational interaction in a more quantitative way from this velocity dependence.

Fastrup and co-workers [15] have observed a similar behavior for some asymmetric Z_1 - Ne collisions. Figure 9 shows their results for N⁺- Ne collisions. Again, a fairly clear threshold depending on $E_0\theta$ (or r_0) together with a clear velocity dependence is observed.

Figure 10 demonstrates similar results for the N⁺- N$_2$ collisions. For there curves, P_{II} reaches values about 5 times larger than were observed for the Ne⁺- Ne and N⁺- Ne collisions. It is very tempting to attribute this to the existence of the unfilled L shell of the nitrogen target, although molecular target effects cannot be ruled out.

These last three figures shown a number of features: a threshold, a velocity dependence, and perhaps a velocity-dependent maximum for P_{II}. All of these features are compatible with a molecular orbital picture. More important, however, is that these data provide the most stringent test yet for this model.

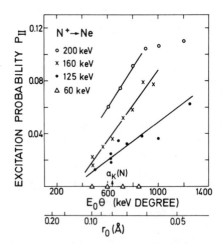

Fig. 9. The excitation probability P_{II}, plotted versus $E_0\theta$, for N⁺- Ne collisions (Fastrup et al. [15]).

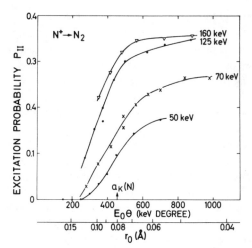

Fig. 10. The excitation probability P_{II}, plotted versus $E_0\theta$ for N^+- N_2 collisions (Fastrup et al. [15]).

It remains to be seen whether molecular orbital theory may be used to calculate the interaction regions and velocity dependent transition probabilities shown in these data.

5. A brief look at the past

It has been firmly established that inner-shell excitations, or vacancies, can be produced by heavy ion-atom collisions. Furthermore is has been shown that these vacancies are produced, not by direct Coulomb interactions, but when electron shells having similar properties are made to interpenetrate. These excitations seems best explained by a quantum molecular model making use of molecular orbitals.

As I have already noted several problems for which further investigations are clearly warranted, I would like to close this report not by looking forward, but by looking backward. Certainly, prior to 1960, people must have pondered many of the same questions. They did, and many of their conclusions were correct.

It was noted earlier in this paper that many atomic physicists were surprised when the laboratories of Fedorenko and Everhart showed that more than six electrons could be removed in a single collision. How many of you knew that in 1912, J.J. Thomson [20] observed mercury atoms in his discharge tube that had lost eight negative corpuscles? And, as Thomson said, "Eight is a very large number of corpuscles to lose." Although I would not care to vouch for his reasoning, he did conclude that these might have been removed by a single atom-atom collision. In 1927 Loeb spoke of the controversy surrounding the question of whether it was possible for positive ions to ionize atoms in binary collisions [21]. He concluded that there must exist a mechanism by means of which the electrons surrouding two atoms could interact and in this manner transfer a portion of the collision's kinetic energy into electronic excitation energy. It is just this sort of a molecular mechanism for inner-shell excitations that Professors Fano and Lichten have made to seem very reasonable. Although Loeb lamented that "To date the new quantum mechanics has been unable to cope with the problem," it was in 1927 that Hund pointed out the quantum mechanical promotion of electronic orbitals. It was also in 1927 that Born and Oppenheimer showed that, under certain conditions, the electronic and nuclear motions of molecules may be considered separately [22].

The first experimental observation of inner-shell excitations produced by heavy ion-atom collisions was made by Coates in 1934 [23]. Using one of Lawrence's newly constructed accelerators, he bombarded several targets with mercury ions having energies as high as 2.4 MeV. By observation of the resulting X-rays, he showed that inner-shell vacancies were produced by these collisions. From the minimum energies required to produce these vacancies, he also deduced that their production did depend on the impact parameter of the collision. From these considerations, he too, suggested that a quasi-molecular model would correctly describe the collision [24].

It seems that our recent recognition of the role played by inner-shell excitation in heavy ion-atom collisions was foreseen some years ago. While we have made great progress in the last decade, clearly our findings would not have surprised these early investigators.

References

[1] For a review of related investigations prior to 1960, see: N.V. Fedorenko, Usp. Fiz. Nauk *68* (1959) 481; [English Transl.: Soviet Phys.-Usp. *2* (1959) 526].

[2] G.H. Morgan and E. Everhart, Phys. Rev. *128* (1962) 667.

[3] V.V. Afrosimov, Yu.S. Gordeev, M.N. Panov and N.V. Fedorenko, Zh. Tekh. Fiz. *34* (1964) 1613, 1624, 1637; [English Transl.: Soviet Phys.-Tech. Phys. *9* (1965) 1248, 1256, 1265].

[4] Q.C. Kessel and E. Everhart, Phys. Rev. *146* (1966) 16.

[5] For a review of the inelastic energy loss data available prior to 1969, see: Q.C. Kessel, in: *Case Studies in Atomic Collision Physics I*, Eds. E.W. McDaniel and M.R.C. McDowell (North-Holland Publ. Co., Amsterdam, 1969) p. 399.

[6] Q.C. Kessel, P.H. Rose and L. Grodzins, Phys. Rev. Letters *22* (1969) 1031.
[7] E. Everhart, G. Stone and R.J. Carbone, Phys. Rev. *99* (1955) 1287.
[8] Q.C. Kessel, A. Russek and E. Everhart, Phys. Rev. Letters *14* (1965) 484.
[9] U. Fano and W. Lichten, Phys. Rev. Letters *14* (1965) 627.
[10] W. Lichten, Phys. Rev. *164* (1967) 131.
[11] F. Hund, Z. Phys. *40* (1926) 742.
[12] C. Snoek, R. Geballe, W.F. van der Weg, P.K. Rol and D.J. Bierman, Physica *31* (1965) 1553.
[13] E.W. Thulstrup and H. Johansen, *VII ICPEAC, Abstracts of Papers,* Eds. L.M. Branscomb et al., Vol. 1 (North-Holland Publ. Co., Amsterdam, 1971) p. 118.
[14] B. Fastrup, G. Hermann, and K.J. Smith, Phys. Rev. A *3* (1971) 1591.
[15] B. Fastrup, G. Hermann and Q. Kessel, *VII ICPEAC, Abstracts of Papers,* Eds. L.M. Branscomb et al., Vol. 1 (North-Holland Publ. Co., Amsterdam, 1971) p. 390; also: Phys. Rev. Letters *27* (1971) 771.
[16] M. Barat and William Lichten, private communication.
[17] E. Everhart and Q.C. Kessel, Phys. Rev. *146* (1966) 27.
[18] Q.C. Kessel, M.P. McCaughey and E. Everhart, Phys. Rev. Letters *16* (1966) 1189; *17* (1966) 1170.
[19] M.P. McCaughey, E.J. Knystautas, H.C. Hayden and E. Everhart, Phys. Rev. Letters *21* (1968) 65.
[20] J.J. Thomson, Phil. Mag. *24* (1912) 668.
[21] L.B. Loeb, Science *66* (1927) 627.
[22] M. Born and R. Oppenheimer, Ann. Phys. (Leipzig) *84* (1927) 457.
[23] W.M. Coates, Phys. Rev. *46* (1934) 542.
[24] After the presentation of this report, Dr. R. Morgenstern kindly brought the following papers to my attention: O. Beeck, Ann. Phys. (Leipzig) *6* (1930) 1001; O. Beeck and J.C. Mouzon, Ibid. *11* (1931) 737 and 858; and W. Weizel and O. Beeck, Z. Phys. *76* (1932) 250. These investigations concern outer-shell excitations in collisions of alkali ions with rare gas atoms and use a molecular orbital model (He-He orbitals) to interpret the results.

EXCITATION OF INNER-SHELL ELECTRONS
BY PHOTONS AND FAST ELECTRONS

M.J. VAN DER WIEL

FOM-Institute for Atomic and Molecular Physics,
Kruislaan 407, Amsterdam/Wgm., Netherlands

This report discusses a few aspects of the excitation of inner-shell electrons: firstly, the determination of total electron-impact cross-sections from the intensity of an Auger electron spectrum; secondly, some recent work on excitation of inner electrons to discrete states; thirdly, the results of various methods for the detection of simultaneous processes in inner- and outer shell, following electron or photon impact.

1. Introduction

When considering excitation of inner-shell electrons it is of interest to discuss the excitation produced by photons or fast electrons, since for these projectiles the mechanism is thoroughly understood [1] and does not present the kind of problems one encounters in the description of heavy-particle collisions. As such, the information obtained from photon or electron experiments is of a quite fundamental nature. For instance, one might think of the determination of energy levels of the target and the possible modes of decay of well-defined inner-shell hole states. This information can then be used as a background for further studies on heavy-particle collisions.

The reason for discussing photon and fast-electron impact together is that these processes are quite closely related. From table 1 it appears that the cross section for photoionization has an essential factor in common with both the differential and the total cross-section for electron impact. This factor df/dE, the continuous oscillator strength, is defined by:

$$df/dE = 2E |\langle \psi(E) | \sum_j r_j | \psi_0 \rangle|^2 \quad \text{(in a.u.)},$$

where E is the energy transfer, $\psi(E)$ the energy-normalized continuum wavefunction (of dimension energy$^{-\frac{1}{2}}$), ψ_0 the ground-state wavefunction and r_j

Table 1
Relations for ionization by photon and electron impact

Photoionization	Small angle electron scattering	Ionization by fast electrons
$\sigma_{\text{photoion.}} = \dfrac{mc}{\pi e^2 h} \dfrac{df}{dE}$	$\dfrac{d\sigma}{d\Omega}(\theta, E) = \dfrac{2}{E} \dfrac{k_n}{k_0} \dfrac{1}{K^2} \dfrac{df}{dE}(K)$	$\sigma_{\text{ion}}(E_{\text{el}}) =$
	in dipole approx.	$[\displaystyle\int_{IP}^{\infty} \dfrac{1}{E} \dfrac{df}{dE} dE] \, E_{\text{el}}^{-1} \ln cE_{\text{el}}$
	$\dfrac{df}{dE}(K) = \dfrac{df}{dE} + aK^2 + \ldots$	

the dipole operator for atomic electron j. As for electron impact, the differential cross-section for scattering through an angle θ at an energy loss E is given in first Born approximation [2] by the formula in the second column of table 1. It contains a few kinematic factors (k_0, k_n and K, the magnitudes of the momenta before and after the collision, and the momentum transfer) and the generalized oscillator strength $df(K)/dE$. For small momentum transfers, i.e. for scattering near zero degree at energy losses much smaller than the primary energy, we can apply the dipole approximation and neglect the higher terms in the expansion of $df(K)/dE$ in powers of K^2. Then only the dipole term df/dE remains.

Finally, the third column of table 1 lists the Bethe formula for the total cross-section for (inner-shell) ionization as a function of the electron impact energy. The proportionality constant of the well-known $E_{\text{el}}^{-1} \ln E_{\text{el}}$ term is given by an integral over the whole df/dE-distribution weighted with a factor $1/E$.

On the basis of these three relations, this report discusses some of the progress that has been made in the field under consideration. Three topics were selected, which concern mainly the primary excitation event, since the decay processes are dealt with in some of the other invited contributions on inner-shell processes:

Sec. 2 — Total cross-sections for ionization of inner shells by fast electrons.

Sec. 3 — Excitation of inner-shell electrons to discrete states.

Sec. 4 — Simultaneous processes in inner- and outer shell.

2. Total cross sections

The usual method for the experimental determination of cross sections for inner-shell ionization is based upon a measurement of the yield of X-rays produced by electron bombardment. In order to obtain a total cross-section for the production of inner-shell holes, one has to know the fluorescence yield. For low-Z elements, with inner-shell binding energies generally below 1 keV, this yield is very small (when compared with the yield of Auger electrons) and is not known with good accuracy. For this reason a new method was introduced by Glupe and Mehlhorn [3,4], which involves the absolute determination of the total intensity of the Auger electron spectrum. The calibration of the analyser transmission — the crucial point in this experiment — was performed with the help of accurate cross-sections for elastic scattering. The method described here assumes an isotropic distribution of ejected electrons. This is correct for intermediate hole configurations with a value of $j=\frac{1}{2}$, for instance a hole in a 1s-shell. However, for values of $j > \frac{1}{2}$, an unequal population of the various magnetic sublevels is to be expected, which may lead to a (small) anisotropy in the distribution of ejected electrons or to a polarization of the emitted photons. The existence of this effect has been demonstrated for Auger electron emission by Mehlhorn and co-workers [5] and its magnitude was found to agree well with a calculation by McFarlane [6].

For K-shell ionization, where no problem arises due to anisotropy, total cross-sections have been measured in Ne, N and O [3,4], with an accuracy claimed to be about 5%. The data for Ne have been plotted in fig. 1 as σE_{el}, versus $\ell n E_{el}$, such that a graphical test of the Bethe relation (table 1) is possible. Concerning this figure a few remarks can be made:

a) In principle the method provides the sum of single inner-shell ionization and simultaneous inner- and outer-shell ionization. In the case of Ne the two contributions can be separated, however, by making use of the data of Krause et al. [7] and Carlson et al. [8] on the ratio of single to double processes as a function of impact energy (for more details see section 4).

b) The straight-line behaviour, predicted by the Bethe approximation for sufficiently high impact energy, appears to set in already at energies only a few times in excess of the threshold energy. This differs markedly from what is known for outer-shell ionization, where the Bethe relation holds only at impact energies above about twenty times the ionization energy (see for instance Schram et al. [9]).

c) The numbers M_K^2 and M_{KL}^2 in fig. 1, i.e. the slopes of the two lines, could be compared with a properly weighted integral of the df/dE-distribu-

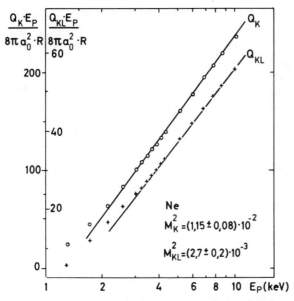

Fig. 1. Absolute cross-sections for K- and KL-ionization in Ne as a function of electron-impact energy (ref. [3] and [4]). The slopes of the lines, i.e. the values of the integral over the df/dE distribution (see table 1, third column), are given by M_K^2 and M_{KL}^2.

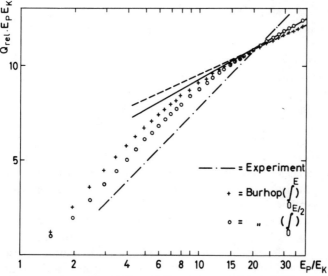

Fig. 2. Relative experimental (ref. [3] and [4] and theoretical (ref. [12]) cross-sections for K-ionization in Ne as a function of reduced electron-impact energy.

tion over the whole K-continuum, as obtained in photoabsorption. This procedure, which provides an independent check of the reliability of the results, has been applied already in a similar case, that of Ar L-shell ionization [10].

d) The double Auger process (see section 2.3), in which the excess energy available in the inner-shell hole is shared by two outgoing electrons, gives rise to a small continuum at energies below that of the lowest Auger line. This contribution was not measured, but was taken into account by a correction according to the data of Carlson and Krause [11].

Finally, Glupe and Mehlhorn [3,4] compared their results with theoretical values from non-relativistic quantum-mechanical [12,13], as well as classical [14] calculations. In all cases studied (see for instance fig. 2), the behaviour of the calculated cross-sections with energy differs from that of the experimental results, notably in the high-energy range.

3. Discrete excitation

As to the excitation of inner electrons to discrete states, one must expect that, just as for an outer shell, there is a series of discrete levels beyond the filled outer shell, which converge to the inner-shell ionization threshold. Figure 3 shows a beautiful example of the fully resolved photoabsorption spectrum of the discrete Ar L-lines, as recorded by Nakamura et al. [15] with dispersed electron-synchrotron radiation. A complete assignment of the lines has been made. It is interesting to note the broadened shape of the lines between the L_{III} and L_{II} thresholds, giving evidence for an autoionization from the discrete L_{II} states to the L_{III} continuum before the Auger decay occurs.

The same energy region has been studied in electron energy loss by van der Wiel and Wiebes [10]. Figure 4 shows the energy-loss spectra of 10 keV electrons, measured in coincidence with the ions Ar^{2+} and Ar^{3+}. Some details concerning the experimental method will be given in section 4. Here it may suffice to remark that the discrete states do not only decay to Ar^{1+}, as one would expect in the case of the normal Auger decay, but at least for a certain fraction to higher charge states. This means the decay is accompanied by additional ionization in the outer shell. A similar process for ionized states of the inner shell was observed earlier by Carlson [16].

In the same electron-ion coincidence experiment the inner-shells of N_2 and CO were studied [17]. Among other things, this study proved that the unusual shape of the broad absorption band in the N_2 K-absorption spectrum measured by Nakamura et al. [18], was due to total absorption of the radiation at 400.8 eV. This conclusion has been confirmed recently by an estimate

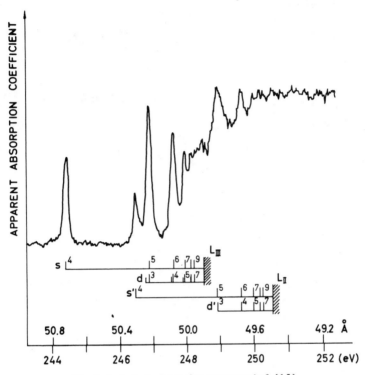

Fig. 3. Ar-L photoabsorption spectrum (ref. [15].

of the oscillator strength for this band by Krause and Wuilleumier [19]. The absorption at the lowest discrete level (or levels, see ref. [20] appears to be quite strong compared with that of the adjoining continuum. Complete spectra of the energy-loss regions of ref. [17], measured in coincidence with the various ionic products, have been presented at this conference [20]. It should also be mentioned, that the discrete excitation of inner electrons can be studied through Auger electron spectrometry [21,22], since the decay of these states produces lines in the Auger spectrum at the high-energy side of the group of normal lines.

Another example of a rather prominent discrete line is found at the K-edge of Ne in a spectral region, which is nearly impossible to study in electron energy loss due to the rapid decrease of the intensity of electron scattering. The spectrum (fig. 5) was taken with dispersed bremsstrahlung by Wuilleumier and Bonnelle [23]. There is a faint indication of absorption to one or a number of doubly excited KL-state(s), which brings us to the last topic of this report.

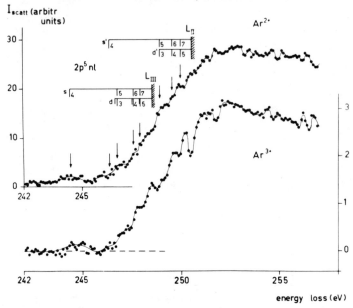

Fig. 4. Ar-L electron energy-loss spectrum, measured in coincidence with Ar^{2+} and Ar^{3+} ions (ref. [10].

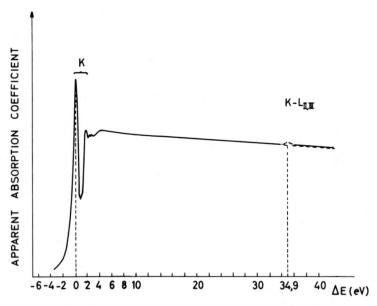

Fig. 5. Ne-K photoabsorption spectrum (ref. [23].

4. Simultaneous processes in inner- and outer shell

As we saw already, each inner-shell process, whether it be the sudden creation or annihilation of an inner-shell hole state, has a certain probability of being accompanied by an additional excitation in the outer shell(s). The mechanism responsible for this is fairly easy to understand in the case of well-separated shells. Then each sudden change in the occupation of an inner shell is experienced by the outer electrons as a sudden change in the effective screening of the nuclear charge. In the subsequent readjustment of the outer electrons to the new situation, there is a probability for one or more electrons to be excited to a discrete or continuum state. The probability is independent of the initial event, provided it is sufficiently rapid. In the case of excitation to a continuum state the process is usually referred to as "electron shake-off". The simple mechanism described here is easily accessible for a theoretical treatment. In this respect a paper by Carlson et al. [24] should be mentioned, which presents an extensive list of shake-off probabilities calculated for a wide range of Z-values. Most of the recent experimental results to be discussed in this section appear to be in quite satisfactory agreement with these calculations. Various methods exist by which electron shake-off can be detected experimentally, and a number of them have been listed in table 2; of each of the methods a representative result will be shown.

a) When using photons as projectile, one can measure the photoabsorption (see fig. 6, Wuilleumier [25]) and observe the well-known inner-shell absorp-

Table 2
Inner-shell ionization

Projectile	Method	Observable		Fig.	Ref.
		Single hole	+ shake-off		
photon	absorption spectrometry	edge + continuum	extra shake-off continuum	6	[25]
	photoelectron spectrometry	line	continuum (high energy part)	7	[26]
electron	Auger electron spectrometry	normal lines	satellite lines	8	[8]
	electron energy loss coincident with ions	edge + continuum	separate shake-off continuum	9	[10]

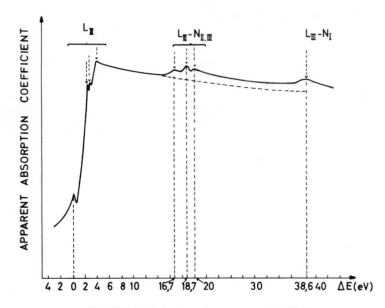

Fig. 6. Kr-L photoabsorption spectrum (ref. [25].

tion edge, followed at higher photon energies by some discrete structure –
due to simultaneous excitation of an inner- and outer electron – and an overall jump representing the onset of the shake-off continuum.

b) As an alternative, photons of a fixed energy can be used if the energy
spectrum of the ejected electrons is recorded. With this method a sharp line is
observed for single electron ejection, whereas in the case of shake-off the
excess energy is shared by two outgoing electrons, such that a continuous
distribution arises [16]. In photoelectron spectrometry only the high-energy
part of this continuum is observed.

The spectrum of Ne K-ionization induced by $Mg-K_\alpha$ photons (fig. 7, Carlson
et al. [26]) shows, besides the main peak due to single ionizations, a series of
discrete lines and a continuum, corresponding to the simultaneous KL-
processes indicated in the figure.

c) With electrons as projectile, inner-shell events can be studied trough the
Auger electrons. The spectrum contains the normal Auger lines as well as the
satellite lines due to multiple hole states. In order to illustrate the use of this
method in the study of electron shake-off, fig. 8 shows the ratio of the intensity of a satellite line to that of a normal line as a function of impact energy
[8]. The result gives evidence for the additional outer-shell process to become

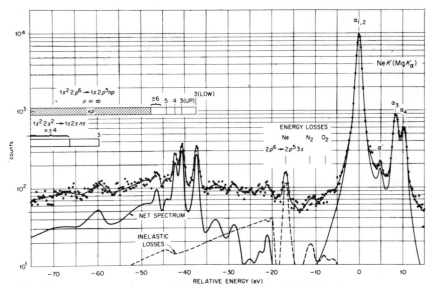

Fig. 7. Photoelectron spectrum of Ne-K ionization, induced by MgK$_\alpha$-photons (ref. [26]).

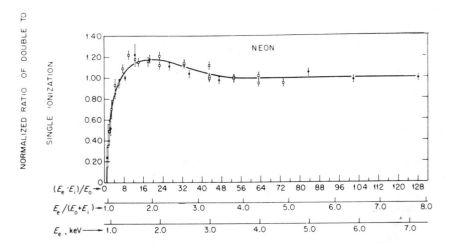

Fig. 8. Normalized ratio of intensities of satellite and normal Auger lines in Ne as a function of electron-impact energy (ref. [8]). E_e is electron-impact energy; E_i is binding energy of the inner-shell electron and E_0 is binding energy of the shake-off electron.

independent of the initial ionization event at sufficiently high impact energy. The ratio between the total intensities of satellite − and normal lines at high impact energy was determined in a separate study [7].

d) Application of the relation for small-angle electron scattering of table 1, enables us to obtain df/dE spectra from a measurement of the differential scattering of fast electrons. This method is particularly useful in that it provides a range of energy transfers that bridges the gap between far-U.V. sources (see Cairns et al. [27] and the characteristic X-ray lines. Furthermore, the intensity is sufficient to work at such low target gas pressures that ions can be extracted and detected in delayed coincidence with the scattered electrons [28, 10]. In this way df/dE spectra for the various charge states are obtained, which provide information on the simultaneous processes complementary to that of the other methods.

One of the results of this experiment is the set of oscillator-strength distributions shown in fig. 9 for L-shell excitation of Ar [10], leading to the final charge states one to four. The peak in fig. 9a at about 245 eV represents the decay of the group of discrete excited states of the 2p electrons to Ar^{1+}. If a 2p electron is ionized in the initial event, the most probable decay product is Ar^{2+} (fig. 9b). Production of Ar^{3+} (fig. 9c) occurs mainly via the shake-off mechanism. At energy transfers between 250 and 280 eV, only a single 2p hole can be formed, but in the subsequent decay the fast Auger electron shares its energy with a second outer electron. The jump in the Ar^{3+} curve between 280 and 300 eV represents the onset of shake-off in the initial ionization event. A double-hole intermediate state is produced, which decays via the normal Auger process to a triply charged final state. More details of the multiply ionizing events observed in this study are described in ref. [10]. Among other things, a simple model allowing for equal shake-off probabilities per outer electron was found to hold remarkably well for shake-off due to the creation of a 2p hole and due to the annihilation of a hole in the Auger decay.

Similar work on Kr and Xe is presently in progress.

In order to evaluate the potentialities of each of the methods discussed here, it is good to consider their limitations. The photoabsorption method is limited in its use not only by the lack of suitable photon sources, but also by the sometimes very small relative height of the edge of the shake-off continuum (see e.g. fig. 5).

As to photoelectron spectrometry, it is often not possible to make a detailed study of the shake-off phenomenon as a function of the primary photon energy. In Auger spectrometry, the problem one meets is that in some cases satellite lines coincide with normal lines.

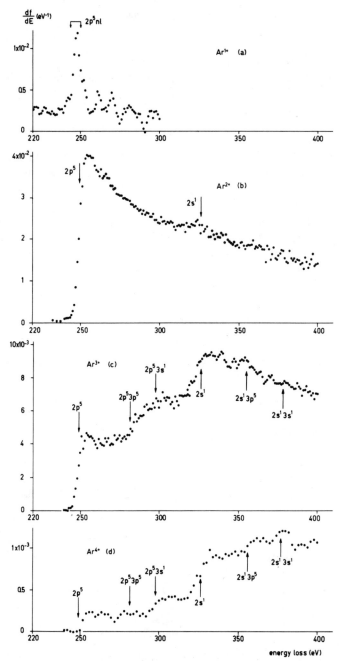

Fig. 9. Oscillator-strength spectra for Ar-L excitation leading to the charge states one to four (from an electron-ion coincidence experiment, ref. [10]).

Finally, the electron-ion coincidence method becomes impracticable at too high energy losses, typically about 500 eV, due to the very rapid decrease of the intensity of scattering, generally at least with the third power of the energy loss.

5. Conclusion

It is worthwile, in the present stage of the work reported here, to consider what future studies on each of the subjects of section 2 would be of fundamental interest.

Firstly, concerning the total ionization cross sections, we may conclude that in view of the accuracy of the experimental values reported, further theoretical work is needed to clear up the discrepancy between existing calculations and experiment, which is especially evident in the high energy behaviour.

Secondly, our knowledge of excitation of inner-shell electrons to discrete levels is still very scanty, and systematic work on aspects as line intensities, linewidths and distributions over possible final states has yet to begin.

Thirdly, for most of the simultaneous processes in inner- and outer shell studied up to now, the sudden approximation appears to give a good description. In contrast to this, it is known [29, 30] that for simultaneous ejection of two electrons from one shell, this approximation fails completely. It would be of interest, therefore, to find cases where two shells are so close that the sudden approximation begins to break down. For this problem, as well as for that mentioned in the second point, it is essential to have a source of energy transfers that is continuously variable over a wide energy range. From this point of view most of the progress should be expected to come from experiments using electron-synchroton radiation or fast electrons in combination with energy loss analysis.

Acknowledgements

This work was performed as a part of the research program of the Stichting voor Fundamenteel Onderzoek der Materie (Foundation for Fundamental Research on Matter) and was made possible by financial support from the Nederlandse Organisatie voor Zuiver-Wetenschappelijk Onderzoek (Netherlands Organization for the Advancement of Pure Research).

References

[1] U. Fano and J.W. Cooper, Rev. Mod. Phys. *40* (1968) 441.
[2] H. Bethe, Ann. Phys. (Leipzig) *5* (1930) 325.
[3] G.Glupe and W.Mehlhorn, Phys.Letters *25A* (1967) 274.
[4] G. Glupe and W. Mehlhorn, J. Phys. (Paris), to be published.
[5] W. Mehlhorn, *VII ICPEAC, Invited Talks and Progress Reports,* Eds. T.R. Govers and F.J. De Heer, (North-Holland Publ. Co., Amsterdam, 1972) p. 169.
[6] S.C. McFarlane, *VII ICPEAC, Abstracts of Papers,* Eds. L.M. Branscomb et al, Vol. 1 (North-Holland Publ. Co., Amsterdam, 1971) p. 406.
[7] M.O. Krause, F.A. Stevie, L.J. Lewis, T.A. Carlson and W.E. Moddeman, Phys. Letters *31A* (1970) 81.
[8] T.A. Carlson, W.E. Moddeman and M.O. Krause, Phys. Rev. A *1* (1970) 1406.
[9] B.L. Schram, F.J. de Heer, M.J. van der Wiel and J. Kistemaker, Physica *31* (1965) 94.
[10] M.J. van der Wiel and G. Wiebes, Physica *53* (1971) 225.
[11] T.A. Carlson and M.O. Krause, Phys. Rev. Letters *14* (1965) 390.
[12] E.H.S. Burhop, Proc. Cambr. Phil. Soc. *36* (1940) 43.
[13] M.R.H. Rudge and S.B. Schwartz, Proc. Phys. Soc. *88* (1966) 563.
[14] M. Gryzinski, Phys. Rev. *138* (1965) A336.
[15] N. Nakamura, M. Sasanuma, S. Sato, M. Watanabe, H. Yamashita, Y. Iguchi, A. Ejiri, S. Nakai, S. Yamaguchi, T. Sagawa, J. Nakai and T. Oshio, Phys. Rev. Letters *21* (1968) 1303.
[16] T.A. Carlson and M.O. Krause, Phys. Rev. Letters *17* (1966) 1079.
[17] M.J. van der Wiel, Th.M. El-Sherbini and C.E. Brion, Chem. Phys. Letters *7* (1970) 161.
[18] M. Nakamura et al. (same authors as [15]), Phys. Rev. *178* (1969) 80.
[19] M.O. Krause and F. Wuilleumier, to be published.
[20] Th.M. El-Sherbini and M.J. van der Wiel, *VII ICPEAC, Abstracts of Papers,* Eds. L.M. Branscomb et al., Vol. 2, (North-Holland Publ. Co., Amsterdam, 1971) p. 1050.
[21] K. Siegbahn, C. Nordling, G. Johansson, J. Hedman, P.F. Hedén, K. Hamrin, U. Gelius, T. Bergmark, L.O. Werme, R. Manne and Y. Baer, *ESCA Applied to Free Molecules* (North-Holland Publ. Co., Amsterdam, 1969).
[22] T.A. Carlson, W.E. Moddeman, B.P. Pullen and M.O. Krause, Chem. Phys. Letters *5* (1970) 390.
[23] F. Wuillemier and C. Bonnelle, C.R. Acad. Sci., Ser. B. *270* (1970) 1029.
[24] T.A. Carlson, C.W. Nestor Jr. and T.C. Tucker, Phys. Rev. *169* (1968) 27.
[25] F. Wuilleumier, Thesis, Paris (1969), unpublished.
[26] T.A. Carlson, M.O. Krause and W.E. Moddeman, J. Phys. (Paris) (to be published).
[27] R.B. Cairns, H. Harrison and R.I. Schoen, Phys. Rev. *183* (1969) 52.
[28] M.J. van der Wiel, Physica *49* (1970) 411.
[29] F.W. Byron and C.J. Joachain, Phys. Rev. *164* (1967) 1.
[30] M.J. van der Wiel and G. Wiebes, Physica *54* (1971) 411.

Physics of Electronic and Atomic Collisions, VII ICPEAC, 1971 − North-Holland (1972)

REVIEW OF FLUORESCENCE YIELDS AND AUGER ELECTRON EMISSION

HANS MARK

Ames Research Center, NASA, Moffett Field, Calif., 94035

A brief review of atomic fluorescence yields in the K, L, and M atomic shells is presented. Selected experimental methods using both characteristic X-ray spectroscopy and Auger electron spectroscopy are described. A discussion of the most recent theoretical work is also included. The state of knowledge of K-shell fluorescence yields both experimentally and in theoretical understanding is excellent. In the case of the L-shell, much progress has been made recently in measuring fluorescence yields of individual L-subshells. Some advances have also been made in measuring Coster-Kronig transition probabilities in the L-shell. The state of our knowledge of M-shell fluorescence yields is still rudimentary.

1. Introduction

Atomic physics, particularly the measurement and understanding of atomic transition rates and atomic branching ratios, has received considerable attention during the last decade. These are three reasons for this development: (1) the enormous drive to understand the structure of the atomic nucleus, which dominated physics between 1930 and 1960, led to the development of instrumentation that could be fruitfully applied to the study of atomic physics; (2) a great many practical reasons to study atomic physics and better understand atomic phenomena became apparent in the decade following 1960; and (3) advanced theoretical techniques and computation machines have made it interesting from a fundamental viewpoint to look once again in greater detail at the problem of atomic structure. In this paper, several developments that seem to be particularly interesting because they illustrate trends in the field will be reviewed from the perspective of a user of the fundamental results for practical purposes. There will be no attempt to be comprehensive.

Atomic transitions between inner shells of atoms play an important role in many practical phenomena so it may be useful to begin by listing some of the most important applications. The use of fluorescence yields in photon transport processes is well understood [1]. The Boltzmann equation describing photon transport contains a term describing the contribution of fluorescence radiation created inside the absorbing medium by atoms whose inner shells have been ionized by the incident beam. This term must be estimated accurately if dose buildup factors due to secondary radiation processes are to be determined with the necessary precision. The stress on the word accuracy is intentional because fluorescence radiation is particularly important in the calculation of dose rates at a point in the medium after the incident radiation has traversed many mean free paths. In such a case the dose rate may be due almost entirely to fluorescence radiation. In a closely related area in radiation physics, the standardization of radioisotope intensities strongly on the evaluation of effects than can be caused by radiationless transitions. The calibration of many modern radiation detection devices is also affected by the existence of fluorescence effects and radiationless transitions. A great many analytical methods based on X-ray fluorescence radiation have found wide practical application in such fields as medical research [2], trace element analyses [3], nondestructive testing and the analysis of geological samples in situ [4]. In trace element detection, extremely sensitive methods depending on X-ray fluorescence have been developed. One report [3] indicates the detection of one part in 10^{12} of heavy-atom trace-element contamination in the atmosphere collected on a carbon foil exposed for one day. The practical importance of such a result is obvious. Compact fluorescence spectrometers have been developed for geological exploration designed for use in the field. Finally, rock samples returned from the surface of the moon by the Apollo 11 and Apollo 12 missions have been analyzed using electron microscope microprobes to produce fluorescence X-rays [5].

In addition to the above examples, which use fluorescence X-rays created by various means, Auger electron spectroscopy and low energy electron defraction (LEED) have found extensive applications in the new field of surface physics. This technique, for example, has been used to detect monolayers of potassium and cesium as thin as one tenth of an atom on germanium and silicon surfaces [6]. Atoms residing on the surface of a sample can be identified from characteristic Auger electron energies and the quantities of such surface deposits can be determined, provided the fluorescence yields or the Auger yields are known.

The study of radiationless transitions is also important from a fundamental viewpoint. Nonradiative transition probabilities seem to be more sensitive to the detailed nature of atomic wave functions than many other measurable atomic quantities. A systematic study of radiationless transitions could therefore lead to information that could be used to improve methods for determining numerical atomic wave functions. Furthermore, a detailed knowledge of radiationless transitions in atoms is necessary for the interpretation of many measurements in atomic and nuclear physics. The relationship between the properties of the atom and nuclear effects due to the phenomenon of internal conversion is also very familiar. Atomic collision cross-sections for processes in which inner shells are excited can often be measured by detecting the characteristic radiations, but the cross-sections can only be calculated from the measured radiation intensities if the fluorescence yields are well known [7]. In addition to these examples there are a number of smaller effects that are important from a fundamental viewpoint. One example is the internal ionization process or the ejection of atomic electrons during nuclear beta decay, which is usually studied by detecting characteristic X-rays of the daughter atom in coincidence with beta particles [8]. The Auger cascade process is another interesting phenomenon that depends strongly on the knowledge of atomic fluorescence yields. An Auger event coming from an inner shell vacancy produces a doubly ionized atom, and successive radiationless transitions can lead to highly ionized atomic states. The possibility of using such a process to produce highly ionized particle beams has recently been seriously considered in the design of heavy ion accelerators.

The list of practical applications outlined above is by no means complete but it does illustrate the force that has been driving new developments in the field. Another matter should be mentioned before discussing some of the more substantive recent results. Almost all of the new experimental results in the last decade are due to the development of new semiconductor devices for the detection of radiation. In the past, high resolution detection of X-rays or energetic electrons has been possible only by sacrificing aperture, i.e., sacrificing intensity. Semiconductor radiation detectors of very high efficiencies have made it possible to obtain high resolution spectra of X-rays or Auger electrons. The importance of this experimental point cannot be overemphazid and illustrative examples will begiven in some of the following sections.

The following material is a condensation of chapters to appear in a forthcoming review article on atomic fluorescence yields and Coster-Kronig transitions [9].

2. K-shell fluorescence yields

From a practical viewpoint, the fluorescence phenomena following the ionization of the K-shell of an atom are by far the most important fluorescence effects. They are also the easiest to describe since the K-shell consists of only one subshell. The fluorescence yield of the K-shell can be defined

$$\omega_K = I_K/n_K \tag{1}$$

where I_K is the number of radiative transitions to a vacancy in the K-shell and n_K is the number of vacancies in the K-shell. Measurements of K-shell fluorescence yield date back more than 50 years. Perhaps the most remarkable series of experiments was that carried out by H. Lay in 1934 [10]. The results of this series were very reliable and recent measurements have confirmed the trends as a function of atomic number. Lay was the first to observe these trends. In his work the number of K-shell vacancies created in the experiment was usually determined by measuring the absorption coefficient of an incident X-ray beam. The number of fluorescence transitions was measured by detecting the so-called fluorescence radiation and, as shown in eq. (1), the fluorescence yield was defined simply as the ratio of these quantities. In much of the more recent work on K-shell fluorescence yield measurements, the methods of Lay were followed except that newer and more accurate radiation detection devices were used in place of the photographic film he employed.

With the introduction of radioactive sources of high purity and large specific activity, and with the detailed understanding of certain nuclear transitions it became possible to use radioisotopes to determine K-shell fluorescence yields more accurately in certain elements. Consider the case of a nucleus possessing an energy level having a very high internal conversion coefficient. If the electron spectrum following the decay of this level is determined, two groups of electrons will be observed, one corresponding to the internal conversion electron emitted in the nuclear transition, and another corresponding to the Auger electron emitted following the radiationless filling of the vacancy created in the internal conversion process. It is obvious that the intensity ratio of these two electron groups is simply proportional to $1/(1-\omega_K)$. Since the same electron detector can be used to measure the intensity of both groups, this method is inherently very precise and several authors have claimed accuracies of better than 1% for measurements of this kind. Figure 1 shows an example of an electron spectrum from which a K-shell fluorescence yield has been calculated using the ratio of internal conversion to Auger electron intensities. It is important to repeat that only the existence of pure and very high specific activity radioisotope sources with well understood nuclear energy level schemes makes this method of determining K-shell fluorescence yields a practical one. It is also a good example of a case where the measurement of Auger electrons rather than the characteristic X-rays gives a superior experimental result. There are several other cases

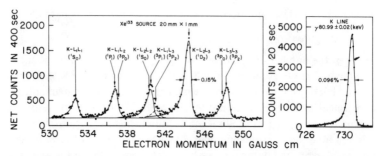

Fig. 1. The K-LL Auger electron spectrum of ^{133}Cs following the β-decay of ^{133}Xe. The 80.99 keV K-conversion line in ^{133}Cs is shown at right and this transition gives rise to almost all the K X-rays and Auger-electron lines from this nuclide. These measurements were made using the Chalk River high resolution (0.07%) spectrometer. (From: R.L. Graham, F. Brown, G.T. Ewan and J. Uhler, Can. J. Phys. *39* (1961) 1086).

where the use of radioisotopes together with special detection techniques provides experimental advantages for securing more accurate fluorescence yields. One case is the use of gaseous isotopes in gas proportional counters. These cases will not be treated in detail; they all depend, again, on the availability of high specific activity radioisotopes. All of the new methods for determining K-shell fluorescence yields will be discussed in detail in a new review article [9].

A theoretical interpretation of K-shell fluorescence yields has also been a topic of interest for more than 50 years. Wentzel's [11] semi-empirical approach, based on the notion that the radiative transition probability depends on the fourth power of the atomic number and that the non-radiative transition probability is roughly independent of the atomic number, leads to the following relation for the K-shell fluorescence yield as a function of Z:

$$\omega_K = (1 + \alpha Z^{-4})^{-1} \qquad (2)$$

where α is a constant having a value of approximately 10^6. This formula was modified by Burhop [12] to account for screening and relativistic effects leading to the three parameter equation

$$\left(\frac{\omega_K}{1-\omega_K}\right)^{1/4} = A + BZ + CZ^3 . \qquad (3)$$

A best fit of the most reliable experimental data gives the following values for the constants A, B, and C [19]:

$$A = -0.007 \quad \pm 0.012$$
$$B = \quad 0.0342 \pm 0.0006 \qquad\qquad (4)$$
$$C = -1.14 \quad \pm 0.10 \times 10^{-6}.$$

In addition to this semi-empirical approach, several attempts have been made to calculate K-shell fluorescence yields from first principles. The most recent contribution is by Kostroun, Chen, and Crasemann [13] who use the matrix elements of the coulomb interactions between the various atomic electrons to calculate the quantum mechanical expression for the fluorescence yields. A number of approximations must be made in such a calculation. In particular it is important to choose wave functions that lead to relatively easy calculations and at the same time provide a desirable degree of accuracy. Kostroun et al. [13] use non-relativistic screened hydrogenic wave functions similar to those used by Burhop [14] in the first calculation of this kind and by Callan [15] in more recent work. Other workers have applied different wave functions, such as relativistic hydrogenic wave functions [16] or self-consistent-field numerical wave functions [17, 18]. In the calculation of the K-shell fluorescence yield it is necessary to sum all of the matrix elements representing transitions between the K-shell and other occupied atomic levels that may give rise to important contributions to the transition rate. One advantage of using non-relativistic hydrogen-like wave functions is that they make it easier to perform the summation in this case. Figure 2 summarizes the more recent theoretical K-shell fluorescence yield calculations, and fig. 3

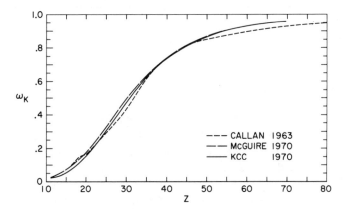

Fig. 2. Theoretical K-shell fluorescence yield as a function of atomic number. The three curves are the results obtained by Callan [15], McGuire [18], and Kostroun et al. [13].

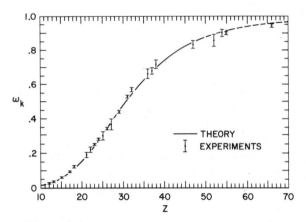

Fig. 3. Theoretical K-shell fluorescence yield as a function of atomic number compared with the best experimental data points. The theoretical curve is taken from Kostroun et al. [13] and the "most reliable" experimental points are taken from Bambynek et al. [9] (From [13].)

shows the theoretical K-shell fluorescence yield given by Kostroun et al. [13] compared with the critically evaluated most reliable data points to be included in the review article by Bambynek et al. [9].

The figures and the results presented here shown that little needs to be added to our understanding of K-shell fluorescence yields. There is much experimental data and the agreement between the best experimental data and theory is excellent (see fig. 3). Finally, a good semi-empirical formula exists (eq. (3)) that makes it possible in practice to calculate the K-shell fluorescence yield for any element using the empirical constants shown in eq. (4).

3. L-shell fluorescence yields

The L-shell of atoms is more complicated than the K-shell since it consists of three separate subshells, each defined by different quantum numbers. A fluorescence yield may be defined for each subshell as in eq. (1). Unfortunately, it is difficult to measure this quantity directly for several reasons. In most experiments, vacancies are created not only in the desired subshell but also in the other two. Consequently, the experimental measurement is an average L-shell fluorescence yield containing contributions of the fluorescence yield of all three subshells. Since the subshell fluorescence yields generally differ, the value of the average L-shell fluorescence yield obtained in this way depends on the manner in which the primary vacancies were distributed among the subshells. Usually it is difficult to isolate the fluorescence yield of an individual subshell in such a measurement. Another problem is the existence of transitions between the subshells of the L-shell. These so-called Coster-Kroning transitions [19] may move a vacancy from one L-subshell to another before the vacancy is filled by an electron making a transition from a higher shell. Thus, even if the primary vacancy distribution among the L-subshells for a given experiment is known, Coster-Kronig transitions will redistribute the vacancies and possibly change the average value of the L-shell fluorescence yield we would expect to measure in that experiment.

From these considerations we see that six quantities must be known to obtain a complete quantitative description of the decay of an excited atom with a vacancy in the L-shell. These six quantities are the three subshell fluorescence yields, ω_1 for the L_1 ($S_{1/2}$) subshell, ω_2 for the L_2 ($P_{1/2}$) subshell, and ω_3 for the L_3 ($P_{3/2}$) subshell and the three Coster-Kronig transition probabilities between the subshells, f_{12}, f_{23} and f_{13}. The quantities f_{ij} are the probabilities that a vacancy will move from the L_i to the L_j subshell. The situation outlined here is described in great detail by Fink et al. [9].

Two circumstances have led to much better experimental information regarding L-shell fluorescence yields during the past decade. The first is again the advent of high resolution X-ray and electron detection devices using solid state diodes as the radiation sensitive elements. These devices have made it possible to separate characteristic X-rays emitted in the rather complex processes that follow the filling of an L-shell vacancy. In many instances a detailed analysis of the spectra obtained by high resolution measuring devices makes it possible to isolate and to determine at least some of the six quantities necessary to describe the phenomenon of L-shell fluorescence. An example of such a high resolution spectrum is shown in fig. 4. The second is the availability of high specific activity radioisotopes.

Several special cases of L-shell fluorescence yield measurements are of particular interest because of their simplicity and because it is possible to obtain some clear cut measurements. One deals with the measurement of ω_3, the fluorescence yield of the highest lying (L_3) subshell of the L-shell. Because this subshell is the least tightly bound of the three L-subshells, it is possible to ionize it without ionizing the other two subshells. Consequently, measurements of ω_3 alone can be made rather easily [20]. The other experimental case involves the measurement of the L-shell fluorescence yield following ionization of the K-shell. A K-shell vacancy is most often filled by transitions from the L_2 and L_3 subshells to the K-shell vacancy. These transi-

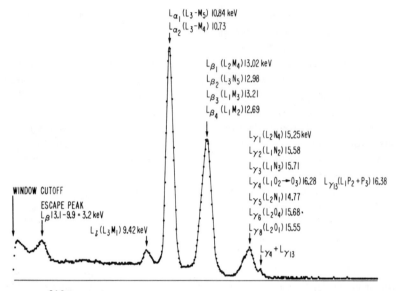

Fig. 4. The ^{210}Pb L X-ray spectrum taken with a Ge (Li) X-ray spectrometer. The resolution of the instrument is 436 eV, full width at half maximum at 14.4 keV. The L
X-rays of this element have quantum energies between 9 and 16 keV. This remarkable
spectrum was obtained by H.U. Freund and R.W. Fink, Phys. Rev. *178* (1969) 1952.

tions give rise to the familiar $K_{\alpha 1}$ and $K_{\alpha 2}$ characteristic X-ray lines. The
transition L_1 to K is forbidden by the angular momentum selection rules;
consequently, processes of this kind lead to L-shell vacancies only in the L_2
and L_3 subshells. Furthermore, the vacancy distribution can be determined
directly by measuring the intensities of the $K_{\alpha 1}$ and the $K_{\alpha 2}$ X-rays. The
L-shell fluorescence yield resulting from this kind of process can then be determined by measuring the coincidence rate between K-shell X-rays and the
resulting L X-rays created by the filling of the vacancies in the L-shell [21]. If
the $K_{\alpha 1}$ and $K_{\alpha 2}$ X-rays can be resolved, then it should, in principle, be possible to determine ω_2 and ω_3 separately, provided the effect of the Coster-
Kronig transition between the L_2 and L_3 shells can be accurately included.
Some recent measurements of ω_2 and ω_3 obtained by the K-shell fluorescence excitation technique and subsequent K to L X-ray coincidence measurements are shown in table 1. The values of ω_2 and ω_3 given in this table
were obtained by Price et al. [22] using the assumption that $f_{23} = 0.13 \pm 0.13$.
The necessity to assume a value for f_{23} as well as the inaccuracy of the present
assumption illustrates the principal limitation of the X-ray coincidence method.

Table 1

A summary of ω_2 and ω_3 values for heavy elements. The 2σ errors of the quantities are also shown. These results are taken from [22].

Z	Element	ω_2	2σ	ω_3	2σ
71	Lu	0.257	0.052	0.251	0.035
72	Hf	0.299	0.046	0.228	0.025
73	Ta	0.270	0.045	0.254	0.025
74	W	0.295	0.052	0.272	0.037
75	Rh	0.310	0.064	0.284	0.043
76	Os	0.328	0.054	0.290	0.030
77	Ir	0.317	0.058	0.262	0.036
78	Pt	0.341	0.053	0.317	0.029
79	Au	0.354	0.052	0.317	0.025
80	Hg	0.408	0.079	0.367	0.050
81	Tl	0.400	0.079	0.386	0.053
82	Pb	0.354	0.057	0.354	0.028
83	Bi	0.380	0.058	0.362	0.029
90	Th	0.473	0.080	0.517	0.042
92	U	0.545	0.081	0.500	0.040

In spite of the difficulties outlined above, important progress has been made in measuring individual L-subshell yields and also Coster-Kronig transition probabilities in many elements. In addition, a number of promising developments make it likely that more and better L-shell measurements will be obtained in the near future. Perhaps the most important of these is the improvement in our ability to calculate atomic ionization cross sections and, therefore, to determine the initial distribution of vacancies among the subshells for given experimental ionization conditions. This theoretical work has been inspired primarily by revived interest in plasma physics and astrophysics. Ionization by protons or by heavy charged particles looks particularly promising. The state of our knowledge of theoretical ionization cross sections for protons is such that very serious consideration should be given to initiating fluorescence yield measurements using energic protons to ionize the inner shells of atoms. Following the theoretical work of Bang and Hansteen [23], who first considered the effect of the deflection of the incident particle by the nucleus in an ionizing collison, Garcia [24] has improved the theory to a point where it is considered reliable for the calculation of vacancies and vacancy distributions created by proton impact. Furthermore, the improvements in the resolving power of new solid state X-ray detectors make it possible to easily observe and resolve the characteristic X-rays produced by the incident proton beam in the L-shell, and in heavy elements, the M-shell as well. It should thus be possible to measure a number of fluorescence yields of various shells and subshells by the proton bombardment method. In the case of heavier incident particles the situation is not quite so favorable. Nevertheless, attention should also be paid to the possible use of heavier particles for the measurement of L-shell fluorescence yields [25]. Finally, it should be mentioned that as in the case of the K-shell, the use of certain specially suited new radioisotopes of high specific activity has been most useful in determining more L-shell fluorescence yields [26].

The recent developments in the determination of Coster-Kronig transition probabilities have also been very significant. These transitions were discovered by careful analysis of the intensities of L-series X-ray spectra [19]. It was difficult, however, from such analysis to determine the rate at which Coster-Kronig processes ocurred. Using X-ray detectors and Auger electron spectrometers that can resolve X-rays or electrons coming from transitions to individual L-subshells makes it possible to perform experiments that yield values of Coster-Kronig transition rates in many instances. Perhaps the most interesting example is the determination of f_{23}. Figure 5 is a partial listing of the recent experimental and theoretical work in determining f_{23} [27]. It is interesting to note that the theoretical values of f_{23} generally are lower than those predicted by theory using both the screened hydrogenic wave function approach of Chen et al. [27], and the self-consistent field wave functions developed by McGuire [28]. This discrepancy has led to the speculation that there is perhaps a radiative component to the Coster-Kronig transition that contributes to the observed value but that has been included in the nonradiative calculations. The radiative dipole L_1 to L_3 Coster-Kronig transition has recently been observed [29]. However, the L_2 to L_3 radiative transitions that would contribute to the value of f_{23} have not been seen. The calculations by Chen et al. [27] indicate that the radiative transition rate for this spin flip magnetic dipole transition is extremely small. Consequently, the difference that is apparent between the theoretical and the experimental values of f_{23} lies elsewhere. It is very likely that an effort to understand this difference will yield

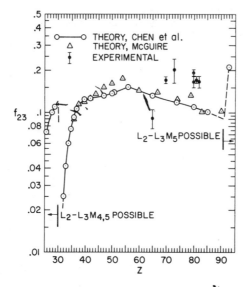

Fig. 5. Theoretical curves for the Coster-Kronig Transition probability f_{23} compared with experimental results. The theoretical values are taken from [27] and the experimental data are the most recent results (1969-1970) from several laboratories.

more accurate atomic wave functions that could be used to good advantage in other atomic physics calculations.

4. M-shell fluorescence yields

The case of the M-shell is even more complex than the L-shell since there are now five rather than three subshells that must be considered. It is an amusing fact that for more than 30 years there existed only one measurement of an M-shell fluorescence yield in the literature and that was a value for the element Uranium given by Lay [10]. As in the case of fluorescence yield determinations for other atomic shells, the advent of better X-ray and electron detection devices has made it possible to make a serious attack on the problem of determining good experimental values for M-shell fluorescence yields. Not enough is known to draw any definitive conclusions with respect to the situation in the M-shell. The available data are listed in table 2 [9] with the hope that more experimental work will be forthcoming in the near future.

Table 2.
A summary of M-shell fluorescence yields and Coster-Kronig yields. The quantities labeled "ν" are defined in [9].

Z	Element	$\bar{\omega}_M$	ω_{LM} (Note a)	ω_{LM} (Note b)	$(\omega_1^M + f_{12}^M \omega_2^M)$	ν_i^M	ω_i^M	Ref.
76	Os		0.013±0.0024	0.016±0.003				[30]
79	Au	0.023±0.001						[31]
79	Au		0.024±0.005	0.030±0.006				[30]
82	Pb	0.029±0.002						[31]
82	Pb		0.026±0.005	0.032±0.006				[30]
83	Bi	0.037±0.007						[32]
83	Bi	0.035±0.002						[31]
83	Bi		0.030±0.006	0.037±0.005				[30]
92	U	0.06						[10]
93	Np				$0.002^{+0.003}_{-0.002}$	$\nu_1 = 0.065\pm0.014$ $\nu_2 = 0.080\pm0.029$ $\nu_4 = 0.062\pm0.005$ $\nu_{4,5} = 0.065\pm0.012$	$\omega_5 \approx 0.06\pm0.012$	[33]
96	Cm				$0.0075^{+0.0089}_{-0.0075}$	$\nu_1 = 0.081\pm0.016$ $\nu_2 = 0.068\pm0.023$ $\nu_3 = 0.062\pm0.019$ $\nu_4 = 0.080\pm0.006$ $\nu_{4,5} = 0.075\pm0.012$	$\omega_2 = 0.0046^{+0.0051}_{-0.0046}$ $\omega_5 \approx 0.075\pm0.012$	[33]

5. Conclusions

It might be well to repeat here that this very brief review has not by any means been exhaustive. In particular, the author has perhaps slighted the work being performed in the field of Auger electron spectroscopy and he must admit to some prejudice here because of his inexperience in electron measurements. Several general conclusions, however, can be drawn. The first is that our knowledge of K-shell fluorescence yields both experimentally and theoretically is excellent and that little more needs to be done in this area. In the case of the L-shell, great progress has been made and many L-subshell yields are now well determined. The same cannot be said for Coster-Kronig transition rates for the L-shell and this seems a fruitful area for further efforts. Much needs to be done in the case of the M-shell before any claim to real understanding can be made. Finally, it should be clear that a continuing development of instrumentation for atomic physics is perhaps the driving factor that will lead to further progress in this very interesting, fruitful, and fundamental field.

References

[1] H. Goldstein, *Fundamental Aspects of Reactor Shielding* (Addison Wesley Publishing Co., Inc., Cambridge, Mass., 1959).
[2] See, for example, L.R. Anspaugh, J.W. Gofman, et al., in: *Proc. Second Symp. Low-Energy X- and Gamma-Ray Source Applications,* ORNL-IIC-10 (1967).
[3] T.B. Johansson, R. Akselsson and S.A.E. Johansson, Nucl. Instr. and Meth. *84* (1970) 141.
[4] R. Fitzgerald and P. Gantzel, Chap. 1 in: *Energy Dispersion X-ray Analysis,* Ed. J.B. Wheeler, ASTM Publ. STD-485 (1970).
[5] H.J. Rose, F. Cuttitta, E.J. Dwornik, M.K. Carrou, R.P. Christian, J.R. Lindsay, D.T. Ligon and R.R. Larson, Science *167* (1970) 520.
[6] R.E. Weber and W.T. Peria, J. Appl. Phys. *38* (1967) 4355.
[7] J.D. Garcia, Phys. Rev. A 1 (1970) 1402.
[8] B. Crasemann and P. Stephas, Nucl. Phys. *A134* (1969) 641.
[9] W. Bambynek, B. Crasemann, R.W. Fink, H.U. Freund, H. Mark, C.D. Swift, R.E. Price, and P.V. Rao, Rev. Mod. Phys. to be published; and R.W. Fink, R.C. Jopson, H. Mark and C.D. Swift, Rev. Mod. Phys. 38 (1966) 513.
[10] H. Lay, Z. Phys. *91* (1934) 533.
[11] G. Wentzel, Z. Phys. *43* (1927) 524.
[12] E.H.S. Burhop, J. Phys. Radium *16* (1955) 625.
[13] V.O. Kostroun, M.H. Chen, and B. Crasemann, Phys. Rev. A 3 (1971) 533.
[14] E.H.S. Burhop, Proc. Roy. Soc., Ser. A *148* (1935) 272.
[15] E.J. Callan, Phys. Rev. *124* (1961) 793.
[16] B. Talukdar and D. Chattarji, Phys. Rev. A 1 (1970) 33.
[17] W. Melhorn, Z. Phys. *208* (1968) 1.

[18] E.J. McGuire, Phys. Rev. A 2 (1970) 273.

[19] D. Coster and R. de L. Kronig, Physica 2 (1935) 13.

[20] H. Küstner and E. Arends, Ann. Phys. (Leipzig) 22 (1935) 443.

[21] R.C. Jopson, H. Mark, C.D. Swift, and T.H. Zenger, Phys. Rev. 124 (1961) 157.

[22] R.E. Price, H. Mark and C.D. Swift, Phys. Rev. 176 (1968) 3.

[23] J. Bang and J.M. Hansteen, K. Danske Vidensk. Selsk. Mat.-Fys. Medd. 31 nr. 13 (1959) 1.

[24] J.D. Garcia, Phys. Rev. A 1 (1970) 280.

[25] F.W. Saris, thesis (University of Leiden, 1971).

[26] See, for example, S. Mohan, H.U. Freund, R.W. Fink and P.V. Rao, Phys. Rev. C 1 (1970) 254.

[27] M.H. Chen, B. Crasemann and V.O. Kostroun, Phys. Rev. A 4 (1971) 1.

[28] E.J. McGuire, Phys. Rev. A 3 (1971) 587.

[29] H.U. Freund, E. Kattunen and R.W. Fink, Bull. Amer. Phys. Soc. 15 (1970) 1305.

[30] R.C. Jopson, H. Mark, C.D. Swift and M.A. Williamson, Phys. Rev. 137 (1965) A 1353.

[31] A.A. Konstantinov and T.E. Sazonova, Izv. Akad. Nauk. SSSR, Ser. Fiz., 32 (1968) 631; [English Transl.: Bull. Acad. Sci. USSR, Phys. Ser. 32 (1968) 581].

[32] H. Jaffe, Bull. Res. Council Israel 3 (1954) 316.

[33] E. Karttunen, thesis (Georgia Institute of Technology, 1971).

AUGER ELECTRON SPECTROSCOPY

WERNER MEHLHORN *

*Institut für Kernphysik, Universität Münster, 44 Münster,
Germany*

Experimental group intensities $I(KL_1L_1)$, $I(KL_1L_{2,3})$ and $I(KL_{2,3}L_{2,3})$, relative to the total intensity $I(KLL)$ are compared with theoretical values calculated non-relativistically. Recent calculations by McGuire are in better agreement with the experiment but are still not satisfactory, especially for $Z < 18$. For the first time, theoretical values of $M_{4,5}NN$ line intensities are compared with experimental values. The basic conditions for a non-isotropic emission of Auger electrons are discussed, and experimental evidence for non-isotropic distributions of the $L_3M_{2,3}M_{2,3}({}^1S_0)$ Auger electrons of argon is given. The application of Auger electron spectroscopy to free molecules is considered. For N_2, as an example, the various Auger transitions and the resulting information on the molecular structure are discussed.

1. Introduction

The basic de-excitation processes after an inner-shell ionization are X-ray emission and Auger electron emission. So Auger electron spectroscopy (AES), like X-ray spectroscopy, is well suited to study the structure of and the dynamics in atoms and molecules, particularly in inner shells. Due to the development of high resolution and high transmission electron spectrometers, AES has become an important research field during the last decade. The main current research activities of AES in atomic and molecular physics are:

a) Determination of energies, intensities and widths of Auger lines. These quantities give information on atomic and molecular structure and serve as a sensitive test for electron wave functions used to calculate these quantities. Applying AES to free molecules gives information on the electronic and, in favourable cases, also on vibrational states of doubly ionized molecules [1–4].

b) Processes such as simple ionization, simple excitation, double ionization,

---

* Now at Fakultät für Physik, Universität Freiburg, 78 Freiburg, Germany.

ionization-excitation, etc. can be distinguished by AES. This gives detailed information on the interaction of radiation or particles with atomic electrons. Absolute inner-shell ionization cross-sections by electron impact [5] or ion impact [6] have been measured by means of AES. In the studies of ion-atom collisions the Auger effect is widely used as an indication of inner-shell ionizations [7–10]. In cases of multiple processes, such as primary double ionization and ionization-excitation or double Auger processes, AES gives information on electron-electron correlation effects and rearrangment processes in the atom or molecule. This has been mainly investigated at Oak Ridge [11–13].

In the following I will report on the progress in some selected fields of AES.

2. Intensities of Auger electrons

Most of the experimental investigations of Auger spectra have dealt with the K-shell. This is true also for theoretical calculations [14–18]. During the last two years new theoretical values became available, not only for the K-shell [19–26a], but also for the L-shell transitions [26b].

2.1. Intensities of KLL Auger lines for $Z \leqslant 56$

It has been pointed out earlier [28a, 28b] that the experimental group intensities $I(KL_1 L_{2,3})/I(KL_1 L_1)$ and $I(KL_{2,3} L_{2,3})/I(KL_1 L_1)$ deviated strongly from theoretical values calculated non-relativistically by Rubenstein [14], Callan [15] and Archard [16] for small atomic numbers Z. New non-relativistic calculations by McGuire [20] with Hartree-Fock-Slater wave functions for bound and continuum electrons agree better with experiment but are still not satisfactory. On the other hand, for large Z, relativistic values calculated earlier by Asaad [17] and Listengarten [18] and recently by Bhalla and Ramsdale [23] are in good agreement with the experimental values.

In figs. 1, 2, and 3 the experimental intensities of the groups $KL_1 L_1$, $KL_1 L_{2,3}$ and $KL_{2,3} L_{2,3}$, relative to the total KLL intensity, are compared with the corresponding theoretical values for $Z \leqslant 56$. I prefer to use these relative group intensities because they give more detailed information on the dependence of the transition probabilities on Z than the relative intensities $I(KL_1 L_{2,3})/I(KL_1 L_1)$ and $I(KL_{2,3} L_{2,3})/I(KL_1 L_1)$ used earlier. Also, the new relative group intensities are independent of any coupling scheme used for the two final vacancies in the L-shell; only configuration interaction will increase the $KL_{2,3} L_{2,3}$ intensity at the expense of the $KL_1 L_1$ intensity [27, 28a]. The experimental intensities $I(KL_1 L_{2,3})/I(KLL)$ and

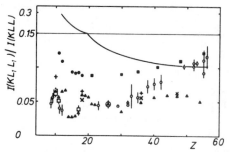

Fig. 1. Comparison of experimental relative intensities $I(KL_1L_1)/I(KLL)$ with theory. Experiment (for references see [28b]): $\dot{Q}$ = solid state target, $\dot{\phi}$ = gaseous target. Non-relativistic theory: —— = Callan [15], X = Rubenstein [14], ● = Archard [16], + = Callan et al. [19], ▲ = McGuire [20]. Relativistic theory: ■ = Bhalla and Ramsdale [23]. All non-relativistic values have been corrected for configuration interaction [27, 28a].

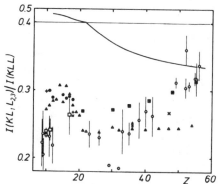

Fig. 2. Comparison of experimental relative intensities $I(KL_1L_{2,3})/I(KLL)$ with theory. For explanation of symbols see fig. 1.

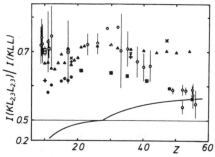

Fig. 3. Comparison of experimental relative intensities $I(KL_{2,3}L_{2,3})/I(KLL)$ with theory. For explanation of symbols see fig. 1.

$I(KL_{2,3}L_{2,3})/I(KLL)$ both show a rather smooth dependance on Z (fig. 2 and 3), while the experimental intensity $I(KL_1L_1)/I(KLL)$ depends much more strongly on Z (fig. 1). Most interesting is the sudden decrease by as much as 40%, extending from $Z=10$ to 11 and 12, which is found when the values for sodium and magnesium, measured with a solid state target [29], are compared with the neon values, found for a gaseous target [30, 13a].

As this strong change in KL_1L_1 intensity can be expected to be a solid-state effect, at least partly, we investigated the KLL spectrum of a sodium atomic beam target [31]. The new KL_1L_1 intensity is indeed not as small as the solid target value, but we cannot exclude the possibility that a KL-LLL satellite line coincides with the Kl_1L_1 line simulating a too large KL_1L_1 intensity. In the case of neon, no satellite line coincides with the KL_1L_1 diagram line; this has been shown by Krause et al. [13a].

For $Z < 25$, theoretical values of the relative KL_1L_1 intensity, except for the values of McGuire [20], are much larger than the experimental values (all non-relativistic values of fig. 1 and 3 have been corrected for configuration interaction). However, the McGuire values show some strange local structure for the KL_1L_1 intensity but not for the other two group intensities (figs. 2 and 3). With increasing Z all experimental group intensities deviate systematically from the non-relativistic values, while they agree better with relativistic values calculated by Bhalla and Ramsdale [23]. Not included in figs. 1−3 are the non-relativistic values of Walters and Bhalla [22] and Kostroun et al. [26a], because the transition amplitudes were not available.

The wave functions used in the various calculations are: screened hydrogenic and analytical Coulomb functions for bound (b) and continuum (c) electrons (Callan [15]), Hartree functions for b and c electrons (Rubenstein [14]), Hartree-Fock functions for b and analytical Coulomb functions for c electrons (Archard [16]), Hartree-Fock functions for b and c electrons (Callan et al. [19]), Hartree-Fock-Slater functions for b and c electrons (McGuire [20], Walters and Bhalla [21, 22]) and relativistic Hartree-Fock-Slater functions for b and c electrons (Bhalla and Ramsdale [23]).

Only the theoretical relative intensities $I(KL_1L_{2,3})/I(KLL)$ can be compared with experimental values without any correction, this being an ideal test for the wave functions used. But here also theoretical values deviate by as much as 20−40% from the experimental ones for $Z < 18$.

2.2. Auger spectra of noble gases

If valence-shell electrons are involved in the Auger transitions, the Auger spectra of free atoms, especially of noble gas atoms, should be investigated to avoid solid-state effects and to take advantage of the high symmetry of the

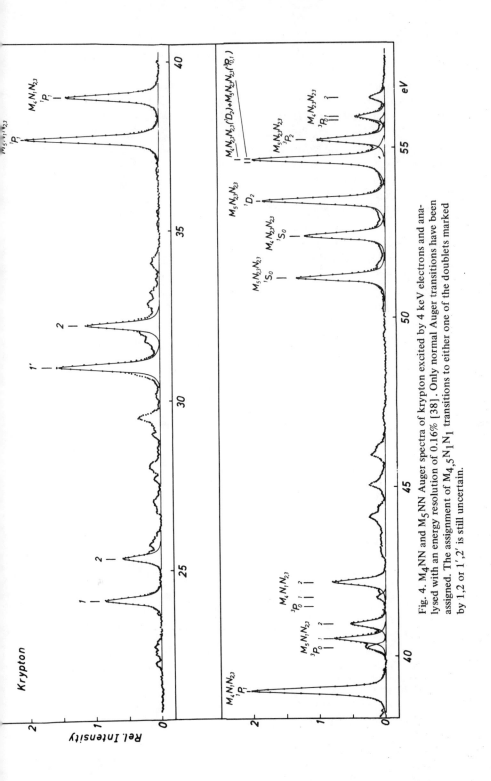

Fig. 4. M_4NN and M_5NN Auger spectra of krypton excited by 4 keV electrons and analysed with an energy resolution of 0.16% [38]. Only normal Auger transitions have been assigned. The assignment of $M_{4,5}N_1N_1$ transitions to either one of the doublets marked by 1,2 or 1',2' is still uncertain.

noble gas atoms. Auger spectra of noble gases, other than neon, have been investigated mainly at Münster (krypton MNN [32, 33], argon LMM [34, 35]) and at Uppsala (argon $L_{2,3}$MM, krypton $M_{4,5}$NN, xenon $M_{4,5}$NN, $N_{4,5}$OO [2, 36]). I will discuss only briefly the M_4NN and M_5NN spectra of krypton (fig. 4 [33]), where theoretical transition amplitudes have been calculated only recently by McGuire [37] using Hartree-Fock-Slater wave functions. In fig. 4 almost all Auger lines are well separated, so that the intensities of lines can be determined with high accuracy. Only the assignment of $M_4N_1N_1$ and $M_5N_1N_1$ transitions to either one of the doublets 1,2 or 1′,2′ is still uncertain [32, 36], although I rather prefer the doublet 1′,2′ [38].

In fig. 5 the experimental intensities are compared with theoretical values; the latter have been calculated assuming jj-coupling for the initial M_4 or M_5 vacancy and intermediate coupling with configuration interaction for the two final vacancies in the N-shell [38]. There are two sets of theoretical values corresponding to the two possibilities of assignment of $M_{4,5}N_1N_1$ transitions. In each case the theoretical values are normalized to the experimental intensities of $M_{4,5}N_{2,3}N_{2,3}(^1S_0)$ doublet lines. The overall agreement is fairly good for many lines, but there are also large deviations, especially for the $M_{4,5}N_1N_{2,3}(^1P_1)$ transitions, showing that theory is not yet in full accord with experiment. A strong non-isotropic angular distribution of $M_{4,5}$NN

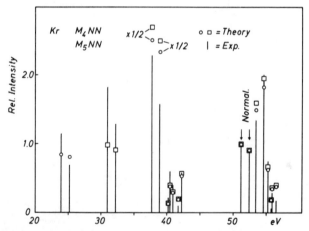

Fig. 5. Comparison of experimental line intensities of M_4NN and M_5NN transitions with theory. Theoretical values have been calculated assuming jj-coupling for the initial vacancies M_4 and M_5 and intermediate coupling and configuration interaction for the final vacancies in the N-shell [37, 38]. The two theoretical sets, given by ○ and □, refer to the two possible assignments of $M_{4,5}N_1N_1$ transitions to the doublets 1,2 and 1′,2′.

Auger electrons of krypton, excited by 4 keV electrons (fig. 4), which could explain the deviations between theory and experiment, has not been found experimentally.

2.3. *Angular distribution of Auger electrons*

It has been predicted earlier [39], that Auger electrons following an inner-shell vacancy with quantum number $j > 1/2$, caused by a directed electron or proton beam, may have a non-isotropic angular distribution. This is due to different ionization probabilities $Q(j, |m|)$ of magnetic sublevels m resulting in an alignment of the ionized atoms relative to the axis of the primary particle beam defining the quantization axis. The angular distribution depends also on the final atomic state of the Auger transition. In order to prove this, we measured the angular distribution of $L_3 M_{2,3} M_{2,3}(^1S_0)$ electrons relative to the $L_2 M_{2,3} M_{2,3}(^3P_{0,1,2})$ electrons excited by electron impact [40, 41]. While theory predicts a simple angular distribution for the $L_3 M_{2,3} M_{2,3}(^1S_0)$ electrons, see eq. (2), the $L_2 M_{2,3} M_{2,3}(^3P_{0,1,2})$ electrons have essentially an isotropic distribution. In addition, both lines are well separated from all other lines and can therefore be measured with high precision (fig. 6).

Assuming the ionization cross-section of the initial magnetic sublevels to be $Q(3/2, |1/2|)$ and $Q(3/2, |3/2|)$ and introducing the parameter

$$a = \frac{Q(3/2, |3/2|) - Q(3/2, |1/2|)}{Q(3/2, |1/2|)}, \tag{1}$$

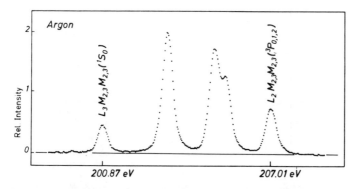

Fig. 6. Selected $L_{2,3} M_{2,3} M_{2,3}$ transitions of argon to measure the angular distribution of $L_3 M_{2,3} M_{2,3}(^1S_0)$ Auger electrons.

the following distribution of $L_3M_{2,3}M_{2,3}(^1S_0)$ Auger electrons results:

$$I(\vartheta) \sim [1 + \tfrac{3}{4}a(1 - \cos^2 \vartheta)]. \qquad (2)$$

Since the ionization cross-sections are energy dependent the parameter a is also energy dependent. In fig. 7 the relative intensities $I_{rel}(\vartheta) = I(\vartheta, L_3M_{2,3}M_{2,3}(^1S_0))/I(\vartheta, L_2M_{2,3}M_{2,3}(^3P_{0,1,2}))$ are plotted for $\vartheta = 30, 90$ and $150°$ and for three different primary electron energies $E_p = 2E(L_3)$, $4E(L_3)$ and $16E(L_3)$. We have normalized all values in such a way that $I_{rel}(\vartheta = 0) = 1$. From fig. 7 it can readily be seen that for primary electron energies which are two or four times the threshold energy $E(L_3)$, we measure non-isotropic distributions with a = -0.10 ± 0.03. For $E_p = 16E(L_3)$ the distribution is isotropic within experimental error.

Only recently the ionization cross-sections $Q(2p, m_\varrho = 0) = Q_0$ and $Q(2p, m_\varrho = \pm 1) = Q_1$ have been calculated by McFarlane [42] for a quantization axis which coincides with the incident electron beam, by means of the Born approximation. The parameter a is given in terms of Q_0 and Q_1 by

$$a = 2(Q_1 - Q_0)/(Q_1 + 2Q_0). \qquad (3)$$

For a the following results can be deduced from the values Q_0 and Q_1 calculated by McFarlane: a) For primary energies of two and four times the threshold energy the parameter a has the values -0.03 and -0.07, respectively.

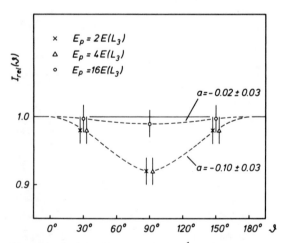

Fig. 7. Relative intensities $I_{rel}(\vartheta) = I(\vartheta, L_3M_{2,3}M_{2,3}(^1S_0))/I(\vartheta, L_2M_{2,3}M_{2,3}(^3P_{0,1,2}))$ for three different primary energies E_p. The values $I_{rel}(\vartheta)$ are normalized to $I_{rel}(\vartheta = 0) = 1$.

b) For energies about 16 times the threshold energy both cross-sections Q_o and Q_1 are equal, thus giving $a = 0$ and an isotropic distribution. c) For the high energy limit a is found to be +0.15 and energy independent. The first two theoretical results agree nicely with our experiment.

Volz and Rudd [6] have also measured angular distributions of the intensity of several L_3MM transitions of argon excited by 300 keV protons, but they did not find any significant deviations from isotropy.

3. AES of free molecules

Recently AES has been applied to simple gaseous molecules at Münster (N_2 [1]), Uppsala (N_2, O_2, NO, CO, CF_4, C_2H_6, C_6H_6 [2] and Oak Ridge (N_2, O_2, CO, NO, H_2O, CO_2 [3, 4]). Though the Auger spectra involving electrons in the chemical bond are more complex than atomic spectra, they offer a new method for determining molecular states. For example, the identification of normal Auger lines gives information on a) the splitting of the initial state of the Auger transitions due to spin coupling of the inner vacancy with partially filled outer orbitals and b) the ground and excited states of doubly ionized molecules via the final states of Auger transitions.

The K-Auger spectrum of N_2 has been most thoroughly studied and best understood of all the molecules. Figure 8 shows the K-Auger spectrum of N_2, excited by 6 keV electrons and measured with an energy resolution of 0.16% [1]. No splitting of the initial state $1s^{-1}$ of N_2 due to spin coupling occurs, because the outer orbitals are filled. The high energy lines marked by D and E are due to auto-ionizing transitions where intially one 1s-electron is excited to the bound but unfilled orbital $\pi_g 2p$ and the final states are the first excited state (A $^2\Pi_u$) and the ground state (X $^2\Sigma_g^+$) of the singly charged N_2. This interpretation has been directly confirmed by Carlson et al. [3]. The Auger

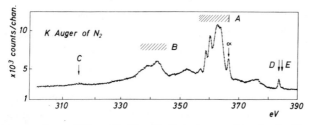

Fig. 8. K-Auger spectrum of N_2 excited by 6 keV electrons and analysed with an energy resolution of 0.16% (from [1]).

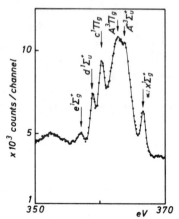

Fig. 9. High energy part of the K spectrum of N_2 (from [1]). The designation of the states of N_2^{2+}, corresponding to the various maxima, is exactly analogous to that used for the isoelectronic molecule C_2.

groups marked by A, B and C correspond to normal Auger transitions where two weakly bound electrons ($\sigma_g 2p$, $\pi_u 2p$, $\sigma_u 2s$), one weakly bound and one strongly bound $\sigma_g 2s$-electron, or two strongly bound electrons $\sigma_g 2s$ are involved. The high energy maximum α of group A can be assigned to the normal Auger line of highest energy having the ground state X $^1\Sigma_g^+$ of N_2^{2+} as the final state. Thus the various maxima of group A correspond to excitations above the ground state of N_2^{2+}. In fig. 9 the Auger group A is shown on an enlarged scale. Using potential-energy curves derived by Hurley [43] for N_2^{2+}, it was possible to assign definite excited states to the maxima. The energy of the state d $^1\Sigma_u^+$ of 7.9 eV relative to the ground state of N_2^{2+} was found to be in excellent agreement with the energy of the only state measured up to that time, by means of UV emission spectroscopy [44].

No distinct vibrational structure has been found in the KLL spectrum of N_2. In general the following conditions must be met to observe vibrational structure of the final states: a) The spacing of the vibrational levels should be larger than the level width of the initial state, which is of the order of 0.10-0.15 eV. b) There should be no splitting of the initial state due to spin coupling. c) There should be a high degeneracy of the $\sigma_g 1s$ and $\sigma_u 1s$ levels in homonuclear molecules. d) Only one vibrational level of the initial state should be excited. Until now clear vibrational structure has been found only in the K-Auger spectrum of carbon in CO [2, 4]. Here we know from the beginning that the first three conditions are satisfied. Thus the observation of vibrational structure seems to indicate that the fourth condition is fullfilled also.

References

[1] D. Stalherm, B. Cleff, H. Hillig and W. Mehlhorn, Z. Naturforsch. 24a (1969) 1728.

[2] K. Siegbahn, C. Nordling, G. Johansson, J. Hedman, P.F. Heden, K. Hamrin, U. Gelius, T. Bergmark, L.O. Werme, R. Manne and Y. Baer, ESCA Applied to Free Molecules (North-Holland Publ. Co., Amsterdam, 1969).

[3] T.A. Carlson, W.E. Moddeman, B.P. Pullen and M.O. Krause, Chem. Phys. Letters 5 (1970) 390.

[4] W.E. Moddeman, T.A. Carlson, M.O. Krause, B.P. Pullen, W.E. Bull and G.K. Schweitzer, J. Chem. Phys. 55 (1971) 2317.

[5] G. Glupe and W. Mehlhorn, Phys. Letters 25A (1967) 274; and a paper presented at the C.N.R.S. colloquium Les Processus Electroniques Simples et Multiples du Domaine X et X-UV, Paris 1970, to be published in J. Phys. (Paris), Colloq. 2 (1971).

g [6] D.J. Volz and M.E. Rudd, Phys. Rev. A 2 (1970) 1395.
      M.E. Rudd, T. Jorgensen and D.J. Volz, Phys. Rev. 151 (1966) 28.

[7] R.K. Cacak, Q.C. Kessel and M.E. Rudd, Phys. Rev. A 2 (1970) 1327.

[9] G.M. Thomson, P.C. Laudieri and E. Everhart, Phys. Rev. A 1 (1970) 1439.

[10] P. Dahl (1971), private communication.

[11] T.A. Carlson and M.O. Krause, Phys. Rev. Letters 14 (1965) 390; and 17 (1966) 1079.

[12] T.A. Carlson, W.E. Moddeman and M.O. Krause, Phys. Rev. A 1 (1970) 1406.

[13a] M.O. Krause, T.A. Carlson and W.E. Moddeman, Manifestation of Atomic Dynamics Through the Auger Effect, paper presented at the C.R.N.S. Colloquium Les Processes Electroniques Simples en Multiples du Domaine X et X-UV, Paris, 1970, to be published in J. Phys. (Paris), Colloq. 2 (1971).

[13b] M.O. Krause, Rearrangement of Inner-Shell Ionized Atoms, paper presented at the C.R.N.S. Colloquium Les Processus Electroniques Simples et Multiples du Domaine X et X-UV, Paris, 1970 to be published in J. Phys. (Paris), Colloq. 2 (1971).

[14] R.A. Rubenstein, Ph. D. Thesis (unpublished), University of Illinois (1955).

[15] E.J. Callan, Phys. Rev. 124 (1961) 793.

[16] G.D. Archard (1963), private communication.

[17] W.N. Asaad, Proc. Roy. Soc., Ser. A 249 (1959) 555.

[18] M.A. Listengarten, Izv. Akad. Nauk SSSR, Ser. Fiz. 25 (1961) 792; and 26 (1962) 182 [English Transl. Bull. Akad. Sci. USSR, Phys. Ser. 25 (1961) 803; and 26 (1962)

[19]] E.J. Callan, T.K. Krueger and W.L. McDavid, Bull. Am. Phys. Soc. 14 (1969) 830.

[20] E.J. McGuire, Phys. Rev. 185 (1969) 1; and A 2 (1970) 273.

[21] D.L. Walters and C.P. Bhalla, Phys. Rev. A 3 (1971) 519.

[22] D.L. Walters and C.P. Bhalla, Phys. Rev. (to be published).

[23] C.P. Bhalla and D.J. Ramsdale, Z. Phys. 239 (1970) 95.

[24] C.P. Bhalla, H.R. Rosner and D.J. Ramsdale, J. Phys. B 3 (1970) 1232.

[25]   C.P. Bhalla, Phys. Rev. A 2 (1970) 722.
[26a]   V.O. Kostroun, M.H. Chen and B. Crasemarn, Phys. Rev. A 3 (1971) 533.
[26b]   E.J. McGuire, Phys. Rev. A 3 (1971) 587.
[27]   W.N. Asaad, Nucl. Phys. 66 (1965) 494.
[28a]   W. Mehlhorn and W.N. Asaad, Z. Phys. 191 (1966) 231.
[28b]   B. Cleff and W. Mehlhorn, Z. Phys. 219 (1969) 311.
[29]   A. Fahlman, R. Nordberg, C. Nordling and K. Siegbahn, Z. Phys. 192 (1966) 476.
[30]   W. Mehlhorn, D. Stalherm and H. Verbeek, Z. Naturforsch. 23a (1968) 287.
[31]   H. Hillig, B. Cleff and W. Mehlhorn, Z. Phys. (to be published).
[32]   W. Mehlhorn, Z. Phys. 187 (1965) 21.
[33]   D. Stalherm, Master Thesis (unpublished), University of Munster (1968).
[34]   W. Mehlhorn, Z. Phys. 208 (1968) 1.
[35]   W. Mehlhorn and D. Stalherm, Z. Phys. 217 (1968) 294.
[36]   K. Siegbahn, C. Nordling, A. Fahlman, R. Nordberg, K. Hamrin, J. Hedman,
        G. Johansson, T. Bergmark, S.-E. Karlsson, I. Lindgren and B. Lindberg, ESCA-
        Atomic, Molecular and Solid State Structure Studied by Means of Electron Spec-
        troscopy. Nova Acta Regiae Soc. Sci. Upsaliensis Ser. IV, Vol. 20 (1967).
[37]   E.J. McGuire, private communication, 1971.
[38]   D. Stalherm and W. Mehlhorn, Z. Phys. (to be published).
[39]   W. Mehlhorn, Phys. Letters 26A (1968) 166.
[40]   B. Cleff and W. Mehlhorn, paper presented at the Meeting of the German Physical
        Society, Section Mass Spectrometry, München, March 1970.
[41]   B. Cleff and W. Mehlhorn, Phys. Letters 37A (1971) 3.
[42]   C. McFarlane, VII ICPEAC, Abstracts of Papers, Eds. L.M. Branscomb et al.
        (North-Holland Publ. Co., Amsterdam, 1971) p. 406; J. Phys. B (to be published).
[43]   A.C. Hurley, J. Mol. Spectrosc. 9 (1962) 18.
[44]   P.K. Carroll and A.C. Hurley, J. Chem. Phys. 35 (1961) 2247.

Physics of Electronic and Atomic Collisions, VII ICPEAC, 1971 — North-Holland (1972)

CHARACTERISTIC X-RAY PRODUCTION
IN HEAVY-ION-ATOM COLLISIONS

F.W. SARIS
*FOM-Instituut voor Atoom- en Molecuulfysica, Kruislaan 407,
Amsterdam, The Netherlands.*

This report aims to show what progress is being made in the understanding of violent atomic collisions by studying ion-induced X-ray production. Total cross-section measurements are discussed as well as high-resolution X-ray spectrometry. Two main conclusions may be drawn from total cross-section data:
- X-ray production by heavy-ion impact is much more efficient than by proton impact;
- resonances occur in the ion-induced X-ray production if there is a matching of electron-energy levels in the two particles.
These experimental findings are qualitatively well understood in terms of quasi-molecule formation and crossings of molecular orbitals during the collision. In addition mean fluorescence yields have been obtained by comparison of X-ray emission cross-sections and Auger-excitation cross-sections. These fluorescence yields appear to be strongly dependent on the defect configuration of the atom involved.

High resolution X-ray spectrometry shows an abundance of satellite lines produced in ion-atom collisions. The observed subshell splittings and line shifts yield detailed information on the complex excitation and de-excitation processes involved.

Finally the main conclusions are summarized along with a discussion of possible further investigations.

1. Introduction

Although the first experimental observation of ion-induced X-ray production was made by Coates in 1934 [1], it had to be re-discovered that, besides electrons, photons and protons, also heavy ions can be employed for X-ray production. In ion-atom collisions it is generally observed that each atomic shell gets readily excited when the collision forces an interpenetration of electron shells of comparable binding energy. The creation of a vacancy in the atomic shells initiates two competing rearrangement processes: an Auger transition may occur which gives rise to the emission of electrons, and a radiative decay may also occur, leading to emission of photons in the (soft) X-ray region.

The aim of this report is to show what progress is being made in the understanding of atomic collision processes by studying X-ray production in ion-atom collisions. Total cross-section measurements will be discussed as well as high-resolution X-ray spectrometry. An outline of the main conclusions, to which the present experimental investigations lead, will be given, rather than a discussion of the various experimental techniques. Although the list of references may serve as a bibliography, it is impossible to go into the details of all these very interesting data. For a review article on ion-induced X-rays one is referred to Khan and coworkers [2].

2. Total cross-sections

2.1. *Experimental results*

Inner-shell ionization and X-ray production by proton impact have received much attention in the theoretical work of Merzbacher and Lewis [3], Bang and Hansteen [4] and more recently Garcia [5], Hansteen and Mosebekk [6] and Basbas et al. [7]. Most of the data and references can be found in Khandelwal et al. [8]

Only recently soft X-ray emission in heavy-ion-atom collisions became a subject of interest. For obvious reasons the first problem solved was: "Do proton impacts differ substantially from those of electron-carrying ions?" [9]. The mechanism responsible for inner-shell ionization by proton impact is believed to be a direct Coulomb interaction between the proton and the inner-shell electron involved. A classical binary-encounter model is found to be in good agreement with experimental cross-section data, see the above refs. [2-7]. At comparable impact energies the cross-sections for proton impacts are 3 to 5 orders of magnitude lower than the cross-sections for heavy-ion impact. This is illustrated in fig. 1 by the results for C K-shell excitation in collisions of $Z^+ \to C$ [10] and in fig. 2 for Ar L-shell X-ray production in collisions of $Z^+ \to Ar$ [11]. From these data we may indeed conclude that the inner-shell-excitation mechanism in heavy-ion-atom collisions is different from that for proton impact, see also [12-14]. In the case of heavy-ion-atom encounters it is supposed that during the collision a short-lived quasi-molecule is formed and inner-shell electrons are promoted because energy-level crossings occur as the projectile approaches the target atom close enough.

If one plots the total cross-section data as a function of the atomic number Z, resonances appear for those collisions in which there is a matching of electron-energy levels in the two particles. This was first observed in 1965 by Specht [15], who provided the first systematic outline of the dependence of

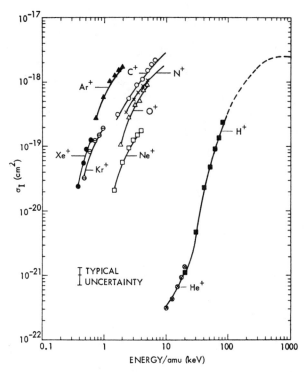

Fig. 1. Carbon K-shell excitation cross-section, σ_I, as a function of incident-ion energy per amu [10].

the X-ray emission cross-section on the overlap of inner-shells involved. He studied X-ray emission from collisions of energetic fission fragments on metal targets, see fig. 3. Similar results have been obtained for the Cu L-shell X-ray production studied in collisions of $Z^+ \rightarrow$ Cu, see fig. 4, or the reverse $Cu^+ \rightarrow$ Z, see fig. 5 [16]. If one plots the data of fig. 2 as a function of Z one obtains fig. 6 [11]. These results can be summarized by stating that resonances appear for symmetrical and quasi-symmetrical cases where the binding energy of the inner-shell under study is about equal to the binding energy of one of the inner-shells of the collision partner. So far two exceptions to this "rule" have been observed: Cairns et al. [17] find maxima in addition to the expected resonances; Datz et al. [18] observe an anomaly for MeV ions which indicates that spin-orbit coupling should be taken into account also. These experimental findings serve as a direct test for the Molecular-Orbital (MO) concept, known as the Fano-Lichten model [19].

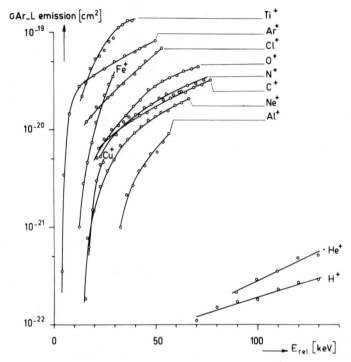

Fig. 2. Cross-section for Ar L-shell X-ray emission in collisions of $Z^+ \rightarrow$ Ar versus the incident ion energy E_{rel} (in the centre of mass system) [11].

2.2. Theoretical investigations

As discussed in previous papers of this volume, [20] and [21], Lichten [22] has constructed energy-level diagrams of MO's of the Ar-Ar and Ne-Ne systems. At various internuclear distances there occur crossings of energy levels. If the distance of closest approach during the collision becomes small enough, then at a crossing an electron may be promoted to a higher energy level. In the Ar-Ar case the numerous crossings of the $4f\sigma$ MO with higher orbitals in a short region of internuclear distances does account for the promotion of Ar L-shell electrons.

Recently Kessel [23, 24] suggested to determine critical internuclear distances from the energy dependence of total X-ray emission cross-sections. In the first approximation, one assumes that the inner-shell excitation is dependent only on the distance of closest approach, r_0, of the two nuclei. Further-

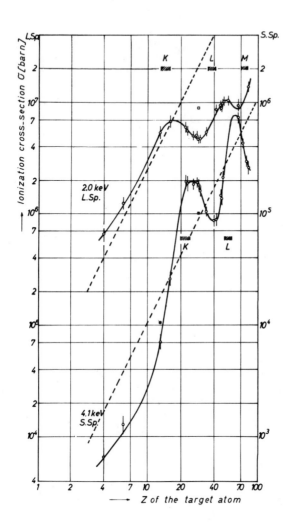

Fig. 3. L-shell ionization cross-sections of light (L.Sp) and heavy (S.Sp) fission fragments as a function of the atmic number of the target atom. The impact energy of the fission fragments is in between 74 and 42 MeV. Dashed lines represent calculations based on the Born approximation. The regions of overlap of binding energies of the K-, L- and M-shells of the target atoms and projectiles are indicated [15].

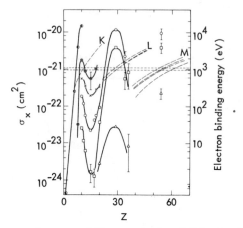

Fig. 4. Cross-sections, σ_x, for copper L X-ray production (left-hand scale) in a thick copper target as a function of the atomic number of the incident ion, for different, fixed, ion energies per atomic mass unit (i.e. fixed ion velocities): Δ 10 keV/amu; □ 2.0 keV/amu; ○ 3.0 keV/amu; × 5.0 keV/amu; ⊗ 10keV/amu; ◖ 50keV/amu. The dashed lines represent ground-state electron binding energies of the target atoms and the horizontal lines represent copper L-shell binding energies (right-hand scale) [16].

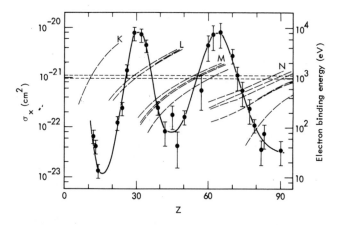

Fig. 5. Cross-sections, σ_x, for copper L X-ray production (left-hand scale) in incident copper ions striking solid metal targets, as a function of the target atomic number. The impact energy is fixed 160 keV (2.5 keV/amu). The dashed lines represent ground-state electron binding energies (right-hand scale) for the target atoms and the projectile [16].

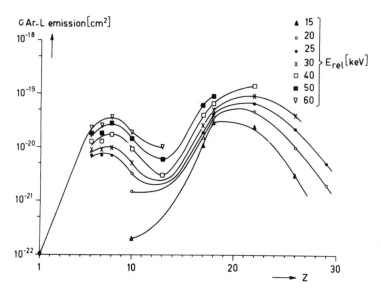

Fig. 6. Cross-sections for Ar L-shell X-ray emission in collisions of $Z^+ \to$ Ar versus the atomic number of the projectile. The data are plotted for a set of impact energies (in c.m. system) [11].

more, it is assumed that excitation occurs only for r_0 smaller than a certain critical internuclear distance r_c and that the excitation probability, P, is constant in this region. If $p(r_c)$ is the impact parameter p at which the distance of closest approach, r_0, equals r_c, then the expression for the inner-shell excitation cross-section is:

$$\sigma_I = P \pi p^2(r_c) . \tag{1}$$

Using a screened Coulomb interaction potential, the impact parameter as a function of the distance of closest approach may be written as:

$$p(r_0) = r_0 [1 - (b/r_0) \exp(-r_0/a)]^{1/2} , \tag{2}$$

where

$$b = Z_1 Z_2 e^2/E_0 , \qquad a = a_0/[Z_1^{2/3} + Z_2^{2/3}]^{1/2} ,$$

Z_1 and Z_2 are the atomic numbers of the atom and ion, e is the elementary charge, E_0 is the kinetic energy of the projectile, a_0 is the first Bohr radius. The energy dependence of the cross section can be found from formulae (1) and (2):

$$\sigma_I(E_o) = P\pi r_c^2 \left[1 - \frac{Z_1 Z_2 e^2}{E_o r_c} \exp(-r_c/a) \right] . \tag{3}$$

The X-ray emission cross section is then given by

$$\sigma_{em}(E_o) = \bar{\omega}\, \sigma_I(E_o) \tag{4}$$

where $\bar{\omega}$ is the mean fluorescence yield, discussed in section 3.

The threshold behaviour of $\sigma_{em}(E_o)$ is sufficient to determine the value of r_c, for the type of emission whose total cross-section is measured; $\bar{\omega}$, the mean fluorescence yield, will be used as a parameter which is determined by the best fit between the curves of the calculated excitation cross-sections and measured emission cross sections. In the case of Ar^+ on Ar many crossings of the $4f\sigma$ orbital with higher levels occur as the internuclear separation becomes smaller than $0.3 \times 10^{-8}\text{\AA}$. So, according to Lichten [22], the probability for Ar L-shell ionization is estimated to be one at such close collisions (see also ref. [21]). Since there are two argon atoms involved, two L-shell electrons

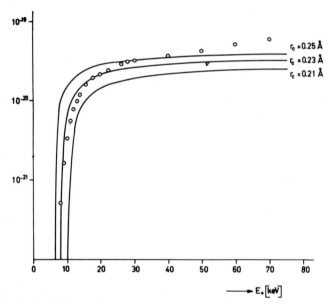

Fig. 7. The Ar-L emission cross-section measurements (O) are compared with the calculated (−) cross section $\bar{\omega} \times \sigma_I(E_e)$ for different r_c: (0.25Å, 0.23 Å, 0.21 Å) in the Ar^+ on Ar case; $P = 2$; $\bar{\omega} = 1.1 \times 10^{-3}$ [25].

will be promoted and P in eq. (3) will be 2 for $r_0 \leqslant r_c$. The energy dependence of the cross-section is calculated using eq. (3) for different values of r_c: 0.25 Å, 0.23 Å, 0.21 Å. The calculated $\sigma_I(E_0)$ is compared with the measured $\sigma_{em}(E_0)$ in fig. 7 [25]. The threshold behaviour of $\sigma_{em}(E_0)$ is best described by $r_c = 0.23$Å, which means that in this model 0.23 Å is the critical internuclear separation of the two Ar particles at which the Ar L-shell excitation takes place. A difference of 10% in r_c is more than enough to give a discrepancy in cross-sections near threshold of an order of magnitude.

The same procedure can be followed in order to determine the critical internuclear distances r_c for Ar L-shell excitation in heteronuclear collisions. In fig. 8 the r_c values for Ar L-shell excitation in collisions of Z^+ on Ar are plotted versus the atomic number Z [11]. A comparison is made with data on the "active r_0 region" where structure in the inelastic energy loss distribution is observed by other investigators [26]-[29]. Going from Cu ($Z = 29$) to Ar ($Z = 18$) the critical internuclear distance increases steadily until $Z = 13$. For $Z = 25, 19, 18, 17, 16, 15$ and 13 the "active r_0 regions" are shown as ob-

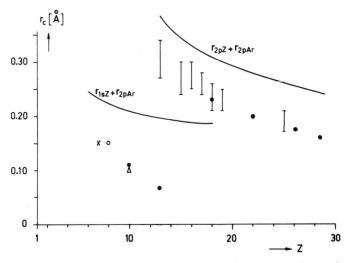

Fig. 8. Critical internuclear distances for Ar L-shell excitations in collisions of Z^+ on Ar plotted versus Z; • from X-ray measurements [11], from structure in inelastic energy loss distributions: I "active r_0 regions" [26], Δ from ref. [27], ○ from ref. [28], × from ref. [29].

The solid lines show the sum of the radii of maximum charge density for the wave functions of 2p electrons of argon and 2p or 1s electrons of the projectile [11].

served by Fastrup et al. [26], who attribute the structure in the inelastic
energy-loss distribution found for $13 \leqslant Z < 18$ to L-shell excitation not of argon
but of the projectile. For Al$^+$ ($Z=13$) on Ar we observe an interesting case: at
large internuclear distances (0.27 Å $\leqslant r_c \leqslant$ 0.34 Å) Al L-shell excitation occurs, whereas for a much smaller value of r_c (= 0.07 Å) the Ar L-shell photon
is observed. The Al L-shell vacancy is produced at internuclear distances small
enough to cause an interpenetration of L-shells of projectile and target atom.
In order to produce an Ar L-shell vacancy we have to force the collision partners to internuclear distances for which the Al K-shell and Ar L-shell overlap.
In fig. 3 the r_c values increase again going from $Z = 13$ to 6/7 where we can
only indicate a lower limit to r_c, but inelastic energy loss measurements give
here $r_c \approx 0.15$ Å [28], [29]. In order to illustrate the geometrical effect of
the shell sizes one can simply add the radii of maximum charge density for
the wave functions of 2p electrons of argon and 2p or 1s electrons of the projectile. This is shown in fig. 8 by the solid lines for $r_{2pZ} + r_{2pAr}$ and $r_{1sZ} +$
r_{2pAr}. The data strongly suggest that the excitation of the Ar L-shell happens
for $Z \leqslant 18$ via interaction of the L-shells of projectile and target atom, whereas
for $6 \leqslant Z < 18$ the excitation is dominated by a K-L overlap. Apparently a
considerable overlap of interacting shells is required before excitation takes
place.

Recently Lichten and Barat [30] have elaborated an extension of the
Fano-Lichten model for asymmetrical systems. Among others they show that
in a correlation diagram the 2p orbital of the atom with the lower atomic
number is correlated with the 4 fσ MO, and several crossings are found. The
2p orbital of the heavier atom is correlated with the 3dσ MO, being much less
coupled to higher MO's. Therefore it is always the L-electron of the lower Z
atom which is promoted. In this way it is explained why in collisions of $Z^+ \rightarrow$
Ar for $Z \geqslant 18$ Ar L-shell X-rays are observed whereas for $Z < 18$ the Ar
L-shell excitation is found to be much reduced. For $Z < 6$ the correlation
diagram does not show any crossing which allows a promotion of Ar 2p- electrons. So the X-ray production cross-section is expected to decrease drastically for $Z < 6$ as is observed for protons in figs. 2 and 6. For an extensive discussion of the Fano-Lichten model for asymmetrical systems one is referred
to Barat and Lichten [30], and Larkins [31].

Finally it should be noted here that the shape of the K-shell and L-shell
excitation functions as determined experimentally appear to be different,
thus showing the difference in coupling mechanism between different MO's.
In contradiction to the C K-shell excitation functions of fig. 1, which gradually increase with impact energy, the Ar L-shell data of fig. 2 rise sharply
over two orders of magnitude beyond the threshold. These K-shell excitations

occur via rotational coupling of the 2pσ and the 2pπ MO's [22]. Since this coupling is strongly velocity dependent, the above velocity-independent model is not expected to be valid. Fortner and co-workers [32] have applied the Landau-Zener formula to calculate the C K-shell excitation probability in collisions of $Z^+ \rightarrow$ C. Although it is not clear why Landau-Zener should be applicable in the case of rotational coupling, the experimental data nicely follow this Landau-Zener type of velocity dependency.

3. Fluorescence yields

Historically, the fluorescence yield of an element was defined in terms of the intensity of fluorescent radiation produced when a sample of material was exposed to a beam of energetic X-rays. More recently, it has been defined in terms of the probability that a vacancy in a given shell results in a radiative transition. An extensive review on atomic fluorescence yields has been published by Fink et al. [33]. Besides photons and electrons, heavy charged particles can also be employed for primary vacancy production. An advantage in using ion bombardment is that the characteristic X-rays produced are free of the usual bremsstrahlung background present when electron bombardment is used. According to eq. (4) the mean fluorescence yield $\bar{\omega}$ can be deduced from $\sigma_I(E_o)$ and $\sigma_{em}(E_o)$ because:

$$\bar{\omega} = \sigma_{em}(E_o)/\sigma_I(F_o). \tag{5}$$

In many cases $\sigma_I(E_o)$ is neither theoretically nor experimentally very well known. However, the inner-shell excitation cross-section is related to $\sigma_A(E_o)$, the cross section for Auger-electron emission, by:

$$\sigma_I(E_o) = \sigma_A(E_o) + \sigma_{em}(E_o). \tag{6}$$

So the mean fluorescence yield can be computed from the X-ray emission cross-section and the Auger-electron emission cross-section because substitution of eq. (6) into eq. (5) yields:

$$\bar{\omega} = \sigma_{em}(E_o)/[\sigma_A(E_o) + \sigma_{em}(E_o)]. \tag{7}$$

As an example we use eq. (7) to calculate the fluorescence yield for the Ar L-shell and Ne K-shell. Cacak et al. [24] evaluated cross-sections for "Auger excitation" by simply integrating the area of the fast electron peak in the secondary-electron cross-section curve. However, after creation of an inner-shell vacancy it is not necessary that an Auger-de-excitation process results in the emission of one and only one fast electron. Many electron de-excitation processes may also occur, although no evidence of this kind was found in a recent coincidence study of $Ar^+ + Ar$ collisions [34]. For σ_A in eq. (7) we may only use the "Auger-excitation" cross-section Cacak et al. [24], if we assume many-electron de-excitation processes to be negligible. These Auger-excitation cross-sections are listed in table 1 together with the results on the Ar L-shell and Ne K-shell X-ray emission cross-sections and the fluorescence yields as calculated with eq. (7). It is very remarkable that both fluorescence yields tend to increase by a factor 2 as the impact energy of the ion, E_0, is doubled. This might be caused by the excitation mechanism, since heavy ion-atom collisions excite states which have many electrons promoted, also of the outer shells. A high degree of excitation or ionization of the outer-shell diminishes the Auger transition rate and increases the radiative transition rate relatively! Larkins [35] was able to calculate the fluorescence yields ω_K and $\omega_{L2,3}$ for various defect atomic configurations of the argon atom by means of a statistical weighting procedure. These calculations show a drastic increase over orders of magnitude for $\omega_{L2,3}$, changes in ω_K are much less as has been discussed also by Burch et al. [36]. This change in fluorescence yield must also explain why in fig. 7 the calculated cross-sections at higher impact energies are always lower than the measured ones which steadily increase with E_0, compare also Cacak et al. [24].

As stated above innner-shell excitation during proton bombardment is believed to be caused by a direct scattering mechanism. Probably this more

Table 1

Mean fluorescence yields, $\bar{\omega}_L$ and $\bar{\omega}_K$, for the Ar L-shell and Ne K-shell respectively, deduced from σ_A and σ_{em} in symmetric collisions.

E_0 [keV]	Ne$^+$ on Ne collision		
	$\sigma_A(E_0)$ [cm^2]	$\sigma_{em}(E_0)$ [cm^2]	$\bar{\omega}_K$
50	0.27×10^{-20}	4.30×10^{-23}	1.6×10^{-2}
100	2.71×10^{-20}	8.95×10^{-22}	3.2×10^{-2}

E_0 [keV]	Ar$^+$ on Ar collision		
	$\sigma_A(E_0)$ [cm^2]	$\sigma_{em}(E_0)$ [cm^2]	$\bar{\omega}_L$
50	3.30×10^{-17}	4.18×10^{-20}	1.2×10^{-3}
100	3.87×10^{-17}	8.20×10^{-20}	2.1×10^{-3}

gentle way of inner-shell excitation leaves the outer-shell more or less undisturbed (see also the next section). Therefore the fluorescence yield in this case is expected to be lower than after excitation with a heavy ion. Volz and Rudd [37] obtained Ar L-Auger-excitation cross-sections in the same way as above for 125-300 keV proton impact on Ar. At 125 keV proton energy σ_A = 6 x 10^{-19} cm^2 and σ_{em} = 3 x 10^{-22} cm^2. So $\bar{\omega}$ = 5 x 10^{-4} and indeed the fluorescence yield is found to be lower than obtained in the Ar$^+$ → Ar experiment (table 1).

4. High resolution spectroscopy

Generally a thin window proportional counter has been used for measuring total yields in the soft X-ray region, which have been discussed in the previous sections. In the ultra-soft X-ray region, however, the use of wavelength dispersion is necessary in order to observe any subshell splitting or X-ray line shift. In the harder X-ray region, energy dispersion is applicable by means of a liquid nitrogen cooled Si(Li) detector. This latter detector has been employed to detect K-shell X-rays produced by MeV proton and oxygen bombardment of Ni, Cu, Ca and V [38]. With a system resolution of 180 eV (FWHM) at 5.9 KeV photon energy, one is able to distinguish K_α from K_β lines. An interesting observation is: relative to proton bombardments the K_α lines produced by oxygen bombardments are shifted ≈ 50 eV, the K_β lines are shifted ≈ 150 eV. The observed effect is interpreted as due to multiple ionization of the outer shell occurring during heavy-ion-atom collisions simultaneously with the inner-shell ionization. The influence of the ionization on the shielding of the nuclear charge causes the line shift. Similar effects have been observed in X-ray spectra of the Al K-shell [39], Si K-shell [40], Fe K-shell [36], Ni, Cu, Zn L-shells [41, 42], L and M X-ray spectra of I [43, 18], Mo, Yb, Au [43].

As shown in fig. 9 the Al K-shell X-ray spectra [39] show an abundance of well resolved satellite lines. It is suggested that the five peaks on the high energy side of the $K_{\alpha 1,2}$ line in the nitrogen excited spectrum are K_α satellite lines from atoms with one through five vacancies in the L-shell. With the nitrogen-ion excitation the integrated K_β satellite spectrum is about 77% as intense as the integrated K_α satellite spectrum. Ordinarily the K_β band is about 1% of the $K_{\alpha 1,2}$ line. This difference must be attributed to the dependence of the fluorescence yield on the degree of ionization as discussed in the previous section. The relative intensities of satellites within the two groups, together with a knowledge of the fluorescence yields and transition rates for multiply ionized states allow determination of the relative probability of

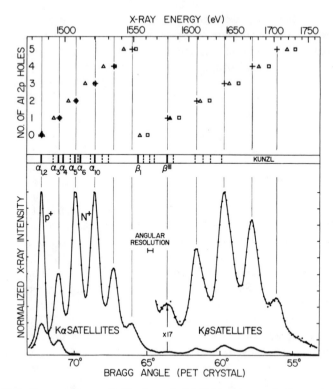

Fig. 9. Al K_α X-ray spectra excited by impact of 5 MeV protons and nitrogen ions on Al metal. At the top, the measured peak energies (+) are compared with X-ray energies obtained from the Herman-Skillman program (□) and a screening-constant program (△). Energies of the $K_{\alpha 1,2}$, K_β, and the satellite lines measured by Kunzl are indicated, with the stronger lines labeled and the weaker satellites shown by dashed lines [39].

producing the various initial multiple vacancy configurations, see for instance Burch et al. [36].

An interesting observation has also been made by Der et al. [41]. Zinc targets have been bombarded with 8, 15 and 20 MeV oxygen ions. As the bombarding energy is increased, the size of the shift in the principle peak relative to the proton case decreases; the same effect has been observed by Burch [44] also. The authors state that the observation is consistent with the expected decrease in cross-section for M- and N-shell ionization as a result of the larger velocities of the projectiles as compared to the 3d-electron velocity. It should be noted here that at these high impact energies the influence of recoil atoms cannot be denied [45]. In addition calculations done by House

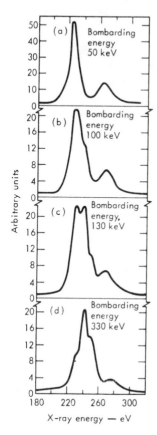

Fig. 10. X-ray spectra observed for several impact energies in $Ar^+ \rightarrow$ Ar collisions [47].

[46] show a small decrease in the K_α-line shift as the 3d-shell is depleted. Such an effect might occur for L_α-lines as well.

Sofar high-resolution X-ray spectra have been obtained from solid targets, with one exception only. Khan's group [47] has been able to measure the Ar L-shell X-ray spectrum emitted during $Ar^+ +$ Ar collisions. Their results are shown in fig. 10. The principle lines shift to higher energies. The main peak consists of one line of energy 224 ± 4 eV at 50 keV incident ion energy, whereas at 330 keV at least three lines with energies 230, 240 and 250 eV may be distinguished. The authors suggest the observation of a double L-shell vacancy as observed also in their MeV work [41]. However calculations made by Larkins [48] show that the $3s \rightarrow 2p$ transition energy shifts from 225 to 250 eV as the charge state of the ion increases from 2+ to 7+. The smaller peak in fig. 10 near 264 eV also shifts to higher energies with increasing impact energy. This line is identified as due to the transitions 4s → 2p and 3d → 2p within the expected neutral Ar atom with one 2p vacancy.

5. Conclusions and possible extensions

Summarizing the present experimental results we see that protons and alpha particles act like point charges, no molecular effects are observed as in the case of heavier projectiles. In heteronuclear collisions it is the inner-shell electron of the lighter atom which is promoted, and resonances occur whenever there is a matching of electron-energy levels. Qualitatively these results can be understood within the frame work of the Fano-Lichten model extended. Critical internuclear distances for inner-shell excitation have been deduced from the threshold of the cross-section. The shape of the excitation function reveals some information on the coupling mechanisms which generally appear to be different for K-shell and L-shell excitations, see also ref. [49]. After this phenomenological approach it is about time for differential cross-section measurements such as have been started by the Jülich group [50].

Mean fluorescence yields have been obtained from X-ray emission cross-sections and Auger excitation cross-sections. These fluorescence yields depend strongly on the configuration of the atom involved. A knowledge of the fluorescence yield for multiple-vacancy configurations allows determination of the state of the X-ray emitting particle from the emitted satellite spectrum. These spectra have given evidence for the creation of multiple vacancies in inner and outer shells occurring simultaneously in heavy ion excitation.

The state of the outer shell largely dominates X-ray production in heavy-ion-atom collisions. This is important to note if one wants to determine X-ray emission cross-sections from thick-targets yields [51]. On the other hand it is expected that comparison [52] of intensities of satellite lines emitted from solid and gaseous targets reveals additional information on the "density effect", i.e. the dramatic difference between charge state distributions resulting from the passage of ions through gases and solids [53]. Since the time between two successive collisions in a solid target is very short, the possibility is opened also to study ion-atom collisions with projectiles having an inner-shell vacancy (the 2p vacancy life-time of argon is about an order of magnitude larger than the collision time). This will cause a hole in one of the MO's during the collision, which increases the probability of promotion of electrons from lower MO's. Such electrons cannot be promoted in single-collision experiments in gases, so we expect X-rays from states which are excited during double collisions in solids which cannot be observed otherwise [54]. Finally these "holes" in MO's may also decay during the collision, thus giving rise to X-ray emission from short-lived quasi-molecular states formed during the collision. At very small impact parameter collisions it might even be possible to observe X-rays from the short-lived united atom [55].

Acknowledgements

This work is part of the research program of the Stichting voor Fundamenteel Onderzoek dat Materie (Foundation for Fundamental Research on Matter) and was made possible by financial support from the Nederlandse Organisatie voor Zuiver-Wetenschappelijk Onderzoek (Netherlands Organization for the Advancement of Pure Research).

References

[1] W. M. Coates, Phys. Rev. *46* (1934) 542.
[2] J. Khan et al., Rev. Mod. Phys., to be published.
[3] E. Merzbacher and H. W. Lewis, *Encyclopedia of Physics,* Ed. S. Flügge, Vol. 34 (Springer Verlag, Berlin, 1958) p. 166.
[4] J. Bang and J. M. Hansteen, K. Danske Vidensk. Selsk. Mat. Fys. Medd. *31* (1959) 13.
[5] J. D. Garcia, Phys. Rev. A *1* (1970) 280; ibid. A *1* (1970) 1402.
[6] J. M. Hansteen and O. P. Mosebekk, Z. Phys. *234* (1970) 281.
[7] G. Basbas, W. Brandt and R. Laubert, Phys. Letters *34A* (1971) 277.
[8] G. S. Khandelwal, B. H. Choi and E. Merzbacher, Atomic Data *1* (1969) 103.
[9] U. Fano, Comments Atomic Molecular Phys. *1* (1969) 1.
[10] R. C. Der, T. M. Kavanagh, J. M. Khan, B. P. Curry and R. J. Fortner, Phys. Rev. Letters *21* (1968) 1731; Phys. Rev. A *4* (1971) 556.
[11] F. W. Saris, Physica *52* (1971) 290.
[12] W. Brandt and R. Laubert, Phys. Rev. Letters *24* (1970) 1037.
[13] P. B. Needham Jr. and B. D. Sartwell, Phys. Rev. A *2* (1970) 27.
[14] M. Terasawa, T. Tamura and H. Kamada, *VII ICPEAC, Abstracts of Papers,* Eds. L. M. Branscomb et al., Vol. 1 (North-Holland Publishing Co., Amsterdam 1971) p. 416.
[15] H. J. Specht, Z. Phys. *185* (1965) 301.
[16] T. M. Kavanagh. M. E. Cunningham, R. C. Der, R. J. Fortner, J. M. Khan, E. J. Zaharis and J. D. Garcia, Phys. Rev. Letters *25* (1970) 1473.
[17] J. A. Cairns, D. F. Holloway and R. S. Nelson, *Atomic Collision Phenomena in Solids,* Eds. D.W. Palmer, M.W. Thompson and P.D. Townsend (North-Holland Publishing Co., Amsterdam, 1970) p. 541.

[18] S. Datz, C. D. Moak, B. R. Appleton and T. A. Carlson, Phys. Rev. Letters 27 (1971) 363.

[19] U. Fano and W. Lichten, Phys. Rev. Letters 14 (1965) 627.

[20] E. Rudd, VII ICPEAC, Invited Talks and Progress Reports, Eds. T. R. Govers and F. J. de Heer (North-Holland Publishing Co., Amsterdam, 1971) 107.

[21] Q. Kessel, VII ICPEAC, Invited Talks and Progress Reports, Eds. T. R. Govers and F. J. de Heer (North-Holland Publishing Co., Amsterdam, 1971) 126.

[22] W. Lichten. Phys. Rev. 164 (1967) 131.

[23] Q. C. Kessel, Bull. Amer. Phys. Soc. 14 (1969) 946, and private communication.

[24] R. K. Cacak, Q. C. Kessel and M. E. Rudd, Phys. Rev. A 2 (1970) 1327.

[25] F. W. Saris and D. Onderdelinden, Physica 49 (1970) 441.

[26] B. Fastrup, G. Hermann and K. J. Smith, Phys. Rev. A 3 (1971) 159.

[27] V. V. Afrosimov, Yu. S. Gordeev, A. M. Polyansky and A. P. Shergin, VI ICPEAC, Abstracts of Papers, Ed. I. Amdur (MIT Press, Cambridge, Massachusetts, 1969) p. 744.

[28] F. W. Bingham, Phys. Rev. 182 (1969) 180.

[29] E.J. Knystautas, Q.C. Kessel, R. Del Boca and H.C. Hayden, Phys. Rev. A 1 (1970) 825.

[30] M. Barat and W. Lichten, to be published.

[31] F. Larkins, to be published.

[32] R.J. Fortner, B.P. Curry, R.C. Der, T.M. Kavanagh and J.M. Khan, Phys. Rev. 185 (1969) 164.

[33] R.W. Fink, R.C. Jopson, H. Mark and C.D. Swift, Rev. Mod. Phys. 38 (1966) 513.

[34] G.M. Thomson, P.C. Laudieri, W.W. Smith and A. Russek Phys. Rev. A 3 (1971) 2028

[35] F.P. Larkins, J. Phys. B 4 (1971) L 29.

[36] D. Burch, P. Richard and R.L. Blake, Phys. Rev. Letters 26 (1971) 1355.

[37] D.J. Volz and M.E. Rudd, Phys. Rev. A 2 (1970) 1395.

[38] P. Richard, I.L. Morgan, T. Furuta and D. Burch, Phys. Rev. Letters 23 (1969) 1009; P. Richard, T.I. Bonner, T. Furuta, I.L. Morgan and J.R. Rhodes, Phys. Rev. A 1 (1970) 1044; D. Burch and P. Richard, Phys. Rev. Letters 25 (1970) 983.

[39] A. Knudson, D. Nagel, P. Burkhalter and K.L. Dunning, Phys. Rev. Letters 26 (1971) 1149.

[40] P. Richard and D. McCrary, Bull. Amer. Phys. Soc. 16 (1971) 847.

[41] R.C. Der, R.J. Fortner, T.M. Kavanagh, J.M. Khan and J.D. Garcia, Phys. Letters 36A (1971) 239.

[42] M. Terasawa, private communication.

[43] P.H. Mokler, Phys. Rev. Letters 26 (1971) 811.

[44] D. Burch, private communication.

[45] K. Taulbjerg and P. Sigmund, to be published.

[46] L. House, Astr. Phys. J. Suppl. 18 (1969) 21.

[47] M.E. Cummingham, R.C. Der, R.J. Fortner, T.M. Kavanagh, J.M. Khan, C.B. Layne, E.J. Zaharis and J.D. Garcia, Phys. Rev. Letters 24 (1970) 931.

[48] F. Larkins, J. Phys. B 4 (1971) 1.

[49] B. Fastrup, G. Herman and Q. Kessel, Phys. Rev. Letters 27 (1971) 177.

[50] H.J. Stein, H.O. Lutz, P.G. Mokler, K. Sistemmich and P. Armbruster, Phys. Rev. Letters 24 (1970) 701.

[51] F.W. Saris and D.J. Bierman, Phys. Letters 35A (1971) 199.

[52] H. Tawara and F.W. Saris, to be published, H. Lutz, H.J. Stein, S. Datz and C. Moak, to be published.

[53] S. Datz, C.D. Moak, H.O. Lutz, L.C. Northcliffe and L.B. Bridwell, Atomic Data 2 (1971) 273.

[54] J. Macek, private communication.

[55] F.W. Saris, W.F. v.d. Weg, H. Tawara, R. Laubert and A. Ratkowski, Phys. Rev. Letters, to be published.

Physics of Electronic and Atomic Collisions, VII ICPEAC, 1971 − North-Holland (1972)

THEORY OF PSEUDO-STATE EXPANSIONS*

R.J.DAMBURG

*Institute of Physics of the Latvian Academy of Sciences,
Riga, Salaspils, USSR*

The development of the close-coupling approximation for the last decade is considered. Attention is given to the role of the minimum principle.
In the approximation the total wave function is expanded in terms of
atomic eigenstates. Only inclusion of open channels is strictly necessary in
the expansion.

The correlation method is a generalization of the close-coupling approximation. In the correlation method closed channels are allowed for through
short-range correlation terms. The correlation method is not always sufficiently effective as regards long-range interactions: 1) the resonances are
better described if atomic eigenstates for the "new" channels are explicitly
taken into account below the thresholds, 2) the behaviour for the elastic
scattering phase shift will be exact at $k \rightarrow 0$ if the pseudo-state is introduced,
3) introduction of the pseudo-states allows to take into account the dipole
polarizability of atomic states for the multi-channel case.

In the intermediate energy range the minimum principle in its present form
cannot be satisfied. In this case the pseudo-states describe approximately
the flux into all open channels.

The applicability of the Born approximation is considered for normalization of cross-sections for excitation of 2p and 2s states at high energies.

1. The close-coupling method

The close-coupling method proposed by Massey and Mohr in 1932 [1] is
the most natural and powerful approximation for solving the electron-atom
scattering problems when the energy is low. In this method (as applied to the
electron-hydrogen scattering problem) the two-electron wavefunction
$\psi_{LM}(\mathbf{r}_1,\mathbf{r}_2)$ is expanded in terms of target eigenstates with unknown scattering coefficients.

---

* Read by title only.

$$\Psi_{LM}(\mathbf{r}_1,\mathbf{r}_2) = \frac{1}{r_1 r_2} \sum_{nl_1 l_2} u_{nl_1}(r_1) F_{nl_1 l_2}(r_2) \mathcal{Y}^M_{L\,_1 l_1 l_2}(\hat{\mathbf{r}}_1,\hat{\mathbf{r}}_2) \pm (1 \rightleftharpoons 2) , \qquad (1)$$

where

$$\mathcal{Y}^M_{L\,_1 l_1, l_2}(\hat{\mathbf{r}}_1,\hat{\mathbf{r}}_2) = \sum_{m_1 m_2} (l_1 l_2 m_1 m_2 | LM) \mathcal{Y}_{l_1 m_1}(\hat{\mathbf{r}}_1) \mathcal{Y}_{l_2 m_2}(\hat{\mathbf{r}}_2)$$

and $\mathcal{Y}^M_{L\,_1 l_1 l_2}(\hat{\mathbf{r}}_1,\hat{\mathbf{r}}_2)$ are orthogonalized angular parts of the two-electron wave function, $(l_1 l_2 m_1 m_2 | LM)$ are Clebsch–Gordon coefficients, $F_{nl_1 l_2}(r) = F_\nu(r)$ is the radial part of the free electron wave function, $u_{nl_1}(r) = u_\nu(r)$ is the reduced atomic radial wave function, L is the total angular momentum of the system of two electrons.

Substituting (1) into the Schrödinger equation (2)

$$(H-E)\Psi(\mathbf{r}_1 \mathbf{r}_2) = \left(-\tfrac{1}{2}\nabla^2_1 - \tfrac{1}{2}\nabla^2_2 - \frac{1}{r_1} + \frac{1}{r_{12}} - E \right) \Psi(\mathbf{r}_1,\mathbf{r}_2) = 0 \qquad (2)$$

then yields the set of coupled integro-differential equations for radial functions derived by Percival and Seaton in 1957 [2] :

$$\left[\frac{d^2}{dr^2} - \frac{l_2(l_2+1)}{r^2} + k^2_\nu \right] F_\nu(r) = 2 \sum_{\nu'} [V_{\nu\nu'}(r) - W_{\nu\nu'}(r)] F_{\nu'}(r) , \qquad (3)$$

where k_ν is the wave number and $V_{\nu\nu'}(r)$ are potential interaction terms and $W_{\nu\nu'}(r)$ exchange interaction terms.

Since one cannot solve an infinite set of coupled equations, the atomic states which enter into the expansions of the total wave function (1) are confined to just a few of the lowest lying states giving rise to a finite set of coupled integro-differential equations. This is called a close-coupling approximation.

The first calculations along these lines were concerned with 1s–2s excitation and neglected the exchange and coupling to all states other than the initial and final states [3].

In the sixties the close-coupling approximation was used by various groups of physicists, including those in Riga [4]. Above all we should mention the thorough and sophisticated calculations which were performed by P.G.Burke and K.Smith and their colleagues [5–7].

The results obtained from the 1s–2s–2p approximation proved to be most interesting [4–9]. It was shown [8] that the coupling between the degenerate states causes the resonances below the threshold and oscillations of the cross-sections above the threshold. The excitation cross-section remains finite in the neighbourhood of the threshold. These theoretical predictions were confirmed experimentally [10–13].

Because of the probable importance of coupling to higher states, Burke and Schey [14] investigated the convergence of the close-coupling approximation by solving the system of 1s–2s–2p–3s–3p equations. The convergence in the method left much to be desired. Schwartz's variational calculations [15], the method of polarized orbitals [16] and Temkin's non-adiabatic method [17] were important for an understanding of the scattering problem, including the close-coupling method.

Notwithstanding the obvious success of the close-coupling method the situation remained not quite satisfactory for a long time. The only method of qualitative estimation of the calculations was comparison of the calculated cross-sections with the experimental results. And it is known that such comparison is not always to be relied upon. The above in no way diminishes the importance of experimental investigations for theoretical physicists as well. The advance of the theory of electron-atom collisions would not have been so rapid, had not the last decade seen great progress of experimental investigations. However, not only contact of theory with experiments was required, but their certain intrinsic independence and intrinsic criteria for the estimation of the quality of the results. It was just this that the close-coupling method and the theory of collisions in general were lacking.

It seems strange now, but even after thorough calculations on the elastic scattering of electrons on atomic hydrogen in the ground state, it was not immediately appreciated that the scattering phase shift obtained in the close-coupling approximation obeys the following relation between the eigenphases δ (see also (5)):

$$\delta_{1s} < \delta_{1s,2s} < \delta_{1s,2s,2p} < \delta_{1s,2s,2p,3s} < \delta_{1s,2s,2p,3s,3p} < \cdots . \qquad (4)$$

It is just (4) which is the basis for the intrinsic criterion for the scattering theory: the minimum principle.

In the general case when there are several open channels, the multi-channel minimum principle also presents a criterion of the relative accuracy of the different close-coupling calculations. The eigenphases can be defined in terms of the R matrix as

$$\tan \delta_i = (A^T R A)_{ii} \qquad (5)$$

where A is the orthogonal matrix which diagonalizes the R matrix, and the index "i" represents a linear combination of channel indices corresponding to a given total L. The minimum principle states that the exact values for $\tan \delta_i$ are upper bounds on any values that may arise from close-coupling calculations in which exact target atom wave functions are used in all open channels, or

$$\tan \delta_i \geqslant \tan \delta_i^{(t)} , \tag{6}$$

provided that $\tan \delta_i^{(t)}$ is on the same branch of the tangent function as in $\tan \delta_i$. Here the superscript "t" designates a particular approximate representation of all the closed channels. Since the tangent function is monotonically increasing, the above inequality implies

$$\delta_i \geqslant \delta_i^{(t)} . \tag{7}$$

Undoubtedly the "discovery" of the minimum principle was helped by the extensive data accumulated as a result of numerical calculations.

Some problems regarding the minimum principle have been treated by Percival [18], Gailitis [19], McKinley and Macek [20]. But the greatest contribution to development and elucidation of this fundamental principle was made by L.Spruch and the New York University group [21].

2. Various modifications of the close-coupling method

The first ideas to modify the close-coupling approximation were prompted by the slow convergence in the method before the minimum principle was formulated. The basic reason for this slow convergence in the close-coupling method is that only a finite (and reasonably small) number of eigenstates may be included in any practical numerical calculation and this means the neglect of all higher excited states including the continuum. It was shown by Castillejo et al. [22] that continuum states in the expansion contribute 18.6% to the polarizability of the hydrogen atom.

Rotenberg [23] proposed a new expansion basis for the two-electron wave function. He introduced the so-called Sturmian basis set which was a complete, discrete but non-orthogonal set excluding the continuum, the first member only of which was the physical ground state, all higher members being pseudo-states. The question as to how fast the Sturmian expansion converges for the problem is still an open one.

In 1962 Burke and Schey [14] first expressed the idea about the possible use of a pseudo-state for taking into account polarizability; however, the concrete function was not obtained.

With the minimum principle the close-coupling method received the mathematical basis which it needed. It became clearer what role is played by open and closed channels. According to the minimum principle, allowance for closed channels can only increase the phase shift or the reaction matrix. If we take into account all open channels the calculated result will be a lower limit. These properties are conserved if we use an algebraic expression for the closed channels, i.e. if $\Psi(\mathbf{r}_1\mathbf{r}_2)$ is represented in the form

$$\Psi(\mathbf{r}_1,\mathbf{r}_2) = \sum_{i=1}^{n} u_i(\mathbf{r}_1)F_i(\mathbf{r}_2) + \sum_{j=1}^{m} c_j\phi_j(\mathbf{r}_1,\mathbf{r}_2) \pm (1\rightleftharpoons 2) , \tag{8}$$

where ϕ_j are functions satisfying the conditions

$$r_1\phi_j \to 0 \quad \text{as} \quad r_1 \to \infty ; \qquad r_2\phi_j \to 0 \quad \text{as} \quad r_2 \to \infty . \tag{9}$$

Equations

$$\int u_i(\mathbf{r}_1)(H-E)\Psi(\mathbf{r}_1,\mathbf{r}_2)\,d\mathbf{r}_1 = 0 , \quad i = 1, 2, ... n \tag{10}$$

and

$$\int \phi_j(\mathbf{r}_1,\mathbf{r}_2)(H-E)\Psi(\mathbf{r}_1,\mathbf{r}_2)\,d\mathbf{r}_1\,d\mathbf{r}_2 = 0 , \quad j = 1, 2, ... n \tag{11}$$

follow from the Kohn variational principle. Substituting expansion (8) into (10) and (11) we obtain a system of n integro-differential and m algebraic equations which can be solved by a non-iterative method. The main contribution to this method, called the correlation method, was made by Burke [14,24]. Burke and Taylor [24] showed that the inclusion into $\phi_j(\mathbf{r}_1,\mathbf{r}_2)$ of correlation terms depending on the inter-electron distance r_{12}, should improve the expansion where it needs it most.

The form adopted for the correlation terms by Burke and Taylor is

$$\phi_j(\mathbf{r}_1,\mathbf{r}_2) = r_1^{p_j}r_2^{q_j}r_{12}^{s_j} \exp\left[-k(r_1+r_2)\right]\mathcal{Y}_{Ll_1l_2}^{M}(\hat{\mathbf{r}}_1,\hat{\mathbf{r}}_2) .$$

The second sum in (8) does not contribute to the long-range forces nor to the scattered flux. But even with a reasonable number of terms it eliminates the main disadvantage of the close-coupling approximation: short-range inadequacy. The correlation method presents a powerful expansion of the close-coupling approximation.

To apply the method, it is in principle sufficient to include only open channels in the first sum of the expansion (8). However, in some cases it is useful to abandon this reservation. Desirability of explicit allowance in the expansion of the total wave function of closed channels just below the threshold was realized long ago and was noted, for example, by Feshbach [25].

So, in the vicinity of the threshold for excitation of the 2s, 2p states (that is the resonance region) the allowance for the 2s, 2p terms in the close-coupling expansion of the total wave function is of the utmost importance. In this way, the long-range degenerate dipole interaction (interaction in the "new" channels), which is the principle cause for the resonances, is taken into account [8].

Representation of long-range potentials by short-range correlation terms is possible in principle, but this is not always the best way to solve the problem.

3. Allowance for the dipole polarizability of atomic eigenstates

The elastic scattering cross-section at low energies is well-known to be strongly influenced by the long-range potential $V \sim \alpha r^{-4}$. Suffice it to mention here the papers on effective range theory of the New York University group. For a polarization potential $V \sim \alpha r^{-4}$, O'Malley et al. [26] have obtained:

$$k^{-1} \tan \delta_0 = -a_0 - \tfrac{1}{3}\pi\alpha^2 k - \tfrac{4}{3}a_0\alpha^2 k^2 \ln k + \dots , \quad l = 0 , \qquad (12a)$$

$$\tan \delta_l = \pi\alpha k^2 /(2l+3)(2l+1)(2l-1) + \dots , \quad l \geqslant 1 . \qquad (12b)$$

Hence it is seen that for $l \geqslant 1$ the elastic-scattering phase shift δ_l for $k \to 0$ is altogether independent of the short-range potential. At $l = 0$, the second term of the expansion in k for $k^{-1} \tan \delta_0$ does not depend on short-range forces. The scattering length a_0 at $l = 0$ is determined both by short-range and polarization potentials; in this case polarization plays a large role too.

It is clear from the paper by Castillejo et al. [22] that it is impossible in the usual close-coupling approximation to take into account completely the long-range polarization potential.

The adiabatic methods, in particular the method of polarized orbitals proposed by Temkin and Lamkin [16], fully account for polarization potentials. However, all adiabatic methods suffer from the "cut-off" procedure of

long-range potentials at short range. Therefore adiabatic methods cannot give
the lower bound for the exact phase of the elastic scattering. It seems doubt-
ful whether one can take account at all of dipole polarizability without loos-
ing the extremum properties for the phase within the framework of one
integro-differential equation. But this can be done by solving two equations
for any total angular momentum L [27].

Starting with the complete set of radially coupled equations, we specialize
at once to the case where the only open channel is that containing the 1s
atomic state. The asymptotic forms of the closed-channel radial functions
may be expressed in terms of the open-channel function, according to Castillejo et al. [22]. When they are substituted into the right-hand side of the
open-channel equation, one obtains the following asymptotic equation which
applies to both singlet and triplet scattering, since the exchange terms, as
other short-range potentials, should be omitted

$$\left(\frac{d^2}{dr^2} - \frac{L(L+1)}{r^2} + \frac{\alpha(1s-p-1s)}{r^4} + k_1^2\right) F_{1s} = 0 , \tag{13}$$

where

$$\alpha = \frac{2}{3} \sum_{n=2}^{\infty} \frac{\langle u_{10}ru_{n1}\rangle^2}{E_n - E_1} = \frac{2}{3} \frac{\langle u_{10}ru_{\overline{2p}}\rangle}{E_{\overline{2p}} - E_1} . \tag{14}$$

We shall find the pseudo-function $u_{\overline{2p}}$ and pseudo-energy $E_{\overline{2p}}$ which will replace the complete set of atomic functions u_{n1} and energies E_n in order to
allow for polarization. One may readily evaluate α by the implicit summation
technique [28]. Here we seek a bound solution of the inhomogeneous equation:

$$\left(-\frac{d^2}{dr^2} - \frac{2}{r} + \frac{2}{r^2} - 2E_1\right) u_{\overline{2p}}(r) = \frac{2(E_{\overline{2p}}-E_1)}{\langle u_{\overline{2p}}ru_{10}\rangle} ru_{10}(r) . \tag{15}$$

The normalized solution and effective energy level in (15) are

$$u_{\overline{2p}}(r) = \sqrt{32/129} \left(\tfrac{1}{2}r^3 + r^2\right) e^{-r} ; \qquad E_{\overline{2p}} = -7/86 . \tag{16}$$

It can be seen that a close-coupling calculation, with exchange, in which the
two basis wave functions for the target system

$$\frac{1}{r} u_{10}(r)\, \mathcal{Y}_{00}(\hat{\mathbf{r}})\,, \qquad \text{and} \qquad \frac{1}{r} u_{\overline{2p}}(r)\, \mathcal{Y}_{1m}(\hat{\mathbf{r}})$$

are included, will have built into it the exact value of the ground-state polarizability.

Independently, Drachman [29] proposed another set of equations which solves the above problem to the same degree of satisfaction. Numerical calculations according to Drachman were performed by the author and by Callaway and his colleagues at the Louisiana State University.

Neither of these methods has an advantage over the other, they allow for short-range potentials of the problem in a different way though both incompletely. However, the applicability of the minimum principle is preserved in both cases, allowing, if necessary, for systematic improvement of the results, for example, by addition of short-range correlation terms.

The usual close-coupling procedure leads to a system of two integro-differential equations for $L = 0$ and one of three equations for $L \geqslant 1$. However, for $L \geqslant 1$ too one can obtain a system of two equations while allowing just as well for dipole polarizability; of course, in this case short-range interactions are less completely allowed for. In this case one should use the quantum numbers L, M, n, l_1, λ instead of L, M, n, l_1, l_2, i.e. replace l_2 by $\lambda = |\mu|$, where μ is the projection of the orbital angular momentum of the target electron on the axis joining the nucleus to the free electron. Such a system is used in the derivation of the adiabatic equation by Temkin [30]. A description of the use of the corresponding system of angular functions $H^M_{Ll_1\lambda}(\mathbf{r}_1, \mathbf{r}_2)$ is given in [31]. It also gives the resulting system of close-coupling equations which was obtained.

We shall now consider the use of pseudo-states in the multi-channel case [32]. We shall consider the vicinity of the $n = 2$ threshold. Any higher threshold can be treated similarly.

As was mentioned before, atomic eigenstates 1s, 2s, 2p should be taken into account exactly. But when $k_2^2 \ll 1$, it is important to have built into the close-coupling equations the exact values of the effective polarizabilities of the 2s and 2p atomic states.

$$\alpha(2s{-}p{-}2s) = \frac{2}{3} \sum_{n=3}^{\infty} \frac{\langle u_{20} r u_{n1}\rangle^2}{E_n - E_2}\,, \tag{17}$$

$$\alpha(2p{-}s{-}2p) = \frac{2}{3} \sum_{n=3}^{\infty} \frac{\langle u_{21} r u_{n0}\rangle^2}{E_n - E_2}\,, \tag{18}$$

$$\alpha(2p-d-2p) = \frac{2}{3} \sum_{n=3}^{\infty} \frac{\langle u_{21}ru_{n2}\rangle^2}{E_n - E_2}. \tag{19}$$

To avoid misunderstanding, we shall note that the polarizabilities needed here are *not* physical polarizabilities of atomic states [in contrast to the polarizability $\alpha(1s-p-1s)$ of the 1s state!]. Indeed, for example, the physical polarizability of the 2s state is mainly due to the 2p atomic state which, owing to the relativistic- and Lamb-splitting, does not coincide exactly with the 2s state. But we neglect these effects in scattering problems.

One may again evaluate α's by the implicit summation technique.

$$\left(-\frac{d^2}{dr^2} - \frac{2}{r} + \frac{2}{r^2} - 2E_2\right) u_{\overline{3p}}(r) = \frac{2(E_{\overline{3p}}-E_2)}{\langle u_{\overline{3p}}ru_{20}\rangle}\{ru_{20}(r)-\langle u_{21}ru_{20}\rangle u_{21}(r)\} ; \tag{20}$$

$$\left(-\frac{d^2}{dr^2} - \frac{2}{r} - 2E_2\right) u_{\overline{3s}}(r) = \frac{2(E_{\overline{3s}}-E_2)}{\langle u_{\overline{3s}}ru_{21}\rangle}\{ru_{21}(r)-\langle u_{10}ru_{21}\rangle u_{10}(r)-$$

$$-\langle u_{20}ru_{21}\rangle u_{20}(r)\} ; \tag{21}$$

$$\left(-\frac{d^2}{dr^2} - \frac{2}{r} + \frac{6}{r^2} - 2E_2\right) u_{\overline{3d}}(r) = \frac{2(E_{\overline{3d}}-E_2)}{\langle u_{\overline{3d}}ru_{21}\rangle} ru_{21}(r) . \tag{22}$$

In terms of these pseudo-states it may be easily verified that the α's become:

$$\alpha(2s-p-2s) = \frac{2}{3} \frac{\langle u_{20}ru_{\overline{3p}}\rangle^2}{(E_{\overline{3p}}-E_2)} ; \tag{23}$$

$$\alpha(2p-s-2p) = \frac{2}{3} \frac{\langle u_{21}ru_{\overline{3s}}\rangle^2}{(E_{\overline{3s}}-E_2)} ; \tag{24}$$

$$\alpha(2p-d-2p) = \frac{2}{3} \frac{\langle u_{21}ru_{\overline{3d}}\rangle^2}{(E_{\overline{3d}}-E_2)} ; \tag{25}$$

The orthonormalized solutions and the effective energy levels in (20), (21) and (22) are:

$$u_{\overline{3p}} = (1/2)(5/26)^{1/2}r^2(1-r^2/30)e^{-r/2} , \qquad E_{\overline{3p}} = -5/104 ; \tag{26}$$

$$u_{\overline{3s}} = (3/2)^{1/2} [57-2/9(4/3)^9]^{-1/2} r\{e^{-r/2}(1-\tfrac{1}{2}r-\tfrac{1}{2}r^2+r^3/12)+(1/2)(4/3)^6 e^{-r}\} ,$$
$$\tag{27}$$

$$E_{\overline{3s}} = [3+(1/9)(4/3)^8] [57-(2/9)(4/3)^9]^{-1} - 1/8 ;$$

$$u_{\overline{3d}} = (1/8)(55)^{-1/2}r^3(1+r/6)e^{-r/2} , \qquad E_{\overline{3d}} = -9/176 , \tag{28}$$

where $u_{\overline{3p}}$ is orthogonal to u_{21}, and $u_{\overline{3s}}$ is orthogonal to u_{10} and u_{20}.

It can be seen that a close-coupling calculation with the exchange in which the six basic wave functions for the target system,

$$\frac{1}{r} [u_{10}(r),u_{20}(r),u_{\overline{3s}}(r)] \, \mathcal{Y}_{00}(\hat{r}), \qquad \frac{1}{r} [u_{21}(r),u_{\overline{3p}}(r)] \, \mathcal{Y}_{1m}(\hat{r}) , \qquad \text{and}$$

$$\frac{1}{r}u_{\overline{3d}}(r) \, \mathcal{Y}_{2m}(\hat{r})$$

are included will have built into it the exact values of the effective polarizabilities of the 2s and 2p states. Besides, it can be verified that the polarizability of the 1s state is also effectively improved by inclusion of the $\overline{3p}$ pseudo-state.

One could suggest before the calculations were made (this is now confirmed) that the use of pseudo-states would be particularly effective at small k_1 or k_2 and for $L \geq 1$. Besides, it may also prove effective in the triplet case for $L = 0$. In the last case the role of long-range potentials increases owing to the Pauli principle. But with increasing energies the role of the short-range interactions becomes more important, and one should use in addition short-range correlation terms.

4. Excitation of 2s and 2p states at intermediate energies

On account of the fact that for all open channels one must use exact atomic states in the expansions of the total wave function, the close-coupling method is of limited applicability in a strict mathematical treatment. Even allowance for six atomic states (some of them could be pseudo-states) represents almost the limit of capability of present-day computers. In e–H scattering one can therefore treat energies at most up to the $n = 4$ threshold, expecting reasonably accurate results only up to the $n = 3$ threshold or even somewhat lower. However, calculations with the use of the 1s–2s–2p close-coupling approximation were made up to energies of ≈ 54 eV [6]. The results for 1s–2s and 1s–2p excitation cross-sections proved to be too high. In some

cases the first Born approximation or its modifications give much better results. A possible agreement between the two approaches should not be regarded as an indication of their validity, contrary to what is sometimes said.
If one wants to be logical, the opposite is true, since the first Born-type
methods can at best be quite good approximations to the close-coupling treatment.

The main drawback of the 1s–2s–2p close-coupling approximation at intermediate energies is that the flux into all open channels is not taken into
account and this cannot be done for some very fundamental reasons.

Burke and Webb approximated the infinity of open channels by including
two pseudo-states in the expansion of the total wave function [33]:

$$\Psi(1,2) = \sum_n u_n(1) F_n(r) \pm (1 \rightleftharpoons 2),$$

where the sum over n includes the 1s, 2s, 2p atomic eigenstates and two
pseudo-states which are designated as $\overline{3s}$ and $\overline{3p}$. At the energies considered,
the minimum principle is not allowed for and in this sense the calculation so
far has no strict mathematical foundation. Of course, the criterion for the
choice of pseudo-states at intermediate energies must be different from that
used at low energies. Long-range interactions are not determinant here since
at such energies electrons can come quite close to the atom. Therefore the $\overline{3s}$
and $\overline{3p}$ pseudo-states here should represent short-range correlations in the
final state. The radial forms of $\overline{3s}$ and $\overline{3p}$ pseudo-states were taken as

$$\overline{3s} = (1.532090 - 1.189309r + 0.157320 r^2) \exp(-0.515998 r), \qquad (29)$$

$$\overline{3p} = (0.612216 r - 0.128908 r^2) \exp(-0.552796 r), \qquad (30)$$

with the appropriate s-wave and p-wave angular terms. The chosen pseudo-
states have about the same range as the 2s and 2p atomic eigenstates. The
linear coefficients were chosen to normalize and orthogonalize the pseudo-
states to the lower atomic eigenstates with the same angular symmetry. The
choice of pseudo-states is somewhat arbitrary. The exponents are slightly different from the value 0.5 associated with the $n = 2$ states of H. They were ad-
justed so that the pseudo-state thresholds coincided with each other and with
the ionization threshold at 13.6 eV.

The summations

$$\sum_{n=3}^{\infty} |\langle \overline{3s}|ns\rangle|^2 \ , \qquad \sum_{n=3}^{\infty} |\langle \overline{3p}|np\rangle|^2$$

were performed over all bound states. This showed that 24.6% of the $\overline{3s}$ state and 28.6% of the 3p state arose from the continuum, while the first terms in these summations were 0.534 and 0.477 respectively. These results of calculations using pseudo-states are in surprisingly good agreement with experiment.

The above authors remark that "with new techniques of solving coupled integro-differential equations there is no reason why more pseudo-states should not be included and the convergence of the pseudo-state expansion studied in greater detail" [33].

Endeavour is also required on the mathematical foundation of the close-coupling approximation for the energy region where not all open channels can be taken into account exactly.

5. On the applicability of the Born approximation

The close-coupling approximation allowing for the short-range correlation terms and for the pseudo-states has led to results which are in a very good agreement with experiments [34]. Those are: series of resonances in the elastic scattering below the $n = 2$ threshold, shapes of the 1s—2s, 1s—2p cross-sections in the vicinity of the threshold, ratio $Q(1s-2s)/Q(1s-2p)$ near threshold, ratio of spin exchange cross-section to total cross-section for 1s—2s excitation, polarization of Lyman-α radiation induced by electron collision. Absolute values of the total cross-sections for excitation are not needed in any of these cases. At present there are no experimental possibilities to measure the absolute values of the total cross-sections for excitation of the 2p and 2s states with a sufficient degree of accuracy. Therefore at energies $\approx 200-700$ eV, relative cross-sections are normalized to the Born approximation (applying cascade corrections).

Rather by deeply rooted traditions than on some rigorous (or calculated) grounds it is considered that at such energies the Born cross-section can be relied upon with great accuracy. However, it turns out that at low energies the cross-sections normalized in this way differ by about 20% from those calculated in the close-coupling approximation [35].

To clarify the situation, Propin and I have treated a simple model. Although pseudo-states are not used here the results obtained bear a relation to the considered problem.

The reason why the Born approximation for total cross-sections improves with increasing energy is that in this case an increasing number of partial cross-sections give a considerable contribution to the total cross-section, while the coupling between the channels becomes weaker with increasing L. We want to show, however, that the Born approximation may become applicable with the expected degree of accuracy at energies much higher than is usually believed. It will mean that the coupling between the channels does not decrease quickly enough.

We have considered the following model. Instead of the close-coupling equations we have taken the system of equations in which one retains interactions which do not decrease faster than $1/r^2$:

$$\left[\frac{d^2}{dr^2} - \frac{L(L+1) + \mathscr{A}}{r^2} + k^2\right] F = \frac{\mathscr{B}}{r^2} F, \tag{31}$$

where $\mathscr{A}$ is the symmetric matrix coupling the degenerate channels 2s and 2p the matrix $\mathscr{B}$ contains elements coupling the channel 1s with channels corresponding to the atomic eigenstate 2p [36]. When solving (31) we put $\mathscr{B}^{L\pm1}_{1s,2p} = 0$ ($\mathscr{B}^{L\pm1}_{2p,1s} \neq 0$), i.e. take into account only the coupling between the degenerate channels 2s and 2p with $k = k_2$. The solution of the system (31) in the given approximation is easily found owing to the possibility of diagonalizing the matrix $L(L+1) + \mathscr{A}$ with the help of the unitary matrix A [36]:

$$A^{-1}[L(L+1) + \mathscr{A}] A = \mu(\mu+1).$$

Cross-sections $Q^L_{L\pm1}(1s-2p)$ and $Q^L(1s-2s)$ are expressed through combinations of integrals of the type $\int_0^\infty \mathscr{J}_{L+1/2}(k_1 r)\mathscr{J}_{\mu_i+1/2}(k_2 r)\, dr/r$ where $\mathscr{J}_s(y)$ are the Bessel functions.

In the chosen model, there are no physically acceptable solutions for $L = 0, 1, 2$ [8,36]. Therefore total cross-sections are defined as

$$Q_{cc} = \sum_{L=3}^{\infty} Q^L. \tag{32}$$

We shall define the Born cross-sections Q_B for the model as usual putting the matrix $\mathscr{A}$ equal to zero, i.e. breaking the coupling between the channels 2s and 2p. For total cross-sections we shall again make use of definition (32).

Table 1 gives the ratios of total cross-section for excitation of the 2p state.

Table 1
Ratio of total close-coupling to Born cross-sections for 2p excitation.

k_1 :	3	5	7	9
ratio :	0.801	0.825	0.846	0.860

It is seen from the table 1 that the ratio indeed tends to 1 with increasing k_1, but slowly. Even at $E \approx 1100$ eV (k_1=9) Q_{cc} is 14% smaller than Q_B.

Table 2
Ratios of partial close-coupling to total Born cross-sections for 2p excitation.

k_1 \ L	3	8	13	18	23
3	0.383	0.894	0.969	0.988	0.995
5	0.292	0.830	0.937	0.970	0.984
7	0.275	0.807	0.923	0.961	0.977
9	0.270	0.797	0.917	0.956	0.974

It is seen from table 2 that with increasing L the partial cross sections for excitation of the 2p state really tend to the Born cross sections. However, for fixed L the coupling between the channels becomes more important with increasing k_1. This is observed at each L given in table 2, particularly at small L. The relative contribution of the first partial cross-sections to the total cross-section decreases with increasing k_1, but even at k_1 = 9 ($E \approx 1100$ eV) the sum of the first eight partial cross-sections (from L = 3 to L = 10) accounts for more than 20%. All this leads to a slow convergence of Q_{cc} to Q_B with increasing k_1.

Let us go back now to the problem of the excitation of the 2p state of the hydrogen atom by electron impact. If one normalizes the experimental cross-section $Q(1s-2p)$ to the results of calculations in the close coupling-approximation at low energies, then at high energies ($E \approx 200-700$ eV) the normalized experimental curve Q_{cc} lies above that for Q_B. In the considered model the curve Q_{cc} is always lower than Q_B. This may be due to the fact that the model does not reflect all the peculiarities of the actual problem. In particular, the first three partial cross-sections are not taken into account, the model potentials are singular at zero and the influence of the other channels is not taken into account. However, the calculations point to the fact that doubts about the grounds for normalization of the cross-section for excitation of the 2p state at energies $E \approx 200$ eV, expressed in Burke's papers [7,35] are quite justified.

The situation with the cross-section for excitation of the 2s state is even more complicated because of the larger role played by cascades from the 3p state.

The merit of the model just described is its simplicity. The solution of the 1s–2s–2p close-coupling approximation in the energy region considered, even without exchange, might be a more fundamental check on the validity of the Born approximation.

References

[1] H.S.W.Massey and C.B.O.Mohr, Proc. Roy. Soc., Ser. A *136* (1932) 289.

[2] I.C.Percival and M.J.Seaton, Proc. Cambr. Phil. Soc. *53* (1957) 654.

[3] B.H.Bransden and J.S.C.McKee, Proc. Phys. Soc. A *69* (1956) 422.

[4] Cf. the papers in: *Atomic Collisions – The Theory of Electron-Atom Collisions* (Acad. Sci. Latvian SSR Institute of Physics Trans. XIII), eds. V.Ya.Veldre, R.Ya. Damburg and R.K.Peterkop (Academy of Sciences of the Latvian SSR Press, Riga, 1961); [English Transl. by M.V.Kurepa, Butterworths, London, 1966].

[5] P.G.Burke and K.Smith, Rev. Mod. Phys. *34* (1962) 458.

[6] P.G.Burke, H.M.Schey and K.Smith, Phys. Rev. *129* (1963) 1258.

[7] P.G.Burke, A.J.Taylor and S.Ormonde, Proc. Phys. Soc. *92* (1967) 345.

[8] M.Gailitis and R.Damburg, Proc. Phys. Soc. *82* (1963) 192.

[9] R.Damburg and M.Gailitis, Proc. Phys. Soc. *82* (1963) 1068.

[10] G.E.Chamberlain, S.J.Smith and D.W.O.Heddle, Phys. Rev. Letters *12* (1964) 647.

[11] J.W.McGowan, J.F.Williams and E.K.Curley, Phys. Rev. *180* (1969) 132.

[12] W.R.Ott, W.Kauppila and W.L.Fite, Phys. Rev. A *1* (1970) 1089.

[13] G.J.Schulz, Phys. Rev. Letters *13* (1964) 583.

[14] P.G.Burke and H.M.Schey, Phys. Rev. *126* (1962) 147.

[15] C.Schwartz, Phys. Rev. *124* (1961) 1468.

[16] A.Temkin and J.C.Lamkin, Phys. Rev. *121* (1961) 788.

[17] A.Temkin, Phys. Rev. *126* (1962) 130.

[18] I.C.Percival, Phys. Rev. *119* (1960) 159.

[19] M.K.Gailitis, Zh. Eksp. Teor. Fiz. *47* (1964) 160; [English Transl.: Soviet Phys. -JETP *20* (1965) 107].

[20] W.A.McKinley and J.H.Macek, Phys. Rev. Letters *10* (1964) 210.

[21] Y.Hahn, T.F.O'Malley and L.Spruch, Phys. Rev. *134* (1964) B911.

[22] L.Castillejo, I.C.Percival and M.J.Seaton, Proc. Roy. Soc., Ser. A *254* (1960) 259.

[23] M.Rotenberg, Ann. Phys. (New York) *19* (1962) 262.

[24] P.G.Burke and A.J.Taylor, Proc. Phys. Soc. *88* (1966) 549.

[25] H.Feshbach, Ann. Phys. (New York) *19* (1962) 287.

[26] T.F.O'Malley, L.Spruch and L.Rosenberg, J. Math. Phys. *2* (1961) 491.

[27] R.J.Damburg and E.Karule, Proc. Phys. Soc. *90* (1967) 637.

[28] A.Dalgarno and N.Lynn, Proc. Phys. Soc. A *70* (1957) 223.

[29] R.J.Drachman, *V.ICPEAC, Abstracts of Papers*, eds. I.P.Flaks and E.S.Solovyov (Publishing House "Nauka", Leningrad, 1967) p. 106.

[30] A.Temkin, Phys. Rev. *116* (1959) 358.

[31] R.J.Damburg and E.Karule, Atomic Scattering IV, ed. V.Veldre (Latv. Acad. Sci., Riga, 1967) p. 5.
[32] R.J.Damburg and S.Geltman, Phys. Rev. Letters 20A (1968) 485.
[33] P.G.Burke and T.G.Webb, J. Phys. B *3* (1970) L131.
[34] S.Geltman, *VII ICPEAC, Invited Talks and Progress Reports,* eds. T.R.Govers and F.J.de Heer (North-Holland Publ. Co., Amsterdam, 1972) p. 216.
[35] S.Geltman and P.G.Burke, J. Phys. B *3* (1970) 1062.
[36] M.J.Seaton, Proc. Phys. Soc. *77* (1961) 174.

Physics of Electronic and Atomic Collisions, VII ICPEAC, 1971 – North-Holland (1972)

APPLICATIONS OF PSEUDO-STATE EXPANSIONS

Sydney GELTMAN

Joint Institute for Laboratory Astrophysics,
National Bureau of Standards and University of Colorado,
Boulder, Colorado, 80302, USA

The various types of pseudo-state expansions which have been applied
to the scattering of a charged particle by atoms are discussed. Of the applications so far made, greater success has been achieved in the case of low
energy electron-hydrogen scattering than for high-energy proton-hydrogen
scattering.

1. Introduction

The most reliable theoretical method for the calculation of low energy
inelastic cross-sections is the close-coupling method. It consists basically of an
expansion of the full scattering wave function in terms of eigenstates of the
target system. The coefficients of these eigenstates are then determined as the
solution of a set of coupled equations, whose number will depend on the
number of eigenstates included in the original expansion.

The close-coupling method is most suited to the situation in which the
initial and final states are close in energy to one another and couple strongly,
while other states are more distant and couple relatively weakly to the initial
and final states of interest. Examples of this are intra-multiplet transitions in
an atom and rotational transitions in diatomic molecules. On the other hand,
for the case of electronic transitions in atoms it is not at all obvious that the
close-coupling method will give good results. If we consider the $1s-2p$ transition in the hydrogen atom, we see immediately that there are an infinite
number of states which lie above the 2p state in the same energy interval
which separates the 2p from the 1s state below. The largest close-coupling
eigenstate-expansion calculations which have been done on the electron-
hydrogen system contain the six basis states $1s, 2s, 2p, 3s, 3p, 3d$, and one is
still not sure of the accuracy of these results because of the infinity of closely
lying states which are not included in the basis set.

216

For this reason much work has been done recently on the development of alternate expansions, in which so-called pseudo states take the place of some of the target system eigenstates. The hope is that a judicious choice of a small number of pseudo states will take account of the major physical effects of the coupling of the initial and final states to the infinity of actual states that exist.

In this paper we will review the various types of pseudo states which have been proposed and then discuss their application to electron (and positron) — atom and proton — atom scattering. Most of the applications to date have been for hydrogen-like target atoms. We will omit applications to the Faddeev equations, as these are in the area of the following paper of this volume [1].

2. Types of pseudo states

There is unfortunately no *a priori* way of choosing pseudo states with the full certainty that they will yield the best possible scattering results. Hence a number of different types have been proposed on the basis of optimizing the input of the physics needed to properly describe certain aspects of the scattering problem.

In all applications it is desirable to retain the exact target eigenstates for all open channels, and only supplement the expansion with pseudo states to take account of the infinity of closed channels. This is necessary to insure that the asymptotic scattering boundary conditions are satisfied so that the S or R matrices (or transition amplitudes in time-dependent treatments) resulting from a close-coupling calculation can be considered correct to second-order accuracy in a variational sense.

Most of the pseudo-state sets which have been proposed are orthogonal sets of functions, and are also chosen to be orthogonal to the open-channel eigenstates included in the expansion. Aside from numerical convenience there is no physical reason for requiring this orthogonality. Since any close-coupling calculation can only be carried out with a relatively small number of basis states, the actual set used is rarely complete.

Also, most of the pseudo states discussed below will correspond to electronic states in a central potential (unless otherwise specified). This will mean that their angular parts are coupled to the angular functions of the scattered particle in the usual way, leaving only the radial functions to be treated differently.

2.1. Sturmian pseudo states

The Sturmian pseudo states were introduced by Rotenberg [2,3]. Their interesting property is that they form a complete set without having a continuum. They are formally defined as the solutions of

$$\left\{ -\frac{d^2}{dr^2} + \frac{l(l+1)}{r^2} + \beta_{nl} V(r) - E_0 \right\} S_{nl}(r) = 0 \tag{1}$$

which vanish at $r = 0$ and $r = \infty$ for $l = 0, 1, 2 \ldots$ and $n = l + 1, l + 2, \ldots$, where E_0 is a fixed negative number and β_{nl} is an eigenvalue. Unlike the usual sets of eigenfunctions which correspond to fixed potential and a spectrum of energies, the Sturmians correspond to a fixed energy and a spectrum of potential strengths. The β_{nl}'s form a discrete spectrum in the range $1 \leqslant \beta_{nl} < \infty$. As β_{nl} gets large, the kinetic energy gets large (since E_0 remains constant) and the number of oscillations in the Sturmian functions increases.

The most important set of Sturmians for problems involving atomic targets is that generated with the Coulomb potential, $V(r) = -2/r$, the so-called Coulomb Sturmians. If we compare the resulting equation with the usual equation defining the radial Coulomb functions,

$$\left\{ -\frac{d^2}{dr^2} + \frac{l(l+1)}{r^2} - \frac{2}{r} + \frac{1}{n^2} \right\} u_{nl}(r) = 0 \, , \tag{2}$$

we note that the choice $E_0 = -1/(l+1)^2$ and $\beta_{l+1,l} = 1$ results in $S_{l+1,l} = u_{l+1,l}$, that is, the first Sturmian state is identical with the lowest lying Coulomb state for a given orbital angular momentum. The analytic form for the general Coulomb Sturmian function is also simply expressible in Laguerre polynomials.

Thus the attractive feature of the Sturmian pseudo states is that they do not contain a continuum. The feeling is that with a small number of them included in the expansion for the total wave function one has a better representation of the exact wave function than is obtainable from the same number of Coulomb states. One must keep in mind, however, that even with the Sturmians one is always omitting an infinite number (though denumerable) of states from the complete basis set.

2.2. Polarization pseudo states

An examination of the asymptotic form of the open-channel radial close-coupling equations for electron-hydrogen scattering for energies in which only elastic scattering is possible shows that the leading potential terms are of order $1/r^4$, $1/r^5$, and so on ($1/r$ for electron-ion scattering). If one increases the energy such that only $n = 2$ excitation is possible one finds that the leading asymptotic potential terms (both direct and coupling) are of order $1/r^2$, $1/r^3$, $1/r^4$, and so on. The terms of order $1/r^2$ arise from the dipole coupling between 1s, 2s, and 2p states and the $1/r^3$ term is the result of the permanent quadrupole moment associated with the 2p state, and these effects are exactly accounted for by the inclusion of the exact open-channel target states.

The terms starting with $1/r^4$ are the result of induced polarizabilities – dipole, quadrupole, etc. – and they depend on coupling to all of the closed channel states, including the continuum. For example, the well known expression for the ground-state dipole polarizability of the hydrogen atom is

$$\alpha_1(1s \to p \to 1s) = 2 \sum_{n=2}^{\infty} \frac{\langle u_{10} r u_{n1} \rangle^2}{E_n - E_1} = 4.5 a_0^3 \,. \tag{3}$$

Damburg and Karule [4] have shown that the 2p pseudo state,

$$\bar{u}_{21} = \left(\frac{32}{129}\right)^{1/2} e^{-r} \, (r^2 + r^3/2) \,, \tag{4}$$

will provide the full ground-state dipole polarizability, that is

$$\alpha_1(1s \to p \to 1s) = 2 \, \frac{\langle u_{10} r \bar{u}_{21} \rangle^2}{\bar{E}_{21} - E_1} \,, \tag{5}$$

where $\bar{E}_{21}$ is the expectation value of the atomic Hamiltonian with respect to $\bar{u}_{21}$. If the hydrogenic u_{21} is explicitly included in the close-coupling expansion, then the first term in the summation in (3) is taken care of and an additional 2p pseudo state (called $\bar{\bar{u}}_{21}$) may be introduced to provide the remaining dipole polarizability ($\Sigma_{n=3}^{\infty}$ in (3)). Also it may be shown that the induced quadrupole polarizability, which is proportional to the quantity

$$\sum_{n=3}^{\infty} \frac{\langle u_{10} r^2 u_{n2} \rangle}{E_n - E_1} \,,$$

is fully accounted for by the use of the single 3d pseudo state,

$$\bar{u}_{32} = \left(\frac{32}{535}\right)^{1/2} e^{-r} \left(\frac{r^3}{2} + \frac{r^4}{3}\right). \tag{6}$$

For scattering energies between the $n = 2$ and $n = 3$ thresholds, the introduction of new open channels leads to the appearance of six new dipole polarizabilities $\alpha_2(nl \rightarrow l \pm 1 \rightarrow n'l)$, which are defined analogously to α_1 in (3). These have been discussed and evaluated by Damburg and Geltman [5]. They find the three pseudo states,

$$\bar{u}_{30} = N_{30}r \left\{ e^{-r/2}(1 - \tfrac{1}{2}r - \tfrac{1}{2}r^2 + r^3/12) + \tfrac{1}{2}(4/3)^6 \, e^{-r} \right\}$$

$$\bar{u}_{31} = N_{31} \, e^{-r/2} \, r^2(1 - r^2/30)$$

$$\bar{u}_{32} = N_{32} \, e^{-r/2} \, r^3(1 + r/6), \tag{7}$$

which yield the full polarizability of all the major α_2's (table 1); the N's are normalization constants. One also has the convenient property that the atomic Hamiltonian is diagonal in the representation of the open-channel eigenstates and these pseudo states. The above hydrogenic polarization pseudo states are being generalized for complex atoms by Lan [6].

Table 1
Effective polarizabilities in $e-H$ scattering just above the $n = 2$ excitation threshold (From [5].

Effective polarizabilities	Exact value (in a_0^3)	Percent contained in 1s, 2s, 2p, 3s, 3p, 3d expansion	Percent contained in 1s, 2s, 2p, $\overline{3s}$, $\overline{3p}$, $\overline{3d}$ expansion
$\alpha_2(1s \rightarrow p \rightarrow 1s)$	1.54	26.0	56.9
$\alpha_2(1s \rightarrow p \rightarrow 2s)$	24.8	61.2	100.0
$\alpha_2(2s \rightarrow p \rightarrow 2s)$	120.0	75.0	100.0
$\alpha_2(2s \rightarrow p \rightarrow 1s)$	4.97	47.8	84.9
$\alpha_2(2p \rightarrow s \rightarrow 2p)$	11.0	77.1	100.0
$\alpha_2(2p \rightarrow d \rightarrow 2p)$	260.0	83.2	100.0

The polarization pseudo states are found as the solutions to certain inhomogeneous differential equations, and can straightforwardly be evaluated for all the α's of hydrogen. The higher multipole polarizabilities can be computed in a similar way. The practical limit to incorporating these into a close-coupling calculation is the computer limitations on the total number of basis states that can be handled. Unless there are special complications in a particular channel, such as a virtual or resonance state, one would expect the dipole polarizabilities to have a major influence on the scattering, particularly at energies just above a new threshold. It is in that region that we would expect polarization pseudo states to be effective. We ŵould certainly not expect them to be useful just below a hydrogenic threshold where resonances are expected and the $\bar{E}_{nl}$'s are a poor approximation to the degenerate energy level E_n of the new threshold.

The introduction of these polarization pseudo states was suggested by the polarized orbital method, which has been used extensively for electron-atom scattering [7]. The difference in the two methods can be illustrated by comparing the wave function expansions for elastic scattering (in a schematic way),

polarization pseudo state: $\Psi(1,2) = u_{10}(1)F_1(2) + \bar{u}_{21}(1)F_2(2)$;

polarized orbital: $\Psi(1,2) = [u_{10}(1) + \phi(1,2)] F_1(2)$.   (8)

Although it turns out that the polarized orbital $\phi(1,2)$ does contain the pseudo state $\bar{u}_{21}$, it is clear from the above forms that the two Ψ's cannot be expected to be very similar, particularly when one understands that F_1 is an open channel oscillatory function while F_2 is a closed channel damped function. Also the original form of the polarized orbital method is not stationary in a variational sense unless the S or R matrix elements are corrected by the term $\int d\tau \Psi (H-E) \Psi$, a term which automatically vanishes in any true close-coupling treatment. An extended form of the polarized orbital method appears to overcome this latter difficulty [8].

2.3. Short-range or correlated pseudo states

We mentioned above that the presence of a virtual or resonance state, or possibly a bound state of nearly zero energy, could have a large influence on the scattering in certain energy regions. Even when not in the energy region of quasi-bound states, the behavior of the short-range part (i.e., small r_1 and r_2) of the effective potentials may be more important in determining the scattering parameters than the long-range polarizability effects. Such short-range flexibility may be put into the assumed total wave function by supplementing a close-coupling expansion with a function $\Phi(r_1, r_2, r_{12})$, where $\Phi \to 0$ as r_1 or $r_2 \to \infty$. Such a term will introduce an additional kernel to the coupled radial equations but this does not as a rule greatly complicate their numerical solution. The function Φ may be of the form $c\chi_b$, where χ_b is a Rayleigh-Ritz variationally determined wave function representing the true bound states or compound states of the projectile-target system. On the other hand, a less restrictive choice for Φ is to allow it to contain parameters which are determined by the variational principle for scattering. It is not clear that a Φ determined in this latter manner would turn out to have the form of $c\chi_b$ since the coupling with the open channels is neglected in the evaluation of χ_b.

Seaton [9] has pointed out that a more consistent treatment of the closed channel part of the scattering wave function should not make a distinction between target- and scattering wave functions, but rather treat both electrons on the same basis. Thus the short-range or correlated pseudo states are different from all of the other types discussed here in that they are wave functions of the composite system (projectile plus target) rather than states of the target alone.

2.4. *"Flux-loss" pseudo states*

A difficulty with most types of pseudo states is that they are useful only in very specific energy regions. For example, the polarization pseudo states, $\bar{u}_{30}$, $\bar{u}_{31}$, and $\bar{u}_{32}$, are expected to give best results within a small energy region (say ≈ 1 eV) above the $n = 2$ threshold. One would expect them to give poor results in the vicinity of the $n = 3$ threshold because their corresponding pseudo thresholds, $\bar{E}_{30}$, $\bar{E}_{31}$, and $\bar{E}_{32}$, are no longer degenerate and are each different from the true threshold energy E_3. Thus real excitations of these pseudo states would not be a physically reasonable situation.

Burke and Webb [10] have introduced pseudo states whose function it is to somehow simulate the actual loss of flux into the infinity of excited states (both bound and continuum) that are energetically accessible at intermediate electron energies (say 1 to 4 Ry). They are of the form

$$\bar{u}_{nl} = \sum_{i} c_i r^i \exp(-\gamma_{nl} r), \qquad (9)$$

where the coefficients were chosen to orthogonalize the pseudo states with the open-channel hydrogenic eigenstates and to yield degenerate pseudo-threshold energies (for a given n) which are made to coincide with the actual ionization threshold. It was felt that the greatest effect of inelastic flux loss would occur at the onset of ionization. Clearly, with a sufficient number of c_i and γ_{nl} parameters there is no difficulty in meeting these conditions, and hence there is no uniqueness associated with the resulting pseudo states.

2.5. *Other pseudo states*

In addition to the above pseudo states, which have been chosen to optimize some physical feature of the scattering problem, a number of calculations have been performed using pseudo states whose only apparent virtue is that they are numerically convenient. These are used in the same spirit as one would use a superposition of many configurations or arbitary functions to find bound-state energies in atoms and molecules. The existence of the upper-bound principle in the energy calculation allows one to systematically approach the correct result by increasing the complexity of the trial wave function. Except for some very restricted cases, one does not have a general bounding principle for the scattering parameters, so the choice of arbitrary pseudo states is of more limited usefulness.

3. Electron-atom scattering

The only use of Sturmian pseudo states in the "electron"-atom problem was by Rotenberg [2] for positron-hydrogen elastic scattering. A close-coupling expansion containing as many as eight Sturmian functions was used. Unfortunately, a numerical error was later found in these results and they were never repeated, so the question of the usefulness of a Sturmian expansion in the "electron"-hydrogen problem has never been answered.

The low-energy elastic electron-hydrogen scattering has been thoroughly investigated with a variety of pseudo states. The results for the ^{1}S and ^{1}P elastic scattering are given in table 2 where they are compared with the "exact" many-parameter Kohn variational calculations of Schwartz [11] and Armstead [12]. The best pseudo-state result for the ^{1}S case is that of Matese and Oberoi [13], who have used a 1s, 2s, 2p eigenfunction expansion supplemented by a short-range pseudo state of the form $c\chi_b(\mathbf{r}_1,\mathbf{r}_2)$. χ_b is a linear combination of products of short-range functions of r_1 and r_2 (no r_{12} included) which minimizes the expectation value of the H$^-$ Hamiltonian, and an appropriate angular function. The next two lines are the results of Burke et al. [14] using 1s, 2s and 1s, 2s, 2p expansions supplemented by the polarization pseudo states $\bar{u}_{21}$ and $\bar{\bar{u}}_{21}$, respectively. As expected, the $\bar{\bar{u}}_{21}$ result is somewhat better than the $\bar{u}_{21}$ result because, although they both contain the full $\alpha_1(1s\rightarrow p\rightarrow 1s)$, the first is a 4-state rather than a 3-state expansion. Note that for the ^{1}P case the polarization pseudo-state results are quite good at low energies compared with the ^{1}S case because the higher angular momenta are more sensitive to the long-range polarization potential. The final line in table 2 gives the 1s, 2s, 2p results of Burke et al. [15] for comparison. It can be seen that the improvements introduced by the pseudo states are substantial.

We may make one additional comparison in elastic scattering at

Table 2

Phase shifts for ^{1}S and ^{1}P elastic $e−H$ scattering. The first line gives the "exact" variational results of [11] and [12]; lines 2−5 give various pseudo-state results [13], [14], [15]. The phase shifts are given in rad; k^2 is the electron energy in Ry. (From [13].)

	^{1}S					^{1}P				
$k^2 = 0.01$	0.09	0.25	0.49	0.64	0.01	0.09	0.25	0.49	0.64
"Exact" [11,12]										
2.553	1.696	1.202	0.930	0.886	0.007	0.017	−0.001	−0.013	−0.004
1s,2s,2p + cx_b [13]										
2.545	1.683	1.187	0.917	0.873	0.006	0.013	−0.008	−0.023	−0.015
1s,2s + $\overline{2p}$ [14]										
2.529	1.657	1.155	0.875	0.823	0.006	0.014	−0.007	−0.026	−0.021
1s,2s,2p + $\overline{2p}$ [14]										
2.532	1.663	1.162	0.881	0.832	0.006	0.014	−0.007	−0.023	−0.017
1s,2s,2p [15]										
2.492	1.596	1.093	0.817	0.773	0.003	0.004	−0.029	−0.059	−0.059

$k^2 = 0.16$ Ry, where the ^{1}S phase shift of Schwartz is 1.4146 rad, while Burke
and Taylor [16] find a value of 1.4143 rad using a 1s, 2s, 2p expansion supplemented by a 16-term correlation pseudo state $\Phi(r_1, r_2, r_{12})$ in which all parameters have been optimized by the scattering variational principle. This is
clearly a much better result than is given by the less elaborate pseudo states
in table 2. They have applied this method also to elastic S-wave e–He$^+$ scattering and also to a few inelastic cases in these systems. Jacobs [17] has used
a set of numerically convenient 2s, 2p, 3s and 3p pseudo states (which are
linear combinations of the Coulomb Sturmians) to evaluate the ^{1}P e–He$^+$
elastic and inelastic scattering wave functions, which were used as the final
states for the calculation of the photoionization cross-sections of the $1\,^1$S
and $2\,^1$S states of He.

If we proceed to somewhat higher energy than is contained in table 2,
but still below the $n = 2$ threshold, we come to the region of elastic resonances.
A number of pseudo-state calculations have been applied to the lowest
$(2s^2)^1$S resonance in the e–H system, which occurs at an energy of 0.703 Ry,
and these results are given in table 3. The lower-bound principle for elastic
phase shifts assures us that the calculated phase shift (for all results given in
table 3) must lie below the exact phase shift. On this basis the best result is
that of Burke and Taylor [16], obtained with a 1s, 2s, 2p expansion supplemented by a 16-parameter correlation pseudo state. Also included in table 3
are the results of calculations with short-range pseudo states, polarization
pseudo states, and pure eigenstate expansions. Matese and Oberoi [13]
have reasoned that the best choice of χ_b in the resonance region would be a
bound state which corresponds to the appropriate compound or autoionizing
state, and have thus evaluated χ_b subject to the constraint that the hydrogenic
ground state is properly projected out. However, if one compares their two

Table 3
Phase shifts for elastic e–H scattering at the lowest ^{1}S resonance (0.703 Ry). The results
are from various pseudo-state calculations, as indicated in the first column. The phase
shifts are given in rad; k^2 is the electron energy in Ry. (From [13].)

1s,2s,2p +	$k^2 = 0.68$	0.69	0.70	0.71	0.72	0.73
Φ (16 terms) [16]	0.929	0.989	1.431	3.765	3.902	3.946
$c\chi_b$ (1s^2) [13]	0.915	0.970	1.288	3.713	3.883	3.932
$c\chi_b$ (2s^2) [13]	0.859	0.924	1.427	3.688	3.825	3.871
$\overline{3s,3p,3d}$ [19]	0.850	0.915	1.423	3.677	3.814	3.864
3s,3p,3d [15]	0.835	0.901	1.393	3.654	3.797	3.844

results (using the $1s^2$ ^1S stable state or $2s^2$ ^1S compound state for χ_b) one
finds a generally better result with the stable H^- state. This is contrary to one's
intuition and perhaps is explainable by the possibility that the determination
of χ_b by an energy-variational method does not tend to yield the same function as if it were determined by the scattering-variational method. Thus
Matese and Oberoi have only the one linear parameter in $c\chi_b$ to optimize for
the scattering calculation while Burke and Taylor have all 16 parameters in Φ
to vary.

Proceeding to the $n = 2$ inelastic threshold, the two pseudo-state calculations which give the best results just above this threshold are the ones of
Taylor and Burke [18] using a 20-parameter correlation Φ and of Geltman
and Burke [19] using the $\overline{3s}, \overline{3p}, \overline{3d}$ polarization pseudo states. In table 4 the
various results just above the threshold are given. The result labeled "best" is a
composite of all the partial cross-sections which correspond to maximum
eigenphase sums. The minimum principle here requires that the exact eigenphase sum be an upper bound to any of these calculated eigenphase sums. On
the basis of this criterion the $\overline{3s}, \overline{3p}, \overline{3d}$ results were found to be "best" for all
symmetry cases except the ^1S, where the correlation results were "best". The
experimental results for the $1s-2s$ and $1s-2p$ excitations close to threshold
[20,21], which are put on an absolute basis by normalization to the Born
approximation at higher energies, generally fall about 20% below the calculated values given in table 4. This discrepancy is much larger than the differences between all the calculated values given in the table. (A new measurement [22] reported at this Conference reduces the discrepancy with theory
to about 5%.) However, a comparison of the experimental ratio $Q(1s-2s)/$
$Q(1s-2p)$ [20,22] with the "best" calculated ratio gives extremely good
agreement (fig. 1).

Burke and Webb [10] have supplemented a $1s, 2s, 2p$ eigenstate expan-
sion with $\overline{3s}$ and $\overline{3p}$ "flux-loss" pseudo states to evaluate the $1s-2s$ and $1s-2p$
excitation cross-section at higher energies. Their results are shown in fig. 2
compared with other calculations and experiment, and are seen to be remarkably good.

4. Proton-atom scattering

In the area of the scattering of heavy charged particles by atoms, the only
applications to date of pseudo-state expansions are for the proton-hydrogen
atom system. This system has been the subject of much theoretical investigation. The energy range of interest lies above 1 keV since, because of the mass

Table 4

Excitation cross-sections (in πa_0^2) for e−H collisions just above the $n = 2$ threshold. The results are from various pseudo-state calculations, as indicated in the first column. k^2 is the electron energy in Ry. (From [19].)

1s,2s,2p +	$k^2 = 0.76$		0.78		0.81		0.83	
	Q(1s−2s)	Q(1s−2p)	Q(1s−2s)	Q(1s−2p)	Q(1s−2s)	Q(1s−2p)	Q(1s−2s)	Q(1s−2p)
3s,3p,3d [15]	0.160	0.264	0.167	0.264	0.208	0.322	0.229	0.381
$\overline{3s,3p,3d}$ [19]	0.146	0.238	0.160	0.246	0.203	0.301	0.222	0.346
Φ (20 terms) [18]	0.141	0.239	0.152	0.233	0.195	0.273	0.212	0.308
"best"	0.146	0.237	0.160	0.244	0.192	0.296	0.222	0.351

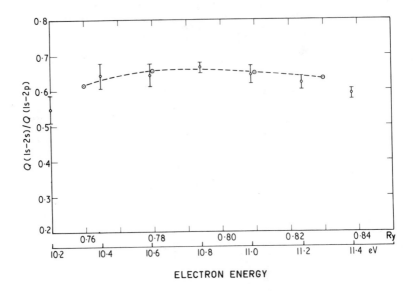

Fig. 1. Cross-section ratio $Q(1s-2s)/Q(1s-2p)$ for the electron-impact excitation of hydrogen just above the $n = 2$ threshold. Comparison of "best" theoretical values (dashed curve) [19] and experiment (points with error bars) [20]. (From [19].)

difference, proton impacts are very inefficient in causing electronic transitions at lower energies. The basic method used is the semi-classical or impact parameter method in which, for the higher energies of interest, one assumes that the relative motion of the two protons may be described by a straight line path with constant velocity. An expansion for the full time-dependent wave function is assumed in terms of atomic eigenstates which may be supplemented by pseudo states. These must include basis functions which are centered on both protons since charge-transfer processes are of interest as well as direct ones. The transition amplitudes are obtained as the solution of a set of coupled first-order equations in the time or distance-along-path variable for a particular velocity and impact parameter, and cross-sections are calculated as integrals over all impact parameters.

The first application of pseudo states to this problem was the use of Sturmian functions by Gallaher and Wilets [23]. They have used the Coulomb Sturmian states with $E_0 = -1/(l+1)^2$, such that the first Sturmian state coincides with the lowest lying hydrogenic state for a given l. Rather than

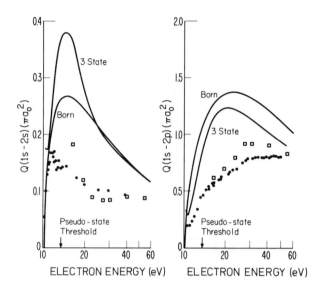

Fig. 2. Cross-sections Q for the electron impact excitation of hydrogen including cascade contributions. Calculation with "flux-loss" pseudo states (open squares) [10], experiment (filled points) [20,21], Born, and 3-state close-coupling results. (From [10].)

having supplemented an expansion containing atomic eigenstates for all the final states of interest, Gallaher and Wilets used a completely Sturmian expansion. This required the projection for the transition amplitudes

$$a(1sA \rightarrow nlmC) = \int dr \psi_{nlmC}(\mathbf{r}) \Psi_{1sA}(\mathbf{r}, t = \infty) ,$$ (10)

where C represents the proton on which the final electronic state is centered (A = target proton, B = incident proton) (cf. fig. 3). The most extensive calculations were carried out with a set of four Sturmian functions — 1s, 2s, $2p_0$, and $2p_1$ (symmetry considerations show that inclusion of the $m = -1$ state is redundant). They have also done some calculations with six-state ($1s,2s,2p_0$, $2p_1,3s,4s$), eight-state ($3p_0,3p_1$) and nine-state (5s) Sturmian expansions.

A calculation in which a 1s, 2s, $2p_0$, $2p_1$ expansion was supplemented by numerically convenient $\overline{3s}$, $\overline{3p_0}$, $\overline{3p_1}$ pseudo states was carried out by Cheshire et al. [24]. The results of various calculations for the process of 2p charge transfer are given in fig. 3. This cross-section is perhaps the most diffi-

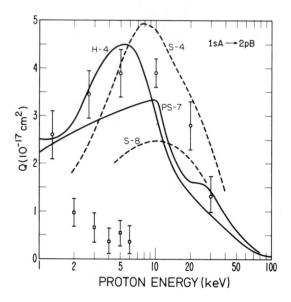

Fig. 3. Cross-section for the charge-transfer excitation to the 2p state in the collision of protons with ground-state hydrogen atoms. The number of basis states centered on each proton is indicated on curves; H-hydrogenic eigenstates [24,27], S-Sturmian pseudo states [23], PS-pseudo states of Cheshire et al. [24]. Experimental points – circles [25] and squares [26].

cult to compute of all the transitions considered since it involves a charge transfer as well as excitation with change in orbital angular momentum. The large disparities between the various calculated curves indicate the sensitivity of the results to the assumed basis functions. The large change in results in going from a four- to an eight-state Sturmian expansion indicates that one has not yet achieved significant convergence in the Sturmian expansion. Thus there is no indication that the use of pseudo states in this problem has produced any improvement over the pure hydrogenic expansion. The two experiments on this cross-section have also yielded very different results, indicating that severe experimental as well as theoretical problems exist for the determination of these cross-sections.

Work is in progress by Wilets, Redding, and Zimmerman [28] using the simple pseudo states $\exp(-\lambda_i r)$ (with λ_i complex). The numerical convenience of exponential functions allows them to include the order of 20 states without unduly increasing the computer time needed. Preliminary results indicate good convergence.

References

[1] J.C.Y.Chen, *VII ICPEAC, Invited Talks and Progress Reports,* eds. T.R.Govers and F.J.de Heer (North-Holland Publ. Co., Amsterdam, 1972) p. 232.

[2] M.Rotenberg, Ann. Phys (New York) *19* (1962) 262.

[3] M.Rotenberg, in: *Advances in Atomic and Molecular Physics,* eds..D.R.Bates and I.Esterman, vol. 6 (Academic Press, New York, 1970) p. 233.

[4] R.J.Damburg and E.Karule, Proc. Phys. Soc. *90* (1967) 637.

[5] R.J.Damburg and S.Geltman, Phys. Rev. Letters *20* (1968) 485.

[6] V.K.Lan, private communication.

[7] A.Temkin, Phys. Rev. *107* (1957) 1004;
A.Temkin and J.C.Lamkin, Phys. Rev. *121* (1961) 788.

[8] J.Callaway, R.W.Labahn, R.T.Pu and W.M.Duxler, Phys. Rev. *168* (1968) 12;
V.K.Lan, J. Phys. B *4* (1971) 658;
N.Feautrier, H.van Regemorter and V.K.Lan, J. Phys. B *4* (1971) 670.

[9] M.J.Seaton, Comments Atomic Molecular Phys. *1* (1970) 184.

[10] P.G.Burke and T.G.Webb, J. Phys. B *3* (1970) L131.

[11] C.Schwartz, Phys. Rev. *124* (1961) 1468.

[12] R.L.Armstead, Phys. Rev. *171* (1968) 91.

[13] J.J.Matese and R.S.Oberoi, Phys. Rev. A *4* (1971) 569.

[14] P.G.Burke, D.F.Gallaher and S.Geltman, J. Phys. B *2* (1969) 1142.

[15] P.G.Burke, S.Ormonde and W.Whitaker, Proc. Phys. Soc. *92* (1967) 319.

[16] P.G.Burke and A.J.Taylor, Proc. Phys. Soc. *88* (1966) 549.

[17] V.Jacobs, Phys. Rev. A *3* (1971) 289.

[18] A.J.Taylor and P.G.Burke, Proc. Phys. Soc. *92* (1967) 336.

[19] S.Geltman and P.G.Burke, J. Phys. B *3* (1970) 1062.

[20] W.R.Ott, W.Kauppila and W.L.Fite, Phys. Rev. A *1* (1970) 1089;
W.Kauppila, W.R.Ott and W.L.Fite, Phys. Rev. A *1* (1970) 1099.

[21] J.W.McGowan, J.F.Williams and E.K.Curley, Phys. Rev. *180* (1969) 132.

[22] D.M.Cox and S.J.Smith, *VII ICPEAC, Abstracts of Papers,* eds. L.M.Branscomb et al., Vol. 2 (North-Holland Publ. Co., Amsterdam, 1971) p. 707.

[23] D.F.Gallaher and L.Wilets, Phys. Rev. *169* (1968) 139.

[24] I.M.Cheshire, D.F.Gallaher and A.J.Taylor, J. Phys. B *3* (1970) 813.

[25] R.F.Stebbings, R.A.Young, C.L.Oxley and H.Ehrhardt, Phys. Rev. *138* (1965) A1312;
R.A.Young, R.F.Stebbings and J.W.McGowan, Phys. Rev. *171* (1968) 85.

[26] D.Gaily and R.Geballe, private communication.

[27] D.Rapp and T.E.Sharp, private communication.

[28] L.Wilets, private communication.

Physics of Electronic and Atomic Collisions, VII ICPEAC, 1971 − North-Holland (1972)

ON THE APPLICATION OF THE FADDEEV EQUATIONS
TO ATOMIC PROBLEMS*

JOSEPH C. Y. CHEN

*Department of Physics and
Institute for Pure and Applied Physical Sciences
University of California, San Diego, La Jolla, California 92037*

Recent results obtained from the application of the Faddeev equations to atomic problems are summarized and discussed. At low energies, the convergence problem is still critical for the separable-expansion method. Application of the Faddeev-Watson multiple-scattering expansion to high-energy atomic problems yields interesting predictions both for elastic scattering and for rearrangement collisions. These high-energy results are compared with the various Born approximations.

1. Introduction

There are two apparent reasons which excite one's imagination and motivate him to study the application of the Faddeev equations to three-body atomic problems.

(a) The Faddeev equations are in a form which is mathematically more rigorous than other equations so far available for a non-relativistic three-body problem with only pair interactions. With a rather weak restriction on the two-body potentials, Faddeev [1] has shown that the kernel of these equations is compact for all but physical values of E. All terms in the expansion of the equations containing five or more two-body T-matrices are bounded for real E and the singularities in the amplitude are branch points near which the amplitude is bounded. Although for Coulomb interaction the analytic behavior of the kernel is not clear, it nevertheless remains true that the kernel of the once-iterated Faddeev equations is connected.

(b) The faddeev equations are in form which allows straightforward computation of the bound- and resonance-states, as well as of the transition amplitude for scattering- and rearrangement collisions, once the off-shell two-

* Research supported in part by the U.S. Atomic Energy Commission Contract No. AT(04-3)-34, PA 196 and by the National Science Foundation Grant No. GP-20459.

body T-matrices for each pair of interactions are explicitly known. For Coulomb interactions, several mathematically well-defined, closed-form representations are available for the off-shell two-body Coulomb T-matrix [2]. This then puts the three-body atomic problems (both the bound and continuum problems) within the realization of a numerical solution.

Whether such an enthusiams is premature remains to be seen. It should nevertheless be noted that the methods which have so far been adopted for solving the Faddeev equations have all met with only a very limited success.

In this progress report, I shall summarize and discuss the recent results obtained in the various attempts to solve the Faddeev equations for atomic problems. No effort will be made in this report to reproduce the theoretical development of the various attempts. For theoretical details, the original publications should be consulted. In sec. 2, the low-energy results are reported. The results for high-energy atomic collisions are reported in sec. 3.

2. The Faddeev equations for low-energy atomic problems

At energies below the three-body break-up threshold, the energy argument of the two-body T-matrix which appears in the kernel of the Faddeev equations is negative. To solve the Faddeev equations for atomic problems below this break-up threshold, all we need is the off-shell twobody Coulomb T-matrix at negative energies [3]. A number of exact alternative expressions are known for the off-shell Coulomb T-matrix at negative energies. Since we are at negative energies, the off-shell Coulomb T-matrix is a well behaved function and has, as it should, an infinite set of simple poles associated with the Coulomb two-body bound states. Thus, the problem is reduced simply to a computational problem.

The Faddeev equations are a set of three coupled integral equations with five variables. By partial-wave decomposition, one may reduce these equations to a set of N coupled integral equations in two variables. This permits the reduction of the number of variables at the expense of increasing the number of coupled equations. For atomic problems such as the ($e^{\pm}$, H) systems, the partial-wave decomposition has a reasonable convergence behavior at low energies due to the favorable mass ratio. The set of coupled partial-wave Faddeev equations in two variables may be truncated under favorable situations.

The separable-expansion method introduced by Ball et al. [3] consists of expanding the partial-wave off-shell two-body Coulomb T-matrix in a sum of terms which is separable in the two variables of the coupled partial-wave

Faddeev equations. This then permits the coupled equations in two variables to be reduced to coupled equations in one variable. For Coulomb interactions, there are two exact term-by-term separable representations of the off-shell Coulomb T-matrix available in terms either of the Sturmian functions [3] or of the Coulomb functions [4]. Consequently, alternative sets of coupled partial-wave Faddeev equations in one variable can be derived. Such sets of equations have been derived in the Sturmian-function representations and in the mixed-mode representation [5]. In the mixed-mode representation, the Coulomb-function representation was adopted for pairs where the interaction potential is attractive, whereas for pairs where the interaction potential is repulsive and the continuum contribution is dominating, the Sturmian-function representation was adopted.

The two-body bound-state poles in the off-shell two-body T-matrix give rise to the threshold branch points for the off-shell three-body amplitude. Three-body bound states will appear in the off-shell three-body amplitude as poles below the first threshold branch point. From the residues at these poles,

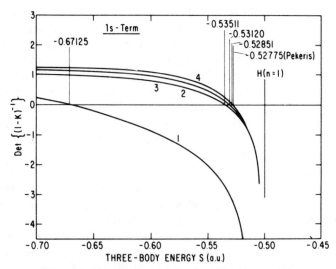

Fig. 1. H$^-$ bound-state calculation (from ref. [6]); the zero in the function det $\{1-K\}$ where K is the matrix representation of the Faddeev kernel (see eq. (3.1) of ref. [6]), gives the position of the pole in the three-body amplitude. In this calculation, the e$^-$–p$^+$ amplitude is approximated by the 1s hydrogen (Coulomb) function only and 1, 2, 3, 4 indicate the number of the Sturmian functions included in the s-wave e$^-$–e$^-$ amplitude, (See also C.L. Pekeris, Phys. Rev. 115 (1959) 1216.

one obtains the three-body bound-state wave functions. The region between
the lowest and the next branch points is the energy region for purely elastic
scattering of a particle by a two-body system in its ground state. A single
inelastic process occurs above the second threshold, and so forth. By solving
the exact coupled equations in one variable, we can obtain, in principle to
any desired accuracy, the bound-state and resonance energies and wave functions as well as transition amplitudes below the three-body breakup threshold
[3, 5–9]. In practice it is always necessary to truncate the separable sums for
the two-body Coulomb T-matrix and to limit the number of partial waves

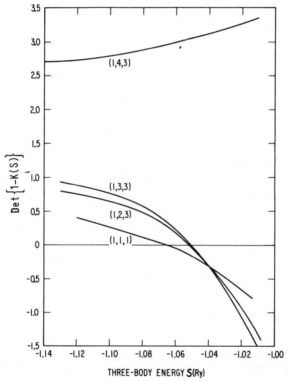

THREE-BODY ENERGY S(Ry)

Fig. 2. Investigation of the three-body (e^+, e^-, p) bound state (from ref. [7]). The zero
of det $\{1 - K(s)\}$ corresponds to the three-body bound-state pole in the three-body
amplitude at energies below the elastic threshold at -1 Ry. The symbol $(1, x, 3)$ denotes
that the result is obtained by taking 1s Sturmian-function term for the (e^-, p^+) pair; 1s,
2s, and 2p Sturmian-function terms for the (e^+, e^-) pair, and an x number of Sturmian-
function terms for the (p^+, e^+) pair. The Sturmian functions are counted in the hydrogenic order.

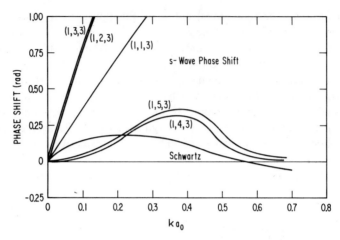

Fig. 3. Energy dependence of the s-wave positron hydrogen scattering phase shift (from ref. [7]); κ^2 is the center-of-mass energy of the projectile in a.u. The positronium-formation threshold is located at $ka_0 = 0.707$. The symbol $(1, x, 3)$ denotes that the result is obtained by taking only 1s S–F terms for the (e^+, e^-) pair and 1s, 2s and 2p s-F terms for the (e^-, p^+) pair and an x number of Sturmian-function terms for the (p^+, e^+) pair. The Sturmian functions are counted in the hydrogenic order. For "Schwartz", see C. Schwartz, Phys. Rev. *124*, (1961) 1468.

in the coupled equations; this then leads to the problem of convergence with respect to the inclusion of the remaining terms.

In figs. 1 and 2 two samples of the convergence behavior in the determination of three-body bound-state poles [6, 7] are given for the (e^-, H) and (e^+, H) systems in the mixed-mode and Sturmian-function representations, respectively. It is seen that the three-body bound state predicted using only the first few terms converges for the (e^-, H) system to the Pekeris value in fig. 1 and disappears for the (e^+, H) system in fig. 2 when more terms are included in the separable sum. The calculated energy dependence of the phase shift for elastic (e^+, H) scattering [7] is shown in fig. 3. The result exhibits an oscillatory behavior similar to that observed in the determination of resonance states and phase shifts in the (e^-, H) system [3, 5]. This slow, oscillatory convergence behavior prevents the separable-expansion method from yielding accurate predictions. Unless some perturbation scheme or variational techniques may be devised to improve the convergence the separable-expansion method in the present form is limited to describing qualitative features of atomic collisions.

3. The Faddeev-Watson multiple-scattering expansion for high-energy atomic collisions

For high-energy atomic collisions, the iterative solution of the Faddeev equations may be used. This iterative solution in the form of a multiple-scattering expansion is identical [10] to that obtained from a set of coupled equations developed by Watson [11] for the scattering of a particle by a system of N bound particles when $N = 2$. The Faddeev-Watson multiple-scattering expansion does not contain any disconnected diagrams. Physically, this implies a possibly better convergence for these expansions than, for example, the Born series which are obtained by iterating the corresponding Lippmann-Schwinger equation. The difficulties with the Born series have long been recognized [12]. It would, therefore, be of interest to compare the Faddeev-Watson multiple-scattering (FEMS) expansion with the Born series.

In the FWMS expansion the successive terms are expressed in terms of the off-shell two-body Coulomb T-matrices, instead of the bare Coulomb potentials. At energies above the three-body breakup threshold, care must then be taken in treating the branch-point singularities in the Coulomb T-matrix [13, 14]. In addition to the normal continuum (unitarity) cut, the Coulomb T-matrix contains cuts on the initial and final half of the energy shell. It is the latter on-shell Coulomb cuts which make the Coulomb interaction much different [14, 15]. I shall return to this point later in connection with rearrangement collisions.

I shall now first consider the application of the first-order FWMS approximation to several elastic-scattering problems [16]. It is well known that the first-order Born approximation does not distinguish elastic electron scattering from position scattering. When the two-body target is made of equal-mass particles (having charges which are equal but opposite in sign) the first-order Born approximation predicts a zero for the elastic scattering independent of the incident particle [16]. This anomalous behavior does not appear in the first-order FWMS approximation, because in the latter approximation the two bare Coulomb potentials are replaced by two off-shell two-body Coulomb T-matrices. This then allows us to take into consideration the contributions from the intermediate two-body poles and branch-point singularities, and also modifies the contributions from the poles in the initial and final two-body bound-state wave functions.

The exact first-order FWMS approximation has been evaluated numerically by Sinfailam and Chen [17] for the elastic $(e^\pm, H)$ scatterings and for elastic $(p^+, e^- e^+)$ and $(e^+, e^- e^+)$ scattering. The results for the differential cross-section are given in fig. 4 and 5. In fig. 4 the results for the elastic scattering

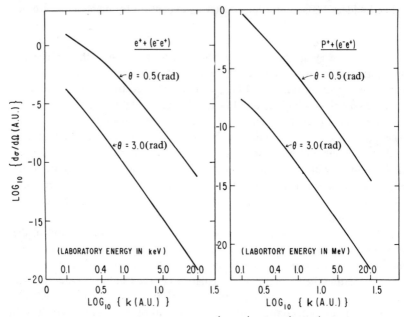

Fig. 4. The energy dependence of the elastic (e^+, e^-e^+) and (p^+, e^-e^+) differential scattering cross-section in the first order FWMS approximation (θ and k refer to C.M. system). κ^2 is the center-of-mass of the projectile in a.u.

of p^+ and e^+ by positronium are shown. Here the first-order Born approximation gives zero contribution. A comparison of the energy dependence of the differential elastic ($e^\pm$, H) scattering cross sections in the first-order FWMS and Born approximations is given in fig. 5 for two fixed scattering angles. It is seen that significant differences are predicted in the first-order FWMS approximation at rather high energies and large scattering angles.

It has long been generally believed that at sufficiently high energies the first-order Born approximation would be accurate. The Born results in the energy range between $E = 100$ to 500 eV have been used extensively to normalize the relative experimental measurements for electron scattering by atoms (or molecules). The result shown in fig. 5 calls for the need to examine quantitatively how high the energy should be for the first-order Born approximation to be accurate. The energy for the first-order Born approximation to be accurate can be determined experimentally by locating the energy above which the difference between the (e^-, H) and (e^+, H) scattering data ceases to be appreciable.

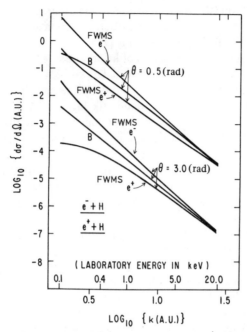

Fig. 5. Comparison of energy dependence of the (e^-,H) and (e^+,H) elastic differential scattering cross section in the first-order FWMS approximation with the Born approximation at two fixed scattering angles (from ref. [17]) (θ and κ refer to C.M. system). κ^2 is the center-of-mass energy of the projectile in a.u.

The application of the FWMS expansion to three-body rearrangement collisions is perhaps more interesting. To clarify the problems involved in the rearrangement collisions, I would like first to give a very brief review of the controversies concerning the energy dependence and the role of the proton-proton interaction in (p^+, H) electron-transfer collisions.

Following the work of Oppenheimer [18], Brinkman and Kramers (BK) have argued in 1930 that the proton-proton interaction should not effectively contribute to the electron-transfer cross-section [19]. The neglect of proton-proton interaction is justified in the high-energy region of validity of the first-order Born approximation by the large proton-electron mass ratio which allows a classical description of the collision process. This was, however, questioned by Bates and Dalgarno [20] and by Jackson and Schiff (JS) [21]. The latter have shown that this interaction is not only non-negligible, but that it has the same energy dependence (E^{-6}) at high energies as the rest of the first-order Born term (the electron-proton interaction). The inclusion of the proton-proton interaction reduces the BK cross-section at all energies, and by a factor of 0.661 in the high-energy limit [21].

These results spurred investigation of higher-order terms in the Born series for the (p^+, H) electron-transfer collisions. Drisko [22] has found that the second-order Born terms cancel the first-order terms and give rise to an $E^{-5.5}$ energy dependence for the cross-section in the high-energy limit. Thus, the second-order Born approximation does not converge to the first-order Born approximation. Mapleton [23] has also investigated the second-order Born terms and has found agreement with Drisko's result for small-angle scattering. However, he was unable to determine whether the second-order Born terms yield convergent amplitudes when all the intermediate states are summed over. Indeed, the convergence of the Born series for rearrangement collision in general is in doubt.

According to the first-order FWMS approximation, the proton-proton interaction is not simply given by the bare Coulomb potential; instead it is given by the off-shell Coulomb T-matrix. It is not unreasonable to expect that the effect of the proton-proton interaction would be reduced in the high-energy limit if the off-shell Coulomb T-matrix is taken into consideration [24, 25]. By going into the complex plane, it can be shown [14] that in the first-order FWMS approximation the additional three-body amplitude consists of contributions coming from (a) the two-body asymptotic poles in the initial and final bound-state wave functions; (b) the intermediate two-body anti-bound-state poles; and (c) the branch-point singularities on the off-shell T-matrix for proton-proton interactions.

Chen and Hambro [25] have argued that in the high-energy limit the on-shell contribution dominates. Thus, the contributions coming from the intermediate bound-state poles and the branch-point singularities associated with the continuum (or unitary) cut are small in comparison with the contributions coming from the asymptotic bound-state poles (which are the on-shell contributions). Based on the asymptotic bound state-pole contributions, Chen and Hambro have shown that the cross-section converges to the BK cross-section in the high-energy limit. This result is, however, not correct because the Coulomb T-matrix has also cuts on the energy shell (in addition to the normal continuum cut) which were neglected. In the high-energy limit, the on-shell Coulomb cuts actually give rise to the leading contribution [15]. The on-shell cuts were also neglected in the work of Shastry et al. [24].

The appearance of the cuts on the energy shell is a consequence of the absence of the long-range Coulomb distortion in the plane-wave momentum representation. The convenience of adopting a representation in which the free Green's function is diagonal is obtained at the expense of having the on-shell Coulomb cuts. Thus, these cuts are a part of the package deal of the plane-wave momentum representation for the Coulomb interaction and cannot be neglected by appeal to properties of the screened Coulomb potential.

The complete first-order FWMS approximation for the (p^+, H) electron-transfer collisions has later been evaluated numerically by Chen and Kramer [15]. The results for the differential and total cross-sections are shown in figs. 6, 7, and 8. It is seen from fig. 6 that the exact cancellation of the contributions coming from the bare attractive and repulsive interaction which causes the JS differential cross-section to dip to zero at a forward angle is removed in the first-order FWMS approximation. At high energies the first-order FWMS approximation approaches the JS differential cross-section from above at forward angles (fig. 7). As the scattering angle increases, the cross-section gradually crosses the JS cross-section and then lies below it. The inclusion of the pure p^+-p^+ interaction to all orders thus shifts the cross-section

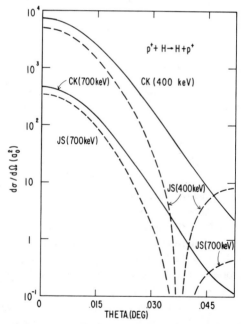

Fig. 6. Comparison of the Jackson-Schiff (JS, ref. [21]) and first-order FWMS (CK, ref. [15]) approximations to the differential cross-section in atomic units as a function of the c.m. scattering angle for the (p^+,H) electron-transfer rearrangement collisions at two fixed laboratory energies (in keV).

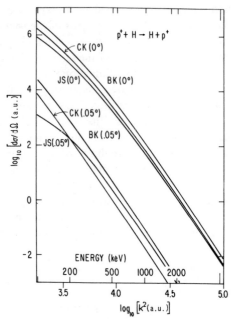

Fig. 7. Comparison of the Brinkman-Kramers (BK, ref. [19]), Jackson and Schiff (JS, ref. [21]) and the first-order FWMS (CK, ref. [15]) approximations to the differential (p^+,H) electron-transfer rearrangement cross-section as a function of the center-of-mass energy k^2 (the corresponding laboratory energy of the projectile is also given in keV) at two fixed center-of-mass scattering angles.

back from the JS cross-section towards the BK cross-section (fig. 8) but asymptotically ($E>$2MeV) it returns to the JS cross-section (fig. 7). Thus in the high-energy limit, the proton-proton interaction still provides a significant contribution to the electron-transfer cross-section in comparison with the contribution coming from the bare $e^- - p^+$ interaction.

This suggests that perhaps the leading term for the electron-transfer amplitude may not be given by the bare electron-proton interaction but rather is given by a higher-order term as was suggested by Drisko [22] on the basis of the Born series. The Drisko result was supported by the work of McCarroll and Salin [26], based on the Faddeev equations. This work was, however, disputed by Coleman [27]. Carpenter and Tuan [28] have shown, using the second-order FWMS expansion, that the electron-transfer cross-section converges to the second-order Born cross-section and has an $E^{-5.5}$ energy dependence. In the Carpenter-Tuan work, one of the off-shell Coulomb T-matrices

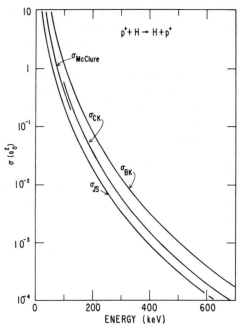

Fig. 8. Comparison of the Brinkman-Kramers (BK, ref. [19]), Jackson-Schiff (JS, ref. [21]) and the first-order FWMS (CK, ref. [15]) approximations to the total cross-section with experimental results (McClure, C.W. McClure, Phys. Rev. *148* (1966) 47) in atomic units as a function of the laboratory energy of the projectile in keV for the (p^+, H) electron-transfer rearrangement collisions.

in the second-order FWMS approximation was, however, taken to be the bare Coulomb potential. When the complete second-order FWMS approximation is evaluated, Chen et al. [14], have shown that both the second-order Born term considered by Drisko [22] and the truncated second-order FWMS term considered by Carpenter and Tuan [28] get cancelled. In view of the first-order FWMS results, it is conceivable that the remaining of the second-order FWMS term could converge to the second-order Born term at perhaps an even higher energy (than the energy for the first-order case) where the nonrelativistic approximation would certainly no longer be valid. Further investigation of the second-order FWMS terms is desirable. Experimental measurements of the total and differential electron-transfer cross-sections at such high energies are needed.

In conclusion, I would like to show the interesting result for the $(e^+ e^- e^+)$ electron-transfer cross-section obtained in the first-order FWMS approximation by Chen and Kramer [15]. This equal-mass problem in certain respects displays an interesting departure from the results of the (p^+, H) and other

systems, such as the (e^+,H) and $(p^+,e^-\mu^+)$ systems at corresponding velocities, investigated by them. In fig. 6 for the (p^+,H) system, it is seen that the
JS differential cross-section dips to zero for some scattering angle (due to the
cancellation between contributions coming from the e^--p^+ and p^+-p^+ interactions), then returns to briefly overshoot the first-order FWMS differential
cross-section before becoming a monotonically decreasing function of scattering angle. This implies that p^+-p^+ knock-out contribution to the electron-
transfer amplitude is not appreciable at these energies.

Figure 9 shows the behavior of the JS and first-order FWMS differential
cross-section for the (e^+,e^-e^+) system. In this case, after returning from the
dip, both the JS and first-order FWMS values do not begin to decrease but,
instead, steadily increase to $\theta = 180°$. The differential cross-sections at $\theta =$
$180°$ is actually larger than they were at the forward angle $\theta = 0°$. This indicates that there are considerable e^+-e^+ knock-out contributions to the $(e^+,$
$e^-e^+)$ electron-transfer cross-section. This knock-out effect shows up most
significantly in fig. 10: the total cross-section for this equal-mass system has

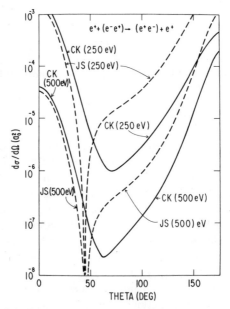

Fig. 9. Comparison of the Born (JS, ref. [15]), and the first-order FWMS (CK, ref. [15])
approximations to the differential cross-section in atomic units as a function of the c.m.
scattering angle for the (e^+, e^-e^+) electron-transfer rearrangement collisions at two fixed
laboratory energies.

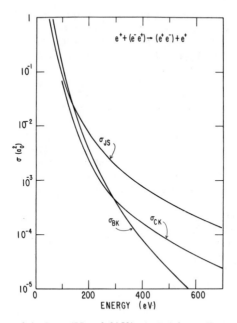

ENERGY (eV)

Fig. 10. Comparison of the Born (JS, ref. [15]), the Brinkman-Kramers (BK, ref. [15]) and the first-order FWMS (CK, ref. [15]) approximations to the total cross-section in atomic units as a function of the laboratory energy of the projectile in eV for the (e^+, e^-e^+) electron-transfer rearrangement collisions.

an E^{-3} energy dependence in the high-energy limit rather than the E^{-6} energy dependence shown by the other above-mentioned systems. The BK approximation which does not account for the e^+-e^+ interaction still predicts and E^{-6} energy dependence.

References

[1] L. D. Faddeev, *Mathematical aspects of the three-body problem in the quantum scattering theory,* The Israel Program for Scientific Translations, Jerusalem, 1965.

[2] For a review, see: J.C.Y. Chen and A.C. Chen, in: *Advances in Atomic and Molecular Physics, Vol 8.* Eds. D. R. Bates and I. Estermann, (Academic Press, New York, 1972) (to be published).

[3] J. S. Ball, J.C.Y. Chen and D.Y. Wong, *V ICPEAC, Abstracts of Papers,* Eds. I.P. Falks and E.S. Solovyov (Publishing House "Nauka". Leningrad, 1967) p. 20; Phys. Rev. *173* (1968) 202.

[4] J. C. Y. Chen and T. Ishihara, J. Phys. B 2 (1969) 12; Phys. Rev. 186 (1969) 25.

[5] J. C. Y. Chen, K.T. Chung and P.J. Kramer, Phys. Rev. 184 (1969) 64.

[6] J. C. Y. Chen and K.T. Chung, Phys. Rev. A 2 (1970) 1449.

[7] P. J. Kramer and J.C.Y. Chen, Phys. Rev. A 3 (1971) 568.

[8] G. Banerji, S.N. Banerjee and N.C. Sil, J. Phys. B.B 4 (1971) L5.

[9] S. Radhakant, C.S. Shastry and A.K. Rajagopal, Phys. Rev. A 3 (1971) 234.

[10] J. C. Y. Chen and C.J. Joachain, Physica 53 (1971) 333.

[11] K. M. Watson, Phys. Rev. 89 (1953) 575; 103 (1956) 489; 105 (1957) 1388.

[12] R. Aaron, R.D. Amedo and B.W. Lee, Phys. Rev. 121 (1961) 319; S. Weinberg, Phys. Rev. 130 (1963) 776;
     M. Scadron, S. Weinberg and J. Wright, Phys. Rev. 135 (1964) B202.

[13] J. Nuttall and R.W. Stagat, Phys. Rev. A 3 (1971) 1355.

[14] J. C. Y. Chen, A.C. Chen and P.J. Kramer, Phys. Rev. A 4 (1971) 1982.

[15] J. C. Y. Chen and P.J. Kramer, Phys. Rev. letters 27, (1971) 899; Phys. Rev. A5 (1972).

[16] A. C. Chen, J.C.Y. Chen, A.-L. Sinfailam and L. Hambro, Phys. Rev. A 4 (1971) 1988.

[17] A. -L. Sinfailam and J.C.Y. Chen, Phys. Rev. A 5 (1972) .

[18] J. R. Opppenheimer, Phys. Rev. 31 (1928) 349.

[19] H. C. Brinkman and H.A. Kramers, Proc. Acad. Sci. Amsterdam 33 (1930) 973.

[20] D. R. Bates and A. Dalgarno, Proc. Phys. Soc. A 65 (1952) 919.

[21] J. D. Jackson and and H. Schiff, Phys. Rev. 89 (1953) 359.

[22] D. R. Drisko, Thesis, Carnegie Institute of Technology (1955) (unpublished).

[23] R. A. Mapleton, Proc. Phys. Soc. 91 (1967) 868.

[24] C. S. Shastry, L. Kumar and J. Callaway, Phys. Rev. A 1 (1970) 1137.

[25] J. C. Y. Chen and L. Hambro, J. Phys. B 4 (1971) 191.

[26] R. McCarroll and A. Salin, Proc. Roy. Soc., Ser. A 300 (1967) 202.

[27] J. P. Coleman, J. Phys. B 1 (1968) 315 (letter to the Editor, followed by reply from R. McCarroll and A. Salin).

[28] C. P. Carpenter and T.F. Tuan, Phys. Rev. A 2 (1970) 1811.

Physics of Electronic and Atomic Collisions, VII ICPEAC, 1971 – North-Holland (1972)

USE OF THE GLAUBER APPROXIMATION
IN ATOMIC COLLISIONS

A PROGRESS REPORT

E.GERJUOY*

*Department of Physics, University of Pittsburgh,
Pittsburgh, Pennsylvania 15213, USA*

Progress in the use of Glauber Theory in atomic collisions is reviewed.
The Glauber approximation is described and its underlying basis discussed,
for potential scattering and for inelastic collisions. Actual calculations
using the Glauber approximation then are compared with experiment, and
with alternative approximations, particularly the Born and the Vainshtein.
It appears that the Glauber approximation is reliable for electron-hydrogen
elastic scattering and excitation at incident energies exceeding about 30 eV.
For more complicated atomic collisions, the utility of the Glauber approximation has not yet been significantly tested.

1. Introduction

I shall review recent progress in the use of the Glauber Approximation to
estimate atomic collision cross-sections. In so doing, I think a very brief
historical introduction is in order, because to my knowledge this paper,
which covers the period up to – but not including – the present Conference,
is the first attempt at a reasonably comprehensive status report on the use of
Glauber Theory in atomic collisions [1]. In fact, this whole subject of the application of Glauber or Glauber-like approximations to atomic collisions is
unusually contemporary, especially in comparison with most of the topics
being reviewed at this Conference. Particularly noteworthy is the fact that at
the MIT meeting of this Conference only two years ago, there was but a single

* Supported in part by the Advanced Research Projects Agency under Contract No.
DA 31-124-ARO-D-440 and by the National Aeronautics and Space Administration
under Contract No. NGL 39-011-035.

paper (by Byron [2]) in any way related to Glauber Theory. This fact is to be contrasted with the situation at the present Conference, where there are a sizeable number of contributed papers on Glauber and Glauber-related approximations, in addition to my progress report.

On the other hand, although the use of the Glauber approximation is a new development in atomic collision theory, applications of Glauber theory to nuclear physics and to high energy physics have been performed since about 1955, by Glauber and others. Glauber's earlier papers are not very transparent, but a reasonably understandable exposition of his approximation was given by Glauber [3] in 1959, at which time he himself pointed out that the origins of his theory are traceable to work by Moliere [4] as early as 1947. It is clear from Glauber's 1959 discussion [3] that the Glauber approximation can be regarded as an improved high-energy approximation, yielding the same predictions as the Born approximation at those large incident energies where the Born approximation is valid, but generally differing from the Born approximation (and hopefully an improvement on it) when the Born approximation fails. Therefore, the fact that the Glauber approximation has been employed in atomic physics only during the past few years also is noteworthy, and is indicative of the increasing fragmentation of physics research. However, it must be admitted that part of the reason for this relatively late appearance of Glauber's name in the atomic physics literature is the fact that his formula for the scattering amplitude involves a quite complicated multi-dimensional integral, which at first sight seems intractable even for the standard trial horse of atomic collision theory, namely electron-atomic hydrogen collisions. To Victor Franco [5], a student of Glauber's, belongs the credit of first recognizing (in 1968) that the Glauber amplitude for the elastic scattering of electrons by atomic hydrogen can be reduced to a tractable form. A similar reduction was performed independently by Birman and Rosendorff [6].

Thus the use of Glauber Theory in atomic collisions began with Franco's 1968 article [5]. Since then it has become clear that for the simple case of electron collisions with atomic hydrogen, Glauber Theory can provide good estimates of elastic and excitation cross-sections in an intermediate incident energy range heretofore not conveniently accessible to theory, namely at energies too low for the Born approximation to be valid, yet so high that reliable close-coupling calculations are impractical because very many states are energetically accessible and must be included in the close-coupling expansion. Moreover, the Glauber estimates of these electron-hydrogen cross-sections can now be performed with very little more effort than is required to compute the Born estimates of the same cross-sections. The Glauber elastic and excitation cross-sections are equally easily computed for proton collisions with atomic hydrogen, and look hopeful, but their reliability in this case cannot be confidently inferred from the available data. For more complicated targets, as, e.g., in electron collisions with He or Li, neither the practicality nor the accuracy of the Glauber approximation has yet been established. Developing methods for readily and reliably predicting elastic and excitation cross-sections in electron and proton collisions with light atoms unquestionably is the major present task facing the would-be Glauberizer; until such methods are developed, the Glauber approximation will have to be considered an interesting tool – but not yet a major advance – in atomic collision theory. It also should be mentioned that even in the afore-mentioned comparatively very simple proton-hydrogen and electron-hydrogen collisions, easily computable Glauber formulas for electron exchange, electron capture or ionization cross-sections have not been derived.

2. The Glauber formula

The above has been a brief summary of the history of Glauber theory in atomic collisions, and of the conclusions which fairly can be drawn from this history. In what follows, I shall expand on this summary, mainly by describing the results of various Glauber calculations. First of all, let me quote, without any attempt at derivation or justification, Glauber's formula for the collision amplitude. It is convenient to do so in two steps, beginning with the least complicated case, namely potential scattering. Here the Glauber amplitude for scattering of a particle having mass m, from initial momentum $\hbar k_i = m v_i$ to final momentum $\hbar k_f$, is [3]

$$A(k_i \rightarrow k_f) = \frac{ik_i}{2\pi} \int d^2b \ e^{iq \cdot b} \ \Gamma(b) \tag{1}$$

$$\Gamma(b) = 1 - e^{i\chi(b)} \tag{2}$$

$$\chi(b) = -\frac{1}{\hbar v_i} \int_{-\infty}^{\infty} dz' V(b + z'\hat{\kappa}) \tag{3}$$

where the potential $V(r)$ is usually, but not necessarily, spherically symmetric; $q = k_i - k_f$ is the momentum transfer (in units of $\hbar$); $\hat{\kappa}$ is the unit vector along the direction $k_i + k_f$; b is a vector in the plane through the origin perpendicular to $\hat{\kappa}$; and d^2b is the element of area in this plane. Moreover, with this choice of $\hat{\kappa}$, the momentum transfer q automatically has no component along $\hat{\kappa}$, i.e., lies entirely in the plane containing b, so that

$$\mathbf{q} \cdot \mathbf{b} = qb \cos(\phi_b - \phi_q) \tag{4}$$

where ϕ_b, ϕ_q are azimuthal angles locating $\mathbf{b}$, $\mathbf{q}$ respectively in this plane.

I shall not derive the Glauber amplitude formula (1) here, but I shall comment on its physical basis and justification. From its derivation, and from its structure, the Glauber approximation is seen to belong to the class of so-called eikonal approximations, and is just one example of the many possible quantum mechanical approximations in this class. More specifically, eikonal approximations in classical optics [7] — and in quantum mechanical potential scattering [8] — give the solution to the wave equation in terms of path integrals along the geometric rays perpendicular to the wave fronts. Thus eikonal approximations tend to be valid at short wave lengths and high energies. For each scattering angle, (3) shows that the Glauber formula (1) is approximating the actual ray path by a single straight line along a direction making equal angles with the initial and final particle velocities. For wide angle scattering this Glauber path differs considerably from the actual ray path. Correspondingly, the Glauber approximation (1) usually is regarded as primarily valid at small scattering angles. For small angle scattering only, $\hat{\kappa}$ in eq. (3) can be replaced by the direction of the incident velocity $\mathbf{v}_i$, in which $\mathbf{b}$ can be identified with the impact parameter vector specifying the actual trajectories.

I cannot discuss here the various alternative forms of the eikonal approximation which have been proposed for potential scattering, and which supposedly are superior to the Glauber at wide angles or at low energies. Descriptions of such alternatives to the Glauber, along with additional references to the literature, may be found in papers (dating from 1956 to the present) by, e.g., Saxon and Schiff [9], Feshbach [10], Levy and Sucher [11], Blankenbecler and co-workers [12], Abarbanel and Itzykson [13], Wilets and Wallace [14], and Lebedeff [15]. However, the particular eikonal potential scattering approximation (1) favored by Glauber does have some special properties worth mentioning. First of all, the Glauber version (1) is one of the simplest eikonal approximations, a feature not too significant in the potential scattering case, but extremely important when attempting to evaluate eikonal scattering amplitudes for more complicated collisions. Secondly, with $\hat{\kappa}$ along $\mathbf{k}_i + \mathbf{k}_f$, the Glauber amplitude (1) is consistent with the requirements of time-reversibility [3], i.e., is consistent with detailed-balance requirements, and moreover obeys unitarity [3,8], i.e., satisfies the optical theorem expressing conservation of particle flux. Thirdly, at all scattering angles the Glauber approximation (1) is identical with the Born approximation in the limit that the incident velocity $\mathbf{v}_i$ becomes very large [3,16]; in fact, when the exponential exp $(i\chi)$ in eq. (2) is expanded in powers of χ, i.e., in inverse powers of the incident velocity, the leading term in eq. (1) becomes precisely the Born approximation amplitude. Fourthly, the path integral $\chi(\mathbf{b})$ diverges for a pure Coulomb interaction, but if evaluated for a screened Coulomb interaction, it turns out that in the limit where the screening vanishes, the Glauber scattering amplitude (1) is exactly correct, both in phase and in magnitude at all incident velocities and all scattering angles [16] ; this Glauber result is another one of the marvelously unexpected properties of the Coulomb field we keep stumbling upon, and may be compared with the equally marvelous fact that in the limit of vanishing screening the Born approximation scattering amplitude becomes exact in magnitude, though not in phase [17].

The preceding remarks indicate that for potential scattering the simple Glauber approximation (1) may be valid over a wider range of energies and scattering angles than originally anticipated, especially for Coulomb and Coulomb-like interactions. Thus there is the possibility that the Glauber approximation is particularly suitable for atomic collisions, although of course any atomic collisions of actual interest (e.g., our stand-by electron-hydrogen or proton-hydrogen collisions) involve at least three particles and therefore are too complicated to be understandable in terms of merely a potential scattering model. To deal with such multi-particle collisions we require a suitable generalization of the potential scattering eikonal-type approximation (1). Various generalizations are arguable; I shall quote, again without derivation or justification, the generalization given by Glauber [3], applicable to multi-particle two-body reactions not involving breakup or rearrangement (e.g., to the electron excitation of He or Li, neglecting exchange). One first computes what may be termed a frozen elastic amplitude, using the same formula (1), but holding fixed the positions of the bound particles. This frozen amplitude is a function of the bound particle coordinates by virtue of the fact that the interaction $V(\mathbf{r})$ seen by the incident particle depends on the instantaneous positions of the bound particles. Then, according to Glauber [3], the actual elastic- or excitation amplitude is obtained by folding the frozen elastic amplitude between the initial and final bound states.

Specifically, in $e^{-}-H(1s)$ collisions, with the origin at the proton and neglecting proton recoil, the Glauber amplitude for scattering from an initial bound state u_i to a final bound state u_f, neglecting exchange, is [18]

$$A_{fi}(\mathbf{k}_i \rightarrow \mathbf{k}_f) = \frac{ik_i}{2\pi} \int d\mathbf{r}_1 d^2b \, u_f^*(\mathbf{r}_1) \, e^{i\mathbf{q}\cdot\mathbf{b}} \, \Gamma(\mathbf{b},\mathbf{r}_1) u_1(\mathbf{r}_1) \tag{5}$$

$$\Gamma(\mathbf{b},\mathbf{r}_1) = 1 - \exp[i\chi(\mathbf{b},\mathbf{r}_1)] \tag{6}$$

$$\chi(\mathbf{b},\mathbf{r}_1) = -\frac{1}{\hbar v_i} \int\limits_{-\infty}^{\infty} dz' V(\mathbf{b}+z'\hat{\mathbf{\kappa}},\mathbf{r}_1) \tag{7}$$

$$V(\mathbf{r},\mathbf{r}_1) = -\frac{e^2}{r} + \frac{e^2}{|\mathbf{r}-\mathbf{r}_1|}. \tag{8}$$

In eqs. (5)–(8), $\mathbf{r}_1$ is identified with the coordinate of the initially bound electron, and eq. (4) is retained, i.e., the momentum transfer vector $\mathbf{q}$ still is supposed to lie in the plane containing $\mathbf{b}$ and perpendicular to $\hat{\mathbf{\kappa}}$.

The derivation of the Glauber multi-particle formula [as illustrated by eq. (5) for e⁻–H(1s) collisions] has been examined by a number of investigators, including Glauber himself [3,19], Birman and Rosendorff [6], Osborn [20], Feshbach and co-workers [21], Harrington [22], and Byron [2,23]. Not all these workers take precisely the same point of view concerning the assumptions underlying the multi-particle formula, but there is general agreement that the momentum transfer and energy transfer should be small compared to their incident values. However, even these favorable circumstances do not make the justification of the Glauber multi-particle formula straightforward. For electron-atom collisions, the Glauber folding procedure illustrated by (5) appears to be a special case of a theorem due to Chase [24], and probably can be justified in a useful range of incident energies and scattering angles, granted the Glauber amplitude (1) is a good estimate of the elastic scattering from the frozen atomic particles. For proton-atom collisions, considerations urged by Reading [25] suggest the justification may be more difficult, owing to complications induced by atomic recoil. In fact, cross-sections for rotational excitation of molecules by electrons of less than 1 eV have been quite accurately computed [26] via the aforementioned folding procedure, recognizing that it is necessary to compute the elastic scattering from the frozen molecular particles without the aid of the Glauber elastic formula (1), which formula of course is unlikely to be valid at such low incident energies.

Feshbach and co-workers [21], and independently Byron [2,23], have attempted to derive the Glauber multi-particle formula by making eikonal-type approximations in the complete untruncated set of close-coupling equations. The validity of these approximations is difficult to assess; nevertheless, from the point of view of this interesting approach, at high energies, where an accurate close-coupling expansion must include a large number of states, the Glauber multi-particle formula – which corresponds to an approximate solution of the complete set of close-coupling equations – would seem more hopeful than presently practical close-coupling treatments, which can handle accurately only a severely truncated sub-set of these same equations.

I remark that for inelastic collisions the Glauber bound state formula (5) is not consistent with the requirements of time-reversibility, which is one indication that the Glauber approximation for collisions of composite systems is not as well-founded theoretically as is the Glauber approximation (1) for potential scattering. Indeed, because of vagueness in the approximations leading to the Glauber multi-particle formula, the direction of path integration $\hat{\kappa}$ in eq. (7) often is taken along the incident velocity $\mathbf{v}_i$, or along the vector $\mathbf{k}_i + \mathbf{k}_f$ [in analogy with the potential scattering choice of $\hat{\kappa}$ in eq. (3)]. However, as has not always been recognized in the literature, when the exponential $\exp(i\chi)$ in eq. (6) is expanded in powers of χ, the leading term in eq. (5) has the desirable property of being identical with the Born approximation amplitude only when $\hat{\kappa}$ is perpendicular to $\mathbf{q}$ at every $\mathbf{q}$, which for inelastic scattering is not the same as choosing $\hat{\kappa}$ along $\mathbf{k}_i + \mathbf{k}_f$.

The formula (5) for A_{fi} is a five-dimensional integral. For electron-helium scattering, with two bound electrons, the Glauber formula involves an eight-dimensional integral; for electron-lithium scattering, we have an eleven-dimensional integral, unless the integrations over the core electrons somehow can be bypassed for collisions exciting only the outer 2s electron. These remarks make it obvious that successful employment of the Glauber approximation in electron collisions with atomic hydrogen need not imply the approximation will be practical in electron collisions with heavier atoms; for collisions involving two or more bound electrons a reliable means of reducing the associated multi-dimensional Glauber integral must be found.

Even for electron-hydrogen collisions, the integral in eq. (5) for A_{fi} looks very complicated. To illustrate, for 1s–2s excitation [18], in atomic units, with $n = e^2/\hbar v_i$,

$$A_{2s,1s}(\mathbf{q}) = \frac{ik_i}{2\pi} \frac{1}{4\pi\sqrt{2}} \int_0^\infty ds \int_0^\infty db \int_{-\infty}^\infty dz_1 \int_0^{2\pi} d\phi_s \int_0^{2\pi} d\phi_b \, bs(2-r_1)$$

$$e^{-3r_1/2} e^{i\mathbf{q}\cdot\mathbf{b}} \left[1 - \left(\frac{|\mathbf{b}-\mathbf{s}|}{b} \right)^{2in} \right] \tag{9}$$

where $\mathbf{s}$ is the projection of the vector $\mathbf{r}_1$ on the plane containing $\mathbf{b}$, here the x, y plane, so that

$$r_1 = \sqrt{s^2 + z_1^2} \tag{10}$$

and

$$|\mathbf{b}-\mathbf{s}| = [b^2+s^2-2bs\,\cos(\phi_b-\phi_s)]^{1/2} \tag{11}$$

with ϕ_s the azimuth angle of s in the plane containing **b**. However, following procedures introduced by Franco in his aforementioned paper [5] on the elastic scattering of electrons by atomic hydrogen, Tai et al. [18] in 1969 reduced the five-dimensional integral in eq. (9) to the one-dimensional integral

$$A_{2s,1s}(\mathbf{q}) = \frac{2^{10}ik_i}{3^6\sqrt{2}} \int_0^{\pi/2} d\theta\,\sin^3\theta\,\cos\theta$$

$$\frac{[-2\sin^4\theta+\tfrac{56}{9}q^2\cos^2\theta\,\sin^2\theta-\tfrac{128}{81}q^4\cos^4\theta]}{[\sin^2\theta+\tfrac{4}{9}q^2\cos^2\theta]^5} \times$$

$$\times \left[1-\frac{|\cos 2\theta|^{2in+1}}{(\cos\theta)^{2in}}\,_2F_1(\tfrac{1}{2}+\tfrac{1}{2}in,\,1+\tfrac{1}{2}in;\,1;\,\sin^2 2\theta)\right] \tag{12}$$

where $_2F_1$ denotes the standard hypergeometric function. Similar reductions to one-dimensional integrals are possible for any direct excitation amplitude in electron-hydrogen and proton-hydrogen collisions [27]. The expressions for 2p, 3s and 3p excitation were given by Tai et al. [18], and apparently were independently derived, at just about the same time, by Sil and his co-workers in India [28,29], who also recently have published the expressions for 1s—3d excitation [30].

The one-dimensional integral in eq. (12), like most one-dimensional integrals involving standard functions, is readily and inexpensively evaluated with the aid of a high speed computer. However, very recently, in a paper still in press, Thomas and Gerjuoy [31] have further shown that the integral in eq. (12), and indeed any direct excitation amplitude in electron-hydrogen and proton-hydrogen collisions, can be evaluated in closed form as a finite sum of hypergeometric functions. For excitation to low lying levels, this sum never involves more than a few terms; for instance, the amplitude from eq. (12) is [31]:

$$A_{2s,1s}(\mathbf{q}) = \frac{4ik_i}{\sqrt{2}} \left(\frac{2}{3}\right)^6 \left(\frac{9}{4q^2}\right)^{1-i n} (i n)\Gamma(1+i n)\Gamma(1-i n) \times$$

$$\times \left\{ 2i n(1+i n)\,_2F_1\left(1-i n,1-i n;1;-\frac{9}{4q^2}\right) + \right.$$

$$+ 4i n(1-i n)^2 \left(\frac{9}{4q^2}\right) \,_2F_1\left(2-i n;2-i n;2;-\frac{9}{4q^2}\right) +$$

$$\left. + (1-i n)^2(2-i n)^2 \left(\frac{3}{2q}\right)^4 \,_2F_1\left(3-i n;3-i n;3;-\frac{9}{4q^2}\right)\right\}, \qquad (13)$$

where Γ now denotes the usual Gamma function. With a computer, using known series expansions for the hypergeometric functions, the Glauber expression (13) for $A_{2s,1s}$ is scarcely more difficult to compute than is the corresponding expression in the Born approximation.

3. Comparison with experiment

Franco's 1968 article [5] compared the Glauber and Born predictions of total elastic scattering cross-sections in e^-–H(1s) collisions. At incident energies above about 100 eV, these Glauber and Born predictions are indistinguishable; as the energy decreases from 100 eV, the Glauber elastic cross-sections lie increasingly above the Born. The only available absolute measurements [32] of these elastic cross-sections are in the energy range between 2 and 10 eV, where the Glauber predictions are a factor of 2 to 3 above the Born. In this energy range, the data lie even above the Glauber values; in other words the only available data for e^-–H(1s) total elastic scattering very decidedly favor the Glauber over the Born. However, the Glauber approximation is not expected to be reliable at energies as low as 10 eV because (as has been explained) it is fundamentally a high energy approximation; also, the exchange amplitude, ignored in this Glauber calculation, should not be negligible below about 30 eV. Moreover, at energies of 10 eV and below, accurate predictions of e^-–H(1s) cross-sections via essentially exact procedures, starting from the full three-particle Hamiltonian, are practical, e.g., by convergent close-coupling expansions [33]. Thus Franco's numerical results [5] actually were not very significant; his real contribution, as I have already pointed out, was his demonstration that Glauber calculations of e^-–H(1s) collisions could be performed without much labor.

Franco's 1968 article [5] was followed by a comparison of Glauber and Born predictions for differential elastic scattering cross-sections in e^-–H(1s) collisions. These calculations, by Tai et al. [34], in 1969, covered the energy range between 50 and 200 eV, and indicated that the Born and Glauber predictions were identical at wide angles; at smaller angles, the Glauber predictions rose above the Born, thereby producing the aforementioned result that the Glauber total elastic e^-–H(1s) cross-sections exceed the Born. There are no absolute measurements of differential cross-sections, but the shapes of the Glauber curves clearly were a better fit to the observed relative differential cross sections than were the Born predictions, especially at 50 eV. Since 50 eV is an energy high enough for Glauber theory to be believable, and since reliable, assuredly convergent close-coupling expansions are not practical at this energy, Tai et al.'s [34] numerical results were significant and provocative. However, the really convincing evidence for the utility of Glauber theory in e^-–H(1s) collisions is provided by the 2s and 2p excitation cross-sections, for which there are good data covering an extended energy range.

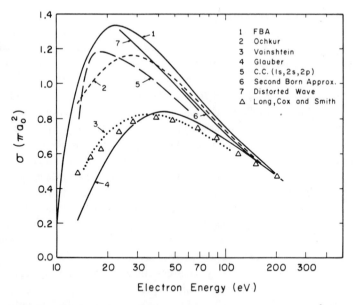

Fig. 1. 1s–2p excitation cross-section in e^-–H(1s) collisions, in units of πa_0^2. The triangles are the data points. The curves show various theoretical estimates of 1s–2p excitation, computed via Glauber and various other approximations discussed in ref. [18]. FBA denotes First Born Approximation; C.C. denotes close-coupling. (From Tai et al. [18].)

As an example, fig. 1, from Tai et al. [18], shows predicted and observed 1s–2p excitation cross-sections in e⁻–H(1s) collisions. There is no need to discuss here the detailed origins of the various theoretical curves, which are explained in ref. [18]. The significant features of fig. 1 are that all the theoretical curves are essentially identical above 200 eV, and that at lower energies the Glauber (curve 4) is a distinctly better fit to the data points than the Born (curve 1), or than a close-coupling expansion limited to 1s–2s–2p states (curve 5). The failure of the Glauber curve at energies below 30 eV is understandable on the grounds previously mentioned in connection with Franco's elastic scattering calculation (5). It is true that the close coupling results can be improved and made competitive with the Glauber, as Burke and Webb [35] recently have shown, but the computational effort is arduous, and has been carried out only at energies below 54 eV. It is further true that in fig. 1 curve 3, based on an approximation originally introduced by Vainshtein et al. [36] in 1964, also is competitive with the Glauber and is not more difficult to compute than the Glauber. However, this Vainshtein curve in fig. 1 includes a rough estimate of the exchange contribution, not contained in the Glauber curve. When this exchange contribution is removed, the Vainshtein is somewhat inferior to the Glauber in the energy range above about 30 eV, as Sheorey et al. [37] very recently have shown.

These authors [37] also have examined the Vainshtein predictions for the angular distribution of the scattered electrons following excitation of the $n = 2$ levels of atomic hydrogen, and find that at large angles these Vainshtein predictions are essentially the same as the Born. Fig. 2, also from Tai et al. [18], shows that at large angles the Glauber predictions for such inelastically scattered electrons are markedly superior to the Born, and therefore to the Vainshtein as well. Again there are no absolute measurements of differential cross-sections; in each case the data are normalized to the theory at 21°. At the energies of fig. 2, no close-coupling calculations have been reported for e⁻–H(1s) excitation. The designation Born-Oppenheimer in fig. 2 means that to the usual Born amplitude has been added an estimated exchange amplitude, which proves to be utterly negligible at angles less than 80°. The fact that the Born and Glauber predictions at large angles differ so markedly for this inelastic process, though they agreed at large angles for elastic scattering, is understandable. At large angles the observed angular distributions in fig. 2 are very close to pure Coulomb scattering, as is easily verified. As Tai et al. [18] discuss, this empirical observation is consistent with the expectation that large angle scattering of the electron, whether elastic or inelastic, results primarily from collisions which bring the incident electron very close to the proton; the atomic electron has too small a mass (alternatively, has too

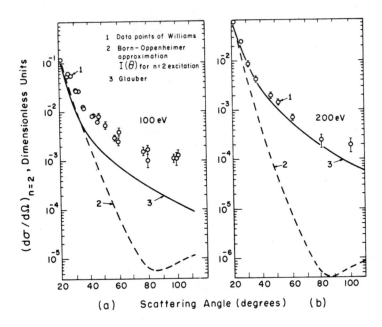

Fig. 2. Differential cross-sections for excitation of the $n = 2$ levels of atomic hydrogen
(a) at 100 eV; (b) at 200 eV. The circles (1) are the data points. Curves 2 and 3 are
theoretical angular distributions, all normalized to the experimental data points at
$\theta = 21°$. Curve 2 (dashed): the Born-Oppenheimer approximation; curve 3 (solid): the
Glauber approximation. (From Tai et al. [18].)

spread-out a wave function) to give large deflections to the incident electron.
For elastic collisions, therefore, the actual large angle scattering is primarily
prduced by the proton alone, and even at quite low energies is predicted
correctly and identically by both the Born and the Glauber, because of the
previously explained marvelous properties of Coulomb interactions. For the
inelastic collisions of fig. 2, however, the deflection produced by the interaction $-e^2/r$ between the incident electron and the proton vanishes in the overly
simple Born approximation, because of orthogonality between the initial and
final bound state functions. Consequently the Born angular distribution of
fig. 2 are in effect being produced only by the electron-electron interaction,
and thus are far too low at large angles. In the Glauber approximation the
scattering of the incident electron by its interaction with the proton is not
eliminated by orthogonality. This orthogonality effect also means that the
linear term in the previously discussed expansion of exp $(i\chi)$ is not really the

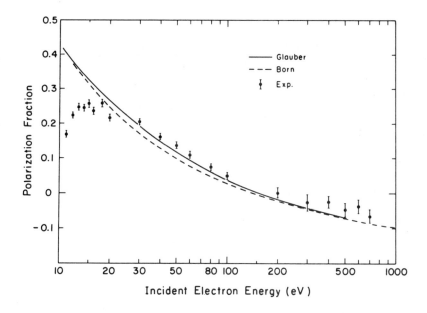

Fig. 3. Polarization fraction for Lyman-α radiation emitted following e^-—H(1s) excitation, observed at an angle 90° to the incident electron beam. Solid line, Glauber; dashed line, Born; circles, experiment. This figure, from Gerjuoy et al. [38] does not show their computed Vainshtein polarization fraction predictions, which also lie quite close to the experimental points.

dominant term in the inelastic Glauber integral at high energies and large scattering angles, thus explaining the fact that in fig. 2 the large angle Glauber and Born curves actually are farther apart at 200 eV than at 100 eV.

Fig. 3, from still unpublished work by Gerjuoy et al. [38], shows that the polarization of the Lyman-α radiation following 1s—2p excitation also is well predicted by Glauber theory, although for this purpose the differences between the Glauber, Born and Vainshtein predictions are not very marked. In effect, figs. 1—3 taken together indicate that at intermediate energies the Glauber approximation simultaneously estimates accurately the sum and the ratios of the excitation probabilities to the various magnetic substates of the 2p level. Note that the Glauber curve in fig. 3 is computed with the path integral direction $\hat{\kappa}$ perpendicular to the momentum transfer vector $\mathbf{q}$ at every $\mathbf{q}$, as originally specified in eq. (7); if $\hat{\kappa}$ had been chosen along the incident direction $\mathbf{v_i}$, the predicted polarization fraction would be -0.27 independent of energy [18,23], i.e., completely at variance with the experimental observations.

The foregoing comparisons thoroughly justify the conclusion, stated earlier, that Glauber theory is a reliable practical means of predicting e^-–H(1s) elastic and excitation cross-sections in an intermediate energy range. Once one goes past e^-–H(1s) collisions the situation is less clear, and can be quickly summarized. In proton collisions with atomic hydrogen, the Glauber expressions are formally the same as in electron-hydrogen collisions; it only is necessary to change the scale of the momentum transfer vector q. Glauber proton-hydrogen calculations have been performed by Franco and Thomas [27], and by Sil's group [30,39]. Fig. 4, from Franco and Thomas [27], compares the Glauber predictions with recent close-coupling predictions, computed far more tediously by Cheshire et al. [40]. There are only a few experimental points in the energy range above about 20 keV where the

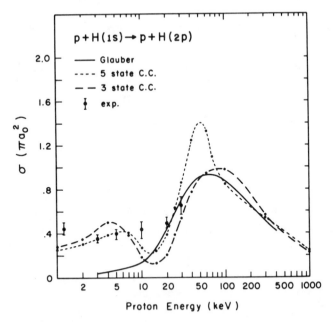

Fig. 4. Cross-sections for 1s–2p excitation of atomic hydrogen by protons, from Franco and Thomas [27]. Solid line, Glauber; short dashes, close coupling using a three state expansion; long dashes, close-coupling using a five state expansion. The close-coupling results are taken from Cheshire et al. [40].

incident proton velocity begins to exceed the bound electron velocity, and where therefore the Glauber approximation may be expected to become valid. In this energy range the Glauber is competitive with the close-coupling, but obviously no firm conclusions can be drawn about the accuracy of the Glauber without measurements at higher energies. It can be said that at 20–30 keV the Glauber is distinctly superior to the Born, whose predictions are a factor of 3–4 too high at these energies.

For targets more complicated than atomic hydrogen, the collision amplitudes no longer can be written in terms of readily computable one-dimensional or closed form expressions such as eqs. (12) and (13). For electron-helium elastic scattering, Franco [41], using an approximate product-type helium ground state wave function, has reduced the eight-dimensional integral for the collision amplitude to a three-dimensional integral, which then was evaluated numerically. Related but cruder Glauber calculations of electron and proton elastic scattering from helium also have been reported by Johnson and Brolley [42]. In the 100–500 eV range, the e⁻–He elastic differential cross-sections obtained in this way by Franco were somewhat closer to observation than the Born predictions. However, the agreement between the Glauber and the data is not really good, and the use of a particular eigenfunction, together with the heavy reliance on a powerful computer, makes it very difficult to assess the significance of the results. For instance, it is difficult to assess Franco's finding that the Glauber and Born electron-helium elastic scattering predictions differ by a factor of 2 at an energy of 500 eV and a momentum transfer q^2 of 10 a.u., whereas in his 1968 electron-hydrogen calculations [5], at the same energy and momentum transfer, he understandably found that the Born and Glauber predictions were essentially identical. For a more definitive assessment of the Glauber approximation in e⁻–He collisions, calculations of excitation cross-sections are needed; judging by the e⁻–H(1s) results, the differences between the Glauber and the Born should be more marked in He excitation than in elastic scattering. Excitation calculations of this sort are in progress in several groups [43]. However, irrespective of the future results of such He calculations, I am convinced that further reduction of the Glauber multiple integral is essential if the Glauber approximation is to herald a major advance in the theory of collisions involving multi-electron target atoms.

A procedure for such reduction has been proposed in a very recent article by Franco [44], based on an integral representation derived by Thomas and Gerjuoy [31] for their closed form evaluation of the Glauber e⁻–H(1s) collision amplitude. However, I doubt the utility of this reduction procedure of Franco's, which leads to very awkward looking expressions, and which he has

not employed in actual calculations. Of course, by simply ignoring the multi-
electron features of the target atom, the necessity of having to reduce the
Glauber multi-dimensional integral always can be avoided. This approach has
been taken for 2s–2p excitation in e^-–Li collisions by Mathur et al. [45],
who wholly disregarded the core 1s electrons. Their Glauber results again are
an improvement over the Born approximation, but the agreement with experimental data again is not very good. In any event, Mathur et al's treatment of
the core electrons is so crude that their results have little bearing on the expected validity of Glauber calculations which would replace the actual multi-
electron target atom by a more believable model atom with one electron. A
more realistic approach to a one-electron model for e^-–Li scattering might be
to lump the core electrons and Li nucleus into a single screened Coulomb potential, but this would mean having to develop new procedures for reducing
the five-dimensional Glauber amplitude integral to a tractable form. The
present procedures [5,18,31] for this reduction, particularly the procedure
of Thomas and   Gerjuoy [31], make very strong use of the special properties
of the Coulomb interaction and hydrogenic eigenfunctions.

This concludes my report on recent progress in the use of the Glauber approximation in atomic collisions. It will add the final remark that – in view
of time limitations and   my desire to concentrate on Glauber calculations – I
perforce have had to ignore many interesting eikonal-type atomic collision
calculations not strictly of the Glauber sort, including calculations by Miller
[46]; Chen and Watson [47]; Byron et al. [48], and Callaway [49].

References

[1] A very brief survey of Glauber theory, especially as applied to e^-–H(1s) collisions,
    was recently presented as part of a status report on the three-particle problem in
    atomic physics, Cf. E.Gerjuoy, in: Atomic Physics 2 (Proc. 2nd Int. Conf. Atom.
    Phys), ed. P.G.H.Sandars (Plenum Press, London, 1971) p. 271.
[2] F.W.Byron, Jr., VI ICPEAC, Abstracts of Papers, ed. I.Amdur (MIT Press, Cambridge,
    Mass., 1969) p. 644.
[3] R.J.Glauber, in: Lectures in Theoretical Physics, Vol. I, eds. W.E.Brittin and L.G.
    Dunham (Interscience Publishers, New York, 1959) p. 315.
[4] G.Moliere, Z. Naturforsch. 2A (1947) 133.
[5] V.Franco, Phys. Rev. Letters 20 (1968) 709.
[6] A.Birman and S.Rosendorff, Nuovo Cim. 63B (1969) 89. These authors also made
    some numerical computations of e^-–H(1s) elastic scattering cross-sections.
[7] P.Franck and R.von Mieses, Die Differential- und Integralgleichungen der Mechanik
    und Physik, Vol. 2 (Mary S.Rosenburg, New York, 1943) pp. 860–861;
    H.Goldstein, Classical Mechanics (Addison-Wesley Publishing Co., Reading, Mass.,
    1950) pp. 310–312.

[8] K.Gottfried, *Quantum Mechanics*, Vol. 1 (W.A.Benjamin Inc., New York, 1966) pp. 113–117.

[9] D.S.Saxon and L.I.Schiff, Nuovo Cim. *6* (1957) 614;
D.Saxon, Phys. Rev. *107* (1957) 871;
L.I.Schiff, Phys. Rev. *103* (1956) 443; see also: W.M.Brown, *An Approximation Method for Large-Angle Scattering of High Energy Scalar and Vector Waves,* thesis, University of California at Los Angeles (1959), unpublished.

[10] H.Feshbach, in: *International School of Physics "Enrico Fermi" Course 38* (Academy Press, New York, 1967) p. 183.

[11] M.Levy and J.Sucher, Phys. Rev. *186* (1969) 1656.

[12] R.Blankenbecler and M.L.Goldberger, Phys. Rev. *126* (1962) 766;
R.L.Sugar and R.Blankenbecler, Phys. Rev. *183* (1969) 1387.

[13] H.D.I.Abarbanel and C.Itzykson, Phys..Rev. Letters *23* (1969) 53.

[14] L.Wilets and S.J.Wallace, Phys. Rev. *169* (1968) 84;
S.J.Wallace, *The Eikonal Expansion,* preprint (May 1971).

[15] S.A.Lebedeff, J. Phys. B *4* (1971) in press.

[16] R.J.Moore, Phys. Rev. D *2* (1970) 313.

[17] Cf. e.g., L.I.Schiff, *Quantum Mechanics* (McGraw Hill Book Co., New York, 1955) pp. 116 and 170.

[18] H.Tai and R.H.Bassel, Bull. Amer. Phys. Soc. *14* (1969) 937;
H.Tai, R.H.Bassel, E.Gerjuoy and V.Franco, Phys. Rev. A *1* (1970) 1819.

[19] R.J.Glauber, in: *High-Energy Physics and Nuclear Structure*, ed. S.Devons (Plenum Press, New York, 1970) p. 207.

[20] T.A.Osborn, Ann. Phys. (New York) *58* (1970) 417.

[21] H.Feshbach and J.Hufner, Ann. Phys. (New York) *56* (1970) 268;
W.H.Bassichis, H.Feshbach and J.F.Reading, Ann. Phys. (New York), to be published;
H.Feshbach, A.Gal and J.Hufner, Ann. Phys. *66* (1971) 20.

[22] D.R.Harrington, Phys. Rev. *184* (1969) 1745;
D.R.Harrington, *Theory of Multiple Diffraction Scattering* (1970) unpublished.

[23] F.W.Byron, Jr., *The Excitation of Atomic Hydrogen and Helium in the Eikonal Approximation* (1970) unpublished.

[24] D.M.Chase, Phys. Rev. *104* (1956) 838. Glauber's multi-particle formula has been justified on this basis by M.Mittleman, Phys. Rev. A *2* (1970) 1846.

[25] J.F.Reading, Phys. Rev. A *1* (1970) 1642.

[26] E.S.Chang and A.Temkin, J. Phys. Soc. Jap. *29* (1970) 172;
See also: D.E.Golden, N.F.Lane, A.Temkin and E.Gerjuoy, Rev. Mod. Phys. (1971) in press;
S.Hara, J. Phys. Soc. Jap. *27* (1969) 1592.

[27] V.Franco and B.K.Thomas, Phys. Rev. A *4* (1971) 945.

[28] A.S.Ghosh, P.Sinha and N.C.Sil, J. Phys. B *3* (1970) L58.

[29] A.S.Ghosh and N.C.Sil, Indian J. Phys. *43* (1969) 490.

[30] K.Bhadra and A.S.Ghosh, Phys. Rev. Letters *26* (1971) 737.

[31] B.K.Thomas and E.Gerjuoy, J. Math. Phys. *12* (1971) 1567.

[32] R.T.Brackmann, W.L.Fite and R.H.Neynaber, Phys. Rev. *112* (1958) 1157;
R.H.Neynaber, L.L.Marino, E.W.Rothe and S.M.Trujillo, Phys. Rev. *124* (1961) 135.

[33] Cf., e.g., N.F.Mott and H.S.W.Massey, *The Theory of Atomic Collisions* (Oxford University Press, London, 1965) p. 540.
[34] H.Tai, P.J.Teubner and R.H.Bassel, Phys. Rev. Letters *22* (1969) 1415.
[35] P.G.Burke and T.G.Webb, J. Phys. B *3* (1970) L131.
[36] L.Vainshtein, L.Presnyakov and I.Sobel'man, Zh. Eksp. Teor. Fiz. *45* (1963) 2015; [English Transl.: Soviet Phys. -JETP *18* (1964) 1383].
[37] V.B.Sheorey, E.Gerjuoy and B.K.Thomas, J. Phys. B *4* (1971) 657.
[38] E.Gerjuoy, B.K.Thomas and V.B.Sheorey, submitted to J. Phys. B.
[39] A.S.Ghosh and N.C.Sil, to be published.
[40] I.M.Cheshire, D.F.Gallaher and A.J.Taylor, J. Phys. B *3* (1970) 813.
[41] V.Franco, Phys. Rev. A *1* (1970) 1705.
[42] J.D.Johnson and J.E.Brolley, Prog. Theor. Phys. (Japan) *44* (1970) 1700. I am indebted to Dr. M.Inokuti for bringing this publication to my attention, and for comments concerning it.
[43] N.C.Sil, private communication.
[44] V.Franco, Phys. Rev. Letters *26* (1971) 1088.
[45] K.C.Mathur, A.N.Tripathi and S.K.Joshi, Phys. Rev., to be published.
[46] W.H.Miller, J. Chem. Phys. *53* (1970) 3578.
[47] J.C.Y.Chen and K.M.Watson, Phys. Rev. *174* (1968) 152; and *188* (1969) 236; J.C.Y.Chen, C.-S.Wang and K.M.Watson, Phys. Rev. A *1* (1970) 1150.
[48] F.W.Byron, Jr., R.V.Krotkov and J.A.Medeiros, Phys. Rev. Letters *24* (1970) 83.
[49] J.Callaway and A.F.Dugan, Phys. Letters *21* (1966) 295; J.Callaway, in: *Lectures in Theoretical Physics, Vol. XI-C: Atomic Collision Processes,* eds. S.Geltman, K.T.Mahanthappa and W.E.Brittin (Gordon and Breach, Science Publishers, New York, 1969) p. 119.

Physics of Electronic and Atomic Collisions, VII ICPEAC, 1971 – North-Holland (1972)

T-MATRIX EXTRAPOLATION METHODS

J.NUTTALL

Department of Physics, Texas A&M University,
College Station, Texas 77843, USA

We outline the difficulties of applying standard methods, such as the Kohn variational method and the Watson-Faddeev integral equations, to the calculation of amplitudes for $e^{\pm}-H$ scattering at energies where ionization is possible. The method of extrapolation from complex energies is discussed as an alternative, and results for s-wave $e^{\pm}-H(1s)$ elastic scattering are given. It is shown how, in principle, the method may be applied to other processes. In conclusion, it is speculated that a more extensive use of analyticity might lead to new and more efficient ways of solving atomic three-particle scattering problems.

1. Introduction

The theorist wishing to engage in the calculation of atomic collision cross-sections must at the outset make a choice between two broad alternatives. On the one hand, he can study systems involving many electrons and admit from the beginning that it is hopeless, except for certain limiting cases, to expect to be able to make really accurate calculations of anything. In many applications, however, extreme precision is not required, and work in this direction is of great value. The other type of problem is one where only a few particles are involved, and there is the possibility that, with the help of modern computers, the partial differential equations describing the problem might be solved to any reasonable required accuracy. The challenge here, which is particularly acute in atomic physics with its long-range interactions, is to overcome the mathematical difficulties and then find the most efficient way of calculating the required cross-section.

Here, we are concerned with the second type of problem, and since the time required to carry out an "exact" calculation probably varies exponentially with the number of particles, we are quite content at present to restrict our attention to the simplest non-trivial problem, the three-body problem.

The rest of this report will be devoted to the scattering of electrons (or positrons) from atomic hydrogen, a subject that has attracted the attention of generations of atomic theorists. It is hardly necessary in this setting to justify the effort that continues to go into this endeavor, but, apart from the intrinsic value of a knowledge of e–H cross-sections, it is very useful to have a proving ground for approximations to be applied to larger systems.

The degree of difficulty of carrying out an "exact" calculation of e–H scattering depends critically on the total energy E of the system. If E is low enough, only a few channels are energetically accessible (open), which leads to the possibility of important simplifications in the calculation. This point has been exploited with considerable success in the past, but it is not our object to describe this work here. We are concerned with scattering at somewhat higher energies, at which excitation to any one of an infinite number of levels, and also ionization, are possible, but which are not high enough to apply one of the methods valid in the limit of infinite energy. This intermediate range, stretching upwards perhaps 100 eV from near the ionization threshold, is undoubtedly the most difficult one for the theorist to attack, as is shown by the paucity of calculations performed there. The purpose of this report is to discuss the methods which may be employed to compute cross-sections in the intermediate energy range, to summarize recent progress in this area, and to point out the many places where more work remains to be done.

We shall begin by describing the drawbacks of two standard methods, the Kohn variational method and the Watson-Faddeev integral equations, and go on to survey the advantages and problems of the technique of extrapolation from complex energies. Some speculations about directions for possible progress in the future conclude the report.

2. Two standard methods

2.1. *The Kohn method*
The Coulomb potential takes on such a beautifully simple form in coordinate space that it is natural to turn in this direction when considering how to set up an e–H scattering calculation. In fact at lower energies, when just a few channels are open, the most succesful results have been achieved by the application of some derivative of the Kohn variational method. The calculation of s-wave elastic scattering below the first inelastic threshold, carried out by Schwartz [1] 10 years ago, first demonstrated the power of the Kohn method.

To describe a version of the Kohn method convenient for our purposes, we introduce the initial state ϕ_{1s} given by

$$\phi_{1s} = \frac{e^{-r_2} \sin k_1 r_1}{2\pi k_1 r_1} \tag{1}$$

and the outgoing part of the complete scattering wave function χ, with

$$\chi = \lim_{\epsilon \to 0} (E - H + i\epsilon)^{-1} QV\phi_{1s} . \tag{2}$$

Here, the total energy $E = k_1^2 - 1$, H is the Hamiltonian for the system

$$H = -\nabla_1^2 - \nabla_2^2 - \frac{2}{r_1} - \frac{2}{r_2} + \frac{2}{r_{12}}$$

and

$$V = -\frac{2}{r_1} + \frac{2}{r_{12}} .$$

The operator $Q = (1 \pm P_{12})/\sqrt{2}$ symmetrizes as necessary. (Atomic units are used throughout, unless specified otherwise.)

The amplitude for s-wave elastic scattering from $H(1s)$ is given formally by T, with

$$T = (Q\phi_{1s}|QV\phi_{1s}) + \lim_{\epsilon \to 0} (\phi_{1s}|VQ(E-H+i\epsilon)^{-1}|QV\phi_{1s}) , \tag{3}$$

and the Kohn method states that $[T]$, given by

$$[T] = (Q\phi_{1s}|QV\phi_{1s}) + (\phi_{1s}VQ|\chi_t) + (\chi_t'|QV\phi_{1s}) - (\chi_t'|(E-H)\chi_t) , \tag{4}$$

is stationary with respect to variations of trial functions χ_t, χ_t' about their exact values $\chi_t = \chi$ and $\chi_t' = \chi^*$. At this point $[T] = T$, so that (4) provides an estimate of T accurate to second order if χ_t, χ_t' are accurate to first order. An important restriction is that the trial functions must represent explicitly those parts of χ, χ' that do not fall off rapidly at large distances. Each open channel will give rise to such a contribution. Thus, if we are working below the $n = 2$ threshold, χ_t is often written as

$$\chi_t = bQ\theta_{1s} + Q \sum_{l+m+n \leqslant M} c_{lmn} r_{12}^l r_1^m r_2^n \exp\left[-\tfrac{1}{2}a(r_1+r_2)\right] \qquad (5)$$

where

$$\theta_{1s} = e^{-r_2} \frac{e^{ik_1 r_1}}{r_1} \left(1-e^{-\tfrac{1}{2}ar_1}\right). \qquad (6)$$

The parameters a, b, c_{lmn} are varied after (5) has been substituted into (4) to obtain an estimate of T.

Schwartz, using an approach along the above lines, obtained results accurate to three figures. The Kohn method for this case is relatively straightforward to program and does not take up a great deal of computer time. To extend the technique to the ionization region is unfortunately not so simple. We must add to χ an infinite number of terms θ_{nl} corresponding to the excited states of the atom, and also must include another part describing ionization. The relevant asymptotic form has been discussed by Peterkop [2], who showed that

$$\chi \sim F(\hat{\boldsymbol{\rho}}/\rho)\, e^{i\sqrt{E}\rho}\, \rho^{-\tfrac{5}{2}+i\eta} \quad \text{as} \quad \rho \to \infty, \qquad (7)$$

where

$$\hat{\boldsymbol{\rho}} = (\mathbf{r}_1, \mathbf{r}_2) \quad \text{and} \quad \eta = -\frac{\rho}{2\sqrt{E}}V_0, \qquad V_0 = -\frac{2}{r_1} - \frac{2}{r_2} + \frac{2}{r_{12}}.$$

To include all these terms in χ_t involves much complication, and such a calculation has not yet been attempted.

It might be noted that the form given in eq. (7) is not correct if any of the three interparticle distances is not large, but we have made some progress towards remedying this [3]. If it should prove necessary to have to include the modification to (7) in the trial function, the Kohn method would become even more unwieldy. There is little known about just how much detail about the asymptotic form need be inserted into χ_t before the Kohn method will converge, and this seems to be a subject that could profitably be studied by someone with mathematical inclinations. At present, the only rigorous discussion has been restricted to the scattering of a single particle in a short-range potential, where it was shown that the Kohn method converges in measure [4].

2.2. Momentum-space integral equations

If it is decided to forgo the advantages of coordinate space and to attempt a solution of the problem by the Watson-Faddeev momentum-space integral equations [5], there are some formidable problems to be overcome before a calculation in the ionization region has any chance of succeeding. The main difficulty is concerned with the existence of a solution to the equations. If the total energy appearing in the kernel of the equations is made complex, then, although the two-body T-matrices in the kernel are still singular for forward scattering [6], it is not too difficult to show that the kernel, while not L^2, is compact in a suitable Banach space, so that there is a unique, well-behaved solution. However, even if we are really interested in elastic scattering, the equations involve as an intermediate step the computation of what would be, for short-range potentials, ionization amplitudes. By this we mean quantities such as

$$T_I(\mathbf{q}_1,\mathbf{q}_2) = (\mathbf{q}_1,\mathbf{q}_2|Q\{1+V_0(E-H)^{-1}\}QV|\phi_{1s}) , \qquad (8)$$

where $|\mathbf{q}_1,\mathbf{q}_2\rangle$ is a state in which the electrons are described by plane waves of momentum $\mathbf{q}_1, \mathbf{q}_2$. By relating T_I to the Fourier transform of a quantity involving χ, we may deduce that T_I is singular as $E \to \mathbf{q}_1^2 + \mathbf{q}_2^2$ with the behavior [7]

$$T_I \sim (E-\mathbf{q}_1^2-\mathbf{q}_2^2)^{-i\eta}\, \bar{T} + (\text{terms} \to 0) . \qquad (9)$$

The quantity $|\bar{T}|^2$ is proportional to the observed ionization cross-section, but the solution of the integral equations, T_I, is not well-defined for physical, positive values of E.

The straightforward way to obtain equations that are better behaved would be to substitute (9) into the Watson-Faddeev equations, and find an equation for $\bar{T}$. This has not yet been done, but Veselova and Faddeev [8] have done something like this to take out similar (but two-body) singularities in the equations describing the scattering of an electron from a bound pair with a net charge. The complications of this line of attack seem to be at least as great as those of the Kohn method.

3. Extrapolation from complex energies

The problems outlined in the previous section encourage us to consider alternative ways of attempting calculations in the intermediate energy range.

One of these, suggested by the fact that, for complex total energy E, the calculation resembles that for a bound state (and thus is considerably easier), is the main subject of this report. This is the method of extrapolation from complex energies which aims to calculate the elastic amplitude (3), for example, by determining T at a number of complex values of E and extrapolating to find the limit required in (3). A method of this sort was first introduced by Schlessinger and Schwartz [9], but they attempted to extrapolate from real values of E below the $n = 1$ threshold. Their technique is fairly successful in predicting scattering in the elastic region, but appears to have little chance of succeeding in the more distant ionization region.

The procedure we have used falls into two parts, the computation of T at complex E and the extrapolation to real energy. These are treated separately below.

3.1. Computations at complex E

We shall illustrate the technique by discussing the example of s-wave elastic scattering, where we wish to calculate $T(E)$ given by

$$T(E) = (Q\phi_{1s}|QV\phi_{1s}) + (\phi_{1s}|VQ(E-H)^{-1}|QV\phi_{1s}) \qquad (10)$$

with $E = p_1^2 - 1$ complex but with the k_1 used in the definition of ϕ_{1s} real. Those parts of the asymptotic form of χ corresponding to θ_{nl} and (7) will now fall off exponentially, since, for example, in (6) the quantity k_1 should be replaced by p_1. The same principle (4), which now might be called the inhomogeneous Rayleigh–Ritz principle, may be used to calculate $T(E)$, but there is no need to include anything more than the Hylleraas terms in (5). However, since for small $\mathrm{Im}\, p_1$, some of the θ_{nl} will not decrease very fast, we have found it worthwhile to include in our calculations θ_{1s}, θ_{2s} and θ_{2p}. They lead to a significant improvement in the accuracy with which $T(E)$ can be estimated for a given value of M in (5).

There are parts of χ that do not fall off exponentially for complex E. This must be the case, since $(E-H)\chi = V\phi_{1s}$ does not do so. These parts may be found by a method used by Temkin [10], and the leading term of χ from this source is

$$\frac{-Q(2+r_2)r_2\, e^{-r_2}\, \sin k_1 r_1}{4\pi k_1 r_1^3}. \qquad (11)$$

These terms are all square-integrable and do not have to be included explicitly in χ_t, but the rate of convergence should increase if they are, and we are now engaged in including the most important of them in our calculation.

Schwartz [11] and Delves [12] have started to develop a theory of variational approximations, of which the aim is to predict the asymptotic behavior of the estimate as $M \to \infty$. It appears that the behavior is related to the form of the wave function χ at its various singular points in coordinate space, in this case the point at infinity probably being the most important. Progress in this direction would be helpful in reducing the effort needed to obtain a given accuracy.

3.2. Extrapolation to real E

If we were discussing short-range potentials, $T(E)$ would be analytic in a region including the physical value of $E = E_0$, and the extrapolation would presumably cause no great difficulty. However, with Coulomb potentials, T is singular at $E = E_0$, as we have seen in the case of ionization, and more care is needed.

In the case of s-wave elastic scattering from the 1s state, the singularity is rather weak, and the leading terms in an expansion about $p_1 = k_1$ read

$$T_{1s,1s}(x) = T_{1s,1s}(0) + a_1 x + a_2 x^2 - \frac{3ix^3 \ln x}{4k_1} \operatorname{Im} T_{1s,1s}(0) + \dots , \qquad (12)$$

with $x = p_1 - k_1$. However, for excitation to the $n = 2$ levels, the singularity is stronger, and although the limit as $p_1 \to k_1$ exists, the first derivative is infinite. We have determined, using expansions similar to (11) and unitarity, that the leading terms in the expansions of $T_{2s,1s}(x)$, $T_{2p,1s}(x)$ are

$$T_{2s,1s}(x) = T_{2s,1s}(0) - \frac{3ik_1}{k_2^2} x \ln x \operatorname{Re} T_{2p,1s}(0) + \dots$$

$$\qquad (13)$$

$$T_{2p,1s}(x) = T_{2p,1s}(0) + \frac{3ik_1}{k_2^2} x \ln x \operatorname{Re} T_{2s,1s}(0) + \dots$$

where $k_1^2 - 1 = k_2^2 - 1/4$.

An important point that seems to apply to these expansions (although we have not proved it) is that the coefficients of the singular terms for excitation to a level with a given n can be written in terms of the amplitudes for excitation to the levels with that n and their derivatives. This knowledge should be of considerable assistance in extrapolating excitation amplitudes, provided that we consider all amplitudes for a given n together. Spruch and his collaborators [13] have shown with their work on the threshold behavior for problems with long-range potentials where similar types of singularity arise, that, if enough is known about the nature of the singularity, then the extrapolation can be successfully performed. It is possible in principle to calculate ionization amplitudes with the energy-extrapolation method by multiplying by the inverse of the singular factor in (9) before extrapolating [7].

3.3. Results

We have carried out calculations of s-wave ground state elastic scattering of both electrons [14] and positrons [15] from the hydrogen atom at energies in the ionization region up to $E = 1.25$ Ry, using the method described earlier in this section. In the least favorable case, $e^- - H$ scattering in the singlet spin state, with $M = 8$ (95 trial functions) we can obtain estimates of that appear to be accurate to 0.02% at $k_1 = 1.1$, $p_1 = 1.1 + i0.15$. The error increases rapidly as $\text{Im} \, p_1$ decreases and slowly as $\text{Re} \, p_1 = k_1$ increases. The values of $T(p_1)$ that can be calculated with reasonable precision lie on smooth curves, not far from straight, as $\text{Im} \, p_1$ is varied. Fig. 1 shows some of these curves with our extrapolation into $\text{Im} \, p_1 = 0$. The singularity in (12) is so weak as to be insignificant in this case.

For triplet $e^- - H$ scattering our procedure appears to converge well even at $\text{Im} \, p_1 = 0$. The reason for this is no doubt that there is very little inelastic scattering in this state, so that the lack of all the θ_{nl} in χ_t is not serious. This view is borne out by applying the optical theorem to our calculated amplitude, which shows that at least 98% of the total cross-section comes from elastic scattering. The case of $e^+ - H$ scattering has a difficulty between the two examples above.

Some of our results are shown in table 1. The triplet results agree well with close coupling calculations [16] at $k_1 = 1.1$. It is of some interest to note that our results, along with those of Schwartz [1], show that $k_1 \cot \delta$ (where δ is the real part of the triplet phase shift) is very close to a linear function of k_1^2 from $k_1 = 1.5$ down to near $k_1 = 0$.

At $k_1 = 1.1$, our prediction for the singlet $e^- - H$ s-wave partial cross-section is 0.30 (in units of πa_0^2), which compares with 0.19 for the best close-coupling calculation [16] and 0.23 for close-coupling with correlations [17].

The elastic-scattering calculations appear to be fairly successful, but we can expect that, with stronger singularities to deal with in the extrapolation, more difficulty will be encountered with excitation and ionization. Computations for examples of these cases are now in progress.

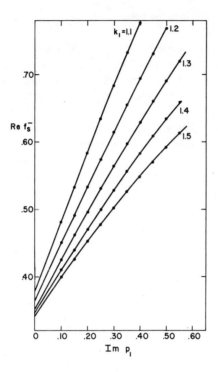

Fig. 1. Extrapolations of Re f_S^- = $-k_1$ Re T for the e$^-$–H s-wave singlet state from the values calculated at $p_1 = k_1 + i \operatorname{Im} p_1$, shown by the solid circles. Note that the size of the circles is not related to the expected error.

Table 1

Estimates from the energy extrapolation method of the triplet and singlet e$^-$–H s-wave scattering amplitudes f_t^-, f_s^-, and the e$^+$–H amplitude f^+, where $f = k_1 T$, so that $f = e^{i\delta}$ sin δ in the elastic region.

k_1	Re f_t^-	Im f_t^-	Re f_s^-	Im f_s^-	Re f^+	Im f^+
1.1	0.232	0.939	0.37	0.47	−0.20	0.05
1.2	0.298	0.893	0.35	0.45	−0.22	0.07
1.3	0.350	0.845	0.34	0.43	−0.24	0.09
1.4	0.386	0.795	0.33	0.42	−0.25	0.10
1.5	0.422	0.749	0.33	0.41	−0.28	0.12

4. Speculations on directions for future progress

The complex energy-extrapolation method avoids the need for explicitly determining what is going on in all open channels, if we are just interested in calculating scattering in a pair of channels, those of the initial and final states. If enough information is inserted about these two channels, the problem can be reduced to the extrapolation of a function with an arbitrarily large number of derivatives. A big challenge is to find a way of preserving the advantage of the method (a description of an infinite number of open channels not needed) while at the same time removing the need for extrapolation.

Another way of approaching this subject is to consider the amplitude $T_1(q_1, q_2)$ discussed in connection with the Watson-Faddeev equations. Presumably (it would be nice to have a proof) this function is analytic in the components of q_1 and q_2 in a region including real values except for singularities corresponding to the various channels, which will occur at

$$E - q_1^2 - q_2^2 = 0 \text{ (ionization channel)}$$

$$E - q_1^2 + \frac{1}{n^2} = 0 \text{ (channel with electron number 2 in a level with quantum number } n)$$

and two other similar sets. What may be an important point is that, if the integral operator corresponding to a Coulomb potential in momentum space is applied to a function of momenta analytic save at one point, the result has a singularity (of a different type) at the same point, but is analytic elsewhere.

Suppose that we are dealing with elastic scattering in the 1s state. Then we are clearly forced to work at the singularity at $E - q_1^2 + 1 = 0$, but the above property of the potential tells us that perhaps all the other singularities have nothing to do with this one. We should look for an integral equation in which the integrals are carried out over complex values of q_1, q_2 that avoid all singularities but $E - q_1^2 + 1 = 0$. Indeed in multi-channel two-body problems with long-range forces, this idea can be carried out, and it also works for a three-body problem with particles of arbitrary mass but with no interaction between one pair of particles. It is not known whether the full three-body problem can be solved this way.

Perhaps it is of interest in this connection to point out that analyticity in momentum space provides a powerful way of deriving results about the three-body problem with short-range potentials. For instance, the techniques of Rubin et al. [18] enable us to reproduce much more easily most of the mathematical results of Faddeev [19] (although for a more limited class of potentials), and incidentally prove that the multiple scattering series converges at high energy.

One more property of the problem that has not yet been employed is the analyticity of the potential, and hence the wave function, in the coordinates. We [20] have recently shown that the use of coordinate-space analyticity provides an efficient way of calculating cross-sections for n–d scattering with Yukawa potentials. The application of this tool is virgin territory in atomic physics.

Although the atomic three-body problem has been studied for more than 40 years, it would not be surprising if we were to see some exciting new developments before too long. I wonder what they will be.

Acknowledgements

The author is grateful to many colleagues, in particular G.D.Doolen, G.D. McCartor, F.A.McDonald and R.W.Stagat, who have shared in developing the ideas and performing the work reported here. The support of the U.S.Air Force Office of Scientific Research, Office of Aerospace Research, grant No. 71-1979, is much appreciated. The author would also like to thank the organizing committee of VII ICPEAC for the opportunity to present this report and a grant to help with expenses.

References

[1] C.Schwartz, Phys. Rev. *124* (1961) 1468.
[2] R.K.Peterkop, Izv. Akad. Nauk SSSR Ser. Fiz. *27* (1963); [English Transl.: Bull. Acad. Sci. USSR, Phys. Ser. *27* (1963) 987].
[3] G.D.Doolen and J.Nuttall, J. Math. Phys. *12* (1971) 2198.
[4] J.Nuttall, Ann. Phys. (New York) *52* (1969) 428.
[5] see J.C.Y.Chen, *VII ICPEAC, Invited Talks and Progress Reports,* eds. T.R.Govers and F.J.de Heer (North-Holland Publ. Co., Amsterdam, 1972) p. 232.
[6] This singularity may be one reason why the approach of replacing the two-body *T*-matrices with an operator of finite rank is not more successful.
[7] G.D.McCartor and J.Nuttall, Phys. Rev. A *4* (1971) 625.
[8] A.M.Veselova, *Two-Body Coulomb Singularities in the Equations for Charged Particles,* preprint, Kiev (1969); L.D.Faddeev, *The Three-Body Problem,* eds. J.S.C.McKee and P,M.Rolph (North-Holland Publ. Co., Amsterdam, 1970) p. 154.
[9] L.Schlessinger and C.Schwartz, Phys. Rev. Letters *16* (1966) 1173; see also S.C.Pieper, J.Wright and L.Schessinger, Phys. Rev. D *3* (1971) 2419.

[10] A.Temkin, Phys. Rev. *126* (1962) 130.

[11] C.Schwartz, in: *Methods in Computational Physics,* Vol. 2, eds. B.Alder, S.Fernbach and M.Rotenberg (Academic Press, New York, 1963) p. 241.

[12] L.M.Delves and K.O.Mead, *On the Convergence Rates of Variational Methods,* preprint; see also
L.M.Delves, *Variational Techniques in the Nuclear Three-Body Problem* to appear in *Advances in Nuclear Physics.*

[13] O.Hinckelman and L.Spruch, Phys. Rev. A *3* (1971) 642; and references contained therein.

[14] F.A.McDonald and J.Nuttall, Phys. Rev. A *4* (1971) 1821; Phys. Rev. Letters *23* (1969) 361.

[15] G.D.Doolen, G.D.McCartor, F.A.McDonald and J.Nuttall, Phys. Rev. A *4* (1971) 108.

[16] P.G.Burke, Proc. Phys. Soc. *82* (1963) 443.

[17] P.G.Burke and A.J.Taylor, Proc. Phys. Soc. *88* (1966) 549.

[18] M.H.Rubin, R.L.Sugar and G.Tiktopoulos, Phys. Rev. *159* (1967) 1348.

[19] L.D.Faddeev, *Mathematical Aspects of the Three-Body Problem* (Daniel Davey Inc. New York, 1965).

[20] J.Nuttall and H.L.Cohen, Phys. Rev. *188* (1969) 1542; also
F.A.McDonald and J.Nuttall (in preparation).

Physics of Electronic and Atomic Collisions, VII ICPEAC, 1971 — North-Holland (1972)

POSITRON SCATTERING THEORY

Richard J. DRACHMAN

Theoretical Studies Branch, Goddard Space Flight Center,
Greenbelt, Maryland 20771, USA

Recent progress in the theory of positron-atom scattering is discussed. The point of view is taken that the positron-hydrogen system should be used to test approximate methods which can then be applied to heavier atoms, particularly helium, for which experiments are more practicable. Various approximations are discussed and compared with the essentially exact results in hydrogen below the inelastic threshold. The best of these are extended to elastic positron-helium scattering. Annihilation in helium is also reviewed. The much more difficult problem of positronium formation is discussed briefly, both for hydrogen and helium. The question of bound states and scattering resonances is also mentioned.

1. Introduction

In discussing recent progress in low-energy positron theory, I would like to present a certain consistent viewpoint: that we can test our theoretical methods on the one-electron system and then apply them to the two-electron system. From McGowan's paper it appears that the positron-helium scattering system is now reasonably tractable from the experimental point of view [1]. At the moment (and for some time to come) we cannot make that statement about the positron-hydrogen atom system. But it is precisely the latter which has been best treated by the theoreticians. Although another 2-electron system, molecular hydrogen, is now coming under investigation [2], it is even harder to treat theoretically than helium because of its lack of spherical symmetry. Of course, there has been theoretical work reported on positron scattering from lithium [3], and neon and argon [4], but they are less completely examined and we will not discuss them here.

Before beginning the discussion of calculational techniques and results, I would like to place the problem of positron-atom systems in a clearer perspective. At first sight it differs very little from the corresponding problem of electron-atom scattering: the interaction potential involving the projectile simply changes sign. But qualitatively this change of sign is important. Firstly, the scattering of a positron from an undistorted atom (the static approxima-tion) corresponds to a repulsive interaction, while the effect of the distortion or polarization of the atom is mostly attractive, so a good deal of cancellation occurs when one tries to compute the phase shifts. Secondly, a new inelastic threshold appears at the energy where positronium formation is allowed. This threshold is at 6.8 eV for hydrogen and 17.8 eV for helium – in each case below the threshold for excitation of the first excited state of the target atom, which is the first inelastic threshold seen in electron scattering. (In fact, the positronium channel is always open for positron-alkali scattering, due to the loose binding of the valence electron.)

Perhaps a more important difference between positron and electron scatter-ing lies in the fact that the positron is distinguishable from the target elec-trons. As it penetrates the region occupied by the electrons, the details of its effect on the atomic wave function remain important, while in the electron scattering case the Pauli principle dominates in the inner region.

Finally, we should remember that whenever the positron is sufficiently close to one of the atomic eleectrons, it has a certain chance of annihilating with the emission of two 0.5 MeV gamma rays, whose angular correlation can be measured. The annihilation rate and the width of the correlation pattern offer additional tests of our theoretical understanding of positron scattering dynamics.

Let me first discuss the one-channel problem below the positronium thresh-old, to which most theoretical analyses are restricted, and then briefly review the much less satisfactory situation in the inelastic region.

2. Elastic scattering of positrons in hydrogen

The first successful calculation of elastic positron-hydrogen scattering was the Kohn variational calculation performed by Schwartz [5]. He used an ex-tensive expansion in Hylleraas form to describe the correlation between the incoming particle and the atomic electron, and he restricted his analysis to s-wave scattering. The main part of his paper concerned electron scattering, and almost as an afterthought he gave results for positrons. He merely remarked that the lack of exchange symmetry in the positron case made it necessary to include more terms in the expansion to reach a given order of approximation.

For a long time this pioneering work was considered to be definitive. It was followed some time later by a similar calculation for p-waves by Armstead

[6] ; the kinematics of p-wave scattering requires twice as many terms in the correlation function for a given order than s-waves, but the results again seem to be fairly reliable. No similar work has been done for higher partial waves.

Before I describe some recent work on this subject, let me outline the Kohn variational method as applied by Schwartz [5]. One assumes a trial function of the form

$$\Psi_T = [\psi_1 + \tan \eta_T \psi_2] + \Phi , \tag{1}$$

where η_T is the trial value of the phase shift,

$$\Phi = e^{-\gamma(x+r)} \sum_i C_i x^l r^m \rho^n$$

and where ψ_1 and ψ_2 have the proper asymptotic forms to describe elastic scattering. The index i refers to the triplet (l,m,n), x is the positron coordinate, r is the electron coordinate and ρ is the interparticle distance, the C_i's are linear parameters, and γ, α, and δ (cf. (3)) are non-linear parameters. One looks for the stationary value of the variational expression

$$\tan \eta_V \equiv \tan \eta_T + \frac{1}{4\pi} \int \Psi_T [H-E] \Psi_T \, d\tau , \tag{2}$$

under variations of all the C_i as well as $\tan \eta_T$; the error in the variational phase shift $\tan \eta_V$ is quadratic in the trial-function error.

At zero energy, this method gives an upper bound [7] on the scattering length a, which can be improved by increasing the expansion length and varying γ. Schwartz reported a value of $a_V < -2.10$ with an estimated error of no more than 0.01. Recently, Houston and I [8] recomputed the scattering length by this method using 84 terms in the expansion but generalizing the exponential function to contain three non-linear parameters:

$$\Phi = e^{-[\alpha\rho + \gamma r + \delta x]} \sum_i C_i x^l r^m \rho^n . \tag{3}$$

We searched fairly carefully for the best values for these parameters and obtained an upper bound on the scattering length of $a_V < -2.10278$. Extrapolation to $N = \infty$ gave the estimate $a = -2.1036 \pm 0.0004$, in full agreement with Schwartz's earlier result. (All scattering lengths are in units of a_0, the Bohr radius for hydrogen; N is the number of trial functions.) The accelerated convergence produced by the use of three non-linear parameters was responsible for the rather small error that we quote.

One technical point must be mentioned before I go on to discuss finite-energy scattering: an additional term describing the long-range polarizability of the target must be included to obtain the good convergence I described. This requirement was satisfied by Schwartz in his original paper, and we re-tested the convergence both with and without the extra term. We agree completely with his results.

Schwartz's s-wave results at finite energies were not so straightforward. He found singularities in $\tan \eta_V$ for certain values of the non-linear parameter. This may not be surprising since there exists no theorem concerning the boundedness of phase shifts obtained by the Kohn variational method. Almost any value can be obtained for a suitable expansion length and non-linear parameter. But Schwartz supposed that the phase shifts obtained for values of the non-linear parameter lying well away from singularities are significant; these plateau values increase with N and seem to converge well. For ten years they have been considered to be definitive, at least to the accuracy of 10^{-3} rad quoted; the p-wave results of Armstead [6] are similar in character.

Hahn et al. [9] and Gailitis [10] have, however, given formulations of the scattering problem which are applicable to positron-hydrogen elastic scattering and which give rigorous lower bounds to the phase shifts. These bounds hold below the energy of the first inelastic threshold or (if there is one) of the first resonance below threshold. The same sort of correlation function appropriate to a Kohn calculation may be used. The critical difference concerns the form of the open-channel part of the function:

$$\Psi_T = \frac{u(x)}{x} \phi_{1s}(r) + Q\Phi \, , \tag{4}$$

where ϕ_{1s} is the ground-state wave function of the hydrogen atom, and where $u(x)$ must now satisfy a certain integro-differential equation. Using this formulation, Bhatia et al. [11] have recently reported lower bounds on the s-wave phase shifts, in reasonable agreement with Schwartz's [5] but at some energies outside his estimated error.

The method, briefly, is as follows: we used the generalized Hylleraas correlation function discussed before but orthogonalized it to the hydrogen ground state $|1s\rangle$ by using the projection operator Q:

$$Q \equiv 1 - |1S\rangle\langle 1S| \ . \tag{5}$$

We then approximately diagonalized the Hamiltonian in the projected Q-space, obtaining eigenvalues $\mathcal{E}_\lambda$ and eigenfunctions Φ_λ from Rayleigh–Ritz principle:

$$\delta \frac{\langle \Phi Q H Q \Phi \rangle}{\langle \Phi Q^2 \Phi \rangle} = 0 \ . \tag{6}$$

The scattering equation to be solved is then

$$\left[\frac{d^2}{dx^2} - 2e^{-2x} \left(1 + \frac{1}{x} \right) + k^2 \right] u(x) - \sum_{\lambda=1}^{N} \frac{V_\lambda(x)\langle V_\lambda u \rangle}{E - \mathcal{E}_\lambda} = 0 \tag{7}$$

where

$$V_\lambda(x) = - \int d\mathbf{r} \left[Q\Phi_\lambda(\mathbf{r},x) \left(\frac{2}{|\mathbf{r}-\mathbf{x}|} \right) \phi_{1s}(r) \right] \ .$$

For each set of non-linear parameters the potentials V_λ were recomputed along with the $\mathcal{E}_\lambda$ and the equation solved iteratively. An exhaustive preliminary search failed to find any $\mathcal{E}_\lambda$ lying below the inelastic positronium threshold at 6.8 eV, which indicates that no compound state or "Feshbach" [12] resonances seem to exist in the elastic region. The scattering results are shown in table 1.

The rigorous lower bounds of Bhatia et al. [11] are shown in column 2, and are consistent with Schwartz's [5] except at $k = 0.7$. After extrapolation and correction for long-range effects, the three values marked with an asterisk disagree by more than Schwartz's estimated error of 10^{-3} rad. The new values must be considered more reliable because they were obtained from a lower-bound calculation. The last column shows some recent results of Doolen et al. [13], which are equivalent to a variational calculation with 120 terms. No bound property has been proven for this method, but the agreement is seen to be very good. I think we can say that the s-wave positron-hydrogen scattering problem is just about solved.

In the next two figures I show the forest of approximate calculations of s-wave positron-hydrogen scattering which has appeared in the recent literature.:. Each of them has some element of simplicity, elegance, or originality to justify our interest, but it is perfectly clear that most of them represent the correct

Table 1

Phase shifts for positron-hydrogen scattering in various approximations. k is the positron momentum. Column a is the Kohn variational calculation of Schwartz [5], column b is the lower bound ($N=84$) result [11] which is extrapolated to $N = \infty$ in column c. The $N = 120$ result [13] is in column d. (N is the number of trial functions.) The asterisks mark values which are in error by more than 10^{-3} rad.

k (a.u.)	Phase shift (rad)			
	a	b	c	d
0.1	0.151*	0.1479	0.1483	0.1481
0.2	0.188	0.1875	0.1877	0.1876
0.3	0.168	0.1672	0.1677	0.1671
0.4	0.120	0.1196	0.1201	0.1199
0.5	0.062	0.0619	0.0624	0.0623
0.6	0.007*	0.0030	0.0039	0.0034
0.7	−0.054*	−0.0524	−0.0512	−0.051

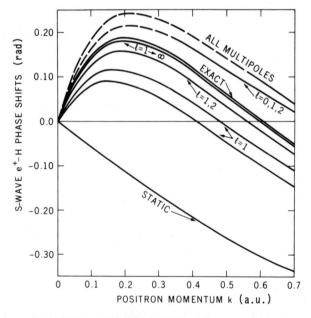

Fig. 1. s-wave positron-hydrogen phase shifts. Except for the static and exact [11] curves, all the others are adiabatic with different multipoles included. "All multipoles" and $l = 1 \to \infty$ are from [14] ; $l = 0, 1, 2, l = 1, 2$, and the upper $l = 1$ curves are from [16]. The lower $l = 1$ curve [18] uses a certain cutoff to simplify the potential.

answer so poorly that they are of no use at all to the experimentalist. In fig. 1 is a comparison of most of the published non-variational results. The "exact" result was discussed before. The lowest curve is the static result which actually is a lower bound, although an outstandingly poor one. In the good old days before computers it was piously hoped that this might be a fair approximation! Notice that all the other curves have the same shape; that comes from the struggle between repulsion, represented by the static potential, and attraction, due to polarization of the target. The crossing point is perhaps the critical element in the s-wave phase shift; if one doesn't include the correct amount of attraction, this zero occurs at the wrong energy and falsifies the cross-section.

All these approximations are essentially of the polarized-orbital type. They assume a wave function of the form

$$|\Psi\rangle = \chi(\mathbf{x})[1 + G(\mathbf{x},\mathbf{r})] |1s\rangle , \tag{8}$$

where the correlation function is

$$G = \sum_n \frac{|n\rangle\langle n|V}{E_{1s} - E_n} , \tag{9}$$

where V stands for those parts of the potential which involve the positron. The scattering equation is obtained from the non-variational Ansatz

$$\langle 1S| [H-E] |\Psi\rangle = 0 , \tag{10}$$

and results in the simple differential equation

$$-\nabla^2\chi + [V_1 + V_2 - k^2]\chi = 0 . \tag{11}$$

Here V_1 is the static potential and V_2 is the second-order adiabatic potential:

$$V_1 \equiv \langle 1s|V|1s\rangle$$

$$V_2 \equiv \langle 1s|VG|1s\rangle . \tag{12}$$

Each of the curves in fig. 1 corresponds to a different truncation of the sum (9). The top curve [14] employs a complete sum over all hydrogen states (except 1s) using the elliptical coordinate technique of Dalgarno and Lynn [15]. The fourth contains all but s-states; the monopole distortion has been

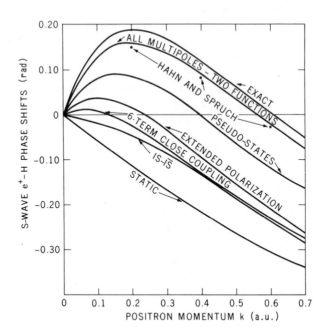

Fig. 2. Lower bound s-wave positron-hydrogen phase shifts. The static and exact [11] curves are the same as in fig. 1. "All multipoles-two functions" [24] refers to eq. (13). Hahn and Spruch [22] expanded in Legendre polynomials. Perkins [19] and Fon and Gallaher [21] used pseudo-states. "Extended polarization" [23], close coupling [17] and 1s–1̄s [18] are quite poor.

suppressed. Various other truncations of the sum have been examined by Bransden and Jundi [16], and are also shown here. I think you can see the general features: the addition of successive multipoles produces gradual convergence, but the monopole spherical distortion must be suporessed or the exact answer is exceeded.

In fig. 2 I have collected several results, all of which give rigorous lower bounds for the phase shift. Each one treats the correlation part of the wave function differently, but none of them uses the Hylleraas coordinates that led to the "correct" results that I described before; the latter, along with the static results, are shown again for comparison. The six-state close-coupling calculation of McEachran and Fraser [17] reflects the slow convergence in relative partial waves or multipole order that is generally found in positron calculations; only s, p and d states were included in their expansion, which was truncated after $n = 3$. The two-state expansion including the 1s ground-state of positronium is slightly poorer [18] . Perkins [19] did a three term close-coupling calculation but allowed the exponents of the 2p and 3d wave functions to be variational parameters; his much-improved results are shown, also. This technique is a "pseudo-state" expansion of one type. Another pseudo-state form which may be called the "closely-coupled polarized orbital" method was introduced by Damburg and Karule [20] to give the exact polarizability for each multipole term retained. Fon and Gallaher [21] reported results using this method at the present meeting, and they differ very slightly from those of Perkins [19] . Hahn and Spruch [22] used a direct expansion in Legendre polynomials up to $l = 5$, including several terms for each l; a total of 53 terms was retained. The convergence was slow, but an extrapolation to infinite l could be made and it gave results in agreement with the exact ones.

Since the best non-variational results came from an adiabatic, polarized-orbital method, it is interesting to use the same type of wave function variationally to obtain bounds. The results are not very good if all multipoles are included; a simplified form of this approximation is the "extended polarization" method of Callaway et al. [23] which is far too repulsive. Another idea is to treat the Dalgarno–Lynn correlation function [15] as a pseudo-state, letting

$$|\Psi\rangle = [\chi(\mathbf{x}) + F(\mathbf{x})G(\mathbf{x},\mathbf{r})]\,|1s\rangle \ . \tag{13}$$

and solving two coupled equations for χ and F. I introduced this method [24] in the hope that the second function $F(\mathbf{x})$ could compensate, at small x, for defects in the adiabatic correlation term. (Recently, Matese and Fung [25] have clarified the relationship between this method and the general optical potential formalism.) The results are fairly good as you see in fig. 2, and the method can be easily extended to the helium problem.

Fig. 3 shows a similar assortment of results for p-wave scattering, including the static result and Armstead's 70-term Kohn calculation [6] . In this case, the polarized-orbital type of calculation (which was over-attractive for s-waves) is not attractive enough at higher energy. We can trace this defect to the fact that the most general p-wave correlation function, as used by Armstead, contains two distinct types of terms:

$$\Phi = \sum_i e^{-\gamma(x+r)} \, [C_i \hat{x}^l r^m \hat{\mathbf{x}} + D_i x^m r^l \hat{\mathbf{r}}]\, \rho^n \ . \tag{14}$$

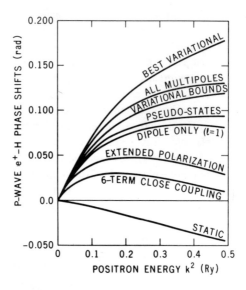

Fig. 3. p-wave positron-hydrogen phase shifts. All references are the same as in figs. 1 and 2 except "best variational" [6] and "variational bounds" [34].

Only the first type is represented in the polarized orbital method, which therefore omits some important short-range terms. In fact, a rigorous lower-bound calculation [26], containing only C-type terms, agrees well with a polarized orbital calculation that includes all multipoles. We will return to this point later in connection with helium.

But before I go on to the application of these methods to the positron-helium system, I would like to mention an important problem recently solved or almost solved. No calculation has ever even suggested (to my knowledge) that a stable bound state of the positron-hydrogen system exists, but interest in that possibility seems to persist. By Rayleigh–Ritz variational methods one can obtain only an upper bound to the total energy of the system, which has never indicated binding. Rotenberg and Stein [27] in this way have shown that a "positron" of mass greater than 2.2 times its actual mass is certainly capable of being bound to the hydrogen atom. Although their calculation seems very complete, there was always some question as to whether this limit could be lowered enough to allow the binding of real positrons. Now, however, Aronson et al. [28] have shown, by a modification of the adiabatic method, that no binding is possible since the effective interaction between atom and positron is too weak. Their numerical result is not absolutely rigorous, but it removes the last reasonable doubts as far as I can see.

3. Elastic scattering and annihilation of positrons in helium

Now that we have examined the situation in positron-hydrogen scattering theory, we should be ready to choose one or more techniques to use in the helium problem. A Kohn variational calculation and perhaps some form of polarized-orbital method might be our first choices. In fact, there is very little else; no rigorous bounds using Hylleraas coordinates have been tried.

We face a special problem, however. The Kohn method presupposes knowledge of the asymptotic form of the wave function, and that requires knowledge of the target wave function. Of course, only variational approximations to the helium ground-state wave function are known, and the good ones are much more complex than the hydrogen function. The universal first choice is the hydrogenic function

$$\phi(r_1,r_2) = \frac{Z^3}{\pi} e^{-Z(r_1+r_2)} , \tag{15}$$

where Z is a variational parameter. This is clearly a crude approximation, lacking any inter-electronic correlation.

The question to ask next is: what do we mean by E appearing in the Kohn variational principle, eq. (2)? The boundary conditions would not be satisfied if we used the exact energy with an approximate ground-state wave function, so some calculations have used the expectation value of H_0:

$$E = \langle H_0 \rangle + k^2 . \tag{16}$$

Houston and Moiseiwitsch [29] examined the zero-energy positron-helium problem in this way, with results that seemed to converge erratically. Houston [30] later showed that the upper bound property does not hold in this case, and that most simple ground-state functions do not give convergent results.

Another method is to replace the atomic Hamiltonian by a model Hamiltonian of which the approximate wave function is an eigenfunction. That is, we assume that

$$\bar{H}_0\phi = \bar{E}_0\phi ; \qquad \bar{E} = E_0 + k^2 ; \qquad H = \bar{H}_0 + V , \tag{17}$$

where $\bar{H}_0$ is the model Hamiltonian. The interaction potential is unchanged. With this new Hamiltonian all the boundedness theorems hold, and convergence is regular. In principle, a sequence of increasingly accurate approximate helium wave functions generates a sequence of models, and their phase shifts converge in some sense to the exact answer. In practice, only the simplest such models have been examined.

You will recall that the non-variational polarized-orbital method, with all multipoles except the monopole, gave good results for s-wave hydrogen scattering. It was also used [31] for helium by employing the model corresponding to the hydrogenic wave function of eq. (15). That calculation of mine was the first to suggest that the existing experimental cross-section near the positronium threshold [32] was significantly in error, low by a factor of five. The present experimental situation implies, ironically enough, that near threshold the theoretical cross-section is now low by about a factor of two [33]. But good agreement is obtained at low energies where the s-wave is dominant; the error is probably in the higher-l partial waves.

This is just what we saw in the hydrogen case, where the adiabatic theory gave too little short-range attraction in the p- and d-waves. I would like to show you a semi-empirical adjustment of the theory that is based on the analogy between positron-hydrogen and positron-helium scattering. Monopole suppression worked well for s-wave positron scattering in hydrogen, so we adopted it for s-waves in helium also. For the higher partial waves, an enhancement in the adiabatic monopole potential can be used to supply the needed extra attraction. By increasing the monopole potential in hydrogen to 3.5 times its adiabatic value, we can get agreement with Armstead's p-wave results [6]. An increase by a factor of 23 gives agreement for d-waves [34]. Using these same factors in helium, we get the total cross-section curve shown in fig. 4; it is compared there with the unenhanced value. The single experimental value [33] lies on the new curve. I think this procedure ought to be considered reasonable at the present stage and useful for design of experiments, but it is clearly not a fundamental theory by any means. Two more fundamental s-wave calculations have also been transferred from the hydrogen case: the polarized-orbital lower bound method, eq. (13), and the Hylleraas correlation method treated variationally [24,8]. I won't go into the details here, except to say that they agree well, and that the sensitivity of the phase shifts to the helium wave function is small, provided that the value of $\langle r^2 \rangle$ is close tõ the exact one. This is a way of saying that the size and softness of the ground-state are most important for the scattering. The extended polarization method [23] also agrees, but we saw that it was quite poor in the hydrogen case. It gives large negative s-wave and small p-wave phase shifts near the positronium threshold.

Once we have a scattering wave function $\Psi(\mathbf{r}_1,\mathbf{r}_2,\mathbf{x})$, preferably obtained variationally, we can compute annihilation rates and the angular correlation between the annihilation γ-rays. The appropriate formulae are [35,36]:

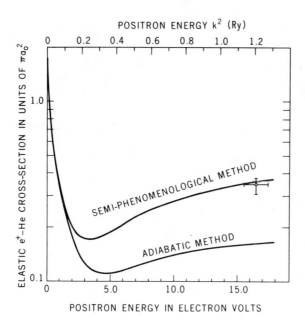

Fig. 4. Elastic positron-helium cross-section compared with experiment [33]. The upper curve is modified, as explained in the text, from the work [31] resulting in the lower curve.

$$Z_{eff} = 2 \int d^3r \int d^3x |\Psi(\mathbf{r},\mathbf{x},\mathbf{x})|^2 \qquad (18)$$

$$P(q_3) \propto \int\limits_{-\infty}^{\infty} \int dq_1 dq_2 \int d\mathbf{r} |\int d\mathbf{x}\, e^{i\mathbf{q}\cdot\mathbf{x}} \Psi(\mathbf{r},\mathbf{x},\mathbf{x})|^2 . \qquad (19)$$

The "effective electron number", Z_{eff}, is related to the annihilation cross-section as follows:

$$\sigma_a = Z_{eff} \frac{c}{V} \alpha^4 \cdot \pi a_0^2 , \qquad (20)$$

where α is the fine-structure constant $e^2/\hbar c$, and where the angle between the two outgoing γ-rays is

$$\theta = \pi - \frac{\hbar q_3}{mc} . \qquad (21)$$

(The function P is the distribution of one component of the momentum ($\hbar$g) of the electron-positron pair at the instant of annihilation.) The two variational methods give Z_{eff} = 3.7 and 4.3 respectively at zero energy, while the experimental values [37] lie near the former value. [The discrepancy of 15% between these two values is perfectly consistent with the 1.3% disagreement in scattering length, which is a variational quantity; the annihilation rate is not.] The width of the angular correlation pattern is found to be 9.5 × 10⁻³ rad [38] compared with Stewart's experimental value [39] of 9.2 ± 0.2 × 10⁻³ rad; the agreement is again fairly good. But again, nothing much is known at energies above thermal.

4. Scattering and re-arrangement above the positronium threshold

Once we raise the positron bombarding energy above the threshold for re-arrangement or positronium formation, we face a new and much more difficult problem. The two open channels require the solution of more equations, but it is the non-orthogonality of the ground-states of hydrogen (or helium) and positronium that is the source of most of the trouble. In addition, both systems are polarizable, and we saw that polarizability was an important part of the description of scattering below threshold. The positronium atom is eight times as polarizable as the hydrogen atom, and so the cruder approximations will probably fail above threshold. Much more work is needed before this two-channel problem is reasonably well understood. Nevertheless, there has been a fairly active research effort directed at solving the problem, mostly in hydrogen so far. In a Progress Report like this, it is necessary to review this work both critically and with admiration.

The history of calculations of the positronium formation cross-section in hydrogen begins, as usual, with the Born approximation [40]. There are no surprises here – the cross-section rises to a maximum of $4\pi a_0^2$ at about one volt above threshold and then decreases slowly and smoothly. There is, of course, no way for any of the higher thresholds to affect the results. All Born calculations for re-arrangement processes are now thought to be unreliable, even beyond the post-prior ambiguity.

The next approximation is a two-state expansion which retains the ground-states of both hydrogen (1s) and positronium ($\overline{1s}$). The trial function is

$$\Psi_{BJ} = F(\mathbf{x})\phi_{1s}(r) + G(\mathbf{R})\phi_{1s}(\rho) , \qquad (22)$$

where

$$R = \tfrac{1}{2}(x+r)$$

and

$$\rho = x - r \; ;$$

these two new coordinates are the center-of-mass and the relative coordinates of the positronium system, respectively. The two equations which must be solved for F and G are

$$\int dr\phi_{1s}(r)[H-E]\,\psi_{BJ} = 0 \; , \tag{23}$$

and

$$\int d\rho\phi_{\overline{1s}}(\rho)[H-E]\,\Psi_{BJ} = 0 \; .$$

Because of the mixed coordinate system, these are integro-differential equations. They have been solved numerically by Bransden and Jundi [41], for several partial waves, although the omission of polarization makes the results unlikely to be quantitatively correct. I will come back to this later.

Fels and Mittleman [42] simplified the problem by choosing a simpler, but less natural, coordinate system. They write

$$\Psi_{FM} = F(x)\phi_{1s}(r) + G(x)\phi_{\overline{1s}}(\rho) \cdot e^{\frac{1}{2}k_F \hat{x} \cdot \rho} \tag{24}$$

and, since the two unknowns are both functions of the positron coordinate, simpler differential equations result. The exponential factor is needed to correct the asymptotic form. It is clearly irrelevant which of these coordinate systems is used to describe the exact solution, but for approximations one would expect the former to be better. The results of these two approximations are quite radically different with Bransden and Jundi's cross-section for positronium formation [41] being very much the larger. Fels and Mittleman [42] point out that their choice of coordinates introduces an extra centrifugal-like potential which seems to dominate.

Both of these calculations have also been extended by the addition, non-variationally, of polarization potentials for hydrogen and positronium. The results again are quite different. Fels and Mittleman [42] find that the elastic scattering is sensitive to the polarization while the positronium formation is not. Bransden and Jundi [41] find indications of a resonance just below the threshold; this is almost certainly a result of the non-variational method [43, 11,27]. Doolen et al. [13] used an extrapolation in the complex k-space to obtain complex s-wave phase shifts above threshold. Again, these do not look much like the other results. I am obviously not being very optimistic about these calculations; the approximations are not yet convincing.

Dirks and Hahn [44], however, have begun a program that should result eventually in reliable results in the two-channel problem for hydrogen. Using Hahn's generalized variational bound method [45], they have derived approximate values for the s-wave partial cross-sections above threshold. These are still not quantitative because only very few correlation terms were included, but I think they are very encouraging.

Fels and Mittleman [42] found, as their most important result, that positronium formation is some 40 times smaller than in the Born approximation. In another paper [46] they apply their method to helium and find an even more extreme reduction. So small is their predicted formation cross-section in helium, that it may actually be in disagreement with experiment. But using their helium results, they have recently shown [47] that above the positronium threshold almost all the annihilation is from positronium and almost none is annihilation of free positrons in flight.

One more topic of interest is the question of positron-scattering resonances lying below the $n = 2$ hydrogen threshold. Using the same general principles as in the electron-hydrogen case [48], it was shown by Mittleman [49] that an infinite series of resonances is also to be expected for positrons. The effect is due to the long-range $1/r^2$ potential resulting from 2s–2p degeneracy. The short-range effects — exchange (for electrons) and positronium formation (for positrons) — cannot eliminate the resonances but can change their positions. Seiler et al. [50] have now reported a calculation in the close-coupling 1s–2s–2p approximation on the position and width of the first three such resonances. This calculation is welcome and overdue; it shows that the resonances are reasonably far below the $n = 2$ threshold and very narrow. Unfortunately, the complicated positronium channel was omitted, and more work is necessary.

5. Conclusions

It now seems that the hydrogen atom has served well to test methods to be used for positron elastic scattering in more complex atoms. The situation in the region where two channels are open is clearly much more primitive, but progress is being made there as well. An interesting start is being made also in the three-electron, one-positron problem, represented by the positronium-helium system [51], while the chemistry of the positronium-hydride molecule is under investigation [36,52]. There is every reason to expect sig-;ant nificant progress in these interesting problems by the time of our next conference.

References

[1] J.W.McGowan, *VII ICPEAC, Invited Talks and Progress Reports*, eds. T.R.Govers and F.J.de Heer (North-Holland Publ. Co., Amsterdam, 1972) p. 295.
[2] J.G.Lodge, J.W.Darewych and R.P.McEachran, Can. J. Phys. *49* (1971) 13.
[3] B.T.Dai and A.D.Stauffer, Can. J. Phys. *49* (1971) 2527.
[4] R.E.Montgomery and R.W.LaBahn, Can. J. Phys. *48* (1970) 1288.
[5] C.Schwartz, Phys. Rev. *124* (1961) 1468.
[6] R.L.Armstead, Phys..Rev. *171* (1968) 91.
[7] L.Spruch and L.Rosenberg, Phys. Rev. *117* (1960) 143.
[8] S.K.Houston and R.J.Drachman, Phys. Rev. A *3* (1971) 1335.
[9] Y.Hahn, T.F.O'Malley and L.Spruch, Phys. Rev. *128* (1962) 932.
[10] M.Gailitis, Zh. Eksp. Teor. Fiz. *47* (1964) 160; [English Transl.: Soviet Phys. -JETP *20* (1965) 107].
[11] A.K.Bhatia, A.Temkin, R.J.Drachman and H.Eiserike, Phys. Rev. A *3* (1971) 1328.
[12] H.Feshbach, Ann. Phys. (New York) *5* (1958) 357.
[13] G.Doolen, G.McCartor, F.A.McDonald and J.Nuttall, Phys. Rev. A *4* (1971) 108.
[14] R.J.Drachman, Phys. Rev. *138* (1965) A1582.
[15] A.Dalgarno and N.Lynn, Proc. Phys. Soc. A *70* (1957) 223.
[16] B.H.Bransden and Z.Jundi, Proc. Phys. Soc. *89* (1966) 7.
[17] R.P.McEachran and P.A.Fraser, Proc. Phys. Soc. *86* (1965) 369.
[18] W.J.Cody, J.Lawson, H.S.W.Massey and K.Smith, Proc. Roy. Soc., Ser. A *278* (1964) 479.
[19] J.R.Perkins, Phys. Rev. *173* (1968) 164.
[20] R.Damburg and E.Karule, Proc. Phys. Soc. *90* (1967) 637.
[21] W.C.Fon and D.F.Gallaher, *VII ICPEAC, Abstracts of Papers*, eds. L.M.Branscomb et al., Vol. 2 (North-Holland Publ. Co., Amsterdam, 1971) p. 939.
[22] Y.Hahn and L.Spruch, Phys. Rev. *140* (1965) A18.
[23] J.Callaway, R.W.LaBahn, R.T.Pu and W.M.Duxler, Phys. Rev. *168* (1968) 12.
[24] R.J.Drachman, Phys. Rev. *173* (1968) 190; *V ICPEAC, Abstracts of Papers*, eds. I.P.Flaks and E.S.Solovjov (Publishing House "Nauka", Leningrad, 1967) p. 106.
[25] J.J.Matese and A.C.Fung, Phys. Rev. A *3* (1971) 928.
[26] A.K.Bhatia, private communication (1971).
[27] M.Rotenberg and J.Stein, Phys. Rev. *182* (1969) 1.
[28] I.Aronson, C.J.Kleinman and L.Spruch, Phys. Rev. A *4* (1971) 841.
[29] S.K.Houston and B.L.Moiseiwitsch, J. Phys. B *1* (1968) 29.
[30] S.K.Houston, unpublished (1969).

[31] R.J.Drachman, Phys. Rev. *144* (1966) 25.

[32] S.Marder, V.W.Hughes, C.S.Wu and W.Bennett, Phys. Rev. *103* (1956) 1258;
W.B.Teutsch and V.W.Hughes, *ibid* 1266.

[33] D.G.Costello, D.E.Groce, D.F.Herring and J.W.McGowan, preprint (1971).

[34] C.J.Kleinman, Y.Hahn and L.Spruch, Phys. Rev. *140* (1965) A413.

[35] R.A.Ferrell, Rev. Mod. Phys. *28* (1956) 308.

[36] S.M.Neamtan, G.Darewych and G.Oczkowski, Phys. Rev. *126* (1962) 193.

[37] C.Y.Leung and D.A.L.Paul, J. Phys. B *2* (1969) 1278;
G.F.Lee, P.H.R.Orth and G.Jones, Phys. Letters *28*A (1969) 674;
S.J.Tao and T.M.Kelly, Phys. Rev. *185* (1969) 135.

[38] R.J.Drachman, Phys. Rev. *179* (1969) 237.

[39] C.V.Briscoe, S.-I.Choi and A.T.Stewart, Phys. Rev. Letters *20* (1968) 493.

[40] I.M.Cheshire, Proc. Phys. Soc. *83* (1964) 227;
H.S.W.Massey and C.B.O.Mohr, *ibid* A*67* (1954) 695.

[41] B.H.Bransden and Z.Jundi, Proc. Phys. Soc. *92* (1967) 880.

[42] M.F.Fels and M.H.Mittleman, Phys. Rev. *163* (1967) 129.

[43] R.J.Drachman, Phys. Rev. *171* (1968) 110.

[44] J.F.Dirks and Y.Hahn, Phys. Rev. A *2* (1970) 1861; *3* (1971) 310;
Y.Hahn and J.F.Dirks, *ibid 3* (1971) 1513.

[45] Y.Hahn, Phys. Rev. C *1* (1970) 12.

[46] M.F.Fels and M.H.Mittleman, Phys. Rev. *182* (1969) 77.

[47] M.F.Fels and M.H.Mittleman, Phys. Rev. A *3* (1971) 1827.

[48] A.Temkin and J.F.Walker, Phys. Rev. *140* (1965) A1520.

[49] M.H.Mittleman, Phys. Rev. *152* (1966) 76.

[50] G.J.Seiler, R.S.Oberoi and J.Callaway, Phys. Rev. A *3* (1971) 2006.

[51] P.A.Fraser and M.Kraidy, Proc. Phys. Soc. *89* (1966) 533;
P.A.Fraser, J. Phys. B *1* (1968) 1006;
M.I.Barker and B.H.Bransden, J. Phys. B *1* (1968) 1109; *2* (1969) 730;
R.J.Drachman and S.K.Houston, J. Phys. B *3* (1970) 1657.

[52] C.F.Lebeda and D.M.Schrader, Phys. Rev. *178* (1969) 24;
D.M.Schrader and T.Petersen, Phys. Rev. A *3* (1971) 61.

Physics of Electronic and Atomic Collisions, VII ICPEAC, 1971 — North-Holland (1972)

POSITRON EXPERIMENTS TODAY:
SCATTERING FROM HELIUM

J.William McGOWAN

*Department of Physics, University of Western
Ontario, London, Canada*

Considerable sophistication has developed in instrumentation associated with the swarm techniques which permit studies of the annihilation
of a free positron with a bound electron, ortho-positronium quenching,
measurements of the cross-sections for total momentum transfer at energies well below the positronium-formation threshold, measurements of
Z_{eff}, and so on. However, swarm techniques become less effective as the
velocity of the colliding positron approaches that for the formation of positronium.
    Recently, it has been shown that a source of positrons can be fabricated
which gives a narrow energy distribution [FWHM = 1.0 eV]. As a result,
complimentary beam experiments can be attempted. In this progress report
(e^+,He) scattering experiments and -results are reviewed as an example of
work possible using both swarm- and beam techniques.

1. Introduction

One of the primary problems we have in electron scattering is to test the
effects of the electron exchange force between the bombarding electrons and
the electrons in the target atom or -molecule, since these electrons are completely indistinguishable. One way to eliminate the problem is to replace one
electron with an anti-electron, i.e. a positron. This is perhaps most meaningful
in the elastic-scattering region, below the onset of any inelastic processes.
However, even this study is somewhat complicated theoretically by the fact
that the mean static interaction of an atom with a positron is repulsive while
the long-range polarization is attractive so that the two effects oppose rather
than combine as in the case of electron scattering. Furthermore, we do not
yet know if (e^-,e^+) pair annihilation has a direct effect upon scattering cross-
sections. Although we have eliminated exchange, at higher scattering energies

there are the unique problems of positronium formation both in the ground- and excited state, and the formation of compound states which must be added to those of excitation and ionization of the target atom or -molecule.

Theoretically, the most tractable system is (e^+,H) [1]; experimentally, (e^+,Ar) has proven more manageable [2,3]. For the moment, (e^+,He) has become the compromise system for which considerable theory [1] and complementary experimental data are now available. It is this system which will receive the most detailed review in this report. Limited work has been reported on positron collisions with neon, krypton, xenon, nitrogen, hydrogen and a large number of organic and inorganic compounds. See refs. [3–9] for an introduction to this work.

Essentially, two types of experiments have been carried out. The first type includes variations on swarm experiments which the atomic-scattering community readily associates with electron scattering. The second type is a beam experiment involving the collision of energy-resolved positrons with a gas target. This is a new method, and while only one experiment is as yet reported, several others will be reported soon. Clearly, in the future, there will be many more swarm- and complementary beam experiments covering energies from the elastic-scattering region, i.e.,

$$e^+ + He \rightarrow e^+ + He \, , \tag{1}$$

through the onsets of the inelastic channels (cf. fig. 1):

$$e^+ + He \rightarrow Ps + He^+ - 17.8 \ eV \quad \text{(charge transfer or positronium} \atop \text{formation)} \tag{2}$$

$$\rightarrow e^+ + He(2^1S) - 20.6 \ eV \quad \text{(helium excitation of first} \atop \text{singlet state)} \tag{3}$$

$$\rightarrow Ps(n=2) + He^+ \quad \text{(excited positronium formation)} \tag{4}$$

$$\rightarrow e^+ + He^+ + e - 24.6 \ eV \quad \text{(ionization)} \, , \tag{5}$$

possibly:

$$e^+ + He \rightarrow (He,e^+) \text{ compound state} \rightarrow He^* + e^+ \, , \tag{6}$$

and so on. Competing with all of these processes is the direct annihilation of the positron with the bound electron in the atom,

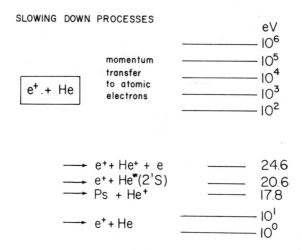

Fig. 1. Slowing down processes for positrons in helium gas, the energy ranges over which they apply, and the threshold energies for the processes involved.

$$e^+ + He \rightarrow \text{gamma rays} + He^+ . \tag{7}$$

2. Swarm experiments

Conceptually, the electron- and positron swarm experiments are similar, but as you will see, in many ways the positron swarm studies are much richer. One may introduce a pulse of electrons into the typical gas-filled electron drift tube [10] at $t = 0$ by flashing a photo-cathode or otherwise gating an electron source. One then measures the time t it takes for the electrons to traverse the gas cell, as a function of gas pressure, p, and axial electric field, E. In these experiments the drift velocity is proportional to E/p. Normally the pressure range studied is $0.1 \leqslant p \leqslant 20$ Torr.

In order to determine the total momentum-transfer cross-section, σ_{TMT}, it is necessary to solve the diffusion equation,

$$\partial f(v)/\partial t = F[\sigma_{TMT}, v, f(v)] . \tag{8}$$

where F refers to a complicated functional dependence, in order to determine the electron-velocity (energy) distribution function $f(v)$ and derive σ_{TMT}

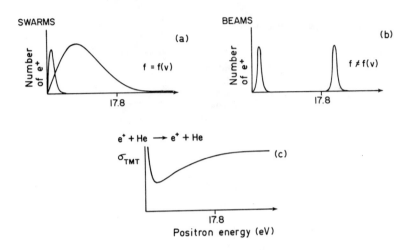

Fig. 2. Representative changes in energy (velocity) distributions of positrons as a function of the mean energy of the positrons (a) for swarms (b) for beams. In both cases, a low and high energy case is shown. The predicted shape of the (e^+,He) total momentum-transfer cross section through the Ramsauer-like dip is given in (c).

from the analysis. At low mean velocities, $f(v)$ is very narrow. As the electron velocity is increased through an increase of E/p or of gas temperature, $f(v)$ broadens rapidly [10]. This behavior, shown schematically in fig. 2, represents one of the prime characteristics of a swarm experiment.

A variation on this type of experiment allows the study of the formation and destruction of (X,e^-) complexes as a function of E/p and p [11]. In these cases, the negative ions X^- are usually detected by means of a mass spectrometer and a gating system which enables an experimentalist to measure accurately the number of ions present and their velocity distribution after a given period of time, t.

With positrons the situation is similar in that there is a drift tube with an axial electric field E, but normally the pressure range covered is much higher, $1 \leqslant p \leqslant 100$ atm. (Note: the unit used in positron drift experiments is the amagat — 1 amagat = 1 mol/22.4 litre = 4.46×10^{-5} mol/cm^3.) But unlike the electron-swarm case, positrons do not come from sources which have a reasonably narrow energy distribution or are convenient for drift studies as far as their half-life is concerned (cf. table 1). Normally, they are obtained from either long-lived natural radioactive sources like ^{22}Na, ^{64}Cu, ^{58}Co, or short-lived machine-made sources like ^{11}C, which has a 22.5 min natural lifetime toward β^+ decay, or from the conversion of bremsstrahlung into a (e^+,e^-)

Table 1

Characteristics of positron sources

Source	Half life	Percent β^+ decay	Method of production
^{11}C	20.5 min	100	^{11}B(p,n)^{11}C, ^{12}C(γ,n)^{11}C
^{22}Na	2.6 yr	89	^{27}Al(^{3}He,2α)^{22}Na
^{55}Co	18.2 hr	60	^{58}Ni(p,α)^{55}Co, ^{56}Fe(p,2n)^{55}Co
^{57}Ni	36.0 hr	50	^{56}Fe(^{3}He,2n)^{57}Ni
^{58}Co	71.3 days	15	^{58}Ni(n,p)^{58}Co, ^{55}Mn(α,n)^{58}Co
^{64}Cu	12.7 hr	19	^{63}Cu(n,γ)^{64}Cu
^{68}Ge–Ga	280 days	85	
^{90}Nb	14.7 hr	54	^{90}Zr(p,n)^{90}Nb, ^{90}Zr(d,2n)^{90}Nb

pair. The source of the radiation may be a LINAC or an electron Van de Graaff. To-date and to my knowledge, no bremsstrahlung source has been used in swarm studies. Shortly, other accelerator sources may be available such as that proposed for Wayne State University, where proton bombardment of ^{11}B will produce e$^+$ through the sequence

$$p + {}^{11}B \rightarrow {}^{11}C \rightarrow {}^{11}B + n + e^+ + \text{neutrino} .$$

From radioactive sources, let's say ^{22}Na for example, the energy distribution of e$^+$'s is typically broad (FWHM>0.1 MeV) with a maximum energy of 0.54 MeV, a peak intensity near 0.17 MeV and a spectrum which reaches down to very low energies. In other words, most positrons are produced with energies much in excess of those needed to study low-energy elastic- and inelastic processes. As a consequence, the high pressures referred to above are first needed to moderate the positron energy.

The action of thermalizing high-energy positrons (fig. 1) requires many collisions. From the MeV to keV range, slowing down is essentially described by the Spencer–Fano [12] theory of momentum-sharing between the positron and atomic electrons. Below this, the various inelastic channels summarized by eqs. (3) and (5), and perhaps (6), take over. Notice in fig. 1 that elastic scattering is neatly separated from the positronium-formation threshold and that there is 2.8 eV between the positronium-formation threshold and the first allowed transition. (Note: the 2^3S state cannot be excited readily, since there is no electron exchange possible). In cases like (e$^+$,Li) the positronium formation threshold is at 0 eV. For (e$^+$,He) below 17.8 eV, positrons can only slow down through momentum-transfer collisions. Once thermalized in dense gaseous targets in a time $\leqslant 10^{-10}$s, the positron can be accelerated in the field E in a gas chamber at pressure p, and the lifetime λ of the free positron can be measured readily.

One danger with high pressures is that a large variety of processes that have a second- or perhaps even higher-order dependence on gas pressure, may occur. The list of second-order processes known already includes the quenching of excited positronium states due to electron-exchange collisions, (X,e^+), compound state formation- and destruction, etc.

The usual positron swarm experiment calls for the measurement of the e^+ destruction or annihilation rate as a function of $E/p, p$, impurity content, etc. If a ^{22}Na positron source is used, accompanying the birth of each positron and delayed by only 10^{-12}s is a 1.28 MeV gamma-ray coming from the de-excitation of the excited ^{22}Ne which is formed during the β^+ decay process, cf. fig. 3.

Also shown in fig. 3 is a very rough schematic diagram of the typical swarm apparatus. Counter #1 is tuned to the 1.28 MeV gammas. When one is detected, $t = 0$ is set in the time-to-amplitude converter. A time t later, counter #2 detects a 0.51 MeV gamma-ray associated with the annihilation of the positron in the gas. Nearly all the useful data are drawn from the analysis of the resulting lifetime spectrum.

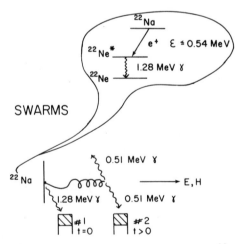

Fig. 3. A schematic representation of a swarm apparatus in which a ^{22}Na positron emitter is used. In the baloon, the decay scheme for ^{22}Na is given.

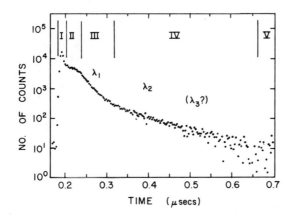

Fig. 4. A representative time spectrum for positron annihilation in argon for $E/p = 0$ and $p = 8.9$ amagat. I, prompt peak; II, shoulder region which is sensitive to E/p; III, annihilation of the free positron with atomic electrons; the apparent annihilation rate is a function of E/p and gas temperature; IV, annihilation of 1^3S state of o-Ps; slope is a function of p; V, background of random coincidences.

In fig. 4, I show a typical lifetime spectrum for (e^+, Ar). I chose this instead of the (e^+, He) system because the usually recognizable features are more pronounced. These features include:

Region I: A prompt peak at $t = 0$ which includes a) annihilations in the source, b) annihilations of fast positrons in the process of being slowed down by collisions with gas atoms, c) unresolved two-gamma annihilations of para-positronium with electron- and positron spins anti-parallel, lifetime $t_p \approx 1.25 \times 10^{-10}$ s, and, d) possible annihilation of (Ar, e^+) complexes.

Region II: A broad shoulder which is sensitive to E/p and which reflects the σ_{TMT} cross-section and the Ps formation cross-section.

Region III: An exponential decaying section which is attributed to annihilation of the free positron in flight through the gas cell. The apparent decay rate (reflected in the slope of the exponential) is found to be both a function of E/p and of the gas temperature.

Region IV: An exponential decay attributed to the annihilation of the 1^3S state of Ps. Angular momentum considerations indicate that this is three-gamma decay. The decay rate is pressure dependent and is thought to reflect the quenching of ortho-positronium primarily through electron exchange $(o\text{-}Ps) + Ar \rightarrow (p\text{-}Ps) + Ar^*$.

Region V: A background due to random coincidences of counts in counter #1 and counter #2.

It is generally felt that the time spectrum associated with regions III, IV, and V can be fitted with a curve of the form $n = n_{10} \exp(-\lambda_1 t) + n_{20} \exp(-\lambda_2 t) + b$, where n_{10} is the amplitude of free component extrapolated to $t = 0$; n_{20} is the amplitude of o–Ps extrapolated to $t = 0$; and b is the constant background.

From the exponential portion III associated with the annihilation of the free positron, if the spins of the free positron and the bound electron which make up the annihilation pair are antiparallel, the free-singlet annihilation rate λ_1 is shown to be:

$$\lambda_1 = 4.51 \times 10^9 \ (\rho/M_A)Z_{eff}(s^{-1}) , \tag{9}$$

where Z_{eff} is the effective number of annihilation electrons available in the atom (or molecule) of molecular weight (mass units) M_A. As expected, the probability that the electron and positron are at the same point in the atom is zero when the gas pressure or density ρ is zero, cf. refs. [2,6,13–18]. The results of various experiments for e+ in helium are summarized in table 2. As too often is the case, the uncertainties associated with each experiment are sometimes smaller than the variation between the different measurements. This probably reflects a systematic error associated with impurities in the gaseous targets which, through much effort, has been minimized in the most recent investigations, which tend to agree.

It was not realized in earlier experiments in argon, as well as in helium, that a shoulder was present (region II of fig. 4) in the time spectrum, so sufficient care may not have been taken to account for the non-exponential character of the curve in this region.

An unweighted average of the three most recent measured values [16–18] of Z_{eff} for helium at room temperature gives $Z_{eff} = 3.7 \pm 0.1$, in excellent agreement with the variational calculation of Drachman [23], but in poorer agreement with the most recent calculations by Houston and Drachman [27] based upon the Harris method. A similar analysis of the last three measurements for argon [2c,d,e] gives $Z_{eff} = 26.4 \pm 0.5$. As the energy of the positron is increased, the value of Z_{eff} must approach the number of electrons in the atom.

Calculated values of Z_{eff} are very sensitive to the theoretical model used, therefore a comparison of measured and calculated values of Z_{eff} is a good test of the theory. It has been demonstrated both theoretically and experimentally that Z_{eff} is a decreasing function of E/p. Lee et al. [28] and Leung

Table 2

Experimental and theoretical (e$^+$,He) scattering cross sections. σ_{TMT} is the total momentum-transfer cross-section and σ_{TS} the total scattering cross-section; both are indicated in units of πa_0^2. The data are from the references indicated in the corresponding column.

Energy (eV)	Experimental					Theoretical σ_{TS}		
	σ_{TMT}			σ_{TS}				
	[4,5]	[19]	[17]	[20,21]	[22]	[23,24]	[25]	[26]
Thermal			1.05					
2			0.10	0.17 ±0.06		0.17		0.28
4			0.13	0.12 ±0.06		0.12		0.30
10			0.20			0.14		0.36
14			0.22		0.36 ±0.04	0.16		0.37
16.5	0.023 ±0.006	0.26 ±0.03	0.22	0.35 ±0.04	0.36 ±0.04	0.17	0.42 Upper limit	0.36
19.3				0.60 ±0.16			s,p,d- wave	1.94
21.3				1.0 ±0.15				2.22
26.1				1.24 ±0.27				2.2

and Paul [17] have shown that Z_{eff} falls more than 10% as the average energy of the positrons is increased to 1 eV. In the case of argon it has further been shown [2f] that Z_{eff} is a function of the gas temperature in a way which suggests that the dependence is similar to that found when E/p is varied.

One may also derive from a measurement of λ_1 an annihilation cross-section per atom:

$$\sigma_a = (c/(137)^2 v) Z_{eff} \pi a_0^2 , \qquad (10)$$

where c is the velocity of light. This cross-section is seen to be small even for positrons in equilibrium with liquid He. Near 4K, $\sigma_a \approx 5\pi a_0^2$.

Measurements of λ_2, the ortho-positronium quenching rate associated with the portion of the time spectrum labelled IV, are a function of the pressure p as one would expect. Upon extrapolation to $p = 0$ one obtains values which are reasonably consistent from one experiment to another: $\lambda_2 \cong 7.5\ \mu s^{-1}$. There is an exciting group of studies on o–Ps formation in high-density He gas and in liquid He, associated with what is called bubble formation. For an excellent introduction to the literature of this field refer to the 1968 review by Fraser [29].

There has been some suggestion by Leung and Paul [17] that region IV of the time spectrum may contain a third exponential term with a deactivation rate λ_3 associated perhaps with the quenching of the long-lived 2s state of ortho-positronium. This is an interesting possibility but, as the authors point out, highly speculative.

What is known of σ_{TMT} in the region below the threshold of positronium formation, i.e. below 17.8 eV for the (e$^+$,He) system, comes from the solution of the diffusion equation (cf. ref. [17] for example),

$$\frac{\partial f(v,t)}{\partial t} = \frac{1}{v^2}\frac{\partial}{\partial v}\left[\alpha(v,\sigma_{TMT})\frac{\partial f(v,t)}{\partial v} + \beta(v,\sigma_{TMT})f(v,t)\right] - \left[r_a(v) + r_f(v)\right]f(v,t),$$

through regions II and III of the lifetime spectrum. Here the mean velocity v is proportional to E/p, α and β are complex functions of $\bar{v}$ and the total momentum transfer cross-section σ_{TMT}, r_a and r_f are the rates of positronium annihilation and formation which are zero for $v \ll \bar{v}$, the threshold velocity for positronium formation.

The values of σ_{TMT} derived from an analysis of the diffusion equation for higher velocities are very model-dependent. However, a detailed knowledge of the general shape of the cross-section curve and its approximate magnitude make possible a computer fit of the diffusion equation to the time spectrum. This has effectively been done by Leung and Paul [17] for helium, while Orth and Jones [2d] have analytically been able to derive the distribution function $f(v)$ as a function of E/p for argon. Leung and Paul used several models. Their final results closely parallel but exceed the theoretical results of Drachman [23] through most of the energy interval from the thermal region to the positronium-formation threshold.

In table 2, I have listed the available experimental cross-sections for total momentum transfer, σ_{TMT}, and for total scattering, σ_{TS}, related through the differential elastic scattering cross-section, $\sigma(\theta)$, in the following way:

$$\sigma_{TS} = 2\pi \int \sigma(\theta)\sin\theta\ d\theta \tag{11}$$

and

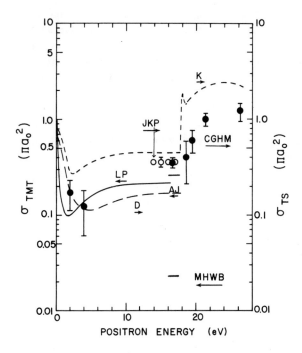

Fig. 5. Measured values of σ_{TMT} where MHWB [4] and AJ [19] are data from similar swarm experiments. In both instances the gray area is an indication of the uncertainty. The σ_{TMT} swarm data by LP [17] are also given. Measured values of σ_{TS} by CGHM [20,21] (closed circles) and JKP [22] (open circles) are shown in comparison with two very different theoretical results D [23,24] and K [26].

$$\sigma_{TMT} = 2\pi \int \sigma(\theta)\,(1-\cos\theta)\sin\theta\,d\theta \ . \tag{12}$$

In fig. 5, I have plotted the experimental and some theoretical values of σ_{TMT} and σ_{TS}. Note that the first data reported by Marder et al. [4], based on the analysis of Teutsch and Hughes [5], are more than an order of magnitude below theory and recent experiments at the positronium formation threshold. This was a dilemma for many years. As time has passed, measured values have increased, in fact theory and experiment are converging rapidly in the elastic-scattering region [30].

It is not at all surprising that there has been difficulty in obtaining good values of σ_{TMT} just below the positronium threshold, since in the analysis of the diffusion equation one assumes that positronium formation and -destruction are negligible, thus restricting one to choose mean velocities corresponding to ≈ 5 eV, far removed from 17.8 eV. The number of positrons in the high energy tail of the distribution is small so that the solution of the diffusion equation must be relatively insensitive to the choice of σ_{TMT} at higher energies.

The strength of the swarm technique lies in the determination of cross-sections as a function of E/p at low energies. In these cases the energy distribution is narrow, the approximation that positronium production and -loss are negligible is strictly adhered to, and virtual positronium most likely makes an insignificant contribution. As I will report below, it appears that both virtual positronium- and positronium formation make a large contribution to total scattering cross-sections at higher energies.

For (e^+, Ar), it is clear from the data of Jones and his collaborators, and of Paul et al., that the variation of the shoulder width with E/p is consistent with a σ_{TMT} function which is somewhat similar in shape to that found for electron-inert gas scattering i.e., it shows a Ramsauer character, with a minimum in the cross-section at low energies.

Nearly all investigators of the (e^+, He) system have remarked on the extreme effect of impurities on their measurements of σ_{TMT}, Z_{eff},o-Ps lifetime and shoulder width. It was also clear in the one beam experiment reported by Costello et al. [20,21] that σ_{TS} was very sensitive to impurities.

3. Beam experiments

For the purpose of this progress report, I have chosen as the primary characteristic of beam experiments that the electron- or positron velocity distribution function, $f(v)$, is not a strong function of the energy of interaction of the projectile and target (cf. fig. 2). Furthermore, one normally considers the gas targets to be thin so that multiple scattering is not a problem.

In principle, electron- and positron beam experiments are the same; the largest difference lies in the electron- and positron sources. Relatively large numbers of electrons of reasonable energy spread are readily available, whereas positrons in small numbers come with an enormous energy spread. In 1958 W.H.Cherry [31] reported in his thesis that positrons from ^{22}Na, when moderated by mica with a thin layer of chromium, gave an apparently narrow peak of positrons with energies less than 5 eV which could serve as an excellent source of positrons for beam studies (cf. fig. 6). This lay dormant until Groce et al. [21,32] re-discovered the effect for a number of moderating sys-

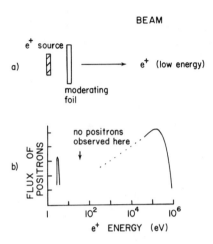

Fig. 6. a) Schematic representation of e$^+$ source and moderator. b) Characteristic representation of positrons coming through a moderator.

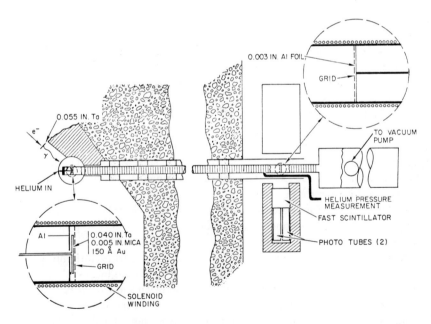

Fig. 7. Time-of-flight apparatus used in the General Atomic beam experiment, showing the time of flight spectrometer (collision chamber), details of the e$^+$ source and -moderator, and details of the annihilation foil.

Table 3
Systems used to moderate positrons in beam experiments. a) A negative value corresponds
to a positron coming from the surface with energy; b) The accuracy of this measurement
is small due to experimental factors; however, the higher value may reflect the CsBr-sub-
strate since the gold-foil is thin.

Material	Values of negative work function[a]		
	Experimental (eV)	Theoretical (ev)	Refs.
Gold	–	–2.26	[33]
Mica (150 Å) gold	–0.75 ± 0.5	–	[32]
(≥1000 Å) gold	≤0	–	[22]
CsBr (150 Å) gold	–2.90 ± 1.0[b]	–	[32]
Al (200 Å) gold	–1.25 ± 0.5	–	[32]
Mica-chromium	>–5	–	[31]
Polyethylene	–20.7	–	[34]
Graphite	~–1.5	–	[22]
Cu	–	–3.1	[33]

tems where the source of positrons was pair production with a 35 MeV
LINAC as the source of bremsstrahlung (cf. fig. 7).

In table 3, I have listed all systems thus far studied. Also given are values
of the peak energies of the positrons emitted from the surfaces plus some calculated values [33]. In the experiments of Costello et al. [32], no positrons
could be found with energies in the interval 2–100 eV. The above findings
have now been verified by the group at the University of Toronto [22] who
have used gold-covered mica as the moderator of ^{22}Na positrons. The group
at the University of Western Ontario has further demonstrated that not only
the mica-gold moderator but gold and aluminum moderators work as well
while the efficiency for copper now appears to be considerably worse. Along
with Tong [33] who has done the only theory, Groce et al. [21,32] have
described the phenomenon as the "negative work function".

Now we have a narrow energy-band of low-energy positrons, but only a
few of them. Approximately one out of every 10^7 positrons born in the
source survive the trip through the moderator sandwich and emerge in the
low-energy bundle. These particles, because they are in a narrow-energy
bundle, can be biased to whatever energy is desired. The full width at half
maximum is ≈1 eV, with the peak in the distribution coming between 0.5

and 5 eV (cf. ref. [32]). Laboratories at University College, London, University College, Swansea, University of Toronto, Wayne State University, and our own at the University of Western Ontario, are already designing, building and even operating scattering experiments dependent upon positron sources based upon the negative work function. As scattering experiments proceed, complementary experiments dealing with the yield from the moderator, the energy distribution of the positrons in the low-energy peak, the angular distribution of the emitted particles, and the effect of moderator temperature on the energy distribution of the emitted positrons, etc., are under way.

In the next few paragraphs, I have summarized some of the qualities of and problems associated with positron beam experiments:

I. Long-term stability. There is definite merit associated with the elimination of hot filaments from an electron scattering experiment, since filament stability is often a problem. However, one replaces the problems of short-term stability of electron emitters with problems of very long term stability of electronics, positron emitting surfaces, surfaces of lens elements, apparatus temperature and so on.

II. Detection of positrons. Because there are so few positrons, one would like to detect them with high efficiency. At first one imagines this is no problem because so much energy (1.02 MeV) is available for detection when a positron annihilates. But there are problems:

(a) Detection of annihilation γ-rays in coincidence [32]. To conserve momentum, a ground-state para-positronium annihilates releasing two 0.51 MeV γ-rays which, when identified and detected in coincidence, provide a flawless way to detect a positron. However, the efficiency is normally between 2 and 10 percent because of geometric effects and the finite thickness of the scintillators. Furthermore, it is necessary to drive the low-energy positrons into a surface to overcome the negative work function and to minimize reflection which appears to be large. Two geometries have been used which preferentially detect low-energy positrons. In the first, an annihilation foil of aluminum is used with a thickness such that fast positrons pass through while low energy ones are stopped in it. In the second, a biased rod is used to attract low energy positrons while allowing higher energy particles to pass by.

(b) Well detector [35]. A higher-efficiency method of detection is the well of scintillant like NaI, where the total energy associated with the annihilation γ-rays is absorbed in the scintillator. The original efficiency is good, and the discrimination against degraded or infested γ-rays is excellent because one can preferentially detect the 1.02 MeV peak. Well-type Ge(Li) detectors may be available in the near future.

(c) Electron multiplier. Pendyala et al. [36] have successfully used a channel

electron-multiplier to detect slow positrons even though the CEM is sensitive
to γ-rays. The use of the CEM apparently increases the detection efficiency
by a factor of 10 to 20 over the detection of annihilation γ-rays in coincidence.

III. Background. The gamma-ray background is one of the most serious problems in positron beam experiments. For long-lived sources, there are the
gammas which come from annihilation in the source or from cascade or other
decay modes in the source. In some machine sources, where time-of-flight
energy analysis is used, there is the problem of gamma flash [21,32]. Finally,
there is the problem of the reflection of positrons in the vacuum system with
subsequent annihilation near the detector. Large distance from the source,
sufficient lead shielding, care that positrons do not reflect freely throughout
the system, will minimize background. In pulsed high-energy electron systems
which produce short-lived sources like ^{11}C, one can carry on the experiment
in the time between pulses, thus eliminating the gamma flash [37].

Only (e^+, He) total scattering through the energy intervals 1–40 eV and
17–26 eV has thus far been measured by beam techniques. For this experiment, first reported by Groce et al. [21] and Costello et al. [20], a high
current 55 MeV LINAC was used in the pulsed mode (20 ns) to produce
bremsstrahlung which subsequently was used to produce (e^+, e^-) pairs in a 0.04
inch tantalum target (cf. fig. 7). As mentioned earlier in this report, several
moderators were used (cf. table 2), but for the final results a mica slab, 0.005
inch thick, with a 200 Å gold coating, was used. The bulk of the positrons
which come from the moderator-gold sandwich have an energy near 1 eV
which could be changed by biasing the moderator with respect to the 3 m
long time-of-flight spectrometer which was filled with gas and used as the
collision chamber. Extreme care had to be taken to assure the purity of the
helium gas.

In the 17 to 16 eV energy interval, one obtains a spectrum simply and
directly by measuring the attenuation of the positrons as a function of gas
pressure. In the energy interval from 1 to 4 eV, a correction had to be made
to allow for the trapping of particles in the axial magnetic field. As a result of
the trapping, they reached the annihilation foil at longer times corresponding
to lower energies. The correction was made by using the scattering phase
shifts reported by Drachman [24]. With these phase shifts, Costello et al.
[20,21] determined, as was suspected by Drachman, that the monopole term
had to be completely suppressed. Further, it was demonstrated that Drachman's calculations of σ_{TS} at low energies are nearly correct, in agreement
with the recent swarm measurements of σ_{TMT} reported by Leung and Paul
[17]. The results are summarized in table 3 and fig. 5. At the positronium-

formation threshold, the Drachman calculations [23,24] are too low; however, when this p- and d partial waves are scaled to the known excact (e^+,H) case, the agreement is excellent [38]. Above the positronium formation threshold at 17.8 eV, the cross section begins to rise and at 19.3 eV it is nearly a factor of two larger than that below 17.8 eV. At 26.1 eV it has increased by nearly a factor of four. This is generally in accord with the calculations of Kraidy [26] who has included the polarization of positronium by He^+ as a primary factor in his model. The p-wave resonance predicted by Kraidy were not found perhaps because of the large energy intervals used in the experiment. The recent and as yet unpublished data of Jaduszliwer et al. [22] support these results. They are obtained with a mica-gold moderated ^{22}Na source where the estimated low-energy positron yield was near 3×10^{-8} slow positrons per fast ^{22}Na positron.

4. Future of positron scattering

Swarms. The near future should bring a reduction of the background with an accompanying increase in the accuracy of low-energy measurements of σ_{TMT} and Z_{eff}. There should be an accompanying increase in the accuracy of o-Ps destruction measurements with a verification of the quenching of excited Ps. More sophisticated analytical and numerical techniques will also help. Better time resolution will allow studies of p-Ps formation and -collisional destruction. Swarm experiments will make major contributions in Ps collision studies, a field which may not be studied by beams for many years.

Beams. Positron beam studies are in the era analogous to the nearly Ramsauer studies of total electron scattering, i.e., equivalent to the early thirties. One can predict that the next few years will herald the development of both short-lived artificial and long-lived natural sources, and a more thorough understanding of positron energy moderation. With more efficient sources many atoms, X, and molecules, XY, will be studied. At first, total scattering measurements,

$$e^+ + X \rightarrow e^+ + X$$

will be made through the onsets of inelastic thresholds. These, no doubt, will be accompanied by positron energy-loss studies,

$$e^+ + X \rightarrow e^+ + X^* \qquad \Delta E_{e^+} \neq 0 \, ,$$

differential scattering measurements,

$$e^+ + X \to e^+(\theta) + X \ ,$$

ground state- and excited positronium formation studies,

$$\to Ps^* + X^+ \ ,$$

attachment processes analogous to dissociative electron attachment,

$$e^+ + XY \to (e^+,X) + Y \ ,$$

annihilation,

$$e^+ + X \to \text{gamma rays} + X^+ \ ,$$

and so on.

All of the above beam- and swarm studies will give accurate information about target atoms and -molecules. In fact, with only a little imagination one can predict that e^+ scattering will continue to develop as one of the basic atomic and molecular spectroscopies.

Acknowledgements

This report and continuing studies at the University of Western Ontario have been supported through the generosity of the University, NASA—Goddard grant NGR 42-029-006 and the National Research Council of Canada. My general appreciation goes out to the many people who have discussed problems with me.

References

[1] R.J.Drachman, *VII ICPEAC, Invited Talks and Progress Reports.* eds. T.R.Govers and F.J.de Heer (North-Holland Publ. Co., Amsterdam, 1972) p. 277.
[2] a) W.R.Falk, P.H.R.Orth and G.Jones, Phys. Rev. Letters *14* (1965) 447.
b) D.A.L.Paul, Proc. Phys. Soc. *84* (1964) 563.
c) S.J.Tao and J.Bell, *Positron Annihilation,* eds. A.T.Stewart and L.O.Roellig (Academic Press, New York, 1967) p. 393.
d) P.H.R.Orth and G.Jones, Phys. Rev. *183* (1969) 7.

e) S.J.Tao, Phys. Rev. A 1 (1970) 1257.

f) D.B.Miller, P.H.R.Orth and G.Jones, Phys. Letters 27 A (1968) 649.

[3] H.S.W.Massey, J.Lawson and D.G.Thompson, Quantum Theory of Atoms, Molecules and the Solid State, ed. P.D.Lowdin (Academic Press, New York, 1966) p. 203.

[4] S.Marder, V.W.Hughes, S.C.Wu and W.Bennett, Phys. Rev. 103 (1956) 1258.

[5] W.B.Teutsch and V.W.Hughes, Phys. Rev. 103 (1956) 1266.

[6] P.E.Osmon, Phys. Rev. 138 (1965) B216.

[7] P.E.Osmon, Phys. Rev. 140 (1965) A8.

[8] D.A.L.Paul and C.Y.Leung, Can. J. Phys. 46 (1968) 2779.

[9] S.J.Tao, Phys. Rev. A 2 (1970) 1669.

[10] J.L.Pack and A.V.Phelps, Phys. Rev. 121 (1961) 798.

[11] H.S.W.Massey, Electronic and Ionic Impact Phenomena, Electron Collisions with Molecules and Photoionization, Vol. 2, eds. H.S.W.Massey, E.H.S.Burhop and H.B. Gilbody (Oxford at the Clarendon Press, 1969).

[12] L.V.Spencer and U.Fano, Phys. Rev. 93 (1954) 1172.

[13] T.B.Daniel and R.Stump, Phys. Rev. 115 (1959) 1599.

[14] B.G.Duff and F.F.Heymann, Proc. Roy. Soc., Ser. A 270 (1962) 517.

[15] L.O.Roellig and T.M.Kelly, Phys. Rev. Letters 15 (1965) 746.

[16] V.I.Goldenskii and I.Levin, referred to in: B.G.Hogg, G.M.Laidlaw, V.I.Goldenskii and V.P.Shantarouich, Atomic Energy Review 6 (1968) 149.

[17] C.Y.Leung and D.A.L.Paul, J. Phys. B 2 (1969) 1278.

[18] S.J.Tao and T.M.Kelly, Phys. Rev. 185 (1969) 135.

[19] B.Albrecht and G.Jones, unpublished paper, presented at the Second International Conference on Positron Annihilation, Kingston, Canada, September 1971.

[20] D.G.Costello, D.E.Groce, D.F.Herring and J.Wm.McGowan, Can. J. Phys. 50 (1972) to be published.

[21] D.E.Groce, D.G.Costello, J.W.McGowan and D.F.Herring, Bull. Amer. Phys. Soc. 13 (1968) 1397; and VI ICPEAC, Abstracts of Papers, ed. I.Amdur (MIT Press, Cambridge, Mass., 1969) p. 757.

[22] B.Y.Jaduszliwer, W.C.Keever and D.A.L.Paul, unpublished paper presented at the Second International Conference on Positron Annihilation, Kingston, Canada, September 1971.

[23] R.J.Drachman, Phys. Rev. 173 (1968) 190.

[24] R.J.Drachman, Phys. Rev. 144 (1966) 25.

[25] R.J.Drachman, private communication.

[26] M.Kraidy, Ph. D. Thesis, University of Western Ontario, London, Canada (1967).

[27] S.K.Houston and R.J.Drachman, Phys. Rev. A 3 (1971) 1335.

[28] G.F.Lee, P.H.R.Orth and G.Jones, Phys. Letters 28 A (1969) 674.

[29] P.A.Fraser, in: Advances in Atomic and Molecular Physics, eds. D.R.Bates and I.Estermann, Vol. 4 (Academic Press, New York, 1968) p. 63.

[30] In ref. [19], Albrecht and Jones reported the results of an experiment which duplicated that of Marder et al. [4], using the analysis of Teutsch and Hughes [5]. They find that the average value of σ_{TMT} up to the positronium-forbidden threshold is $0.260 \pm 0.020 \, \pi a_0^2$ in excellent agreement with recent experiment and theory. They associate the earlier results with impurities in the helium gas.

[31] W.H.Cherry, Ph. D. Thesis, Princeton University, 1958.

[32] D.G.Costello, D.E.Groce, D.F.Herring and J.Wm.McGowan, Phys. Rev. B 15 (1972) to be published.

[33] B.Y.Tong, Phys. Rev. B *15* (1972) to be published.
[34] J.M.J.Madey, Phys. Rev. Letters *22* (1969) 784.
[35] J.H.Neiler and P.R.Bill, in: *Alpha-, Beta-, and Gamma-Ray Spectroscopy,* ed. K. Siegbahn, Vol. 1 (North-Holland Publ. Co., Amsterdam, 1965) p. 262 (see especially section 3.2). Also a good summary is available in *Proceedings of the Total Absorption Gamma-Ray Spectometry Symposium,* Gatlinburg, Tennessee, May 10–11, 1960, U.S. AEC Office of Technical Information Report TID-7594.
[36] Pendyala, P.H.R.Orth, Zitzewitz and J.Wm.McGowan, unpublished.
[37] B.Y.Jaduszliwer, B.J.Bowden and D.A.L.Paul, Bull. Am. Phys. Soc. *15* (1970) 785.
[38] R.J.Drachman, submitted for publication.

Physics of Electronic and Atomic Collisions, VII ICPEAC, 1971 – North-Holland (1972)

ELECTRON SPIN POLARIZATION BY INELASTIC SCATTERING AND BY PHOTOIONIZATION

J. KESSLER

Physikalisches Institut, University of Münster, 44 Münster, Germany

New developments in electron spin polarization caused by spin-orbit interaction are reported. First, spin polarization resulting from inelastic electron scattering is discussed. In particular, the polarization caused by excitation of the $6\,^1P_1$ and $6p'^3P_1$ states of mercury at various primary energies has been studied. The second part of the paper deals with the Fano effect, i.e. spin polarization due to photoionization by circularly polarized light. With a cesium vapor jet as target a polarization of 100% has been obtained in this way. Polarised electrons have also been produced by photoionization of a solid cesium target.

1. Introduction

Spin polarization effects in electron collision processes have been a topic of this conference only for a couple of years. The increasing importance of this field is demonstrated by the fact that the number of contributions on spin polarization in the proceedings of this meeting has been rapidly increasing from volume to volume. And also in the new edition of the well-known book of Massey and Burhop (1) on impact phenomena, several sections now deal with spin effects, whereas they were not even mentioned in the preceding edition.

I shall discuss an aspect of this field, where there has recently been much progress: the conspicuous effects caused by the relatively small forces of spin-orbit interaction. I shall focus the emphasis on the latest developments which concern inelastic processes, such as inelastic electron scattering and photoionization.

2. Spin polarisation in electron scattering

2.1. *Earlier experiments involving elastic electron scattering*

I shall first summarize some results which have been found up to the last

315

conference. These earlier studies were concerned with spin effects due to
elastic scattering of electrons. Figure 1 shows an example. The polarization *P*
is defined as

$$P = (N_\uparrow - N_\downarrow)/(N_\uparrow + N_\downarrow) ,$$

where $N_\uparrow$ and $N_\downarrow$ are the numbers of spin-up and spin-down electrons in the
electron beam. Up and down always refer to the preferential direction of the
experiment. In a scattering experiment this preferential direction is given by
the normal to the scattering plane. Figure 1 therefore means that near $\theta = 99°$
most of the scattered electrons have their spins perpendicular to the scattering plane, namely parallel to the normal of the scattering plane, whereas near
$\theta = 101°$ most of the electrons have their spins anti-parallel to that direction.

These polarization effects are due to spin-orbit interaction and have been
quantitatively explained. The basic idea is as follows. An unpolarized electron
beam can always be considered as a mixture of equal numbers of spin-up and
spin-down electrons. If such a beam impinges on an atom, the force on the
electrons depends on their spin direction due to spin-orbit interaction. That
means that we have different scattering cross-sections for the two kinds of
electrons. The numbers of spin-up and spin-down electrons scattered into a
certain direction are different from each other. In other words: the scattered
beam is polarized.

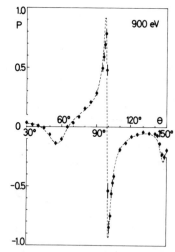

Fig. 1. Polarization vs. scattering angle of 900 eV electrons scattered elastically by mercury atoms. Experimental and theoretical values.

Since spin-orbit interaction increases with increasing atomic number, the polarization of the scattered electrons is significant particularly for heavy atoms, as studies with many different target atoms have confirmed. The experimental results on spin polarization in elastic scattering have been very well explained theoretically at energies above 100 eV, whereas below this energy theory becomes difficult. Spin polarization of the scattered electrons has also been observed in elastic scattering from various molecules, yielding interesting information on these molecules. All these experiments on spin polarization in elastic electron scattering at low energies have been made mainly in two groups [2] : the group at Mainz and the group at Karlsruhe which is presently moving to Münster.

2.2. Recent experiments involving inelastic electron scattering

This was the general background very briefly summarized. Now let us consider the latest developments in the field. An interesting question was: how about inelastically scattered electrons, can they also have a spin polarization? Or put differently: are the electrons in a Franck-Hertz experiment polarized? Dr. Eitel end Mr. Hanne [3] answered this question with the apparatus of fig. 2.

An electron beam crosses a mercury atomic beam which is the target. The primary energies range from 25 to a few hundred eV. The scattered electrons

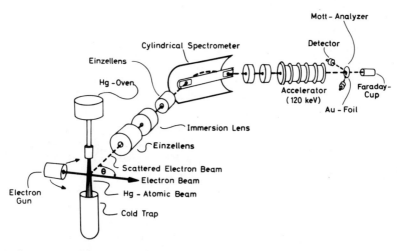

Fig. 2. Apparatus for measuring the polarization of inelastically scattered electrons (from [3b]).

are focused into a cylindrical mirror analyzer, where those electrons which
have excited a certain state of the Hg atom are selected. The overall energy
resolution is 0.8 eV, the angular resolution $\pm 1°$. The polarization of the inelastically scattered electrons is measured by a Mott-analyzer, after the electrons have been accelerated to 120 keV: by means of the left-right-asym-
metry of the intensity scattered by the gold foil into the detectors, the polarization can be determined in a well-known way.

There were two difficulties in the experiment. Firstly, the inelastic cross
sections are a factor of 10 to 100 smaller than the elastic ones. The intensity
in this double scattering experiment is therefore very low. And secondly one
has to be very careful in order to avoid double or plural scattering: it turns
out that – for example – a small angle inelastic process at one atom plus a
large angle elastic process at another atom is a very likely combination to
occur. These plural scattering processes have to be avoided, since they cannot
be distinguished from the inelastic scattering by a single atom which is to be
studied. At each energy the reliability of the results was therefore checked by
systematic variation of the target density over a large range.

Figure 3 shows the results for primary energies of 180 and 50 eV. The
experimental points in the upper half denote the polarization of electrons
which have excited the 6^1P_1 state of Hg; the energy loss is 6.7 eV. So we see
quite clearly: also inelastically scattered electrons can be polarized. The degree of polarization can be larger than 50%. – It is quite interesting to compare these curves with the elastic ones shown in the lower half of fig. 3. They
look very similar at these energies.

This changes, however, when the energy is further reduced, as shown in
fig. 4. Here the polarization of electrons scattered into the same inelastic
channel is shown, but the primary energies are now 30 and 25 eV. It is quite
evident, that the polarization of the inelastically scattered electrons is rather
low at these energies; at 25 eV the values are 10% or smaller. The elastic
curves look quite different, they show still high degrees of polarization.

Another interesting information is obtained by variation of the scattering
channel at a fixed primary energy. For a primary energy of 180 eV, fig. 5
shows the polarization of electrons which had an energy loss of 11.05 eV.
That means excitation of an inner electron leading to the autoionizing state
$6p'^3P_1$.

Compared with the other curves at this energy, the polarization has again
decreased. But on the whole the curves look very similar.

So we can say: it does not matter very much, whether we have elastic scattering, where the atom remains in its groundstate (cf. fig. 6), or an inelastic
process involving the transition of a 6s or a 5d electron. The polarization
curves of the scattered electrons look very similar at this primary energy.

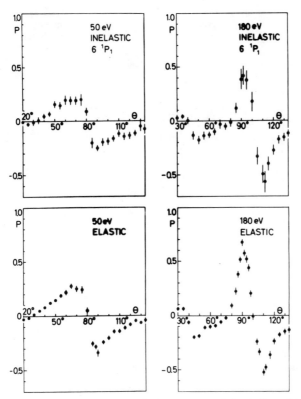

Fig. 3. Polarization vs. scattering angle of electrons scattered elastically and inelastically by Hg atoms (excitation of $6\,^1P_1$ state, energy loss 6.7 eV). Primary energies 180 and 50 eV (from [3b]).

This example serves to elucidate the following statement: *it is not the particular channel as such, but rather the fraction of the lost energy which affects the polarization of the scattered electron.* At small primary energies this fraction is large, and we have no similarity between elastic and inelastic polarization curves. At large primary energies this fraction is small, and we have great similarity between elastic and inelastic curves.

2.3. Interpretation of experimental results.

Can the above results be understood theoretically? The similarity between elastic and inelastic polarization curves at higher energies suggests that coupling between elastic and inelastic channels plays an important role. This can

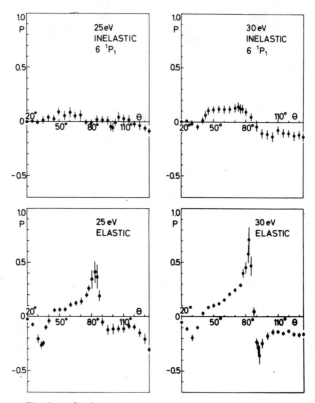

Fig. 4. As fig. 3, primary energies 30 and 25 eV (from [3b]).

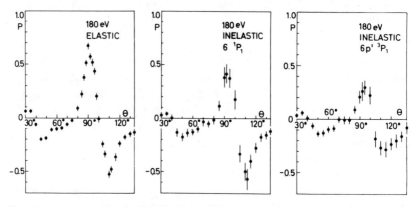

Fig. 5. Polarization vs. scattering angle of electrons with a primary energy of 180 eV after excitation of the $6p'^3P_1$ state (energy loss 11.05 eV).

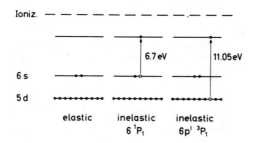

Fig.6. Transitions of the Hg atom being discussed.

be pictured by a very crude physical model as follows. The incident electron first loses energy in exciting the atom. This event will approximately leave the electron still travelling in the forward direction because of the strong peaking about the incident direction for inelastic scattering. The electron will then undergo large angle elastic scattering in the field of the same atom which now is in an excited state.

One might, therefore, hazard the guess that the differential cross section for the whole process would be proportional to the product of the amplitude for inelastic scattering in the forward direction times the elastic amplitude evaluated at the scattering angle. It is the elastic part of the double process which determines what happens at large angles, and we see therefore that the particular inelastic channel involved is not very important. If the energy loss in the inelastic part of the double process is small compared with the incident energy, the electron has nearly its full primary energy in the elastic part of the double process, so that the results obtained are very similar to those of pure elastic scattering.

The model discussed here is nothing but an interpretation of the second Born approximation. Along this line, Bonham [4] from Indiana University has recently given a quantitative description of inelastic scattering, yielding the basic facts I gave here. At present, however, he has not yet obtained numerical results for comparison with our data.

There is one other calculation available, which has been made by Madison and Shelton [5] from Florida State University. These authors used the distorted wave approximation including exchange of the incident electron with the atomic electrons. They calculated numerical values for the 6^1P_1 channel at the energies we used in our measurements. Figure 7 shows that at 50 eV the agreement between theory and experiment is quite satifactory. At 180 and 30 eV at least the general trends of the results are the same, whereas at 25 eV there is no similarity left between experimental and theoretical data.

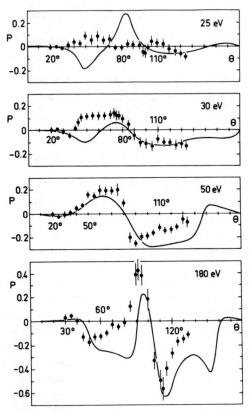

Fig. 7. Comparison of experimental and theoretical results for electron spin polarization resulting from inelastic electron-mercury scattering (energy loss 6.7 eV): −− calculated [5]) ⦚ experimental [3].

Taking account of the dielectric polarization of the atomic charge cloud did not improve the agreement.

But we must remember that spin-polarization due to inelastic electron scattering is a very new field, experimentally as well as theoretically. In elastic scattering it took several years before the polarization effects had been explained as perfectly as demonstated by fig. 1. So we will need some time to understand the details of the more complicated inelastic polarization effects.

3. Electron spin polarization in photoionization

3.1. Photoionization of gaseous targets

What I am going to discuss now seems, at first sight, to be something quite different. It concerns electron spin polarization due to photoionization by circularly polarized light, the Fano effect. What would you answer if somebody asked you: "Where does the spin angular momentum of the photons go, when atoms are ionized by circulary polarized light?"? The correct answer is, of course: "We generally find the spins of the absorbed photons in the orbital angular momenta of the photoelectrons." For example, s-electrons go into p-states just as described by the selection rules for l and for the magnetic quantum numbers.

So it is the orbital angular momentum of the photoelectrons which in general takes care of the conversation of angular momentum, and — as a rule — the preferential orientation of the photon spins in circularly polarized light does not cause a preferential orientation of the spins of the photo-electrons produced. In particularly favourable cases, however, it may happen that the coupling between spin- and orbital angular momentum of the electrons does produce an orientation of the electron spins in the experiment discussed.

This is illustrated by fig. 8. Without spin-orbit interaction it would not make a difference whether we photoionize with ordinary light or with circularly polarized light; the result would be the same in the two cases. Taking spin-orbit interaction into account, we obtain a difference between the cross-section for producing electrons with spins in the direction of the spins of the circularly polarized photons and the cross-section for producing electrons with spins opposite to that direction. Different numbers of spin-up and spin-down electrons mean, however, a polarized electron beam!

This polarization can be quite significant, if we irradiate the target with wavelengths near a minimum of one of these curves (such a minimum is typical for the alkali vapors). In this case we obtain practically only electrons of one spin direction, that means a large polarization as shown in fig. 8, lower half. So again the relatively weak spin-orbit interaction produces a significant effect, quite similar to what we saw in electron scattering. At wavelengths where there are equal numbers of spin-up and spin-down electrons the polarization is zero, and at even shorter wavelengths P is negative, since more spin-down than spin-up electrons are produced.

The polarization curve of fig. 8, which holds for a cesium atom, has been calculated by Fano [6]. Raith [7] and co-workers at Yale found a very nice way for getting information on these spin-up and spin-down cross-sections. And we [8] measured the polarization of the photoelectrons directly.

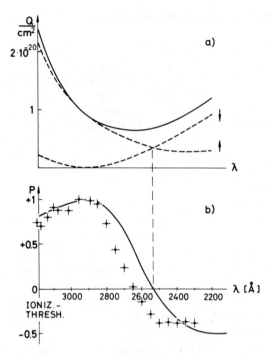

FIg. 8. (a) Cross sections vs. wavelength for photoeffect at the cesium atom. $---$ Photo-electron spin in and opposite to direction of photon spin, respectively. $\underline{\quad\quad}$ Sum of the dotted curves. (b) Spin polarization P of the photoelectrons. Theory [6] and experimental points [8].

The main components of the apparatus are shown in fig. 9: light source, monochromator, circular polarizer, oven for producing a vapor jet which is of course unpolarized. The photo-electrons which are produced here are extracted, accelerated and directed into the Mott-detector which allows the measurement of their polarization.

The experimental polarization data are also shown in fig. 8. Without going into any details I shall indicate what these measurements are good for.

Firstly, they provide information on the influence of spin-orbit interaction on photoabsorption which is much more detailed than that obtained from cross-section measurements. This influence is described by a simple function of the transition matrix elements, and the experiments yield this function. Secondly, the Fano effect is a promising way of producing polarized electrons. The main intensity of a mercury high-pressure arc lamp is concentrated

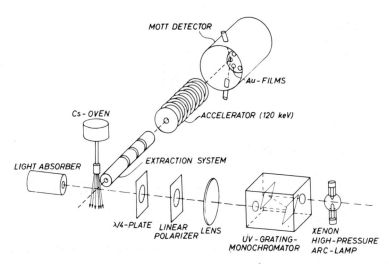

Fig. 9. Apparatus for measuring the polarization of photoelectrons coming from an unpolarized atomic beam.

in the wavelength-range of maximum polarization of fig. 8. With such a lamp and without a monochromator we obtained an average value of the polarization of $81 \pm 3\%$ at a current of 10^{-11}A, although our apparatus was not built to have a strong source of polarized electrons, but rather to get quantitative data on the Fano effect. In Bonn, however, people do try to build a source of polarized electrons on the basis of the Fano effect: Koch and Walther [9] use laser light and it is very likely that they get much higher intensities of polarized electrons than with the old method of photoionizing polarized atomic beams.

3.2. Photoionization of solid targets

Let me conclude with our latest experiment, where we substituted the cesium atomic beam by a solid cesium target. Figure 10 shows that also in this case the photoelectrons were polarized, though the polarization is much lower. The polarization peak is shifted into the visible range, which is even more convenient, experimentally. I cannot say, that we have already understood this curve, theoretically. It is quite clear, however, that here typical solid state considerations play a role. We have some ideas, but in order to check them we have to evaluate our measurements being made now at other solid alkali targets.

When all this will be better understood, one will not only have much bet-

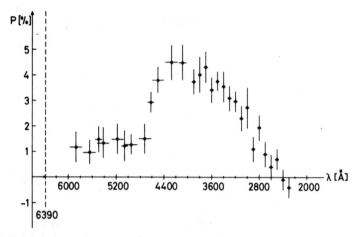

Fig. 10. Spin polarization of photoelectrons from solid cesium by circulary polarized light.

ter knowledge of the mechanisms playing a role in photoionization of solid targets. Also for applications as a source of polarized electrons it would be useful to have a theoretical guide, which targets to choose in order to get higher polarization. For it goes without saying that the intensity we obtained from solid targets is by sevral orders of magnitude larger than that from atomic beams. We therefore plan to continue these studies with solid targets although I don't feel so sure whether these results would be within the scope of an atomic collisions conference.

References

[1] H.S.W. Massey and E.H.S. Burhop, *Electronic and Ionic Impact Phenomena* (Oxford University Press, London, 1952 and 1969)

[2] For detailed references cf. J. Kessler, Rev. Mod. Phys. *41* (1969) 3

[3] W. Eitel and J. Kessler, (a) Phys. Rev. Letters *24* (1970) 1472; (b) Z. Phys. *241* (1971) 355; (c) F. Hanne and J. Kessler, to be published.

[4] R.A. Bonham, preprint (1971); private communication.

[5] D.H. Madison and W.N. Shelton, preprint (1971)

[6] U. Fano, Phys. Rev. *178* (1969) 131.

[7] G. Baum, M.S. Lubbel and W. Raith, Phys. Rev. Letters *25* (1970) 267.

[8] U. Heinzmann, J. Kessler and J. Lorenz, Phys. Rev. Letters *25* (1970) 1325; Z. Phys. *240* (1970) 42. The ordinate of fig. 4 of that paper is wrong.

[9] U. Koch and H. Walther, private communication.

Physics of Electronic and Atomic Collisions, VII ICPEAC, 1971 – North-Holland (1972)

INELASTIC COLLISIONS OF FAST CHARGED PARTICLES
WITH ATOMS AND MOLECULES –
THE BETHE THEORY REVISITED*

Mitio Inokuti

Argonne National Laboratory,
Argonne, Illinois 60439, USA

The current understanding is summarized from a unified point of view, which Bethe initiated four decades ago and which enables one to put a variety of theoretical and experimental data into a coherent picture. Emphasis is placed on certain properties of the generalized oscillator strength. Although the contents of this lecture are largely excerpts from another, more comprehensive, review article [Rev. Mod. Phys. 43 (1971) 297], a few additional remarks also are included.

1. Introduction

Let me start by defining the subject "inelastic collisions of fast charged particles with atoms and molecules". By the term "inelastic" I mean "resulting in electronic excitations including ionization". Thus, the elastic collision and the purely rotational or vibrational excitation are outside the scope of my discussion. By "charged particles" I mean any charged particles so long as they may be regarded as structureless. For brevity and convenience, however, I shall refer to electron collisions most of the time. The term "fast" also needs to be explained. When I say that an incident particle is fast, I mean that it is fast compared to the orbital velocity of the atomic electrons that are pertinent to the inelastic process under consideration. A five keV electron, for example, is fast with respect to almost any excitation of He, but it is not fast with respect to the K-shell ionization of Ar.

As you may have heard many times, the first Born approximation is believed to be adequate for fast collisions. The first Born approximation is

---

* Work performed under the auspices of the U.S. Atomic Energy Commission.

nearly as old as the quantum mechanics and is explained in many textbooks. Nevertheless, a number of physically important consequences of the first Born approximation do not seem to be thoroughly appreciated. In particular, a systematic examination of all these consequences, started by Bethe [1,2], provides many aims of worthwhile study, both experimental and theoretical, even now in 1971.

For the past several years I have tried to evaluate the current knowledge about fast collisions as thoroughly as possible, and have written a review article [3]. Following are some excerpts from it, together with a few additional remarks.

Why does one seriously study an old theory? The answer is that it is still good and useful within its range of applicability, which is now being defined sharper and sharper year by year. In short, the Bethe theory is quite adequate for the description of the *majority* of fast inelastic collisions, and contains a great deal of physics involved in the subject. Also, it provides a unified framework of sound understanding.

Let me emphasize that knowing a good framework of understanding is completely different from knowing numerical answers to all problems of interest in individual cases. Therefore, a great deal of work in the future is needed even within the Bethe theory.

2. The generalized oscillator strength

Consider an inelastic collision of a fast electron having velocity v (thus having kinetic energy $T = mv^2/2$) with an atom, which makes a transition from the initial state 0 (most often the ground state) to an excited state n (either discrete or continuum). Suppose that the incident electron changes its momentum by an amount $\hbar K$, the numerical value of which may be easily calculated from the scattering angle and the excitation energy E_n involved. (Sometimes one calls E_n the energy transfer of the collision.) The cross-section $d\sigma_n$ for the inelastic collision expressed in terms of the magnitude $\hbar K$ of the momentum transfer is

$$d\sigma_n = \frac{4\pi a_0^2}{T/R} \cdot \frac{f_n(K)}{E_n/R} \cdot d[\ln(Ka_0)^2] , \tag{1}$$

where a_0 is the Bohr radius and R is the Rydberg energy. The quantity $f_n(K)$ is the generalized oscillator strength (GOS) for the transition $n \leftarrow 0$, an important property of the atom representing its internal dynamics relevant to the inelastic collision.

The expression (1) was in effect foreseen by Bohr [4], who developed a theory of stopping power before the advent of the modern quantum mechanics. Some of his arguments may be sketched below. If for the moment one disregards the binding of atomic electrons to the nucleus and supposes that these electrons, whose total number is Z, were free and stationary, then the cross-section expressed in terms of $\hbar K$ is

$$d\sigma = \frac{4\pi a_0^2}{T/R} \cdot \frac{Z}{(Ka_0)^2} \cdot d[\ln (Ka_0)^2] \ . \tag{2}$$

Actually, this expression is nothing more than the Rutherford cross-section, which may be derived from classical mechanics as well as from quantum mechanics. In this simplified but hypothetical situation, the energy transfer is uniquely determined by the momentum transfer through elementary two-body kinematics. For collisions with a real atom, however, a definite amount $\hbar K$ of momentum transfer still leaves the atom with a choice of the resulting degree of internal excitation. Thus, in place of the middle factor $Z(Ka_0)^{-2}$ of eq. (2), one must have a function of the momentum transfer $\hbar K$ and the energy transfer E_n. This function represents the conditional probability that the atom makes the transition to state n upon receiving momentum transfer $\hbar K$. For traditional reasons one expresses this function by $(R/E_n)f_n(K)$, and thus arrives at eq. (1).

Bohr [4] indeed discussed several general properties of this function, but had no method for evaluating it from atomic dynamics. Bethe [1] gave an expression for it on the basis of the first Born approximation. That is,

$$f_n(K) = (E_n/R)(Ka_0)^{-2} \left| \left(n \left| \sum_{j=1}^{Z} e^{i\mathbf{K}\cdot\mathbf{r}_j} \right| 0 \right) \right|^2 \ , \tag{3}$$

where $\mathbf{r}_j$ is the position of the jth atomic electron and $(n| \ |0)$ represents a matrix element taken between the atomic eigenstates n and 0.

What does one know about the important quantity $f_n(K)$? This is the central question of my lecture. Let me first discuss some general properties. Already Bohr [4] recognized, on the basis of his correspondence principle, a crucial fact that the average of the energy transfer to the atom over all modes of internal excitation should be the same as the energy transfer to Z free electrons at each value of the momentum transfer $\hbar K$. Expressed in our notation, this means that

$$\sum_n f_n(K) = Z . \tag{4}$$

This expression is the Bethe sum rule, which can be proved from eq. (3) under quite general conditions. Another general property concerns the limit

$$\lim_{K \to 0} f_n(K) = f_n , \tag{5}$$

which is called optical (dipole) oscillator strength and is equal, apart from a universal constant, to the cross-section for the absorption of a photon of energy E_n. As is evident from kinematics, large values of K occur for collisions resulting in large scattering angles, and small values of K occur for collisions resulting in small scattering angles. For any inelastic collision, however, the limit $K \to 0$ is never precisely realized even for zero scattering angle. The smallest K value at fixed E_n and T occurs for zero scattering angle and is given for $E_n \ll T$ by

$$(Ka_0)^2_{min} \cong E_n^2/(4RT) . \tag{6}$$

Thus, the relationship between photoabsorption and inelastic collisions becomes closer and closer, as one goes to greater and greater T and to smaller and smaller scattering angles.

3. The Bethe surface

As seen from eq. (1), it is appropriate to use the variable $\ln (Ka_0)^2$ for consideration of the K dependence of $f_n(K)$; the integrated cross-section σ_n for excitation of the state n is then given, apart from the factor $4\pi a_0^2 (R/T)(R/E_n)$, by the area under a curve for $f_n(K)$ plotted as a function of $\ln (Ka_0)^2$, as first pointed out by Miller and Platzman [5] . Fig. 1 shows such a plot for the excitation of the $n = 2$ level of atomic hydrogen. For the 2p excitation, which is optically allowed, the GOS is a monotonically decreasing function of $\ln (Ka_0)^2$ and the decline for $(Ka_0)^2 \gg 1$ is quite steep. For the 2s excitation, which is optically forbidden, the GOS shows a maximum around $(Ka_0)^2 \approx 1$ and is nearly vanishing for other regions.

For transitions into the continuum, i.e., for ionization, the excitation energy is a continuous variable E that takes all real values greater than the ionization energy I. One considers then the density of the cross-section $d\sigma/dE$ per unit range of E. The differential cross-section $d (d\sigma/dE)$ expressed in terms

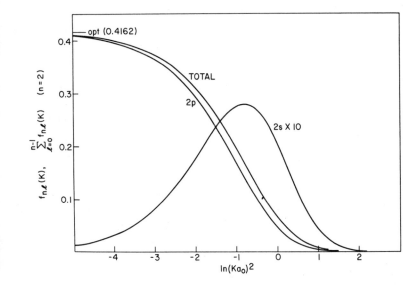

Fig. 1. The GOS for the transitions from the ground state to the $n = 2$ level of atomic hydrogen. The curve labeled "TOTAL" represents the sum $f_{2p}(K) + f_{2s}(K)$. The line labeled "opt" shows the optical oscillator strength f_{2p}. (Taken from ref. [3].)

of $\ln (Ka_0)^2$ is given by the same form as eq. (1), except that $f_n(K)$ is now replaced by the density $df(K,E)/dE$ of the GOS. Fig. 2 shows a plot of $df(K,E)/dE$ of atomic hydrogen for various values of E. For lower values of E, the curves are similar to the curve labeled as TOTAL in fig. 1, but show a broad maximum. For higher values of E, the maximum becomes increasingly more pronounced. This situation is even more apparent in fig. 3, which shows $df(K,E)/dE$ for very high values of E. The peak is located around $E/R = (Ka_0)^2$ and reflects the fact that, for collisions with large E and $\hbar K$, the momentum transfer and the energy transfer become correlated nearly as if atomic electrons were free. Since the atomic electrons are not quite free, the peak has a finite width of the order of $(B/E)^{1/2}$ on the $\ln (Ka_0)^2$ scale, where B is the binding energy of the atomic electrons.

The GOS for all excitations of an atom or molecule may be represented most comprehensively by a three-dimensional plot. If one plots $df(K,E)/dE$ as a function of $\ln (Ka_0)^2$ and of E, then one obtains a surface that may be called the Bethe surface. Fig. 4 shows the Bethe surface for atomic hydrogen.

The Bethe surface embodies all information concerning inelastic collisions

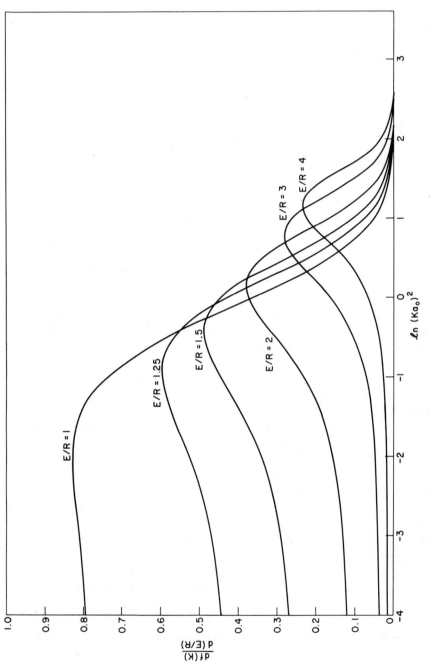

Fig. 2. Density of the GOS per unit range of excitation energy E for the transitions with $1 \leqslant E/R \leqslant 4$ from the ground state into the continuum of atomic hydrogen. (Taken from ref. [3].)

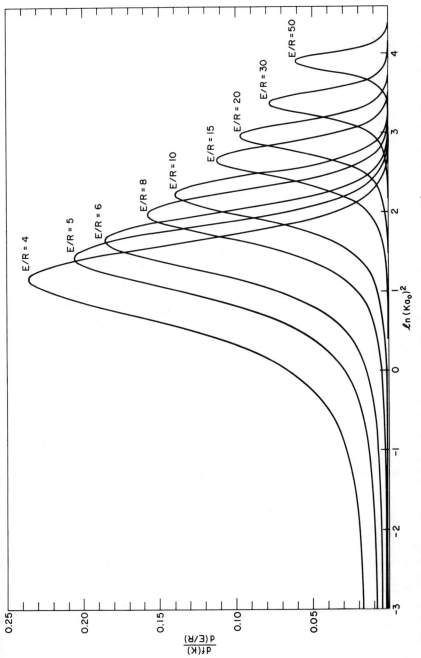

Fig. 3. Density of the GOS per unit range of excitation energy E for the transitions with $4 \leqslant E/R \leqslant 50$. Note the change of vertical scale from that of fig. 2. (Taken from ref. [3].)

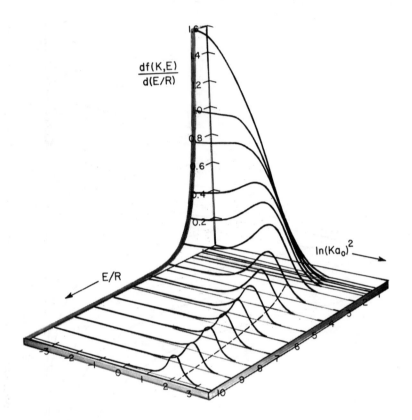

Fig. 4. A plastic model of the Bethe surface for atomic hydrogen. The horizontal axes for
E/R and $\ln (Ka_0)^2$ define the base plane. The vertical axis represents $Rdf(K,E)/dE$. The
two plates placed at $E/R = 3/4$ and $8/9$ represent the discrete spectrum, in which case
the vertical scale corresponds to $\frac{1}{2}n^3f_n(K)$, n being the principal quantum number. While
the model shows the major portion, the surface indefinitely extends as a plateau toward
smaller $\ln (Ka_0)^2$. (Taken from ref. [3].)

of fast charged particles. Recent years have seen impressive advances in experimental studies pertinent to our subject. Modern techniques permit one to
produce initial electron beams having high resolution in energy and angular
collimation and to analyze scattered electrons in great detail [6–9]. When an
experimentalist determines the differential cross-section $d\sigma_n$ for fast electrons,
he is in effect exploring the Bethe surface of the target atom or molecule over
a region of E_n and $\ln (Ka_0)^2$ of his observation. Indeed, for the current knowl-

edge of the Bethe surface of atoms and molecules except for atomic hydrogen, one owes much to experiments by Lassettre and his coworkers, Simpson and his coworkers, Geiger, and other investigators. Sometimes, a theoretician is able to construct wave functions for the atomic or molecular eigenstates and to compute the GOS according to eq. (3). Such a calculation is another means of learning about the Bethe surface, yet within the (usually modest) accuracy of the atomic models used.

The stopping power (more precisely the stopping cross-section $\Sigma_n E_n \sigma_n$) corresponds, apart from the factor $4\pi a_0^2 R^2/T$, to the volume under the Bethe surface extended over a region of E_n and $\ln (Ka_0)^2$ defined by kinematics. Fig. 4 clearly indicates the well-known fact that the stopping power includes two major contributions, one from collisions with small E_n and small $(Ka_0)^2$ ("optical collisions") and the other from collisions with large E_n and large $(Ka_0)^2$ (nearly binary-encounter collisions).

Presently available data, both theoretical and experimental, permit construction of the Bethe surface for He, perhaps within an accuracy of several percent. The result will be similar to the Bethe surface of atomic hydrogen, except for the vertical and horizontal scales. (Also, double excitations in He will be seen as minor structures.) For atoms and molecules such as Ne, Ar, Kr, H_2, N_2, and O_2, the major portions of the Bethe surface are known somewhat more crudely, and improvements of our knowledge are expected in the coming few years. For atoms and molecules that do not usually exist in the gaseous phase, experimental studies are just beginning. Theoretical calculations on atoms other than H and He are now being performed by several workers in a systematic way. Most of the existing calculations are based upon one-electron models, but the importance of electron correlation in the GOS calculations is being examined in several instances. (For references of the topics of this paragraph, see secs. 3.4 and 3.5 of ref. [3].)

4. Minima of the GOS

For some transitions the matrix element in eq. (3) changes its sign at a certain value of $(Ka_0)^2$. The GOS then takes a zero-value minimum. Examples of such a minimum are shown in figs. 5 and 6.

The minimum of the GOS is significant in several respects. First, a departure from exact zero in the measured GOS may indicate a failure of the first Born approximation. Second, within the validity of the first Born approximation, the position of the minimum is closely related to the nodes of the orbitals of the active electron, and therefore provides a stringent test of

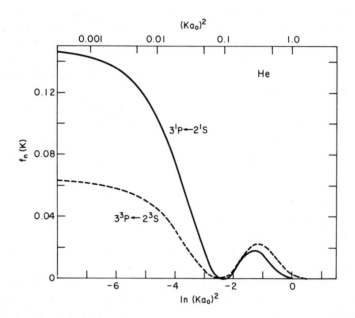

Fig. 5. The GOS for the $3^1P \leftarrow 2^1S$ and $3^3P \leftarrow 2^3S$ transitions in helium. (Taken from ref. [3].)

calculated wave functions of an atom or molecule. Third, minima of the same nature occur in a wide variety of atoms and molecules [10]. Finally, analogues of the minimum are observed in the inelastic-scattering form factors for Coulomb excitation of nuclei [11].

In general, the minimum is not necessarily a zero, even within the first Born approximation. Consider a p ← s transition in an alkali atom, and suppose that the matrix element calculated without account for the spin-orbit coupling changes its sign at a certain value of $(Ka_0)^2$. If one takes the spin-orbit coupling into account, then the radial wave functions for the p orbital will be different depending upon the total angular momentum j, which is $1/2$ or $3/2$ in this example. The combined contributions to the GOS thus will never precisely vanish at any Ka_0. The same argument also implies that the excited atom left behind after an inelastic scattering corresponding to the vicinity of the minimum will be spin-polarized. (In the case of ionization, the ejected electron will be spin-polarized.) An analogue of this phenomenon in photoabsorption has been predicted [12] and has in fact been observed [13].

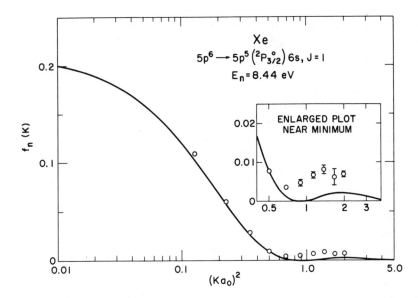

Fig. 6. The GOS for the 8.44 eV transition in xenon. The curve shows the result of a calculation based on Hartree-Fock wave functions. The circles represent electron-scattering data. (Taken from ref. [10].)

5. Concluding remarks

Another important item in the Bethe theory deals with the integrated cross-section σ_n, which is obtained as a result of integration of eq. (1) over all kinetically possible values of $\ln (Ka_0)^2$. The major result is that the dependence of σ_n upon the electron kinetic energy T is universally expressed in the form

$$\sigma_n = A_n T^{-1} \ln T + B_n T^{-1} + C_n T^{-2} + ... , \tag{7}$$

where the coefficients A_n, B_n, C_n, ... are all determined uniquely from the $f_n(K)$. This expression suggests that a plot of $T\sigma_n$ as a function of $\ln T$ will show an approach to a straight line for sufficiently high T. This plot, first proposed by Fano [14], is extremely powerful in analyses of experimental data. In particular, the coefficient A_n is simply related to the optical oscillator strength f_n. The second coefficient B_n depends upon the $f_n(K)$ for non-vanishing values of Ka_0. The two coefficients A_n and B_n virtually exhaust the meaningful content of the first Born approximation, in the sense that the coefficients C_n and others contain in general contributions from effects not included in the first Born approximation. More details on this topic are found in secs. 4.1–4.4 of ref. [3].

A few final remarks concern the applicability of the first Born approximation. It is well known indeed that true cross-sections at velocities not greatly exceeding the velocities of atomic electrons depart from the prediction of the first Born approximation. But the precise way in which the departures occur remains only poorly understood at present.

Traditionally, the departures have been discussed most often in connection with the velocity dependence of the integrated cross-section σ_n. The differential cross-section $d\sigma_n$, however, provides in general more conclusive evidence in this respect.

Suppose that an experiment has given a set of $d\sigma_n$ at several values of T and several values of $\hbar K$ (or, equivalently, at several scattering angles) for a definite transition $n \leftarrow 0$. If one substitutes experimental $d\sigma_n$ values into the left-hand side of eq. (1), one can solve eq. (1) for the GOS, all other quantities being either observable variables or universal constants. The resulting "apparent" GOS will be in general a function of K and T and may be denoted by $\dagger_n(K,T)$. A necessary (though not sufficient) condition for the validity of the first Born approximation is that the $\dagger_n(K,T)$ actually turns out to have the same K dependence, independent of T. For sufficiently large T, this will indeed be the case. This criterion assumes no theoretical knowledge of the GOS and thus can be used entirely operationally as soon as experimental data on $d\sigma_n$ are at hand. If the $\dagger_n(K,T)$ depends upon T, then a departure from the first Born approximation is evident.

If the apparent GOS turns out to be independent of T, then one is in a position to compare it with any theoretical result based upon eq. (3).

This rigorous procedure of testing the first Born approximation has been applied by Lassettre and coworkers to several cases of interest. (See refs. [3] and [7].) An important result is the recognition that the validity of the first Born approximation depends not only upon the ratio E_n/T but also upon the symmetry of the states n and 0. More specifically, the first Born approximation becomes valid for a transition between states with the same symmetry at much greater T than it does for other kinds of transitions. Lassettre [15] recently has advanced a theoretical explanation of this observation.

Another piece of general knowledge is the Lassettre theorem of the limiting GOS [16]. On a quite general basis, one can show that

$$\lim_{K \to 0} \dagger_n(K,T) = f_n \qquad \text{(for any } T\text{)}. \tag{8}$$

The content of this theorem should be sharply distinguished from eq. (5); the statement refers to "any T" and is not subject to the validity of the first Born approximation. While the theorem gives a theoretical justification of the determination of f_n from electron-scattering data, an application of the theorem is not always straightforward, because the limit $K \to 0$ is never physically attainable.

The Lassettre theorem seems to imply that the first Born approximation is applicable to small-angle scattering for even moderately fast electrons. For large-angle scattering, in contrast, we have several indications of notable departures from the first Born approximation. First of all, one has known for years that the electron-exchange effect is significant for large-angle scattering. Recent theoretical work [17,18] seems to show the importance of the interactions between the incident electron and the atomic nucleus; these interactions give vanishing contributions within the first Born approximation but modify large-angle scattering even at large velocities, according to refs. [17] and [18].

References

[1] H.Bethe, Ann. Phys. (Leipzig) 5 (1930) 325.

[2] H.Bethe, in: Handbuch der Physik, eds. H.Geiger and K.Scheel, Vol. 24/1 (Springer Verlag, Berlin, 1933) p. 273.

[3] M.Inokuti, Rev. Mod. Phys. 43 (1971) 297.

[4] N.Bohr, Phil. Mag. 25 (1913) 10; 30 (1915) 581.

[5] W.F.Miller and R.L.Platzman, Proc. Phys. Soc. A 70 (1957) 299.

[6] C.E.Kuyatt, in: Methods of Experimental Physics; Vol. 7: Atomic and Electron Physics, Atomic Interactions Part A, eds. B.Bederson and W.L.Fite (Academic Press, New York, 1968) p. 1.

[7] E.N.Lassettre, Can. J. Chem. 47 (1969) 1733.

[8] L.Kerwin, P.Marmet and J.D.Carette, in: Case Studies in Atomic Collision Physics I, eds. E.W.McDaniel and M.R.C.McDowell (North-Holland Publ. Co., Amsterdam, 1969) p. 525.

[9] S.Trajmar, J.K.Rice and A.Kuppermann, in: Advances in Chemical Physics, Vol. 18 (Interscience Publishers, New York, 1970) p. 15.

[10] Y.-K.Kim, M.Inokuti, G.E.Chamberlain and S.R.Mielczarek, Phys. Rev. Letters 21 (1968) 1146.

[11] T.deForest, Jr. and J.D.Walecka, Advan. Phys. 15 (1966) 1; ibid. 15 (1966) 491.

[12] U.Fano, Phys. Rev. 178 (1969) 131; ibid. 184 (1969) 250.

[13] J.Kessler and J.Lorenz, Phys. Rev. Letters 24 (1970) 87;
J.Kessler, VII ICPEAC, Invited Talks and Progress Reports, eds. T.R.Govers and F.J.de Heer (North-Holland Publ. Co., Amsterdam, 1972) p. 315.

[14] U.Fano, Phys. Rev. 95 (1954) 1198.

[15] E.N.Lassettre, J. Chem. Phys. 53 (1970) 3801.

[16] E.N.Lassettre, A.Skerbele and M.A.Dillon, J. Chem. Phys. *50* (1969) 1829.
[17] H.Tai, R.H.Bassel, E.Gerjuoy and V.Franco, Phys. Rev. A *1* (1970) 1819.
[18] S.Geltman and M.B.Hidalgo, J. Phys. B *4* (1971) 1299.

Physics of Electronic and Atomic Collisions, VII ICPEAC, 1971 − North-Holland (1972)

VIBRATIONAL AND ROTATIONAL EXCITATION
OF DIATOMIC MOLECULES WITHIN
AN ELECTRONIC TRANSITION

J.P. DOERING

Department of Chemistry
The Johns Hopkins University
Baltimore, Maryland 21218, U.S.A.

Recent experiments have shown that vibrational and rotational excitation of diatomic molecules within electronic transitions induced by positive ion or electron impact is a universal phenomenon which can be observed under the proper conditions in almost all systems. As a general rule, ion impact is found to produce non-equilibrium vibrational and rotational energy distributions when the projectile ion laboratory velocity is less than 10^8 cm s^{-1}. Vibrational excitation can also be observed in low energy electron impact experiments, but it is not clear whether significant rotational excitation by electrons also takes place. Recent improvements in the traditional optical excitation apparatus and the development of inelastic ion scattering experiments have allowed a great deal of new information to be obtained about these phenomena. In addition, it has been recently found that pure vibration-rotation transitions induced by positive ion impact are a very important class of phenomena. Possible production mechanisms for the observed excitations as well as future prospects in this area are discussed.

1. Introduction

This report discusses our laboratory's recent progress in the study of vibrational and rotational excitation in ion-molecule collisions. As there have been a number of investigations in this area in the past few years, a complete review of the field will not be possible. This report will, therefore, deal only with our work and comparisons of our results with those of other investigators.

The phenomena to be discussed are the production of vibrational and rotational excitation simultaneously with a electronic transition in collisions of positive ions and electrons with diatomic molecules. All such excitation processes have the common feature that some of the translational energy of the colliding system is converted into internal electronic, vibrational, or rotational excitation of the collision products.

The traditional method for the study of such energy transfer collisions has been the use of optical emissions from the collision products as a probe of the final state of the system. If the collison leaves the products in an excited electronic state from which an allowed electronic transition to a lower state accompanied by an emission in the ultraviolet spectral region can occur, the lifetime with regard to radiation of the collision products will generally be much shorter than the lifetime for relaxation through collisions with the background gas provided there are no special quenching processes to be considered. Under these conditions, the emitted radiation provides a good probe of the energy distribution of the collision products. The requirement of a convenient optical emission, which can be used to study the collison products, has made nitrogen the most widely used target molecule. Charge transfer to excited states of the N_2^+ ion occurs in a significant fraction of collisions of positive ions with nitrogen, and the N_2^+ first negative system in the near ultraviolet is easily detected and analyzed to determine the rotational and vibrational energy distribution. Rotational excitation within an electronic transition can be detected by comparison of the observed rotational energy distribution with that predicted from a Boltzmann distribution of energy among rotational states at the ambient gas temperature. Vibrational excitation appears as a deviation of the relative vibrational band intensities in the optical emission system from those predicted by the Franck-Condon principle.

Unfortunately, only a few excited states of some target molecules emit a suitable optical band system with sufficiently "open" rotational and vibrational structure to allow the energy distributions to be accurately determined under the weak signal conditions which are usually found in collision experiments. For this reason, most of the experimental data in this area have been taken using N_2, CO, and a few other targets. The use of inelastic scattering experiments to study vibrational excitation, which will be described later in this report, is a promising new technique which is not subject to the same restrictions as optical experiments. However, this technique cannot, at present, be used for the study of rotational excitation.

For convenience, the present report is divided into sections dealing with optical experiments on positive ion and electron impact followed by a discussion of our inelastic ion scattering experiments. This division is arbitrary, scientifically, since both types of experiments refer to the same phenomena, but is convenient for organizational purposes since the two types of experiments are very different in construction and operation.

2. Optical Studies

2.1 *Apparatus*

The optical excitation apparatus, which we have used to study collisions of positive ions and electrons with nitrogen, has been described in the literature [1] and bears a close resemblance to devices used by other investigators. Therefore only those features of our apparatus which are unusual will be discussed in this report.

The first important feature which we developed was the multistaging of the ion beam energy. Ions are withdrawn from the ion source, mass analyzed, and conveyed to the collision chamber at a fixed energy of 10 keV and then decelerated to the desired final energy just before traversing the interaction region. This arrangement has allowed us to obtain very large ion currents at the collision chamber − of the order of 100 μA of the desired species after mass analysis. The second important feature was the use of a grating spectrometer of good resolving power with very long entrance and exit slits. Our 1 meter Fastie-Ebert spectrometer has 5 cm long entrance and exit slits which are illuminated by the positive ion beam as it passes through the target gas in the collision chamber about 1 cm above the entrance slit. This close-coupled arrangement eliminates the need for any optical system to transfer the emitted radiation and allows us to take full advantage of the long slits. Most of our rotational excitation experiments were performed with 0.2 Å resolution or better. Finally, we used a good photomultiplier tube cooled to −40°C as a detector. The photomultiplier had a dark current count rate of only a few counts per second.

In order to investigate the effect of the initial rotational energy distribution on the collision products, we constructed a collision chamber in which the target gas could be cooled to 100 K during the experiment [2]. For the study of electron excitation, a simple electron gun replaced the ion source-mass spectrometer assembly.

The net gain in signal to noise ratio of this system, as compared to a conventional optical excitation apparatus, was about one order of magnitude.

2.2 *Positive ion excitation of nitrogen*

Figure 1 shows the N_2^+ first negative (0,0) band at 3914 Å excited by 1000 eV H_2^+ ion impact. This spectrum illustrates both the signal to noise ratio achievable with our apparatus and the remarkable appearance of these bands when the emitting ions are rotationally excited as a consequence of a low energy ion-molecule collision. We have described the features of this spectrum in detail previously [1] so only a few of the major points will be mentioned

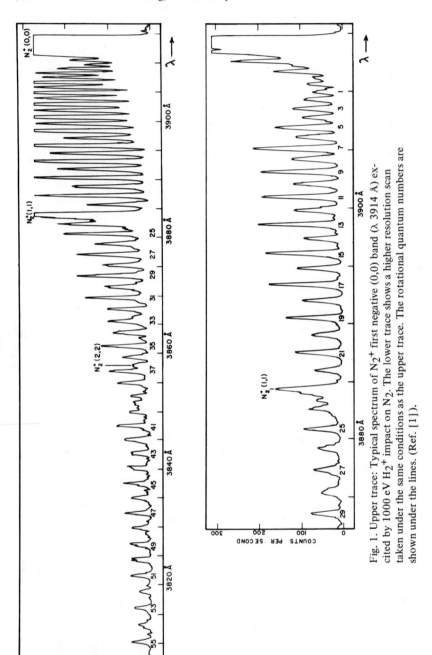

Fig. 1. Upper trace: Typical spectrum of N_2^+ first negative (0,0) band (λ 3914 Å) excited by 1000 eV H_2^+ impact on N_2. The lower trace shows a higher resolution scan taken under the same conditions as the upper trace. The rotational quantum numbers are shown under the lines. (Ref. [1]).

here. First, there is obviously a long, high-energy tail on the rotational energy distribution since rotational lines can be observed up to $K' = 56$. For a Boltzmann distribution at room temperature, only the first 22 rotational lines are normally detectable under the weak-signal conditions usually found in collision experiments. Second, it can be seen that for the rotational lines above $K' = 20$, the characteristic odd–even 2:1 intensity ratio, which is observed in the normal spectrum, is not maintained. Consideration of the effects of overlap of the high-energy lines from the P branch on the R branch lines leads to the conclusion that disturbances of the usual intensity ratio are to be expected when high rotational states of the emitting molecules are populated.

In order to test for a Boltzmann distribution, the data from spectra of this type were plotted in the form of a traditional rotational temperature plot as shown in fig. 2. Note that the observed intensities cannot be fitted to a Boltzmann distribution even when the effects of overlapping branches are taken into account. Furthermore, if only the first 22 lines are included in the plot and a best straight line is drawn, a rotational temperature in the range of 300 to 500 K is obtained. The fact that rotational excitation in Non-molecule collisions shows up as a long high-energy tail on the rotational energy distribution is what has made this phenomenon so hard to study in the past. Many investigators have attempted to deduce the presence or absence of rotational excitation from plots of the intensities of the first 22 lines; but as can be seen from fig. 2, these first few lines can give completely misleading results. Polyakova and co-workers [3,4,5] have studied rotational excitation by measurements of the first 22 lines, but their work has been extremely precise. Unless great pains are taken to assure very accurate measurement of the relative line intensities, no attempt should be made to deduce the presence or absence of rotational excitation effects from the first 22 lines of the band system.

Our investigations of other systems using different projectile ions incident on N_2 have disclosed some differences between the effects for atomic and molecular projectile ions [6]. Molecular ions generally caused a greater amount of rotational excitation. Polyakova et al. [4,5] have found similar differences between various projectile ions. The onset of rotational excitation appears to be at a projectile ion laboratory velocity of about $10^8 \mathrm{cm\ s^{-1}}$. Above this velocity, there appears to be little or no measurable perturbation of the Boltzmann distribution of energy in the rotational states. However, the excitation effects appear to increase monotonically below $10^8 \mathrm{cm\ s^{-1}}$. In contrast to the above results, Mickle et al. [7] have found that the highly excited rotational state populations produced in Li^+–N_2 and Na^+–N_2 collisions could be well described by a Boltzmann distribution.

We were unsuccessful in attempts to calculate the observed spectra using a model in which there was an exponentially decreasing probability for transi-

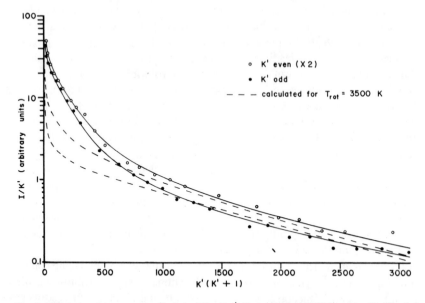

Fig. 2. "Rotational temperature" plot of the N_2^+ first negative (0,0) band excited by 0.4 keV H_2^+. The dashed lines are calculated for a Boltzmann distribution having a characteristic temperature of 3500 K. Note that the measured intensities of the K'-even lines have been multiplied by two. (Ref. [1].)

tions with increasing $|\Delta K|$. Apparently, the transition probability is also a function of K and the probability of a transition with large $|\Delta K|$ increases with K. This functional dependence is what is required to generate the characteristic appearance of these spectra which have a long tail of highly excited rotational lines.

Figure 3 shows spectra of the $\Delta v = -1$ sequence of the N_2^+ first negative band system excited by H_2^+ ions of different energies [8]. These spectra clearly show the dramatic increase in the intensities of the vibrational bands originating from higher vibrational energy levels as the projectile ion velocity is decreased. Data from a number of different spectra similar to those in fig. 3 are shown in fig. 4. Here we have plotted both the band intensity ratios as well as the relative populations of the vibrational states for the first four members of the $\Delta v = -1$ sequence of the first negative system excited by impact of various ions on N_2. Notice that the differences between the behavior of various projectile ions is small compared to the total effect and that the vibrational excitation increases monotonically to lower energies in our results. The onset of excitation effects is at a projectile ion velocity near 10^8 cm s^{-1}.

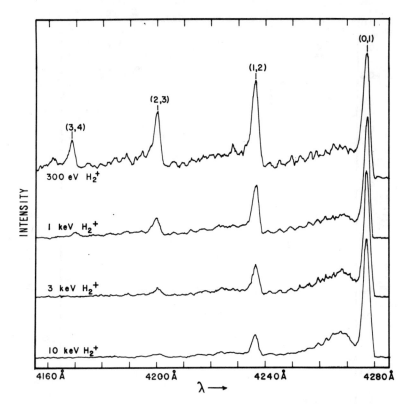

Fig. 3. Typical spectra of the N_2^+ first negative system $\Delta v = -1$ sequence excited by H_2^+ ions of various energies, (Ref. [8]).

These results are similar to those of Polyakova et al. [4,5] except that these investigators found that the effect decreased at a low enough projectile ion velocity and are also of the opinion that the difference in behaviour between various projectile ions is significant. At projectile ion velocities above 10^8 cm s^{-1}, the relative intensities of the members of the sequence agree with the relative intensities calculated from the Franck-Condon factors. These calculated "normal" intensities are indicated in fig. 4.

2.3. Optical results – electron impact

It has been obvious for some years that compared to the effects observed in positive ion impact, vibrational and rotational excitation of molecules in electron collisions is small. For projectile electron energies above 100 eV, there is no measurable transfer of energy from translation to internal degrees

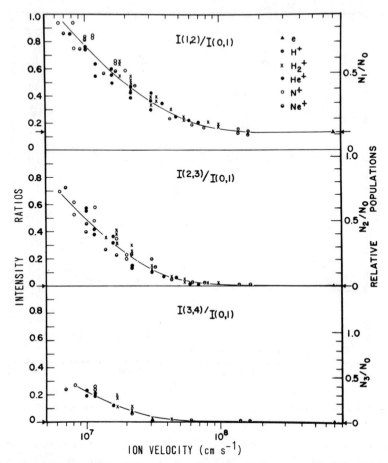

Fig. 4. Intensity ratios and relative vibrational level populations vs. projectile ion laboratory velocity calculated from measurements of the N_2^+ first negative system $\Delta v = -1$
sequence for various projectile ions at different energies. The arrows show the relative
intensities and populations predicted by the Franck-Condon principle (Ref. [8]).

of freedom since emission spectra from nitrogen excited under these conditions show that the observed intensities in the emitted optical spectrum are in
agreement with those predicted by the Franck-Condon principle for vibration
and are consistent with a room temperature Boltzmann distribution of energy
among rotational states.

There have been some reports of rotational excitation by electron impact at lower energies. However, we have never been able to find any effect. Using the cooled collision chamber to reduce the rotational energy distribution to the first 11 states, we found that there was no departure from a Boltzmann distribution at the ambient temperature near 100 K for impact energies as low as 30 eV [2]. The latest results of Fogel' and his co-workers are in agreement with this result [9]. We therefore conclude that if there are any observable rotational excitation effects in electron impact excitation, the effects must be very small and confined to a small energy region very close to threshold.

The situation with regard to vibrational excitation is more interesting. Recent work in our laboratory on vibrational excitation by electron impact in the production of the N_2^+ first negative system by low energy electron impact on nitrogen has shown that the relative population of the 0 and 1 vibrational states of the N_2^+ ions in the $B^2\Sigma_u^+$ state produced by electron impact approximately doubles as the electron energy is decreased from 50 to 25 eV [10]. This effect is in good agreement with results of Fogel' et al. [9,11].

In summary, it now appears that vibrational excitation occurs in electron impact ionization of N_2 in the energy range near threshold, but rotational excitation does not. Furthermore, the general results of these experiments are that such excitation in electron impact is weak compared to the observable phenomena in ion-molecule collisions. Part of the explanation for this difference may be due to the different projectile velocities since electrons are traveling much faster at the energy threshold than ions of many hundreds of eV energy. The differences between electron and positive ion impact will furnish an interesting area for further investigation in the years ahead.

2.4. Optical results – Summary

The above discussion has been restricted to excitation effects associated with production of electronically excited N_2^+ ions by electron and ion impact. For comparison, we can summarize briefly the available results for other processes in nitrogen besides ionization and consider the available data for other target molecules.

In order to determine whether vibrational and rotational excitation was present in excitation of N_2 to excited electronic states of the neutral molecule, we examined the emissions from the N_2 second positive system [8]. Our results for proton impact at various energies and 100 eV electron impact showed no excitation; however, we have concluded that, in these cases, the singlet-triplet transitions leading to production of this band system are produced mainly by low energy secondary electron impact. The secondary electrons are produced either by ionization of the target gas in collisions with the projectile ion or electron beam or by interaction of the beam with metal surfaces in the vacuum system. The second positive excitation cross section is so large in the region between 10 and 20 eV that all of the observed radiation apparently comes from this secondary process. We concluded that optical studies of excitation of the second positive band system must be accepted with caution because of possible effects of secondary electrons. We did not examine the first positive system; however, it is undoubtedly affected by the same difficulties. The other available emission systems in N_2 would be considerably more difficult to study.

There have been some studies of other target molecules, particularly CO, in other laboratories [12]. The results appear to be rather similar to our nitrogen results although there are some differences in the exact excitation effects. Polyakova et al. [13] have also studied collisions involving fast inert gas atom impact on nitrogen and have found even greater excitation of vibration and rotation than for positive ion impact.

In summary, it seems likely that rotational and vibrational excitation effects will be found for all classes of collisions with low enough projectile velocities. Unfortunately, however, the number of possible systems which can be studied by optical means is very limited. We will, therefore, turn to a discussion of the inelastic scattering experiments we have developed in an attempt to study a wider variety of systems.

3. Inelastic scattering experiments

Inelastic electron scattering experiments have been performed for many years. In such an experiment, the energy loss of the projectile is measured after collision with the target gas. Transitions to bound states of the neutral target atom or molecule can be detected as discrete peaks in the spectrum. Energy resolution is, generally, good enough to allow the vibrational components of an electronic transition to be separated. Transitions which involve ionization do not appear as discrete peaks in the spectrum because the production of an electron with a range of possible energies causes an ionization continuum to be produced in the inelastic scattering spectrum.

In order to use an inelastic scattering experiment to detect vibrational excitation of the target molecule in collisions, it would be necessary to either resolve the vibrational components of the electronic transition or, at least, have a good measure of the envelope of the transition if resolution was not sufficient to resolve the individual vibrational components. These conditions have been met by electron scattering experiments for a number of years; however, with a few exceptions, little or no vibrational excitation has been observed in electronic transitions to bound states of the target molecule. In most cases, the vibrational components have relative intensities which agree with those predicted by the Franck-Condon factors [14]. However, we felt that if such an apparatus could be adapted to positive ion scattering experiments, it might be possible to observe vibrational excitation effects similar to those observed with optical methods. We have, therefore, constructed a positive ion scattering apparatus which performs essentially the same experiment as an electron scattering apparatus using a positive ion as the projectile.

3.1. Apparatus

To perform a positive ion scattering experiment, one must produce a mass analyzed beam of positive ions of well defined energy and measure the energy loss on collision with the target gas. The low brightness of positive ion sources and the large energy spread of the emitted ions make a monochromatic ion beam considerably more difficult to produce than an electron beam of corresponding energy half-width and intensity.

The apparatus is shown schematically in fig. 5. Energy multistaging techniques have been used freely in this design. The ions are energy-analyzed at a fixed low energy of 12 eV in order to achieve sufficient energy dispersion with practical size deflectors. The scattered ion analyzer is articulated so that it can be rotated to look at various scattering angles. In practice, we have achieved a positive ion beam of most any easily produced ionic species of

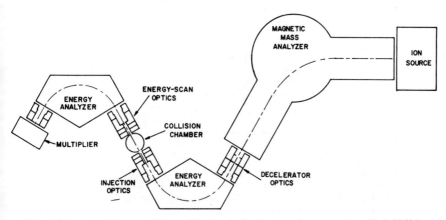

Fig. 5. Schematic diagram of the positive ion inelastic scattering apparatus. (Ref. [16].)

about 10^{-9} A intensity in the collision chamber with an energy half-width of approximately 100 meV. The scattered signal from a strong inelastic transition is typically of the order of a few hundred counts per second with a collision chamber pressure of the order of 10^{-3} Torr.

It must be understood that since the scattered ions must be analyzed electrostatically, such an apparatus can only be used to study processes which involve inelastic scattering of the projectile ion without charge transfer by bound states of the neutral target molecule. Obviously, the presently available resolution of 60 meV, at best, does not allow the study of rotational excitation within an electronic transition.

3.2. Inelastic scattering results – electronic transitions

Our inelastic scattering results have not yet been carried out over a very large energy range because of insulation problems in the apparatus. However, we have accumulated a number of clear examples of vibrational excitation within electronic transitions of the neutral target molecule. Fig. 6 shows a typical example for the N_2 transition a $^1\Pi_g \leftarrow X \, ^1\Sigma_g^+$ near 9 eV. The bars represent the relative Franck-Condon factors for the vibrational components of the transition which are unresolved in this case. The relative Franck-Condon factors have been normalized to the peak of the transition. The excess excita-

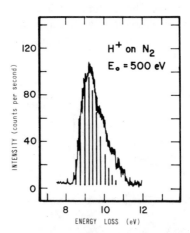

Fig. 6. Inelastic scattering spectrum of 500 eV H^+ on N_2 in the 8-12 eV energy loss region. The bars are the relative intensities of the vibrational bands of the N_2 a $^1\Pi_g \leftarrow X \, ^1\Sigma_g^+$ transition calculated from the Franck-Condon principle and normalized to the peak of the experimental curve to show the excess excitation of high vibrational states (Ref. [16].).

tion to high vibrational levels of the target is quite obvious. Other investigators [15] have observed vibrational excitation of N_2 by H_2^+ and Ar^+ projectiles. We have found similar effects with CO and other target molecules [16]. These results demonstrate that anomalous vibrational excitation occurs in excitation of electronic transitions in the neutral molecule. Improved energy resolution will greatly enhance the usefulness of this technique.

3.3. Vibration-rotation transitions

Through the use of positive ion scattering experiments, a remarkable new class of transitions produced by positive ion impact has come to light in the past several years [17]. In examining the forward proton scattering from H_2 at 500 eV incident energy, we were surprised to observe what appeared to be very strong inelastic structure spaced approximately 0.5 eV in energy loss below the unscattered peak. Figure 7 shows an example of these spectra. Further investigation and substitution of deuterium for hydrogen as the target gas established clearly that we were observing proton-induced vibration-rotation transitions within the ground electronic state of H_2. These effects have now been observed in a number of systems at lower impact energies [18,19,20].

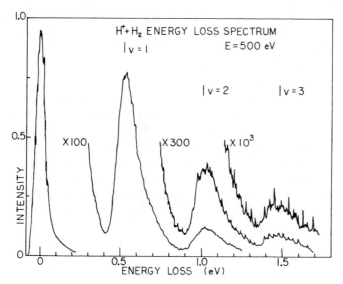

Fig. 7. Typical spectrum of 500 eV H^+ scattered from H_2. The positions of the first three excited vibrational states of H_2 are shown.

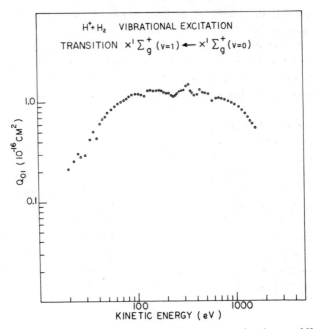

Fig. 8. Cross-section vs. energy for excitation of the first vibrational state of H_2 by proton impact. Above approximately 60 eV, all scattered ions are collected so Q_{01} represents the total cross-section. Below this energy, there is appreciable scattering outside the analyzer acceptance angle so Q_{01} represents the forward scattering cross-section for $\theta_{LAB} \leqslant 1.5°$.

We have recently determined the cross-section for some of these processes [21]. Figure 8 shows the cross-section vs. energy for excitation of the $v' = 1$ level of H_2 by proton impact. The maximum cross-section is several orders of magnitude larger than the cross-section for the corresponding process produced by low energy electron impact. These excitation effects also appear to be larger than those observed within an electronic transition. It is only because of the ease of optical study of excitations effects that vibrational excitation was first discovered within an electronic transition.

4. Conclusions

The basic question to be answered about vibrational and rotational excitation in charged particle collisions concerns the mechanism for production of the observed excitation. There have been a few theoretical attempts to date to explain the observed phenomena. Liu [22] has suggested that rotational excitation occurs as a consequence of conservation of angular momentum in inelastic collisions. A number of other investigators [23], including ourselves, have suggested that vibrational excitation arises from the perturbing effects of the projectile ion on the electronic structure of the target molecule. Since the Franck-Condon principle does not appear to hold in such excitation collisions, it seems likely that the collisional excitation involves an electronic transition in which the transition is between states which are represented by perturbed wave functions which differ considerably from the isolated target molecule wave functions. On the whole, it appears that vibrational excitation is rather easier to study experimentally than rotational excitation and understanding of vibrational excitation may come first.

The most striking feature of the experimental results in this area is that excitation phenomena have been observed in almost every system which has been studied. The critical dividing point for ion-molecule collisions appears to be a projectile ion laboratory velocity of about 10^8 cm s^{-1}. For velocities greater than this value, there appears to be no diversion of translational energy into other degrees of freedom. But for every system studied, lower projectile ion velocities produced collisions in which vibrational and rotational excitation could be detected.

With regard to optical measurements of vibrational and rotational excitation, it appears that the main areas to be cleared up for those systems which are accessible to study are the exact effects of the chemical nature of the projectile ion and the extension of the data to lower projectile ion velocities. Besides N_2 and CO there may be a few other target molecules which have sufficiently simple vibrational and rotational fine structure in strong emission bands to allow this type of study, but much work will be required to perform such experiments.

It is because of these difficulties that we feel the direct inelastic scattering experiments are very promising for the future. We do not foresee any immediate improvements which will make possible the study of rotational excitation, but it is clear that vibrational excitation can be studied with existing apparatus. Such techniques have also opened up the very important class of phenomena involving direct vibration-rotation transitions excited by ion impact which are a much more intense and, potentially, more important class of phenomena than excitation within an electronic transition.

References

[1] J.H. Moore, Jr. and J.P. Doering, Phys. Rev. *174* (1968) 178.

[2] J.H. Moore, Jr. and J.P. Doering, J. Chem. Phys. *50* (1969) 1487.

[3] G.N. Polyakova, V.I. Tatus', S.S. Strel'chenko, Ya.M. Fogel' and V.M. Fridman, Zh. Eksp. Teor. Fiz. *50* (1966) 1464; [English Transl. Soviet Phys.-JETP *23* (1966) 973].

[4] G.N. Polyakova, V.I. Tatus' and Ya.M. Fogel', Zh. Eksp. Teor. Fiz. *52* (1967) 657; [English Transl. Soviet Phys.-JETP *25* (1967) 430].

[5] G.N. Polyakova, Ya.M. Fogel', V.F. Erko, A.V. Zats and A.G. Tolstolutskii, Zh. Eksp. Teor. Fiz. *54* (1968) 374; [English Transl. Soviet Phys.-JETP *27* (1968) 201].

[6] J.H. Moore, Jr. and J.P. Doering, Phys. Rev. *182* (1969) 176.

[7] R.E. Mickle, H.I.S. Ferguson and R.P. Lowe, *VII ICPEAC, Abstracts of Papers*, Eds. L.M. Branscomb et al., Vol. 1 (North-Holland Publishing Co., Amsterdam, 1971) p. 384.

[8] J.H. Moore, Jr. and J.P. Doering, Phys. Rev. *177* (1969) 218.

[9] Ya.M. Fogel', private communication.

[10] J. Kiefer, Jr. and J.P. Doering, unpublished data.

[11] G.N. Polyakova, Ya.M. Fogel' and A.V. Zats, Zh. Eksp. Teor. Fiz. *52* (1967) 1495; [English Transl.: Soviet Phys.-JETP *25* (1967) 993].

[12] G.N. Polyakova, V.F. Erko, A.V. Zats, Ya.M. Fogel' and G.D. Tolstolutskaya, ZhETF, Pis. Red. *11* (1970) 562; [English Transl.: Soviet Phys.-JETP Letters *11* (1970) 390].

[13] G.N. Polyakova, V.F. Erko, Ya.M. Fogel', A.V. Zats and B.M. Fizgeer, Zh. Eksp. Teor. Fiz. *56* (1969) 1851; [English Transl. Soviet Phys.-JETP *29* (1969) 994].

[14] E.N. Lassettre, Can. J. Chem. *47* (1969) 1733.

[15] F.D. Schowengerdt and J.T. Park, Phys. Rev. A *1* (1970) 848.

[16] J.H. Moore, Jr. and J.P. Doering, J. Chem. Phys. *52* (1970) 1692.

[17] J.H. Moore, Jr. and J.P. Doering, Phys. Rev. Letters *23* (1969) 564.

[18] T.F. Moran and P.C. Cosby, J. Chem. Phys. *51* (1969) 5724.

[19] P.C. Cosby and T.F. Moran, J. Chem. Phys. *52* (1970) 6157.

[20] H. Udseth, C.F. Giese and W.R. Gentry, J. Chem. Phys. *54* (1971) 3642.

[21] F.A. Herrero and J.P. Doering, to be published.

[22] C. Liu, J. Chem. Phys. *53* (1970) 1295.

[23] M. Lipeles, J. Chem. Phys. *51* (1969) 1252.

Physics of Electronic and Atomic Collisions, VII ICPEAC, 1971 – North-Holland (1972)

REACTIVE SCATTERING OF ATOMS AND MOLECULES: CROSSED MOLECULAR BEAM EXPERIMENTS

YUAN TSEH LEE †

The James Franck Institute and Department of Chemistry
The University of Chicago, Chicago, Illinois, 60637, U.S.A.

ABSTRACT:

Recent developments in the study of the dynamics of chemical reactions by the crossed molecular beams method are discussed. The topics include the analysis of the quantum state distributions of reaction products, the vibrational, rotational and translational excitation of reagents and new varieties of chemical reactions under investigation.

1. Introduction

The increased discussion of "chemical processes" at a conference on the "Physics" of Electronic and Atomic Collisions is further evidence of the rapidly disappearing boundary between Physics and Chemistry in recent years, especially where collisions of atoms and molecules are involved.

In this paper, the discussion will be limited to the study of reactive scattering of atoms and molecules by the crossed molecular beams method.

In crossed molecular beams experiments, information on the dynamics of a chemical reaction is usually derived from measurements of the angular distribution and kinetic energy distribution of reactively scattered product molecules. The angular distribution can often provide information on the lifetime of the collision complex, the disposal of angular momentum and the preferred orientation of reactant molecules with respect to the relative velocity. On the other hand, the extent of internal excitation of product molecules is simply related to the difference between the total energy of the system and the measured kinetic energy of the products [1]. This dynamic information is essential in the understanding of "molecular physics of atomic transfer", which is usually referred to as "dynamics of chemical reactions" by chemists.

The field of the study of molecular dynamics of chemical reactions by the crossed molecular beams method has been developing very rapidly in the last few years [2]. In what follows, the discussion will be concentrated on the progress made in

A. The analysis of quantum state distributions of reaction products;

B. The vibrational, rotational and translational excitation of reagents;

C. New varieties of chemical reactions under investigation.

2. The analysis of quantum state distributions of reaction products

In contrast to chemiluminescene experiments [3] which have provided detailed information on vibrational-rotational state distributions of hydrogen halides formed in many exoergic reactions, crossed molecular beam experiments, although providing valuable information on angular distributions of product molecules, do not directly provide information on the partition of internal energy between rotational and vibrational excitation from the measured translational energy of the products. In some cases, additional kinematic restrictions, such as conservation of angular momentum, enable one to predict the extent of rotational excitation of the products [1a], but accurate information on internal excitation depends on further experimental analysis by various methods.

Experimental determination of average rotational excitation of alkali halides formed in the reaction of alkali atoms and halogen containing molecules has been made in the past from the measurement of the deflection of these molecules in an inhomogeneous electric two-pole (Stern-Gerlach) deflection field [3a, 3b]. The paradox of experimental results involving CH_3I and HBr is now understood to be due to polarization of the rotational angular momentum of the reaction products perpendicular to the initial relative velocity vector [3c]. Recently, a more sophisticated measurement of the rotational state distribution of RbBr formed in the Rb + Br_2 reaction was performed by the focussing of various rotational quantum states (j,m) of velocity-defined RbBr in a quadrupole inhomogeneous electric field [4]. As to vibrational energy distribution, fruitful results have started to appear from the measurement of molecular beam electric resonance spectra of reaction products. In Cs + SF_6 → CsF reactions [5], the observed Stark spectrum of CsF arises from transitions between space-quantized components $(M_J \rightarrow M_J,)$ of particular rotation-vibration (J,v) states, and thus provides information on internal excitation. New work of this type was reported at this conference [6]. So far, all of the experimental analysis of product excitation by inhomogeneous electric field deflection or molecular beam electric resonance is on alkali halides, which can be easily detected by surface ionization, but we can expect that in the near future these methods will also be applied to many other systems.

In some cases, when kinematic relations are favorable, it is possible to identify product vibrational states directly from the structure in angular- and velocity distributions. For example, in the $F + D_2$ reaction [7], as illustrated in fig. 1., the exoergicity of 31.5 kcal/mol (1.37 eV) is just about enough to excite DF the fourth vibrational state. Since the energy spacing of vibrational states is large, ≈ 8 kcal/mol, and the energy spread in the distribution of rotational excitation is expected to be smaller even if the estimated typical total angular momentum of the system ($\approx 10\,\hbar$) all entered as rotational excitation of DF, the spread of translational energy of each vibrational state will also be smaller than the vibrational spacings. As a result, in center-of-mass coordinates, products of each vibrational state can be expected to be moving with a narrow velocity range well separated from other vibrational states[7b, 8]. Furthermore, this reaction has an activation energy [9] and the linear configuration has the lowest activation energy of ≈ 1 kcal/mol [8b, 10]. At low collision energies, the reaction will mainly take place through collinear collisions; consequently, DF formed will mainly be scattered backward with respect to the motion of the F atom. From the preceeding argument and the Newton diagram shown in fig. 2., it is quite obvious that if beams of F and D_2 with narrow velocity and angular spread are crossed, products with different vibrational states should appear at different laboratory angles. We have carried out this experiment [8] with a velocity selected F atom-and a supersonic D_2 beam in an experimental arrangement shown in fig. 3. The angular distribution of DF was measured by a rotatable mass spectrometric detector.

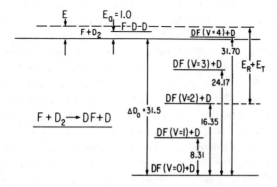

Fig. 1. Energetics of the reaction $F + D_2 \rightarrow DF + D$ (energies in kcal/mol).

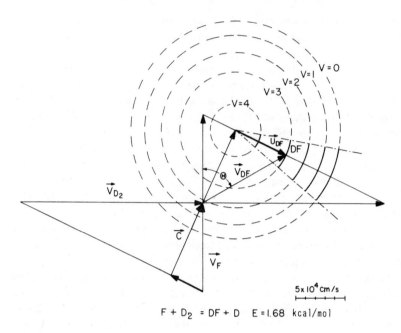

F + D$_2$ = DF + D   E = 1.68 kcal/mol

Fig. 2. Kinematics of the reaction of F with D$_2$ at a relative kinetic energy of 1.68 kcal/mol. The dashed circles indicate the maximum DF velocity in each vibrational state allowed by energy conservation.

The experimental results and the contour map of the product distribution in velocity space is shown in fig. 4a and 4b, for several collision energies. As expected, at the lowest energy, 0.8 kcal/mol, almost all the products are scattered backward and the major products DF(v=4) and DF(v=3) are clearly separated in the angular scan. When the collision energy is gradually increased, more and more products moved to a forward direction with respect to the F velocity. For reactions with activation energy, it has been shown in theoretical calculations [11] and in experiments [12] that the products shift to a smaller angle as the collision energy is increased; but the most striking phenomenon observed in this experiment is the drastic difference between angular distributions of products in different vibrational states as a function of collision energy. In the energy range in which this experiment was carried out, a marked forward shifting for highest vibrationally excited DF(v=4) is observed, but the angular distribution of DF(v=3) remains relatively unchanged. At higher energies as the Newton diagram stretches wider and the recoil velocity for DF(v=4) increases, the separation of DF(v=4) and DF(v=3)

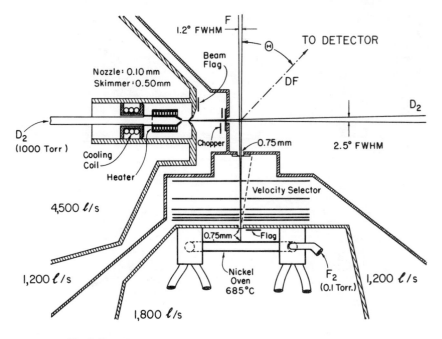

Fig. 3. Experimental arrangement for the study of the F + D$_2$ reaction.

in the angular scan is no longer possible, but it is still possible to distinguish them in a velocity scan of the products, which will be performed in the near future. The ratio between DF(v=4) to DF(v=3) is found to be about 0.75 at the lowest collision energy in agreement with the result obtained by the chemiluminescene method [7b].

This reaction, at least at collision energies near the activation energy, shows a strong kinematic coupling in the reaction dynamics. It seems to suggest that as bent configurations become important at higher collision energy, the larger impact parameters associated with a bent configuration favor production of the highest vibrationally excited state, DF(v=4), as indiacted by the forward shift in the angular distribution. This kinematic coupling could partly result from the fact at low collision energy, if DF(v=4) is formed, the energy left for translational, rotational motion can only excite a few rotational states of DF(v=4). Since product orbital angular momentum will also be small for low recoil velocities, the small total angular momentum implies that only collisions with small impact parameters can produce DF(v=4) as a consequence of the conversation of angular momentum. Experimentally, we did

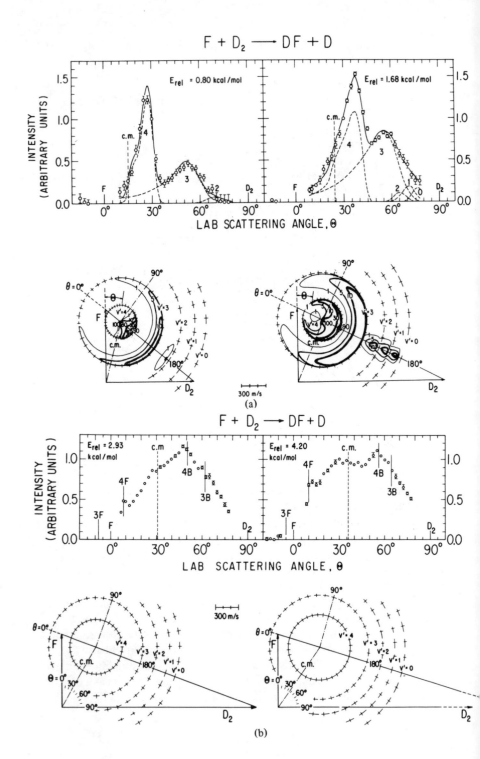

F + D₂ ⟶ DF + D

(a)

F + D₂ ⟶ DF + D

(b)

observe that the angular distribution of DF(v=4) is narrower than that of DF(v=3) at the lowest collision energy. The restriction on the impact parameter imposed by angular momentum conservation for DF(v=4) production is a strong function of the total energy available. As the collision energy increases, the critical impact parameter for DF(v=4) production becomes larger and larger. Similar phenomena were also observed in the transfer of D atoms from hydrocarbons; in the reactions F + CD_4 [13] and F + C_2D_4 [14], only DF(v=4) is observed in the forward direction with respect to F velocity.

3. The vibrational, rotational and translational excitation of reagents

In the last few years some significant progress has also been made in the extension of reactant energies to higher values for both the internal and the kinetic energy. For internal excitation, it is not surprising that laser excitation has started to play an important role in crossed molecular beam experiments. By using CO_2 and HCl chemical lasers, scattering of vibrationally excited SF_6 [15] and HCl[16] with alkali atoms has been investigated recently. Although detailed dynamic information on the effect of vibrational excitation is yet to be obtained in these experiments, in the study of K + HCl$^+$ mentioned above, the reactive cross-section for HCl(v=1) has been shown to be orders of magnitude greater than that of the slightly endoergic reaction with HCl(v=0). The effect of rotational excitation on reaction dynamics has been studied theoretically [17], but the experimental studies have yet to be performed. In a beam produced by supersonic expansion of molecules such as hydrogen halides, a large fraction of the molecules can be excited directly by a laser to a given vibration-rotation state, because the rotational temperature of the molecules will be lowered by relaxation and the state distribution for most of

Fig. 4. (a) Above: laboratory angular distributions of DF intensity (number density) for average relative kinetic energies of 0.80 and 1.68 kcal/mol. ○, experimental points; — , calculated total intensity; - - -, calculated in intensity of DF in particular vibrational states. Below: corresponding Cartesian contour plots of [DF flux (c.m.)] / [DF c.m. velocity]² in velocity space. The dashed circles denote the largest DF velocity for each vibrational state allowed by energy conservation.
(b) Above: Laboratory angular distributions of DF number density for average relative kinetic energies of 2.93 and 4.20 kcal/mol. The vertical lines indicate the angular limits for DF in particular vibrational states directly forward (F) or backward (B) in the c.m. frame. Below: corresponding Newton diagrams with dashed circles denoting the largest DF velocity for each vibrational state allowed by energy conservation.

the molecules will be limited to only the few lowest rotational levels of the ground vibrational state. We can expect in the near future detailed study of the reaction dynamics of chemical reactions using vibration-rotation-state-specified reactant molecules.

For non-polar molecules, laser excitation will not be feasible, but an attempt to produce highly vibrationally excited molecules by the combination of atoms in a jet may offer some interesting results. The vibrational excitation of atomic alkali molecules produced by supersonic expansion has been shown to be as high as 60 to 80% of the dissociation energy [18]. Many reactions of these vibrationally excited alkali molecules have been studied recently [19]. But, unfortunately, no comparison can be made with the reaction of alkali molecules in low internal energy, since the recombination through supersonic expansion is the only way to produce beams of diatomic alkali molecules. An attempt at producing highly vibrationally excited I_2 molecules by this method is now under investigation [20].

For extension in translational energy, the development has reached the point where substantially endothermic reactions can now be studied in the hyperthermal energy range. There are three different methods which are commonly used in producing hyperthermal energy molecular beams. Many experiments have been carried out by using beams produced by the charge exchange method [21], in which the accelerated charged particles are neutralized by resonant transfer prior to reaction. In the energy range which is of interest in chemical reactions, up to ≈ 20 eV, this method does not provide nearly enough beam intensity to make product angular distribution measurements feasible, due to space charge limitation on the ion current. Almost all the processes studied by this method involve either ionization or electronic excitation, since ions and photons can be detected easily. The newly developed sputtering beam source [22] has been shown to produce metallic atom beams with intensity several orders of magnitude larger than that of the charge exchange method for energies up to ≈ 30 eV. Many interesting results were obtained by this method recently [22a, 23]. For reactions of heavy atoms and molecules, the most promising method probably is the seeded beam method [24]. A high energy beam of heavy molecules can be obtained through supersonic expansion of a gas containing a small fraction of heavy molecules mixed with light molecules at high temperature. Since both heavy and light molecules will reach the same terminal velocity in the high pressure supersonic expansion, the energy ratio between the heavy and the light molecules in the ratio between their molecular weights. The actual energy of the heavy molecules is determined by the ratio between the molecular weight of the mixture and by the gas temperature prior to expansion. For example a Xe beam produced by expanding 1%

of Xe and 99% of H_2 at $1000°C$ will have an energy of 10eV. The most attractive features of a seeded supersonic beam source are the narrow velocity distribution and the high intensity, typically in excess of 10^{18} molecule sr^{-1} s^{-1}, which is 10^8 to 10^{10} times greater than that produced by the charge exchange method.

Until very recently, the study of reactive scattering as a function of collision energy has been limited to exoergic reactions in the thermal energy range. With the advent of the seeded supersonic beam, not only can the reactions studied at thermal energy be observed in the hyperthermal range [32], but reactions with substantial activation energy or endoergicity also become possible. A negative result showing that the kinetic energy alone is not sufficient to allow the HI + DI → HD + I_2 reaction to proceed was reported in the past [25]. We have recently carried out experiments on collision-induced dissociation of alkali halides by high energy xenon [29] and also measurements of the angular distribution of the products of the substantially endothermic chemical reaction I + CH_3Br, by seeding CH_3Br in H_2 [13]. Production of HI and IBr, which are both endothermic by 25 kcal/mol (1.08 eV) was observed, and their angular distribution is shown in fig. 5, but CH_3I, which is only endothermic by 12.5 kcal/mol (0.54 eV), was not observed. The same chemical specificity, the transfer of H or the halogen atom to the attacking halogen atom, rather than that of the CH_3 radical, is well known in exoergic reactions. The angular distribution of HI, the sharp forward-backward peaking shown in fig. 5, is characteristic of a reaction in which orbital angular momentum dominates and the complex lifetime is longer than or comparable to a rotational period [26]. If the I atom has to enter along the direction of the C-H bond, it is easy to understand this, since the heavy bromine atom is not collinear with C-H-I and there is always a finite impact parameter and a large orbital angular momentum involved. In addition, the transfer of a light hydrogen atom between heavy particles does not change the reduced mass appreciably. The sharp forward-backward peaking along the relative velocity vector also enables us to distinguish HI($v=1$) and HI($v=0$). It is not surprising that the vibrational state distribution is not inverted in this endoergic reaction. IBr formed in this reaction peaks slightly backward.

Actually, the observation of the fact that a substantially endothermic reaction can proceed rather efficiently by kinetic energy alone is interesting. The reactive scattering of potassium and laser-excited HC1 mentioned before, the application of microscopic reversibility to many exothermic reactions studied [27], and theoretical trajectory studies [28] all point to the conclusions that for substantially endothermic reactions, vibrational excitation in the bond which is to be broken increases the rate constant by orders of magnitude, and

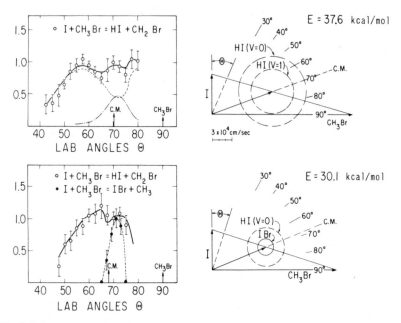

Fig. 5. Laboratory angular distributions of product number density and Newton diagrams for the reaction I + CH$_3$Br at average relative kinetic energies of 37.6 kcal/mol (1.63eV) and 30.1 kcal/mol (1.31 eV). o, experimental points for HI; ●, experimental points for IBr. ----, HI angular distributions calculated by assuming forward: backward ratio of 3:1 for HI(v=o) for both energies. The peak in the center of the HI angular distribution at 37.6 kcal/mol is attributed to HI(v=1).

that translational energy of the reactants is far less effective than vibrational energy in producing reaction. However, all the experimental evidence which substantiates these conclusions is strictly speaking only applicable to endoergic reactions at energies just above threshold, since the application of microscopic reversibility to an exoergic reaction studied at thermal energy only provides information for the reverse endoergic reaction which produces products of thermal energy. Near the threshold of an endoergic reaction, in addition to the consideration of the nature of the potential energy surface, the law of conservation of angular momentum tells us that it is impossible to transfer all the kinetic energy to potential energy during the collision unless the impact parameter is zero. But when the kinetic energy of the reactants is substantially higher than the endoergicity, this kinematic restriction will not play an important role. This is so because even for collisions with larger impact parameters, the fraction of kinetic energy converted to potential energy during the collision is sufficient to overcome the activation energy or endo-ergicity. How effective the translational energy will be in producing endoergic reaction will then be determined only by the nature of the potential energy surface for the reaction with respect to where the barrier to reaction lies [28]

The collision-induced dissociation studies of CsI + Xe → Cs$^+$ + I$^-$ + Xe [29] have shown that when the collision energy is near the threshold of this endoergic reaction ($\approx$4.5 eV), the dissociation cross-section σ increases drastically with increase in internal excitation, as expected, but when the collision energy is substantially higher than the endoergicity, the dissociation becomes very efficient ($\sigma\approx$10 Å^2) and depends very little on vibrational excitation. The I + CH$_3$Br reaction mentioned above similarly provides another evidence of the "adequacy of translational energy" in endoergic reaction. It is erroneous to believe that vibrational excitation of the bond to be broken is required for all endoergic reactions.

4. New varieties of chemical reactions under investigation

The new chemical reactions of alkali metals now involve diatomic alkali molecules. So far, reactions with hydrogen atoms, halogen atoms and halogen molecules have been investigated. In the reactions Cl + Na$_2$ → NaCl + Na and Cl + K$_2$ → KCl + K [19b], electronically excited Na(3^2P) and K(4^2P) were produced with a cross-section of 10 to 100 Å^2. The larger cross-section for direct excitation found in these reactions is consistent with theoretical predictions obtained from estimates of the ionic-covalent curve crossings [30] and from a statistical model [31]. The studies carried out on the reactions of halogen molecules and diatomic alkali molecules [19b] have shown that these reactions do not form two alkali halides. Some of this work has been reported at the conference [19c]. Although new reactions of alkali metals are moving on to alkali dimers, the experimental studies of alkali atom reactions cannot be regarded as exhausted. As experimental techniques advance, better-defined initial conditions can yield more detailed dynamic information, especially on the energy dependence of reaction dynamics, which has just begun to be explored [32].

It is not surprising that when the experimental studies of reactive scattering had gone beyond the reactions of alkali atoms through the use of a sensitive mass spectrometric detector, the first series of reactions studied involved halogen atoms and hydrogen atoms. The dissociation energies of halogen and hydrogen molecules range from 37 to 104 kcal/mol (1.6 to 4.5 eV); consequently, by choosing proper oven materials, beams of hydrogen and halogen atoms can readily be obtained by thermal dissociation. The reactions of these atoms with hydrogen, halogens and hydrogen halide molecules produce new hydrogen, halogens and hydrogen halides. These three-atom systems containing hydrogen and halogens have been investigated by various groups in the last three years, and were listed together with other three-atom systems in the paper presented by D.R. Herschbach [2] during the conference on Potential Energy Surfaces in Chemistry last year. Two new halogen atom halogen molecule reactions studied since then are $F + Cl_2 \rightarrow ClF + Cl$ [33] and $I + F_2 \rightarrow IF + F$ [13]. Most of the available energy in the last reaction appears as internal excitation of IF.

In addition to the three atom systems containing hydrogen and halogen molecules, two types of reactions of organic molecules have been under extensive investigation. The first is the transfer of a hydrogen or halogen atom from organic molecules to hydrogen or halogen atoms [13, 14, 34]. Some of these experiments were mentioned briefly above. The second is the formation of a carbon-halogen bond in the reaction of halogen atoms with olefin molecules [14, 35, 36, 37]. These reactions are of particular interest to chemists for various reasons. In simple atom-molecule reactive scattering, the crossed molecular beams method provides information on the "dynamics" of well-known chemistry, but in the reactions of halogen atoms with olefin molecules, chemical information such as reactivity, specificity as a function of the substituents on the olefin molecule, and favored product channel can also be obtained. These reactions also provide an excellent opportunity to study the reaction of unimolecular decomposition and reveal the nature of intramolecular energy transfer, by virtue of the fact that when halogen atoms react with olefins, the excess energy of the complex is localized where the new carbon-fluorine bond is formed, namely, the location of the double bond in the olefin, and the interaction is strong enough (in excess of 2 eV) to form a long-lived complex. The situation is especially favorable for a fluorine atom, since the C-F bond is the strongest single bond of any between carbon and other elements. The excess energy is sufficient to break the carbon-carbon bond, carbon-hydrogen bond or other carbon-halogen bonds. We have carried out a systematic study of angular distributions and energy distributions of more than twenty of these multichannel decomposition reactions [37] in the past year. Figure 6 shows reactions of fluorine and cis-butene-2. In addition to two reaction channels resulting from the decomposition of the collision complex, the other reaction channel is the direct transfer of a hydrogen atom to the fluorine atom. In the $F + C_2D_4$ reaction [14], we have studied formation of DF and C_2D_3F through different mechanisms. The reaction is expected to be sterospecific; our experimental results may imply that if F ap-

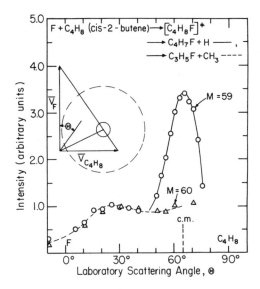

Fig. 6. Laboratory angular distributions and Newton diagram for the F + C$_4$H$_8$ (cis-2-butene) reactions. O, Mass 59, the ion (C$_3$H$_4$F$^+$) produced by both products, C$_4$H$_7$F and C$_3$H$_5$F. Δ, Mass 60, from C$_3$H$_5$F. ⎯⎯ corresponds to the angular distribution of C$_3$H$_5$F, and ⎯⎯⎯⎯⎯ corresponds to C$_4$H$_7$F, as verified from the angular distribution of Mass 74 (C$_4$H$_7$F$^+$).

proaches C$_2$D$_4$ in the plane of the molecule, especially along the C-D bond, highly vibrationally excited DF (mostly in v=4) will be formed through direct transfer of the deuterium atom to fluorine. On the other hand, if F approaches C$_2$D$_4$ perpendicular to the molecular plane, a long-lived complex will be formed by interaction of the F atom with the delocalized π electrons of C$_2$D$_4$, producing C$_2$D$_3$F.

Since the interesting chemiluminescence work on reactions of alkaline earth atoms with various molecules forming halides [38] and oxides [39], much attention has been paid to the measurement of the angular distributions of these reactions. In addition to the work on Ba + O$_2$, presented at this conference [40], at least three more groups are working on the reactions of alkaline earths with various molecules [41]. The fact that alkaline earth atoms are divalent will provide very interesting new information. Of course the electronic state of oxides formed in these reactions will be interesting.

Reactions with CH$_3$ radicals are also under investigation [15, 42]. These reactions, together with oxygen atom and other free radical reactions, will be the next to flourish.

Acknowledgements

It is a pleasure to thank those colleagues who kindly provided information for this paper. The experiments done at The University of Chicago were supported by the U.S. Atomic Energy Commission and performed by J.M. Parson, T.P. Schafer, K. Shobotake, P.E. Siska, F.P. Tully and Y.C. Wong. We have also benefitted from the use of facilities provided by the Advanced Research Projects Agency for materials research at The University of Chicago. The revision of the manuscript by P.E. Siska, T.P. Schafer, and J.M. Parson is gratefully acknowledged.

Refe;ences

[1] a) D.R. Herschbach in: *Molecular Beams (Adv. Chem. Phys. Vol. 10)*, Ed. J. Ross, (Interscience Publishers, New York, 1966) p. 319.
  b) J.P. Toennies in: *Chemische Elementarprozesse*, Eds. H. Hartmann, J. Heidberg, H. Heydtmann and G.H. Kohlmaier, (Springer-Verlag, Berlin, 1968) p. 157.
[2] D.H. Herschbach, *Proc. Conf. Potential Energy Surfaces in Chemistry*, Ed. W.A. Lester Jr. (IBM Research Laboratory, San Jose, California, 1971) p. 44.
[3] C. Maltz and D.R. Herschbach, Disc. Faraday Soc. *44* (1967) 176;
  b) C. Maltz, Ph.D. Thesis, Harvard University, 1969;
  c) Neil Weinstein and D.R. Herschbach, private communication.
[4] R. Grice, J.E. Mosch, S.A. Safron and J.P. Toennies, J. Chem. Phys. *53* (1970) 3376.
[5] S.M. Freund, G.A. Fisk, D.R. Herschbach and W. Klemperer, J. Chem. Phys. *54* (1971) 2510.
[6] H.G. Bennwitz, R. Haerten, O. Klais and G. Müller, *VII ICPEAC, Abstracts of Papers*, Eds. L.M. Branscomb et al., Vol. 1 (North-Holland Publishing Co., Amsterdam, 1971) p. 29;
[7] The F + D_2 reaction has been studies recently by
  a) *Chemical laser*: J.H. Parker and G.C. Pimentel, J. Chem. Phys. *51* (1969); 91;
  b) *Chemiluminescence*: J.C. Polanyi and D.C. Tardy, J. Chem. Phys. *51* (1969) 5717;
  K.G. Anlauf, P.E. Charters, D.S. Horne, R.G. MacDonald, D.H. Maylotte, J.C. Polanyi, N.J. Skrlac, D.C. Tardy and K.B. Woodall, J. Chem. Phys. *53* (1970) 4091;
  c) *Trajectory calculations*: J.T. Muckerman, J. Chem. Phys. *54* (1971) 1155; R.L. Jaffe and J.B. Anderson, J. Chem. Phys. *54* (1971) 2224.
[8] a) T.P. Schafer, P.E. Siska, J.M. Parson, F.P. Tully, Y.C. Wong and Y.T. Lee, J. Chem. Phys. *53* (1970) 3385;
  b) T.P. Schafer, Y.T. Lee, J. Chem. Phys. to be published.
[9] P.D. Mercer and H.O. Pritchard, J. Phys. Chem. *63* (1959) 1468.
[10] J.T. Muckerman and M.D. Newton, Private communication.
[11] M. Karplus and K.T. Tang, Disc. Faraday Soc. *44*, (1967) 56.

[12] J.D. McDonald, P.R. LeBreton, Y.T. Lee and D.R. Herschbach, J. Chem. Phys., to be published.

[13] Y.C. Wong and Y.T. Lee, J. Chem. Phys. to be published.

[14] John M. Parson and Y.T. Lee J. Chem. Phys. to be published.

[15] John Ross, private communication.

[16] T.J. Odiorne, P.R. Brooks and J.V.V. Kasper, J. Chem. Phys. (1971) in press.

[17] a) J.T. Muckerman, J. Chem. Phys. *54* (1971) 1155.
b) Roberta Saxon, Ph.D. Thesis, University of Chicago, 1971.

[18] a) R.J. Gordon, Y.T. Lee and D.R. Herschbach, J. Chem. Phys. *54* (1971) 2393;
b) W.S. Struve and D.R. Herschbach, private communication.

[19] a) Y.T. Lee, R.J. Gordoin and D.R. Herschbach, J. Chem. Phys. *54* (1971) 2410;
b) W.S. Struve, T. Kitagawa and D.R. Herschbach, J. Chem. Phys. *54* (1971) 2759; and private communication;
c) C.M. Kendall, P.B. Foreman and R. Grice, VII ICPEAC, Abstracts of Papers, eds. L.M. Branscomb et al., Vol. 1 (North-Holland Publishing Co., Amsterdam, 1971) p. 23.

[20] D.R. Herschbach, private communication.

[21] a) M. Hollstein and H. Pauly, Z. Phys. *196* (1966) 353;
b) N.G. Utterback and G.H. Miller, Rev. Sci. Instrum. *32* (1961) 1101.

[22] a) V. Kempter, Th. Kneser and Ch. Schlier, J. Chem. Phys. *52* (1970) 5851;
b) J. Politiek, P.K. Rol, J. Los and P.G. Ikelaar, Rev. Sci. Instrum. *39* (1968) 1147.

[23] A.P.M. Baede, A.M.C. Moutinko, A.E. de Vries and J. Los, VI ICPEAC, Abstracts of Papers, Ed. I. Amdur (M.I.T. Press, Cambridge, Mass., 1969) p. 592.

[24] a) N. Abuaf, J. B. Anderson, R.P. Andres, J.B. Fenn and D.G.H. Marsden, Science *155*, (1967) 997;
b) N. Abuaf, Ph. D. Thesis, Princeton University (1966);
b) J. B. Anderson, Entropie *18*, (1967) 33.

[25] S. B. Jaffe and J.B. Anderson, J. Chem. Phys. *51* (1969) 1057.

[26] a) W.B. Miller, S.A. Safron and D.R. Herschbach, Disc. Faraday Soc. *44* (1967) 108;
b) G. A. Fisk, J. D. MacDonald and D.R. Herschbach, ibid. *44* (1967) 228;
c) E. A. Entemann and D. R. Herschbach, ibid. *44* (1967) 289;
d) W. B. Miller, S.A. Safron, G.A. Fisk, J.D. McDonald and D.R. Herschbach, J. Chem. Phys., to be published.

[27] K. G. Anlauf, D.H. Maylotte, J.C. Polanyi and R.B. Bernstein, J. Chem. Phys. *51* (1969) 5716.

[28] J. C. Polanyi and W.H. Wong, J. Chem. Phys. *51* 1439 (1969).

[29] F. P. Tully, Y.T. Lee and R.S. Berry, Chem. Phys. Letters *9* 80 (1971).

[30] J. L. Magee, J. Chem. Phys. 7, 652 (1939 iscussion following a paper by E.P. Wigner, p. 646); *8* 687 (1940).

[31] P. Pechukas, J.C. Light and C. Rankin, J. Chem. Phys. *44* 794 (1966).

[32] R.B. Bernstein M.E. Gersh and A.M. Rulis, *VII ICPEAC, Abstracts of papers*, eds. L.M. Branscomb et al., Vol. 1 (North-Holland Publishing Co., Amsterdam, 1971). p. 34.

[33] P. E. Siska and Y. T. Lee, to be published in J. Chem. Phys.

[34] S. Datz, private communication.

[35] J. D. McDonald, Ph. D. Thesis, Harvard University (1971).

[36] D. Cheung and D.R. Herschbach, private communication.

[37] J. M. Parson, K. Shobotake, Y.T. Lee and S.A. Rice, to be published in J. Chem. Phys.

[38] C. D. Jonah and R.N. Zare, Chem. Phys. Letters 9 65 (1971).

[39] C. D. Jonah, R. N. Zare and Ch. Ottinger, to be published in J. Chem. Phys. (1971).

[40] J. Fricke, B. Kim and W.L. Fite, *VII ICPEAC, Abstracts of Papers,* eds. L.M. Branscomb et al., Vol. 1 (North-Holland Publishing Co., Amsterdam, 1971). , p. 37.

[41] Bernstein's group at Wisconsin; Herm's group at Berkeley and Herschbach's group at Harvard.

[42] A. E. Grosser, private communication.

Physics of Electronic and Atomic Collisions, VII ICPEAC, 1971 – North-Holland (1972)

COLLISIONAL BROADENING OF SPECTRAL LINES

H.VAN REGEMORTER

Observatoire de Paris, 92-Meudon, France

A brief review of the basic principles of line broadening theory is given.
When the impact approximation is valid, the line broadening problem is
simply an application of collision theory. In this case and otherwise, the
study of line profiles is a way to obtain information on long-range, and
even short-range, potentials for binary interactions between an atom and
an electron or a heavy particle.

1. Introduction

In all international conferences on plasma physics or on astrophysics many
papers on line broadening are presented. A few are now presented at the conferences on atomic collisions. The line broadening theory has in fact been
considerably stimulated by the needs of plasma physicists and astrophysicists,
but the same is true for atomic collision theory. Nevertheless, until recently,
there has been some misunderstanding between people working in line braod-
ening theory and people specialized in collision theory. This problem did not
exist in the days of Lorentz and Holtsmark, but originated with the development of plasmaphysics two decades ago. The literature on line broadening
theory is difficult to read for somebody who is interested in individual processes. Emphasis is given to the many body problem. Binary interactions are
reduced to long-range interactions and to fluctuating fields. Complicated
operators take care of the time evolution of the radiating atom perturbed by
all the perturbers surrounding it. The statistical problem, specific to line
broadening theory, hides completely the quantum mechanical problem of the
interaction between the radiating atom and one perturber. At the end, the
statistical problem is simplified anyway, so that it may be solved, and mirac-
ulously the results are given in terms of cross-sections and of scattering amplitudes, or at least in terms of binary interactions.

Of course a line profile cannot give direct information on a given cross-section Q and can only give the average $\langle n v Q \rangle$; but since it always involves the perturbation of an excited state, it offers a way to obtain information on cross-sections involving excited states (elastic cross-sections, inelas.ic cross-sections, etc.). The profile of a spectral line can yield information on the relevant potential curves and coupling schemes in a way similar to that by which one can study the relaxation of excited states by measuring the polarization of radiation following collisional excitation or the fluorescence induced by excitation transfer.

2. The line shape

The theory of pressure broadening involves two distinct problems. The first is the study of the interaction between the radiating atom and one perturber. The second, which is typical to pressure broadening, is the statistical problem of combining the effects of a large number of perturbers.

For a dipolar transition, the absorption coefficient and the spontaneous emission within the line are proportional to:

$$F(\omega) = \lim_{T \to \infty} \frac{1}{2\pi T} \int_0^T dt \, e^{i\omega t} \left| \langle \Psi_f(t) | \mathbf{d} | \Psi_i(t) \rangle \right|^2 . \tag{1}$$

We refer to $F(\omega)$ as the line shape, or the normalized profile

$$\int_{-\infty}^{+\infty} F(\Delta\omega) d(\Delta\omega) = 1 ,$$

where $\Delta\omega = \omega - \omega_0$ is the frequency separation measured from the line center. Ψ_f and Ψ_i are the final and initial total wave functions and $\mathbf{d}$ the electrical dipole of the whole radiating system.

It is usual to write the line shape in function of its Fourier transform

$$\Phi(s) = \int_{-\infty}^{+\infty} e^{-i\Delta\omega s} F(\Delta\omega) d\omega , \tag{2}$$

to calculate $\Phi(s)$ first — because one has to solve the statistical problem — and then to come back to $F(\omega)$:

$$F(\Delta\omega) = \frac{1}{\pi} \mathrm{Re} \int_0^\infty e^{i\Delta\omega s}\, \Phi(s)\, ds \ . \tag{3}$$

The statistical problem can only be solved in very simple cases. In fact it is necessary to assume that the perturbers contribute to the line shape independently, and that for N perturbers in the emitting volume V

$$\Phi(s) = \langle \phi(s) \rangle^N \ , \tag{4}$$

where $\langle\phi(s)\rangle$ is the average autocorrelation function relative to one perturber.

There are situations in which the statistical problem does not arise: those where the perturbation is due only to the nearest perturber — as e.g. far in the wings of the line.

There are situations in which the statistical theorem (4) is verified, for example for fast particles, at low densities, when the moving perturbers act one after another in the time sequence of their closest approach to the radiating atom.

3. Characteristic times

The time intervals which are important in computing $\Phi(s)$ are of the order of $s \cong \Delta\omega^{-1}$. Assuming classical paths for the perturbers with impact parameter ρ, the collision time is $\tau_c = \rho v^{-1}$.

If $s \gg \tau_c$ the interaction is completed in a time which is very short compared to the time of interest. The interaction is a "collision" and the line broadening problem is just an application of collision theory. For each type of interaction, one must have:

$$\Delta\omega \ll v\rho_e^{-1} \tag{5}$$

where ρ_e, given by $Q = \pi\rho_e^2$, defines the effective impact parameter.

If n is the perturber density, $\gamma = n\langle vQ\rangle$ is the probability that the atom experiences a collision. The time between two collisions is then $\tau_i = \gamma^{-1}$, γ being precisely the half-width. When $\gamma^{-1} \gg \rho_e v^{-1}$ each collision acts individually, one after another. It is the same to say that the collision volume ρ_e^3 is very small compared to the volume per perturber n^{-1}. This is the impact approximation for which evidently the statistical problem can be solved using (4). In the wings of the line, condition (5) is not always fulfilled. The results are not given in terms of collision cross sections. For $\Delta\omega$ very large, s can be so small that during s the perturber does not have time to move: this is the so-called quasi-static limit.

The impact approximation is valid for light particles and for short range interactions. For example it is generally valid for neutral H or neutral atoms but not for protons because of the long range nature of the Cr^{-2} potential. The impact approximation is always valid for electrons in the case of the so-called – non hydrogenic – "isolated lines", but not for the electron contribution to the broadening of many hydrogenic lines (because of the Cr^{-2} field).

4. The impact approximation [1–5]

Most of the calculations have been performed by means of the semi-classical approach. The Ψ in eq. (1) is the wave function of the radiating atom perturbed by all the perturbers surrounding it. The total time evolution operator which transforms $\Psi(0)$ into $\Psi(t)$ is a simple product of one-perturber time-evolution operators as soon as theorem (4) is valid, as in the impact approximation. In the interaction picture, one has

$$\Psi_i(t) = \sum_j U_{ij}(t)\Psi_j(0) \exp\left(-iE_j t/\hbar\right),\tag{6}$$

where the time evolution operator U can be written as

$$U = \theta \exp\left(-i/\hbar\right) \int_{-\infty}^{t} V(t')\,dt';\tag{7}$$

θ is a time ordering operator. When the time intervals of interest in integration (1) or (3) are very large compared to ρv^{-1}, the collision time, the upper limit can be replaced by ∞ and U is simply the S-matrix. This is the usual impact approximation in which all the results can be given in terms of cross sections or scattering amplitudes. Use is generally made of second order perturbation theory, but some authors simply drop the operator θ from (7) and use an approximate S-matrix whose advantage is to remain unitary. This procedure is not better than the use of a proper cutoff ρ_1 below which the perturbation theory – or the pure exponential form for S – breaks down.

In fact, in the case of the broadening of isolated lines by electrons, a comparison of semi-classical calculations [6] with recent quantum calculations [7,8] and also with experiments, shows that the semi-classical approach may give good results even when strong collisions are important. This is probably because whereas for strong close collisions ($\rho < \rho_1$, roughly the "Weiskopff" radius for which the exponent in (7) is of the order of unity) the perturbation treatment is wrong for each cross section, the half width of a line is proportional to infinite sums of cross sections $\Sigma_j Q_{ij}$ (the quantum results are extrapolations of close coupling results averaged over resonances).

As is well known, the results for γ are very sensitive to the polarization field — the only one in fact retained in the adiabatic Lindholm picture. At energies just above the threshold of the level it is necessary to take the distortion of the atomic orbitals into account (polarized orbitals) or to use many-channel close-coupling results. Consequently, there are situations in which a line profile can yield supplementary information about the validity of the model or the method used to solve the collision problem.

5. The broadening of hydrogenic lines [9–11]

Whereas for non-hydrogenic isolated lines ($\gamma \ll \Delta E_{ij}$ for levels differing only by L) the quadratic Stark effect due to the protons is very small (the contribution of the protons to the broadening is of the order of 20% of the contribution of the electrons), for hydrogenic lines one faces the difficult problem of a linear Stark effect (the static approximation is used for protons) combined with the electron effects. The theory is not yet very satisfactory but comparison with experiments gives some confidence in the model used, in which the electron induces phase shifts and transitions between Stark sublevels.

But in this case the usual impact approximation is not always valid for the electrons (eq. (5) is not satisfied mainly because ρ_e is large as a consequence of the long-range interaction). At first the impact approximation was corrected in an empirical way [12]. Recently the Anderson and Talman [13] adiabatic result, in which the proper operator $U(t)$ is used instead of the S-matrix, has been generalized to the many-channel case and to the dipole potential Cr^{-2}. This is the so-called "unified theory" of line broadening, in which the statistical approximation (4) is used throughout, and with which one can hope to obtain good agreement with experiments for the whole profile, from the impact regime to the "static" wings [14,15].

In fact, if theorem (4) is true for the two regimes and in between, the problem is to treat the binary interaction correctly: accurate quantum calculations can be performed for one perturber within or beyond the usual impact approximation (16), and it is possible to show that from the quantum standpoint the impact approximation is equivalent to the use of the asymptotic perturber wave function χ instead of the exact value of χ.

In solving (1), scalar products of the form

$$|\langle \chi_{fk'} | \chi_{ik} \rangle|^2$$

appear. When the r of interest in the integrals is much bigger than the range of the potential, use can be made of the asymptotic form: results are given in terms of cross sections. For broadening of hydrogenic lines by electrons, this is not true and correct χ functions must be used. The results are always sensitive to the exact value of the long range potential [17] and seem to be sensitive to close collisions as well [18].

The astrophysicists are not only interested in Lyman α and low Balmer lines, but also in lines involving highly excited states for which the impact approximation is not valid for electrons, particularly at the low densities of interest [11]. They also have to know the pressure broadening of radio frequency transitions between highly excited H states [19].

6. Pressure broadening due to neutral atoms [20,21]

In the Sun the pressure broadening of an isolated line is not due to charged particles but to collisions with neutral hydrogen ($n_H > 10^3 n_e$).

This leads us to the problem of pressure broadening by foreign gases, an old problem for which there is a new interest since there is experimental [22] and theoretical evidence [23] that the long range Van der Waals potential Cr^{-6} is not the important part of the potential in the broadening process. For light perturbers with small polarizabilities such as H and He, the repulsive part of the potential is the more important, as is the case for example in transfer of excitation $J \rightarrow J'$: Therefore, from the width and shift – two pieces of information – or eventually, when the impact approximation is not valid (no Lorentz shape); from the entire profile, one can guess the possibility of obtaining information on the "potential curves" involving the radiating atom – in an excited state – and the perturber. Calculations have been carried out for NaH molecular potentials [24]. From the correlation between the half-width of a line and the elastic scattering between an electron and the perturber (there is an analogous correlation between transfer of excitation

$P_{1/2} - P_{3/2}$ and the processes: perturber +e), one can assume that the interaction A (excited) + B does in fact take place between B and the valence electron of A which behaves as a quasi free particle [25,26]. The exchange repulsive potential has been estimated in this way and the model has recently been applied to the line broadening problem [27]. The study of pressure broadening appears as a technique complementary to other studies of the relaxation of excited states: depolarization of resonance lines, fluorescence after transfer of excitation, level crossings, double resonance ... [28]. But if in a controled laboratory plasma, pressure broadening can be the more important feature of a line, in astrophysical situations, one has always to remember that the line shape can be essentially sensitive to the motions of the emitting region, to the interaction with the radiation field, to the mode of the scattering of the quantum, or to other parameters one wants to deduce from the line profiles also!

References

[1] M.Baranger, in: *Atomic and Molecular Processes,* ed. D.R.Bates (Academic Press, New York, 1962) p. 493.
[2] M.Baranger, Phys. Rev. *111* (1958) 481, 494; ibid. *112* (1958) 855.
[3] L.A.Vainshtein and I.I.Sobelman, Opt. Spektrosk. *6* (1959) 440; [English Transl.: Opt. Spectrosc. *6* (1959) 279.]
[4] S.Sahal-Bréchot, Astron. and Astrophys. *1* (1969) 91.
[5] S.Sahal-Bréchot, Astron. and Astrophys. *2* (1969) 322.
[6] J.Chapelle and S.Sahal-Bréchot, Astron. and Astrophys. *6* (1970) 415.
[7] O.Bely and H.R.Griem, Phys. Rev. *1*A (1970) 97.
[8] K.S.Barnes and G.Peach, J. Phys. B *3* (1970) 350.
[9] H.R.Griem, A.C.Kolb and K.Y.Shen, Phys. Rev. *116* (1959) 4.
[10] P.Kepple and H.R.Griem, Phys. Rev. *173* (1968) 317.
[11] E.Ferguson and H.Schütler, Ann. Phys. (New York) *22* (1963) 351.
[12] N.Lewis, Phys. Rev. *121* (1961) 501.
[13] P.W.Anderson and J.D.Talman, Conf. Broadening of Spectral Lines, Pittsburgh (1955) (unpublished).
[14] E.W.Smith, J.Cooper and C.R.Vidal, Phys. Rev. *185* (1969) 140.
[15] D.Voslamber, Z. Naturforsch. *24a* (1969) 1458.
[16] H.Van Regemorter, Phys. Letters *30A* (1969) 365.
[17] H.R.Griem, Comments on Atomic and Molec. Phys. *2* (1970) 53.
[18] C.R.Vidal, J.Cooper and E.W.Smith, J. Quant. Spectrosc. Radiat. Transfer *10* (1970) 1011.
[19] H.R.Griem, Astrophys. J. *148* (1967) 547.
[20] S.Y.Chen and M.Takeo, Rev. Mod. Phys. *29* (1957) 20.
[21] S.J.Tsao and B.Curnutte, J. Quant. Spectrosc. Radiat. Transfer *2* (1962) 41.
[22] W.R.Hindmarsh, Monthly Not. Roy. Astron. Soc. *119* (1959) 11.

[23] E.Roueff and H.Van Regemorter, Astron. and Astrophys. *1* (1969) 69.
[24] E.L.Lewis, L.F.McNamara and H.H.Michels, Phys. Rev. A *3* (1971) 1939.
[25] V.A.Alekseev and I.I.Sobelman, Zh. Eksp. Teor. Fiz. *49* (1965) 1274; [English Transl.: Soviet Phys. -JETP *22* (1966) 882].
[26] B.M.Smirnov, Zh. Eksp. Teor. Fiz. *51* (1966) 466; [English Trans.: Soviet Phys. -JETP *24* (1967) 314].
[27] E.Roueff, Astron. and Astrophys. *7* (1970) 4.
[28] A.Omont, in: *Physics of the One- and Two-Electron Atoms*, eds. F.Bopp and H.Kleinpoppen (North-Holland Publ. Co., Amsterdam, 1966) p. 777.

APPLICATIONS IN AERONOMY

A.DALGARNO

Harvard College Observatory
and Smithsonian Astrophysical Observatory,
Cambridge, Massachusetts, 02138, USA

A discussion is presented of the application of atomic collision processes to the interpretation of some selected phenomena occurring in the
atmospheres of the planets. The topics are the terrestrial tropical ultraviolet dayglow, the composition of the Jovian ionosphere and some aspects of the chemistry of the stratospheric and tropospheric regions of
the Earth's atmosphere.

1. Introduction

Aeronomy is the study of the physics and chemistry of the atmospheres of
the planets as they respond to the absorption of solar radiation. The atomic
and molecular collision processes through which the incident solar energy is
converted to luminosity, to ionization and to heat are critical elements of
that study.

At an earlier conference, Donahue [1] presented a comprehensive review
of the collision processes that are relevant to the atmosphere of the planet
Earth. A recent series of articles published as a report in the July 1971 issue
of the Transactions of the American Geophysical Union largely achieves the
same purpose and I propose instead to select for discussion a few of the current problems whose resolution involves aspects of the physics of electronic
and atomic collisions. The problems relate to phenomena occurring in the atmospheres of the planets Earth, Mars, Venus and Jupiter.

2. The tropical ultraviolet nightglow

Far ultraviolet emissions were detected by Hicks and Chubb [2] at altitudes of less than 500 km in the equatorial zone using photometers aboard

the OGO 4 polar-orbiting satellite. The emissions appear symmetrically located in positions 12°–15° on both sides of the magnetic dip equator and completely encircle the Earth. A subsequent study by Barth and Schaffner [3] using a scanning spectrometer also on OGO 4 established that the tropical nocturnal airglow consists of the 1304 Å and 1356 Å lines of atomic oxygen. The Lyman–Birge–Hopfield bands of molecular nitrogen are not detected nor are the ultraviolet lines of atomic nitrogen. The ratio of the 1356 Å line to the 1304 Å line varies about an average value of 0.56 and the total intensity of the two lines may approach 2 or 3 kilorayleighs (1 kR = 10^9 photons cm^{-2} s^{-1}). Before these data can be useful in aeronomy, it is necessary to identify the collision mechanisms responsible for the excitations.

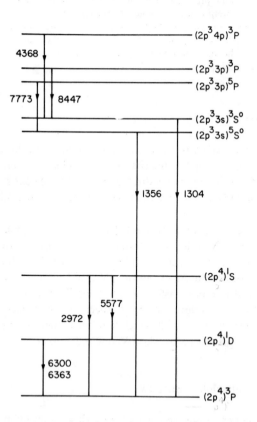

Fig. 1. Energy level diagram for atomic oxygen.

A partial energy level diagram of atomic oxygen is reproduced in fig. 1. The 1304 Å line arises from the allowed resonance transition $(2p^3 3s)^3 S^0 - (2p^4)^3 P$ and the 1356 Å line from the forbidden transition $(2p^3 3s)^5 S^0 - (2p^4)^3 P$. The $(2p^4)^1 S$ level in fig. 1 is the upper level of the oxygen green line at 5577 Å and of an ultraviolet line at 2972 Å and the $(2p^4)^1 D$ level is the upper level of the oxygen red lines at 6300 Å and 6363 Å.

The large energy of at least 9.5 eV involved in producing the excited $^3 S^0$ and $^5 S^0$ states severely restricts the possible sources. The location of the tropical ultraviolet glow appears to coincide with an anomalous enhancement of the electron density [4] and the excitation mechanisms are presumably related either directly or indirectly to the increased ionization.

A direct relationship is obtained by the postulate of electron-ion recombination. The energy requirements rule out dissociative recombinations of NO^+ and O_2^+ ions in their ground states. Metastable $O_2^+(^4\pi_u)$ ions are produced during the day by photoionization and by reactions of metastable $O^+(^2 D)$ ions with O_2 and they can provide a daytime source of the excited oxygen atoms. It seems unlikely that sufficient metastable ions can survive to contribute to the ultraviolet nightglow.

A direct relationship is also obtained by the postulate of radiative recombination [5]:

$$O^+ + e \rightarrow O^* + h\nu . \tag{1}$$

If our theoretical understanding of the process is correct, the suggestion encounters severe quantitative difficulties [3]. We expect a rate coefficient, α, for capture into the $^3 S^0$ and $^5 S^0$ states at atmospheric temperatures of about 5×10^{-13} cm^3 s^{-1}. The peak electron density at a time when the ultraviolet intensity was 3 kR was 3×10^6 cm^{-3} leading to a volume emission rate of 4.5 cm^{-3} s^{-1}. The altitude extent of the emitting region is unlikely to exceed 200 km and the predicted maximum ultraviolet intensity is accordingly 90 R. The observed intensity is sometimes 30 times larger.

The interpretation of the 1356 Å/1304 Å intensity ratio is complicated by the atmospheric absorption of the resonance line to which the atmosphere is optically thick. (The observed variations in the ratio may be a consequence of changes in the 1304 Å scattering efficiency, produced by different atmospheric altitude profiles; they cannot be attributed to the radiative recombination mechanism except by postulating implausibly large changes in the ambient electron temperature.)

If the emissions originate above the optically thick region, the local intensity ratio is 1.1, double that measured. Meier and Prinz [5] suggest that 0.84

is more appropriate to the OGO 4 measurements. The rate predicted from radiative recombination is uncertain but probably it is somewhat larger than
the value, 1.7, given by the ratio of the statistical weights [3].

   Further observational tests can be made. Thus radiative recombination
produces emission continua. Capture to the ground state is associated with a
continuum with its edge near 910 Å [6] and capture to the $^5S^0$ and $^3S^0$ excited states with continua with edges at respectively 2772 Å and 3026 Å
[3,8]. The $^5S^0$ and $^3S^0$ continua fall within the spectral region spanned by
the scanning spectrometer but they were not detected [3]. Their expected
intensities are, however, close to the sensitivity limit of the detector [3].

   Line emission following radiative recombination has apparently been observed by Tinsley [9] who detected a line at 4368 Å following evening twi-
light. The line results from the $(2p^34p)^3P - (2p^33s)^3S^0$ transition of atomic
oxygen. Tinsley derived a rate coefficient of 3.5×10^{-14} cm^3 s^{-1} for populating the ^3P level, a value that is probably in harmony with theory. An explicit calculation would be valuable.

   The rate coefficient derived by Tinsley, taken in conjunction with theory,
implies that a process in addition to radiative recombination is populating the
$^3S^0$ and $^5S^0$ levels. A natural suggestion is dielectronic recombination [7]:

$$O^+ + e \rightarrow O^\dagger \rightarrow O^* + h\nu . \tag{2}$$

Dielectric recombination (inverse autoionization) differs from radiative recombination in that capture occurs into a resonating state. Dielectronic recombination of O^+ ions and electrons was discussed by Bates [10] who concluded that at atmospheric temperatures it would not significantly augment
radiative recombination. In any case, the most likely capture at thermal
velocities is to the $(2s^22p^3(^2D^0)3p)^3D$ state which radiates preferentially to
the $(2s^22p^3(^2D^0)3s)^3D^0$ state emitting a diffuse line at 8232 Å. The $^3D^0$
state decays mostly to the ground state emitting a sharp line at 989 Å and it
is unlikely that dielectronic recombination can enhance the population of the
$^3S^0$ and $^5S^0$ levels.

   Hicks and Chubb [2] have proposed that the excited $^3S^0$ and $^5S^0$ levels
are excited by a flux of soft low energy electrons. The energy must be low in
order that the electrons do not penetrate deeply into the atmosphere where
they could produce molecular nitrogen emissions.

   Detailed calculations of the absorption of electrons in atomic oxygen have
been carried out [11] from which fig. 2 may be constructed. Fig. 2 shows the
1356 Å/1304 Å ratio as a function of the initial energy of an electron absorbed in a weakly ionized gas of atomic oxygen. It takes full account of

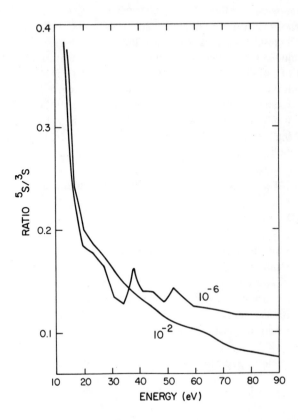

Fig. 2. The ratio of the excitation efficiencies of 1356 A to 1304 A as a function of the initial energy E of an electron absorbed in a weakly ionized gas of atomic oxygen. The curves are labelled by the fractional ionization.

secondary ionizations and of the discrete nature of the energy losses through excitation. The important excitation function data for exciting the $^3S^0$ and $^5S^0$ levels are taken from Stone and Zipf [12].

The calculated 1356 Å/1304 Å intensity ratio tends to a limiting value near 0.12 at high energies, a value that is not inconsistent with the ratio, 0.19, measured by Barth and Schaffner [3] during auroras when the trapping and absorption of the 1304 Å photons is taken into account. At low energies, the ratio necessarily increases to large numbers since the 1356 Å line has a lower threshold energy than does the 1304 Å line. To obtain an intensity ratio not less than 0.56, the electron energies must not exceed 12 eV. To produce 2 kR ultraviolet emission, the flux of such electrons must be 4×10^{10} eV cm^{-2} s^{-1}. The heat deposited into the ambient electron gas by such a flux is 4×10^9 eV cm^{-2} s^{-1}. The resulting substantial rise in the electron temperature is apparently excluded by the electron temperature experiment on OGO 4 [3].

The flux of soft electrons also excites the O^1S and O^1D levels. The resulting excitation rates are 3×10^8 cm^{-2} s^{-1} and 3×10^9 cm^{-2} s^{-1}. The measured spectral range includes the 2972 Å line originating in the O^1S level but its intensity is not yet known. A correlation between the red line emission at 6300 Å and the ultraviolet airglow has been observed (cf. [2]) but such a correlation would be established by the increased electron density with which the ultraviolet glow is associated.

Knudsen [8] has suggested that the process of mutual neutralization,

$$O^+ + O^- \rightarrow O' + O'' , \tag{3}$$

is responsible for the tropical ultraviolet airglow. The cross section has been measured using merging beam techniques and the thermal rate coefficient at 1200°K is $(1.5 \pm 0.5) \times 10^{-7}$ cm^3 s^{-1} [13]. Considerations based upon a Landau–Zener curve-crossing description suggest that reaction channels with end products leading to $O(^5S^0)$ and $O(^3S^0)$ atoms are the most probable and that the resulting quintet-triplet ratio is not inconsistent with the observed ratios [4].

The negative ions may be produced by radiative attachment,

$$e + O \rightarrow O^- + h\nu , \tag{4}$$

with a rate coefficient of about 1.3×10^{-15} cm^3 s^{-1} [15] and destroyed by (3) and by associative detachment,

$$O + O^- \rightarrow O_2 + e , \tag{5}$$

with a rate coefficient of about 1.9×10^{-10} cm^3 s^{-1} [16].

An upper limit to the production of ultraviolet photons is provided by the production of negative ions from (4), with which is associated a continuum emission with its short wavelength edge at 8463 Å. Reaction (4) has long been recognized as a source of nightglow continuum [17].

Nocturnal emission in the spectral range between 6000 Å and 8500 Å has been detected at altitudes above 300 km [18]. In addition to the attachment continuum (4), oxygen lines at 8447 Å and 7773 Å (that are produced preferentially by mutual neutralization (5) according to [14]) and at 6300 Å and

8323 Å appear in this spectral range. The observed intensity is at most 50 rayleighs, which, if the mutual neutralization theory has been correctly described, implies an ultraviolet intensity from altitudes above 300 km that is surely less than 50 rayleighs and probably less than 25 rayleighs. The theoretical analyses of Knudsen [8] and Hanson [19] show that mutual neutralization cannot produce sufficient excited atoms at lower altitudes to bridge the gap between the total ultraviolet intensities and the red emission intensity at high altitudes. Similar arguments can be used to exclude the soft electron hypothesis. Hanson [19] has used the theoretical analysis to argue that as a source of ultraviolet emission mutual neutralization is comparable to but always less efficient than radiative recombination. His argument rests heavily on quantitative estimates of the rates of the various reactions.

The discrepancy between the observed intensities and the predicted intensities resulting from radiative recombination and mutual neutralization persists. If the experimental calibration is not at fault, it seems there must be a mechanism as yet unidentified.

3. The ultraviolet dayglow and Mars and Venus

The Mariner 6 and 7 spacecraft to Mars carried ultraviolet spectrometers. The observed spectra with some identifications [20,21] are reproduced in figs. 3 and 4. The main features are the ultraviolet and Fox–Duffendack–Barker bands of CO_2^+, the Cameron bands of CO and the ultraviolet multiplet at 2972 Å of atomic oxygen. Properly interpreted, these observations can yield a wealth of detailed information about the composition and structure of the atmosphere of Mars.

The CO_2^+ bands can be produced by photoionization of neutral carbon dioxide:

$$hv + CO_2 \rightarrow CO_2^+(\tilde{B}^2\Sigma_u^+) + e \quad \lambda \leqslant 686\,\text{Å} ,$$

$$hv + CO_2 \rightarrow CO_2^+(\tilde{A}^2\pi_u) + e \quad \lambda \leqslant 716\,\text{Å} ,$$

(6)

by impact excitation by fast photoelectrons of energy E:

$$e + CO_2 \rightarrow CO_2^+(\tilde{B}^2\Sigma_u^+) + e + e \quad E \geqslant 18.1\,\text{eV},$$

$$e + CO_2 \rightarrow CO_2^+(\tilde{A}^2\pi_u) + e + e \quad E \geqslant 17.3\,\text{eV},$$

(7)

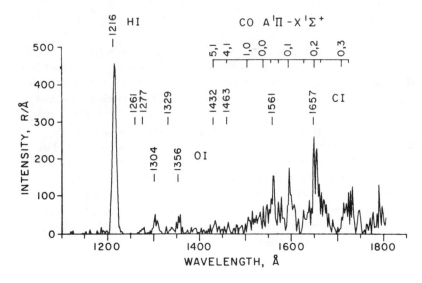

Fig. 3. The ultraviolet spectrum of Mars 1100 Å – 1800 Å (reproduced from [21]).

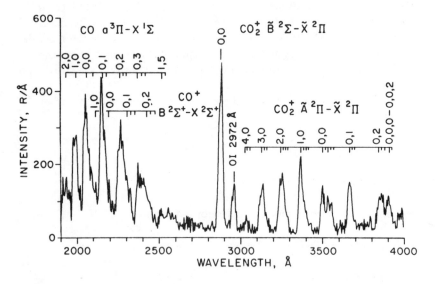

Fig. 4. The ultraviolet spectrum of Mars 1900 Å – 4000 Å (reproduced from [21]).

and by fluorescent scattering of solar radiation by pre-existing CO_2^+ ions:

$$h\nu + CO_2^+(\tilde{X}^2\pi_g) \to CO_2^+(\tilde{B}^2\Sigma_u^+) \qquad \lambda = 2890\,\text{Å}\,,$$
$$h\nu + CO_2^+(\tilde{X}^2\pi_g) \to CO_2^+(\tilde{A}^2\pi_u) \qquad \lambda \leqslant 3507\,\text{Å}\,, \tag{8}$$

[22,23]. Similar processes leading to CO_2^+ ions in the more highly excited $\tilde{C}^2\Sigma_g^+$ state followed by cascading also populate the $\tilde{A}$ and $\tilde{B}$ states.

If the energetic electrons in (7) are produced by photoionization of CO_2, the original solar photons must be at wavelengths shorter than 400 Å. Taking into account the small flux of short wavelength photons and the electron impact cross-section data [24] that show that most of the electron impact ionization events leave the CO_2^+ in its ground state, we may easily demonstrate that (7) is not a major source of excitation.

To analyze (6) properly, we require data on the photoionization cross sections for populating specific vibrational levels of the different excited electronic states. Fixed angle photoelectron spectroscopy has been carried out with helium resonance lines photons at 584 Å [25] and optical measurements of the radiation resulting from the absorption of 584 Å photons by CO_2 show that the emissions are isotropic at that wavelength [26]. In view of its critical importance to the construction of a model for the upper atmosphere of Mars (and of Venus), an extension of the laboratory studies to other wavelengths and other angles is desirable. In the absence of data, it has been assumed [22, 23,27] that the branching ratios are independent of wavelength.

To analyze (8) properly, we require essentially the absorption oscillator strengths from the ground vibrational level $v'' = 0$ of the $\tilde{X}^2\pi_g$ state to the excited vibrational levels v' of the $\tilde{A}^2\pi_u$ and $\tilde{B}^2\Sigma_u^+$ states together with the emission branching ratios for the (v',v'') bands. With certain assumptions [22], the data can be obtained from the lifetime measurements of Hesser [28] and the relative transition probability measurements of Poulizac and Dufay [29]. More extensive laboratory studies would be valuable.

Calculations [22,23] show that both (6) and (8) probably contribute substantially to the CO_2^+ emissions on Mars and Venus, (6) being more important for the B state and (8) for the $\tilde{A}$ state. The processes can be distinguished observationally because the emission resulting from (6) follows the neutral CO_2 altitude distribution and emission resulting from (8) follows the ionized CO_2^+ altitude distribution. Not only do the relative intensities of the two band systems vary with altitude but so do the relative band intensities within a single band system. Thus it was expected that bands originating in $v' = 0$ and 1 of the $A^2\pi_u$ state would become relatively more intense with increasing

altitude than bands originating in $v' = 2$ [22] as is apparently the case [21].
Also, according to Barth et al. [21], the scale height of the $\tilde{A}^2\pi_u - \tilde{X}^2\pi_g$
emission is larger than the scale height of the $\tilde{B}^2\Sigma_u^+ - \tilde{X}^2\pi_g$ emission, as
would be expected from an atmosphere in which the CO_2^+ density decreases
more slowly with increasing altitude than does the CO_2 density. However,
Stewart [27] has reported that the measurements yield a scale height of
24 km for the $\tilde{A}^2\pi_u - \tilde{X}^2\pi_g$ emission and 25 km for the $\tilde{B}^2\Sigma_u^+ - \tilde{X}^2\pi_g$ emission. There are considerable uncertainties in these scale heights but they are
clearly much smaller than the 45 km scale height of the measured electron
density [30]. Thus the ultraviolet emission intensities and scale heights imply
that CO_2^+ is not the major ion on Mars. A plausible alternative is O_2^+ [27,31],
the O_2^+ ions being produced from the CO_2^+ ions by collisions of CO_2^+ with
atomic or molecular oxygen in the reactions [32]

$$CO_2^+ + O_2 \rightarrow O_2^+ + CO_2 , \tag{9}$$

$$CO_2^+ + O \rightarrow O_2^+ + CO , \tag{10}$$

$$CO_2^+ + O \rightarrow O^+ + CO_2 ,$$

$$O^+ + CO_2 \rightarrow O_2^+ + CO . \tag{11}$$

(These reactions severely limit the possible abundance of CO_2^+ in the terrestrial
atmosphere.) There is no direct evidence that atomic and molecular oxygen
are present in sufficient concentrations to achieve the conversion of a substantial fraction of the CO_2^+ ions to O_2^+.

The Mariner observations of the Cameron bands of CO are of considerable
interest. The Cameron bands arise from the forbidden $(a^3\pi - X^1\Sigma)$ transition
and they are much more intense than the fourth positive band system of CO
that arises from the allowed $(A^1\pi - X^1\Sigma)$ transition. The Cameron bands cannot be produced on Mars by fluorescent scattering of solar radiation or by
photoelectron impact. Apart from the problem of producing sufficient intensity without violating the observations of the fourth positive system, the observed vibrational distribution corresponds to neither process [33]. It seems
that the bands must originate with CO_2.

The possible mechanisms are dissociative recombination,

$$CO_2^+ + e \rightarrow CO + O , \tag{12}$$

electron impact dissociation,

$$CO_2 + e \rightarrow CO + O + e \qquad E \geqslant 11.5 \, eV, \tag{13}$$

and photodissociation,

$$CO_2 + h\nu \rightarrow CO + O \qquad \lambda \leqslant 1082 \, \text{Å}. \tag{14}$$

The vibrational distributions resulting from (12) and (14) are unknown whilst that resulting from (13) has recently been measured for 20 eV electrons [21] and is very like the Mars distribution. McConnell and McElroy [31] have used the measured cross-sections for production of the $a^3\pi$ metastable molecules to predict the production rate in the Martian atmosphere. They computed a limb intensity of about 250 kR, a computation that implies a very high efficiency for converting solar photons into Martian photons, since electrons with sufficient energy to excite the $a^3\pi$ level of CO in an atmosphere of CO_2 require solar photons with wavelengths shorter than 490 Å.

The measured intensity is nearly 600 kR [21] and it seems that (12) and (14) must also contribute strongly. According to Stewart [27], it is difficult to produce the observed intensity if the major ion is not CO_2^+, but there are several sources of uncertainty in the various arguments, not least of which are the atomic and molecular data.

The large flux in the Cameron bands demonstrates the existence of a large supply of oxygen atoms and of carbon monoxide and raises in a more severe form the question of the subsequent removal mechanisms. The large flux with its implication of a high efficiency for conversion of short wavelength solar radiation into luminosity must also have important consequences on the thermal structure of the planet.

Many other issues remain concerning the interpretation and implications of the Mariner data. I shall discuss briefly that involving the determination of nitrogen abundance in the atmosphere. The fractional abundance of nitrogen relative to carbon is a critical parameter in studies of the evolution of the planet.

The presence of nitrogen in the atmosphere of the planet Earth would be easily established by a remote observer by the detection of the various molecular band emissions. None of these appears in the Mariner spectra. Many may be obscured by the strong CO_2^+ and CO emissions. Detailed calculations of the effects of photoelectron impact [34] show that of the band systems the Vegard–Kaplan and first negative systems are perhaps the best means of detection of nitrogen but neither is promising.

Lines of atomic nitrogen may provide a more sensitive indication [35]. Molecular nitrogen is ionized according to

$$N_2 + h\nu \to N_2^+ + e , \tag{15}$$

$$N_2 + h\nu \to N + N^+ + e , \tag{16}$$

and it recombines by dissociative recombination,

$$N_2^+ + e \to N + N , \tag{17}$$

or is transformed to CO_2^+ by charge transfer,

$$N_2^+ + CO_2 \to N_2 + CO_2^+ , \tag{18}$$

$$N^+ + CO_2 \to N + CO_2^+$$

$$\to NO^+ + CO . \tag{19}$$

The atomic nitrogen is not readily removed. With sufficient O_2, it can form NO through

$$N + O_2 \to NO + O , \tag{20}$$

after which

$$N + NO \to N_2 + O \tag{21}$$

may occur. This is a slow process and high in the atmosphere where (17) proceeds more rapidly than (18), nitrogen must be almost entirely in the atomic form. The resonance lines of atomic nitrogen near 1200 Å are not apparent in the Mariner spectra.

4. The ionosphere of Jupiter

The atmosphere of Jupiter consists largely of molecular hydrogen with lesser amounts of methane and ammonia and possibly hydrogen sulphide. Helium has not been detected but may be present; its abundance relative to hydrogen is an important cosmogonic parameter. There is some dissociation of H_2 and of CH_4 and NH_3, and atomic hydrogen is the major constituent high in the atmosphere. Model atmospheres have been constructed by Trafton [36], Gross and Rasool [37], Hunten [38], Prinn [39] and Shimizu [40].

The models of the ionosphere are based on electron production by photo-ionization:

$$hv + H \rightarrow H^+ + e ,$$

$$hv + H_2 \rightarrow H_2^+ + e ,$$

$$hv + H_2 \rightarrow H + H^+ + e , \tag{22}$$

$$hv + He \rightarrow He^+ + e .$$

Despite the simplicity of the constituents, the subsequent chemistry is uncertain. The H_2^+ will usually be removed rapidly by the fast reaction

$$H_2^+ + H_2 \rightarrow H_3^+ + H , \tag{23}$$

which has a rate coefficient of 2×10^{-9} cm^3 s^{-1} [41].
At great heights,

$$H_2^+ + H \rightarrow H_2 + H^+ \tag{24}$$

may play a role. Dissociative recombination

$$H_2^+ + e \rightarrow H + H \tag{25}$$

is slow with a rate coefficient that is probably less than 10^{-9} cm^3 s^{-1}, and it can be neglected on Jupiter. The rate coefficient for dissociative recombination of H_3^+,

$$H_3^+ + e \rightarrow H_2 + H , \tag{26}$$

is unknown. A value of 10^{-8} cm^3 s^{-1} is usually adopted.
The He$^+$ ions can be removed only slowly by radiative recombination

$$He^+ + e \rightarrow He + hv . \tag{27}$$

The rate coefficient is about 6×10^{-12} cm^3 s^{-1} at 150K. In the case of capture into the ground state of helium, the emitted photon can ionize H, H_2 and He. When capture occurs into the excited states, the discrete emission photons can ionize H and H_2. However, the helium ions are more probably removed by chemical reactions, such as the radiative charge transfer processes

$$He^+ + H \rightarrow He + H^+ + h\nu \; , \tag{28a}$$

$$He^+ + H \rightarrow HeH^+ + h\nu \; . \tag{28b}$$

The calculated rate coefficient [42] at 150K is 0.7×10^{-15} cm^3 s^{-1} for (28a) and 1.2×10^{-15} cm^3 s^{-1} for (28b). Charge transfer without radiation,

$$He^+ + H \rightarrow He + H^+ \; , \tag{29}$$

is presumably very slow.

Analogous reactions may occur in collisions with H_2:

$$He^+ + H_2 \rightarrow He + H_2^+ + h\nu \; , \tag{30}$$

$$He^+ + H_2 \rightarrow HeH_2^+ + h\nu \; , \tag{31}$$

$$He^+ + H_2 \rightarrow He + H_2^+ \; , \tag{32}$$

$$He^+ + H_2 \rightarrow HeH^+ + H \; . \tag{33}$$

The sum of the rate coefficients for (32) and (33) is smaller than 10^{-13} cm^3 s^{-1} [43]. They may be larger if the molecular hydrogen in the Jupiter atmosphere is vibrationally excited. The rate coefficients for (30) and (31) are unknown.

The HeH$^+$ ions and HeH$_2^+$ ions produced by (29), (31) and (33) presumably undergo dissociative recombinations but again the rates are unknown and may be slow.

The H$^+$ ions apparently do not react with He or H_2. They can recombine radiatively:

$$H^+ + e \rightarrow H + h\nu \; , \tag{34}$$

but the process is slow. For an electron density of 5×10^5 cm^{-3}, the mean recombination time is four days. A more probable fate is downward diffusion followed by the three-body reaction

$$H^+ + H_2 + H_2 \rightarrow H_3^+ + H_2 \; , \tag{35}$$

which has a rate coefficient of about 3×10^{-29} cm^6 s^{-1} [44]. With Hunten's model [38], (35) is more rapid than (34) at altitudes below 250 km. A similar reaction may be significant in determining the He$^+$ ion balance.

The presence of a small amount of some minor constituent such as atomic oxygen could drastically modify this conventional description of the iono-sphere. If atomic oxygen were present at 250 km with a fractional abundance exceeding 10^{-7}, a more rapid removal sequence would be:

$$H^+ + O \rightarrow H + O^+ , \tag{36}$$

followed by

$$O^+ + H_2 \rightarrow OH^+ + H , \tag{37}$$

$$OH^+ + e \rightarrow O + H . \tag{38}$$

The conventional picture may also require modification of the ionization source function. In the polar cap regions of the Earth, energy deposition into the ionosphere from the solar wind and from the extreme ultraviolet are com-parable, but it is expected that on Jupiter the solar wind contribution is dominant [45]. The ultraviolet ionizing flux at Jupiter is about 0.1 erg cm^{-2} s^{-1} over the planet. The solar wind energy deposited on the polar cap, which occupies an area of a few per cent of Jupiter, could be as large as 100 erg cm^{-2} s^{-1}.

5. Trophospheric and stratospheric photochemistry

For my final topic, I shall return to Earth and mention briefly some as-pects of the chemistry of the troposphere and stratosphere. Large amounts of carbon monoxide are continuously deposited into the atmosphere and yet the ambient concentration is at worst increasing only slowly. A mean resi-dence time of 0.1 year [46] or 0.2 year [47] are the most recent estimates. A natural sink must exist. There is evidence to suggest that certain soil con-stituents may provide a major sink [48] and the atmosphere may provide another [49]. As Bates and Witherspoon [50] pointed out, the reaction

$$CO + OH \rightarrow CO_2 + H \tag{39}$$

removes carbon monoxide in the stratosphere. The hydroxyl radical is pro-duced in the stratosphere by

$$O_3 + H \rightarrow OH + O_2 . \tag{40}$$

Levy [49] has noted that ozone is present near the ground in a fractional concentration that averages 5×10^{-8} at a summer latitude of $34°$ and he has suggested the chain

$$O_3 + h\nu \rightarrow O(^1D) + O_2 , \tag{41}$$

$$O(^1D) + H_2O \rightarrow OH + OH , \tag{42}$$

$$OH + CO \rightarrow H + CO_2 . \tag{43}$$

The $O(^1D)$ atoms are rapidly quenched in collisions with the major constituents N_2 and O_2, but the ground state $O(^3P)$ atoms then rapidly form O_3 which produces $O(^1D)$ again. The ozone photolysis is also a large source of metastable $O_2(a^1\Delta_g)$ molecules.

When the naturally occurring nitrogen oxides and methane are included in the chemistry, more complicated molecules such as formaldehyde, methylperoxyl radicals [49] and nitric and nitrous acids [51] can be created and may exist in the atmosphere in substantial concentrations. The important effects of the nitrogen oxides on the normal ozone balance have been stressed by Crutzen [52]. A large natural source of stratospheric nitric oxide is provided by [53]

$$O(^1D) + N_2O \rightarrow NO + NO . \tag{44}$$

The ozone balance is critical to life on this planet. Nitrogen oxides are pollutants in automobile and power plant exhausts [54] and they play a significant role in photochemical smog. Nitric oxide is a component of jet aircraft exhausts and the potential consequences on the ozone balance of the nitric oxide injected into the stratosphere by supersonic transport planes have been explored recently by Johnston [55]. Thus the reaction

$$NO + O_3 \rightarrow NO_2 + O_2 \tag{45}$$

is a natural sink for nitric oxide that also destroys ozone. The injection of water vapour also disturbs the ozone equilibrium, not only through reactions such as (42), but because water vapour affects the nitrogen oxide chemistry.

The problems presented by atmospheric contamination are extremely complicated in their solutions and partial analyses tend to be misleading. An extensive quantitative understanding of simple atomic collision processes is an essential element of the much more comprehensive approach that is required if progress is to be assured.

References

[1] T.M.Donahue, V ICPEAC, Invited Papers, ed. L.M.Branscomb (JILA, Boulder, Colorado, 1968) p. 32.
[2] G.T.Hicks and T.A.Chubb, J. Geophys. Res. 75 (1970) 6233.
[3] C.A.Barth and S.Schaffner, J. Geophys. Res. 75 (1970) 4299.
[4] cf. L.Thomas, J. Atmos. Terrest. Phys. 30 (1968) 1631.
[5] R.R.Meier and D.K.Prinz, J. Geophys. Res. 76 (1971) 4608.
[6] W.B.Hanson, J. Geophys. Res. 74 (1969) 3720.
[7] D.R.Bates and A.Dalgarno, in: Atomic and Molecular Processes, ed. D.R.Bates (Academic Press, London, 1962) p. 245.
[8] W.C.Knudsen, J.Geophys. Res. 75 (1970) 3862.
[9] B.A.Tinsley, J. Geophys. Res. 75 (1970) 3932.
[10] D.R.Bates, Planet. Space Sci. 9 (1962) 77.
[11] A.Dalgarno and G.Lejeune, Planet. Space Sci. (1971) in press.
[12] E.J.Stone and E.C.Zipf, Phys. Rev. Letters A 4 (1971) 610.
[13] R.E.Olson, J.R.Peterson and J.Moseley, J. Chem. Phys. 53 (1970) 3391.
[14] R.E.Olson, J.R.Peterson and J.Moseley, J. Geophys. Res. 76 (1971) 2516.
[15] L.M.Branscomb, D.S.Burch, S.Smith and S.Geltman, Phys. Rev. 111 (1958) 504.
[16] F.C.Fehsenfeld, A.L.Schmeltekopf, H.I.Schiff and E.E.Ferguson, Planet. Space Sci. 15 (1967) 373.
[17] cf. A.Dalgarno, Ann. Geophys. 14 (1958) 241.
[18] J.E.Sparrow, E.P.Ney, G.B.Burnett and J.W.Stoddart, J. Geophys. Res. 75 (1970) 5475.
[19] W.B.Hanson, J. Geophys. Res. 75 (1970) 4343.
[20] C.A.Barth, W.G.Fastie, C.W.Hord, J.B.Pearce, K.K.Kelly, A.I.Stewart, G.E.Thomas, G.P.Anderson and O.F.Raper, Science 165 (1969) 1004.
[21] C.A.Barth, C.W.Hord, J.B.Pearce, K.K.Kelly, G.P.Anderson and A.I.Stewart, J. Geophys. Res. 76 (1971) 2213.
[22] A.Dalgarno and T.C.Degges, in: Planetary Atmospheres, I.A.U. Symposium No. 40, eds. C.Sagan, T.C.Owen and H.J.Smith (Springer-Verlag, New York, 1971) p. 337.
[23] A.Dalgarno, T.C.Degges and A.I.Stewart, Science 167 (1970) 1490.
[24] H.Nishimura, J. Phys. Soc. Jap. 21 (1966) 564;
J.W.McConkey, D.J.Burns and J.M.Woolsey, J. Phys. B. 1 (1968) 71;
J.M.Ajello, J. Chem. Phys. (1971) 55 (1971) 3169.
[25] D.W.Turner and D.P.May, J. Chem. Phys. 46 (1967) 1156.
R.Spohr and E.von Puttkamer, Z. Naturforsch. 22a (1967) 705;
J.L.Bahr, A.J.Blake, J.H.Carver and V.Kumar, J. Quant. Spectrosc. Radiat. Transfer 9 (1969) 1359.
[26] T.S.Wauchop and H.P.Broida, J. Geophys. Res. 76 (1971) 21.
[27] A.I.Stewart, J. Geophys. Res. 76 (1971) in press.
[28] J.E.Hesser, J. Chem. Phys. 48 (1968) 2518.
[29] M.C.Poulizac and M.Dufay, Astrophys. Letters 1 (1967) 17.
[30] G.Fjeldbo, A.Kliore and B.Seidel, Radio Sci. 5 (1970) 381.
[31] J.C.McConnell and M.B.McElroy, J. Geophys. Res. 75 (1970) 4290;
M.B.McElroy and J.C.McConnell, J. Geophys. Res. 76 (1971) 6674.
[32] F.C.Fehsenfeld, D.B.Dunkin and E.E.Ferguson, Planet. Space Sci. 18 (1970) 1267.

[33] C.A.Barth, Appl. Opt. 8 (1969) 1295.
[34] A.Dalgarno and M.B.McElroy, Science 170 (1970) 167.
[35] L.E.Goad, private communication (1971).
[36] L.M.Trafton, Astrophys. J. 147 (1967) 765.
[37] S.H.Gross and S.I.Rasool, Icarus 3 (1964) 311.
[38] D.M.Hunten, J. Atmos. Sci. 26 (1969) 826.
[39] R.G.Prinn, Icarus 13 (1970) 424.
[40] M.Shimizu, Icarus 14 (1971) 273.
[41] R.H.Neynaber and S.M.Trujillo, Phys. Rev. 167 (1968) 63.
[42] K.M.Sando, J.Cohen and A.Dalgarno, VII ICPEAC, Abstracts of Papers, Vol. 2, eds.
     L.M.Branscomb et al. (North-Holland Publ. Co., Amsterdam, 1971) p. 973.
[43] F.C.Fehsenfeld, A.L.Schmeltekopf, P.D.Goldan, H.I.Schiff and E.E.Ferguson, J.
     Chem. Phys. 44 (1969) 4087.
[44] T.M.Miller, J.T.Moseley, D.W.Martin and E.W.McDaniel, Phys. Rev. 173 (1968) 115.
[45] cf. N.M.Brice and G.A.Ioannadis, Icarus 13 (1970) 173.
[46] B.Weinstock, Science 166 (1969) 224.
[47] B.Dimitriades and M.Whismon, Environ. Sci. Technol. 5 (1971) 219.
[48] L.S.Jaffe, J. Air. Pollut. Contr. 18 (1968) 534;
     R.E.Inman, R.B.Ingersoll and E.A.Levy, Science 172 (1971) 1229.
[49] H.Levy II, Science 173 (1971) 141.
[50] D.R.Bates and A.E.Witherspoon, Monthly Not. Roy. Astron. Soc. 112 (1952) 101.
[51] M.Nicolet, Ann. Geophys. 26 (1970) 531.
[52] P.J.Crutzen, J. Geophys. Res. 76 (1971) in press.
[53] M.B.McElroy and J.C.McConnell, J. Atmos. Sci. 28 (1971) 1095.
[54] A.C.Stern, Air Pollution (Academic Press, New York, 1968).
[55] H.F.Johnston, Science 173 (1971) 517.

Physics of Electronic and Atomic Collisions, VII ICPEAC, 1971 — North-Holland (1972)

DEVELOPMENT OF COMPUTING METHODS
WITH PARTICULAR EMPHASIS ON
MOLECULAR STRUCTURE CALCULATIONS

Enrico CLEMENTI

IBM Research Laboratory,
San Jose, California, 95114, USA

The field of quantum chemical computations is arbitrarily sub-divided into computations concerning atoms, small molecules, large molecules and macromolecules. It has been shown that low-Z atomic computations for correlated wave functions can be obtained for systems containing up to 10 electrons. For systems requiring full correlation of more than 10 electrons, present techniques are not suited. However, many problems do require much less than full correlation.

For macromolecules, we have restricted the analysis to chain molecules. Two problems are considered. The first is the statistical determination of possible conformations. The second is the determination of electronic band structures. After having indicated that formal solution, computer programs and examples are already available, it is stressed that there is a need to use proper basis sets in order to avoid improper descriptions of the electronic energy bands in polymers.

1. Introduction

The task to cover the ground implied by the above assigned title, can be mastered in a review of limited length only but omitting a substantial number of contributions and by attempting to highlight only the main trends. To partially amend for the deficiencies of such a limited exposition, I refer to two excellent bibliographies for ab initio computations. The oldest is the one by M.Krauss [1], and the most recent is the work by W.G.Richards, T.E.H. Walker and R.K.Hinkley [2].

The main goal in the field of molecular computation is fairly well understood by many of the workers in the field: to build a theoretical analytical and computational framework such that one can, as routinely as possible, accurately simulate and, therefore, (likely) understand and predict the structure of molecules. Actually, this is only the first part of the goal, since there is little reason, per se, to spend time for the accurate prediction of molecular structures. The justification is that the individual and collective properties of molecules are dependent on the molecular structure.

Arbitrarily, I shall divide the molecules into four groups: atoms, small molecules (up to 15–20 electrons), large molecules (20–200 electrons) and macromolecules. In the following, I shall make a few comments on each of the above groups, but I shall emphasize mainly the computations for large molecules and macromolecules, since here likely lies the present frontier in the computations of molecular structures.

2. Atomic computations

Let us distinguish between low-Z atoms and high-Z atoms: this distinction is equivalent to classifying atoms by their dominant coupling scheme (L-S or J-J) or by recognizing the need of introducing relativistic corrections. If we take the standard non-relativistic Hartree–Fock model, we know that we are accepting two strong approximations: one is the neglect of the many-body correction (correlation-energy correction); the other is the neglect of relativistic effects (relativistic correction). Whereas in the first row of atoms (Li or Ne) the relativistic correction is smaller than the correlation correction, the opposite is true in the second-row atoms (the turning point is around $Z = 12$) [3]. However, if we are not interested in variations of the inner-shell energy (like inner-shell excitation processes or collisions with very high energy), then we can neglect the relativistic corrections up to $Z \approx 30$. That is to say, that the non-relativistic description of the electrons (excluding the innermost shell) is not a too inaccurate simulation of the true atom. By the time $Z \approx 50$, not only the innermost shell but also the 2s and 2p shells are drastically effected by the relativistic correction. For $Z \approx 80$ and higher values of Z, the non-relativistic description is hopelessly inadequate even on a qualitative ground. Whereas atomic computations of relativistic Hartree–Fock functions for closed shells have been available for some time, only very recently relativistic Hartree–Fock computations for open shells are being pursued [4].

For low-Z atoms non-relativistic Hartree–Fock computations are available [5], or can be obtained with trivial effort. The same can be stated for partially correlated wave functions. Much effort has been devoted to obtain highly correlated functions. The work of Nesbet [6] is worth considering in this context. His formulation of the correlation correction to the Hartree–Fock

Table 1

Correlation energies (in a.u.) for $O(^3P)$, computed by Nesbet [7]. The experimental value is -0.2539 a.u.

Σe_i	$-0.003\ 849$	
Σe_{ij}	$-0.040\ 178$	for KK
Σe_{ij}	$-0.018\ 795$	for KL
Σe_{ij}	$-0.187\ 306$	for LL
Total	$-0.250\ 127$	

Table 2

First ionization potentials (in a.u.) for the second-row elements. Comparison of the data computed by Nesbet [8], using the pair-approximation, and Clementi [9], using the S.C.F. Hartree−Fock approximation, with experimental values.

	S.C.F. [9]	Nesbet [7]	Exptl. [8]
$Na(^2S)$	0.1818	0.1896	0.1888
$Mg(^1S)$	0.2403	0.2870	0.2809
$Al(^2P)$	0.2022	0.2353	0.2199
$Si(^3P)$	0.2814	0.3232	0.2995
$P(^4S)$	0.3691	0.4208	0.4042
$S(^3P)$	0.3318	0.4063	0.3806
$Cl(^2P)$	0.4334	0.5124	0.4781
$Ar(^1S)$	0.5428	0.6300	0.5790

functions has been implemented by a computer program and a sufficient number of atoms have been studied so that one can attempt few conclusions. In table 1, Nesbet's results (for the electron-pair approximation limit to his Bethe−Goldstone formalism [6]) are reported for the oxygen atom in the ^3P state: the agreement with experimental data is excellent. In table 2, Nesbet's data for the second period are reported: in this table, the first ionization potential is computed as the energy difference between the ground state for the atom and the ground state of the corresponding ion [8]. As one can see from table 2, whereas the computed ionization potentials are in good agreement with experimental data for the atoms at the beginning of the period, the agreement decreases rapidly by increasing Z, leading to rather poor results for the ionization potential of the argon atom. Indeed, the computed ionization potentials are not much better than those one can obtain, most trivially, by using the Hartree−Fock method [9]. These results of Nesbet provide a computational demonstration that the pair approximation does not sufficiently describe the many-body effects, for the case of more than 6 to 7 pairs of electrosn in an atom. This result was expected on the basis of *Hartree–Fock computations alone and comparison with experiments* (more accurately, the breakdown of the pair approximation in an atom was expected for the cases of 9 or more electron-pairs) [10]. It is noted that this comment could be made for Sinanoğlu's pair-theory [11] if actual and accurate computations for nontrivial cases would have been performed by Sinanoğlu and co-workers. It is noted, in addition, that the computational scheme proposed by Nesbet, is very expensive in terms of machine time (of the order of several dozen of hours on an IBM 360/91 for a full computation of an atom with more than 8 electrons). The conclusions here are rather obvious: if an atomic problem (involving low-Z atoms) can be expected to involve no more than about 10 electrons (or less, out of a total of about 30 or less), then present computing hardware and computer programs are available to solve the problem with accuracy. For computations requiring *full* correlation treatment for more than 10 electrons, the present situation is till rather   hopeless. On the other hand, there are relatively few examples in atomic physics, where one *has* to take into exact account more than 10 electrons, since, often the atomic shells of an atom can be treated with different degrees of accuracy. An example of what can be done by a selective strategy, rather than by a frontal assault to the correlation correction problem, can be found in Bagus et al. [12], in the determination of the term splitting for the 6, 7 and 8 electron isoelectronic sequence. These authors did use only a limited amount of configurations (less than 10) and the results are in good agreement with experimental data. Another example is given by the work of Weiss [13] in explaining anamalous behavior of the Rydberg series in the aluminum atom.

3. Small molecules

These have been defined as those molecules containing up to 20 electrons. The definition is clearly only indicative, since not only the number of electrons, but also the number of nuclei should be considered.

As for the case of atoms, highly correlated wave functions for 2- to 4-electron systems can be obtained nearly in a routine fashion; for systems up to 10 electrons 70% to 80% of the correlation can also be obtained easily. For more electrons the situation becomes rapidly complicated by the *size* of the computation. For molecules we resort in general to some form of configuration interaction: namely, the wave function is expanded in terms of many

Slater determinants in addition to the Hartree—Fock determinant. The electronic configurations added to the Hartree—Fock configuration represents single, double, and multiple electronic replacement. The convergency of the series is rather slow, and today 500 to 1000 configurations are added routinely.

The methods used are clearly not suitable for extension to larger molecules, since the number of required configurations would easily go into many thousands. In addition, with such large configurations, it is difficult to analyze carefully the results and this fact tends to oppose that type of analysis that might lead to more proper selections of configurations (i.e., shorter but more efficient expansions).

As for the case of atoms, however, much can be done with *not fully correlated functions* or even simply with Hartree—Fock functions. For example, recently Mayer [14] has computed the vertical ionization potential for H_2O using the Pseudo-Natural-Orbital technique proposed by Edmiston and Krauss [15]. His data, reported in table 3, are in excellent agreement with experimental data.

However, very reasonable data for the ionization potential can be obtained in the Hartree—Fock approximation, as indicated in table 4, for the CH_4 molecule [16,17]. Equivalently, the water-water study by Dierksen [18] or the formic acid dimer study by Clementi and Von Niessen [19] are indication that much can be done with the Hartree—Fock model, if one chooses carefully the problem.

Table 3

Ionization potentials and energies for H_2O. The values computed by Meyer [14] using the pseudo natural orbital technique are compared with experimental data [16].

Energy separated atoms	−76.1101	} Experimental
Energy of molecule	−76.4314	(a.u.)
S.C.F. energy	−76.0627	} Computed
Independent pair	−76.4208	

Vertical ionization potentials (eV)

	Exptl.	P.N.O.-CI
$1a_1$	19.835	19.830
$2a_1$	1.183	1.185
$3a_1$	0.541	0.535
$1b_1$	0.464	0.454
$1b_2$	0.682	0.688

Table 4
Vertical ionization potentials for CH_4 (in eV). The Hartree–Fock values computed by
Clementi and Popkie [16] are compared with experimental data.

Case	Exptl.	Computed
CH_4	0.0	0.0
$CH_4^+(\phi_3)$	13.77 ± 0.05	13.64
$CH_4^+(\phi_2)$	23.1	24.22
$CH_4^+(\phi_1)$	290.7 ± 0.3	290.88
$CH_4^{+2}(\phi_3^2)$	–	38.80
$CH_4^{+2}(\phi_3\phi_4)_{tripl.}$	–	36.32
$CH_4^{+2}(\phi_3\phi_4)_{singl.}$	–	39.11

4. Large molecules

With the exception of many gaseous species, large molecules and macromolecules encompass the entire matter. A solid, crystalline or amorphous, or
liquid (or a solution) can be treated as a single molecular system [20] .

The basic limitation that we encounter in computing wave functions for
large molecules is that we have to perform a most complex computation.
Today, we describe the molecular orbital with an expansion into basis sets of
analytical functions (LCAO-MO-SCF). This way, matrix elements between
orbitals are transformed into matrix elements between basis sets. Each of such
matrix elements is a multi-dimensional integral of various degrees of complexity. The number of integrals to be computed in a Hartree–Fock computation of an N-electrons system is proportional to $(KN)^4$, where K is a number
between 2 and 5 (in general). It is therefore clear that we have to compute
millions or billions of integrals in a large molecule. This brings about two
basic problems, a) the computer time for the computation of the integrals; b)
the computer storage for the integrals. A concomitant problem is the retrieval
of the integrals from their storage location (this, too, takes time). Faced with
this problem, a number of solutions have been attempted. The most obvious
one is to take $K = 1$ and, when this is not enough, to neglect many of the
electrons in the system so that an N-electron system is treated as an N'-elec-
tron system with $N' \ll N$.

Often, a third drastic step is taken and, not only one reduces the problem
from $(KN)^4$ to $(N')^4$, but most of the $(N')^4$ integrals are approximated rather

than accurately computed. The above simplifications often bring the problem to a tractable one (but its significance is open to questions).

On the other hand, the reduction from $(KN)^4$ to $(N')^4$ is deceiving, since there are many molecular systems where $(N')^4$ is still too large a number. Therefore, taking a long-range point of view, we have attempted for the past several years to attack the problem in a frontal way, and to avoid the use of semi-empirical methods.

The following assumptions have been made: 1) the cost per operation in computers will decrease drastically, so that the problem can be solved from an economic point of view; 2) the cost of peripheral storage devices will decrease and the retrieval process will be faster; 3) the speed of operation in computers will increase; 4) by attacking the problem directly, we shall learn how to solve it (sooner or later) because both the computer program organization and the numerical analysis can be continuously improved; 5) the problem is not $(KN)^4$ as often stated but rather $\Sigma_i(K_iN_i)^4$; 6) the correlation problem can be solved with statistical methods; so, we can concentrate our effort in solving Hartree—Fock functions for the large molecules.

The *first three assumptions* are self-evident. As proof of the *fourth assumption,* we would like to notice that a number of techniques so far introduced (like the use of "contracted" functions [21], the use of "move", "add", "subtract", and "merge" techniques [22], the use of the "adjoint functions" [23]) have allowed performance of computations of such dimensions that would have been simply impossible, if one would have relied only on hardware improvements. In addition, in the last few years, communication media specifically designed for exchange of programs and programming algorithms have appeared [24], which allow for better exchange and might avoid duplication of efforts.

The *fifth assumption* is that for sufficiently large molecules, the number of non-zero integrals is not $(KN)^4$ but $\Sigma_i(K_iN_i)^4$ where $\Sigma_iK_iN_i < KN$. This is rather obvious, since when the physical molecular dimension exceeds the dimension of the space covered by a given basis, then a number of integrals will be zero. In practice, this is the case for non-overlapping functions. It might be therefore very important to find what is the size for molecules where the $(KN)^4$ dependency decreases to $\Sigma_i(K_iN_i)^4$. By numerical experimentation, we can state that the molecular system of the dimension of benzene is still well within the $(KN)^4$ dependency, and that a molecular system of the dimension of three connected benzene rings is at the beginning of the $\Sigma_i(K_iN_i)^4$ dependency.

For example, we have recently computed [25] with equivalent basis sets the ground state of carbazol $(C_{12}NH_9)$ and for 2:4:7 tri-nitro-fluorene

($C_{13}N_3O_7H_5$). The first computation requires 42.98×10^6 two-electrons integrals, whereas the second computation requires 280.64×10^6 integrals. Both computations were done with the same numerical accuracy; in view of the ratio of the number of integrals to be computed in the two molecules, the computation for the 2:4:7 tri-nitro-fluorene should have required a computational time equal to the computational time used for carbazole times 6.53. On the other hand, in the larger molecule we are already outside the $(KN)^4$ dependency and in the $\Sigma_i(K_iN_i)^4$ dependency: as a result, the ratio of computer time in the two computations was not 6.53 but only 2.1.

If we have accurate data (obtained via computations) on the condition where we have the transition from a $(KN)^4$ dependency to a $\Sigma_i(N_iK_i)^4$ dependency, then we can estimate a point in time (a date) when it will be possible in an economical and practical sense, to compute routinely large molecules, as above. By assuming a moderate improvement in the computer technology (and by assuming a limited but steady gain in our economy) on the basis of present information, I would like to place this intersection point as occurring at a time between 1976 and 1979. It did require about ten years to reach the present status in small molecules, it will require 5 to 8 years to reach an equivalent position for large molecules computations.

In table 5, some data supporting our reasoning are provided. The first example is the computation (with minimal basis set) of the N_2 molecule. This molecule was first computed (on a desk computer) by Scherr [26]. The molecule was then computed on a first generation computer (UNIVAC-1103), on a second generation computer (IBM-7094) and on a third generation computer (IBM 360/195), with programs written by McLean–Yoshimine–Weiss [27a], McLean–Yoshimine [27b] and McLean–Yoshimine–Bowen–Bagus [27c], respectively. The gain in speed since 1959 is a factor of 10^5 (or 10^7 if we start counting from 1955). As a second example, we take the HCl mole-

Table 5

Examples of computational time.

Case		Machine	Year	Ref.	Time (min)	Program name
N_2	10 basis	(C.Scherr)	1955	[26]	5.25×10^5	–
N_2	10 basis	UNIVAC-1103	1959	[27a]	3.00×10^3	McL.-Y.-Weiss
N_2	10 basis	IBM-7094	1965	[27b]	2.00×10^{-2}	"ALCHEMY"
HCl	16+27+3 basis	IBM-91	1968	[28]	4.35	IBMOL-4
HCl	16+27+3 basis	IBM-91	1970	[28]	1.30	IBMOL-5(A)
HCl	16+27+3 basis	IBM-91	1971	[28]	0.45	IBMOL-5(B)

cule (using 16 s-type, 27 p-type and 3 d-type Gaussian functions) [28]. This example indicates a gain in speed (more indicative than typical for other molecules) of about a factor of 9 obtained by *improvements in the code,* only.

The sixth assumption postulates (in order to obtain accurate energies in large molecules) a different approach to the correlation problem than presently used for atoms and for small molecules. In 1934 Wigner [29] proposed that the correlation correction can be obtained as a simple function of the electronic density ρ. The relation has the form $E = \alpha_1 \int \rho^{4/3} (\alpha_2 + \rho^{1/3})^{-1} d\rho$. This idea was taken up in the field of nuclear computations and in solid state, but has not been considered in molecular computations. There are a number of difficulties with that relation (see for example Clementi [30]) which however can be solved without greater labor or ingenuity. Let us consider the following molecules: N_2, HF, H_2O, NH_3 and CH_4 in their ground state. The correlation correction associated with these systems in the ground state and at equilibrium geometry is 0.380 a.u., 0.378 a.u., 0.366 a.u., 0.361 a.u. and 0.304 a.u. respectively. The use of the above relation for the correlation energy yielded [31]: 0.380 a.u., 0.366 a.u., 0.352 a.u., 0.339 a.u., 0.326 a.u., respectively. This agreement of better than 90% with the exact correlation energy, was obtained by using a value of α_1 equal to α_1 for $C(^1S)$ in CH_4, equal to α_1 for $Ne(^1S)$ in Ne, and interpolation of these two values for HF, H_2O and NH_3. This is a very crude way to transfer the value of α_1 from atoms to molecular computations. (The value of α_2 is the one used for all atoms.) These computations can be performed in the order of a few seconds or minutes on a large computer. For C_2H_6, using the value of α_1, which yields 0.304 a.u. in CH_4, the correlation energies both for the staggered and eclipsed configurations (see later in this paper) is 0.556 a.u. This is in full agreement with experimental data. The above data are presented as partial reason for our confidence that the correlation corrections to large molecules can be obtained without resorting to computation of extreme complexity.

5. Macromolecules

We shall limit ourselves to polymers and co-polymers, and in particular to chain molecules.

5.1. *Conformational analysis*
A chain molecule can exist in several geometrical configurations depending on: 1) its electronic configuration [32] and 2) the interactions with neighboring molecules.

Clearly, the mechanical properties of the polymer, as well as the optical and electronic properties and the chemical reactivity depend also on the statistical distribution of configurations. The stability of each geometrical configuration in itself is the result of the distributions of the electrons, described by the electronic density, ρ, in the field of the nuclei (and vice versa). How can we describe this complex system quantum-mechanically? For practical reasons, one performs a two-step analysis. The first step is essentially a statistical analysis so as to obtain a statistic of the most important conformations. Then, in order to describe the first step more accurately, one performs a quan- tum-mechanical analysis on each configuration.

Whereas the latter simplification is rigorous in a statistical sense, the former simplification is the consequence of practical necessity and it is carried out in a non-rigorous way. Let us recall briefly the reason for this statement. We know from quantum mechanics that for a given electronic density, and a given geometrical distribution of the nuclei, there is an energy, E, for that system. In the following we shall neglect exchange effects, since these can be considered as a quantum-mechanical correction to the classical effect (see Slater [33]), and shall use classical physics arguments. The potential V at a point R due to a density distribution ρ is given by the integral over the entire space (where $\rho \neq 0$) of the ratio of the density at a point r (denoted as $\rho(r)$) divided by the distance between R and r, i.e., $V = \int (\rho(r)/|R-r|) \, d\rho$. This potential is associated to a field F given, in the Coulomb approximation, by the relation $F = \int ([\rho(r)(R-r)/|R-r|^3) \, dr$. (Quantum-mechanically, we have to introduce a correction in F due to the exchange effects; this can be done for example by retaining the functional form of F and by varying the value of $\rho(r)$.) The energy E of the system associated with the field F is then given by the relation $E = (1/8\pi) \int F \cdot F \, dR$.

It is known that both classical- and quantum physics requires knowledge of the density in order to define an energy. If we consider an initial configuration with density ρ_I and a final configuration with density ρ_F, then the energy difference between the initial and final configuration is clearly related to $\rho_I - \rho_F$. In the conformational analysis of chain molecules there are a number of implicit or explicit approximations in obtaining the energy difference between initial and final (or better, any two) configurations.

The first approximation replaces the density ρ and the distribution D of the nuclei, with a distribution ρ' where ρ' *includes the nuclei* and implicitly assumes that ρ' is a function only of the nuclei coordinates. That is to say, that, if a nucleus goes from position R to position R', the electronic density associates with that nucleus, follows the nucleus without change in its distribution. The advantage of this approximation is to reduce the problem from one of many nuclei and even more electrons, to one of only many centers (one for each nucleus).

The second approximation is the one whereby the densities ρ' around each nucleus are considered independent of the density around any other nucleus. (This approximation is an extension of the previous approximation.) As a sequence, energy differences associate with the motion of atoms in "model molecules", like energies of internal rotations, can be used to compute the energy difference in a different molecule, as long as the motion under consideration relates to the same atoms as in the "model molecule". This second approximation can be stated differently, for example it can be equated to a statement of very short range forces.

For what seem contradictory reasons, a third assumption is made: namely, that long range forces are very important, and these are generally designated as "non-bonded interactions".

Much has been done with those approximations, see for example: Birchstein and Ptitsyn [34], Flory [35], Gotlieb [36], Lifson and Roig [37], Mark [38] and Nagai [39]. In the following, we briefly recall some of the formulation obtained in the spirit of the above approximations. We shall follow Flory's formulation and notation [35].

As noted, one of the main concepts used in the determination of the statistical distribution of sterical configurations of a chain molecule (in a given environment and at given temperature and pressure) is one which associates an energy barrier with rotations. It is well known that two chemical groups R_1 and R_2 interconnected by a so-called single bond have the possibility to rotate "independently" around the bond.

An approximate representation for the potential energy variation of the barrier of rotation is the relation:

$$E(\phi) = (E^\circ/2)(1 - \cos \eta \phi) \qquad (1)$$

where $E(\phi)$ is the potential energy, E° the height of the rotational barrier, ϕ the angle of rotation and $360^\circ/\eta$ the periodicity.

For example, in the ethane molecule, $CH_3 - CH_3$ (see fig. 1) the above relation is:

$$E(\phi) = (E^\circ/2)(1 - \cos 3\phi) ,$$

since the rotation has periodicity of 120° (to a first, but good approximation).

In general, however, there are many rotational degrees of freedom to be considered; if we consider the rotations as independent of the other, then we

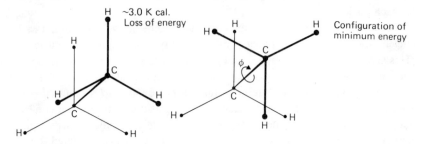

Fig. 1. Staggered and eclipsed configuration for the ethane molecule, C_2H_6.

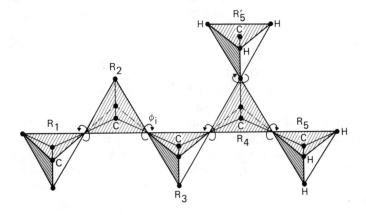

Fig. 2. Idealized configuration in polyethylene. A rotation of 120° around the axis connecting R_3 to R_4, brings R_5 into R_5'.

would have a potential expressed as:

$$E\{\phi\} = \sum_i (E_{\phi_i}^\circ/2)(1-\cos\eta_i\phi_i) \,. \tag{2}$$

In fig. 2, we take as an example polyethylene: the CH_2 groups are indicated as R_1, R_2, R_3, R_4, R_5, etc. A rotation of 120° around the axis interconnecting R_3 and R_4 can bring R_5 to R_5'. Clearly, the interaction between R_5 and R_2 is different from the interaction between R_5' and R_2. Thus, eq. (2) must be corrected by adding a term to $E\{\phi\}$. This correction is referred to as "nonbonded interaction" and $E\{\phi\}$ now has the following form:

$$E\{\phi\} = \sum_i (E^o_{\phi_i}/2)(1-\cos\eta\phi_i) + \sum_{k,l} [a_{k,l}\exp(-br_{k,l})-c_{k,l}/r^6_{k,l}] \ . \tag{3}$$

The indices k and l refer to atom pairs at distance r_{kl}; $a_{k,l}$, b and c_{kl} are in essence empirical parameters.

We have not defined what is a "link" in the chain. In fig. 1, R_1 and R_2 are the CH_3 groups, in fig. 2 R_1 and R_2 are the $-CH_2-$ groups. If we consider a polypeptide group (fig. 3), then we can assume the R_1, R_2 etc. to be the $-NH-CHR-CO$ residues. This assumption is equivalent to state that the $-NH-CHR-CO-$ residues are practically rigid, (ξ and η are fixed in fig. 3 where $\phi = \xi = 0°$). Rotations within the residues are important, rotations between residues are not important in considering energy differences between conformations. Thus, eq. (3) can be simplified as:

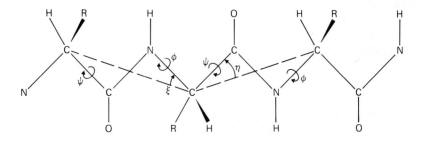

$$E(\phi,\psi)=(E^o_\phi/2)(1-\cos 3\phi)+(E^o_\psi/2)(1-\cos 3\psi)+\sum_{k\ell} E_{k\ell}(\phi,\psi)+E_c$$

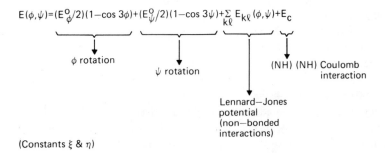

Fig. 3. Polypeptide chain. The residual groups are identified with the $-NH-CHR-CO$ residues. In this figure, ξ and ϕ are both equal to $0°$.

$$E(\phi,\psi) = (E_\phi^o/2)(1-\cos 3\phi) + (E_\psi^o/2)(1-\cos 3\psi) + \sum_{k,l} E_{kl}(\phi,\psi) + E_C \qquad (4)$$

where $E_{k,l}$ includes nearest neighbor interactions and where E_C is the Coulomb interaction between NH groups.

With proper parameterization, eq. (4) is sufficient to yield meaningful energy contour maps, like those given by Brant et al. [40]. Thus, a very complex quantum-mechanical problem can be numerically simulated with proper parameterization and the use of empirical data; thus, the *first* step, namely the possibility to predict the statistical distribution of a chain molecule, is more and more under control. There are, however, implicit limitations: 1) the method depends on availability of experimental data for rotational barriers and non-bonded interactions; 2) the method answers statistical data and as today formulated, it cannot be expanded to give information on the electronic distribution and their variations.

The second step, the quantum mechanical study of the electronic density of a chain molecule at a *given* geometrical configuration, is therefore needed in order to *understand* the statistical distribution of a chain molecule at a deeper level.

We shall discuss three points: 1) computations of barriers of rotation; 2) computation of non-bonded interactions; and 3) computations of the electronic wave functions for polymers with translational symmetry.

5.2. Computations of rotational barriers

We shall discuss the barrier of rotation with reference to a specific example: C_2H_6 [41].

In table 6, the total energy for the eclipsed and staggered configurations (as well as the computed barriers) are reported for computation performed in the self-consistent-field approximation; the limit of this approximation is the Hartree–Fock functions [42–47]. The last computation reported in table 6 is very near to this limit. The spread of the computer energies is rather large about 0.25 a.u., and the corresponding spread of computer barrier height is about 0.0018 a.u. In fig. 4, the computed total energies for the staggered configurations and the computed barrier heights are given. From table 6 and fig. 4, we can reach the following conclusions: the Hartree–Fock model contains a reasonable explanation of the barrier. The staggered configuration is correctly computed as more stable than the eclipsed configuration by an amount of 0.005 ± 0.0005 a.u. (the experimental barrier is 0.0047 a.u.) [48].

The Hartree–Fock limit is very near to the energy obtained by Clementi

Table 6

Total energies and barrier heights for C_2H_6. The first 7 lines represent Hartree–Fock computations, the last one gives experimental results.

Author	Total energies eclipsed config. (a.u.)	Total energies staggered config. (a.u.)	Barrier (a.u.)	Ref.
Pedersen and Morokuma (1967)	−78.564 90	−78.570 40	0.005 50	[42]
Pitzer and Lipscomb (1963)	−78.985 93	−78.991 15	0.005 22	[43]
Clementi and Davies (1966)	−79.102 47	−79.108 24	0.005 77	[44]
Fink and Allen (1967)	−79.143 77	−79.147 78	0.004 01	[45]
Clementi and von Niessen (1971)	−79.198 147	−79.203 142	0.004 99	[41]
Veillard (1969)	−79.231 88	−79.237 70	0.005 82*	[46]
Clementi and Popkie (1971)	−79.252 878	−79.258 24	0.005 36*	[47]
Weiss and Leroi (1968) (exptl.)	−79.843 04	−79.847 60	0.004 66	[48]

* When the nuclear geometry is optimized with respect to the C–C distances and H–C–H angles, the agreement with the experimental barrier is better: 0.00489 in [46] and 0.00511 in [47].

and Popkie [47] but the determination of the difference between computed Hartree–Fock and experimental barriers has not been fully settled: this can be done only by computing an energy within 0.0001 a.u. of the Hartree–Fock limit, a claim that we certainly cannot make. However, it seems reasonable to expect that by narrowing the total energy error in the computation to within 0.001 a.u. of the Hartree–Fock limit, the resulting computed barrier will be within 0.0001 a.u. of the Hartree–Fock barrier.

Thus, let us conclude this section on the barrier of rotation by stating that the Hartree–Fock model is capable of predicting rotational barriers within 3% to 5% of the experimental values; this accuracy seems to be sufficient for eq. (3). *Hence, the barrier can be either obtained from experimental data or from computational data.*

The second point we wish to make in this section concerning barriers of rotation, is that the Hartree–Fock model provides a reasonable physical picture of the "origin" of the barrier. Quantum mechanically, as emphasized, the "origin" is simply that during rotation at a given point r, the electronic density changes from $\rho(r)$ to $\rho'(r)$; the quantities $\Delta\rho(r) = \rho(r) - \rho'(r)$ at any value of r and the new positions of the nuclei *are the "origin"*. We can plot (or tabulate) $\Delta\rho(r)$, but this likely will not be too useful since it is not obvious low to pass from a plot of $\Delta\rho(r)$ to the value for ΔE. Therefore, we

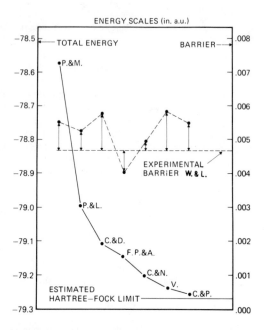

Fig. 4. Computed barrier of rotation for C_2H_6. The energy scale on the left is for total energy in the eclipsed configurations (the authors of the various computations reported in the figure can be obtained from table 6. The energy scale on the right is for the computed height of the energy barrier.

shall make use of decomposition in the total energy. It can be proved [49] that the total energy corresponding to a Hartree–Fock function can be formally decomposed as follows:

$$E = \sum_A E_A + \sum_{A,B} E_{AB} + \sum_{A,B,C} E_{ABC} + \sum_{A,B,C,D} E_{ABCD} \qquad (5)$$

where the subscripts A, B, C, D refer to atoms or groups of atoms and where each summation includes all the terms which are not included in the preceding summations of eq. (5).

In a previous paper [41] we have analyzed the barrier of rotation in C_2H_6 with the help of eq. (5). (The analysis has been called Bond Energy Analysis, B.E.A.) If we consider the C_2H_6 molecule as built of two CH_3 groups, then

Table 7
Decomposition of the rotation barrier of C_2H_6 by grouping (bond energy analysis [41]).

$$(H_3)_A-(C-C)-(H_3)_B$$

Type	Energy (a.u.)
(C_1-C_2) (1×)	0.016 889
$(H_3)_A$(2×)	0.038 668
$(H_3)_A-(C_1-C_2)$ (2×)	−0.034 066
$(H_3)_A-(H_3)_B$ (1×)	0.008 089
$(H_3)_A-(C_1-C_2)-(H_3)_B$ (1×)	−0.024 585

$$(H_3C)_A-(CH_3)_B$$

$(H_3C)_A$(2×)	−0.086 174
$(H_3C)_A-(H_3C)_B$ (1×)	0.091 169
Total	0.004 995

from the B.E.A. we learn that during rotation the $\Delta\rho(r)$ within each of the two groups and the nuclear rearrangements are responsible for a ΔE about 19 times larger than the barrier and of opposite sign, whereas the ΔE associated with the interaction of the two CH_3 groups is about 20 times the barrier and of the same sign. Thus, we can conclude that the barrier is the result of the cancellation of those two opposing effects (see table 7).

In more detail, we can consider the C_2H_6 molecule as built from three groups, two H_3 and one C_2. In this case, during rotation we have obtained that the $\Delta\rho$ within each of the two H_3 groups is responsible for a ΔE somewhat less than 4 times the barrier (and of the same sign), that of the H_3-H_3 interaction is responsible for a ΔE of somewhat less than twice the barrier (and of the same sign), and that the ΔE associated to the $\Delta\rho$ in the $(C-C)$ group is responsible for a ΔE somewhat more than 3 times the barrier (and of the same sign). The $(H_3)-(C_2)$ interaction and the $(H)_3-(C_2)-(H_3)$ interaction (two- and three-center interactions in the sense of E_{AB} and E_{ABC} of eq. (4) are responsible for a ΔE about 12 times the barrier (and of opposite sign).

This type of analysis was extended to different types of grouping [41]. A variety of models are obtained in this way, each more specific than the preceding one, each containing the previous, and all pointing out that there is a $\Delta\rho(r)$ at any point r in space. Thus, one chooses a model which responds to specific needs.

5.3. Non-bonded interactions

The second group of terms needed in eq. (3) to describe the ΔE for different conformations in a chain molecule represent the "non-bonded interactions". Again, these quantities can be obtained from the bond-energy analysis of a Hartree–Fock function.

Let us, for example, consider two molecules of water in the field of a lithium positive ion. Let us position one molecule of water, designated as W_1, in the energetically most favorable position with respect to Li^+ (this is at an Li-O distance of 3.55 a.u. and with the geometry as shown in fig. 5). Then, let us take the second molecule of water, designated as W_2, and place it in a variety of positions with respect to the W_1–Li^+ group. For example, we can place W_2 so that the W_1–W_2–Li^+ system has all the atoms in a plane. Fig. 5 gives the Hartree–Fock energy surface for such a system. With the bond-energy analysis we can ask the question: what is the interaction between W_1

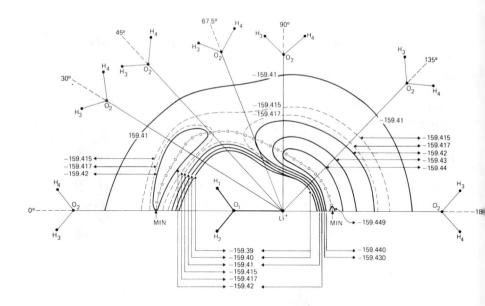

Fig. 5. Hartree–Fock energy surface of the planar $(H_2O)_2$–Li^+ complex. The Li^+ ion and one of the H_2O molecules are kept in a constant geometry relative to each other. The second molecule of water is positioned so as to have all the atoms of the $(H_2O)_2$–Li^+ complex in a plane. The computations are done for an O_1–Li–O_2 angle of $0°$, $45°$, $67.5°$, $90°$, $135°$, and $180°$, at various Li–O_2 distances.

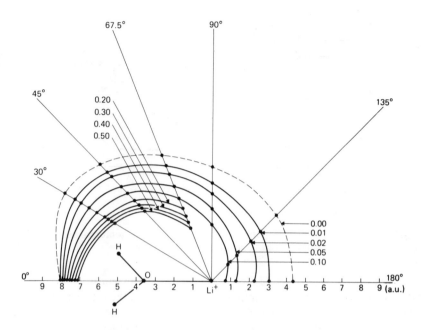

Fig. 6. Non-bonded interaction for two water molecules in the presence of the Li^+ field.

and W_2, since the total energy E of the system $(W_1-W_2-Li)^+$ can be decomposed as:

$$E = E(W_1) + E(W_2) + E(Li) + E(W_1-Li) + E(W_2-Li) + E(W_1-W_2) +$$

$$+ E(W_1-W_2-Li) .$$

Fig. 6 gives the energy surface for $E(W_1-W_2)$. This is an energy map of what goes under the name of "non-bonded interactions". Thus, we have indicated how the non-bonded interaction terms can be obtained from Hartree—Fock computations [50].

Eq. (3) has terms which are dependent explicitly on the rotation (the terms in $\cos \eta \phi_i$) and terms which depend only on the distances between a pair of atoms. Let us comment on both types of terms in the spirit of the bond-energy analysis. We shall consider as an example the case of *one* molecule of water, indicated as W, and one lithium positive ion. Let us consider the case where all the four nuclei of the $[H_2O-Li]^+$ system are in a plane.

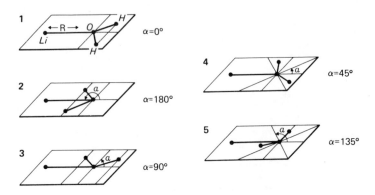

Fig. 7. Planar $[Li-H_2O]^+$ configurations: different values of the rotational angle α for which Hartree–Fock energies were computed.

Fig. 7 shows (for a given O–Li distance) a number of possible orientations, for which energies have been computed as a function of the rotation of an angle α. In fig. 8, the Hartree–Fock energies are given for various values of $R(Li-O)$ and various values of α. Fig. 8 reports the computed variation of the energy of the system for different $R(Li-O)$ distances at the same α whereas fig. 9 illustrates the variation of the energy of the system for different α but within the same value for the $R(Li-O)$ distances. Clearly, E is a function of both $R(Li-O)$ and α; for large R the energy is mainly a function of R, for small R the energy is mainly a function of α.

On the basis of this numerical experimentation, we can now return to analyze eq. (3) (where each summation contains no term present in a preceding summation). It is easy to show that within the framework of the bond-energy analysis, one can derive an energy expression equivalent to eq. (3). Thus, the bond-energy analysis of Hartree–Fock functions (or of more approximated or more accurate wave functions) can be used as a link between the empirical formulation of the energy difference which follows configurational variations (eq. (3)) and the non-empirical formulation.

5.4. Band structure in periodic chains

As noted at the beginning of this paper, a chain molecule can have translational periodicity. Detailed computations of the electronic density can and have been recently performed.

Why compute the electronic structure of polymers? Up to the present, the

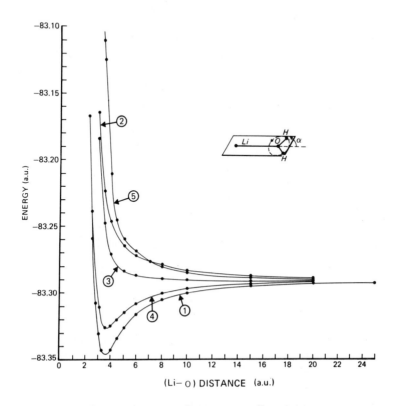

Fig. 8. Planar $[Li-H_2O]^+$ configurations: Hartree–Fock energies for the cases given in fig. 7 at various Li–O distances (in a.u.).

main emphasis in polymer and copolymer chemistry has been the study and exploitation of the mechanical properties. It is hoped that more emphasis will be given to the synthesis of polymers having unique electronic and/or magnetic characteristics.

Since the bonds between atoms in a polymer are not too dissimilar from the bonds between atoms in a smaller molecule, it makes sense, to a first approximation, to describe the polymers with those techniques which seem to work for molecules, and from which we have obtained a good deal of insight in the electronic structure of molecules. That means, we shall use the LCAO approximation (tight-binding approximation) and attempt to make the best of it (SCF–LCAO, at first, Hartree–Fock as soon as feasible). It is noted that there is nothing new, in principle, in this approach.

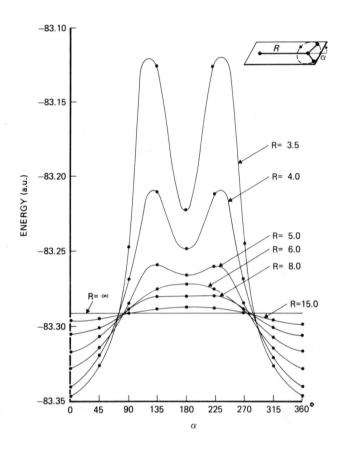

Fig. 9. Hartree–Fock energies for the cases given in fig. 8 as a function of the rotational angle α.

Up to now, the success of the tight-binding approach has been questionable, not because of difficulties in principle, but because of difficulties in practice. The first difficulty is due to the great deal of labor in setting up the integrals; the second difficulty is associated with the large number of integrals needed before a sufficient number of nearest neighbors are taken into account so as to have a converging solution for an infinite system.

Fortunately, we know how to compute large numbered integrals. In addition, a good formulation designed to achieve self-consistent field orbitals in the tight-binding approximation has been developed, for example, by Ladik and Biczo [51]. Recently, André [52] has developed in our laboratory, a program which translates most of Ladik and Biczo's theory into a working computer program.

In the rest of this paper, we shall briefly comment on the results obtained from band computations for Polyene $(-CH-CH)_n$ and polyethylene $(-CH_2-CH_2-)_n$, as presented by André and co-workers [53]. These authors have compared computations done with ab initio techniques and semi-empirical techniques. It is noted that the main differences between the two techniques is related to the integral evaluations. In ab initio computations, the integrals are correctly computed for a basis set which however, *might or might not* adequately describe the electronic density.

It is also noted that the computation of the energy gap and of spectral transitions and ionization potentials are still open to questions because of the theoretical formalism adopted. For occupied bands, the computations are correctly representing (if an appropriate basis set is used) the field of the N electrons of the polymer in the ground state. However, the computations of the energy gap, electronic excitations and electron affinity are open to the same type of criticism as previously pointed out, for example, in the case of the C_4 molecule [54]. The reason is that often present computations make use of "the virtual orbitals" in determining the empty energy bands. The virtual orbitals are the lowest roots immediately above the self-consistent orbitals. These virtual orbitals are not the proper self-consistent solutions for excitation, since the field is obtained self-consistently only for the occupied electrons, nor are the proper solutions for the field of N + 1 electrons, since the iterative corrections in the self-consistent technique explicitly make use only of the representation of the density for the N-electron problem. The virtual orbital therefore cannot account for the electronic rearrangement which follows ionization or excitation of an electron.

With this in mind, it is not surprising to find that there are strong discrepancies in the computations of the band structure when different approximations are used. Thus, André and co-workers [53] report an energy gap for polyethylene which varies from 0.699 a.u. to 0.585 a.u., 0.454 a.u., and 0.691 a.u. for an ab initio computation with small basis set, for a second ab initio computation of very small basis set, for an "extended Huckel" and for a CNDO ("complete neglect of differential overlap") computation, respectively. The data for other properties like ionization, electron affinity, band location and band width show nearly equal scattering of data.

The drastic effect of the basis-set limitations can be perhaps appreciated by considering a simple example of a linear chain, obtained by placing two lithium atoms per unit cell, and considering an *infinite linear* chain of lithium atoms [55]. We shall use a unit cell of dimension (along the chain direction) of 13 a.u. (other dimensions have been analyzed). The two lithium atoms are placed symmetrically with respect to the midpoint of the unit cell and we have computed the infinite chain for a pair of atoms separated by 4.0 a.u., 4.5 a.u., 5.0 a.u., 5.5 a.u., 6.0 a.u. and 6.5 a.u., respectively. Since the cell length has been chosen at 13.0 a.u., a separation of the two lithium atoms of 6.5 a.u. corresponds to an infinite chain of lithium atoms each at 6.5 a.u. from the others. The other distances correspond to an infinite chain of lithium "molecules" with internuclear distances of 4.0 a.u., 4.5 a.u., 5.0 a.u., 5.5 a.u. and 6.0 a.u., respectively.

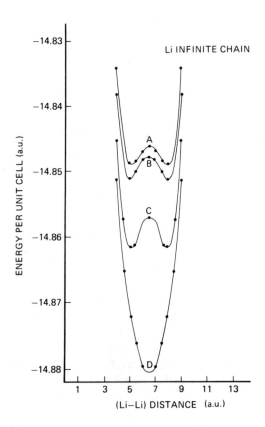

Fig. 10. Effect of the basis set on the potential energy of an infinite chain of pairs of Li atoms. Curves A, B, C, D are obtained with increasingly complete basis sets (see text).

The physical picture emerging from the computation varies drastically if different basis sets are chosen. We have selected a basis containing 11 s-type functions for each lithium atom, plus a number of 2 p-type functions for each lithium. In fig. 10 the computed energy is given for a basis set containing no 2p function (curve A), for a basis set with one 2p function per lithium atom (curve B), two 2p functions (curve C) and three 2p functions (curve D). It is apparent that the four basis sets give *qualitatively* different results (for each computation, 5 nearest neighboring cells were taken into explicit account in the computation). Curves A, B and C have an energy minimum for Li—Li separation of about 5.0 a.u. and a relative maximum at an Li—Li distance of 6.5 a.u.; on the other hand, curve D has the energy minimum for an Li—Li distance of 6.5 a.u. Thus, if a too limited basis set is used, one would conclude that the lithium chain is made from diatomic molecules of lithium atoms, rather than from equally separated lithium atoms (as given by curve D). This example illustrates the need of using adequate basis sets in order to avoid qualitatively incorrect conclusions.

To conclude this section, we can state that numerical techniques and computer programs are available to describe the electronic structure of polymers with translational symmetry. It is too early to assess the quantitative value of these techniques for predictive purposes. We are at the equivalent stage where the molecular computation field was in 1959 when the first correctly computed S.C.F. diatomic molecules with minimal basis sets did appear. As known, those computations offered not too much in terms of valuable chemical or spectroscopic information; however, those computations were the *necessary step* to reach today accuracy which can equal or exceed experimental accuracy.

6. Conclusions

During the 1960 decade, the field of molecular computation has made remarkable progress; from minimal basis-set computations of the first row atoms diatomic molecules, to many accurate Hartree—Fock computations for first, second and third row atoms diatomic molecules; from a vague and qualitative appreciation of the magnitude of many-body effects, to quantitative estimates and/or rigorous computations; from crude semi-empirical approximations for aromatic molecules, to all electron computations; from qualitative potential energy surfaces to quantitatively accurate potential energy surfaces. This list can be considerably extended by including pioneering computations in trajectories, in transition rates, in many expectation values other than the total energy, in the computation of the band structure of polymers, etc., etc.

The theoretical bases, the numerical algorithms and computer programs (as well as hardware) are at hand for a continuous growth during the 1970 decade. One can confidently expect that during this decade, the computations will be more and more predictive in nature rather than merely confirmatory on the accuracy and capabilities of the methods. One can confidently expect a continuous extension of the field in the sense that larger or more complex molecular systems will be amendable to good computations. However, perhaps the most important step in molecular computation, from a methodological point of view, will be in the direction of what is sometimes referred to as "artificial intelligence".

The present examples when the computer program selects different algorithms (following the analysis of input-dependent numerical data) or when the computer program interacts with the program users (suggesting solutions) are an unequivocal step in the direction of heuristic programming.

Most likely, this is not only an obvious step but also an unescapable one, since it originates from the same motivations which constitute the rationale for computations in chemistry. Obviously, this step could not have taken place before attaining the present level in computational capabilities.

In parallel, likely the most important step in molecular computation, from the molecular physics point of view (as a science), will consist of the contributions made by present experimental scientists, as soon as they will regard and use numerical simulation as an additional experimental equipment for their laboratory. Slowly, a *unified* theoretical framework is emerging for atomic and molecular physics as well as for solid state and liquid states. Only then we shall have a theory of matter, since at present we have only a fragmentary formulation.

References

[1] M.Kraus, *Compendium of Ab Initio Calculations of Molecular Energies and Properties,* N.B.S. Technical Note 438 (U.S. Government Printing Office, Washington, D.C., 1967).
[2] W.G.Richards, T.E.H.Walker and R.K.Hinkley, *A Bibliography of Ab Initio Molecular Wave Functions* (Oxford University Press, London, 1971).
[3] See for example: H.Hartmann and E.Clementi, Phys. Rev. *133* (1963) 1295.
[4] Private communication from Professor Grant, Oxford University, England.
[5] See for example: E.Clementi, *tables of atomic functions,* IBM Res. and Developm. *9* (1965) 2.
[6] R.K.Nesbet, a) Phys. Rev. *155* (1967) 51; b) Ibid. *155* (1967) 56.
[7] R.K.Nesbet, Phys. Rev. *175* (1968) 2.
[8] R.K.Nesbet, Phys. Rev. A *3* (1971) 87.

[9] E.Clementi, J. Chem. Phys. *38* (1963) 1001.
[10] E.Clementi, J. Chem. Phys. *42* (1965) 2783.
[11] O.Sinanoğlu, J. Chem. Phys. *36* (1962) 707; *36* (1962) 3198.
[12] P.Bagus, N.Bessis and C.M.Moser, Phys. Rev. *179* (1969) 39;
    P.Bagus and C.M.Moser, J. Phys. B *2* (1969) 1214.
[13] A.W.Weiss, Phys. Rev. *178* (1969) 82.
[14] W.Meyer, Int. J. Quantum Chem. *5* S (1971) 296.
[15] C.Edmiston and M.Krauss, J. Chem. Phys. *45* (1966) 1833.
[16] E.Clementi and H.Popkie, J. Am. Chem. Soc. (in press).
[17] E.Clementi and A.Routh, Int. J. Quantum Chem. (in press).
[18] G.H.F.Diercksen, Chem. Phys. Letters *4* (1969) 373.
[19] E.Clementi, J.Mehl and W.von Niessen, J. Chem. Phys. *54* (1971) 508.
[20] E.Clementi, J. Chem. Phys. *46* (1967) 3851; *47* (1969) 2323.
[21] E.Clementi and D.R.Davies, J. Comput. Phys. *2* (1967) 223.
[22] A.Veillard, Special IBM Technical Report (1968);
    E.Clementi, Int. J. Quantum Chem. *18* (1967) 307.
[23] E.Clementi and J.Mehl, IBM Technical Reports RJ 883 and RJ 889;
    E.Clementi, *Proc. Monrepo Seminar on Selected Topics in Molecular Physics,*
    Monrepo, Ludwigsburg, Germany, October 1970 (in press).
[24] See for example: Comput. Phys. Commun, ed. G.P.Burke (North-Holland Publ.
    Co., Amsterdam).
[25] E.Clementi, I.Batra and H.Seki, unpublished data.
[26] C.W.Scherr, J. Chem. Phys. to be published.
[27] a) McLean, J. Chem. Phys. to be published;
    b) McLean and Yoshimine, Tables of Linear Molecular Wave Functions, Supplement
    to the IBM Journal of Res. and Devl. *5* (1967) 321;
    c) Correspondence concerning Alchemy should be addressed directly to Dr. A.D.
    McLean.
[28] E.Clementi and J.Mehl, IBM Technical Report RJ 883 (June, 1971).
[29] E.Wigner, Phys. Rev. *46* (1934) 1002.
[30] E.Clementi, in: *Electronic Structure in Molecules, Espec. in Cyano Compounds,*
    Ch. 1 of book "C≡N" (Intersci. Pub. Div. of John Wiley, New York, 1970).
[31] E.Clementi and H.Popkie, unpublished data.
[32] K.S.Pitzer and E.Clementi, J. Chem. Soc. *81* (1959) 4477.
[33] J.C.Slater, Exchange Potential, J. Chem.Phys. *43* (1965) S228; see also
    J.C.Slater and K.H.Johnson, Phys. Rev. (in press).
[34] T.M.Birchstein and O.B.Ptitsyn, *Conformation of Macromolecules* (Interscience
    Publishers, New York, 1966).
[35] P.J.Flory, *Statistical Mechanics of Chain Molecules* (Interscience Publishers, New
    York, 1969).
[36] Y.Y.Gotlieb, Zh. Tekh. Fiz. *29* (1959) 523; *27* (1957) 707; [English Transl.:
    Soviet Phys. -Tech. Phys. *4* (1959) 465; *2* (1957) 637].
[37] S.Lifson, J. Chem. Phys. *30* (1959) 964;
    S.Lifson and A.Roig, Ibid. *34* (1961) 1963.
[38] J.E.Mark, J. Amer. Chem. Soc. *88* (1966) 4354; *89* (1967) 6829; *88* (1966) 3708.
[39] K.Nagai, see for example: J. Chem. Phys. *38* (1963) 924; *40* (1964) 2818; *45*
    (1966) 838; *44* (1966) 423.

[40] O.A.Brant, W.G.Miller and P.J.Flory, J. Mol. Biol. *23* (1967) 47.
[41] See for example: E.Clementi and W.von Niessen, J. Chem. Phys. *54* (1971) 521.
[42] L.Pederson and K.Morokuna, J. Chem. Phys. *46* (1967) 3941.
[43] R.M.Pitzer and W.W.Lipscomb, J. Chem. Phys. *39* (1963) 1995.
[44] E.Clementi and D.R.Davies, J. Chem. Phys. *45* (1966) 2593.
[45] W.H.Fink, D.C.Pan and L.C.Allen, J. Chem. Phys. *47* (1967) 895.
[46] A.Veillard, Chem. Phys. Letters *3* (1969) 128 and 565.
[47] E.Clementi and H.Popkie, to be published.
[48] S.Weiss and G.E.Leroi, J. Chem. Phys. *48* (1968) 962.
[49] E.Clementi, J. Chem. Phys. *46* (1967) 3842;
     E.Clementi, Int. J. Quantum Chem. *3* S (1969) 179.
[50] E.Clementi and H.Popkie, to be published.
[51] J.Ladik and G.Biczo, J. Chem. Phys. *42* (1965) 1658.
[52] J.-M.André, Polyatom Program (Comput. Phys. Commun)
[53] J.-M.André, G.S.Kapsomenos, G.Leroy, Chem. Phys. Letters *8* (1971) 195.
     Additional references to the same work are available in this reference.
[54] For the use of virtual orbitals in predicting excited states, see for example:
     E.Clementi, J. Amer. Chem. Soc. *83* (1961) 4501; for the use of the Koopman
     theorem in the determination of valency-shell ionization potentials, see for example:
     E.Clementi, J. Chem. Phys. *47* (1969) 4485; for the use of the Koopman theorem
     in the inner-shell's ionization potential, see:
     E.Clementi and A.Routh (ref. [17]).
[55] E.Clementi, to be published (work reported at the Gordon Conference on Quantum
     Chemistry, summer 1969).

Physics of Electronic and Atomic Collisions, VII ICPEAC, 1971 − North-Holland (1972)

THE COMPUTER SIMULATION OF REACTIVE COLLISIONS

P.J. KUNTZ *

Department of Chemistry, University of Manchester,
Manchester, M13 9PL, United Kingdom

A brief account is given of the classical trajectory method of simulating simple gas-phase chemical reactions. The method of calculating a single trajectory is outlined and it is pointed out how cross-sections can be obtained by averaging over many similar trajectories. An indication is given of the extent to which the method has been applied to chemical systems, with special emphasis given to dynamical interpretations in a few cases. Sample trajectories are shown in order to illustrate the effect of two different dynamical mechanisms on angular scattering. Brief comments on the validity of the classical approximation are optimistic about its use in the future studies of chemical reactions.

1. Introduction

The theoretician in the field of chemical kinetics is today confronted with an enormous amount of very detailed information about reactions he studies. Molecular beam experiments [1] and chemiluminescence studies [2] are providing data on elastic and reactive cross-sections, angular and energy distributions of products, and even on correlations between the different types of product energy [3] and between product scattering angles and relative kinetic energy. For some reactions, this information is available over a wide range of relative velocity of the reactants. [4, 5] The large number of available facts provides stringent tests of any theory of chemical reaction. In this paper, I should like to limit myself to the discussion of reactive collisions and in particular to the computer simulation of chemical reactions by means of classical trajectory analysis.

An *ab initio* theory of chemical reaction would start with the Schrödinger equation for all the nuclei and electrons and from this would develop estimates of the cross-sections for the formation of products in their various

---

* Present address: Theoretical Chemistry Institute, University of Wisconsin, 1101 University Avenue, Madison, Wisconsin 53706, U.S.A.

states and scattered into different solid angles. In practice one always applies the Born-Oppenheimer approximation to separate the motion of the nuclei and electrons, and the theory is then concerned with two essentially independent problems, the determination of a potential energy function which governs the motion of the nuclei, and the dynamical behaviour of the nuclei in this potential. I shall deal only with the dynamical problem, assuming that a potential function is available.

The rigorous approach to the dynamical problem is to solve the nuclear Schrödinger equation subject to appropriate boundary conditions, which enable one to identify the cross-sections for processes of interest. This has proven to be a most difficult problem, and one which has not yet been solved for nuclei moving in three dimensions over a realistic potential surface. The easy way out of this situation is to abandon the use of the nuclear Schrödinger equation and to employ the equations of classical mechanics to find the motion of the nuclei in the given potential-energy field. This procedure cannot be completely justified. The masses of the nuclei are small enough for molecules to have zero-point vibrational energies and for there to be appreciable probability for tunnelling through potential barriers, so some quantum effects are likely to exist. Still there is evidence that the classical approximation is good enough to provide a correct overall description of chemical reactions, which will not differ qualitatively from a quantum description. There have been suggestions [6] that quantum effects could be accounted for by semi-classical methods which make use of certain quantities calculated purely by classical mechanics. In this case the classical approximation provides the necessary starting point.

2. The classical trajectory simulation of reactions

It is convenient to discuss the classical trajectory simulation of gas-phase chemical reactions in terms of the simplest transfer reaction A + BC → AB + C, where A, B, and C are atoms, but it is emphasized that the method can be applied to any number of atoms, and recently a six atom calculation on the reaction $T + CH_4 \rightarrow TH + CH_3$ has been reported (see table 1). In any experiment, one deals with enormous numbers of (A,BC) pairs which collide with each other in every possible way. One can describe a particular collision by specifying parameters such as the initial distance of A from the centre of mass of BC, the orientation of BC with respect to A, the magnitude and direction of the velocity of A relative to BC, and the internal motion of BC. Some of the these quantities can be controlled by the experimenter, while others vary randomly over their allowed ranges. In the simulation procedure one selects a sample of these collision parameters which is representive of the large number of collisions occurring in the real reaction. The sample is used to specify a large number of particular collisions, and the outcome of these is found by following the collision trajectories determined by the classical equations of motion. Cross-sections for any process are then proportional to the fraction of the total number of collisions which lead to that process. The simulation procedure can be discussed in two parts: (i) the solution of the classical equations to find the trajectory for a particular collision, and (ii) the calculation of cross-sections from averages over all collisions.

We first consider the calculation of a particular trajectory. If the three particles A, B, and C are represented by mass points in three-dimensional space, then they can be fully described at any instant of time by 9 Cartesian coordinates and their conjugate momenta. Because the potential energy depends only on the relative positions of the three atoms, the centre of mass can be eliminated from the equations of motion by defining new coordinates q_i which are the 6 Cartesian coordinates of A and B relative to C. The Hamiltonian function $H(q_i, p_i)$ may be written in terms of these new coordinates and their conjugate momenta, so that the equations of motion are reduced from a system of 18 equations to one of 12 simultaneous first order differential equations:

$$\dot{q}_i = \partial H/\partial p_i \qquad i = 1, ..., 6$$
$$\dot{p}_i = -\partial H/\partial q_i \qquad i = 1, ..., 6 . \tag{1}$$

The Hamiltonian function is

$$H(q_i, p_i) = \frac{A+C}{2AC}(p_1^2 + p_2^2 + p_3^2) + \frac{B+C}{2BC}(p_4^2 + p_5^2 + p_6^2)$$

$$+ \frac{1}{C}(p_1 p_4 + p_2 p_5 + p_3 p_6) + V(q_1, ..., q_6) , \tag{2}$$

where A, B, C now represent the masses and (p_1, p_2, p_3) and (p_4, p_5, p_6) are the components of the momenta of A and B respectively. The equations of motion (1) may be reduced further by appropriate transformations [7], but then the Hamiltonian function no longer retains the simple form of eq. (2). Although the number of differential equations can be reduced to 6, the computation time could increase because of the increased complexity of the right-hand-side of eq. (1). Also, further reductions involve the elimination of the total angular momentum and energy, quantities which are conserved during the collision; it is very useful not to eliminate these, but to use their

conservation or lack of it as a check on the accuracy of the solution of
eqs. (1).

The simultaneous eqs. (1) are solved numerically in a stepwise fashion. At
some time t the right-hand-sides are calculated and the values of the deriva-
tives $\dot{q}_i$ and $\dot{p}_i$ are used to find the values of the q_i and p_i at a later time $t +$
Δt. This procedure is repeated over and over to generate sets of (q_i, p_i) for
successive time increments until, after a sufficiently long time, the molecules
are separating from one another, have vanishingly small intermolecular forces,
and are in one of the four configurations (i) A+BC, (ii) AB+C, (III) AC+B,
(iv) A+B+C. The four configurations correspond to no reaction, reaction to
form AB, reaction to form AC, and fragmentation, respectively. At the end of
the trajectory, the coordinates and mometa (q_i, p_i) are used to calculate any
dynamical variables of interest. These usually include the relative kinetic energy of the separating products, $E_{T'}$; the vibrational and rotational energies of
the molecule, $E_{V'} E_{R'}$; the rotational angular momentum of the product
molecule, $\mathbf{J}'$; the orbital angular momentum of the products, $\mathbf{L}'$; and the scattering angle, θ. This is defined as the angle between the centre of mass velocity vectors of the product molecule and the reactant atom, so that forward
scattering corresponds to $\theta = 0°$.

To calculate cross-sections, it is necessary to compute many trajectories in
the manner just described in such a way as to simulate the collisions between
reactants in the gas-phase. The conditions of the particular experiment being
simulated determine the ranges and distributions of the parameters which
specify each collision. The collision parameters must be selected in accordance
with these distributions. For example, the impact parameter, b, can vary between 0 and ∞ and is distributed as b itself; i.e. more collisions occur at high
impact parameters than at low ones. At the start of the trajectory the reactants are separated by some arbitrary distance R, so that the range of impact
parameter is $0 \leqslant b \leqslant R$; however, there is usually some maximum impact
parameter, $b_{max} < R$, such that no reactive collisions will occur for $b > b_{max}$;
b_{max} is found by trial and error. The range $0 \leqslant b \leqslant b_{max}$ can then be broken
into equally spaced intervals of width Δb, and trajectories can be selected
from each interval with a frequency proportional to $b_i \Delta b$, where b_i is the
mid-point of the ith interval. To calculate the cross-section for a specific process it is only necessary to count up all of the trajectories which lead to that
process, divide by the total number of trajectories, and multiply by πb_{max}^2.
As an example, consider the cross-section for scattering of molecules AB and
AC into a range $\Delta\theta$ about the angle θ_i. Let the number of trajectories for
which this process occurs be $N_r(\theta_i)$. The cross-section is

$$S_r(\theta_i) = \frac{N_r(\theta_i)}{N\Delta\theta} \pi b_{max}^2 , \qquad (3)$$

The differential cross-section $\sigma(\theta_j)$ is obtained from this by dividing by $2\pi \sin \theta_j$. The total reactive cross-section is

$$\sigma_r = \sum_{i=1}^{n_\theta} S_r(\theta_j) \Delta\theta = \frac{N_r}{N} \pi b_{max}^2 \tag{4}$$

where N_r is the number of trajectories for which reaction occurs. Cross-sections for more complicated processes, such as "the scattering of molecule AB into a range $\Delta\theta$ about the angle θ with AB having vibrational energy in a specified range $\Delta E_{V'}$ about $E_{V'}$." can be computed in exactly the same fashion: all trajectories which comply with the definition of the process are summed, divided by the total number of trajectories and multiplied by πb_{max}^2. All the dynamical information is contained in the cross-sections. If rate constants are desired, they can be obtained by suitable averages over the relevant cross-sections expressed as functions of the reactants' relative kinetic energy.

3. Trajectory calculations for various chemical systems

The trajectory analysis technique has been applied to a fairly large number of chemical systems [8-39]. Which reactions are studied is to a large extent dictated by two considerations: (i) the availability of an accurate potential-energy function, and (ii) the amount of detailed experimental data available for comparison with the trajectory results. Other trajectory studies [40-42] have been undertaken in conjunction with quantum calculations in order to assess the validity of the classical approximation itself, but discussion of these is deferred until later.

Of the published trajectory studies, only those treating the reactions $H+H_2 \rightarrow H_2+H$ and $H^++H_2 \rightarrow H_2^++H$ or H_2+H^+ (and their isotopic variants) have made use ot reliable potential surfaces. Until recently, the theoretical calculations for H_3 could only be compared with experimental measurements of rate constants. This meant that large numbers of cross-sections had to be calculated [13] and suitably averaged, a procedure which masks much of the detailed nature of the dynamics. Moreover, rate constants are sensitive to the value of cross-sections near the energy threshold for reaction, and it is in this region where the classical method is most likely to be inadequate [40, 42]. Nevertheless, rate constants from trajectory calculations agreed with experiments to within a factor of two or three. In recent years molecular beam angular distributions for the reaction $D+H_2 \rightarrow HD+H$ have appeared [43], and it is encouraging that the trajectory calculations [37] compare very favour-

Table 1
Some chemical systems treated by trajectory analysis
(M = alkali atom, X = halogen atom, R = inert group)

Chemical system	Number of mass points in simulation	References
$H + H_2 \rightarrow H_2 + H$	3	[8, 10, 13, 30, 37, 40, 42]
$H^+ + H_2 \rightarrow H_2 + H^+, H_2^+ + H$	3	[25, 39]
$H + X_2 \rightarrow HX + X$	3	[11, 14, 18, 41]
$Cl + HI \rightarrow HCl + I$	3	[24]
$Cl + Br_2 \rightarrow BrCl + Br$	3	[33]
$M + XR \rightarrow MX + R$	3	[9, 12, 16]
$M + XRR' \rightarrow MX + RR'$	4	[15]
$M + X_2 \rightarrow MX + X$	3	[22, 23, 26, 27]
$T + HR \rightarrow TH + R, TR + H$	3	[34]
$T + CH_4 \rightarrow TH + CH_3$	6	[31]
$H + HF \rightarrow H_2 + F$	3	[29]
$X + H_2 \rightarrow HX + H$	3	[32, 36, 38]
$H_2 + D_2 \rightarrow 2HD$	4	[17]
$H_2 + I_2 \rightleftharpoons 2HI$	4	[32]
$O + CS_2 \rightarrow SO + CS$	4	[19]

ably with these. That such good agreement can be obtained by the classical method even when light masses are involved, suggests that quantum effects will not completely alter conclusions based on classical studies, and the classical method will surely be an adequate approximation for heavier atoms and molecules.

Calculations on the H_3^+ system have been done [25] using a potential surface obtained from an *ab initio* calculation [44]. Unfortunately, these only considered the thermoneutral reaction $D^+ + H_2 \rightarrow DH + H^+$ and failed to account for the endothermic ($\Delta H \approx + 1.85$ eV) reactions which form the products $DH^+ + H$ or $H_2^+ + D$. However, recent calculations [39] on a diatomics-in-molecules surface [45] allow local non-adiabatic transitions to occur as the products separate and can account very well for the formation of these extra products. This is a very interesting case where a quantum effect (transitions from one potential surface to another) which is ignored at one's peril, can be isolated and satisfactorily taken into account within the framework of a classical calculation. Calculations were done in the normal way exept that, in the region of the surface crossing, trajectories were allowed to continue on both surfaces and were assigned weights proportional to the probability of crossing or remaining on the lower surface. This procedure was repeated for each branch of the trajectory until the products had separated. The relative cross-sections for formation of the various ions are in good agreement with experiment [39, 46]. The H_3^+ system is likely to be a useful testing ground for theoretical methods in the near future.

Potential-energy surfaces for other chemical systems are not as reliable as those of H_3 and H_3^+. Most trajectory calculations are therefore performed with the aid of semi-empirical or empirical functions, such as the London-Eyring-Polanyi-Sato (LEPS) function [14]. Essentially these are formulae which interpolate between the reactant and product molecules' diatomic potential curves for which spectroscopic information is often available. Adjustable parameters are used to alter the shape of the surface and to achieve 'correct' barrier heights for reactions being studied. Such surfaces have been particularly useful in calculations whose objective was to study the change in the reaction dynamics as the shape of the potential function is changed. The method of diatomics-in-molecules [47] has also been used in the H_3^+ work [39, 45] (where it gives a good representation of the surface). This method is also semi-empirical, and because it utilizes the excited state curves of diatomic molecules, it is thereby capable of approximating both excited-state and ground-state surfaces. This potential may find increased favour in future investigations, especially of reactions which involve surface crossings (e.g. in ion-molecule reactions $X^+ + H_2 \rightarrow XH^+ + H$) or which can produce electronically excited products, (e.g. $Cl + Na_2 \rightarrow NaCl + Na^*$ [48]).

Trajectory calculations utilizing semi-empirical surfaces appear in the literature for several different families of reactions. Some of these are listed in the table along with references. Of these studies, some are devoted entirely to the calculations of experimentally observable properties such as rate constants or product angular and energy distributions, some also investigate dynamical behaviour, and others are investigations of the effect of the potential-energy surface on both the observable properties of the products and on the energetic requirements of the reaction. An example of this last type is the study [28, 35] which illustrates that the position of a potential-energy barrier on a "diagnostic" potential surface determines the kind of reactant energy needed to promote reaction. The "diagnostic" surfaces were collinear for 3-atom reactions; planar for 4-atom reactions. Barriers in the 'entrance valley' require reagent translational energy to promote reaction, while those in the 'exit valley' require reagent vibrational energy. Such studies are very useful because they interpret the reactive encounters in terms of qualitative features of the potential surface which are not simply artifacts of the particular semi-empirical function employed. An *ab initio* potential surface will share many of these same features, and therefore would lead to similar reaction dynamics. Also, such trajectory studies allow experiments with reagents excited in different ways to shed some light on the main features of the potential surface.

As an example of the study of dynamical behaviour, I shall first consider the reaction $K+Br_2 \rightarrow KBr+Br$ which I studied with Professor Polanyi and his group at the University of Toronto [26,27]. The dynamical problem here is how to explain the experimental observations [1] of the predominantly forward scattering and large vibrational excitation of product KBr in a way which is consistent with the electron-jump model, which explains so well the large cross-section for this reaction. We found that at the experimental energies used, a 'stripping' model would not be satisfactory, because even though a large number of direct encounters did occur, there were a significant number of trajectories for which the would-be 'spectator' atom could not avoid subsequent collisions with the newly formed KBr molecule. If K were not allowed to react with the retreating Br atom, these collisions were repulsive and prevented KBr from scattering into the forward direction. However, if K was allowed to detach itself from the first Br and bond to the second Br, then the collisions were attractive and the resulting product KBr could be scattered forward. According to our investigations, a single direct interaction mechanism cannot satisfactorily account for the main experimental observations, and there are two or three mechanisms which can operate. Since the relative number of collisions exhibiting each type of mechanism changes in a complicated way with relative kinetic energy and mass combination, it is very difficult to generalize the existing trajectory results to other reactive systems in the same family. An attempt at constructing models for the different mechanistic types succeeded only in the case of the direct interaction mechanism. The direct trajectories could be correlated very well by the model, which leads to analytical expressions for product translational energy and angular distributions[49]. These may prove useful if a chemical reaction is found which *truly* goes by a near direct mechanism in some energy region. The reaction $K + ICH_3 \rightarrow KI + CH_3$ is a likely candidate, for the CH_3 group is very light compared with the I atom, and any repulsion between the two will ensure that the CH_3 group will retreat fast enough to avoid subsequent collision with the newly-formed KI. Present low energy experiments [1] give a backward-peaked angular distribution which can be fit very well by the direct interaction model. The fit is not sensitive to the model parameter, which can be determined from the mean amount of translational energy in the products. However, the energy distributions are far too narrow to agree with experi-

ment, and if any direct interaction mechanism applies in this case, this disagreement might indicate a variation of the repulsive force on CH_3 with molecule orientation.

It should be emphasized that the potential function used in the trajectory
calculations on the $M+X_2$ systems was very crude. Other groups have also
studied this system using different potentials [22,23]. In particular the potential used by Blais [23] relied upon attractive forces between the non-
reactive Br atom and the K^+ and Br^- ions to produce forward scattering.
Collisions were slightly more complex and took about half a rotational period
of the MX_2 aggregate, a result which suggests that the attractive forces pull
the unreactive X atom around and eject it in the backward hemisphere. Apparently more than one mechanism can lead to the desired result, and better
estimates of the potential functions are needed to distinguish between them.

Studies in which I participated with Wong, Nemeth and Polanyi on the
hot-atom reactions of tritium atoms with methane [34] proved somewhat
complicated dynamically, even at the high energies. The tritium atoms could
abstract a hydrogen atom, T + HR → TH + R, or could *displace* the H atom,
T + RH → TR + H. At low energies abstraction is favored, but as energy increases, displacement becomes predominant until at very high energies fragmentation occurs at the expense of displacement. The dynamics of these
processes were studied by following the change in the interatomic forces with
time. The force plots showed a remarkably complicated interplay of forces
which occurred during the course of a trajectory, and revealed that despite
the high energies, the outcome of particular reactive encounters depended on
a delicate balance between repulsive forces and was no easier to predict than
for thermal reactions. These two examples of dynamical studies underline the
fact that even direct interactions can not always be interpreted in terms of a
simple mechanism.

4. An example of a classical trajectory

To illustrate some typical results of a trajectory analysis, I have included
some diagrams showing two trajectories taken from a preliminary study of
the ion-molecule reaction $Ar^+ + D_2 \rightarrow ArD^+ + D$ [50]. An empirical potential
surface for this reaction was constructed by adding ion-induced dipole attraction terms to an LEPS potential for the isoelectronic reaction $Cl + D_2 \rightarrow$
$DCl + D$. The latter reaction is slightly endothermic and its angular potential
energy surface, shown in fig. 1, is repulsive at all angles of approach for
$Cl-D_2$ distances less than about 3 Å. In sharp contrast, the exothermic

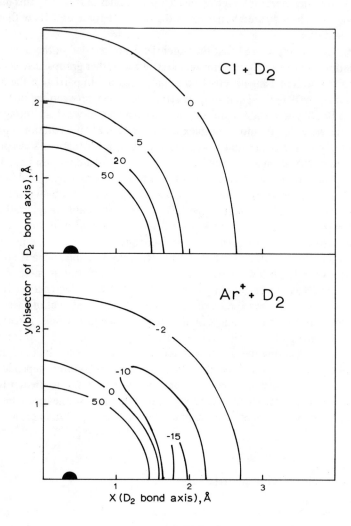

Fig. 1. Angular potential-energy surfaces for Cl + D_2 (LEPS) and Ar^+ + D_2 (LEPS + ion-induced dipole potential). The D_2 molecule lies on the abscissa with its centre at the origin; the heavy dot shows the position of one of the D atoms. Distances are in Å and energies are in kcal mol^{-1}.

($\Delta H \approx -20$ kcal mol^{-1}) ion-molecule reaction has an angular surface which is attractive at long range, and only becomes repulsive at Ar$^+$–D$_2$ distances of less than about 1.5Å. It is instructive to compare trajectories with exactly the same initial conditions on each of these surfaces. In fig. 2 is shown a single trajectory on the Cl + D$_2$ surface. The masses of A, B, and C are 40, 2 and 2 a.m.u. respectively, and the relative kinetic energy is 50 kcal mol^{-1}, most of this being invested in the motion of BC. The trajectories start from the positions marked A, B, C and proceed along the directions indicated by the arrows. The solid black dots mark successive positions of B and C, but since A is so heavy, only the initial and final positions are marked. In the lower part of the figure is a plot of the three interatomic forces as a function of time, the successive black dots along the time axis corresponding to those on the trajectory plot. Up to position 4, there is increasing repulsion between A and

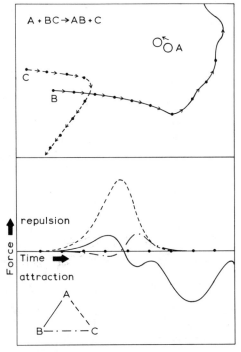

Fig. 2. Planar trajectory and force plots for a relative kinetic energy of 50 kcal mol^{-1}. Masses A, (40 a.m.u.), B (2 a.m.u.) and C (2 a.m.u.) move on the LEPS surface for Cl + D$_2$. Black dots show successive corresponding positions and times for the atoms.

both B and C while the BC bond is mildly resisting being pulled apart. The AC repulsion is very strong and is enough to deflect atom C through a very large angle. From position 5 onwards, B is attracted to A and a repulsi.e force operates between B and C to push them further apart. The trajectory is direct, giving a product molecule AB scattered into the backward hemisphere. Note that B always remains closer to A than C does. Fig. 3 shows that the trajectory for the same mass combination, initial conditions, and energy on the ion-molecule surface behaves in a very different fashion. This time it is atom B which interacts first strongly with A, and half-way between positions 2 and 3 repulsive forces operate between all pairs. When B and C push slightly apart, A at first becomes strongly attracted to B, but then passes through an isosceles configuration so that the roles of B and C are interchanged, and A becomes strongly attracted to C. The product molecule is scattered into a very forward direction. This forward scattering is greatly enhanced by the ability

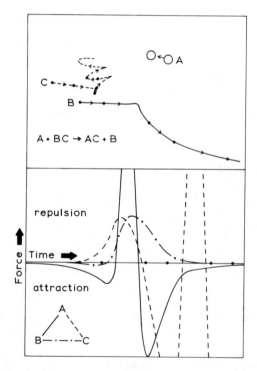

Fig. 3. Planar trajectory and force plots as in fig. 2, but masses move on the $Ar^+ + D_2$ surface.

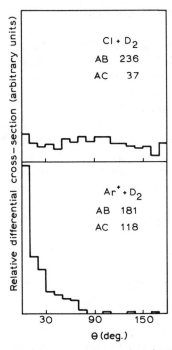

Fig. 4. Distributions of centre of mass scattering angles obtained from 512 trajectories on each potential surface. Forward scattering is $\theta = 0°$. The numbers after AB and AC refer to the number of reactive trajectories yielding AB and AC products respectively.

of A to hop from B to C and by the "focussing" effect of the strong short-range A-B attraction on the outgoing leg of the trajectory. The angular distributions which result from averaging over 512 such trajectories (varying the collision parameters at $E = 50$ kcal mol^{-1}) are shown in fig. 4. The very strong forward peaking for $Ar^+ + D_2$ at this energy is consistent with molecular beam results [4]. The number of trajectories forming AB product and AC product are contrasted for the two surfaces, and the results clearly show that the ability to switch from AB product to AC product in the course of reaction greatly enhances forward scattering. This phenomenon is probably a general one, and not too dependent on the details of the potential surface (with the reservation that the potential determines whether the mechanism will operate at all). Some evidence for this comes from some hard-sphere model calculations of George and Suplinskas [51], who find that the direction of scattering is very different for preferred AB formation or preferred AC formation.

5. The validity of the classical approximation

Several other classical trajectory studies have been carried out in conjunction with quantum mechanical calculations in order to assess the validity of the classical approximation, and to see how the classical variables should be chosen to effect a better representation of the quantum results. The studies of Light and his co-workers on the $H + Cl_2$ reaction [41] revealed the same kind of trends as the classical trajectories: more attractive surfaces produce more HCl vibrational excitation: attraction is particularly effective if it occurs up until the curvature of the reaction path is a maximum. They found that the classical results became more accurate as the total energy increased, and that to achieve best agreement with quantum energy distributions, the Cl_2 molecule should be initially assigned the zero-point vibrational energy and averaged over vibrational phase.

Comparison calculations by Mortensen [40] on an LEPS surface of the reaction probabilities for $H + H_2 \rightarrow H_2 + H$ indicate that the classical results are too low, and this is interpreted in terms of quantum mechanical tunnelling. A very interesting time-dependent quantum mechanical calculation has been recently published by McCullough and Wyatt [42]. They considered the motion of a wave-packet across a semi-empirical potential representing the $H + H_2$ reaction. The time development of the packet is followed and the results graphically displayed by perspective plotting techniques which clearly show the formation of transmitted and reflected wave-packets. Classical trajectories calculated for comparison display many of the same features as the quantum calculations, especially during the first half of the interaction, but they underestimate the size of the transmitted wave-packet and the reaction time. However, as the relative kinetic energy of the reactants is increased, the classical probabilities come closer to the quantum ones. From calculations such as these it is probably fair to say that classical mechanics is competent to estimate many of the dynamical features of chemical reactions. It is obvious that it cannot account for effects such as the existence of zero-point energies, and the above evidence suggests that it will fail in the calculation of cross-sections near threshold, but it appears likely that the gross shape of angular and energy distributions of products can be closely approximated by the trajectory method. There has also been work on semi-classical treatments [6] which use the classical trajectories in order to calculate action integrals which can then be used in a quantum formulation to calculate cross-sections of interest. This method has proved useful in the calculation of elastic and inelastic cross-sections [6, 52] and ought to be useful for reactive collisions as well. Quantum effects such as undulations in the differential cross-section arise because of the interference of waves from two or more different reactive events which both contribute to products at the same energy and scattering angle. This semi-classical method might also be applicable to direct interaction models since the action integrals can easily be calculated; a nice comparison between classical and quantum models could be achieved, since the classical energy and angular distributions are known analytically.

The trajectory analysis technique has been successfully applied to a variety of chemical systems; it has given useful pictures of the dynamics of molecular collisions; and it can be easily extended to the study of systems with more than 3 atoms. The method has proved its worth in chemistry, and should continue to do so.

References

[1] D.R. Herschbach in: *Molecular Beams (Advan. Chem. Phys. Vol. 10)*, Ed. J. Ross, (Interscience Publishers, New York, 1966) p. 319; Numerous studies have been made since this; for examples see: T.P. Schafer, P.E. Siska, J.M. Parson, F.P. Tully, Y.C. Wong and Y.T. Lee, J. Chem. Phys. *53* (1970) 3385;
G.H. Kwei, J.A. Norris and D.R. Herschabch, J. Chem. Phys. *52* (1970) 1317;
V. Kompter, Th. Kneser and Ch. Schlier, J. Chem. Phys. *52* (1970) 5851;
Y.T. Lee, P.R. LeBreton, J.D. McDonald and D.R. Herschbach J. Chem. Phys. *51* (1969) 455.
[2] K.G. Anlauf, P.E. Charters, D.S. Horne, R.G. MacDonald, D.H. Maylotte, J.C. Polanyi, N.J. Skrlac, D.C. Tardy and K.B. Woodall, J. Chem. Phys. *53* (1970) 4091.
[3] J.C. Polanyi and D.C. Tardy, J. Chem. Phys. *51* (1969) 5717.
[4] M. Chiang, E.A. Gislason, B.H. Mahan, C.W. Tsao and A.S. Werner, J. Chem. Phys. *52* (1970) 2698.
[5] P.M. Hierl, Z. Herman and R. Wolfgang, J. Chem. Phys. *53* (1970) 660.
[6] W.H. Miller, J. Chem. Phys. *53* (1970) 1949; ibid 54 (1971) 5386; R.A. Marcus, ibid *54* (1971) 3965.
[7] E.T. Whittaker, *A Treatise on the Analytical Dynamics of Particles and Rigid Bodies* 4th ed. (Cambridge University Press, London, 1964).
[8] F.T. Wall, L.A. Hiller, Jr. and J. Mazur, J. Chem. Phys. *29* (1958) 255; ibid 35 (1961) 1284.
[9] N.C. Blais and D.L. Bunker, J. Chem. Phys. *37* (1962) 2713; ibid *39* (1963) 315;
D.L. Bunker and N.C. Blais, ibid *41* (1964) 2377.
[10] F.T. Wall and R.N. Porter, J. Chem. Phys. *39* (1963) 3112.
[11] J.C. Polanyi and S.D. Rosner, J. Chem. Phys. *38* (1963) 1028.
[12] M. Karplus and L.M. Raff, J. Chem. Phys. *41* (1964) 1267; L.M. Raff and M. Karplus, ibid. *44* (1966) 1212.
[13] M. Karplus, R.N. Porter and R.D. Sharma, J. Chem. Phys. *40* (1964) 2033; ibid *43* (1965) 3259; ibid *45* (1966) 3871.
[14] P.J. Kuntz, E.M. Nemeth, J.C. Polanyi, S.D. Rosner and C.E. Young, J. Chem. Phys. *44* (1966) 1168.
[15] L.M. Raff, J. Chem. Phys. *44* (1966) 1202.

[16] M. Karplus and M. Godfrey, J. Amer. Chem. Soc. 88 (1966) 5332.

[17] K. Morokuma, L. Pederson, and M. Karplus, J. Amer. Chem. Soc. 89 (1967) 5064.

[18] K.G. Anlauf, P.J. Kuntz, D.H. Maylotte, P.D. Pacey and J.C. Polanyi, Disc Faraday Soc. 44 (1967) 183.

[19] I.W.M. Smith, Disc. Faraday Soc. 44 (1967) 1964.

[20] J.V. Dugan, Jr., and J.L. Magee, J. Chem. Phys. 47 (1967) 3103.

[21] J.V. Dugan, Jr., J.H. Rice, and J.L. Magee, Chem. Phys. Letters 2 (1968) 219; ibid 3 (1969) 323.

[22] M. Godfrey and M. Karplus, J. Chem. Phys. 49 (1968) 3602.

[23] N.C. Blais, J. Chem. Phys. 49 (1968) 9.

[24] K.G. Anlauf, J.C. Polanyi, W.H. Wong and K.B. Woodall, J. Chem. Phys. 49 (1968) 5189.

[25] I.G. Csizmadia, J.C. Polanyi, A.C. Roach and W.H. Wong, Can. J. Chem. 47 (1969) 4097.

[26] P.J. Kuntz, E.M. Nemeth, and J.C. Polanyi, J. Chem. Phys. 50 (1969) 4607.

[27] P.J. Kuntz, M.H. Mok and J.C. Polanyi, J. Chem. Phys. 50 (1969) 4623.

[28] J.C. Polanyi and W.H. Wong, J. Chem. Phys. 51 (1969) 1439.

[29] J.B. Anderson, J. Chem. Phys. 52 (1970) 3849.

[30] A. Tweedale and K.J. Laidler, J. Chem. Phys. 53 (1970) 2045.

[31] D.L. Bunker and M.D. Pattengill, J. Chem. Phys. 53 (1970) 3041.

[32] L.M. Raff, L.B. Sims, D.L. Thompson and R.N. Porter, J. Chem. Phys. 53 (1970) 1606;
R.N. Porter, D.L. Thompson, L.B. Sims, and L.M. Raff, J. Amer. Chem. Soc. 92 (1970) 3208.

[33] N.C. Blais and J.B. Cross, J. Chem. Phys. 52 (1970) 3580.

[34] P.J. Kuntz, E.M. Nemeth, J.C. Polanyi and W.H. Wong, J. Chem. Phys. 52 (1970) 4654.

[35] M.H. Mok and J.C. Polanyi, J. Chem. Phys. 53 (1970) 4588.

[36] R.L. Jaffe and J.B. Anderson, J.Chem. Phys. 54 (1971) 2224.

[37] P. Brumer and M. Karplus, J. Chem. Phys. 54 (1971) 4955.

[38] J.R. Muckermann, J. Chem. Phys. 54 (1971) 1155.

[39] J. Krenos, R. Preston, R. Wolfgang and J. Tully, Chem. Phys. Letters 10 (1971) 17.

[40] E.M. Mortensen, J. Chem. Phys. 49 (1968) 3526

[41] D. Russell and J.C. Light, J. Chem. Phys. 51 (1969) 1720.

[42] E.A. McCullough, Jr. and R.E. Wyatt, J. Chem. Phys. 54 (1971) 3578; ibid 54 (1971) 3592.

[43] J. Geddes, H.F. Krause, and W.L. Fite, J. Chem. Phys. 52 (1970) 3296.

[44] I.G. Csizmadia, R.E. Kari, J.C. Polanyi, A.C. Roach and M.A. Robb, J. Chem. Phys. 52 (1970) 6205.

[45] R.K. Preston and J.C. Tully, J. Chem. Phys. 54 (1971) 4297.

[46] J. Krenos and R. Wolfgang, J. Chem. Phys. 52 (1970) 5961; W.B. Maier II, J. Chem. Phys. 54 (1971) 2732.

[47] F.O. Ellison, J. Amer. Chem. Soc. 85 (1963) 3540.

[48] W.S. Struve, T. Kitagawa, and D.R. Herschbach, J. Chem. Phys. 54 (1971) 2759.

[49] P.J. Kuntz, Trans. Faraday Soc. 66 (1970) 2980.

[50] P.J. Kuntz, J.C. Polanyi and A.C. Roach (unpublished work).

[51] T.F. George and R.J. Suplinskas, J. Chem. Phys. 54 (1971) 1037.

[52] R.P. Marchi and F.T. Smith, Phys. Rev. 139 (1965) A1025.

Physics of Electronic and Atomic Collisions, VII ICPEAC, 1971 – North-Holland (1972)

COMPUTER METHODS AND PACKAGES IN
ELECTRON-ATOM COLLISIONS I

Kenneth SMITH*

*Dept. of Physics, University of Nebraska,
Lincoln, Nebraska, 68508, USA*

The purpose of this Progress Report is to survey those software packages for electron-atom collision processes which are readily available to the physics community. The theoretical foundations of these packages and the objectives (experimental results) which they set out to achieve are briefly reviewed. We conclude the Report with a discussion of the numerical problems encountered in implementing this software.

1. Introduction

The scope of this paper is defined by the key-word "Packages" appearing in the title. Numerous computer codes have been written to simulate the scattering of electrons by atomic systems – it is not my intention to produce a catalogue. My objective is to inform you of those codes which can be obtained from their authors as transferable software packages which can then be run to produce *new* results. A word or two of caution about possession of such packages:

1. the preparation of input data and the analysis of output is a major problem in data handling;

2. all packages have parameter regions where various algorithms break down;

3. the more lines of code in a package, the greater the probability of errors which may have gone undetected by the tests and production runs. In other words, in major computer codes it is impossible to ensure that the code is perfect, one can only increase the confidence limits as more and more tests are run.

---

* Postal address 1971–'72: Centre for Computer Studies, University of Leeds, Leeds, England.

The principal interest in software packages is in the transferability of a scientific contribution to knowledge. Without such transferability, there is too much redundancy, re-discovery and costly duplication, thereby negating one of the principles of the scientific method: communication. With the existence of such packages, programs and results can be tested in the same way it has been done for 300 years in theoretical developments, and scientists can advance the discipline by building on the successes of the past.

As far as electron-atom collisions are concerned, transferable software packages exist only within the so-called close-coupling approximation. In sec. 2, we define the desired scope of computer packages for electron scattering by atomic systems, and the related photoionization process, by reviewing some highlights of present experimental knowledge. In sec. 3, we itemize the available software packages and their range of applicability. In sec. 4 we conclude with a discussion of the computer methodology employed in these packages.

2. Electron-atom collisions

2.1. *Theoretical background*

In this paper, the scattering of electrons by atomic systems will be considered only within the framework of non-relativistic Schrodinger wave mechanics. We shall exclude from our discussion classical and semi-classical theories. Furthermore, we shall not consider the effects of including spin-orbit coupling terms in the Hamiltonian. With these restrictions in mind, we are still left with the impossible task of solving the many-dimensional partial differential equations presented in eq. (1), subject to various boundary conditions:

$$\left\{ \sum_{i=1}^{N+1} \left[\frac{\hbar^2}{2m} \nabla_i^2 - \frac{Ze^2}{r_i} \right] + \sum_{i>j} \frac{e^2}{|r_i - r_j|} - E \right\} \tilde{\Psi}(\Gamma':E:x_1 x_2 ... x_{N+1}) = 0 , \tag{1}$$

where Γ' represents the complete set of quantum numbers needed to specify the system in its initial state, and where N is the number of target electrons and Z is the nuclear charge.

To find a solution to eq. (1) we have to determine the real function $\tilde{\Psi}$ for all values of its variables $x_1, ..., x_{N+1}$ where x_i denotes the spin and spatial coordinates of electron "i".

$$\tilde{\Psi}(\Gamma':E:x_1x_2...x_{N+1}) \underset{r_{N+1}\to\infty}{\cong} (N+1)^{-1/2} \sum_\Gamma \psi(\Gamma;x_1x_2...x_N;\hat{x}_{N+1})k_\Gamma^{-1/2}$$

$$\times [\delta_{\Gamma'\Gamma} \sin\theta_\Gamma + R_{\Gamma'\Gamma}(E)\cos\theta_\Gamma] \, r_{N+1}^{-1} . \tag{2}$$

In eq. (2) we exhibit the asymptotic form of $\tilde{\Psi}$ demonstrating the appearance of the reactance matrix $R_{\Gamma'\Gamma}(E)$ from which we calculate the electron-impact cross-sections. In other words, we really need $\tilde{\Psi}$ only in the asymptotic domain in order to compute electron scattering by atomic systems. (The phase angle θ_Γ is defined later in eq. (9).)

In eqs. (3) and (4) we present the formulae for calculating the photoionization cross-section of an atomic system from an initial state LSΠ to a final state Γ in the dipole velocity approximation, where L denotes the total orbital angular momentum of the target atomic system, wave function Φ, S the total spin and Π the total parity. The z-components of L and S are M_L and M_S, while the three components of the dipole velocity operator, $\mathbf{V}$, are identified by m_1.

$$\sigma_v(E,LS\Pi,\Gamma) = [2\pi e^2\hbar^2/m^2 c\nu 2(2L+1)(2S+1)]$$

$$\times \sum_{M_L M_S m_1} \left| \langle\Psi(\Gamma,E,\tau) \sum_{i=1}^{N+1} \nabla_i^{m_1} \Phi(LSM_L M_S\Pi,\tau)\rangle \right|^2 \tag{3}$$

where τ denotes collectively all the electron variables, and the final state wave function, Ψ, is related to the scattering wave function $\tilde{\Psi}$ by

$$\Psi(\Gamma,E,\tau) = \sum_{\Gamma'} (2/\pi)^{1/2} [-i\delta + R(E)]_{\Gamma'\Gamma}^{-1} \tilde{\Psi}(\Gamma',E,\tau) . \tag{4}$$

These formulae require the solution to eq. (1) for all values of the coordinates, not just in the asymptotic domain. The existence of eqs. (3) and (4) enable us to put approximation schemes for generating $\tilde{\Psi}$ to a wider range of tests, thereby offering the opportunity of increasing our confidence limits in the validity of our approximations.

The most important point to note about eq. (1) is that the Hamiltonian is known exactly! We do not have to guess at the nature of Coulomb forces — we know them for all distances between the reactants.

All practical methods for calculating approximate solutions to eq. (1) involve assumptions on the separation of variables in $\widetilde{\Psi}$. In other words, $\widetilde{\Psi}$ is expanded in one form or another in an infinite number of terms. The competition between the various methods reduces to deciding which terms to retain in an expansion. But, what are the guiding criteria? Other than for the simplest collision problem, electrons by hydrogen-like target systems, we have no rigorous mathematical criteria for deciding that one approximation is superior to another. We must compare with experiment.

2.2. Research philosophy

There are experiments of the 1930's, there are experiments of the 1950's, of the '60's and now of the '70's. As the resolution of the apparatus has improved, the amount of data to be interpreted by theoretical models has increased phenomenally. We are now in a position to state the *Publication Law of Experiments*. This law has significant consequences for theoretical models, although they are so often ignored. These consequences can be synthesized into the *Credibility Law of Theoretical Models*.

Publication law of experiments:
Physical systems which yield structure-free data do not excite scientific inquiry.

Credibility law of theoretical models:
Approximation schemes which do not reproduce accepted experimentally determined structures have no credibility when applied to systems where no experiments exist.

Among the non-accepted structures we would include
1. the 0.45 eV resonance in electron-helium scattering reported by Schulz [1];
2. the oscillations in electron-helium scattering observed by Golden and Zecca [2];
3. the pair of autoionizing states in 0^- observed by Edwards, Risley and Geballe [3].

However, such UFO's (unidentified fysical objects) do provide considerable stimulus to exploratory theoretical investigations, as opposed to either repetitive production, or symbolic manipulative theoretical publications.

2.3. Experimental-data structures

In the remainder of this section we shall present a selection of results to illustrate the present experimental position in regard to electron-atom, and related photon-atom, collisions in order to provide a background against which we discuss the computer software simulating these processes.

In fig. 1 we present the experimental results of McGowan et al. [4] on the

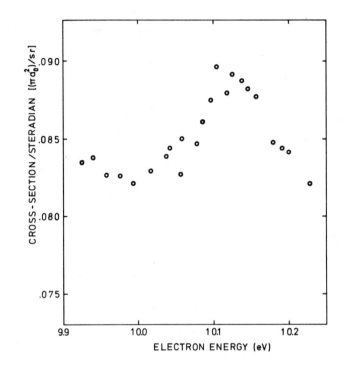

Fig. 1. Experimental cross-section [4] for the elastic scattering of electrons by atomic hydrogen.

scattering of electrons by atomic hydrogen observed over a narrow cone at 90°. Fig. 2 shows the inelastic 2s ← 1s cross-section for electrons on He$^+$ ions as observed by Dance et al. [5] and Daly and Powell [6]. We recall, see eq. (3) that the wave functions generated in e−He$^+$ calculations can be used as the final-state wave functions for photoabsorption in helium; in fig. 3 we remind the reader of the classic results of Madden and Codling [7] which provide a stringent test of the theoretical model.

In fig. 4 we present the experimentally determined spectra for excitation of the 2^3S of helium by electrons at 30°, 60° and 90°, see Ehrhart et al. [8].

We conclude this representative survey of well-established structures by presenting the photoabsorption spectra for nitrogen, (Comes and Elzer [9]) and sulphur (Tondello [10]) in figs. 5 and 6 respectively.

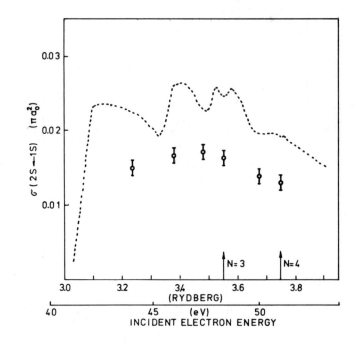

Fig. 2. Experimental cross-sections for the electron impact excitation of the 2s state of He$^+$. Circles with error-bars: Dance et al. [5]; dashed line: Daly and Powell [6].

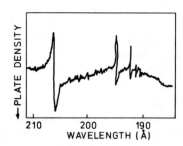

Fig. 3. Densitometer trace of the absorption spectrum of Helium showing the anomalies to have Beutler–Fano shapes (from [7]).

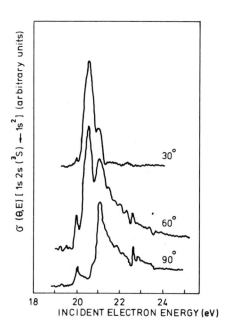

Fig. 4. Spectra for electron excitation of the 2^3S state of Helium at 30°, 60° and 90° (from [8]).

3. Software packages

In fig. 7 we present a chronological survey of the use of computers in electron-atom collisions over the last twenty years, although we must not forget the use of an analogue computer by Morse and Allis in the early 1930's. Until 1960 every computer code was a "one-off" calculations of a specific process, the only physically varying input parameter being the incident electron energy.

Let us remind ourselves that a computer code is the translation into machine language of the mathematical model of a physical system. In other words, running the code is simulating the physical system. In order to simulate

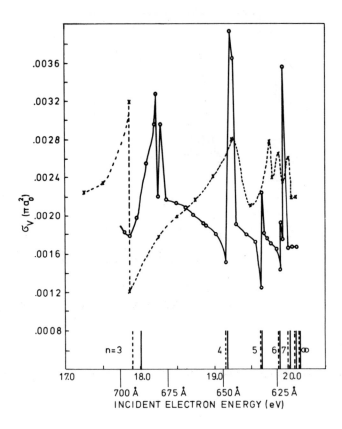

Fig. 5. Cross-section for photoionization of atomic nitrogen. Dashed line: experimental data [9]; solid line: theoretical close-coupling results [28]. The positions of the auto-ionizing levels are taken from Caroll et al. Astrophys. J. *146* (1966) 553.

the physical system under a variety of conditions, the mathematical model must express these conditions. Eq. (1) is an impractical mathematical model.

3.1. *SCATCODE*

The first practical mathematical model to allow us to investigate the scattering of electrons by hydrogen-like systems in any quantum state was formulated by Percival and Seaton [11]. This formulation was translated into a

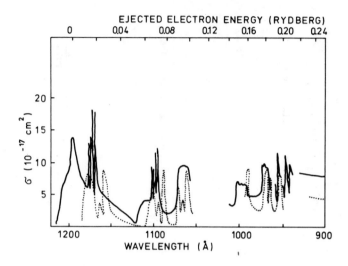

EJECTED ELECTRON ENERGY (RYDBERG)

WAVELENGTH (Å)

Fig. 6. Photoionization cross-section of Sulphur from its $3p^4\ ^3P$ ground state. Solid line: experimental data from Tondello [10]; dashed line: ATOMNP prediction [16].

software package, called SCATCODE, over a five year period by Burke, Schey, Smith, McVicar and Ormonde. Regretably this code has yet to be added to the Program Library of Computer Physics Communications but copies can be obtained from either Burke or Ormonde. A comprehensive discussion is found in Ormonde et al. [12].

3.2. ATOMNP

The success of SCATCODE, and the availability of the giant computers STRETCH and ATLAS encouraged the development of the code ATOMNP which simulates the scattering of electrons by those atomic systems with configurations [13]:

$$\text{either } 1s^2 2s^2 2p^q \quad \text{or} \quad 1s^2 2s^2 2p^6 3s^2 3p^q .$$

This code then computes the photoionization cross-section (see [14]) from the target with configuration p^{q+1}. The software package ATOMNP is available from the program library of Computer Physics Communications [15].

K. Smith, Computer methods and packages

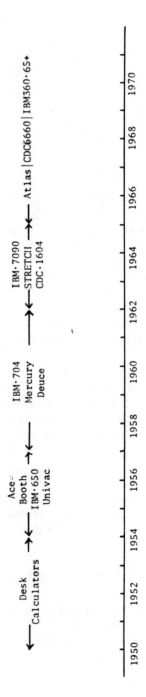

Fig. 7. Chronology of the parallel development of computers and electron-atom software packages.

Just how good is ATOMNP? In fig. 6 we presented a comparison of the *predictions* of ATOMNP (see [16]) compared with the latest observations of Tondello [10] for the photoionization of sulphur from its $3p^4(^3P)$ ground state. We see that there is general agreement between theory and experiment although the precise positions of the resonances and shape parameters are not in good agreement and the absolute value of the photoionization cross-section is somewhat higher than theoretical predictions. In view of the complicated nature of these structures we are tempted to consider the agreement remarkable in view of the nature of the approximations made in these *ab initio* calculations of such a complex target.

A competitor to ATOMNP has been developed by Saraph et al. [17]; more about this package is mentioned in the Report by Eissner [18].

3.3. *ADES*

A three-electron code was developed by Burke et al. [19] to complement the experimental data being collected at the National Bureau of Standards in 1965 on electron-helium scattering. This code, whose mnemonic is ADES, has been adapted to simulate the scattering of electrons by Ca^+ and Mg^+, see Burke and Moores [20] in order to compare with the autoionized states of calcium as observed by Garton and Codling [21]. This package is available from the authors, and a comprehensive description is found in Ormonde et al. [22].

3.4. *SEBAS*

The general theory of the scattering of electrons by any atomic systems was developed by Smith and Morgan [23] and includes all the previously mentioned approximations as special cases. A description of the computer code, SEBAS, based on this analysis is found in [22] and the first results for multi-configuration close-coupling calculations of the autoionizing states of atomic nitrogen are found in Smith and Ormonde [24]. This same code has been used to calculate the resonant structure of lithium between the 2^3S and 2^1P thresholds, see Cooper et al. [25]; other systems have been investigated and were reported on at this conference [26]. In fig. 8 we present a schematic energy-level diagram for electrons incident on O^{++} showing the position of autoionizing states of O^+ as predicted by SEBAS and by Eissner et al. [27], the pair of dotted short horizontal lines labelled (3s).

In fig. 5 we presented the first theoretical calculation of photo-absorption involving an excited configuration of the residual system as carried out by Smith et al. [28]. This software package is currently running on large-scale IBM-360 computers and CDC-6600's and is available from Ormonde.

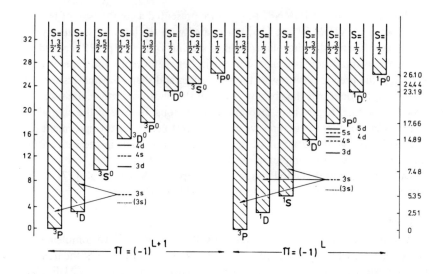

Fig. 8. Schematic energy level diagram of the target atomic terms of the configurations $1s^2 2s^2 2p^2$ and $1s^2 2s2p^3$. The terms are grouped together for the same total parity. The arrows indicate into which continua the autoionized states must decay. L is the total orbital angular momentum of the target.

3.5. DIRAC

The preparation of input data and the analysis of output from large scale atomic scattering codes, run in the production mode, presents a formidable logistics problem. DIRAC, Dynamic Information Retrieval of Atomic Codes is the mnemonic of a computer system which relieves the physicist of these problems. An essential component in the DIRAC system is an interactive graphics device. The system permits the user to view and manipulate his data in the familiar forms of graphs and tables and to generate new data from production codes using a simple Query language. It is hoped that this system will be generally available in the near future [29].

A data bank of all the physics data, experimental or theoretical, is maintained on backing store and interrogated via five directories. If new runs are instigated, producing new data, then the data bank and the appropriate directories are updated automatically. The parameters included in the data bank are R-matrices, eigenphase shifts, electron-impact cross-sections and photon absorption cross-sections. As an option, the data points can be fit to a cubic spline function and a continuous curve drawn on the screen. An interactive resonance routine is available for fitting parameters to the electron scattering-wave phase-shifts and to the photo absorption cross-sections. Hard copies of the results are obtained by "dumping" the screen onto a Calcomp and/or by photographing the screen directly.

4. Computer methodology

4.1. Differential equations

Within the framework of the independent-particle model (Hartree−Fock formalism, close-coupling approximation), see ref. [23], eq. (1) reduces to a system of coupled second order ordinary integro-differential equations as in eq. (5):

$$\left[\frac{d^2}{dr^2} + k_i^2 - \frac{l_i(l_i+1)}{r^2} - \frac{2Z}{r}\right] F_i(r) = \sum_{j=1}^{n} \left[V_{ij}(r)F_j(r) + \int_0^\infty K_{ij}(r,s)F_j(s)\,ds\right]. \quad (5)$$

where V_{ij} and K_{ij} are the direct and exchange potentials respectively, n is the number of channels, while k_i and l_i are the channel wave number and orbital angular momentum respectively.

The whole of the computer methodology is concerned with inventing algorithms leading to the numerical solution of eq. (5) subject to the asymptotic boundary conditions implied by eq. (2) and the requirement that the solutions be physically significant.

Table 1

Numerical techniques for solving systems of coupled second order ordinary integro-differential equations (eq. (5)).

Technique	Authors
1. Iteration	
a. $^{(n+1)}F'' = \int_0^\infty K(r,s)^n F(s)\,ds$	Smith [30]
b. Green's function	McEachran and Fraser [31]
2. Variation-iteration	Sheory [32]
3. Non-iterative	Marriott [33]
4. Matrix	Robertson [34]
5. 2-point boundary value	Feautrier et al. [35]
6. Derivative matrix	Burke [36]

In table 1 we present a comprehensive list of the techniques which have been developed for solving systems of equations as in eq. (5). Data structures are most often found in those regions where some of the k_i^2 are negative, associated with the closed channels:

$$F_i(r) \underset{r \to 10}{\sim} e^{-|k_i|r}, \qquad k_i^2 < 0.$$

One of the most difficult numerical problems is to exclude the unwanted increasing exponential solution. This was solved by Smith and Burke [37] by performing integrations from the origin and from the asymptotic domain and matching at some intermediate point.

The step-by-step numerical integration of eq. (5) has been carried out by numerous methods including the Runge-Kutta, Numerov, Fox—Goodwin, de Voglaraere, etc. A comprehensive survey of these methods in regard to accuracy, computer storage requirements, and CPU efficiency has been carried out by O'Shea [38].

As remarked in the preceeding section, the most flexible computer package available is SEBAS. Within this code, the exchange terms are expressed in terms of y-functions, see eq. (6), which themselves satisfy ordinary differential equations, eq. (7), thus converting the systems of integro-differential equations to an extended set of differential equations only.

$$y_\lambda(A,r) = r^{-\lambda} \int_0^r A(s)s^\lambda \, ds + r^{\lambda+1} \int_r^\infty A(s)s^{-(\lambda+1)} \, ds \tag{6}$$

$$\left[\frac{d^2}{dr^2} - \frac{\lambda(\lambda+1)}{r^2} \right] y_\lambda(A,r) + \frac{(2\lambda+1)}{r} A(r) = 0. \tag{7}$$

4.2. Potential computation

The explicit forms of $V_{ij}(r)$ and $K_{ij}(r,s)$ in eq. (5) involve complicated products of the functions of Racal Algebra, known as generalised re-coupling coefficients. Altorithms have been invented for evaluating these coefficients, see Ormonde et al. [22] and Burke [39].

The r-dependent factors in the direct- and exchange potentials, V and K, involve the assumed known Hartree—Fock orbitals, $P_{nl}(r)$, of the bound electrons of the target system. The existing packages for electron-atom collisions use either the results of the analytic SCF functions of Roothaan and collaborators [40] or the numerical functions of Froese-Fischer [41]. One of the outstanding problems in electron-atom scattering is the generation of accurate bound orbitals for arbitrary electronic configurations. There has been little investigation of the dependence of collision parameters on bound orbitals. In other words, as approximations for the latter are improved, what is the effect on calculated cross-sections?

A problem, related to the choice of $P_{nl}(r)$, is the question of which target atomic term values should be used. For consistency, the theoretical values obtained in the eigenvalue problem which generates $P_{nl}(r)$ should be used. However, the error involved, i.e. comparing refs. [40] and [41] with Moore [42], is usually sufficiently large to shift computed resonance spectra significantly away from the experimentally observed spectra. Consequently, it is common practise to use the hybrid mix of theoretical $P_{nl}(r)$ with experimental term values, $E_{L_1 S_1}$.

4.3. Asymptotic expansions

From eq. (2) we see that we need the asymptotic form of $F_i(r)$ to compute the electron collision cross-sections (but we require the function at all r to compute photoabsorption); in sec. 4.1 we stated that we started inward numerical integration out in the asymptotic domain where eq. (8) is valid.

$$\left[\frac{d^2}{dr^2} +k_i^2 -\frac{l_i(l_i+1)}{r^2} +\frac{2Z}{r}\right] F_i(r) + \sum_{j=1}^{n} \sum_{\lambda=1}^{\Lambda} \frac{a_{ij}^{\lambda}}{r^{\lambda+1}} F_j(r) = 0 . \tag{8}$$

Consequently, it is of cardinal importance to generate accurate asymptotic solutions. Burke and Schey [43] proposed a descending polynomial expansion for neutral systems which was generalized to charged systems by Burke, McVicar and Smith [44]. Norcross and Seaton [45] have proposed a method based on the WKB method which under certain conditions is more reliable than [44]. However, at thresholds and in their vicinity, the radial functions are not linear combinations of $\sin \theta_i$ and $\cos \theta_i$ where

$$\theta_i = k_i r - \eta_i \log 2|k_i|r + \sigma_{l_i} - i\pi/2 . \tag{9}$$

The analogue to this inadequate asymptotic form in the neutral single channel problem is equivalent to using the trigonometric function to approximate a straight line. The correct asymptotic forms at $k_i^2 \approx 0$ have been given by Smith [46] in terms of Bessel–Clifford functions.

At the present time, none of the available software packages have a totally reliable algorithm for computing cross-sections at, and in the vicinity of, thresholds. Consequently, it is not possible to investigate directly an important class of data structures — the threshold laws.

Acknowledgements

This work was supported by the National Science Foundation. The author is most grateful to Stephan Ormonde for his help in putting this paper together.

References

[1] G.J.Schultz, *IV ICPEAC, Abstracts of Papers,* eds. W.L.Fite et al. (Science Bookcrafters, Inc., New York, 1965) p. 117.

[2] D.E.Golden and A.Zecca, Phys. Rev. A *1* (1970) 241.

[3] A.K.Edwards, J.S.Risley and R.Geballe, Phys. Rev. A *3* (1971) 583.

[4] J.W.McGowan, E.M.Clarke and E.K.Curley, Phys. Rev. Letters *15* (1965) 917; *17* (1966) 66;
J.W.McGowan, Phys. Rev. *156* (1967) 165.

[5] D.F.Dance, M.F.A.Harrison and A.C.H.Smith, Proc. Roy. Soc. *290* (1966) 74.

[6] N.R.Daly and R.E.Powell, Phys. Rev. Letters *19* (1967) 1165.

[7] R.P.Madden and K.Codling, Astrophys. J. *141* (1965) 364.

[8] H.Ehrhardt and K.Willmann, Z. Phys. *203* (1967) 1;
H.Ehrhardt, L.Langhans and F.Linder, Z. Phys. *214* (1968) 179.

[9] F.J.Comes and A.Elzer, Phys. Letters *25*A (1967) 334.

[10] G.Tondello, Astrophys. J. (1971) to be published.

[11] I.C.Percival and M.J.Seaton, Proc. Cambridge Phil. Soc. *53* (1957) 654.

[12] S.Ormonde, W.Whitaker, W.Huebner and P.G.Burke, Report No. AFWL-TR-67-10 (1967) unpublished.

[13] K.Smith, R.J.W.Henry and P.G.Burke, Phys. Rev. *147* (1966) 21;
K.Smith, M.J.Conneely and L.A.Morgan, Phys. Rev. *177* (1969) 196.

[14] R.J.W.Henry and L.Kipsky, Phys. Rev. *153* (1967) 51.

[15] M.J.Conneely, L.Lipsky, K.Smith, P.G.Burke and R.J.W.Henry, Comput. Phys. Commun. *1* (1970) 306.

[16] M.J.Conneely, K.Smith and L.Lipsky, J. Phys. B *3* (1970) 493.

[17] H.E.Saraph, M.J.Seaton and J.Shemming, Proc. Phys. Soc. *89* (1966) 27.

[18] W.Eissner, *VII ICPEAC, Invited Talks and Progress Reports,* eds. T.R.Govers and F.J.de Heer (North-Holland Publ. Co., Amsterdam, 1972) p. 460.

[19] P.G.Burke, J.W.Cooper and S.Ormonde, Phys. Rev. *183* (1969) 245.

[20] P.G.Burke and D.L.Moores, J. Phys. B *1* (1968) 575.

[21] W.R.S.Garton and K.Codling, Proc. Phys. Soc. *86* (1965) 1067.

[22] S.Ormonde, B.W.Torres and K.Thomas, Report No. AFWL-TR-70.37 (1970) unpublished.

[23] K.Smith and L.A.Morgan, Phys. Rev. *165* (1968) 110.

[24] K.Smith and S.Ormonde, Phys. Rev. Letters *25* (1970) 563.

[25] J.W.Cooper, M.J.Conneely, K.Smith and S.Ormonde, Phys. Rev. Letters *25* (1970) 1540.

[26] S.Ormonde, K.Smith and B.W.Torres, *VII ICPEAC, Abstracts of Papers,* eds. L.M. Branscomb et al., Vol. 2 (North-Holland Publ. Co., Amsterdam, 1971) p. 1025.

[27] W.Eissner, H.Nussbaumer, H.E.Saraph and M.J.Seaton, J. Phys. B *2* (1969) 341.
[28] K.Smith, S.Ormonde and K.Thomas, Phys. Rev., to be published.
[29] A.R.Davies, K.Smith and K.L.Kwok, Comput. Phys. Commun., in preparation.
[30] K.Smith, Phys. Rev. *120* (1960) 845.
[31] R.P.McEachran and P.A.Fraser, Can. J. Phys. *38* (1960) 317.
[32] V.B.Sheorey, Proc. Phys. Soc. *92* (1967) 531.
[33] R.Marriott, Proc. Phys. Soc. *72* (1958) 121.
[34] H.H.Robertson, Proc. Cambridge Phil. Soc. *52* (1959) 538; also see:
M.J.Seaton, *Conference Digest Computational Physics* (Institute of Physics, 1970) p. 19.
[35] N.Feautrier, P.Feautrier and Vo Ky Lan, C.R.Acad. Sci., Ser. A *267* (1968) 1.
[36] P.G.Burke, *Conference Digest Computational Physics* (Institute of Physics, 1970) p. 9;
P.G.Burke, A.Hibbert and W.D.Robb, J. Phys. B *4* (1971) 153.
[37] K.Smith and P.G.Burke, Phys. Rev. *123* (1961) 174.
[38] B.B.O'Shea, Ph. D. thesis (London, University, 1970).
[39] P.G.Burke, Comput. Phys. Commun. *1* (1970) 241.
[40] C.C.J.Roothaan and P.S.Kelly, Phys. Rev. *131* (1963) 1177.
[41] C.Froese-Fischer, Comput. Phys. Commun. *1* (1970) 151.
[42] C.E.Moore, *Atomic Energy Levels* (NBS Circular 467) U.S.Govt. Printing Office, Washington, D.C., 1949 (Vol. 1), 1952 (Vol. 2), and 1958 (Vol. 3).
[43] P.G.Burke and H.M.Schey, Phys. Rev. *126* (1962) 163.
[44] P.G.Burke, D.D.McVicar and K.Smith, Proc. Phys. Soc. *83* (1964) 397.
[45] D.Norcross and M.J.Seaton, J. Phys. B *2* (1969) 731.
[46] K.Smith, unpublished preprint (1970).

Physics of Electronic and Atomic Collisions, VII ICPEAC, 1971 — North-Holland (1972)

COMPUTER METHODS AND PACKAGES
IN ELECTRON-ATOM COLLISIONS II

W. EISSNER

University College London, Department of Physics,
Gower Street, London W.C. 1, England

Fast general-purpose computer programs are described which provide
data on atomic structure and on the excitation of atoms and ions by electron impact. The target wave functions are obtained in a statistical-model
central field. Two further classes of programs are discussed: they are used
to handle R-matrix data pooled on tapes, and to calculate collision strengths
and finestructure terms. We give some typical results obtained with the
programs.

1. Introduction

This progress report is on computer programs for excitation of atoms and
ions by electron impact and about auxiliary programs for supplying and for
processing data. It is confined to a package that has been developed at University College, London. Our interest lies mainly in the excitation of light- to
medium-heavy atoms (up to around Fe) and their ions at low energies, that is
in the near-threshold region. A partial-wave treatment suits this purpose. The
two collision programs, APEX and IMPACT in fig. 1, both use this method.
ASAR, the first program in the figure, computes atomic-structure data in a
statistical-model central field. Large sections of its code are incorporated in
APEX, which computes electron-collision data in a distorted-wave (DW) approximation. This report concentrates on these two programs. They are fully
automatic general-purpose computer programs, allowing for configuration
mixing which is important for highly ionized systems (Layzer [1]); "general
purpose" stands for not specific for certain ions or isoelectronic sequences.
Distorted-wave results are satisfactory for more than two- or three times
ionized atoms; then the Coulomb force dominates. For lower stages the
partial wave systems of coupled integro-differential equations should be solved
exactly, at least for small total orbitals. IMPACT serves this purpose.

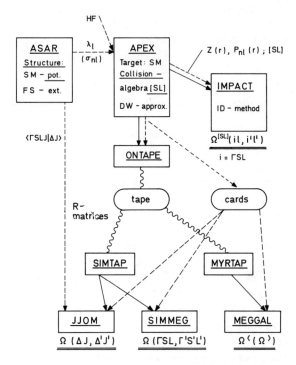

Fig. 1. Computer programs described in this report and their relation to each other. Connecting lines: —— magnetic (disk) link; ∼∼∼ magnetic tape; - - - - data card input. Two lines leading *to* the same point: alternative data link. SM stands for "statistical model", FS for "finestructure", DW for "distorted wave", ID for "integro-differential", and HF for "Hartree–Fock". $\Omega^{\langle}(\Omega^{\rangle})$ indicates that collision strengths below threshold are computed by using those above threshold.

ONTAPE, SIMTAP and MYRTAP are programs for storing $\mathbf{R}$-matrix data, e.g. APEX output, on tape, and for selectively calling it from tape for further processing. SIMMEG, JJOM and MEGGAL compute collision strengths from $\mathbf{R}$-matrix data. We express cross-sections in terms of collision strengths, $\Omega(i,i')$:

$$Q(i\rightarrow i') = \frac{\pi}{k_i^2 g_i}\, \Omega(i,i') \ . \tag{1}$$

Ω is symmetric in i and i', g_i is the statistical weight of the initial state i. We use Rydberg units (Ry) for energies, and the Bohr radius a_0 as unit of length. Eq. (1) maintains its form with this re-definition, but k_i^2 can be interpreted as the energy of the incident electron in Ry.

We are now going to describe the programs in detail.

2. ASAR: computation of term energies and radiative-transition data

ASAR, "*A*tomic *S*tructure *A*nd *R*adiation", is a general purpose program which computes term energies and radiative-transition data of atoms and positive ions using a scaled statistical-model (Thomas–Fermi–Dirac) potential. The standard version, for terms S_iL_i, has been described by Eissner and Nussbaumer [2]. Jones [3] has extended this program to include relativistic effects as a perturbation. This improves the positions S_iL_i markedly for more highly ionized states, where the original version gives less satisfactory results, and it allows for fine-structure splitting resulting in terms J_i.

The minimum input is a list of configurations C one wants to include, and one card for each element of the isoelectronic sequence one wants to compute; apart from the atomic number Z one specifies on this card the number M of lowest terms to be minimized (see eq. (9)). Further input, such as starting values λ_l^0 for the scaling parameters – from previous experience – and initial screening coefficients, σ_{nl}^0 (see eq. (8)), are optional and reduce computer time. The input data may be looked up in fig. 2, which shows the principal overlay structure of the program.

The algebra – the first primary branch, supervised by routine ALGEB – is performed completely automatically from the list of C's. The problems which one encounters when dealing with equivalent electrons, can easily be overcome by using Slater-state expansions. Reducing the angular part of expectation values of one- and two-particle operators then involves little more than products of Clebsch–Gordon coefficients, but numerous summations over Slater states $|j\rangle$ and over particle numbers $(1...N)$. However, present-day computers perform this sort of slave work fairly economically, except perhaps for heavy atoms with some ten open-shell electrons.

In ALGEB1 we construct states tM_SM_L of total SL belonging to configurations C,

$$t = C\beta SL \qquad (2)$$

from Slater states $|j\rangle$, which form our internal frame of reference. The parameter β allows for degenerate SL. Slater-ordered Slater-states are set up in a first

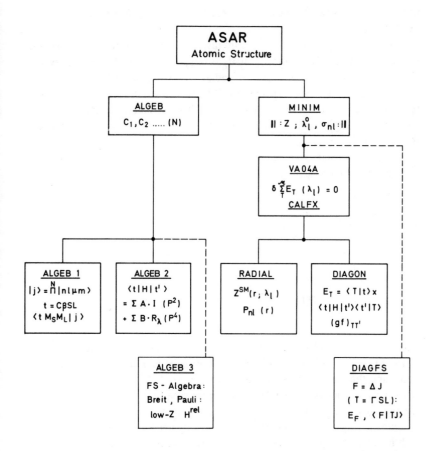

Fig. 2. Flow diagram of the atomic structure program ASAR. Boxes carry the name of the leading subprogram; they may also contain subroutines called by routines at higher level of the overlay structure. Broken lines: finestructure (FS) extension of the standard version.

step by a fast routine (called from ALGEB1) that handles equivalent electrons in a straightforward way, and are stored in integer arrays. Integers can be used throughout by storing twice the angular quantum numbers; incidentally, this meets the requirements of the very efficient Copenhagen package [4] of coupling-function routines. In the N kets $|nl\mu m\rangle$ forming $|j\rangle$ in block ALGEB1 of fig. 2, μ stands for m_s and m for m_1; indices $i(=1...N)$ are omitted. The total spin number S is understood to stand for multiplicity $(2S+1)$, with a minus sign if C is of odd parity; see table 1, e.g. $SL = -3P$ for $CSL =$ $1s^2 2s2p\ ^3P^o$.

For calculating SL terms one could dispose of Slater states with total magnetic quantum numbers other than $M_L = 0$, and $M_S = 0$ or $1/2$, respectively. More are needed in computations of radiative decay and of fine-structure terms. Vector coupling coefficients $\langle tM_SM_L | j \rangle$ come out as the elements of the equivalence transformation that diagonalizes S^2 and L^2 simultanously. An alternative approach to the Slater-state method has been developed by Bordarier [5], and is based on Jucys graphs.

In ALGEB2, matrix elements to the non-relativistic Hamiltonian for N electrons in an electric nuclear field Z,

$$H = \sum_{i=1}^{N} \left\{ h_i + \sum_{j<i} \frac{2}{r_{ij}} \right\}, \tag{3}$$

where

$$h_i = -\frac{d^2}{dr^2} + \frac{l(l+1)}{r^2} - \frac{2Z}{r}, \tag{4}$$

are reduced. For each element $\langle t|H|t' \rangle$ one obtains a sum over Slater integrals $R_\lambda(nl,n'l';n''l'',n'''l''')$ and $I(nl,n'l)$ with coefficients A and B. These coefficients and the arguments of the integrals are stored. Also reduced matrix elements for electric dipole- and quadrupole transitions between the t's are worked out and stored.

Jones [3] approaches the problem from the non-relativistic limit dealt with in the embryonic program, by including the most important parts of the low-Z Hamiltonian as a perturbation. Terms of higher order in the Breit interaction than $Z^4\alpha^2$ and $Z^3\alpha^2$, are neglected. The angular parts are reduced in ALGEB3, in a representation fM_J where

$$f = C\beta SLJ . \tag{5}$$

One recouples tM_SM_L to fM_J with Clebsch–Gordan coefficients.

In the second primary branch of fig. 2, headed by MINIM, at first radial functions $P_{nl}(r)$ are integrated numerically,

$$\left[\frac{d^2}{dr^2} - \frac{l(l+1)}{r^2} + \frac{2Z(\lambda_l;r)}{r} + \epsilon_{nl} \right] P_{nl}(r) = 0 , \tag{6}$$

a scaled Thomas–Fermi–Dirac potential $V(\lambda_l;r) = 2Z(\lambda_l;r)/r$ having been obtained by numerical integration (the λ_l's are scaling parameters). An alternative approach to this statistical-model potential (S.M.) is Klapisch's [6] parametric potential. Clearly the boundary conditions are

$$\lim_{r\to 0} Z(\lambda_l;r) = Z , \qquad \lim_{r\to\infty} Z(\lambda_l;r) = Z - N + 1 . \tag{7}$$

One integrates the eigenvalue equation (6) starting with $Z(\lambda_l^0;r)$ and a tentative eigenvalue

$$\epsilon_{nl}^0 = \frac{(Z-\sigma_{nl}^0)^2}{n^2} . \tag{8}$$

If $M \neq 0$, the program varies the λ's in order to minimize the energy sum of the target states T:

$$\delta \sum_T^M g_T E_T(\lambda_l) = 0 , \tag{9}$$

where

$$g_T = (2S_T+1)(2L_T+1) \tag{10}$$

is the statistical weight. The term energies E_T are computed in DIAGON as the eigenvalues of the H-matrix $\langle t|H|t'\rangle$. The scaling parameters λ_l are close to unity (default value $\lambda_l^0 = 1.0$). One may use different scaling parameters for functions $P_{nl}(r)$ corresponding to different angular quantum numbers l, according to input specifications. Applying the variational principle to the energy does not necessarily give good results for other atomic data obtained with these functions. We shall make use of them as target functions in atomic scattering. A crucial criterion is to check radiative results. How much correlation one might have to allow for in electric-dipole transition probabilities can be seen from Sinanoğlu's comments [7].

The components $\langle t|T\rangle$ of the eigenvector to the eigenvalue E_T form the target states

$$T = \Gamma SL \tag{11}$$

as an expansion of pure configuration terms t:

$$|T\rangle = \langle t|T\rangle|t\rangle . \tag{12}$$

In spectroscopy one is used to put the main contributor "C" in place of Γ; this makes sense for not too highly ionized stages: see Layzer's theory [1]. The case of C III in fig. 4 may serve as an example: mixing with the quasi-degenerate configuration $1s^2 2p^2$, which is the least one has to do, results in the following composition of the ground state $''1s^2 2s^2{}''{}^1 S$:

$$|''1s^2 2s^2{}''{}^1 S\rangle = 0.9610|1s^2 2s^2\ {}^1 S\rangle + 0.2767|1s^2 2p^2\ {}^1 S\rangle .$$

In DIAGFS the matrix $\langle f|H^{\mathrm{rel}}|f'\rangle$, constructed with radial functions that satisfy eq. (9), is diagonalized. This gives eigenvalues E_F to levels

$$|F\rangle = \langle f|F\rangle|f\rangle . \tag{13}$$

We introduce a parameter Δ similar to Γ of eq. (11):

$$F = \Delta J . \tag{14}$$

If sensible one may name Δ by the main contributor $C\beta SL$. The matrix

$$\langle \Delta J|\Gamma SLJ\rangle = \langle \Delta J|t\rangle\langle t|\Gamma SLJ\rangle \tag{15}$$

may be used for recoupling to intermediate wave functions of total angular momentum J. This is done in program JJOM for obtaining more refined collision data from mere $[SL]$-reactance matrices — as indicated by an arrow in fig. 1.

Both DIAGON and DIAGFS also compute gf-values for radiative transitions, as described by Eissner and Jones [8].

3. Partial-wave treatments by APEX and IMPACT

3.1. APEX

This program computes **R**-matrices for excitation of systems as described before by electron collisions in a distorted-wave (DW) method. It is based on the representation of the incident electron by a partial-wave expansion. Non-relativistic Coulomb interaction is assumed between target and electron. The flow diagram, fig. 3, reflects the principal overlay structure. The first secondary branches on both primary levels deal with the target problems as de-

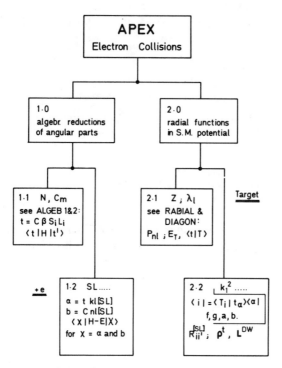

Fig. 3. Overlay structure of the collision program APEX.

scribed in ASAR: block 1.1 requires the same list of configurations C; 2.1 uses scaling parameters λ_l, obtained from running ASAR, to reproduce target wave functions P_{nl} that satisfy the variational principle for the term energies of an ion Z; computing time is reduced if σ_{nl} is also supplied.

The other two secondary branches, which deal with the collision process, expect equally little input — again it is quoted as a first line in the boxes concerned in fig. 3: routine 1.2 reads a card for each intermediate state $[SL]$ of the total system of target plus partial-wave electron (and if storage is exhausted, it skips the rest which must then be run separately). Square brackets are used to indicate that we have states other than target states in mind. Block 2.2 requires a list of the collision energies k_1^2 one is interested in (the subscript indicates reference to the ground term of the target), and information on scaling parameters to be used in the DW treatment.

The second algebraic branch, 1.2, starts with a state $[SL]$ by setting up a channel list, and then computes the collision algebra — i.e. the angular coefficients in the systems of coupled integro-differential equations (ID) for radial partial-wave functions, $F_{kl}(r) = \langle kl|r \rangle$. As the algebraic reductions require

$$\int_0^\infty \mathrm{d}r F_{kl}(r) P_{nl}(r) = 0 , \tag{16}$$

we have to separate all those components $P_{nl}(r) = \langle nl|r \rangle$ concerned in a particular $\lfloor SL \rfloor$ by expanding

$$F_{kl}(r) = F_{kl}^0(r) + \sum_n (\int \mathrm{d}r F_{kl}(r) P_{nl}(r)) P_{nl}(r) . \tag{17}$$

This leads to additional terms in the ID system. Their angular coefficients may be found by adding "bound" channels b to the list of ordinary "free" channels α:

$$\alpha = tkl[SL] , \tag{18}$$

$$b = C^{(N+1)}[SL] , \tag{19}$$

where

$$C^{(N+1)} = Cnl \tag{20}$$

is an $(N+1)$-electron configuration. Reduction of $\langle \chi|H-E|\chi' \rangle$, where each of χ and χ' can stand for either α or b, provides a complete set of elements and coefficients for setting up the ID's of $\lfloor SL \rfloor$. Again Slater states are used, for the α's by adding on an electron $|kl\mu m\rangle$ to $|t\rangle$. With Clebsch—Gordan coefficients target states $|tM_S M_L\rangle$ and states $|kl\mu m\rangle$ may be coupled to $|\alpha[M_S M_L]\rangle$ – for one convenient total $\lfloor M_S M_L \rfloor$ of $N + 1$ electrons. This implies that a complete Slater set of the target, with all $(M_S M_L)$'s is available. The algorithm for generating Slater states of "bound" channels is the same as for the target problem.

As usual we write $f_\lambda^{\alpha\alpha'}$ and $g_\lambda^{\alpha\alpha'}$ for the coefficients to multipole potential integrals $y_\lambda(nl,n'l';r)$ and $y_\lambda(nl,k'l';r)$ in the ID's; as before, we omit the nl's on these coefficients. Apart from $\langle \alpha|H-E|\alpha' \rangle$ we have to reduce $\langle \alpha|H-E|b \rangle$. In the notation of Eissner and Seaton [9] b_λ^{ab} are coefficients to Slater integrals R_λ, and a^{ab} those to integrals I (derived from eq. (4)). Finally $\langle b|H-E|b' \rangle$ has the form of the target reductions.

With target energies and mixing coefficients (of eq.(12)) for a value Z and scaling factors λ_l computed in block 2.1, collision data for one or more collision energies k_1^2 are worked out in 2.2. First the algebraic channels α must be transformed to a system of channels i,

$$|i\rangle = \langle t_\alpha | T_i \rangle |\alpha\rangle , \tag{21}$$

in which the channel energy is properly defined (and thus the asymptotic form of the solutions):

$$K_{ii'}^2 = (E - E_{T_i}) \delta_{ii'} . \tag{22}$$

The transformed coefficients $f_\lambda^{ii'}, g_\lambda^{ii'}, \alpha^{ib}, b_\lambda^{ib}$ may be passed on to IMPACT ([SL] on arrow in fig. 1), or they may be processed further in a distorted-wave treatment, as follows. We solve trial functions

$$\left[\frac{d^2}{dr^2} - \frac{l(l+1)}{r^2} + \frac{2Z^{SM}}{r} + k^2 \right] F_{kl}(r) = 0 \tag{23}$$

in a suitable statistical-model potential with asymptotic behaviour:

$$\lim_{r \to \infty} Z^{SM}(r) = Z - N . \tag{24}$$

This gives elastic reactance-matrix elements

$$R_{ii}^t = \tan \xi_i \tag{25}$$

by comparing the phase shifts of the trial function with that of the Coulomb function in the asymptotic region,

$$F_{k_i l_i}(r) \cong \frac{1}{\sqrt{k_i}} \sin(k_i r + \eta^{\text{Coulomb}}(Z, k_i r) + \xi_i) . \tag{26}$$

Whether one uses the same scaling parameters for Z^{SM} in eq. (23) as for the target, or values obtained for atoms one stage less ionized, makes little difference. The small changes in R_{ii}^t are almost exactly compensated by the Kohn correction. The correction terms are dealt with in the more flexible reactance matrix (ρ) formulation of Kohn's variational principle,

$$\delta(\rho - L) = 0 \tag{27}$$

as given by Saraph et al. [10] . On choosing

$$\boldsymbol{\rho}^t = 0 , \tag{28}$$

their phase transformation reads

$$\mathbf{R} = [\sin \xi + \cos \xi \, \boldsymbol{\rho}] \, [\cos \xi - \sin \xi \, \boldsymbol{\rho}]^{-1} \tag{29}$$

with ξ a diagonal matrix; the Kohn correction L in

$$\boldsymbol{\rho}^k = \boldsymbol{\rho}^t - \mathbf{L} \tag{30}$$

is then based on distorted wave functions $F_i(r)$ with the more advantageous normalization of eq. (26). The Lagrange integrals $L_{ii'}$ are computed observing eq. (17) — but the additional terms, from separating-off target components, are added on variationally, thus making use again of eq. (27). The direct potentials $y_\lambda (nl,n'l';r)$ give rise to long-range integrals; they are computed with Belling's routines [11] . Punched R-matrix output (or data on a punch file, which may directly be processed by program ONTAPE) carries $R_{ii'}$ as well as $R_{ii'}^t$ and $\rho_{ii'}$.

Program APEX allows for two special facilities. One might want to suppress terms above a specified term. So channels due to terms arising from pure correlation configurations will always be ignored; those configurations are merely added for improving target functions (see Nussbaumer [12]). Mind that the collision algebra is required for all correlation channels linked in eq. (21) for improving a target term. Another facility is to omit partial waves $l \geqslant$ LCUT; they may already be ignored in the α-channel list.

A third facility, indicated by an arrow labelled HF in fig. 1, makes it possible to employ target functions P_{nl} other than orthonormalized central-field solutions. Clearly this requires the first facility also: Hartree—Fock functions to different terms SL are not properly orthogonal — this is another reason why S.M.-functions are a quite good compromise, except perhaps for persistent cases like He!

APEX produces tabulated output as well as output onto a punch-file. The latter consists of a term list and of R-matrix cards suitable for processing in SIMMEG, JJOM or MEGGAL. In a core partition of 45k words approximately 60 coupled channels can be handled. A small case, say in the Be-sequence with 3 configurations included, takes up less than 30 seconds on a. CDC6600 for 3 energies k_1^2 of one of the bigger systems $[SL]$ of coupled equations (11 channels).

3.2. *IMPACT*

This is a fast program strictly aimed at solving the coupled ID-equations. Partial collision-strengths are printed as output, the input comes from (APEX minus DW application) —see fig. 1. IMPACT has been developed by Seaton, and the ideas it is based on have been sketched by Burke and Seaton [13]. The ID equations are reduced to a system of algebraic equations, by considering the functions as tabulated and applying finite-difference formulae. This is done in a range $0 < r \leqslant r_M$; at $r = 0$ a power series expansion is used. Outside r_M the exponentially decaying exchange integrals can be ignored, and the direct terms, $V_{ii'}$, be treated in a long-range formulation; for $r \geqslant r_M$ Norcross' [14] program is used, and the solutions fitted at two additional points r_{M+1} and r_{M+2} of IMPACT. The tabulation points, typically 4 to 5 per half-period (optional through input), are set up from an approximate solution $kl = k_{max}s$ in a central potential: $Z(r)$ from APEX, as seen in fig. 1. The program allows for variable steplength, securing a maximum change ratio (by an input parameter, typically 1.2) to safeguard numerical stability. If NMX is the number of tabulation points required, and NCHF the number of (free) channels, then a linear system for NMX · NCHF unknowns has to be solved, say 20 · 10 = 200; one ends up with a few more, if orthogonalizations (eq. (16)) with resulting Lagrange parameters are involved, and also if this results in additional bound channels. Efficient matrix inversion routines must be employed, with proper pivoting which is essential for numeric stability. An advantage of the method is that the number of time-consuming operations does not increase for configuration-mixed terms. Storage requirements restrict the method to small energies in all channels – where the distorted wave method is not too good. Time compares favourably with other methods.

4. ONTAPE: storage of and collision strengths from R-matrix data

The program ONTAPE stores sets of R-matrices, such as created by APEX, on a tape file. It opens a new file, or it places them after previously compiled data, having printed a short list of what's on the file: a line for every ion, followed by one line for each intermediate state $[SL] k_1^2$.

The information is very much condensed, although still legible when printed: in 40-character records – as opposed to the 80-character cards punched by APEX. One may process the punch file of APEX directly, if a back-up deck is not required. For recreating the original R-matrix card images program SIMTAP or a suitable derivative such as MYRTAP may be used.

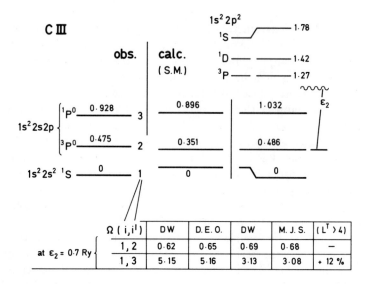

Fig. 4. C III, term energies (in Ry) and collision strengths; top: term schema; left: observed term energies; center: calculations with ASAR, 2 configurations; right: allowing for configuration mixing with $1s^2 2p^2$; bottom: collision strengths for exciting the second and third term from the ground state, with collision energy of 0.7 Ry of the leaving electron. Distorted-wave results (DW, from APEX) are compared with close-coupling calculations: D.E.O. for Osterbrock's results [15], M.J.S. for results obtained with IMPACT. [L] ⩽ 4 included, higher partial wave contributions to optically allowed transitions are estimated assuming a geometric progression.

Big block sizes can be chosen as the program is very small. This assures a big loading factor of the tape, even for big interblock gaps (3/4''). The number of records one can accomodate lies between just under 10^5 and more than 5×10^5, depending upon length (1200' or 2400'), density and number of tracks. CPU time is in the order of 10 seconds, if the data to be recollected (e.g. by SIMMEG) is scattered all over the tape. However, elapse time is considerably larger. On non-timesharing machines data should be arranged on separate files.

Table 1

Sample of results for C III with 3 configurations: C_1, C_2 and C_3 as in fig. 4. Selected print-out produced by SIMMEG and JJOM; top: term list, resulting from ASAR/APEX center: collision strengths (eq. (31)), all $[L-S] < 10$ (in eq. (32)) included, from **R**-matrices computed by APEX; bottom: FS-transitions $\Omega(\Gamma SLJ, \Gamma'S'L'J')$ (eq. (38)) computed with the same **R**-matrices.

C III in 3 configurations: C1 = 1S2 + 2S2, C2 = 1S2 + 2S1 + 2P1, C3 = 1S2 + 2P2

I	S	L	(EI−E1)/RY	CSL
1	1	0	0.0	(C 1) 1S
2	−3	1	0.48603154	(C 2)−3P
3	−1	1	1.03242460	(C 2)−1P
4	3	1	1.26730019	(C 3) 3P
5	1	2	1.41766775	(C 3) 1D
6	1	0	1.77948152	(C 3) 1S

Total collision strengths in SL-coupling

Initial	Final	I	I′	E = 2.486037	1.486037	1.186029
(C 1) 1S	(C 2)−3P	1	2	0.444465	0.614055	0.690465
(C 1) 1S	(C 2)−1P	1	3	4.973769	3.668613	3.567002
(C 1) 1S	(C 3) 3P	1	4	0.015107	0.018031	0.0
(C 1) 1S	(C 3) 1D	1	5	0.250180	0.260868	0.0
(C 1) 1S	(C 3) 1S	1	6	0.014403	0.0	0.0
(C 2)−3P	(C 2)−1P	2	3	1.099927	1.676256	2.198707
(C 2)−3P	(C 3) 3P	2	4	29.747459	22.129697	0.0
(C 2)−3P	(C 3) 1D	2	5	0.896998	1.280424	0.0
(C 2)−3P	(C 3) 1S	2	6	0.099855	0.0	0.0
(C 2)−1P	(C 3) 3P	3	4	0.567131	0.873845	0.0
(C 2)−1P	(C 3) 1D	3	5	20.164249	16.640012	0.0
(C 2)−1P	(C 3) 1S	3	6	5.829131	0.0	0.0
(C 3) 3P	(C 3) 1D	4	5	3.108314	4.304765	0.0
(C 3) 3P	(C 3) 1S	4	6	0.434151	0.0	0.0
(C 3) 1D	(C 3) 1S	5	6	0.627462	0.0	0.0

Finestructure collision strengths for 3C2+

Transition						
Initial CSLJ		Final CSLJ		E = 2.486037	1.486037	1.186029
(C 1) 1S	0.0	(C 2)−3P	0.0	0.049385	0.068228	0.076718
(C 1) 1S	0.0	(C 2)−3P	1.0	0.148155	0.204685	0.230155
(C 1) 1S	0.0	(C 2)−3P	2.0	0.246925	0.341142	0.383592
(C 1) 1S	0.0	(C 2)−1P	1.0	4.932936	3.667048	3.566953
(C 1) 1S	0.0	(C 3) 3P	0.0	0.001679	0.002003	0.0
(C 1) 1S	0.0	(C 3) 3P	1.0	0.005036	0.006010	0.0

W. Eissner, Computer methods and packages

Table 1 (continued)

Transition						
Initial CSLJ			Final CSLJ		E = 2.486037	1.486037	1.186029

Initial CSLJ		Final CSLJ		E = 2.486037	1.486037	1.186029
(C 1) 1S	0.0	(C 3) 3P	2.0	0.008393	0.010017	0.0
(C 1) 1S	0.0	(C 3) 1D	2.0	0.249641	0.260867	0.0
(C 1) 1S	0.0	(C 3) 1S	0.0	0.014403	0.0	0.0
(C 2)−3P	0.0	(C 3)−3P	1.0	0.500070	0.714735	0.808260
(C 2)−3P	0.0	(C 2)−3P	2.0	0.310080	0.338339	0.344072
(C 2)−3P	0.0	(C 2)−1P	1.0	0.122214	0.186251	0.244301
(C 2)−3P	0.0	(C 3) 3P	0.0	0.037298	0.056260	0.0
(C 2)−3P	0.0	(C 3) 3P	1.0	3.139613	2.312504	0.0
(C 2)−3P	0.0	(C 3) 3P	2.0	0.062347	0.089623	0.0
(C 2)−3P	0.0	(C 3) 1D	2.0	0.099666	0.142269	0.0
(C 2)−3P	0.0	(C 3) 1S	0.0	0.011095	0.0	0.0
(C 2)−3P	1.0	(C 2)−3P	2.0	1.321869	1.654165	1.784074
(C 2)−3P	1.0	(C 2)−1P	1.0	0.366642	0.558752	0.732902
(C 2)−3P	1.0	(C 3) 3P	0.0	3.186398	2.312907	0.0
(C 2)−3P	1.0	(C 3) 3P	1.0	2.529190	1.970510	0.0
(C 2)−3P	1.0	(C 3) 3P	2.0	4.006001	3.091009	0.0
(C 2)−3P	1.0	(C 3) 1D	2.0	0.298999	0.426808	0.0
(C 2)−3P	1.0	(C 3) 1S	0.0	0.033285	0.0	0.0
(C 2)−3P	2.0	(C 2)−1P	1.0	0.611071	0.931253	1.221504
(C 2)−3P	2.0	(C 3) 3P	0.0	0.062352	0.089623	0.0
(C 2)−3P	2.0	(C 3) 3P	1.0	4.134727	3.092784	0.0
(C 2)−3P	2.0	(C 3) 3P	2.0	12.080383	9.109110	0.0
(C 2)−3P	2.0	(C 3) 1D	2.0	0.498332	0.711346	0.0
(C 2)−3P	2.0	(C 3) 1S	0.0	0.055475	0.0	0.0
(C 2)−1P	1.0	(C 3) 3P	0.0	0.063015	0.097094	0.0
(C 2)−1P	1.0	(C 3) 3P	1.0	0.189044	0.291282	0.0
(C 2)−1P	1.0	(C 3) 3P	2.0	0.315073	0.485469	0.0
(C 2)−1P	1.0	(C 3) 1D	2.0	19.620320	16.628942	0.0
(C 2)−1P	1.0	(C 3) 1S	0.0	5.818199	0.0	0.0
(C 3) 3P	0.0	(C 3) 3P	1.0	0.604445	0.798112	0.0
(C 3) 3P	0.0	(C 3) 3P	2.0	0.330600	0.380414	0.0
(C 3) 3P	0.0	(C 3) 1D	2.0	0.345368	0.478307	0.0
(C 3) 3P	0.0	(C 3) 1S	0.0	0.048239	0.0	0.0
(C 3) 3P	1.0	(C 3) 3P	2.0	1.498829	1.853338	0.0
(C 3) 3P	1.0	(C 3) 1D	2.0	1.036105	1.434922	0.0
(C 3) 3P	1.0	(C 3) 1S	0.0	0.144717	0.0	0.0
(C 3) 3P	2.0	(C 3) 1D	2.0	1.726841	2.391536	0.0
(C 3) 3P	2.0	(C 3) 1S	0.0	0.241195	0.0	0.0
(C 3) 1D	2.0	(C 3) 1S	0.0	0.625400	0.0	0.0

5. The treatment of collision strengths from R-matrix data by SIMMEG, SIMTAP, MEGGAL and MYRTAP

5.1. SIMMEG

This program has been described by Saraph [16]. It computes collision strengths

$$\Omega(i,i') = \sum_{l,l'} \Omega(il,i'l') \qquad i = \Gamma_i S_i L_i \tag{31}$$

between terms ΓSL from reactance-matrix input. Print-out of partial collision strengths,

$$\Omega(il,i'l') = \frac{1}{2} \sum_{[SL]} (2S+1)(2L+1)|T^{[SL]}(il,i'l')|^2 \tag{32}$$

can also be obtained. We still put intermediate collision states $[SL]$ in brackets. As usual, T is the transmission matrix,

$$T = 1 - S, \tag{33}$$

and S the scattering matrix,

$$S = (i-R)/(i+R). \tag{34}$$

The program performs elaborate checks for completeness of the R-matrix deck, according to heading card instructions, on states $[SL]$, partial l and energies k_i^2 to be expected.

5.2. JJOM

This program* is an extension of SIMMEG. It computes collision strengths for transitions between finestructure terms ΔJ by processing reactance matrices to total $[SL]$ as discussed. The results therefore are approximations. They should be quite good if the finestructure splitting is small enough compared to the distance between terms ΓSL.

The program operates in two modes of approximation: either by transforming the R-matrices to pair coupling using algebraic recoupling coefficients,

---

* Added in proof: H.E.Saraph, Comput. Phys. Commun. 1972, in press. The program has been registered under the name JAJOM.

$$R^{[J]}_{k^2_1} (\Gamma SLJlK, \Gamma'S'L'J'l'K')$$

$$= \quad C([SLJ], SLJ, lK) * R^{[SL]}_{k^2_1} (\Gamma SLl, \Gamma'S'L'\,'l') * C([SLJ], S'L'J', l'K') , \quad (35)$$

where

$$(36)$$

$$C([SLJ], SLJ, lK) = \sqrt{[(2S+1)(2L+1)](2K+1)(2J+1)} \, W([L]lSJ;LK) W([LJ]S^{\frac{1}{2}}_2;[S]K) ,$$

(the W's are Racah coefficients) or with allowance of term coupling in target by employing the coefficients of eq. (15). This becomes important for heavier atoms, when various target -SL's are more strongly mixed. The energy-extrapolation problem for **R**-matrix elements mixed in this transformation would have to be discussed. We simply write

$$R^{[J]} (\Delta JlK, \Delta'J'l'K')$$

$$= \quad \sum_{\Gamma SL, \Gamma'S'L'} \langle \Delta J | \Gamma SLJ \rangle R^{[J]}(\Gamma SLJlK, \Gamma'S'L'J'l'K') \langle \Gamma'S'L'J' | \Delta J' \rangle . \quad (37)$$

Using eq. (33) and related ones, the final result reads:

$$\Omega(XJ, X'J') = \frac{1}{2} \sum_{[J]} [2J+1] \sum_{ll'KK'} |T^{[J]}(XlK, X'l'K')|^2 , \quad (38)$$

where $X = \Gamma SL$ or $X = \Delta$ for the two approximations. In the example of table 1 the Ω's differ by less than 1 per cent for the two methods.

5.3. *SIMTAP*

This program enables SIMMEG and JJOM to be run with tape data alone or with card data as well. No changes other than in job control are required: SIMTAP is run as first step in a job with either program. It generates an output (scratch) file that is a correct input file to the two programs. SIMTAP itself expects the same card input as SIMMEG or JJOM — but with some or all requested **R**-matrices missing. They will be inserted from tape data (see sec. 4) if they are there. Cards override matrices from tape, which readily allows for corrections, particularly with data from more refined methods. SIMTAP prints short messages while searching proceeds: one line if it finds the requested ion, and one line for each of the wanted intermediate states. It should be noted that the intermediate states of any one may be scattered all over the file, separated by data on other ions (or the same ion but with different number of terms etc.). However, mind the comment in sec. 4.

5.4. *MEGGAL*

This program computes partial collision strengths from reactance-matrix data (APEX), taking into account the effects of closed channels near their threshold on accessible transitions. Interpolated collision strengths for requested collision energies can also be obtained. The program has been developed by Hershkowitz [17].

The S-matrix is calculated in a first Born approximation in the reactance matrix — an approximation consistent with the DW method — and reactance matrices ρ — eq. (28) — are chosen for processing. It follows for inelastic transitions that

$$S_{\alpha\beta} = 2i\rho_{\alpha\beta} . \tag{39}$$

Using the notation of eq. (31) we write

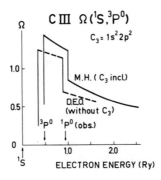

Fig. 5. C III, $\Omega(1s^2 2s^2\ {}^1S, 1s^2 2s2p^3P^0)$ as function of incident electron energy. D.E.O.: Osterbrock's two configuration calculations [15]; M.H.: Hershkowitz's [17] application of MEGGAL, processing (and interpolating) APEX results of the case on the right-hand side in fig. 4 given at 3 energies.

$$\overline{\Omega}^{[SL]}(il,i'l') = \Omega^{[SL]}(il,i'l') + \sum_{l''} \frac{\Omega(il,tl'')\Omega(tl'',i'l')}{\sum_{jl'''} \Omega(tl'',jl''')} \tag{40}$$

for the collision strength below $(<)$ a threshold t, averaged over the resonances (see Gailitis [18] and also Seaton [19]). The program uses Ω's interpolated to the threshold. Fig. 5 contains an application.

5.5. MYRTAP

This program plays the same role as an input editor for MEGGAL as SIMTAP does for SIMMEG and JJOM.

Acknowledgements

I would like to thank M.Hershkowitz, M.Jones, H.E.Saraph and M.J. Seaton for contributions.

References

[1] D.Layzer, Ann. Phys. (New York) 8 (1959) 271.
[2] W.Eissner and H.Nussbaumer, J. Phys. B 2 (1969) 1028.
[3] M.Jones, J. Phys. B 3 (1970) 1571.
[4] J.H.Gunn, Comm. ACM 8 (1965) 217, 492, 493.
[5] Y.Bordarier, thesis (Paris 1970).
[6] M.Klapisch, thesis (Paris 1969).
[7] O.Sinanoğlu, Comments Atomic Molecular Phys. 2 (1970) 73.
[8] W.Eissner and M.Jones, J. Phys. (Paris) C 4 (1970) 149.
[9] W.Eissner and M.J.Seaton, to be submitted to J. Phys. B.
[10] H.E.Saraph, M.J.Seaton and J.Schemming, Phil. Trans. A 264 (1969) 77.
[11] J.A.Belling, J. Phys. B 1 (1969) 136.
[12] H.Nussbaumer, Astrophys. J. 166 (1971) 411.
[13] P.G.Burke and M.J.Seaton, Methods Comput. Phys. Vol. 10 (1971) 1.
[14] D.Norcross, Comput. Phys. Commun. 1 (1970) 88.
[15] D.E.Osterbrock, J. Phys. B 3 (1970) 149.
[16] H.E.Saraph, Comput. Phys. Commun. 1 (1970) 232.
[17] M.Hershkowitz, private communication.
[18] M.Gailitis, Zh. Eksp. Teor. Fiz. 44 (1963) 1974, [English Transl.: Soviet Phys. -JETP 17 (1963) 1328].
[19] M.J.Seaton, J. Phys. B 2 (1969) 5.

Physics of Electronic and Atomic Collisions, VII ICPEAC, 1971 – North-Holland (1972)

COMPUTERS IN EXPERIMENTS

CHRISTOPH G. SCHLIER

*Physics Department, University of Freiburg,
D 7800 Freiburg, German Federal Republic*

An increasing number of collision experiments are connected on-line with a (generally small) computer. Data acquisition, experiment control and data evaluation are its tasks. It allows more complex strategies for signal detection, and feedback from the experimental results to the measuring process which is in progress. It saves some work and gives flexibility in case of changes in the experiment. – This paper discusses the building blocks of the experiment-computer system, possible computer tasks, and trends in software and man-machine communication.

1. Introduction

"Computers in Experiments" is a wide topic. It ranges from the computer-controlled Apollo missions to very simple set-ups, such as a calorimetric experiment in which the thermocouple is connected to a desk-top calculator. Though there are many similiar techniques – e.g. the body temperature of an astronaut will be monitored not much differently than the oven temperature in a beam experiment – there are also many differences in size- and time scale, which prevent me from covering the field of computer-assisted experiments in all its width.

In this paper I will restrict myself in two ways:

(1) I will consider only techniques which are applicable in experiments within the field covered by this conference, and

(2) I will focus very much on experiments where the computer is an integral part of the set-up, which means that it must generally be connected on-line to be considered here. All cases where the computer is only used to post-proces data collected by conventional means are excluded.

I will however, include a section (Sec. 3) about signal detection, since it is my view that if one endeavours to use computer control in an experiment, one should also try to utilize it for better signal-detection schemes. The remaining sections will treat computer hardware (Sec. 2), the three basic tasks of a computer in an experiment, that is: data acquisition (Sec. 4), experiment control (Sec. 5), data evaluation (Sec. 6), and finally software and man-machine interaction (Sec. 7). The paper closes with some remarks about the reception of computers in the laboratory and some indications about the cost of present day's systems. (Sec. 8)

2. Computer hardware and interfacing

The basic building blocks of a computer-controlled experimental set-up can be seen in fig. 1. Functional rather than device-oriented modular blocks are shown. These blocks are, morever, independent of the main alternative, with which one is faced in a big laboratory: shall one give each experiment its own dedicated computer, or use a big time-shared computer for all of them concurrently (cf. sec. 8)?

In fig. 1 the computer proper is made up of the central processing unit (CPU) and its storage. But since it does not work without human interaction,

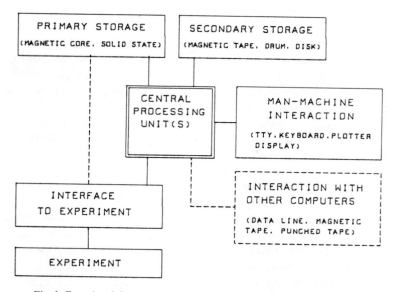

Fig. 1. Functional diagram of a computer-controlled experimental system.

and since manpower is one of the most expensive ingredients of an experiment, the block called man-machine interaction is one of the most important parts of the system (cf. also sec. 7). In small computer systems the ubiquitous component at that place has been a teletype keyboard and printer. Recent technology has produced hardware, which does not have the deficiencies of a mechanical design: purely electronic keyboards and printing mechanisms with only a few moving parts. The latter are either mosaique printers (i.e. the characters are produced from dots in a 5 X 7 matrix, their printing being either thermal [1] or by impact [2]) or impact printers with only one moving print head [3].

Since experimental data are often displayed in graphic form — the reason is man's better ability to read a graph rather than a table of numbers — a computer-controlled plotter will be a useful further option. The basis choice is between plotters driven by a stepping motor (precise but slow, need special interface) and a normal analogue x-y plotter (fast, accuracy $\lesssim 0.1\%$, can be used with the digital-analog converter (DAC) of the experimental interface).

The fastest way to get the computer's answer in a dialog is a display tube, two kinds of which are not so expensive: (a) alpha-numeric displays with character storage in a refreshing memory, and (b) storage oscilloscopes. The latter are, to-date, less easy to read but they have the advantage that they can be programmed for graphics.

Many other possibilities exist for human control, especially in large systems where the overhead cost of employing punched cards or large cathode-ray tube (CRT) displays are easier to bear. In a small system on the other hand, one has another problem: its computing power may not be sufficient to carry out all stages of computing which are needed after the data are collected on-line from the experiment. So an interface to a larger computer, e.g. the university's computing center, is needed. Up to now this interface in most cases has been man, i.e. people have punched printed data in cards and entered those into the big computer. Others have used punched paper tape. Today, when setting up an experiment controlled by a small computer, one should keep in mind that a data-communication line to a large computer is probably the most efficient method. To put the data on a telephone line from your small computer is no longer costly, and the odds that your big computer is equipped to receive them are becoming very high these days. Again, the decision to "satellitize" your small computer may depend much more on the software available than on hardware costs. The devices mentioned so far and others, and their cost are collected in table 1, which has been prepared from manufacturers' material and ref. [4].

Speaking of computerized experiments, the most important interaction to

Table 1
Prices (in $) of small computer system components

A) CPU + 4 K storage	5.000 – 12.000
Hardware multiply	1.000 – 1.500
Floating point processor (if available)	10.000
B) Additional core storage 4 K	2.600 – 6.000
C) Secondary storage	
Small disk	6.000 – 20.000
Cartridge magnetic tape	3.000 – 7.000
D) Computer-computer-interface	
Paper tape (reader + punch)	4.000 – 6.000
"Compatible" magnetic tape	5.000 – 11.000
Data line interface (one side of line)	1.500 – 2.500
E) Computer-man-interface	
Printer + keyboard (TTY)	1.500 – 1.800
Mosaique printer + keyboard	2.500 – 3.500
Ruggedized TTY	ca. 5.000
Alphanumeric display + keyboard	ca. 4.000
Storage oscilloscope + coupler	ca. 6.000
Analog plotter + coupler	2.000 – 4.000
F) Computer-experiment interface	
Basic cost	0 – 2.000
I/O register (12–16 bits)	100 – 500
Clock	250 – 500
DAC (pair of)	800 – 2.500
ADC (10 bit, 50 kHz)	1.000 – 3.000

describe in this chapter is certainly that of the computer with the experiment. This interaction takes place through what is generally called *the* interface.

Figure 2 shows which types of circuits it may contain. Remember that the computer can only interact with the experiments electrically. Every computer-controlled movement in your apparatus has to be actuated by magnet or motor, and every reading of a parameter of the machine relies on the measurement of a voltage or a current which is in some way modulated (provided with a "code") by the parameter value.

The usual codes representing information, which is to be exchanged between computer and experiment are (1) digital values, i.e. bits or parallel strings of bits, (2) analog values, i.e. the voltage or current value itself, or (3) pulses, where the simplest code is given by counting their number serially.

Thus we find 3 ports by which information flows to or from the experi-

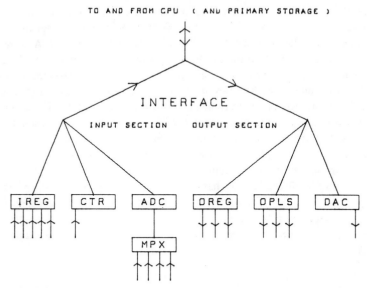

Fig. 2. Main building blocks of computer-experiment interface (CPU = central processing unit, IREG = input register, CTR = pulse counter, ADC = analog-digital converter, MPX = multiplexer, OREG = output register, OPLS = output pulser, DAC = digital-analog converter).

ment: (1) registers, i.e. parallel storage cells (flipflops) for digital information, (2) analog-digital and digital-analog converters, and (3) pulse counters and output pulsers.

It is only a few years ago, that the experimentalist who wanted to interface his experiment to a computer, had to construct all of this interface himself. The computer ended in a bus directly connected to its CPU, where a lot of timing conditions had to be fulfilled in order to have the circuit work. Nowadays many of the minicomputer firms provide registers and analog-conversion equipment as an option to their computer. Pulse handling modules are seldom offered, which is a pity since many of our detectors give their information primarily as pulses. Moreover, voltage-to-frequency conversion (output-pulse rate proportional to voltage input) is very often to be preferred to normal, sampled, analog-digital conversion. Output pulses, too, are frequently needed, but in many cases they can be produced without a special pulser by setting a one-bit register for a fixed time.

Of course the picture drawn so far is too simple. Since the voltages needed by experimental equipment or produced by it are not standardized, a second stage of interfacing is necessary: conversion of the voltage (or current) levels between the interface of fig. 2 and the apparatus. Since operational amplifier are inexpensive this is no serious problem for the experimentalist. A more serious one is the fact that for anything approaching complete computer control many *mechanical* movements and pointers have to be interfaced to electrical ones. Many different types of actuators and transducers for angle, position, force, pressure etc. have to be chosen from a large variety. This is one of the few points where the experimentalist needs an engineer very much. Only for those experiments, where the main machine is manufactured rather than built in the lab (e.g. optical spectrometers or mass-analysers) will these controls in the near future be available commercially with the apparatus.

In conclusion it can be said that the interfacing of those parts of the experimental set-up which are electrically controlled anyhow, no longer represents a problem and that it should not prevent one from using computer control. The complete control including mechanical parts, however, is still engineering work.

3. Signal detection

It is a common observation that a physicist in our field always tries to improve his apparatus by increasing his beam intensity [5]. This is, however, in many cases wrong. What he really should maximize is the signal-to-noise ratio, where "signal" is what he wants to measure. This is sometimes, but not always, improved by an increase of beam intensity: it depends very much on how the noise is increased simultaneously.

A convenient way to discuss an experimental set-up with respect to its signal and noise properties, is to treat it as a communication channel [6] by which nature communicates certain quantities to us. (The noisiness of that channel corresponds to the fact that every measurement is prone to errors. Hence any induction from experiment has to employ some statistical hypothesis, an idea already reflected by J. Bernoulli.)

Figure 3 shows how a molecular beam scattering apparatus might look from this point of view. Both beams s_1 and s_2, are necessarily modulated. (This modulation may be produced by a chopper wheel, but may also be the on-off performed manually at 1 Hz, which is sometimes called "student's modulation".) The cross-section to be determined comes in here as the degree of modulation m of s_1 by s_2. Noise comes in at different places, of which only two have been drawn. At the end, the ultimate signal, which is m, has to be extracted, generally by some kind of synchronous demodulation (be it only with paper and pencil).

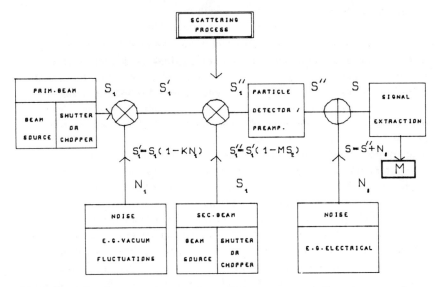

Fig. 3. Signal flow in a scattering experiment. Only two representative noise sources have been drawn, a multiplicative one (n_1) and an additive one (n_0). The degree of modulation m is proportional to the effective scattering cross-section.

What has all this to do with computers? This is answered in the following two statements:

1. The possibilities to use better detection schemes to improve on the signal-to-noise ratio of the quantity to be determined have largely not been exploited in the field of atomic collisions, exept for the use of look-in (= synchronous) detectors and signal averagers. In other fields the situation is a little better, cf. the use of Fourier-transform techniques in NMR [7] and optical spectroscopy.

2. Any such improvement will be practicable only by the use of a computer in the experiment. This is because (a) the detection schemes tend to be complex, and (b) the modulation frequencies (of s_1 and s_2) have to be high, say 10 or 100 Hz or more, instead of the 0.1 or 0.01 Hz which can be handled manually. The reason is that the noise-power spectrum of (probably) any beam apparatus is not flat, but rather of the $1/f$ type [8].

4. Data acquisition

We come now to the three tasks which a computer has to perform in a computer-assisted experiment. The simplest such task, and in many existing systems the only one, is data acquisition: the counting of pulses, the sampling of analog signals, or the reading of data pre-registered in some external device.

There are three reasons to use computer-based data acquisition. The first one is often convenience, especially when the data shall be further processed by computers. The next argument is the sheer *number* of data bits which modern measurement strategies generate. These data have to be reduced by computer anyhow, and doing this "in real-time" (i.e. concurrently with the acquisition of further data) can save much storage and makes experimental results available to the experimenter at an early time.

Finally, the *rate* at which data are generated (measured in bits/s) may exclude any kind of acquisition other than storage on magnetic tape or in a computer core. This is most important if the measuring device works in a burst mode, e.g. with pulsed light sources or in time-of-flight applications. The maximum data rates which can be handled depend very much on the amount of special electronics outside of the computer. The following are typical values obtainable:

Time Averaging (Analog Sampling):

With direct memory access (DMA), fast analog-digital conversion (ADC), and all channel advance electronics outside of computer: up to 10^6 samples (of 10 bits) per second.

With programmed input/output (I/O), computer-supplied ADC, and programmed channel advance: about 5×10^4 samples (of 10 bits) per second.

Multi-scaling:

Maximum reasonable counting rate without excessive dead time losses: 30 MHz.

Maximum channel advance rate with DMA and much external electronics: 1 MHz.

Maximum channel advance rate with programmed I/O, and programmed channel advance control: ca. 50 kHz.

The computer is presently the most powerful data acquisition tool existing. Nevertheless it has limits which can only be extended with excessive expense. Limits on the data *rates* have been shown; limits on the *amount* of data are set by memory cost or processor speed, because data have to be stored or concentrated after acquisition. In the bulk of today's collision experiments these limits will not easily be reached.

5. Apparatus control

Even if the main reason to buy a computer for connection with an experiment may be data acquisition, more advanced systems will certainly use the computer to control the apparatus as well. It's almost free, as long as the operation involved is of the on-off type (e.g. relays, valves, beam shutters), or controlled be equipment which the manufacturer has made "programmable". Other quantities are more difficult to control, and it will certainly be an exceptional case if the task of filling the liquid-nitrogen trap is transferred from man to computer.

A few useful applications of computer control shall be mentioned: First of all, it will generally save some of the experimenter's time by taking charge of tasks as the supervision of machine parameters, periodic calibration procedures, and parameter changes in multi-parameter experiments. Secondly, it gives the possibility to use feedback from the results just obtained to the data acquisition running. E.g. the duration of a single measurement may be made result-dependent, or out-of-range values may be automatically remeasured. Signal search is another possibility, and finally it has already been mentioned in sec. 3 that complex kinds of synchronous detection can only be implemented with a computer.

There are no general rules stating to what extent computer control is sensible, since this depends on the whole milieu of the experimenter's laboratory.

6. Data evaluation

Since most experimentalists have the goal to ultimately publish the results of their measurements in readable form, data evaluation is indispensable, and there are few experiments nowadays, where a computer does not enter somewhere into this procedure. If a computer-based experiment employs a time-shared large computer, there is nothing more to say here. If a small computer is used, the evaluation of an experiment is usually divided into two stages: first comes *data reduction,* i.e. concentration to essential (less redundant) data by simple algorithms, and then a stage of *data evaluation* (in the narrow sense), where complex algorithms and intelligent intervention of the scientist are employed. Lack of memory space and of well supported man-machine communication often prevent one from performing this second stage on the small experiment-computer. In this case easy data transmission to some larger computer is mandatory (cf. also Sec. 8).

Hardly any general statement can be made about the schemes used for data reduction. In planning a system one should, however, keep in mind that it is this stage, where processor word length, the availability of multiplication (and, possibly, floating point-) hardware, software support, and processor speed play a much more important role than in the acquisition part of the game.

7. Software and man-machine communication

This brings us to another important point in the discussion of computer-based experiments: computers have to be programmed. Now in a good school programming of numerical problems in a language like FORTRAN is generally taught. But the problems are not purely numerical here. At least the I/O operations of the experiment interface must be programmed in another language. At present this will generally be some assembler language. Higher languages for process control are offered by some manufacturers [9] and discussed by computer scientists [10]. For experiment control, especially if the data rates are high, these languages will probably not suffice, because they are designed for industrial process control, where the time scale is generally much slower than in our experiments. Moreover, the storage requirements to compile the "bigger" of these languages are large, so they will not fit into a small "stand-alone" computer. (So far, compilers for many of them do not exist anyhow.)

Now the scientist endeavouring to use computer-based apparatus will have to learn a few things, e.g. electronics, in any case. Thus, assembly language will not generally be unacceptable to him, if it can be utilized conveniently enough. Ideally this would mean the existence of a small operating system (requiring in turn some secondary storage) plus some simple means to connect these assembler programs to others written in a higher language.

If speed is not too much at stake, it appears to be a good compromise (offered by some manufacturers) to use the BASIC language [11] as a general frame to which assembler programs handling input and output from the experiment, have been added as language extension or can be called by a CALL statement. Since BASIC is usually interpreted and not compiled, this will not work when the experiment exhausts the processor speed.

Software must not only be written but also be brought into the computer memory and checked there. In addition, programs which actually control an experiment must be accessible by the experimenter's instructions. So the best programming language is worthless if there are no convenient means of man-machine communication. Hardware requirements have been discussed

(Sec. 2), software must as well be provided, e.g. editing programs, debugging programs and the like.

The deficiencies of existing software form one of the greatest handicaps for easy computer control of experiments. This will, however, change in the next few years. Cheaper storage will allow higher languages and better operating systems to spread. Man-machine-connecting hardware will become more reliable and faster. So the amount of manpower needed to computerize an experiment can be expected to decrease substantially.

8. Should we computerize?

Many laboratories nowadays are contemplating to use computers in experiments or do already so. A small personal enquiry showed that in the subfield of heavy-particle scattering, about every third laboratory has an on-line computer now, and many others will buy one soon. At the moment most of these people do not use much experiment control, however. Only in one case a time-shared computer is used [12].

Yet there is some reluctance to employ a computer in the laboratory too. Since these people would not hesitate to employ a new type of oscilloscope or vacuum gauge, their concern must be specifically about computers. My feeling is that unfamiliarity with the way in which hardware and software interact, and the "open-endedness" of a software-programmed system make the uninitiated hesitate.

On the other hand are the promises: faster data acquisition, more complex measurement strategies, concurrent evaluation of results and feedback to decide what to measure, more comfort to the experimenter, and above all: unrivalled flexibility to change strategies and algorithms whenever you want to do it.

There is one real difficulty which computer-based experimenting shares with experimenting in general: there is no systematic literature to learn it. In our case the situation is aggravated by the fact, that even the existing literature is so much scattered in special journals, unpublished reports, and manufacturers' literature [13], that nobody can know more than a small fraction of it. A new student should e.g. read refs. [14, 15], update it with manufacturers' literature [e.g. 13], look for the few systems described from time to time is Rev. Sci. Instrum. and J. Phys. E, draw his analogies from computer-controlled nuclear-physics experiments regularly discussed in the IEEE Transactions on Nuclear Science, and finally try to solve specific questions by consulting ref. [16].

In this paper only a few further remarks can be made in addition to what has already been said. One big problem which is discussed much in my country is whether one should buy small "dedicated" computers or one large computer which is time-shared by many experiments. There are some pros and cons for each kind of system: (1) the price per instruction performed in the computer is cheaper by about a factor ten in small computers; (2) the experiment interface will be cheaper for a small computer; (3) the small computer is self-sustained, there are no negotiations necessary about priorities and availability; (4) the large computer generally possesses more software and simpler man-machine interaction, (5) the large computer has larger storage sometimes needed for the evaluation of results, (6) the cost of peripherals is shared in large systems.

Since dedicated computers can be quite small if they are there just to handle one job (and not to make your laboratory autonomous in computing), and if they are backed by some large computer (which is becoming inexpensive nowadays, cf. Sec. 2), it is my feeling that direct control and acquisition by a time-shared computer is not the most efficient way.

Let us finally see what computer control costs. Table 1 has already been mentioned. Adding up, one finds that an experiment may be computerized starting with a minimum of $ 10.000, and paying $ 25.000 and more for a large system. In preparing the budget one should not forget how many signal averagers, scalers, pulsers, controllers, timers etc. can be saved by having one computer.

9. Concluding remarks

Nothing can better show the evolution taking place in collision laboratories with the installation of computers than the words from a letter of one of my friends: "The only problem has been that [the computer] provides data so easily as to entirely shift the focus of our work. Actually, the shift is of course to where we really wanted it to be all along, interpretation of results . . ."

Acknowledgements

I am grateful to the Deutsche Forschungsgemeinschaft for the support of our work with laboratory computers.

References

[1] e.g. Texas Instrument "Silent" terminal.
[2] e.g. Digital Equipment's "Decwriter".
[3] e.g. IBM "Selectric" Typewriter.
[4] "Auerbach Minicomputer Reports" by Auerbach Info, Inc., Philadelphia, Pa.
[5] cf. the motto of ch. 13 in: N. F. Ramsay, *Molecular Beams,* (Oxford University Press, London, 1956): *"It's all a Matter of Intensity"* – S. Millman.
[6] Communications Theory and Random Noise Theory are covered in many books, e.g.: D. Middleton, *Introduction to Statistical Communication Theory,* (McGraw-Hill Book Co., Inc., New York, 1960);
J. B. Thomas, *An Introduction to Statistical Communication Theory,* (John Wiley & Sons, Inc., New York, 1968);
D. J. Sakrison, *Communication Theory,* (John Wiley & Sons, Inc., New York, 1968).
[7] e.g. R. Freeman, J. Chem. Phys. *53* (1970) 457, and references therein.
[8] A measurement in one of our machines has been made. See J. Meissburger and Ch. Schlier, Report BMwF-FB W68-02 (Bundesministerium fur wissenschaftliche Forschung, Bonn, 1968).
[9] e.g. INDAC by Digital Equipment Co., OLERT by Honeywell, Inc.
[10] D. Bensen et al., Comput.Bull (Dec. 1967) 202;
H. E. Pike, Proc. IEEE *58* (1970) 87;
J. D. Schoeffler and R. H. Temple, Proc. IEEE *58* (1970) 98;
J. Gertler, Comput. J. *13* (1970) 70;
J. Brandes et al., Elektronische Datenverarbeitung *12* (1970) 429.
[11] e.g. J. G. Kemeny and T. E. Kurtz, *Basic Programming,* (John Wiley & Sons, Inc., New York, Second Edition 1971).
[12] G. E. Busch, J. F. Cornelius, R. T. Mahoney, R.I. Morse, D. W. Schlosser and K. R. Wilson, Rev. Sci. Instrum. *41* (1970) 1066.
[13] One must not necessarily buy one of its computers, but one should read Digital Equipment's *"Handbooks".*
[14] B. W. Stephenson, *Digital Computer User's Handbook,* Eds. M. Klerer and G. A. Korn (McGraw Hill Book Co., Inc., New York, 1967), Ch. 4.10.
[15] Ch. Schlier, Messtechnik *76* (1968) 147 and 216.
[16] Computer & Control Abstracts (monthly), cf. especially chapter codes 75 and 88.

Physics of Electronic and Atomic Collisions, VII ICPEAC, 1971 — North-Holland (1972)

ON-LINE DATA BANK IN ATOMIC AND MOLECULAR PHYSICS

Francis J. SMITH

The Queen's University of Belfast,
Belfast 7, N. Ireland

The advent of multi-access systems pioneered by project MAC and the availability of massive on-line storage will make possible conversational retrieval from large computer data banks in a few years' time. But such retrieval will be ineffective and too costly unless care is taken to use the hardware efficiently. Using some tricks learned from the compiler writers, we have been studying the design of efficient on-line retrieval systems in Belfast, and we have built two pilot conversational retrieval systems: one for the retrieval of numerical data and the other for the retrieval of references. Pilot models of these two systems were demonstrated at the conference; the visual display unit was connected to the Queen's University ICL 1907 Computer in Belfast over the telephone network through an accoustic coupler.

1. Introduction

Within a few years terminals linked to computers will be readily available and will be used frequently by scientists and others. Many scientists will have terminals beside their own desks and they will use them as casually and as often as they use a telephone today. Computing costs will be lower and the cost and size of on-line storage will have improved considerably over what is available now. For example, it is predicted that by the end of the decade on-line holographic storage of 10^{13} bits should be possible at a cost of 10^{-7} cents per bit [1]. In Belfast at present we have a 2.4×10^9 bit disc file at a cost below 10^{-2} cents per bit, but already larger files, at costs below ¼ of this, are on the market. Thus it will be possible to store large data banks on -line at costs much less than today. The scientist of tomorrow will want to be able to retrieve the data he needs from these data banks easily, quickly and at an acceptable cost. Our research at Belfast is aimed at studying this problem [2].

2. Reference retrieval

To examine the problem more clearly, let us put ourselves in the position of a scientist of the future in Amsterdam who has an information problem in atomic and molecular physics. He will switch on his terminal, and after typing his name, account number, password, etc. (unless his terminal does all this automatically for him) he types "Information". The resulting conversation will begin as follows:

Scientist:	*Information*
Reply:	Subject?
Scientist:	*Atomic and molecular physics*
	(short delay)
Reply:	You are being connected to the Data Bank on Atomic and Molecular Physics at Belfast.
Belfast:	Are you familiar with the Belfast system?
Scientist:	*Yes*
Belfast:	Data, References or Authors?
Scientist:	*References*
Belfast:	Years?
Scientist:	*1971–1974*
Belfast:	Such a search will cost about $25 including telephone costs from Amsterdam. Is this acceptable?
Scientist:	*Yes*
Belfast:	Keys?
Scientist:	*Electron-impact dissociation*
Belfast:	173 references
Belfast:	More keys?
Scientist:	*Molecular nitrogen*
Belfast:	New key; 526 references
:	Previous key; 173 references
:	Intersection; 15 references
:	Union; 684 references
:	N, P, I or U?
Scientist:	*I*
Belfast:	More keys?
:	
:	
:	etc.

Such reference retrieval from a set of 1000 papers taken from the INSPEC tapes (from which Physics Abstracts are published) was demonstrated at the conference using a WESTREX visual display linked to the University ICL 1907 computer in Belfast over the ordinary telephone network. The scientist of the future is likely to follow-up such a search with an on-line request to his local library computer to have copies of the papers he retrieves sent to him. One of these papers may be ordered automatically on an inter-library loan if the local library does not have it. (But such facilities are still further in the future.)

On-line reference retrieval will be of benefit to the scientist of the future primarily because it will enable him to search the available literature quickly and at great depth. For example, at present we index each paper with all sig-nificant words in its title and abstract. In a second or two the scientist can find all papers with any two word stems occurring either close together or far apart (as required) in the title and abstract. Such searches would be virtually impossible manually.

3. Numerical data retrieval

Although on-line reference retrieval will be an important tool to the scien-tist, it is often not the paper he wants but rather some numerical data con-tained in the paper. This will often not be given in the units he wants or in a form suitable to him: he may work in atomic energy units and need a table of data buts he finds the data in the paper to be in cal/mol and in graphical form. But he cannot remember how to convert from cal/mol to atomic units and he cannot find the conversion factor. When he finds it he does the com-putation incorrectly. Such simple things may hold the scientist back an hour or two, and worse still, if he makes a mistake, it may waste a month or two, Surely it is possible to do such things with the aid of a computer and save the wastage of valuable time which so often occurs.

With this as our starting point we began storing inter-atomic potentials at Belfast for retrieval on-line. Our purpose was to explore what was possible and to design a useful system at as low a cost as possible. We aimed at making the following available:

1. The original potentials as they were taken from the literature with the references;
2. The "best" potential obtained from the available data over as wide a range as possible;
3. This "best" potential would be in the units specified by the scientist;
4. It would be in any of the following forms:
   (a) a table at points to be specified,
   (b) a curve-fit (i.e. a formula fitting the potential over the range required),
   (c) an approximate graph drawn on the terminal,

(d) an accurate graph (or several graphs together) to be drawn on the
graph plotter of the computer and posted to the scientist the next
day,

(e) a subroutine to generate the potential for the scientist, written in
FORTRAN. This could either be printed out on the terminal or
punched automatically on a set of cards and posted to him.

We demonstrated 1, 2, 3, 4a and 4c at the conference. 4b, 4d and 4e are
partly programmed and, as far as we can see, they should present no difficulty. We should be able to demonstrate pilot versions of these facilities by the
end of the year. We have stored for demonstration about 500 potentials and
we have another 500 almost ready for storage. We should have stored most of
the potentials in the literature within a year.

4. Generation of data

If no data is stored for the potential requested, the present system prints
out: "sorry no data available" and asks if the user wants another potential. In
the future we intend to build into the system various rules and approximate
formulae which will enable the program, in many cases, to ask the user if an
approximate generated potential would be acceptable and, if so, to give it to
him in the form he requires. This extra facility will require us to store other
data such as oscillator strengths, polarizabilities, ionization potentials, etc.
When no potential data is available, the new data system will search the other
data in the data bank for relevant information and then generate a potential
from that data when possible. For example, the long-range r^{-6} Van der
Waals coefficient could be calculated from atomic dipole polarizabilities or
oscillator strengths when these are known.

We also intend to include programs which can compute data from the
potentials: data such as deflection angles, phase shifts, elastic total and differential cross-sections, transport proporties, etc. Thus it will be possible for a
scientist who is doing an experiment, say, on the collisions of Li^+ ions with Li
to ask the system for the approximate differential cross-sections at some energies and angles and to be given the results within about fifteen minutes. I
estimate that the cost of this will be about $100 two years from now, and it
may be much less by the end of the decade.

We also intend storing data which can be computed from potentials and
thus build a complex data system with inter-atomic potentials at the base. We
will build on this related data and include dynamically the relations between
the data. It should then be possible to use the system to display the data easi-

ly and quickly and thus to examine the data for consistency, checking its accuracy and improving it where possible.

I am convinced that we can accomplish all but some of the work in the last paragraph within two years, and we may be able to demonstrate these facilities at the next conference. Our biggest problem is getting good scientists to extract the data from the literature and to authenticate it.

5. Volunteers

In the coming year or two we would welcome some volunteers who have available teletype-compatible terminals linked to the telephone network, and who are willing to use the system occasionally, to put up with the failures and shortcomings of the systems in their early stages and to make constructive criticisms. Any comments or criticisms or corrections to the pilot system demonstrated at this conference would also be welcome. If you have a reprint or a preprint in which a potential is given we would appreciate it if you would send us a copy.

Acknowledgement

This work was supported in part by the Office of Scientific and Technical Information, London.

References

[1] W. J. Rolph, Datamation (1970) p.28.
[2] L. D. Higgins and F. J. Smith, Comput. J. *14* (1971) 249–53.